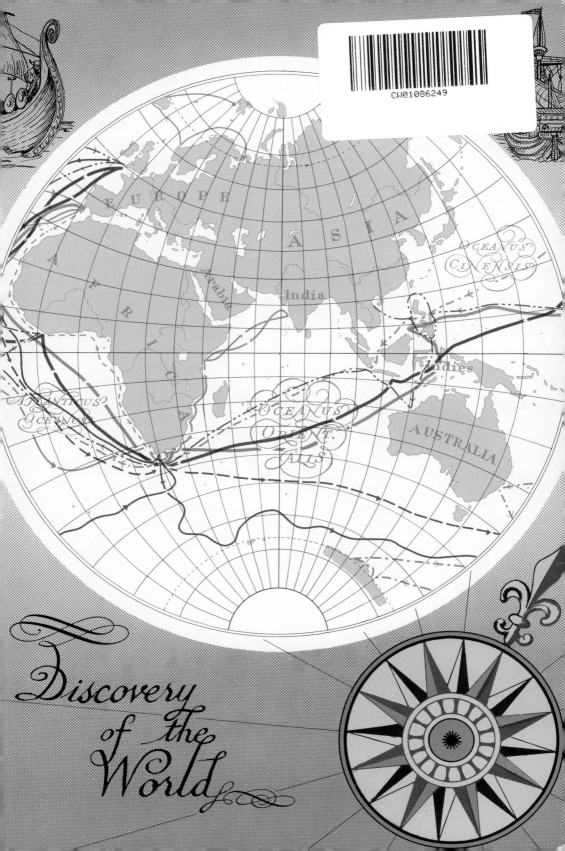

CW01086249

EUROPE

ASIA

AFRICA

Arabia

India

OCEANUS CHINENSIS

Indies

ATLANTICUS OCEANUS

OCEANUS ORIENT. ALIS

AUSTRALIA

Discovery
of the
World

Longman Illustrated Companion to World History

Longman Illustrated Companion to World History

Edited by Grant Uden

Longman

in association with

Kestrel Books
London and New York

Longman Group Ltd.,
(in association with Kestrel Books)
London
Associated companies, branches and
representatives throughout the world

Published in the United States of America by Longman
Inc. New York

ISBN 0 582 20520 4
First published 1976

Phototypeset by Oliver Burridge Filmsetting Ltd., Crawley, Sussex
Printed in Hong Kong by Sheck Wah Tong Printing Press

Library of Congress Cataloging in Publication Data
Main entry under title:

Longman illustrated companion to world history.

Bibliography: p.
Includes index.
I. History-Dictionaries. I. Uden, Grant.
D9. L8 903 75–35742
ISBN 0–582–20520–4

Contents

Editor: Grant Uden
Associate Editor: John S. Wingate-Saul

Illustrations: Anthony Colbert
Cartography: Volume I, John Flower
Volume II, Keith Morton
Index: Sally Bicknell

Picture Research: Sandra Assersohn
with Anne Fisher
and Jane Dorner
Book Lists: R. J. Hoare

CONTRIBUTORS

W. J. Baker
Frederick Buckle, D.S.C., M.A.
Philip A. Burgoyne
Aileen Hamilton Burslem
Charles Chenevix Trench, M.C., B.A.
R. J. Claye, B.A.
P. Collister, M.A.
Tom Corfe, M.A.
Marcus Crouch, B.A., F.L.A.
John Dobie
Phyllis A. Downie, M.A., F.L.A.
Wilfred J. Fance, F.Inst.B.B.
Paul Fincham, B.A.
R. S. Fitton, Ph.D.
W. W. French, M.A.
A. W. Fuller
Max H. Fuller, M.A.
R. M. Gard, M.A.
John F. Goodchild
Hugh Gregor, M.A.
E. E. Y. Hales, C.B.E.
Fernau Hall
Sylvia Haymon
Mark Haymon
E. G. Heath
A. G. L. Hellyer, M.B.E., F.L.S.

J. W. Hunt, M.A.
John F. Leech, M.B.E.
John Marsh, M.A.
Zoë Marsh, B.A., M.Ed.
Brigadier P. W. Mead
Winifred F. Pretty, M.A.
David V. Proctor, M.A., D.I.C.
Peter H. Rogers, B.A., Dip.Ed.
Joan M. Saunders
Hugh Shearman, Ph.D.
Christine Smale, A.R.C.A.
Ernest W. Sockett, B.A.
Frank Staff
H. M. Stedman
B. G. Stone, O.B.E., M.A.
J. J. Sullivan, K.S.G., B.Sc.(Econ.)
Elfrida Vipont
Annesley Voysey, B.Sc.
Arthur H. Waite
Marjorie Weemys
Barry Williams, B.A.
John S. Wingate-Saul, M.A.
Barbara Winstanley, B.Sc., F.M.A.
B. K. Workman, M.A.
Dorothy F. H. Wrenn
Paul Zec, M.A.

Secretary: Mary Chick

Preface

When this project was first launched, it was suggested to contributors that, since most world histories published in this country have been English history in a world setting, a determined effort must be made, not only to look outwards, but to stand outside Britain altogether for a viewpoint, even though this would involve the omission, or at least the playing down, of many familiar names, events and places. This may explain the apparent omission of some old text-book friends, though they may well appear in articles grouping such topics together.

The Companion is not intended to be primarily a work of quick reference, though it may often serve this useful purpose. Rather, it is hoped that it will be congenial to browse in, sometimes for instructional purposes, sometimes simply because it is interesting to do so "Companion" in fact, should imply companion-ability; and, while a good deal of solid fare has been provided, it is hoped that the reader will find much that is outside the range of mere academic convention.

In pursuit of these aims, contributors of very varied background and experience were invited to collaborate. They have come not only from school and university; but also from the world of commerce, the law, the colonial service, agriculture, libraries, museums and technical organisations. A number have lived and worked in the countries about which they write.

The Index provides a detailed system of cross-referencing. As well as listing the entries themselves, it also lists people, places, events etc. which appear within entries, but which do not have entries to themselves. The cross-referencing system used within the text has deliberately been kept simple. For instance, cross-references to other entries are grouped together at the end of an entry and appear thus: *see also* AUSTRIA; CHARLES V; etc. In both the Index and the Colour Sections, references to named articles are shown in **bold**. Where suggestions for further reading are made they appear as follows: ¶ JONES, DAVID and PAULINE. *Hadrian's Wall* (Jackdaw). 1958. The suggestions for further reading are intended mainly for young people, though readable adult books are not excluded.

The Companion has been seven years in the making. Though sustained efforts have been made to keep entries up to date, it is almost inevitable that, in some cases, events have overtaken the text. A well-known contemporary politician has observed that a week in politics is a long time. A week in world history is even longer.

No work of this kind can come to fruition without a great deal of help and advice. In this connection, the editor is especially grateful to F. A. Buckle, Dr. J. L. Henderson, C. P. Hill, J. W. Hunt, J. B. Hope-Simpson and John Marsh. Sally Bicknell's final supervision and preparation of the Index has been a considerable task unostentatiously performed; and, though she looks upon it as all in the day's (or on this case several years') work, I cannot permit the name of Treld Bicknell, the Art Editor, to be excluded from the acknowledgements.

The editor could echo the sentiments of a great historian whose work is recorded in these pages and who, at the end of seventeen years' labour, said "I will not dissemble the first emotions of joy in the recovery of my freedom", but found that joy overcast by a sober melancholy at taking leave of "an old and agreeable companion". I hope that for many people this will prove an agreeable Companion; and, indeed, even become an old one.

G.U. 1975

L

Lace: open-work fabric incorporating ornamental designs. It can be made of linen, cotton, silk, wool, synthetic fibres or even of gold or silver thread. Lace in this sense dates from the beginning of the 16th century.

There are three different kinds of hand-made lace – needlepoint, pillow and crochet. The first, as its name implies, is done with a needle. Pillow lace is really a specialised form of weaving. The parchment pattern is fastened to a pad or pillow with pins which prick out the design. The threads – of which there may be dozens – are held by bobbins and are twisted round the pins and interwoven with each other as the pattern dictates. Crochet may have a longer history than the other two, for it is done with a hook of a kind used from very early times for making netting.

The best of the early laces came from northern Italy, especially Venice, and from Flanders. France and England, by importing Venetian workers, acquired lace-making industries of their own. The first machine for making lace was invented in 1768.

La Fayette, Marie-Joseph, Marquis de (1757–1834): French general who began his career in the French army and was so stirred by the American struggle for independence that he went to Philadelphia and offered his support. At that time a wealthy nineteen-year-old nobleman, he was immediately commissioned by Congress as a major-general. He quickly won the respect and friendship of George Washington and was entrusted with the task of negotiating with France for naval support against the British. His achievement of this task was a great help to the

colonists, and a grateful emerging nation showered praise and rewards upon him. When America entered World War I in 1917 General Pershing visited La Fayette's grave in Paris, removed his cap and said "La Fayette, we are here".

Lake Dwellings: primitive dwellings built over lakes and marshes. During the Neolithic and Bronze Ages in Europe, numbers of these human settlements appear to have been made on wooden platforms either over the waters at the edge of a lake, or over bogland. They were supported on piles, and some settlements, existing over a long period, may at various times have been successively over dry land, over open water and over bogland. The historian Herodotus refers to dwelling platforms erected in the 5th century BC. It would appear from this reference and from physical remains that the communities living in these settlements could be of some size and of some degree of civilisation.

The existence of lake dwellings was first brought to the attention of the archaeological world in the middle of the 19th century. Noteworthy examples have been identified in Scotland and Ireland and in Swiss and Italian lakes.

Lancaster, House of: line of English kings founded by John of Gaunt (Shakespeare's "time-honoured Lancaster" and third surviving son of Edward III) by his first marriage to Blanche, heiress of the Duchy of Lancaster (1359). Their eldest son, Henry Bolingbroke, was exiled (1398) by his cousin Richard II, who later seized the vast Lancastrian lands on Gaunt's death. Bolingbroke returned to claim his lands but found Richard II so unpopular that he claimed the throne as well, forced his cousin to abdicate and was proclaimed as Henry IV (1399). He

Above: John of Gaunt, Duke of Lancaster, dining with the King of Portugal.

King Henry V.

was succeeded by his famous son Henry V (1413–22) and his grandson, the unhappy Henry VI (1422–61), in whose reign the Wars of the Roses broke out.

John of Gaunt also had three sons and a daughter by the mistress he later married; this Beaufort family was afterwards legitimised but debarred from succeeding to the throne. Henry VII, through his mother Lady Margaret Beaufort, was descended from this line.

¶ STOREY, R. L. *The End of the House of Lancaster.* 1966

Land reclamation: the recovery of derelict or submerged land. The reclamation of land for agricultural and other purposes, involving the irrigation of wastes, the draining of marshes and the reclamation of land on the edge of a sea, a lake or a river, has been practised from pre-Christian times. An early example is recorded in an inscription on the tomb of a queen of ancient Egypt: "I constrained the mighty river to flow according to my will and let its waters fertilise lands that had before been barren and without inhabitants."

In Europe, low-lying lands on both sides of the North Sea were reclaimed extensively from the 17th century, the engineers being paid either by the grant of newly reclaimed land or by a salary from a body of commissioners. On some of these reclaimed lands, silt-bearing waters were allowed on to the land at certain times of the year, so that its level was both raised and enriched. This process was known in England as warping.

The experience of the Dutch in land reclamation led to their engineers being regarded as the most expert in the world. At home, they carried out increasingly ambitious projects, culminating in the Zuider Zee scheme, by which an area of over half a million acres [203,430 hectares] was recovered from the sea. In the United States of America, irrigation farming proved highly successful in the more barren of the states. Though there were earlier small schemes, the pioneers of modern irrigation methods in the United States were the Mormons, who began their ultimately very extensive irrigation farming in Utah just before the middle of the 19th century. In England, great areas of the East Anglian fens have been successfully drained, including Whittlesey Mere, the largest lake in the country, six miles [9·66 kilometres] long.

Landscape painting: the painting of inland scenery.

In the field of the arts landscape painting

was fairly late in starting. Stone Age paintings depicted wild animals and, occasionally, the men who hunted them, but made no attempt to place either in their natural setting. The first artists to take all nature as their domain were Chinese. Over many centuries they evolved a subtle and lively art, based on brushwork and line. Their landscapes have no perspective in the Western sense, yet the works of the great Chinese landscape artists – notably those of the Sung dynasty (960-1280) – have a realism that transcends exact representation.

Few Greek or Roman paintings have survived the passage of time. So far as we can judge, both the ancient Greeks and the Romans were more interested in the human figure than in landscape. Nevertheless, wall paintings such as those in the villa of Livia, at Prima Porta near Rome, show the existence in the classical world of landscape painters of skill and imagination.

Modern landscape painting, grounded in an interest in nature for its own sake, dates from the 15th century. The Italians, Masaccio (c. 1401-28) and Giovanni Bellini (c. 1430-1516), and the Flemish painter Jan van Eyck (c. 1390-1441), were among the first to practise this new approach. Even so, landscape remained literally in the background. Not until the 17th century were pictures painted in which nature had pride of place, with figures, when any were included, subordinated to it.

There were two great 17th-century schools of landscape painting – the French and the Dutch. The French painters – of whom the best known are Claude Lorraine (1600-82) and Nicolas Poussin (1594-1665) – specialised in picturesque landscapes which existed only in their imaginations. The Dutch, more homely, took nature as they actually found it. The famous painting of the avenue of poplars

at Middelharnis by Meindert Hobbema (1638-1709) typifies the best Dutch landscape painting of this period.

In the early 19th century it was England's turn to produce landscape painting of the highest quality. John Constable (1776-1837) and the artists of the Norwich School distilled the essence of the English countryside into pictures which are a balm to the eye and the spirit. John Mallord William Turner (1775-1851) gave us landscapes full of light and movement – paintings which influenced the French Impressionists, that group of late 19th-century artists whose aim it was to capture in a swift impression a fleeting moment of light and shade.

The French painter Paul Cézanne (1839-1906), building on both the freedom of the Impressionists and the discipline of the Old Masters, produced paintings, many of them landscapes, which revolutionised not only painting but the very way we look at the world about us. Since his day, while many painters have continued to paint landscapes representationally, others, such as Henry Matisse (1869-1954), Pablo Picasso (1881-1973) and Georges Braque (1882-1923), have used nature as a point of departure for pictures which make no pretence to photographic accuracy or even recognisability. Others, like the English artist Ben Nicholson (b. 1894), have pared landscape to its barest essentials of colour and form.

See colour section.

¶ CLARK, KENNETH. *Landscape into Art.* 1956

Language: organised system of speech, usually of human beings. Language has been described as "the most wonderful creation of the mind of man".

Noah Webster (1758-1843), the American lexicographer, defined language as "the expression of ideas", adding: "Language, as well as the gift of speech,

Above: View of Hampstead *by John Constable. Below:* Trees at the Jas de Bouffon *by Paul Cézanne.*

was the immediate gift of God." Thus, he tried to put his finger on the one thing hidden from us, the origin of language.

Another definition comes from C. K. Ogden (1889-1957), whose *Basic English Dictionary* defines language as "words and their use". Certainly language is the means by which we communicate ideas to each other and in a manner far and away beyond the primitive forms of communication used by other species. Philologists (literally, those who love words) investigate language scientifically and many of them believe that differences of speech may have come about through variations in man's physical structure: primitive people with short upper lips, for example, using consonants such as "f" and "k" rather than "p" which comes more naturally to those with long upper lips. We do not know whether language has a common origin.

It seems likely that speech came before writing and that its invention came about through man's impulse to communicate his wishes and feelings. It is, of course, possible to communicate simple wishes without uttering a syllable, as is done in small communities in which a vow of silence is taken. But life in general as now organised and lived would be impossible without speech and writing.

Among the earliest sounds uttered by man were cries of joy and pain; the war-cries of warriors; the decoy sounds of the huntsmen; and the many noises made in imitation of animals and natural phenomena.

Though by "language" we mean all communication, the very word, derived from French *langue* and Latin *lingua,* meaning "tongue", indicates the greater part played by speech in human communication. But the voice lacked the permanence of writing. We do not know how writing began, but it was probably in the form of crude and simple pictures of objects which served the purpose at the time as tokens or symbols of what men wanted and desired to say. We call them pictographs, a word made up by putting together a Latin and a Greek word: *pictus,* artistic, and *grapho,* I write. The religious markings on the monuments and tombs of the ancient Egyptians are called hieroglyphs, another made-up word contrived by putting together two Greek words: *hieros,* sacred, and *glyphé,* carving.

The invention of writing, and later its extension by the invention of the alphabet, was an enormous step forward in human communication, making it possible to preserve records and events and to send messages by a more reliable method than by speech. Similarly, in modern times, the invention of wire and tape recording of sound has enabled us, by recording conversation, to give a degree of permanence to the voice. This must appreciably increase our store of knowledge and affect to an unpredictable extent the speech of generations to come.

It is estimated that more than half the population of the world can be reached by thirteen of the 3,000 living languages. Of these English is second to Chinese in the number of its speakers, followed by Hindi, Russian, Spanish, Japanese, German, French, Italian, Malay, Bengali and Portuguese. The first recorded language is Sumerian. The oldest living language is Chinese.

The problem of communication between different nations with different languages has long given rise to a desire for a universal language – as is said to have existed before the Tower of Babel was built when, according to the Bible story, "the whole earth was of one language and of one speech". This desire runs counter to the pride which nations take in their own language, a pride which has helped to restore national status previously lost – as with the Czechs, the Irish and the Jews. But a compromise idea is gaining ground, and that is to establish an international second language which shall be used by all the nations side by side with their national tongues. C. K. Ogden believed that this international second language could be English and devised a system, which he called Basic English, for that purpose. The best known artificial language is Esperanto, invented in 1887 by the Polish linguist Doctor Zamenhof.

¶ BARBER, CHARLES. *The Story of Language.* 1964
See also ESPERANTO; HANDWRITING; SHORTHAND, etc.

Laos: kingdom in south-east Asia enclosed by China on the north, Vietnam on the east, Cambodia on the south, and Thailand and Burma on the west. Laos and much of the surrounding country is mainly inhabited by Buddhist Thais or peoples closely resembling them. French, Japanese, Chinese, Americans and Russians have influenced the defining of the confused boundaries. Communications within the country are too poor to bind the inhabitants into strong nationhood.

Laos became an independent kingdom as far back as the 14th century, though it has since suffered invasion and conquest from many sides. At the end of the 19th century it became part of Indo-China and, after World War II, regained independence within the French Union, later being declared a neutral state. In the 1960s the country was torn by outbreaks of civil war, and recently, during the Vietnam War, it was bombed by US forces as a result of being used as a supply route by the Viet-Cong.
See also VIETNAM, etc.

Lao-Tse or **Lao-Tzu** (*c.* 604–*c.* 531 BC): title given to Li Erh, who worked in the imperial library of the Chow dynasty and founded Taoism, one of the three great religions of China. His teachings, expressed in his (reputed) book, the *Tao-te-king,* were mystical and obscure in meaning, but he believed in the strength

Lao-Tse and his disciples.

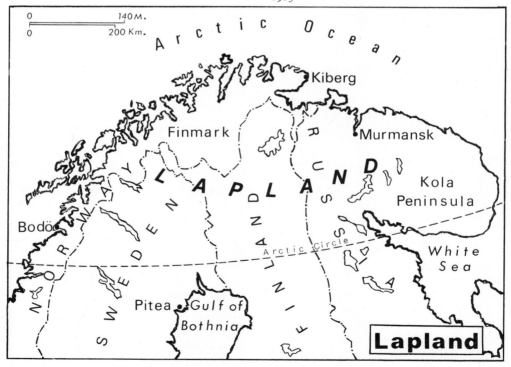

of quietness as a way to virtue, *tao* meaning, roughly, "the way". The religion developed in the centuries after his death, with its many gods and its magic, bears little relation to his original teaching, and the system of worship, with its temples and monasteries, was largely borrowed from Buddhism.

Lapland: region, mostly above the Arctic Circle, comprising parts of Norway, Sweden, Finland and Russia (Kola Peninsula). The Swedish name for the inhabitants – Lapps – means nomads. Lapland was still little known as late as the 16th century and the single incursion of its people into European affairs occurred when they were recruited into the armies of Gustavus Adolphus of Sweden (ruled 1611–32). Lapland has been subjected to many masters and its population has now been largely absorbed by neighbouring countries.

La Salle, René Robert Cavelier, Sieur de (1643–87): French explorer who was one of the first Europeans to enter central North America. Arriving in New France (now Quebec Province, Canada) in 1666, he established a fur trading post near Montreal and spent the years between 1669 and 1671 exploring the Ohio and Great Lakes region. After the existence of a water highway from the St Lawrence to the Gulf of Mexico had been established, La Salle determined to extend French power southwards to the Mississippi delta. Louis XIV of France made him grants of land and "a patent to build forts, trade and explore". Between 1679 and 1682 he descended the Mississippi River to its mouth and claimed the whole valley for France, naming it Louisiana in honour of the French king. La Salle died in 1687, murdered by his own troops, in the territory now known as Texas.

¶ SIBLEY, DAVID. *With La Salle Down the Mississippi.* 1965

Latin America: the countries of North America (except French-speaking Canada), Central and South America where French, Spanish and Portuguese are spoken. The 200 million people include many races: native and European, African Negro and Asiatic Indian, and many of mixed origins. Most speak either Spanish or Portuguese, because for 300 years these lands were ruled by Spain and Portugal. At the end of the 18th century new ideas of freedom and equality began to challenge the control of overseas colonies by European monarchies, especially after Napoleon invaded Spain and Portugal. Brazil declared itself independent of Portugal in 1822. All the Spanish territories, except Cuba and Puerto Rico, gained their independence in a series of ferocious wars between 1810 and 1825, and as a result about twenty new republics were formed. Some of the leaders of these revolutions, like Simon Bolívar (1783–1830), had hoped to form a United States of South America. But local rivalries prevented leaders from co-operating, and the geographical obstacles of mountain and jungle hindered easy trade and communications. Unfortunately, quarrels between these twenty new nations began as soon as the wars for independence ended. They have remained divided ever since, and their weakness has often attracted interference from outside, as in 1862 when Napoleon III tried to take over Mexico. The 19th-century wars of independence too often only gave the local Spanish landowners freedom to rule without interference from Spain, and many peoples of Latin America are today still waiting for freedom.

Latin language: originally the tongue of the Romans and the tribes of the surrounding district of Latium. It belongs to one of the groups of Indo-European languages and conveys its meaning to a large extent by inflection (changes in the endings of words).

As the language of the Roman Empire and of the Western Church, it had a powerful influence on many modern European tongues, especially those of the Romance group, which includes French, Italian and Spanish, and has left many traces in our own. Until comparatively recently Latin was the means by which ideas were spread in western Europe, and it is still much used in legal, medical and botanical terms.

Laud, William (1573–1645): archbishop of Canterbury. He was educated at Reading School, being born in that town, and at St John's College, Oxford, of which he later became president. He was bishop successively of St David's, Bath and Wells, and London, which last appointment he combined with the Chancellorship of Oxford University. In 1633 Charles I promoted him to Canterbury.

Laud's support of the Court of Star Chamber (*see* separate entry) and other arbitrary methods of government; his insistence on the forms of worship laid down in the Prayer Book in England – and, with less success, in Scotland; and the people's strong suspicion that the archbishop was, in fact, a papist, roused enmities which even Charles, who supported him, could not resist. He was imprisoned by Parliament in 1641, but not brought to trial until 1644, and executed on a charge of high treason on 10 January 1645.
See also CANTERBURY, ARCHBISHOPS OF.

Lavoisier, Antoine-Laurent (1743–94): French chemist, perhaps best known for his recognition that oxygen is an element and that combustion is the process of combining with oxygen, a discovery that helped lay the foundations of modern chemistry. To provide money for his researches he became one of the government collectors of revenue. For this he was brought to trial during the Revolution and condemned to the guillotine, one of the charges against him being that he had "put water in the tobacco". He appealed in vain for a fortnight's respite to finish some experiments.

¶ In SHEPHERD, WALTER. *Great Pioneers of Science.* 1964

Lawrence, Sir Henry Montgomery

(1806–57): soldier and hero of the Indian Mutiny, the fourth of six sons of a colonel in the service of the East India Company. Although he distinguished himself more than once as a soldier, he is chiefly remembered for his ability and devotion in political and administrative matters, particularly in the Punjab. A strong Christian belief was the inspiration of everything he undertook. On the outbreak of the Mutiny in 1857, Lawrence found himself charged with the defence of Lucknow, where he died of wounds soon after the siege began.

¶ In KAMM, JOSEPHINE. *They Served the People.* 1954

Lawrence, John Laird Mair, first Baron Lawrence (1811–79): Viceroy of India, the sixth of the brothers mentioned above and the only one to join the Company's service as a civilian. Like his brother, he distinguished himself in the Punjab, though unfortunately they quarrelled over questions of policy; and it was his hold over the area that enabled the British gradually to gain the upper hand in the Mutiny. He was made Viceroy of India (1864–69).

¶ In KAMM, JOSEPHINE. *They Served the People.* 1954

Lawrence, Thomas Edward, known as "Lawrence of Arabia" (1888–1935): British archaeologist and soldier. After extensive travels in Syria and Mesopo-

T. E. Lawrence, known as "Lawrence of Arabia".

tamia and excavations at Carcemish (1910–14), he helped, during the war, to promote and lead an Arab revolt against Turkey (1916–18) which protected the right flank of the British advance into Syria. He told the story in *The Seven Pillars of Wisdom*. In 1922, disgusted by what he regarded as the betrayal of the Arabs, he changed his name to Ross (later to Shaw), to avoid publicity, and joined the RAF as a mechanic. He was killed in a motor-cycle accident in 1935. Several recent books, plays and films have rekindled interest in a controversial figure, about whose character, motives and achievements there is much division of opinion.

¶ BARBARY, JAMES. *Lawrence and His Desert Raiders.* 1965; THOMAS, JOHN. *Lawrence of Arabia.* Muller 1973

League of Nations: an international organisation which was born at the end of the first World War and which

effectively died at the beginning of the second. Its purpose was "to prevent future wars . . . and to promote co-operation . . . between the nations of the world". Membership was open to all self-governing states. The League's main institutions were: the Assembly, consisting of delegations from all member states; the Council, consisting of permanent and non-permanent representatives; and the Secretariat, which was the administrative body, working under a Secretary-General. In addition, there was set up the Permanent Court of International Justice at the Hague. Under the covenant of the League, member states undertook not to go to war until all possibilities of a peaceful settlement had been exhausted; to register treaties publicly with the League; and to collaborate in promoting action in such fields as labour conditions, public health and colonial and minority problems.

Although the League did much useful work of social and economic reconstruction, it was powerless to prevent war. The military adventures of Japan, Italy and Germany in the 1930s and their withdrawal from the League (the USA never joined) meant that by 1939 it was an irrelevant and broken institution. Statesmen and peoples had expected much from the League, but it was betrayed through the determination of governments to put "vital" national interests above all else, and their failure to grant the League the power to bite as well as to bark.

¶ GIBBONS, S. R. and MORICAN, P. *The League of Nations and UNO.* 1970

Lease-Lend Bill: US legislation approved by President F. D. Roosevelt on 11 March 1941, drawn up primarily to help Britain, and any other country fighting Germany and her allies, to obtain essential war supplies. Lease-Lend enabled any country whose defence the President deemed vital to that of the United States to receive arms and other equipment by sale, transfer, exchange or lease. The total Lease-Lend for World War II amounted to fifty billion dollars.

Lebanon, Republic of: republic in western Asia at the eastern end of the Mediterranean, between Syria to the north and east and Israel to the south. The inhabitants speak Arabic and are mostly of Arab race.

Like other parts of this Levantine coast, Lebanon shared in the sea trade of goods crossing the land bridge between the Persian Gulf and the Mediterranean. Tripoli, Beirut, Byblos (now called Jubail), Sidon and Tyre are very ancient ports where routes through the mountains reach what is still the main highway north and south. Phoenicians, Egyptians, Romans, Venetians and others used these centres of trade, which, situated on peninsulas or on islands just off shore, are protected by the sea on at least three sides.

After long domination by the Ottoman Empire, Lebanon became autonomous in 1861 after a massacre of Christians had brought about intervention by European powers. Following a period under French mandate (1920) and as a republic (1926), Lebanon was occupied by British as well as French troops during World War II. The country became an independent republic in 1944 and joined the Arab League and the United Nations in 1945.

Main sources of wealth are still east-west trade, as of old, especially now that the pipelines bring Iraqi and Saudi-Arabian oil to Tripoli and Saida (Sidon). Prosperity is threatened by general Middle East hostility between Israelis and Arabs. *See* ISRAEL and SAUDI ARABIA for map.

¶ SALIBI, KAMAL S. *The Modern History of Lebanon.* 1965

Lebensraum: living-space; a slogan of German imperialism which referred in the early 20th century to the need for colonies overseas to solve the (alleged) problem of Germany's over-population; later used by Hitler in *Mein Kampf* (1923) and subsequently to justify the idea of German expansion in Europe, especially towards the east.

Le Corbusier (Charles Eduard Jeanneret-Gris, 1887–1965): French architect of Swiss birth and one of the most influential of modern times, as well as being author, painter and sculptor. Le Corbusier was interested in the total urban environment. He prepared town-planning schemes for many important cities – among them Algiers, Sao Paulo, Rio de Janeiro, Buenos Aires, Barcelona, Geneva, Antwerp. He designed a new capital city for the Punjab at Chandigarh and was one of the consultants employed on the design of the New York headquarters of the United Nations. Two of his best known works are in France – the housing scheme at Marseilles known as the *Unité d'Habitation* (1947–52) and the chapel at Ronchamp (1955).

See also INTERNATIONAL STYLE.

Right: Unité d'Habitation, *Le Corbusier's housing scheme in Marseilles. Below: Chapelle Notre Dame du Haut at Ronchamp.*

Lee, Robert Edward (1807-70):
commander-in-chief of the Confederate
forces in the American Civil War. He was
commissioned in the engineers in 1829
but by 1855 had assumed command of
cavalry on the Texas frontier. In 1859 he
commanded the troops which put down
John Brown's raid on the military arsenal
at Harper's Ferry. At the outbreak of the
Civil War he declined field command of
the US Army offered by Abraham Lincoln, accepting instead that of Virginia's
military forces. His brilliant leadership
brought many unexpected successes for
the South, but his defeat at Gettysburg
was the turning point of the war. He
surrendered to Grant at the Appomattox
courthouse (9 April 1865) and advised the
South to create a future within the Union.
¶ In WALTON, J. *Makers of the USA.* 1943
See also AMERICAN CIVIL WAR.

*A portrait of Thomas Coke of Holkam with the
famous breed of sheep which is associated with
him.*

**Leicester of Holkham, Thomas
William Coke, Earl of** (1752-1842):
agricultural improver. Popularly known
in his lifetime and to posterity as Coke of
Norfolk, Coke was the son of a Norfolk
squire and was for many years a member
of parliament for his native county, in the
Whig interest. He was among the leaders
of the agricultural revolution of the 18th
century. The poor land which formed his

Holkham estate was improved by such
measures as the use of fertilisers and the
proper rotation of crops, and both the
produce of the soil and the quality of his
farm livestock were increased to such an
extent that his Holkham estate rental is
reputed to have risen from £2,200 to over
£20,000 a year. In old age, in 1837, he
was created Earl of Leicester of Holkham.
See also AGRICULTURAL IMPROVERS.

Lenin (1870- 1924): the name adopted by
Vladimir Ilyich Ulyanov to hide his
identity from the police; Russian revolutionary and founder of the Soviet Republic. An event that considerably influenced him in early years was the
execution of his eldest brother for his part
in an unsuccessful attempt on the life of
Alexander III (1891). Another great influence was Karl Marx (*see* separate entry),
whose writings he studied deeply. He
began writing and organising himself,
and in 1895 founded in St Petersburg
(afterwards renamed Leningrad in his
honour) an illegal society called "the
Union for the Liberation of Working
Classes". In a few months he was arrested,
and spent the next three years in prison
and exile.

One of the landmarks of his career – and
of world history – came in 1903 when at a
conference of the Russian Social Democrats in London the party split into
Bolsheviki ("majority men") led by Lenin,
and the more moderate, now outvoted
Mensheviki ("minority men"). Thereafter
the Bolsheviks and Mensheviks became
bitterly opposed to each other. After a
long period abroad Lenin returned to
Russia in 1917 and overthrew the government that had been set up by Aleksander
Kerenski and for the rest of his life was
virtual dictator, putting down all opposition to the Bolsheviks, now renamed the
Communist Party, with great ruthlessness.
"There is room for other parties," he said,

Lenin with Joseph Stalin.

"only in jail." His exertions laid the foundations of Russia's strength as a great world power.

¶ LIVERSIDGEE, DOUGLAS. *Lenin.* 1970; *Lenin and the Revolution.* 1972

Leningrad: second city of the USSR, founded in 1703 by Peter the Great on swampy land conquered from the Swedes. Named St Petersburg, it became his capital in 1712 and, with only a short interval, remained capital of Russia till 1918. St Petersburg was Russia's outlet to the Baltic and attracted much industry, including shipbuilding. It was the scene of the revolutions of 1917. Renamed Petrograd in 1914, it became Leningrad in 1924. In World War II Leningrad was besieged by the Germans 1941–44, and 900,000 died. Peace brought extensive rebuilding.

¶ MILLER, WRIGHT. *Leningrad.* 1970

Leonardo da Vinci (1452–1519): Italian artist and scientist. Few men in history have displayed such breadth of knowledge, skill and inventiveness, and, with this, great charm of character. He has been called "the Universal Man".

Born in Florence, he was patronised as a young man by Lorenzo de' Medici, but later moved to Milan, where he executed one of his most famous pictures, "The Last Supper". This, now sadly deteriorated, can still be seen on the wall on which it was painted.

From 1499, always in demand, he was moving between Rome, Florence, Venice and Milan, until, in 1518, King Francis I persuaded him to settle in France. He died at Amboise, supported, it is said, in the King's arms. He had brought with him an even more famous picture, his portrait of a woman generally known as "Mona Lisa", which is now in the Louvre, Paris.

His mathematical and mechanical skill brought him fame as a civil and military engineer, and evidence for his versatile abilities lies in the volume of annotated drawings with his curious right-to-left writing, now in the Royal Collection at Windsor Castle. *See colour section.*

¶ GILLETTE, H. S. *Leonardo da Vinci: pathfinder of science.* 1963

See also FIFTEENTH CENTURY; FRESCO; RENAISSANCE.

A design by Leonardo da Vinci, for a flying machine based on the wing of a bird; and containing an example of his right to left writing.

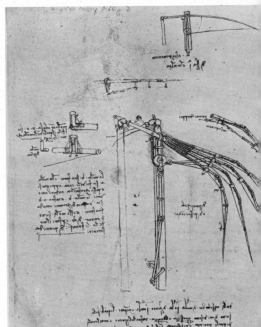

Leopold II (1835-1909): King of the Belgians 1865-1909; son of Leopold I. As a young man he served in the army and travelled widely in the East and in Africa. In 1876 he formed the Association Internationale Africaine and proceeded to exploit the little-known region of the Congo as his personal property. Growing criticism prompted him to set up a commission to inquire into the administration of the area; its report in 1905 revealed serious inefficiency and corruption, and in 1908 Leopold handed over the Congo to the state. At home his reign was remarkable only for the domestic scandals in which his family was involved.

Lepanto, Battle of (1571): naval victory of the West over the Turks. Ever since the fall of Constantinople (1453) the Turks had been pressing forward, both by land and by sea, against the states of Western Europe, whose disunity often prevented effective resistance. At length, however, the exertions of Pope Pius V brought a combined fleet of over 300 Spanish and Venetian galleys and other craft under Don John of Austria face to face with about the same number of Turkish ships in the narrows of the Corinthian Gulf. At first the Turks were successful on the right and left flanks. Then the Christians broke the centre, capturing the commander-in-chief's galley and smashing his squadron. Lepanto was the last great battle in history to be fought with oar-driven ships. The Turks lost an estimated 25,000 men, the Christians 8,000. Some 15,000 Christian slaves were set free from the Turkish galleys. G. K. Chesterton gives a striking picture of the battle in his poem "Lepanto". *See colour section.*

Lesseps, Ferdinand Marie, Vicomte de (1805-94): French canal engineer. He was responsible for the Suez Canal, completed in 1869, which enabled ocean-going ships

Ferdinand de Lesseps (second from right) and his helpers in Alexandria in 1865.

to pass between the Mediterranean and Red Seas. His project for the Panama Canal, between the Atlantic and Pacific Oceans, was not put in hand until after his death and was completed only in 1914.
¶ In CROWTHER, J. G. *Six Great Engineers.* 1959
See also SUEZ CANAL.

Letter of marque: licence or commission granted by a country at war to a private owner, authorising him to use his vessel as a ship of war or privateer. The letter of marque system attracted many captains in hope of rich profits. The Congress of Paris (1856) declared that "privateering is and remains abolished".

Levant: the coastal lands of the eastern Mediterranean, especially Lebanon and Syria. The name derives from French *lever,* to rise, indicating the east and the rising of the sun. In earlier centuries the Far East was known as the High Levant.

Liberia: independent Negro republic on the west coast of Africa. One hundred and fifty years ago a group in the USA formed the American Colonisation Society to return freed Negro slaves to their homeland. A pioneer settlement was established on the border of Sierra Leone and named Liberia – the free state. The early settlers had a hard struggle, but by 1847 they numbered over 30,000 and felt

sufficiently established for President Joseph Roberts, their first Negro leader, to issue a Declaration of Independence. This was recognised by the major European countries, including England, where he was received by Queen Victoria, who sent him home in a naval sloop. It was not till 1926 that relative prosperity came with the leasing of one million acres [406,860 hectares] to the Firestone Tyre and Rubber Company to produce rubber for the US government. Gold and diamond fields have recently been discovered in the interior. Liberia has been a member of the United Nations since 1945.
See AFRICA for map.

Libraries: places set apart to contain books for reading, study, reference or borrowing. There is evidence that from earliest times scholars found places to store the material they required. In the beginning this was not in the form known to 20th century readers. Inscribed tablets, cylinders of baked clay and scrolls of parchment were the forerunners of the printed book. When few could read, these precious documents were kept for scholars' use in temple, colonnade or hall, or in libraries beside the Roman baths.

In the Middle Ages most libraries were found in monasteries. Reading and writing had a special place in the rule of each religious order, especially that of the Benedictines. The number of books was small, but it was increased by the monks' diligent hand-copying. On the dissolution of the monasteries in Britain many libraries were destroyed or their contents dispersed abroad. The manuscripts which survived, often beautifully illuminated, are now treasured in national, cathedral, university and private archives. Books are no longer fastened to reading desks with chains, at first an essential practice but one which was discontinued when, with the invention of printing in the late 15th

The Chained Library of Hereford Cathedral.

century, books grew plentiful; a few examples of chained libraries survive, e.g. in Hereford Cathedral, England.

By the end of the 18th century the collecting of books, which had been the province of the rich, became fashionable among a wider section of the more literate population. The growth of public and private libraries was fostered by the development of publishing and the success of the book trade. Compulsory education in the late 19th century encouraged reading, and the need to provide more books in universities and schools, as well as for the use of the general public, was increasingly recognised. Subscription libraries from which books could be borrowed for a fee became popular.

Today the world is full of libraries – public libraries in cities and towns; state and county libraries providing a wide range of services; libraries attached to institutions of learning, cathedrals, universities, colleges and schools; libraries in ships, hospitals, factories, government offices, banks and industrial concerns. It would be difficult to find an organisation which does not have a need for books and does not somehow find the means to provide them.

"To every scholar his boke", is a wish which can now be fulfilled and he need not journey far to find it. In some countries, under national lending schemes, readers can borrow from libraries hundreds of miles away. Using photographic processes, librarians can also send microfilm copies of books and articles wherever they are required, even overseas.

From being mere custodians guarding their treasures chained to desks, librarians, albeit still curators, have become the means of propagating and exploiting the world's literature. The names of some have already passed into history and are remembered with other benefactors in the libraries they founded; e.g. Sir Thomas Bodley (1543-1616), scholar of Oxford, whose library was made available in 1602; John Rylands of Manchester, a rich man whose widow built a library in his memory and opened its collection of

The Reading Rooms of two of the world's most complete libraries. Above: The British Museum in London. Below: The Library of Congress in Washington.

treasures to the public in 1899; Sir William Osler, whose books on the history of medicine were bequeathed to McGill University, Montreal, Canada, in 1919; Henry Clay Folger (1857-1930), collector of Shakespeareana, who built the Folger Library in Washington, D.C., to house his collection; Henry Huntington, commemorated in the Huntington Library, Los Angeles; and, foremost in the public library service, Sir Andrew Carnegie (1835-1919), whose wealth endowed free libraries in the United States, Canada and Britain.

History has seen the destruction and recreation of many libraries. The Vikings are known to have pillaged monasteries in England, taking the books for the value of their jewel-encrusted covers. Libraries were considered lawful booty in war; for instance, the *Bibliotheca Palatina* in Heidelberg was removed during the Thirty Years War, and later presented to the Pope. Gustavus Adolphus confiscated several libraries which he sent back to Sweden to enrich the University of Uppsala. The Royal Library in Stockholm was similarly augmented by captured books. In recent wars libraries have played a varied part, sustaining the morale of prisoners of war through libraries in prison camps, lending books to people in air raid shelters and hospitals. Many libraries were, however, bombed and burnt or had their contents scattered or destroyed for other reasons. Sometimes it seemed the damage could never be repaired. But when war ended, the printing presses came to life again, libraries were re-stocked and continued to fulfil their centuries-old rôle.

¶ IRWIN, RAYMOND. *The Origins of the English Library.* 1958

Libya: North African kingdom bounded by the Mediterranean Sea, Egypt to the east, Chad and Niger to the south and Algeria and Tunisia to the west. Libya was occupied by a succession of colonisers and conquerors, including Phoenicians, Greeks, Romans, Arabs, and Turks. The country was annexed by Italy after war with Turkey in 1911, the Arabs of the interior being put down with great brutality by Graziani's forces. After the defeat of Italy in World War II, a British military caretaker administration ruled the country until 1951 on behalf of the United Nations, after which it became independent under the Emir Mohammed Idris al-Senussi as king. Treaties of friendship were signed in 1953 between Libya and Great Britain, and in 1954 with the USA on financial and military matters, and substantial aid was given by the two Western powers. In 1970 King Idris was deposed following a military coup, and Britain and the USA were asked to withdraw their forces from Libyan territory. *See* AFRICA for map.

Lifeboats: craft, based on shore, designed for rescue work near the sea coast. Any boat can be used to save lives, but the lifeboat proper is specially built to seek out and meet conditions that other craft try to avoid.

The first known boat to be specially made or adapted for saving life at sea was the work of an English coach-builder, Lionel Lukin, who converted a small fishing coble into an "unimmergible" (i.e. unsinkable) boat by fitting it with a number of hollow, watertight spaces to give it greater buoyancy and replacing some of the heavy woodwork with cork. This coble was stationed in 1786 at Bamburgh Castle, Northumberland, and saw good service on that storm-swept, rocky coast.

Four years later, in 1790, as the result of a competition organised by a group of English north country gentlemen, the first boat designed and built as a lifeboat was launched on the River Tyne.

Christened the *Original*, it was constructed by Henry Greathead of South Shields from a clay model. In the next fourteen years Greathead built another thirty-one lifeboats, eight of which went abroad to other countries. Greathead used some of the ideas of another South Shields man, a singing master named William Wouldhave, whose memorial in the church at South Shields describes him as "Clerk of this Church and inventor of that invaluable blessing to mankind, the Lifeboat". Who, then, was the real inventor of the lifeboat? The answer seems to be that Lukin first converted a boat for life-saving purposes; that William Wouldhave designed the first self-righting boat, i.e. a craft that, even if it were overturned in rough weather, would immediately come upright again; and that Greathead was the first successful builder on a considerable scale.

Twenty-one years after his first experiment, Lukin built the first sailing lifeboat, a forty-foot craft to serve among the sand dunes off the east coast of the British Isles. The first powered lifeboat was not used till 1890 – the fifty-foot steel-built *Duke of Northumberland,* which lasted over thirty years.

The year 1834 saw the foundation in England of "The Royal National Lifeboat Institution for the Preservation of Life from Shipwreck". The man chiefly responsible was Sir William Hillary, who, after a distinguished career as a soldier, turned his energies to the problems of saving life at sea. He himself shared in the rescue of over 300 lives and was three times awarded the Gold Medal of the Lifeboat Institution, the highest award it can bestow. A noteworthy feature of his conception of a lifeboat service was that it must extend to ships of all nations, whether at peace or war, irrespective of race, colour and creed.

The British lifeboat service, despite

| USSR | 72 lifeboats and tenders |
| | 14 salvage tugs |

The modern tendency, with the development of air rescue services, is to reduce the number of stations in favour of a smaller number equipped with more powerful, longer-ranging craft.

¶ ASHLEY, BERNARD. *The Men and the Boats: Britain's Lifeboat Service.* 1968; UDEN, GRANT. *Life-Boats: a survey of their history and present state of development.* 1962

Lighthouses and lightships: strategially placed beacons on land and sea serving as navigational aids to ships. The original lighthouse or Pharos, built by Ptolemy off Alexandria, Egypt, *c.* 280 BC, was lit by wood fires. Subsequent illuminants were coal fires, tallow candles (as in Eddystone Light, south-west of Plymouth, England, 1756), oil-burning wicks (introduced by Swiss inventor Argand, 1784), vaporised oil and electricity, followed in the 1960s by mercury and high pressure arc lamps.

One of the earliest institutions concerned with lighthouses, Trinity House, London, received its first charter from Henry VIII in 1514. This fraternity organised pilotage and was responsible for erecting and maintaining lighthouses and navigational marks around the British Isles. Today it continues to provide this service together with similar organisations in Scotland and Ireland. Local authorities are responsible for lights within their harbour boundaries.

Lightships are moored in shallow waters to indicate shoals and sandbanks such as the Goodwin Sands area in the English Channel. They are also placed off important harbours to indicate the entrance channel as in the case of the Ambrose lightship off New York and the Bar lightship in Liverpool Bay.

Light Lists published by the governments of most countries give full descriptions of lights in use. For identification

The launching of the Shoreham, Sussex, lifeboat.

some periods of financial difficulty, has always been independent of government control and is supported entirely by voluntary contributions. The same is true of a number of other countries. A survey made in 1961 showed that Germany, the Netherlands, Sweden and Uruguay were completely financed by voluntary subscriptions. Others had state and municipal subsidies: a third group, among them Canada, Denmark, India, the USA and the USSR, were state financed.

The size of lifeboat fleets naturally varies with such factors as the length of coastline, the volume of shipping using its ports and the money available. Some idea of the variety may be gathered from a few examples from the 1961 returns made by lifeboat societies throughout the world:

Country	Strength of fleet
Denmark	24 motor lifeboats
	19 pulling and sailing lifeboats
Iceland	3 motor lifeboats
	4 patrolling rescue cruisers
	14 pulling surf boats
	1 ambulance aircraft
Japan	30 motor lifeboats
	67 pulling lifeboats
India	2 motor lifeboats
Italy	3 lifeboats
USA	1,335 motor boats
	1,508 pulling boats

*The famous Eddystone Lighthouse built origi-
nally in 1698. It stands on a small and dangerous
rock near Plymouth, England. It was destroyed
many times but always rebuilt and the lighthouse
stands today on the same spot.*

*The Ambrose Offshore Light Structure in New
York Harbour. It is manned by a resident US
coastguard crew.*

purposes, either by day or night, the
mariner requires to know the height,
colour, visibility range, characteristics,
e.g. group of three white flashes every ten
seconds, and, in poor visibility, details of
fog signals. Today most of the strategi-
cally placed lights act as radio beacons,
and navigation in confined waters can be
assisted with the many electronic aids
available.

¶ CHADWICK, LEE. *Lighthouses and Lightships.* 1971

Lima: capital city of Peru, situated six
miles [9.66 kilometres] from the Pacific
coast on the River Rimac. It was founded
in 1535 by Francisco Pizarro, the conqueror of the Incas. He personally supervised the lay-out and building of its broad
avenues, spacious gardens and massive
public buildings, and was himself buried
in its magnificent cathedral. The city was
rebuilt on its original foundations when
destroyed by an earthquake in 1746. From

Lima the Spanish Viceroy ruled over most
of South America, until in 1824 it became the capital of the new independent
republic. The various wars and revolutions
that have racked Peru have left their
mark on the capital. When the country
was at war with Chile (1879-94) the
Chilean army occupied the city for nearly
three years and ruthlessly despoiled its
buildings and its collections of literary,
artistic and scientific treasures. The present
city is a mixture of old and new.
See also PIZARRO, FRANCISCO.

Lincoln, Abraham (1809-65): sixteenth
president of the USA. Born into an
illiterate and wandering frontier family,
he eventually settled at New Salem,
Illinois, where he ran a store, served as
postmaster and studied law. He was
admitted to the Bar in 1836 and moved to
Springfield, where he became an outstanding lawyer and served four terms in
the state legislature, representing Illinois
as a Whig in Congress from 1847 to 1849.

Lincoln joined the Republicans in 1856 and two years later campaigned strongly, though unsuccessfully, for the Senate. He quickly emerged, however, as the leading candidate for the Republican presidential nomination. He became president in 1860, largely because of splits amongst the Democrats. As a result of his election, seven slave states seceded before he assumed office in March 1861. A month later the Civil War broke out. As a war leader he was at first fumbling and indecisive. What caused the change has never been clear; but from July 1862 he suddenly emerged as master of the situation, assuming direct control, appointing and dismissing his own generals, and protecting them from civilian interference. As president his greatest qualities were the skilful handling of his party and his generals, his personal integrity and ability as a speaker, the best example being the famous Gettysburg Address in 1863, in which he urged the nation's dedication to a new freedom and spoke of "government of the people, by the people, and for the people". The historical legend that represents him as fighting to free the

Abraham Lincoln photographed by Matthew Brady in February 1861.

slave population is misleading. Even as late as August 1862 he said: "My paramount object is to save the Union, and not to save or destroy slavery". A week after the surrender of the main Confederate army, he was shot by John Wilkes Booth in Ford's Theatre in Washington on Good Friday 1865, dying the next morning (15 April).
See colour section.
¶ LATHAM, FRANK B. *Abraham Lincoln.* 1972
See AMERICAN CIVIL WAR; AMERICAN PRESIDENTS; GETTYSBURG; SLAVERY etc.

Lingua franca: jargon or mixed language used between people of different nations; originally basically Italian with Spanish, French, Greek and Armenian and used as the common speech of the Mediterranean Sea and its ports.

Linnaeus, Carolus (Carl Linné, 1707–78): Swedish botanist who originated the binomial (two-name) classification of plants, i.e. the name of the genus, group or class, and the specific name of the individual plant. The system was widely accepted throughout much of the world and, with considerable modifications, is still in use today. The adjective *Linnaean* derives from the botanist's name, which is the Latin form of the Swedish.
¶ DICKINSON, ALICE. *Linnaeus.* 1970

Lisbon: capital of Portugal and major port at the mouth of the River Tagus, the lower plain of which is so fertile that wheat was said even in medieval times to grow in forty days.
Lisbon became the capital in the mid-13th century and flourished as an entrepôt for spices and other goods from the Levantine coast *en route* to Holland and the Hansa cities, from about AD 1300. When the Turks broke the monopoly of Venice after 1453, Henry the Navigator explored the Cape route to India. This

The ruins of Lisbon after the earthquake of 1755.

brought Mediterranean trade to the Atlantic and greater profit to Lisbon. After a devastating earthquake in 1755 had destroyed half the city, it was replanned in magnificent symmetrical style by the Marquis de Pombal, foreign secretary 1750-77. When Napoleon invaded Portugal and the royal family fled to Brazil (1808) the city began to decline and did not climb to importance again till after 1850. Various revolutions in this century have brought considerable damage, but Lisbon remains one of the finest cities of Europe.

¶ WRIGHT, CAROL. *Lisbon.* 1971
See also PORTUGAL.

Lister, Joseph, first Baron Lister (1827–1912): English surgeon and pioneer of antiseptic surgery. Anaesthesia had made the work of surgeons easier, but many patients died because gangrene and blood poisoning attacked them after an operation. Doctors believed that infection was carried to open wounds by the air, but Lister studied the researches of Pasteur and was convinced that germs caused it.

Lister tried soaking dressings and bandages in dilute carbolic acid to kill germs, but the acid often destroyed tissues as well. He then insisted on the disinfection of the hands and instruments of the surgeons, and sterilised his hospital with a carbolic spray. His methods greatly reduced the risk of post-operational infection.

¶ CARTWRIGHT, F. F. *Joseph Lister, the man who made surgery safe.* 1963

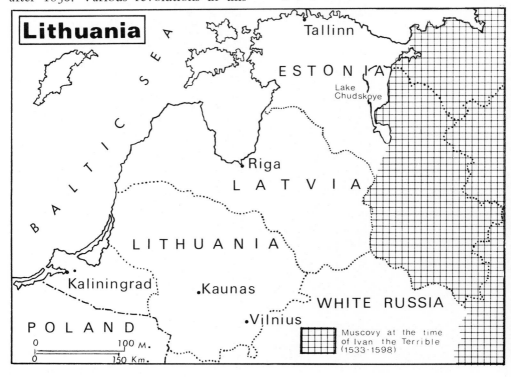

Lithuania

BALTIC SEA

Tallinn

ESTONIA

Lake Chudskoye

Riga

LATVIA

LITHUANIA

Kaliningrad

.Kaunas

WHITE RUSSIA

.Vilnius

POLAND

0   100 M.
0   150 Km.

Muscovy at the time of Ivan the Terrible (1533-1598)

Lithuania: constituent republic of the USSR. The state of Lithuania dates from the 13th century, emerging from Slav tribes settled along the eastern shore of the Baltic Sea. By the 15th century it stretched from the Baltic to the Black Sea, and north to Muscovy. In 1385 Lithuania's Grand Duke, Jagiello, was elected hereditary king of Poland, the two countries being formally united in the Polish Commonwealth in 1569. Russia acquired most of present day Lithuania by the 1795 partition of Poland. Independent from 1919, the state was annexed by Stalin in 1939 and today remains part of the USSR.

Liverpool: second largest port of England, on the estuary of the River Mersey, Lancashire. Settlements existed in the 8th century and trade developed with Ireland, France and Spain. The rise of Lancashire industries greatly increased this trade and extended it to the West Indies and the Americas. Liverpool also profited from slave-trading in the century 1709-1807. In 1618 the Privy Council declared Liverpool to be dependent on Chester, but the volume of water evacuated on the ebb tide scoured the basin by contrast with Chester, which silted up. Engineering work added to these natural advantages and a major dock development occurred in the 18th and 19th centuries. In 1800 the total tonnage of ships entering Liverpool was 450,060. In the next 120 years it rose to over 30 million tons [30,483,000 tonnes] coming from every part of the world, and carrying a great variety of commodities. The trade with America has been the most important, with cotton ranking as the chief import. The port is also an important outlet for the manufactures of Lancashire and the West Riding of Yorkshire.
¶ BORER, MARY CATHCART. *Liverpool.* 1971

Livingstone, David (1813-73): Scottish explorer and missionary; joined London Missionary Society 1838, qualified as medical doctor 1840; posted to Kuruman Mission, N. Cape Colony 1841; married Mary Moffat, daughter of Robert Moffat, founder of the mission in 1844. To his staunch Christianity was added a passion for exploration, and he gloried in blazing the trail for other missionaries. In 1849, with Oswell, he discovered Lake Ngami, and in 1850 followed the Zambesi to its source at Mwinilunga, continuing west to the Atlantic coast at Luanda. In 1855-56 a journey down the Zambesi led to his discovering the Victoria Falls. Later explorations included the discovery of Lakes Nyasa and Shirwa. He died at Ilala 1 May 1873 and, after his body had been carried by natives across Africa to Zanzibar and conveyed thence to England, was buried in Westminster Abbey in 1874.
¶ MATHEWS, B. *Livingstone the Pathfinder.* 1960

Livy (Titus Livius, 59 BC-AD 17): Roman historian. He was born and died at Patavium (Padua) in Lombardy. His *History of Rome*, from the foundation of the city (traditionally 753 BC), is said to have taken forty years to complete and to have amounted to 142 books, of which only thirty-five have survived.

Lloyd George, David, first Earl Lloyd George (1863-1945): British Liberal statesman. The son of a Welsh school-teacher, he entered Parliament in 1890 and in 1905 joined the Liberal government, becoming Chancellor of the Exchequer in 1908. In 1916 he replaced Asquith as leader of the wartime coalition government, thus splitting and hastening the decline of his own party. After his defeat in the 1922 election he never again held office, becoming an elder statesman of occasionally eccentric opinions. He is most remembered for the social legislation, including provision for old-age pensions and national insurance, which he piloted through parliament in the years 1908-11 and for his vigorous wartime leadership, as well as for his fiery oratory and colourful personal life.

¶ In WHITTLE, J. *Great Prime Ministers*. 1966

Lloyd's of London: an association which began in the City of London in the 17th century for the insurance of ships and cargoes. It was named after Edward Lloyd (1688-1726) who kept a coffee-house where the shipowners and merchants met the insurers. In return for a premium the insurers undertook to pay an agreed sum if a ship were lost or damaged. News of the movement of ships was collected from the docks and published in *Lloyd's News* which still appears and is now known as *Lloyd's List*. The society flourished and today Lloyds of London is a world centre for shipping intelligence and insurance.

¶ GIBB, D. E. W. *Lloyd's of London*. 1957

A busy day in Lloyds Coffee House in Lombard Street; 18th century.

Locke, John (1632-1704): English philosopher. He was educated at Westminster School and Christ Church, Oxford, and became secretary to the politician who was later created Earl of Shaftesbury. On the latter's disgrace, he fled to Holland and remained there until James II had quitted the throne.

In all his thought and writing he placed great emphasis on reason and reasonableness, with an acknowledgement that, in matters of religion, some things are by nature unknowable. As a result he stood for toleration and broadmindedness. His most famous philosophical work is the *Essay concerning Human Understanding* (1690).

¶ In THOMAS, H. and THOMAS, D. L. *Great Philosophers*. 1959

Lollard: in English history, a follower of John Wyclif (*see* separate entry), the religious reformer who, with the help of his friends, translated the Bible into English. The derivation is doubtful, but perhaps is from the German *lollen,* to sing, from their custom of singing hymns, or from the Dutch *lollaert,* a mumbler. The term is also applied to a 14th-century Dutch heretical sect.

Lombards: name originating from the Lombardy region of northern Italy, where the Teutonic people known as Lombards settled in the 6th century, but applied in medieval times particularly to Italian merchants and bankers. As the Canon Law forbade Christians to lend money on interest, finance in England was largely in the hands of the Jews until their expulsion in 1290. They were succeeded by Italian merchants and bankers from Piacenza, Siena, Lucca and Florence, all known in England as Lombards. They first arrived in Henry III's reign, and were finally banished by Elizabeth I. They played a large part in the state finances of both England and France. Edward II repaid his father's debt of £56,000 to the Frescobaldi, and both Edward III and Henry V pledged their jewels to the Lombards to raise money. Lombard Street in the City of London commemorates their residence there.

London: capital of England and chief city of the Commonwealth. The Greater London Council administers an area of 616 square miles [1595 square kilometres], home of 7,763,800 people (1948). This vast urban sprawl is less a city than a collection of villages which have been sucked into the maw of the metropolis, yet still obstinately retain something of their former character. London abounds in important buildings – the Houses of Parliament, St Paul's Cathedral, the Tower, Westminster Abbey, palaces, concert halls, museums – but despite the efforts of such architects as Nash and Wren little is systematically planned. It grew up haphazardly, and this is a great part of London's charm.

The city's beginning was a remote outpost of the Roman Empire called Londinium, established at that particular spot because it was the lowest point where the Thames could be crossed and was also the tidal limit of the river. Over the centuries, despite sackings by Vikings, plagues, fires and Hitler's blitz, that favourable geographical position across lines of communication by land and water has ensured London's growth into one of the most important trading centres of the world.

The nucleus of its prosperity, the City of London, is a square mile, the boundaries of which have not changed since the 13th century. Here are the Bank of England, the Stock Exchange and commercial and financial institutions on which the economic wellbeing of the country in large measure depends. Half a million workers pour into that square mile daily,

An aerial view of modern London.

but only 4,210 people actually live there. At night the narrow, winding streets are quiet and the City becomes a village, like all the other component parts of London.

¶ HAYES, JOHN. *London from the Earliest Times to the Present Day.* 1959; HAYES, JOHN. *London: a pictorial history.* 1969

See also BANK OF ENGLAND; CLEOPATRA'S NEEDLES; DOWNING STREET; LLOYD'S OF LONDON; TOWER OF LONDON; WREN, SIR CHRISTOPHER, etc.

London Bridge: bridge over the Thames connecting the City of London with Southwark and Bermondsey. There have been many London Bridges, Roman, Saxon, English, the most famous built in the 14th century with houses, shops and a chapel on it. The buildings, much decayed, were demolished in 1675, and the bridge itself replaced in 1831. This bridge (widened 1902–04) has been sold to an American oil company and is being re-erected at Lake Havasu, Arizona (*see below*), while London gets yet another new London Bridge.

¶ JACKSON, PETER. *London Bridge.* 1971

Longitude: an arc of the equator contained between the prime meridian and the meridian passing through a given position on the earth's surface; or, alternatively, the angle subtended at the pole between the prime meridian and that passing through the position. The prime meridian is usually that which passes through Greenwich, London, representing 0° longitude.

The problem of finding an accurate longitude at sea was not resolved until the 18th century. Latitude could be found easily. In the northern hemisphere it was only a matter of measuring the height of the Pole Star above the horizon. The early mariners could sail north or south until the latitude of their destination was confirmed, then proceed east or west to reach their objective.

Finding longitude by "lunar distance" or "timepiece" methods required two vital factors not as yet available, namely accurate predictions of the moon's position and a ship's clock to keep Greenwich time within seconds. The Board of Longitude, inaugurated in London in 1714, offered rewards of up to £20,000 for practical methods of achieving these objectives.

The award eventually went to John Harrison, an Englishman who made a series of special timepieces for use in ships. His Number Four chronometer was tested at sea 1761–65 to the satisfaction of the Board. Another Englishman, Larcom Kendall, produced a copy in 1770 and Captain Cook tested its accuracy during his 1772–75 voyage.

The longitude by timepiece method was thus established through the ingenuity of John Harrison. The *Nautical Almanac,* first published in 1767, provided the necessary astronomical data for the lunar distance method.

See also HARRISON, JOHN; GREENWICH MEAN TIME.

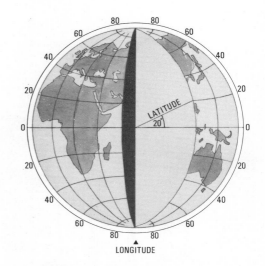

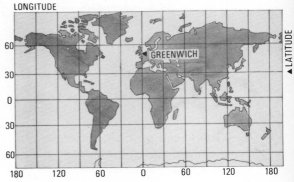

Loom: frame or machine for weaving cloth. Pictures in Egyptian tombs show women working at large looms, consisting of a horizontal beam resting across two upright posts. Long threads – the warps – hung from this beam, kept taut by weights attached to their ends. Thread was fastened to a flat piece of wood or bone – the shuttle – and this was passed under and over the warps, like a threaded darning needle. In this way cloth was woven. All primitive people appear to have used looms, which changed little through the ages, although later looms were flat, resembling bed-frames. The introduction of steam and electric power made the mechanically driven loom a

SYRIAN TREADLE LOOM AND GROUND LOOM FROM PALESTINE
BOTH NOW IN THE BRITISH MUSEUM

time-saving and profitable invention.

¶ ELLACOTT, S. E. *Spinning and Weaving.* 1962
See also COTTON; TEXTILES, etc.

Lorraine: former province of eastern France. Once a duchy of the Holy Roman Empire, it was occupied by France, at first partly, from 1552 till 1766, and then wholly. The Moselle region was annexed in 1871 by Prussia to form Alsace-Lorraine but was officially restored to France in 1918.

Louisiana Purchase (April 1803): the biggest land sale in history, by which the USA bought from France the whole of the Mississippi Valley up to the Rocky Mountains, an area of 828,000 square miles [21,000 hectares]. The price paid was fifteen million dollars. Louisiana had been French until 1762, when it

was ceded to Spain; it was returned to France in 1800. Napoleon, after rejecting the idea of a new American empire, decided to sell the territories, and President Thomas Jefferson was anxious to acquire them. The treaty was negotiated in Paris by the American ambassador, Robert R. Livingston, and by the future president, James Monroe. The agreement left the boundaries ill-defined. While the Gulf of Mexico was fixed as the line to the south and the Mississippi as that to the east, there was no clear understanding as to whether the cession included West Florida and Texas. This was to cause further trouble, especially over Texas. The Senate approved the purchase treaty on 20 October, and formal possession was taken in the last days of the year. William Claiborne was installed as territorial governor in October 1804. In 1812 the state of Louisiana became the first to be admitted to the Union from the new territorial area.

Lourdes: famous place of pilgrimage in south-west France, at the foot of the Pyrenees. In 1858 a peasant girl, later canonised as St Bernadette, had visions of the Virgin in a grotto at this place. At the same time a spring of water appeared, to which miraculous healing powers were attributed. Since then pilgrims in millions have visited Lourdes seeking cures for their ailments, and a magnificent church has been built close to the one which was erected above the grotto. The anniversary of Bernadette's vision is celebrated on 11 February.

Louvre: palace in Paris, once the residence of the kings of France. Today it houses government offices and one of the best art collections in the world. The statue of the Aphrodite of Melos, commonly called the Venus de Milo, and Leonardo da Vinci's portrait of Mona Lisa are only two of the famous works of art on view there. *See colour section.*

The Venus de Milo, Greek 3rd century BC.

Low Countries

Low Countries, Pays-Bas: collective name for Belgium, the Netherlands and Luxembourg (*see* separate entries).

Lucknow: the old capital of Oudh, India, on the River Gumti, a tributary of the Ganges. It was captured by the British after the battle of Buxar, 1764. During the Mutiny, 1857, its Residency, defended by Sir Henry Lawrence (*see* separate entry), who was killed, withstood a three months' siege, until relieved by Havelock.

Luther, Martin (1483-1546): founder of the reformed Protestant Churches in Western Europe. Son of a Saxon miner, he studied philosophy at Erfurt University before entering the order of Augustinian Brothers and being ordained priest. In 1508 he became a lecturer at the new University of Wittenberg.

541

Gradually, however, he found himself growing dissatisfied with some of the teaching of the Roman Church and increasingly critical of its abuses, particularly in the offer of *indulgences,* the partial remission of punishment in the next world, to those who, in this instance, contributed to the rebuilding of St Peter's, Rome. In 1517 he nailed to the door of the principal church in Wittenberg a paper containing ninety-five theses (arguments) denouncing this practice. From now on his writing and preaching emboldened others to protest against what they saw wrong in the Church and to band together in furtherance of their ideas. Although Rome took vigorous steps to condemn the unrest and in 1521 summoned its originator before the Diet of Worms, where he refused to recant, the strength of the new movement, to which more than one of the rulers of the German States lent support, saved him from being put on trial for his life.

In 1524 Luther finally renounced his Augustinian vows and next year married a former nun. He spent the rest of his life in promoting the new faith and trying to preserve unity among its followers.

His translation of the Bible had a profound effect on the development of the German language.

¶ PITTENGER, W. NORMAN. *Martin Luther.* 1972

Luxembourg: Grand Duchy of western Europe. At various times under the rule of Burgundy (1441–1506), Spain (1506–1714), Austria (1714–95) and France (1795–1815), the territory was constituted a Grand Duchy by the Congress of Vienna in 1815 and was recognised as an independent neutral state in 1867. Despite the Duchy's small size (now only 999 square miles [2587 square kilometres], the western part having been incorporated into Belgium), Luxembourg once boasted in its capital (also called Luxembourg) the strongest fortified city in Europe, although the name Luxembourg *(Lutzelburg)* means "little fortress". Opinions differ as to whether it yielded first place to Gibraltar in impregnability, but its situation on cliffs overhanging a river gave it a strong claim. The actual fortress was demolished in 1867, with the recognition of neutrality. *See also* EUROPE.

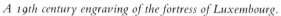

A 19th century engraving of the fortress of Luxembourg.

M

McAdam, John Loudon (1756-1836): road maker. His claim to fame rests chiefly on the improvements he made in the smoothness and durability of roads, by constructing them in layers of broken stones in graded sizes. The use in more recent times of tar to bind the surface produced "tarmacadam" ("tarmac").

¶ In WALTON, J. *Seven Civil Engineers*. 1948

Senator Joseph McCarthy.

McCarthyism: vicious charges against individuals, often without satisfactory evidence, of pro-Communism and un-American activities. During the years immediately following World War II rivalry between America and the USSR led to US politicians using the anti-Communist platform as a vote-getting device. Many Congressmen called for "loyalty oaths" from teachers, civil service employees and government officials. Between 1947 and 1952, such was the hysteria that there were no less than three congressional committees concentrating inquiries into Communism in the US and seeking out subversion in unions, schools, churches, the press and the armed forces. Overshadowing all other investigators was Senator Joseph McCarthy (1909-57), using methods of smear, innuendo and intimidation that many people considered were not in keeping with traditional American liberties. McCarthy and his associates finally overreached themselves, and their methods of investigation became in turn the subject of a Senate inquiry. McCarthy was officially censured, or reproved, by the Senate and lost his influence.

Macedon: ancient kingdom of N.E. Greece, established in about 814 BC by Caranus. Subsequently, under Philip II (ruled 359-336 BC), it rose to dominate Greece and under his son Alexander III (ruled 336-323 BC) defeated the Persian empire. Macedon was annexed by Rome in 146 BC.

See also ALEXANDER III; PHILIP II, etc.

543

Macedonia: (1) mountainous constituent republic of southern Yugoslavia, lying between Greece, Bulgaria and Albania; (2) mountainous region of the Balkan peninsula, consisting of a part of northern Greece, southern Jugoslavia and south-western Bulgaria. The region became part of the Byzantine Empire in 395 and subsequently passed under Bulgarian, Serbian and Turkish control. After the Balkan Wars of 1912–13 it was divided between Greece, Serbia and Bulgaria.

Machiavelli, Niccolo (1469–1527): Florentine statesman and author, famous for his political philosophy which shaped post-medieval politics and diplomacy. His ideas evolved during his work for the Florentine government, when he was sent on diplomatic missions throughout Europe. The adjective "Machiavellian", when applied to politics, has come to mean "unscrupulous", and it is possible that the infamous Cesare Borgia (*see* BORGIA) was the inspiration for Machiavelli's best known work *Il Principe* (The Prince) which asserted the paramount role of the state and its ruler. It taught that any treachery or cunning on the part of a ruler is justified if it upholds his power and security. Following the seizure of Florence by the Medici in 1512 Machiavelli retired from public life, and devoted himself to writing.

Niccolo Machiavelli.

The magnificent terraces of Imtehuatana Hill, near the north of Machu Picchu, the name means the "place to which the sun was tied".

Machu Picchu: mountain fortress of the Incas, north-west of Cuzco, discovered in 1911. It hangs 1,500 feet [457·20 metres] above the Urumbaba River and may have been built to keep out savages from the Amazon forest. The stone buildings and surrounding terraces for farming have survived undisturbed as the Incas left them 400 years ago.

McKinley, William (1843–1901): twenty-fifth president of the USA. Born in Ohio, he served as a major in the Union Army in the Civil War, later becoming an attorney and eventually Governor of Ohio (1891). In 1896 he was elected president on the Republican ticket. His administration saw the highest tariffs in American history and the acquisition of Hawaii, the Philippines, Puerto Rica and Guam. He was re-elected for a second term in 1900 but was assassinated on 6 September 1901.

Madeira: name applied to a collection of islands belonging to Portugal, some 360 miles [578 kilometres] west of the African coast. Madeira (the Island of Woods) is also the name of the principal island. Genoese sailors explored the group before 1400. Its rediscovery in 1419 was one of the first triumphs of Henry the Navigator (*see* separate entry) in his extension of trading routes along the west African coast. It was occupied by the British in 1801 and from 1807–14. The chief local products are Madeira wines, bananas, sugar, fish and handicrafts.

Madison, James (1751–1836): fourth president of the USA. He was born in Virginia and played a prominent part in the politics of the state from 1775 to 1780, when he served in the Continental Congress. He was largely responsible for the content of the American Constitution. He succeeded Jefferson as president in 1809 and served for two terms of office. His fumbling leadership of the Anglo-American War of 1812–14 lost him much prestige. His second administration saw a move towards more central government control of tariffs and banking.

Madras (originally **Fort St George**): third most populous city of India, on the south-east coast, with a fine artificial harbour, and capital of the large Madras Province. Founded by Francis Day in 1640, it became a presidency of the East India Company in 1653, and one of the largest English trading stations in India. In 1746 Madras was captured by the French and remained in their hands for two years. Recaptured by the English, it resisted other attacks by both French and native forces. Its more peaceable progress was marked by the foundation of a bishopric in 1833 and a university in 1857, with important medical, engineering and veterinary colleges. *See also* INDIA.

Madrid: capital and chief commercial centre of Spain, situated on a high plateau almost in the middle of the country. Madrid is mentioned (as Majerit) by 10th-century Arab scribes. It was captured from the Moors by Alphonso VI in 1083 and rose from being a mere hunting lodge of the Spanish kings to become the capital, in 1560, of Philip II. During the Peninsular War (1808–14) it put up a heroic resistance to the French. Among its notable buildings and institutions are the Prado (1785), housing one of the greatest art collections in the world; the Royal Palace and Armoury, containing magnificent collections of armour, furniture, tapestries, clocks, musical instruments etc.; the 17th-century Gothic cathedral; the America Museum; museums specialising in Spanish naval and military history, etc. A more recent memorial is the Valley of the Fallen, thirty miles [48 kilometres] from Madrid, dedicated to those who fell in the Spanish Civil War (*see* separate entry). *See also* PENINSULAR WAR; SPAIN.

Mafia: worldwide network of secret societies, originating in Sicily. *Mafia* (or *Maffia*) is of uncertain origin but may derive from a Sicilian dialect word meaning swaggering and boastful.

Of all the world's secret societies this probably has the most widespread reputation for intimidation and criminal activities. The organisation began in the lawless period of Sicily's history following Napoleon's invasion of southern Italy. Landowners entrusted the safeguarding of their property to unscrupulous ruffians who intimidated the peasant population and formed a league throughout the island which soon turned against the landowners themselves, the Mafia demanding extortionate sums for the "protection" they gave, controlling the sale of lands and crops and establishing a ruthless control far stronger than that of the official administration.

This combination of forces against law and order did not prevent internal quarrels in the Mafia, leading to bitter feuds and ruthless self-imposed justice. Spasmodic efforts were made to stamp out the organisation, but the chief result was to spread its activities and code of criminal conduct to other countries, especially the United States. In October 1890 the New Orleans chief of police was murdered by the Mafia. At the subsequent trial of eleven *mafiusi* the jury was so terrified by the organisation that most were acquitted.

It is one of the things most to the credit of Mussolini and his fascist government that, when they took control of Italy in 1922, they used the dictatorial powers they possessed to root out and exterminate this vicious organisation. Tried in large batches, with the witnesses against them having adequate police protection, many *mafiusi* received life sentences. Nevertheless, such organised evil and the fear it inspires die hard. There is no evidence that the Mafia has been finally extermi-

Part of a cache of rifles and ammunition discovered by police after a raid on a Mafia hideout in Southern Italy, 1969.

nated. The American branch, the *Cosa Nostra,* is still very active, especially in the bribery of city officials. Its own unbreakable traditions that no member victimised by the Mafia shall ever apply for help to the police or give the least assistance in bringing a fellow-member to book, whatever the crime committed, encircles the society with such protection that only great courage and determination can break it. In Sicily, birthplace of the organisation, Carlo Dolci (b. 1925) has dedicated his life to ending the fear, violence and poverty caused by the Mafia.

¶ LEWIS, NORMAN. *Honoured Society: the history of the Mafia.* 1967

Magellan, Ferdinand (*c.* 1480–1521): Portuguese soldier and navigator who served in the East Indies 1505–12 and Morocco 1513–14. Falling into disfavour with King Manuel of Portugal, he renounced his Portuguese nationality and transferred his allegiance to Spain. Charles V put him in command of five ships to seek a westward route to the Moluccas. After steering his fleet for thirty-eight days through the strait named after him, Magellan entered the "Great South Sea" (the Pacific) seen by Balboa in 1513, and continued for another ninety-eight days till he made landfall, probably at Guam, in the Ladrones. In the Philippines he allied himself with the ruler of Cebu against the neighbouring island of Mactan, and was killed there by the islanders in 1521. Of his ships, only the *Vittoria* returned home, the first ship to sail round the world. The chief source for the story of the circumnavigation is the account of Antonio Pigafetta, who was on the voyage and who refers to Magellan as "so great a captain", though he was only a small man and lame from wounds received in Africa.

¶ HONOLKA, KURT. *Magellan.* 1962

Magna Carta, or **The Great Charter** (1215): feudal charter, now regarded as a foundation of English liberties. Barons in opposition to John (ruled 1199–1216) forced him to put his great seal to this charter on 15 June 1215 at Runnymede, near Windsor. Many of its sixty-three clauses dealt with the barons' grievances but some were of wider importance, e.g. no freeman was to be punished without a trial and the king could not demand taxes without the Great Council's consent. So important was it that copies, of which four survive, were sent into every shire. Though John repudiated it, the charter was confirmed by later kings.

¶ JONES, J. A. P. *King John and Magna Carta.* 1972; HOLT, J. C. *Magna Carta.* 1961

Magyars: the dominant racial group in Hungary, who settled there in the 10th century and, under the Hunyadi dynasty in the 15th, became a bastion against the Turks, who frequently occupied much of the country. From the 16th century until 1919 the Austrian emperor was their king, but they retained self-government, and Magyar as their official language.

Maharaja (**Maharajah**): the title of chiefs of high rank in some of the greater states of India, often of those which never came under direct British rule, *maha* meaning "great" and *raja(h)* "ruler"; e.g. the Maharaja of Gwalior, or the Sikh Ranjit Singh, Maharaja of Lahore.

The Old Palace, Gwalior.

Mahrattas, Marathas: a mixed people of central India, welded into a fighting power by Sivaji Bhonsla (1627–80) but splitting during the 18th century into the five states of Baroda, Gwalior, Indore, Nagpur and "the Peshwa's Dominions" (Poona). Generals Lake and Wellesley, in the third Mahratta War (1803–05), were mainly responsible for subduing them.

Maillart, Robert (1872–1940): Swiss engineer who added a new elegance to buildings and bridges in reinforced concrete by integrating the supporting and the supported parts of a structure into a unified whole. The bridge over the Rhine at Tavanasa, Switzerland, where roadway and arch are designed as a

Maillart's bridge over the Rhine at Tavanasa, Switzerland.

single unit, is a typical example of his work.

Mainz: West German city, on the left bank of the Rhine. The site of Celtic and Roman settlement, it became an important medieval city. Gutenberg set up his printing press there in the 15th century. In more recent history Mainz's border position has made it a prime sufferer from Franco-German conflict.

Malagasy Republic, formerly **Madagascar:** island republic in the Indian Ocean about 300 miles [482 kilometres] off the east coast of Africa. The early inhabitants were Indonesians and Indians from the east, mixed with African Muslims from the west. Several countries, including England, attempted to gain a footing but only the French were able to establish themselves, in 1750. Pirates found it a convenient base in the 18th century. It was seized from the Vichy French during World War II to prevent the Japanese occupying it. After its return to France, local uprising led to its independence in 1960.

See MAURITIUS *for map.*

Malaria: infectious, chiefly tropical, disease. The word means "bad air", and the disease was at its worst in marshy areas; hence, it was also termed "marsh fever". In Italy medieval overlords built their castles on the foothills of the Apennines to raise them above the source of infection, which Hippocrates believed to be the vapours from the marsh. This theory persisted until a French doctor, Laverin, discovered malaria "parasites" in 1880, and Italian scientists studied their action in human blood. In 1895 an English scientist, Ronald Ross, found that these parasites developed in certain mosquitoes which bred in the marshes and that their bites infected humans. Malaria is now controlled by spraying the breeding grounds of mosquitoes.

¶ KAMM, JOSEPHINE. *Malaria Ross.* 1955

Malawi (formerly **Nyasaland**): republic in central Africa. In 1859, when Livingstone (1813–73) first saw Lake Nyasa, the fertile land around had been turned into a wilderness by the Arab slave trade which was destroying African tribal society. Slaves were captured to make the long haul of ivory overland. Steamers on the lake would make this unnecessary. Livingstone's reports led to the establishment of mission stations, two of which were named after him; and the African Lakes Company was set up to put down the slave trade and develop peaceful trade. Finally, in 1891, the British government reluctantly took over responsibility for Nyasaland. It remained an agricultural country, many of whose people sought work in the Rhodesias and South Africa. Communications were a big problem, and in order to provide an outlet for Nyasaland's exports a railway was completed in 1915 from Port Herald to

Chindi on the north bank of the Zambesi. Seven years later another was opened, from Beira to the south bank of the river.

In 1953 Nyasaland was federated with the Rhodesias, despite African opposition. Six years later the situation became so serious that a state of emergency was declared. Agitation continued, and in 1963 the Central African Federation broke up. Nyasaland, now called Malawi, became independent under the leadership of Dr Hastings Banda (b. 1905) and, in 1966, a republic within the Commonwealth. *See* AFRICA for map.

¶ ROTBERG, ROBERT. *The Rise of Nationalism in Central Africa: the Making of Malawi and Zambia 1873–1964.* 1966

Malaysia: federation of island and mainland independent states in south-east Asia, established in 1963 and numbering in all about ten million inhabitants.

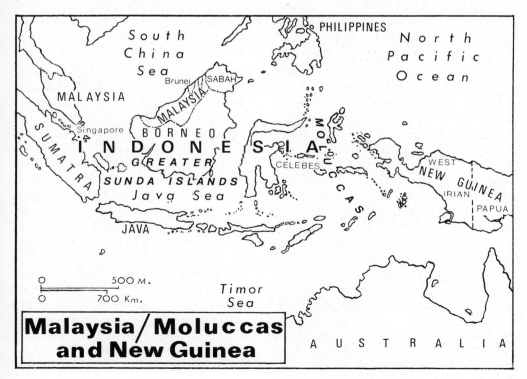

Malaysia/Moluccas and New Guinea

Malays, Chinese and Indians or Pakistanis are the main elements in the population, with Dayaks prominent towards the east. The Chinese tend to increase in numbers and to gain the best jobs. Portuguese and Dutch began to trade and settle in various parts of the present Malaysia during the 16th and 17th centuries. Britain moved into the Straits Settlements (the western area) through the East India Company between 1786 and 1824. This colony was dissolved in 1946. Singapore seceded from the Federation of Malaysia in 1965 and became a republic within the British Commonwealth.

¶ RYAN, N. J. *The Making of Modern Malaysia and Singapore: a history from the earliest times to 1966.* 1970

See also SARAWAK; SINGAPORE.

Mali (formerly **French Sudan**): West African republic bounded in the north by Algeria; east by Niger; south by Upper Volta, the Ivory Coast and Guinea; and in the west by Senegal and Mauritania. In the southern region, irrigated by the upper Niger, cotton, groundnuts, rice, beans, maize and millet are grown. Fish from the Niger find a ready local market, and in the north cattle, sheep, goats and camels are raised by nomadic people, who move on as the grazing is exhausted. Plans are in hand for the damming of the Niger rapids and the building of hydroelectric installations that should enable the development of processing plants for the natural products of the country.

The former colony of the French Sudan comprised Senegambia and Niger. Between 1904 and 1920 it was called Upper Senegal and Niger: then, following various boundary alterations in 1933, 1948 and 1954, the country was granted autonomous republican status within the French community under the name of the Sudanese Republic. In 1959 the country temporarily joined with Senegal in the Mali Federation, leaving this partnership the following year on being granted full independence as the Mali Republic. *See* AFRICA for map.

Malplaquet, Battle of (11 September 1709): the last and most fiercely contested of Marlborough's victories in the War of the Spanish Succession. In this battle, with the help of Prince Eugène, he defeated the French under Villars, who were trying to relieve the siege of Mons.

Malta: island and independent state in the western Mediterranean. Known in ancient times as Melita, Malta has always been of considerable importance. It was colonised by the Phoenicians, the Greeks and the Carthaginians before coming under Roman rule in 201 BC. In AD 60 St Paul was supposedly shipwrecked off the Maltese coast. The island's prosperity declined through successive barbarian invasions, but from 870 to 1090 the Arabs fortified it as a naval base until expelled by Count Roger of Sicily. In the 13th century the island passed from Norman to Angevin rule and subsequently to the rulers of Aragon and Castile. In 1530 Charles V gave Malta to the Knights of St John of Jerusalem in perpetual sovereignty in return for their aid against the Turks. In 1798 the Knights surrendered to Napoleon, but the Maltese accepted British occupation in 1802, and the island became a British possession in 1814. With the opening of the Suez Canal Malta became important as a coaling station, and during the 20th century a vital British air and naval base. In World War II the heroic resistance of the Maltese to constant German and Italian air attack caused George VI to award the George Cross to the island. After the war there were many political crises concerning Malta's constitution; it gained its independence within the Commonwealth in 1964. The running down of Britain's naval dockyard in recent years has brought considerable economic hardship to the island.

See MEDITERRANEAN for map.

¶ BLOUET, BRIAN. *The Story of Malta.* 1972

Mammoths: enormous elephants, now extinct. They resembled the Indian elephant in shape, but their skins were shaggy and their tusks were nine or ten feet long. [3·048 metres]. Mammoths appear to have ranged through northern and central Europe and North America until the end of the Ice Age and were contemporary with early man. The hunters of southern France drew pictures of them on the walls of their caves. In Siberia, USSR, quantities of mammoth ivory have been found. Occasionally, in a warm season, the ice melts to expose a complete mammoth, almost perfectly preserved – and still, apparently, edible.

¶ VEVERS, GWYNNE. *Elephants and Mammoths.* 1968

Manchester: city in Lancashire, England. Manchester grew rapidly in size and importance with the development of the cotton industry in the 19th century. It is now a great commercial centre for the many towns in the area engaged in textiles, chemicals, engineering and atomic energy. Although it is thirty-five miles [56 kilometres] from the sea, the Manchester Ship Canal, which connects the city with the Mersey estuary, makes

The Manchester Ship Canal, Chester to Warrington Section.

Manchester the third largest seaport in Britain. Manchester Airport is the most important in Britain after London. Manchester has a university and some famous libraries.

¶ FRANGOPULO, N. J., editor. *Rich Inheritance: a guide to the history of Manchester.* 1962

Manchuria: historical region of northeastern China. The area had gradually been brought under Chinese rule, but the Mongol invasions of the 13th and 14th centuries partly reversed this process. The Manchus finally conquered China and gave it the imperial dynasty which ruled from 1644 to 1912, joining Manchuria to China until 1932. A frontier with Russia was fixed at the Amur River in 1689. In 1860 China conceded more Manchurian territory to Russia. In 1898, after the Sino-Japanese War of 1894-5, Russia obtained a long lease of the tip of the Liaotung Peninsula, with Port Arthur and Dairen, together with extensive railway rights, administration of territory and substantial trading concessions. With

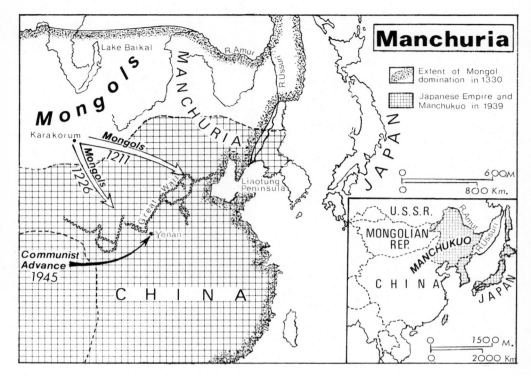

Manchuria

Extent of Mongol domination in 1330

Japanese Empire and Manchukuo in 1939

the close of the Russo-Japanese War in 1905, Russian rights in southern Manchuria were transformed to Japan, which now replaced Russia as the power most dangerous to China. In the disorganisation following the Chinese revolution of 1911, authority in Manchuria was successfully exercised by Chang Tso-lin, a former bandit chief, murdered in 1928. In 1931 Japan occupied Manchuria, setting up in 1932 a new state called Manchukuo, including Jehol and part of Mongolia. This collapsed with the Japanese surrender in 1945 at the close of World War II. Russia regained control of Manchuria, letting it pass, however, to the Chinese People's Republic by the Sino-Russian treaty of 1950 and withdrawing all troops by 1955. In 1969 there were clashes between Russians and Chinese on the Ussuri and Amur frontier rivers, followed by negotiations.
See also CHINA.

Mandarin: name once given by the Portuguese to all public officials of the Chinese empire. The mandarins were an exclusive class selected by severe competitive examination. The word *mandarin* was also applied to the educated Peking dialect of Chinese used for official purposes through the empire.

Mandates: the settlement agreed at Versailles, 1919, and operated under Article 22 of the League of Nations Covenant, of colonial territories taken from Germany and Turkey. Each territory was entrusted to a "Mandatory Power", responsible for developing it in the interests of its native population.

Mandates were of three types (Mandatory Powers in brackets): Class A – Turkish territories, Iraq and Palestine (Great Britain); Syria (France); recognised as provisionally independent, but still requiring assistance.

Class B – German Central African colonies, Tanganyika (Great Britain); Cameroons and Togoland (Great Britian and France); Ruanda (Belgium); mandataries responsible for administration.

Class C – S.W. Africa (South Africa); Samoa (New Zealand); New Guinea (Australia); W. Pacific Islands north of the equator (Japan and Great Britain); under direct rule.

Mandeville, Sir John (14th century): mysterious author of *Travels* which excited Europeans with tales of the Great Khan of Cathay, the Dog-faced People, the Gold-digging Ants and other wonders. Scholars have questioned his existence. A Liège chronicler, Jean d'Outremeuse, reported that Jean de Bourgogne on his deathbed in 1372 revealed himself as Mandeville. The claim of St Albans, England, to his burial place is poorly supported. The *Travels*, concocted from Willian de Boldensele, Odoric, and Albert of Aix's history of the Third Crusade among others, remain a delightful collection of preposterous adventures. The earliest known manuscript, in Paris, is dated 1371.

¶ DENNY, NORMAN and FILMER-SANKEY, JOSEPHINE. *The Travels of Sir John Mandeville.* 1973

Manila: capital of the Philippines in the western Pacific and principal port, industrial and cultural centre of these islands, more than 7,000 in number.

The Spaniards settled at Manila in 1571 and strong Catholic influences were established. Struggles with the Dutch, who also had settlements in the East Indies, spread over the 17th century. The city was captured by the British in 1762 and held for two years, after which it was returned to Spain by treaty.

The Pacific directly links Manila with the USA as it had linked the city with Spain's Mexican possessions. When the USA defeated Spain in 1898 as a result of their quarrel over Cuba, the Philippines (where independence of Spain was being demanded) were transferred to the victors, becoming a republic in 1946.
See also PHILIPPINES.

Mantua: Italian city in the valley of the River Po, sbout seventy-five miles [120 kilometres] from the Adriatic Sea. Its impressive ducal palaces and castles contain fine tapestries and frescoes, some by Andrea Mantegna (1431–1506), who is buried in the Church of St Andrea. The Roman poet Virgil (70–19 BC) was born at Andes, a village in the neighbourhood. Mantua is also the name of the province.

The Castello di San Giorgio, Mantua.

Maori: member of the aboriginal Polynesian race of New Zealand. Europeans who landed after Captain Cook found an advanced Neolithic civilisation, whose members were much given to warfare. Though in 1839 Gibbon Wakefield organised the New Zealand Company for trade and land purchase, the 1840 Treaty of Waitangi guaranteed Maori rights under British rule. The granting of electoral rights and representation in the legislature after the wars of 1860 and 1871 has helped to preserve Maori numbers, skills, customs and traditions. They

553

number about seven per cent of the population of New Zealand and are mainly confined to North Island.

¶ PEARCE, G. L. *The Story of the Maori People.* 1969

A celebration in honour of Mao's re-election as Chairman of the Chinese Communist Party in 1969.

Mao Tse-tung (b. 1893): Chinese statesman and one of the chief founders of the Chinese Communist Party. The son of a yeoman farmer from Hunan, he was greatly influenced by the ideals of Sun Yat-sen (*see* separate entry), and has shown a rare combination of qualities as poet, scholar, political philosopher and guerrilla leader. He organised peasant and industrial unions (1921-26), raised a people's army probably superior to any in China's long history, led the great march from Kiangsi to Yenan (1934-35), and became Chairman of the Central Committee of the Communist Party from 1936. In 1949 he came to virtually supreme power as Chairman of the People's Republic of China when the Kuomintang (or Nationalist Party) under Chiang Kai-shek (*see* separate entry) were driven from the mainland. Although he relinquished the office of Chairman in 1958 he remains the supreme figure in the Republic, not only because of his political stature but through the extraordinary influence of his writings and "thoughts".

In 1966 he launched the Cultural Revolution, which has captured the loyalties of Chinese youth, spread Mao's teachings, kept alive revolutionary fervour and helped the emergence of a new China which can boast, according to an experienced European observer, that every child learns to read and write, and everyone has sufficient to eat.

¶ ROBERTS, E. M. *Mao Tse-tung and the Chinese Communist Revolution.* 1970; ROBOTTOM, J. *Mao Tse' Tung*

Map: from the Latin *mappa*, a tablecloth or napkin; a representation, generally on a plane surface, of the political and physical features of the earth's surface, or part of it, on a greatly reduced scale. Topographical maps show both the artificial and natural features of an area, e.g. roads, railways, telegraphs, canals and towns as well as forests, rivers, highlands and valleys. The one-inch Ordnance Survey maps of the British Isles are excellent examples of the topographical map intended to guide travellers. The so-called cadastral map (from Latin *capistratum*, a register for taxation purposes) is on a larger scale, shows greater details, and is used for management, legal and administrative purposes, since it shows size of fields, boundaries and the like. Many cadastral maps were produced to ease assessments of taxation and were very important in countries like Egypt where the annual Nile floods could easily wipe out boundaries. The general or atlas map has the smallest scale of all. The name "atlas" for a book of maps is supposedly taken from the frontispiece, showing Atlas supporting the earth, of *Atlas: or a Geographical Description of the World* by Gerard Mercator and John Hondt, 1636. A chart is a specialised form of map, of the coast and surrounding areas, showing buoys, soundings, wrecks and lighthouses; or of the ocean.

The oldest existing map is a sketch map

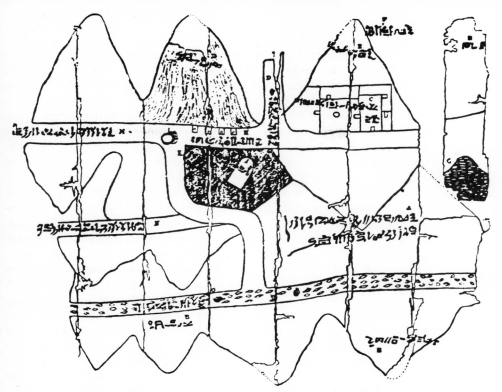

Map of Egyptian gold mine, 1320 BC, the world's oldest existing map.

of access roads to an Egyptian gold mine about 1300 BC. Maps such as those used by Rameses II enabled Eratosthenes (276–194 BC) to measure the distance from Alexandria to Syene by which he estimated the circumference of the earth. The *Geographia* of Claudius Ptolemy, *c.* AD 160, fixed the arrangements of parallels and meridians which form the basis of all map projection. Medieval artists produced maps of biblical, especially Old Testament, stories or ancient myths. Two notable examples are the world map of Mohammed al Idrisi at Palermo, *c.* AD 1150, and the *mappa mundi* of Richard of Haldingham at Hereford, *c.* AD 1300. The monk and chronicler Matthew Paris produced one of the best English maps in about 1250. After 1500 editors of Ptolemy's *Geographia* included up-to-date maps of European countries. Martin Behaim constructed the first modern globe at Nuremberg in 1492.

Excited by stories of the voyages of Amerigo Vespucci, Martin Waldseemüller of Alsace first used the name America on a map in 1507. John Schoner showed many of the new discoveries on paper-covered wooden spheres between 1515 and 1533, and Diego Ribeiro's world map of 1529 gave a reasonably accurate picture of the shape and proportions of the Pacific. Italian publishers, masters of line engraving, dominated map-making to 1570, as the instruments produced at Nuremberg advanced the science of surveying. Flemish craftsmanship and the reputation of Mercator helped to shift the centre of cartography to the Low Countries, and Abraham Ortelius at Antwerp produced the first atlas since Ptolemy, *Theatrum Orbis Terrarum*. The Dutch in turn replaced the Flemings. A map of Asia of 1632 by J. Blaeu is surprisingly accurate, except for the proportions of China, and beautifully illustrated, as are more conventional maps of India in Terry's *A Voyage to East India,* 1655. The English county maps of Christopher Saxton (fl. 1570–96) and John Speed (1552?–1629) are fine examples of artistic craftsmanship. The royal observatories at Greenwich and Paris and Harrison's work on chronometers were of tremendous help in improving the reckoning of longitude, though it was customary to use imagination rather than science to fill empty spaces.

> *Geographers in Afric maps*
> *With savage pictures fill their gaps*
> *And o'er uninhabitable downs*
> *Place elephants for want of towns*
>
> Jonathan Swift

Conventional lettering and signs came generally into use in the 18th century, and towns and physical features began to appear in plan rather than picture. The 18th century, a period of great naval activity, saw a number of mapping achievements, including those of Joseph Desbarres (1722–1824), who published charts of the Atlantic and North American coasts; Thomas Jefferys, whose West Indian and American atlases were published in 1774 and 1778; and James Rennell (1742–1830), the surveyor-general of Bengal, who produced his Bengal Atlas in 1779. With the founding of the English Ordnance Survey towards the end of the 18th century Britain became the best mapped country in the world. During the 19th century almost every other European country completed small-scale maps for their territories.

In 1891 Professor Penck put forward a plan for an International Map of the World (Carte du Monde au Millionème) on a uniform scale – that of one-millionth of nature. The idea made slow progress at first but took a great step forward at the 1908 Geneva Geographical Congress, when the US delegation proposed fixed rules for the production of the map.

Subsequent conferences in Rome, Paris and other centres eventually brought about almost worldwide agreement on this project. *See colour section.*

¶ RAISZ, ERWIN. *Mapping the World.* 1956

Maquis: literally, the Mediterranean coast vegetation, consisting mainly of myrtle, heath, arbutus, rose laurel and oak, but more familiar as the name adopted by the French Resistance Organisation, which carried out guerrilla warfare on the German occupation forces in World War II.

Marat, Jean Paul (1743–93): French revolutionist and member of the Convention, whose inflammatory writings helped to incite the wholesale massacre of political prisoners in September 1792. He was assassinated by Charlotte Corday, who was subsequently guillotined. Marat was described by a contemporary as having "the burning haggard eye of a hyena".

The Death of Marat *painted by Jacques Louis David.*

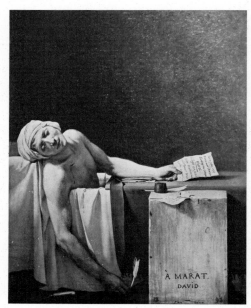

Marathon: district in Attica some twenty miles [32 kilometres] north-east of Athens, where the Greeks defeated the Persian invaders in 490 BC. Meanwhile Pheidippides had set out on his 150-mile [240-kilometre] run to summon aid from Sparta, which he accomplished in two days: from this the term "Marathon Race" is derived. *See also* PERSIAN WARS.

Marconi, Guglielmo (1874-1937): Italian pioneer of radio communication. Born in Bologna, the son of an Italian father and an Irish mother, he was educated in Bologna and Florence, later studying physics under Vincenzo Rosa at Leghorn. He began his experiments in Italy but in 1896 came to London, where the chief engineer of the Post Office gave him facilities for his work. In December 1901 he succeeded in transmitting signals across the Atlantic from Poldhu in Cornwall to St John's, Newfoundland, and, in September 1918, sent the first wireless message from England to Australia. He was a Nobel prize-winner in 1906.

¶ READE, L. *Marconi and the Discovery of Wireless.* 1963

Marengo, Battle of (14 June 1800): defeat of the Austrians by the French under Napoleon Bonaparte in the course of his campaign in northern Italy. Napoleon's white charger which frequently carried him in his later campaigns was named after this important success in his early career.

Maria Theresa (1717-80): Empress of Austria. Despite her importance in the Europe of her time, Maria Theresa seems to have been overshadowed by her archenemy Frederick the Great of Prussia. To maintain her position in face of the hostility of, among others, Prussia and France, she fought the War of Austrian Succession, losing Silesia to Prussia. Maria Theresa gained by participating in the 1772 partition of Poland, and allied Austria with France, marrying her daughter Marie-Antoinette to the future Louis XVI. In overhauling the government of her Empire, she carried out what one historian calls "a political, constitutional and administrative revolution".

Marie-Antoinette (1755-93): queen of France and wife of Louis XVI. A woman of "elevated manner, lofty demeanour and graces of deportment", rather than the physical beauty with which she is often credited, she became intensely unpopular as the centre of reactionary opinion at the French court and of intrigue with foreign powers in an effort to suppress the Revolution. She was imprisoned in 1792 and executed soon after her husband. Though the remark *"Qu'ils mangent la brioche"* ("Let them eat cake") is usually attributed to her when she was told that her people were without bread, the saying is at least 700 years older.

Marie Feodorovna (1847-1928): Empress of Russia 1881-94. The daughter of

557

Christian IX of Denmark, she was happily married to Tsar Alexander III. The Tsarina played no part in politics, other than attempting to warn her son Nicholas II against the influence of Rasputin. She endeared herself to the Russian people by her active interest in philanthropy and education. Visiting England in 1914 (her sister Alexandra married Edward VII) she returned to Russia at the outbreak of war and worked for the Red Cross. The Bolsheviks allowed her to live under close guard in the Crimea, where she remained throughout the German occupation, not choosing to leave Russia until the Armistice of 1918.
See also NICHOLAS II; RASPUTIN.

Marines: soldiers trained for fighting at sea as well as on land. In Great Britain, an Order in Council dated 16 October 1664 authorised 1,200 soldiers to be raised and formed into one regiment for sea service. In 1684 the third regiment of the line was called the Marine Regiment. In 1698 two further marine regiments were raised, and from then onwards the "sea soldiers" became an integral part of the Royal Navy. In 1704 a detachment was landed from Admiral Rooke's ships and played a prominent part in the capture of Gibraltar.

In 1755 the sweeping reforms of Admiral Lord Anson brought the marines under the direct control of the Admiralty, and they were grouped into three divisions at Chatham, Portsmouth and Devonport for training purposes. While afloat they performed the same duties as the seamen, but in action their specialised training adapted them for small arms fighting and landing on enemy shores.

In 1802 the prefix "Royal" was granted in recognition of their fidelity during the naval mutinies. In 1855 they were divided into light infantry and artillery sections and remained as such until 1923, when they became a single force.

In the 20th century the Royal Marines continue to serve ashore and afloat but during World War II and subsequently their primary functions have included the provision of commando units, landing craft crews, special boat sections (frogmen) and detachments for amphibious operations. The corps also provides bands for HM ships and shore establishments.

The United States Marine Corps was founded in 1795, when it consisted of two battalions to assist in the defence of the colonies. Its original organisation and training were modelled on that of Britain and it has remained an integral part of the US naval service, with its headquarters in Washington, where the commandant's house dates from 1805 and captured flags from various battles are on permanent display. Its defined function is "to support the fleet or any part thereof in the accomplishment of its mission"; and in fulfilment of this role the Marine Corps has played a vital part in every war in which the United States has been involved and has also participated in the peacetime occupation of foreign countries, as well as providing routine guards for naval installations, US legations abroad, etc.

Some twenty other countries maintain similar marine organisations.

Marionettes: puppets controlled by strings. The name may come from an Italian word, *morio,* meaning "fool" or "buffoon" or from the French *Mariolettes,* small figures of the Virgin Mary. The former derivation is more likely, because the Italians have always loved both marionettes and puppets.

There is a difference. Puppets are manipulated from below, either by the operator's fingers as glove puppets or by means of rods which can be pushed and pulled to move the figure. Punch and Judy are puppets. Marionettes, on the other hand, are made to move by means of strings or wires attached to the jointed limbs of the dolls, which may be made from wood,

Above : Marionette theatre featuring the favourite characters of the Italian Comedie del' Arte. Below : the strings are pulled by the puppeteer standing behind and above the puppet stage.

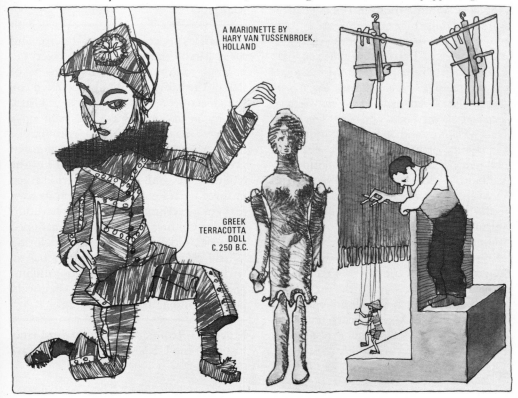

A MARIONETTE BY HARY VAN TUSSENBROEK, HOLLAND

GREEK TERRACOTTA DOLL C. 250 B.C.

wax or plaster. The wires are fastened to thin slats, by moving which the operator can make the marionettes nod, walk or dance.

Marionettes have been found in Egyptian tombs. Greek children played with them. In India and China their shadows, enlarged on to a screen, entertained audiences for generations.

In 16th century England marionette plays of biblical stories were popular. In 1667 Samuel Pepys mentioned a performance of "a puppet play of Patient Grizel", but his puppets were really marionettes, and so was the familiar Pinocchio, who sings "There are no strings on me".

Sicilians still love marionettes. In Palermo there is a marionette theatre where traditional stories from the life of Charlemagne are performed. The figures are quite large – about two feet high [5·08 centimetres] – and heavy. The favourite characters are Roland, Oliver, Turpin and Angelica, and the modern audience gleefully applauds their adventures.

Marlowe, Christopher (1564–93): Elizabethan dramatist. His best known plays are *The Troublesome Reign and Lamentable Death of Edward the Second, Tamburlane the Great* and *The Tragedy of Doctor Faustus*; and, in his finest moments, the beauty of his verse equals, if it does not excel, that of his contemporary William Shakespeare (1564–1616). "Sweet Kit Marlowe", as he was known to his friends, died young, as the result of a drunken quarrel.

¶ HENDERSON, P. *Christopher Marlow*. 1952

Marne: river of northern France, the scene of two decisive battles in World War I. The first was fought in September 1914, when an Anglo-French counter-offensive relieved German pressures on Paris; the second, in July-August 1918,

saw the final German attempt to break through on the western front defeated by the Allies.

Marrakesh or **Marrakech:** one of the four chief towns of Morocco on the north-west side of the High Atlas mountains, and at one time capital of the Moorish Empire. It lies 158 miles [254 kilometres] south-south-west of Casablanca, present capital of Morocco. Founded in the year 1062, Marrakesh reached its heyday in the 14th century. Though much of the ancient town is in decay, modern buildings are rising in and around it, and there are important carpet, textile, leather and food-producing industries.

Marseillaise: the French national anthem, introduced during the French Revolution. It was composed in 1792 by Rouget de Lisle, an army officer, and brought to Paris by soldiers from Marseilles.

Marseilles: second city of France and great Mediterranean port, just over 530 miles [853 kilometres] south-south-east of Paris. Probably originally peopled by Phoenicians, *Massalia* became a Greek colony in about 600 BC and built up a chain of dependencies and commercial links. After a period of decline, the town grew in importance again during the Middle Ages and was at one period ruled in three separate units, each with its own form of government and its own harbour. Most of the medieval buildings, grouped round the old port, were destroyed during World War II. The present city has an ancient university (founded 1409) and important industries, including chemicals, petrol refining and shipbuilding.

Marshall, John (1755–1835): third chief justice of the USA. After taking an active part in the American revolution, he attended law lectures at William and Mary College and was admitted to the Bar in 1783. Marshall was a delegate to the state convention which ratified the Federal Constitution. He declined the position of Attorney General when it was offered to him by George Washington in 1795, but was appointed the chief justice of the US Supreme Court in 1801. His thirty-four years on the bench built up the prestige and power of the court, and he established much important legal precedent by his interpretations of the constitution.

Marshall Plan: name given to the programme launched by US Secretary of State George C. Marshall on 5 June 1947 in an address at Harvard University in which he declared that US policy was directed "not against any country or doctrine but against hunger, poverty, desperation and chaos. Its purpose should be the revival of a working economy in the world so as to permit the emergence of political and social conditions in which free institutions can exist." The plan was primarily designed, by the provision of money and materials, to help the recovery of Europe after the ravages of World War II, but the USSR and the other members of the Eastern Bloc refused to participate.

Martinique: French possession in the Windward Islands group of the West Indies. Its most spectacular feature is Mont Pelée, which erupted in 1902 killing 30,000 people.

Columbus discovered the island in 1502, but settlement by Europeans did not occur until 1637 when the French took it. Martinique figured in the piratical activities of English, Dutch and French during the 17th century but became recognised in 1814 as a possession of France, on whom the island depends for some foods, oil and textiles in exchange for sugar, cotton and fruits. Slavery was abolished in 1848.

Martinique became one of the French overseas departments in 1946.
See CARIBBEAN for map.

Martyrs: those who die for their faith. The term is chiefly used of Christian martyrs and is derived from a Greek word meaning "witness".

The early years of the Church, before it won recognition from the rulers of the Roman Empire, saw the great period of martyrdom. St Stephen was stoned to death very shortly after Jesus had left the earth, and St Peter and St Paul, though not chiefly remembered as martyrs, both suffered death for their faith. The first British martyr was St Alban, who perished during the reign (284–305) of the Emperor Diocletian, which was marked by particularly intense persecutions, though mass martyrdoms occur through history, an instance being the crucifixion of twenty-six Japanese converts of the Jesuits at Nagasaki in 1597.

Section from a medieval panel showing the Martyrdom of Saints.

The Roman Catholic Church continues to this day to bestow sainthood upon its martyrs, though these are not of course its only saints; and the process, known as canonisation, in the case of those who died for their faith in England in the 16th and early 17th centuries is now nearly completed.

The Church of England has never adopted the practice of canonisation, but it holds in reverence those who died for the Reformed Faith in the reign (1553-8) of Queen Mary I, while for many years the Prayer Book made provision for commemorating King Charles the Martyr on the anniversary of his execution (30 January 1649), and there are five churches in England dedicated to him.

Marx, Karl (1818-83): the founder of communism. Born of a German-Jewish family, Marx took up the ideas of revolutionary socialism as a young man, and in collaboration with Engels he set these out in the so-called *Communist Manifesto*, published in 1848. In 1849 he went as a political exile to London, where

Karl Marx.

he spent the rest of his life in near-poverty, relying largely on Engels's support. His most important work was *Das Kapital*, a study of English capitalist society, which with his other works constitutes the "bible" of communism in the 20th century.

Marx interpreted history in terms of economics and the constant struggle of the working classes to secure a better future in the face of capitalist oppression, which he saw as doomed to be overthrown. It was the duty of the workers to hasten this overthrow by every means in their power, especially the strike. His most famous cry, from the *Manifesto* of 1848 was: "The workers have nothing to lose in this world but their chains. Workers of the world, unite!"

¶ KETTLE, A. *Karl Marx.* 1963

Masaryk, Jan Garrigue (1886-1948): Czechoslovak statesman, son of Czechoslovakia's first president. In 1940, after varied diplomatic experience, he became foreign secretary of the Czechoslovak government-in-exile in London, and through frequent broadcasts to his German-occupied country he was a popular choice as foreign secretary after the liberation. Communist pressure made his job increasingly difficult, though he did not resign immediately when the Communists seized power, with Russian support, on 25 February 1948. But on 10 March his body was found under the window of his room at the foreign office, suicide being alleged.

¶ In LARSEN, EGON. *Men Who Fought for Freedom.* 1958

Mason-Dixon Line: boundary line between Pennsylvania and Maryland, USA. In the early days of the establishment of British colonies there were frequent boundary disputes. Perhaps the most contentious of these concerned the boundary between the colonies of Mary-

THE **Mason-Dixon** LINE

Mathematical instruments: early mathematical instruments arose from the practical needs of building and surveying. Simple dividers for dividing lines and angles, and compasses for drawing circles, were of very early origin. On the tomb of a Roman surveyor we find represented the isosceles triangle with a plumb line from the vertex, a square resembling the ordinary carpenter's square, and an object resembling the set square of angles 30, 60 and 90 degrees. With such simple tools the glories of Gothic architecture were achieved.

land and Pennsylvania. It ended in 1767, when the English astronomers Charles Mason and Jeremiah Dixon carried out a survey and plotted the boundary between the two colonies. Later this line took on a larger significance as the boundary between the free states of the North and the slave-owning states of the South.

Perhaps the best known of all early instruments was the astrolabe (*see* separate entry). Although the name is Greek (meaning the taking of the stars), it is thought that the Greeks derived their knowledge of the instrument from the Near East, whence it also spread to China and India. It has been described as the oldest scientific instrument in the world.

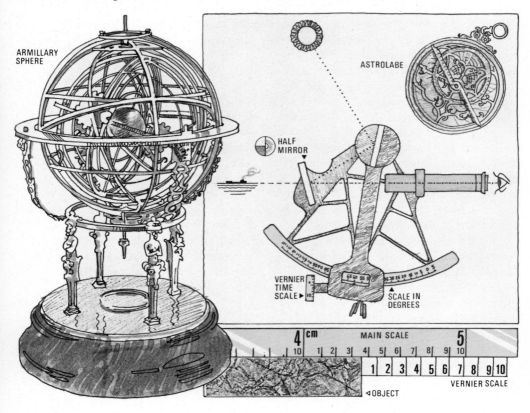

ARMILLARY SPHERE

ASTROLABE

HALF MIRROR

VERNIER TIME SCALE ▶

SCALE IN DEGREES

cm   MAIN SCALE

VERNIER SCALE

◀ OBJECT

It was used in various ways for measuring angles, although its most important applications were in astronomy and also in navigation. There were several types, of which the simplest was the planisphere. This consisted of a circular disc, the circumference of which was marked off in degrees. Attached to the centre of the disc were two movable arms, which could be sighted on distant objects. Another form was the armillary sphere, a three-dimensional version. This got its name from the armillae, or rings, which were arranged concentrically but at right angles to each other. There were usually two, but sometimes three, such circular rings. One ring corresponded with the plane of the equator and the other with the plane of the meridian. The ancient astronomer Ptolemy describes this instrument. Chaucer also wrote a treatise on its use, and a magnificent astrolabe, now to be seen in the British Museum, may have been used by him.

Closely related to the astrolabe was the quadrant, which, as the name implies, used only a quarter of a circle. The protractor, now part of every young student's set of instruments, is obviously of the same derivation, although the date of its appearance is uncertain. One authority gives the date as 1658.

The sextant is said to have originated with Newton, following his invention of the reflecting microscope in 1672, but it was rediscovered by John Hadley in 1731, and it is from this date that its use as a navigational instrument begins.

A device now widely used on micrometer gauges, barometers, cathetometers, theodolites, sextants, telescopes, etc., was invented by the French mathematician Pierre Vernier (1580–1637). Known simply as a Vernier, this is a small auxiliary scale made to slide along the main fixed scale of an instrument, thus enabling smaller intervals to be measured.

A whole range of new mathematical instruments began in 1814 when the first planimeter, a device for measuring an area bounded by an irregular curve, was invented. An instrument much used by engineers is the slide-rule, which, by using the logarithmic scales sliding alongside each other, enables multiplication, division and other mathematical processes to be carried out very quickly.

See also NEWTON, SIR ISAAC; PTOLEMY.

Matthias I Hunyadi or **Matthias Corvinus** (*c.* 1440–90): King of Hungary 1458–90 and of Bohemia 1478–90. Matthias was not crowned King of Hungary until 1464, following a long struggle with the Turks, Bohemia, the Empire and dissenting Hungarian factions. Almost perpetually at war, he was a fine military leader and strategist. In 1468 he conquered Moldavia and Wallachia. In 1478 he made peace with Bohemia, gaining Moravia, Silesia and Lusatia. He captured Vienna, subsequently his capital, and Lower Austria in 1485. A great diplomat, administrator and legislator, his capacity for work rivalled that of Napoleon I. He was a patron of learning, founding the University of Budapest and bequeathing an extensive library.

Mau Mau: secret society in Kenya, drawn mainly from Kikuyu people. A terrorist rising, aimed at driving out white settlers, began in 1952. In the following seven-year struggle more than 2,000 African civilians on both sides were killed, as well a much smaller number of Europeans and Asian civilians. Jomo Kenyatta (b. *c.* 1893), though he has since denied that he was a Mau Mau leader, was imprisoned by the British from 1953 to 1959. With the achievement of Kenyan independence in 1963, little has been heard of the society. Kenyatta is now president of the republic of Kenya.

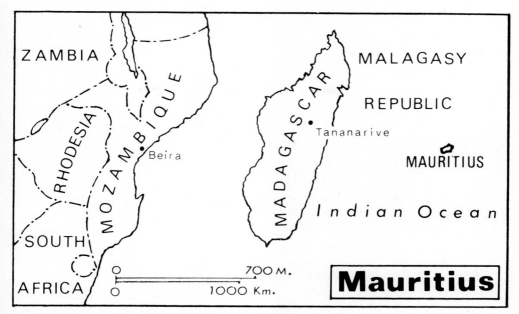

ZAMBIA

RHODESIA

MOZAMBIQUE

Beira

SOUTH

AFRICA

MADAGASCAR

Tananarive

MALAGASY

REPUBLIC

MAURITIUS

Indian Ocean

700 M.

1000 Km.

Mauritius

Mauritius: independent island in the Indian Ocean forming part of the Commonwealth and occupied mainly by former Indian immigrants, with African, European and Chinese minorities. It may well have been visited by Arab traders in the Middle Ages and by Portuguese later, but it became a French possession under the name "Ile de France" in 1715 and still partly maintains the French language and traditions. Being on the route to India the island became a bone of contention between Britain and France until the former seized it in 1810. Cholera, malaria and other epidemics, and cyclones, have caused periods of devastation. Permanent prosperity has been supplied mainly by sugar export.

Maximilian I (1459-1519): King of Germany 1486-1519, Holy Roman Emperor 1493-1519. Attempting to revive the old glories of the medieval Empire, Maximilian caused considerable disorder. However, he carried out military reforms, established the *Reichskammergericht* (Imperial Court of Justice) and patronised the arts. By the marriages arranged for his family the Habsburgs gained vast possessions. Maximilian married Mary, heiress of Burgundy; Philip, their son, married the heiress of Spain; Ferdinand, Maximilian's grandson, married the heiress of Hungary and Bohemia. All these territories were ultimately ruled by Maximilian's grandson Charles V (*see* separate entry).

Maximilian (1832-67): Emperor of Mexico. He was the son of Archduke Charles and brother of Francis Joseph (1830-1916), Emperor of Austria. In the early 1860s Mexico was torn by civil wars, one side being supported by the northern states of USA, the other by the southern states and by Napoleon III, Emperor of France (*see* separate entry). The latter in 1864 persuaded Maximilian to accept the throne of Mexico; but, despite the backing of French troops, later withdrawn, his attempts ended in failure. He was captured and executed by the republicans. His widow became insane but lived until 1927.

May Day: ancient spring festival held on 1 May when people decorated their houses with flowers, danced around the maypole and crowned the May Queen. The festival still survives in some country districts. In most countries of Europe 1 May is now celebrated as Labour Day.

A Mayan carving showing a penitent kneeling before a priest, approximately 709 AD.

Mayan civilisation: an early but advanced civilisation of Central America. The first great cities were on the plains of northern Guatemala, but these were abruptly abandoned during the 6th century BC, the population moving to Yucatan and the highlands of southern Mexico and Guatemala. By AD 1100 a stable civilisation was established under three princely houses, Itza, Xia and Cocom, who dominated the area for two centuries. Thereafter there were three centuries of intermittent civil war, and when the Spaniards arrived they found complete political disorder.

In its earliest known period the Mayan culture had reached a high level. There was writing in a hieroglyphic script and a calendar. Great skill was shown in architecture, stone carving, pottery and textile work. But iron was not known, nor was the principle of the wheel. The great buildings were constructed from unmortared blocks of stone, mostly small, though in a few cases very large blocks were used, and one of the *stelae* (columns) is a single block measuring twenty-five feet [7.62 metres] from the ground. The builders used stone implements for quarrying, facing and carving, and they were ignorant of the principle of the true arch. Many of the buildings were pyramids, not tombs as in Egypt but serving as the bases of high altars.

Religion appears to have been the worship of the forces of nature, with a superior creator god, Quetzalcoatl, whose early emblem was a feathered serpent, which later became a man with serpent and bird characteristics. Human sacrifice probably did not occur in early times but was introduced later from the Aztecs.

¶ GALLENKAMP, CHARLES. *Finding out about the Maya.* 1963

"Mayflower": ship that carried the English Puritans or Pilgrim Fathers to establish a settlement in North America in 1620. Few details are known of the original *Mayflower* but the vessel is assumed to have been a small merchantman of about 180 tons [183 tonnes] and 90 feet [27.4 metres]. The three masts carried square sails on the fore and main and a lateen sail on the mizzen. Steering was by whipstaff. Captain Christopher

A modern replica of the Mayflower *prepares to sail from Plymouth to America.*

Jones sailed *Mayflower* from Southampton, but bad weather forced him into Dartmouth and Plymouth. He finally cleared Plymouth on 16 September 1620 with 102 souls on board. Landfall was made near Plymouth, Massachusetts, on 21 November. *Mayflower* returned to England in 1621.

Mazarin, Jules (Giulio Mazarini, 1602–61): Italian-born French statesman and cardinal. His enemy Cardinal de Retz said, "his strength was to listen. . . . He had brains, an insinuating manner, cheerfulness, style, but his shabby mind spoilt it all." Others commented on his lack of vanity and his immense capacity for work. He became chief minister of France in 1642, extended France's territorial limits and created a powerful central administration, though his policies considerably depleted the royal finances of Louis XIII and XIV.

Mazzini, Giuseppi (1805–72): Italian patriot. Born in Genoa, he founded in 1831 "Young Italy", a revolutionary movement dedicated to the achievement of a united Italian republic. Exiled to Marseilles, then to London, he continued his campaign, returning to Italy in 1848. He helped to set up the short-lived Roman Republic, but with the defeat of the revolutionaries was again exiled. While Cavour and Garibaldi worked to establish the kingdom of Italy, Mazzini remained a strong republican. He was undoubtedly the prophet of a free Italy, as well as an inspiration, through his writings, to liberals in Europe and America.

See also GARIBALDI; ITALY, etc.

Measurement: the science known more academically as metrology. Before we begin to measure anything we must first fix a suitable unit of measurement. Measures of length in early times were largely derived from the human body. Perhaps the most familiar of these, the cubit, was the length of the ulna, or forearm; hence we obtain the English ell and the French *aune*. The cubit was used in ancient Egypt and Babylonia and occurs frequently in the Old Testament. The foot was originally, of course, the length of the human foot. This varied widely from place to place, ranging from the Italian foot of about 275 millimetres to the Olympic foot of 320 millimetres. We read in an early manuscript that the English foot was obtained by selecting "a mickle man, a muckle man and a middling man" and taking the average length of their feet. Both Greeks and Romans used the fingerbreadth and the palm (four fingerbreadths). The fathom was the length of the extended arms, the mile (from *mille*) a thousand double paces. In ancient India the finger was also used but was subdivided into eight breadths of a *yava* or barleycorn. The word "yard" is said to be derived from the Anglo-Saxon *gyrd* (a rod or stick). Its origin can be seen in the method still used for a rough measurement of a length of material, by holding it at arm's length and taking the length from there to the ear as one yard;

hence the "cloth yard shaft" of the English archers. An old chronicle tells us of Henry I "that there might be no abuse in measures, he ordained a measure made by the length of his own arm, which is called a yard". The daily routine of the countryman provided the furlong (the furrow long), the distance the oxen could plough, before they were given a rest, and turned round for the return journey. The acre is thought to have been derived from a morning's ploughing, the cattle being put out to pasture in the afternoon. The continental *morgen* is similarly derived, although in Holland this was about two acres [0·8 hectares], while in Prussia, Norway and Denmark it was about two-thirds of an acre [0·3 hectares].

The origin of the gallon as a unit of volume is obscure. The present British gallon of 277·42 cubic inches was adopted in 1824, replacing two different units, the ale gallon of 282 cubic inches and the wine gallon of 231 cubic inches. The quart is merely the quarter of a gallon. The gill was also a wine measure, derived from the French *gille* or *gelle*.

Another fundamental process of measurement, weighing, is very old. The first weights so far discovered date from about 3400 BC in Egypt, and the wall pictures of the temples show simple balances, usually held in the hand. The shekel (about a quarter of an ounce) was an ancient unit of weight of the Babylonians, and of the Phoenicians and the Hebrews. It was also a silver coin of this weight, and in Exodus we read: "This they shall give, every one that passeth among them that are numbered, half a shekel after the shekel of the sanctuary . . . an half shekel shall be the offering of the Lord." This quotation is also interesting in that it shows that the standard shekel was kept in the Temple.

In ancient Rome the pound was the unit of weight. This was divided into twelve parts (*unciae*); hence the derivation of the

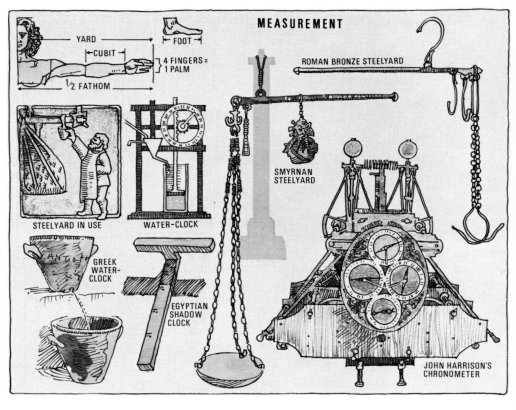

MEASUREMENT

YARD
CUBIT
½ FATHOM
FOOT
4 FINGERS = 1 PALM

ROMAN BRONZE STEELYARD

SMYRNAN STEELYARD

STEELYARD IN USE

WATER-CLOCK

GREEK WATER-CLOCK

EGYPTIAN SHADOW CLOCK

JOHN HARRISON'S CHRONOMETER

word "ounce". In Troy weight there are still twelve ounces in the pound. This system came from the French town of Troyes and is thought to have been introduced by foreign merchants who attended the fairs which played such a prominent part in the commercial life of the Middle Ages. It was probably introduced into England soon after 1250. Troy weight was ultimately replaced by Avoirdupois for most purposes, Troy weight being restricted to the trade of the Goldsmiths. Avoirdupois seems to have been of Spanish origin and to have reached England about 1300. By Elizabeth I's time we are told that "Haberdepoyse is the more usual weight".

When the British Houses of Parliament were destroyed by fire in 1834 the standard pound and the standard yard were lost, and this led to a more scientific definition of them. The new standard yard was manufactured in 1845. The Weights and Measures Act of 1878 defines it as the distance at 62° Fahrenheit between two lines engraved on gold studs embedded in a bronze bar. The pound is defined as the weight *in vacuo* of a cylinder of pure platinum about 1·15 inches [43 millimetres] in diameter and 1·35 inches [50 millimetres] high.

All the units of measurement so far mentioned are of a purely arbitrary nature, but during the 18th century the idea of a "natural" unit became popular. What we now know as the metric system originated from a report made to the French National Assembly by the Paris Academy of Sciences in 1791. As early as 1670 Gabriel Mouton, the vicar of St Paul's Church, Lyons, had proposed as the basic unit of length the length of one second of arc along a great circle of the earth. The unit now decided upon was the metre, which was to be one ten-millionth part of a quarter of a meridian. For this purpose a careful survey was made of the meridian

from Dunkirk to Barcelona, and a platinum bar, the standard metre, was constructed. As it turned out, the measurement was not quite accurate owing to an error in finding the latitude of Barcelona, but the standard as first constructed was not altered. The metre, therefore, is in fact just as arbitrary as the other units we have mentioned. The unit of mass was the gramme, defined as the mass of one cubic centimetre of pure water at the temperature of 4° Centigrade, the temperature at which water attains its maximum density. This new system only gradually replaced the old one and was not made compulsory in France until 1840.

In 1875 the International Bureau of Weights and Measures was established at Sèvres, on land ceded by the French government and declared by them to be international territory. The first task of the Bureau was to construct new standards for the metre and the kilogram and to distribute them to the nations supporting the work. In 1960 an International Conference in Paris adopted a new definition of the metre in terms of the wave length of light. The metric system is now the most widely used system of units.

It is perhaps difficult in these days of standardisation and careful inspection of weights and measures to realise the wide diversity and inaccuracy which once prevailed. To quote only one example, in France, before the introduction of the metric system, there were nearly four hundred different ways of measuring land.

Finally, a brief mention must be made of the measurement of time. Ancient peoples usually divided the day and the night each into twelve equal parts, so that what we should call the hour varied in length from season to season. The earliest method of measuring time was the sundial. This seems to have been first used in Egypt, and Herodotus tells us that it was introduced into Greece from Babylon. It is also thought that the circular rows of stones set up by the Druids were used to mark the sun's path, and to indicate the times and seasons. The need to tell the time at night or when the sun was obscured by clouds gave rise to various other devices, such as the hourglass and the clepsydra (or water clock), while King Alfred is said to have used wax candles enclosed in a horn lantern. Clocks appear to have been introduced in Europe during the 13th century. Salisbury Cathedral has one dating from 1386 and Wells Cathedral one dating from 1392. These were not originally pendulum clocks. The pendulum clock was the invention of Huygens in 1657. Reliable clocks and watches also played a large part in the determination of the longitude of a ship at sea, and in 1714 John Harrison (*see* separate entry) devised a chronometer which won him a prize of £20,000 from the British government. The most modern development in accurate time measurement is the quartz crystal clock, in which a quartz crystal, kept in a state of electrical vibration, replaces the pendulum.

¶ HOGBEN, LANCELOT. *The Wonderful World of Mathematics.* 1968

Mecca: the birthplace of Mohammed (*c.* AD 507) and the most sacred city of Islam. It lies in Arabia about forty-five miles [72 kilometres] from the port of Jidda on the Red Sea and is visited by more than 200,000 pilgrims each year. No non-Mohammedan may enter it.

Medici, Family of: as a personal name, properly written in the Italian form, de' Medici. The family was centred in Florence, but wielded a significant influence over Italian and European history for over three centuries.

It is first found about the year 1200 engaged in the business of banking, on which its fortunes were founded. It is said that the three golden balls which used to hang over the doors of pawnbrokers' shops were taken from the Medici coat-of-arms. Another tradition of the family was that of combining personal wealth and power with sympathy for the cause of the common people.

The greatest days of the family were in the times of Cosimo the Elder (1389–1464), his son Piero (1416–69) and the latter's son Lorenzo the Magnificent (1449–92). Not that these were untroubled years in an age of plottings and jealousies, especially on the part of those opposed to the popular cause. Piero is remarkable for having forgiven those who conspired to take his life; but the vengeance of the people on those responsible for the murder of Giuliano, Lorenzo's brilliant brother, was so savage that Sixtus IV (Pope 1471–84), who was thought by some to have had knowledge of the plot, put Florence for a time under an interdict. During all this period the Medici were virtually lords of Florence, though they rejected any grandiose or formal titles. They introduced a number of enlightened reforms and were generous patrons of scholars and artists, among the latter the painter Botticelli (1444–1570).

The years that followed the death of Lorenzo were a troubled time for Florence and the other states of Italy, but the period saw two of the family become Popes: first Giovanni de' Medici (1475–1521), the second son of Lorenzo, elected Pope in 1513 as Leo X, and second Giulio (1478–1534), the son of Lorenzo's murdered

In the central courtyard of the great mosque in Mecca, stands the Sacred Black Stone believed to have been built by the patriarch Abraham and his son Ishmael.

THE MEDICI FAMILY:
Top row from left to right, Cosimo I, Piero, Lorenzo, called the Magnificent. Left Giuliano, and right Giulio who became Pope Clement VII. Bottom row left to right, Alessandro, Marie and Catherine de Medici.

brother, who became Pope as Clement VII in 1523 and was a patron of Michelangelo and other artists.

Meanwhile, towards the end of this period, Alessandro de' Medici (1511–37), a bastard son of the family, whose parentage is debated, became Duke of Florence in 1532, and with his death the headship of the line passed to another branch of the Medici, which brought about a revival of the power and influence of Florence and in 1569 earned from Pope Pius V the enhanced title of Grand Duke of Tuscany for the head of the family. In somewhat reduced prestige the last grand duke died in 1737, and his sister soon afterwards bequeathed all the Medici treasures to Florence.

It remains to mention two ladies of the family who became queens – and, for a time, regents – of France, where the name is usually spelt de Médicis: Catherine (1519–89), who married Henri II, and Marie (1573–1642), wife of Henri IV and mother of Henrietta Maria, the queen of Charles I of England.

¶ ALLEN, E. *The Story of Lorenzo the Magnificent.* 1961; CHAMBERLIN, E. R. *Florence in the Time of the Medici.* 1972

Medicine: The Egyptians, Greeks and Romans held practitioners of medicine in great respect. In Egypt, Imhotep was said to be the "father of medicine" and was worshipped as a god. Egyptian doctors were priests, and so also were many of the Greek doctors. There was an early link between medicine and religion, and both were revered by ordinary people as mysteries not fully understood by the layman.

In about 400 BC Hippocrates, a Greek physician, founded a school of medicine. He and other doctors exchanged ideas and examined theories of treatment in a scientific manner. Hippocrates taught his pupils the importance of observing and recording the symptoms of disease, and he held that it was impossible to treat one part of the body without some understanding of the functioning of all the other parts. Presentday graduates in medicine still take the oath ascribed to Hippocrates (*see* separate entry), known as the Hippocratic Oath, which regulates medical ethics.

Roman doctors worked in a similar way, and many gained considerable experience while serving as army surgeons with the legions. Some could even supply artificial limbs of wood or ivory to soldiers who had lost an arm or a leg in battle. In the later days of the Roman Empire the city of Rome became greatly overcrowded, and epidemics of typhus and other diseases swept the poorer districts. When Christianity became the official religion of the Empire, public doctors were paid by the state to attend the poor.

The knowledge of medicine declined in Europe after the fall of Rome, although it still flourished in the eastern Empire, kept alive by the Arabs, who trained skilful doctors. In the centuries of warfare and tribal movement which followed the collapse of Roman rule, formal medical training disappeared in Europe, and attempts to cure disease became a matter of charms, spells and magic. In this the Church did little to help, often looking upon illness as being the will of God, inflicted as a punishment for wrongdoing or as a test of faith. Moreover, interest in the body was held by many to be sinful, so that anatomical study was discouraged. In these circumstances, curative medicine became a hit-or-miss affair, usually practised by unskilled persons having a little knowledge of the use of herbs. It is possible that the medieval practice of smearing open wounds with cobwebs and decaying matter could have been the forerunner of penicillin.

One result of the Crusades was the infiltration into Europe of Arabic medical knowledge. Early in the 13th century a medical school was established at Salerno in Italy, where a student had to study for five years and then serve for a period under a recognised physician before he could claim the degree of doctor. But even these men, though they were scholars, remained very ignorant of the internal structure of the human body. It was impossible, for obvious reasons, to study a living body, and the Church forbade the dissection of a dead one, in the belief that it would be rejected at the Resurrection.

It was not until the Renaissance that any serious anatomical study began, initiated by Italian artists who felt that they needed a complete understanding of what they were drawing. Doctors seized this opportunity to make anatomical dissections, and the knowledge thus gained increased their competence. An Italian surgeon, Andreas Vesalius of Padua, was the true founder of modern medicine. He published a book entitled *The Fabric of the Human Body*, which he illustrated with woodcuts full of anatomical detail. Students flocked to his lectures; his audience at the University of Pisa was so great that on one occasion the specially built operating theatre collapsed.

In England and France, although Vesalius's book was studied, there was little development in medical research until the 17th century. Physicians belonged to a trade guild, surgeons were also barbers, and scientific research was of interest to any cultured gentleman. In November 1666 Samuel Pepys mentioned in his diary that he witnessed an experiment when the blood of one dog was let into the body of another, and the following year he saw a "frantic man" who had been calmed by a transfusion of blood from a sheep.

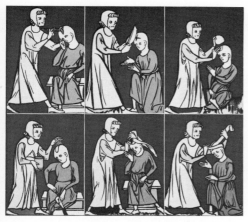

Above: an operation for trepanning in the 13th century, using the ancient Egyptian method. Below: an apothecary's shop in the 15th century.

Above: blood transfusions as practised in the 17th century. Below: a surgical operation in the early days of antiseptic surgery, mid-19th century.

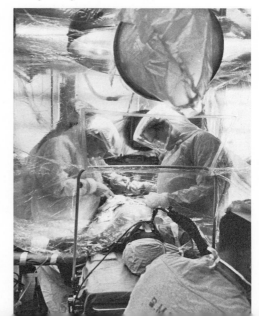

Below: modern germ-free surgery takes place in a vinyl tent filled with sterilized air.

Below: 16th century method of "cauterisation" (sealing a wound with a hot iron).

In 18th century England the world of medicine was dominated by the physicians. Their underlings were the apothecaries and the surgeons. The latter, struggling to break with the Barbers' Guild, were considered too lowly to be awarded any degree. That is why an English physician is addressed as "Doctor", while a surgeon still clings defiantly to the title of "Mister".

But the great British medical schools were established during this century – in Edinburgh by the Munro brothers and Dr Knox, in London by John and William Hunter. In France, too, the Academie de Medicine encouraged medical research. Soon students from America were coming to Europe to train, and taking back their new knowledge to their own country.

Medical science now advanced rapidly in many fields. To name some major contributions, at the end of the 18th century an English country doctor, Edward Jenner, discovered the secret of inoculation against smallpox. At about the same time a revolution began in the sadly ignorant and barbaric treatment of the mentally sick. In a single week the French physician Philippe Pinel (1745–1826) had the chains struck from fifty pitiful creatures who were brought into air and sunlight. His fight for treatment by greater kindness and freedom from harsh restraint was taken up and extended by, among others, William Tuke (1732–1822) and John Conolly (1794–1866) in England, and by Dorothea Dix (1802–87) in the U.S.A.

The use of anaesthetic gases to reduce the pain of operations was pioneered in English by the chemist Humphry Davy (1778–1829) and the physicist Michael Faraday (1791–1867). In America nitrous oxide was successfully used for a tooth extraction in 1842 and, in the same year, ether for a surgical operation. A Scottish physician, James Young Simpson (1811–70) used chloroform to ease childbirth – a method that became respectable when Queen Victoria made use of it.

In France the husband and wife team Pierre (1859–1906) and Marie (1867–1934) Curie made the researches into radioactivity that have resulted in the wide use of the metallic element radium in various medical treatments. The scourge of malaria in tropical regions was partly conquered by two British experts on tropical diseases, Patrick Manson (1844–1922) and Ronald Ross (1857–1932), who identified the mosquito as the agent transmitting the disease to human beings. Insulin, one of the most effective ways of dealing with diabetes, was discovered by the Canadian Frederick Banting and his associates in 1921. Such men as Louis Pasteur (1822–95) had achieved important work in the prevention of infectious disease, but only comparatively recently have there been great advances in the use of antibiotics (Greek *anti*, against and *bios* life). Alexander Fleming (1881–1955) discovered penicillin almost by accident in 1928 and experimented with its uses for some twelve years, his work being furthered by the Australian Howard Florey and the Russo-German Ernst Chain. Streptromycin, another important antibiotic, was discovered by the Russian Selman Waksman, working in the USA. All the last four men named received the Nobel Prize for medicine.

Another group of scientific and medical investigators, known as psychologists, psychiatrists and psychoanalysts, have worked on the problems of human behaviour and the links between mind and physical illness. Though the approaches and objectives may differ the use of the Greek word *psuche* (psyche), meaning the soul or mind, both conscious and unconscious, indicates that much common ground is shared by workers in these fields of medicine. Among the most important names are those of Sigmund Freud (1856–1939), Carl Jung (1875–1961) and Alfred Adler (1870–1937).

Finally, mention should be made of the subject of transplants – the substitution of a healthy organ for a diseased one in the human body. Some work in this field, e.g. in the treatment of kidney trouble, had passed virtually unnoticed. But in 1967 a South African doctor, Christian Barnard, gained worldwide publicity by transplanting a human heart. Many similar operations, most with little success, have since been performed in various countries; but violent controversy has been aroused, not only on medical but ethical grounds – and not only from the general public but within the medical profession itself.

¶ DELGADO, ALAN. *A Hundred Years of Medical Care.* 1970; TAYLOR, BOSWELL. *Medicine.* 1962

See also ALCHEMY; ANAESTHESIA; BARBER-SURGEONS; DENTISTRY; HARVEY, WILLIAM; HIPPOCRATES; HOSPITALS; INOCULATION; JENNER, EDWARD; KING'S EVIL; NIGHTINGALE, FLORENCE; PARACELSUS; PASTEUR, LOUIS; PENICILLIN; PLAGUES; VACCINATION; X-RAY.

Medieval (Mediaeval): pertaining to the Middle Ages, itself a vague term popularised by 17th century historians for the period between the fall of Rome and the Renaissance. The adjective, coined in the 19th century, dates from a time when many artists and writers looked back nostalgically to what seemed to them, rightly or wrongly, a romantic and colourful era. The general use of the term in historical writing now is devoid of these overtones.

Medina, Arabic **Al-Madina:** town in Arabia, 250 miles [402 kilometres] north of Mecca. The years of the Mohammedan era are reckoned from the date of the flight (Hegira) of Mohammed thither from Mecca in AD 622. A railway from Damascus, completed in 1908, was destroyed in World War I, and has not yet been restored.

Mediterranean Sea: sea, 1,145,000 square miles [2,965,500 kilometres] in area, enclosed by the land masses of three continents, Europe, Asia and Africa, with access to the Atlantic by the Strait of Gibraltar. Although it includes several smaller seas – the Aegean, Adriatic, Ionian and Tyrrhenian – it is itself only the small remnant of a vast ocean which in geological times encircled half the globe.

Its name, from Latin *medius*, middle, and *terra*, land, indicates not only its geographical position but its importance as a centre of the ancient world, carrying a vast burden of trade and providing a highway to the East before the discovery of the Cape of Good Hope route. Being almost tideless, it encouraged early seafaring; known currents and the daily alternation of land and sea breezes made coastwise navigation easy; and voyagers from, for example, the Egyptian Delta, could confidently make the round trip via the Syrian coast, south Asia Minor and Crete, and count on the wind from the north to bring them home to the Libyan coast and the mouth of the Nile. This is not to say that seafaring in the Mediterranean was without its hazards, especially out of season. Hesiod, writing *c.* 700 BC, recommended as the best periods for sailing either the spring or "fifty days after the solstice, when the burdensome days of summer come to an end" and counselled "do not wait for the time of the new wine and the terrible blasts of the North Wind which accompany the heavy autumnal rain". There is confirmation of the perils of winter sailing in the Mediterranean in the graphic story of St Paul's shipwreck, *c.* AD 60, as told in the Acts of

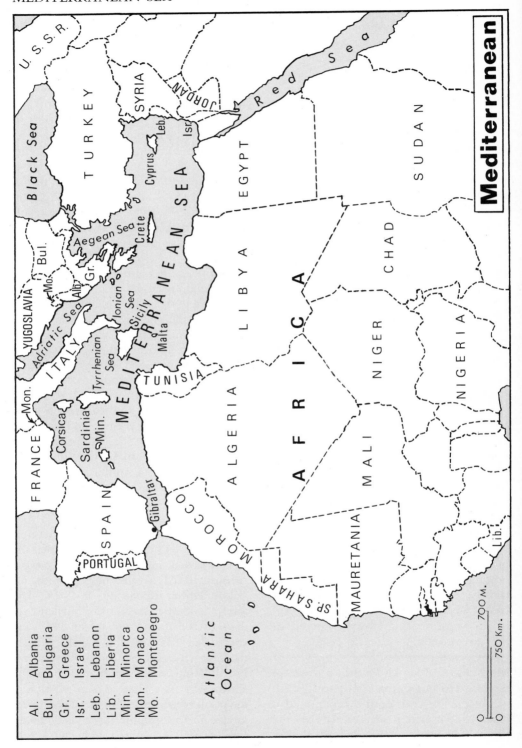

the Apostles, 27: 27. The north-western part of the sea is especially liable to ferocious winter storms.

Throughout the centuries the Mediterranean has been the scene of great sea battles. The year 480 BC saw the decisive defeat of the Persians by the Greeks at Salamis. Two thousand years later Don John of Austria, leading the fleets of Spain and Venice, broke the might of Ottoman seapower at Lepanto (*see* separate entry). In World War II the Allied fleets of steel battleships and aircraft carriers, descendants of the war galleys of the ancient world, fought in the seas of Crete and Sicily and up the coasts of Italy.

The Mediterranean, in fact, despite the spread of the map east, west, north and south, to cover a greater world than the early civilisations dreamt of, has never lost its "middle land" strategic importance. If it has known long periods of political stagnation it has also witnessed sudden abrupt upheavals in the pattern of nations, as in the years 1910–27 when the long stranglehold of Ottoman power was broken and the new states of Egypt, Yugoslavia, Albania and (so changed as to be virtually new also) Greece and Turkey emerged; with, alongside them, new colonies and mandated territories attached to the Great Powers.

¶ PACK, S. W. C. *Sea Power in the Mediterranean: a history from the seventeenth century to the present day.* 1971

Melanchthon (Philipp Schwarzerd, 1497–1560): German scholar and religious reformer. He was largely responsible for putting the Protestant doctrines of Martin Luther (*see* separate entry) into systematic order. The name Melanchthon is the Greek form of his native name, a practice common among scholars of the period.

Memphis: former city of northern Egypt on the west bank of the River Nile, the centre of the worship of Ptah, creator of the world and all living things. Its founder, Menes, was the first Pharaoh. The bull of Apis was housed there, and Memphis was a centre of priestly training. The city lost its importance with the rise of new religions and the foundation by Alexander of Alexandria as his capital. The city of Memphis in Tennessee, USA, was so named because of the supposed similarity of its location.

Mendel, Gregor Johann (1822–84): Austrian monk and botanist who, as the result of his experiments in the garden of the Augustinian monastery at Brünn (Brno), worked out a number of important laws of heredity (the transmission of characteristics and qualities from parent to offspring) in plants and (as was later proved) in animals and human beings. The discoveries that have resulted from his original work are of particular importance in the study of certain hereditary human diseases and abnormalities, such as haemophilia (excessive and too-ready bleeding) which is normally found only in boys and is handed down by their mothers; and colour blindness which, again, is handed down by women but is manifested only in men.

Mendel published his findings in an obscure natural history journal, where they remained largely unknown for sixteen years, when they were rediscovered by other investigators in the same field. Medical scientists afterwards pronounced Mendel's discoveries as the most important in the whole science of life.

¶ SOOTIN, HARRY. *Gregor Mendel.* 1961

Mensheviks: the moderate wing of the Russian Social Democrat Party. At a Party Congress in 1903 the moderates were outvoted and were labelled *Mensheviki* (minority) to distinguish them from the extremists, who were the majority (*Bolsheviki*) on that occasion. Their leader was Martov, a former colleague of Lenin, and Trotsky was associated with them for a short time.

Merchant Adventurers: an organisation of English merchants, with trading factories in Holland and later Hamburg and other German cities. A Merchant Adventurers Company began to operate from England in the reign of Edward III. The earliest charter dates from 1407, though the company was not incorporated until 1553, at a time when Sebastian Cabot (1476-1557) was a governor. The Merchant Adventurers formed a private company to export manufactured articles, mainly cloth, to Europe. Its members were English, unlike the Staplers, who included foreigners in their organisation and traded in unfinished goods, particularly wool. The Merchant Adventurers may have developed from the medieval trading guilds, and it has been suggested that freemen of the Mercers Company of London formed the nucleus of the company. New trading companies formed in the 16th and 17th centuries, such as the East India Companies, were no doubt modelled on the Merchant Adventurers.

From the start the company found itself in competition with the Hansa, a German group which had previously monopolised trade in the North Sea ports and throughout Europe. The 1545 edict of the Emperor Charles V seriously interrupted English trade with the Netherlands and temporarily re-established the Hansa's monopoly in carrying English cloth to Antwerp. Yet commerce with the Low Countries expanded throughout the 16th century. Countermeasures reduced and finally ended the Hansa's special privileges, and in 1598 Elizabeth I of England closed the Steelyard, where the Hansa had its headquarters in London from 1232. The Merchant Adventurers company is thought to have employed up to 50,000 people in the Low Countries at its most prosperous period. The trade in woollen cloths had rapidly overtaken the export of wool in the later Middle Ages. In two centuries, from the middle of the 14th, exported cloths had risen from 500 bales to 100,000, while wool exports had fallen from 30,000 bales to 4,000, to the distress of the Staplers and the merchants of Calais. Inland towns like Colchester, the main entrepôt (i.e. centre for importing and re-exporting), prospered through the activities of the Merchant Adventurers, as did such towns as Braintree, Coggeshall, Norwich and Halstead. The ports through which cloths were shipped, especially London, throve equally on the trade. The annual turnover of Dutch and German trade in the reign of James I has been estimated at one million pounds sterling. Yet the Adventurers clearly encouraged other activities. The Pilgrim Fathers sailed to found the Plymouth Colony under the aegis of the Merchant Adventurers. They differed from the later joint stock companies (e.g. the East India and Hudson's Bay Companies) in that each Merchant Adventurer traded on his own capital in accordance with the company's rules. The joint stock companies traded as a whole, and any profits or losses were distributed among the shareholders.

By the 18th century the Merchant Adventurers had become known as the Hamburg Company, since Hamburg was the central depot for the trade, embracing other German ports. Here the company remained until 1808 when Napoleon's "continental system" and a hostile Europe brought about its dissolution.

¶ LEWENHAK, SHEILA. editor. *The Merchant Adventurers* (Jackdaw). 1967

See also HANSEATIC LEAGUE.

Merchant Navy (Britain); **Merchant Marine** (USA): From a very early period men have engaged in trade and this has involved transport by sea in ships. Because of wars and piracy these "merchant" ships have always had to fight on occasions, and the very distinct division between warships and others is of comparatively modern origin. A primary function of the warship has always been the protection of trade.

Julius Caesar invaded Britain because of the help given by the Britons to his enemies in Gaul, and there was trade across the Channel long before this, indeed as long as the islands had been populated. The Vikings, who invaded Britain after the Romans had left, were keen traders by sea in ships which they sailed and rowed. In the Middle Ages the larger round ships, with a single mast and a square sail, visited Iceland for cod and Spain for wine. Dried and salted cod formed a staple preserved food in the days when the refrigerator was unknown. The same type of ship was used for the export of wool to Flanders. The Hanseatic League was a powerful international combine of merchants which directed this kind of trade in northern waters. From the Mediterranean and such ports as Venice and Genoa great merchant trading galleys brought the spices of the East to Britain and northern Europe.

Fighting fleets or military transports were usually formed by temporarily taking over merchant ships. The Cinque Ports on the south coast of Britain undertook to meet the requirements of the king for a number of ships in this way, in return for special trading privileges.

The 15th and 16th century voyages of discovery by Portuguese and Spanish traders encouraged English merchants to seek distant markets and to fight for special benefits. But in time of war trade was stopped by embargoes, and many merchant seamen were impressed by the state to man its warships.

In time of peace commerce flourished. Merchant companies, such as the English Muscovy Company and the East India Company, were formed and traded in new commodities in the newly discovered regions of the world. Certain ships were designed for particular trades. The colliers from Newcastle, the whalers from Hull and the stately Indiamen out of London are cases in point. The richer trades encouraged the building of finer ships; the East Indiaman of 1,000 tons [1,016 tonnes] laden with spices was larger than the West Indiaman of 500 tons [508 tonnes] bringing home the sugar. Otherwise ships differed little in appearance except in size, and the warship was very like the merchant ship, distinguished only by the many more guns and men carried. Trade rivalry was the cause of many wars, and the big merchant trading companies such as the East India Companies of England, Holland, France and Portugal had their own fighting fleets to settle local rivalries.

The seaman was a breed apart, used to being cooped up in ships, familiar with other parts of the world, able to mix with foreigners and jealous of his freedom when faced with the discipline of a warship. He suffered from old salt meat and sour beer on long voyages, but found compensation on his travels over the oceans of the world and did not envy his fellows tied to the land, farm, smallholding or town office.

In the 19th century ships grew larger; steam power and iron replaced sail and wood. The glamorous days of the Anglo-American rivalry in the tea trade, with tea clippers racing home with the first crops of tea, lasted only some twenty years, 1850-70.

Before the 1860s ship owners were often small groups of persons, perhaps owning one ship divided into sixty-four shares. One of the owners might well be a seaman

The Clipper ship Nightingale.

and the master in command. This system was replaced in the latter half of the 19th century by shipping companies, which often proved more remote from ships and men. The ship master was now the servant of the company. Regulations, such as the British Merchant Shipping Acts, from 1851 onwards laid down conditions for the construction of vessels, the provision of navigation lights and the training of men, but the sailor's lot was nevertheless often far from easy. In the 1870s Samuel Plimsoll waged a campaign in the British Parliament which led to the successful establishment of a load line for ships (*see* PLIMSOLL LINE).

In the United States, despite the interruption and interference of warfare, the merchant marine grew rapidly in the 18th century. Not only was there flourishing trade with Europe, the Mediterranean and Spanish America but in 1784 the merchantman *Empress of China* reached the Far East and forged commercial links with the Orient. By the beginning of the 19th century there were over one million tons [1,016,050 tonnes] of American shipping on the trading routes of the world, operating from Boston, New York City, Philadelphia and many smaller ports. From about 1803 onwards New Orleans and Baltimore came into prominence as centres of thriving trade with the Latin American countries.

As in Britain, the seaman suffered from severe exploitation, and legislation became necessary to protect him. One of the most effective measures was the Seaman's Act of 1915, sponsored by Robert La Follette, which ensured better working conditions, freedom from oppressive contracts and more life-saving equipment.

In 1968, ignoring vessels of less than 100 tons [101·6 tonnes] gross, barges and sailing craft, the world total of merchant ships was 47,444. In mid-1968 the world's largest merchant fleet was that operating under the flag of Liberia, in West Africa. This fleet consists very largely of foreign ships operating under a "flag of convenience", i.e. using a foreign flag to avoid the payment of taxes in their true home ports.

¶ DAWLISH, PETER. *The Merchant Navy.* 1966
See also EAST INDIA COMPANY, etc.

The Liverpool Bay, *a modern container ship of the Merchant Navy.*

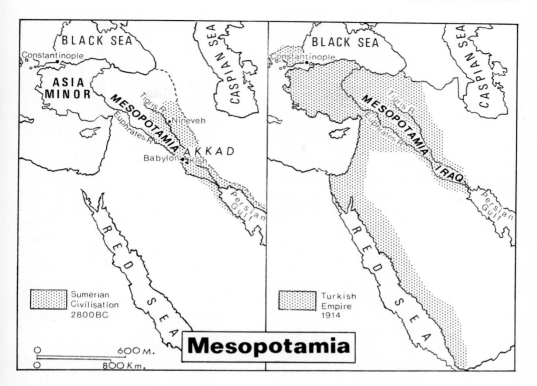

Mesopotamia

Sumerian Civilisation 2800 BC

Turkish Empire 1914

600 M.
800 Km.

Merovingian: pertaining to the line of Frankish kings whose territories included most of what is now modern France and who ruled from 448 to 751. The most important members of the dynasty were Clovis (ruled 481–511) and Dagobert (ruled 628–639). The Merovingians were followed by the Carolingians.

Mesopotamia: the land "between rivers", i.e. the Tigris and Euphrates. From here come mankind's oldest written historical records. The fifth millennium BC was a time of much migration of peoples, and the establishment of villages and primitive agriculture. By the 28th century BC the Sumerians were established in walled cities with satellite towns on the lower Euphrates. Further north, by the end of the third millennium, the Akkad civilisation was established, based on the city of Kish. Sargon (c. 2300 BC) moved the capital to Akkad. The Akkadian language

was Semitic, and cuneiform writing was used in the administration of the Akkadian Empire, superseding the Sumerian language and pictograph writing. Then a new Semitic people, the Amorites, founded an empire based on Babylon. Hammurabi (c. 1792–50 BC) won control of all Mesopotamia. From the 14th century BC there arose an Assyrian empire, beginning with the city of Ashur and later based on Nineveh. The Assyrian empire expanded over much of the Middle East. Nineveh fell in 612 BC to the Medes, rulers of Iran, but the southern part of Mesopotamia fell under the rule of Babylon and is known as Chaldaea. Cyrus, the Persian, captured Babylon in 539 BC. Greek influence came with the conquests of Alexander the Great in the 4th century BC. Muslim conquest began in AD 633. The Mongol invaders in 1258 looted Babylon, destroying its irrigation canals. In 1534 Mesopotamia became part of the

581

stagnant Turkish empire. The modern Iraq emerged when the Turkish empire broke up in World War I.

¶ COTTRELL, LEONARD. *Land of the Two Rivers.* 1963

Messina: town in north-east Sicily controlling the straits of the same name between the island and the Italian mainland. The site was originally colonised by the Greeks. Its university dates from 1549. In 1908 an earthquake destroyed in a few seconds nearly all its buildings.

Methodism: a system of Protestant faith and worship. Its originators were John Wesley (1703–91) and his brother Charles (1707–88), with whom must also be mentioned George Whitefield (1714–70). It is notable that all these were clergymen of the Church of England, and the movement was at first directed towards purifying the abuses of that Church, from which its chief difference is in its system of government.

The history of Methodism is one of various streams turning aside and some uniting again. In Britain, where the number of supporters approaches one million, most have now come together as the Methodist Church in Great Britain (1932). Of a total of twelve million Methodists in the world, ten million are in the USA.

Methuen Treaty (1703): negotiated between Portugal and Britain by Sir John Methuen, the English Ambassador. Duties on Portuguese wines and English wool were reduced reciprocally. From this period is said to date the English fondness for port wine.

Metternich, Clemens Werzel Lothar, Prince von (1773–1859): foreign minister and chancellor of Austria. This brilliant diplomat was the architect of the Vienna settlement (1815) which recon-structed Europe on conservative lines after the defeat of Napoleon. Exiled to England by the revolutions of 1848 (he lived for a time in a seaside villa in Hove), he returned to Austria in 1849 and was a respected and often influential elder statesman. The "Metternich System", which governed European affairs from 1815 to 1848, tried to restore and preserve the old power of monarchies against the new forces of Liberalism and Nationalism. It ultimately – and inevitably – failed, but not entirely to Metternich's surprise.

Mexico: federal republic of North America. The country secured independence from Spain in 1821 when Augustin de Iturbide (1783–1824), with the support of the Catholic Church and the landowners, proclaimed Mexico a constitutional monarchy. A federal republic was set up in 1824. For the next thirty years the most commanding figure was Antonio de Santa Anna (1797–1876), who tried to centralise the government but was continually faced by internal rebellions and American intrigues. Numerous frontier incidents between 1836 and 1846, and the occupation of Texas in 1845 by the USA, led to the Mexican War of 1846–48. President James K. Polk (1795–1849) sent American troops into a disputed area along the frontier and, when they were attacked, accused Mexico of "shedding American blood on American soil". Monterey and Mexico City were captured, and the war ended in September 1846. By the treaty of Guadeloupe Hidalgo (February 1848) Mexico renounced claims to Texas, recognised the Rio Grande frontier and, in return for fifteen million dollars, ceded New Mexico and California. In 1855 a liberal movement drove out Santa Anna but the country soon became involved in civil war and in the French attempts to set up a Catholic Empire under the Archduke

Maximilian of Austria, who was the nominee of Napoleon III of France. From 1863 to 1867 Maximilian ruled Mexico with the help of French troops but, when they were withdrawn, was overthrown by Benito Juarez (1806–72) and shot at Querataro on 19 June 1867. Thereafter, Mexico made considerable economic progress, especially under Porfirio Diaz (1830–1915). In 1917 a new constitution became the basis for great social reforms. From 1924–35 Mexico was controlled by Plutarco Calles, who improved relations with the USA but alienated the Catholic Church. In 1938 the foreign oil companies were nationalised. In recent years Mexico has striven to enter the main stream of world affairs, her recent sponsoring of the Olympic Games (1968) and the World Association Football Cup (1970) providing evidence of this.

See AMERICA for map, *also* AZTECS, MAYAN CIVILISATION, etc.

Michael Feodorovitch (1596–1645): Tsar of Russia 1613–45, founder of the Romanov dynasty. Born of an old and noble Moscow family of Prussian origin, he was chosen as Tsar by a national assembly. He was content to reign by leaving government largely in the hands of his advisers.

Michael VIII Palaeologus (1224–82): Emperor of the Eastern Roman Empire. In 1261 he drove out of Constantinople the Western usurpers who had occupied the city in 1204, on the pretext of the Fourth Crusade, and established the last line of Eastern emperors which ended when Constantine IX Palaeologus perished in the storming of Constantinople by the Turks in 1453.

The family name still survives. In England there is a 17th century tomb of a Palaeologus at Landulph, Cornwall, and another fought at the battle of Edgehill

(1642); while, as late as World War I, the French ambassador to Russia was a Paléologue.

Michelangelo (Michelangelo Buonarotti, 1475–1564): Florentine artist. His skill as a painter came mainly from his deep knowledge of sculpture, which he always preferred. The disturbed state of Florence after the death of his patron Lorenzo de' Medici (*see* MEDICI FAMILY) in 1492 and personal anxieties induced in Michelangelo a melancholy disposition and a distrust of his fellow men which showed itself in jealousy of Leonardo da Vinci (*see* separate entry) and pursued him through his long life.

After a few years in Rome, where he made the figure of Cupid, now in the South Kensington Museum, London, he returned to Florence and produced his famous statue of David; but in 1508 Pope Julius II induced him to undertake the painting of the ceiling of the Sistine

Right: Michelangelo's Madonna and Child *in the Cathedral at Bruges, Belgium.*

Chapel in the Vatican, Rome, a task which occupied four-and-a-half years and left the artist permanently crippled through having to work on a high scaffold with his head thrown back. His panel showing the Creation of Man is one of the most sublime paintings of all time.

His later years took him back to Florence to work as designer and sculptor in the Medici Chapel and again to Rome (1534) for a further five years of painting, this time on a vertical surface, in the Sistine Chapel. As he approached the age of seventy he turned architect and designed the vast dome which crowns St Peter's today. He continued to work as a sculptor to within a week of his death.
See colour section.

¶ ALLEN, AGNES. *The Story of Michelangelo.* 1953
See also FLORENTINE ART.

Microscope: optical instrument by which objects are so magnified that details invisible to the naked eye can be clearly seen. The simple microscope is merely a magnifying glass, usually a double convex lens. To remedy the colour fringes which occur in the outer parts of the field of view, a modified form, known as the Coddington lens, has been devised.

Of much more importance is the compound microscope. This consists of the objective, which is a lens system of short focal length creating a real image of the object inspected, and the eyepiece, through which this real image is viewed.

The first compound microscope appears to have been invented in 1590 by Zacharias Jansen. He used a convex objective and a concave eyepiece, but its field of view was very limited. This was followed, about 1628, by what is known as Kepler's microscope, although not made by him. This used convex lenses for both objective and eyepiece. In 1684 Christiaan Huygens (*see* separate entry) improved this

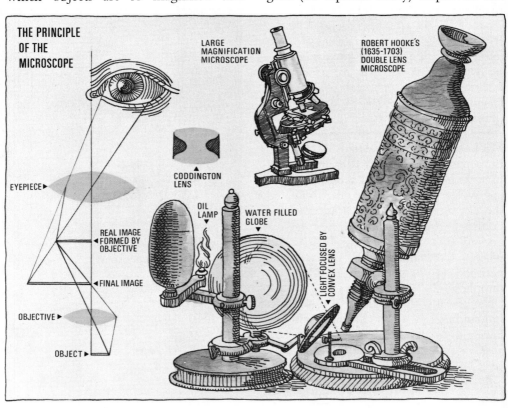

THE PRINCIPLE OF THE MICROSCOPE

EYEPIECE ▶

REAL IMAGE FORMED BY OBJECTIVE ◀

◀ FINAL IMAGE

OBJECTIVE ▶

OBJECT ▶

CODDINGTON LENS

LARGE MAGNIFICATION MICROSCOPE

OIL LAMP ▼

WATER FILLED GLOBE ▼

LIGHT FOCUSED BY CONVEX LENS

ROBERT HOOKE'S (1635-1703) DOUBLE LENS MICROSCOPE

system by devising an eyepiece using two lenses. It was not, however, until the early years of the 19th century that the microscope became a widely used instrument, by which time improved grinding and design of lenses had done much to remove the colours and distortions to which early models were subject.

The electron microscope was first devised by Knoll and Ruska in 1932 and by 1945 this had become a widely used instrument.

Middle Ages: an imprecise term covering the thousand years of western European history from the middle of the 5th century to the middle of the 15th century. Old history books often give 476, the year when Romulus Augustulus, the last Roman emperor in the West, was deposed, as the date when the Middle Ages began and the fall of Constantinople in 1453 as marking the moment they ended. But history is not a slab of cake which divides up into neat slices. Ancient Rome did not fall, any more than the Renaissance began, on any one day. We must guard against viewing the Middle Ages as if they were, so to speak, a walled city in an old tapestry, its inhabitants frozen for all time in quaint and picturesque attitudes. On the contrary, they are part of the stream of history, just as medieval churches and cathedrals are part of contemporary villages and towns.

The first 400 years of the Middle Ages are sometimes further differentiated as the "Dark Ages". As the western Roman Empire crumbled from internal weaknesses and from the pressure of the barbarian hordes surging west and south towards the rich lands beyond the Rhine and the Danube, western Europe did indeed, for a period, go down into darkness. Roman culture was largely submerged, pagan tribes overran wide areas,

and out of the East came a new threat, the rise of Islam.

Most of the barbarian tribes, fortunately, were not savages. Leaving out such exceptions as the Huns and the Vandals, whose names have remained bywords for cruelty and destruction, they were vigorous and adaptable people. Though they destroyed much of the old classical world, they were willing to learn what they could from it.

Heralds of better times were the Frankish kings, Clovis and Charlemagne. Clovis (c. 466–511), who became a Christian in 496, by uniting the Frankish tribes under one rule may be called the creator of modern France. Charlemagne (c. 742–814) carved out an empire stretching from Spain to the Danube. He encouraged learning and the arts and saw himself as the champion of Christendom. On Christmas Day 800, in St Peter's, Rome, Pope Leo III crowned him Emperor of the Romans. While Charlemagne's territorial empire did not survive its founder, the Holy Roman Empire, idea of an earthly counterpart to the spiritual authority of the Pope, lasted – if for long periods little more than a name – for a thousand years. The reign of Alfred (849–?901), King of the West Saxons, warrior, lawgiver, encourager of learning and himself the author of many works, was another milestone on the long road back to ordered government.

For ordinary people, most of them poor peasants, life in those troubled times was precarious in the extreme. Their only hope of security lay in putting themselves, for a price, under the protection of a powerful landowner. The price, according to the time and the circumstances, might consist of military service, agricultural labour, goods or money. Such, reduced to its simplest terms, was the feudal system, the system of land tenure which for hundreds of years shaped

In the Middle Ages, called the Age of Faith, the Church was at the centre of all aspects of life. *Above: The Crusades; Christian Crusaders fight the Saracens at Damietta in 1218. Below: carving of a hawker in a tree by the great stone-mason Peter Wynwode from the stalls of Winchester Cathedral, 1307.*

Superstition and belief in the Devil were also powerful forces in this religious age. *Above: an old woman struggles with a Devil. Below: pilgrimages combined piety with sociability and here weary pilgrims stop to refresh themselves on their journey.*

medieval society (*see* FEUDAL SYSTEM). The system was, as it were, a great pyramid, with the king, who held the kingdom from God, at the top; and at the base, well below the tenants-in-chief and various freeholders, the poor villeins. For the latter it was a harsh and meagre existence, made tolerable, perhaps, by its relative security and by the Church's promise of rewards in the world to come.

At a time when national states were in their infancy the Church was the great unifying influence of western Europe. The Pope, as Christ's representative on earth, commanded the spiritual allegiance of all Christendom. The Middle Ages are sometimes called the Age of Faith. One has only to go into one of the great medieval cathedrals to appreciate something of the tremendous spiritual conviction which could bring into being such exquisite and technically sophisticated structures in an age when so much else was crude and rudimentary.

The Church intervened in almost every field of human activity. The monasteries, which had preserved what remained of the learning of the ancient world, were, for the poor and oppressed, the sole reliable sources of charity and compassion. They served as hospitals and schools. Under the direction of the monks, forests were cleared and marshes drained. When the Church called for volunteers to join a crusade to free the Holy Land from the Mohammedans, men in their thousands forsook their daily occupations to "take the cross".

The Crusades, not one of which attained its object other than temporarily, in many ways illustrate the Middle Ages and what, to us, appear its strange contradictions. Many who went on them did so out of religious faith, yet they were bloodstained expeditions, disfigured by treachery and acts of cruelty hard to reconcile with either Christianity or the medieval code of chivalry, which was intended to humanise the conduct of war. Not only Turks and Jews were slaughtered by the Crusaders – that, in the context of the time, was to be expected – but fellow-Christians as well.

The Crusades had the unlooked-for result of greatly increasing western Europe's trade with the East. Missionaries and merchants pushed ever deeper into Asia, returning with new trade goods, new knowledge and new ideas. The closed medieval world was opening out.

The growing merchant class and the expanding towns were outside the old system of bartering land for services. For trade, money was the key. In 1348 the bubonic plague, known as the Black Death, which wrought dreadful havoc across Europe, further undermined the old order. With labour in short supply, labourers, for the first time, found themselves in a favourable bargaining position.

As time passed, even the Church found itself challenged. Reformers like John Wyclif (*c.* 1320–84) tried to bring it back to its ancient simplicity. In Prague in 1415 Jan Hus (*c.* 1373–1415) died at the stake in the same cause (*see* separate entries under both these names).

Men, in fact, had begun to question their place in the universe. They were no longer content to accept the Church's teaching that life was nothing more than a preparation for heaven. Painters like Giotto (*c.* 1266–1337) began to paint figures which seemed to be made of flesh and blood instead of being merely decorative motifs; sculptors like Donatello (1386 –1466) turned away from the elongated saints of the medieval cathedrals to the realistic sculpture of ancient Rome, itself Hellenistic in origin and tradition. Chaucer (*c.* 1340–1400) wrote poems full of an affectionate and humorous regard for human frailty.

Once such men had begun to demonstrate that human life had its own dignity and worth, the days of the Middle Ages were numbered. *See colour section.*

¶ ROWLING, MARJORIE. *Everyday Life in Medieval Times.* 1967; SOBOL, DONALD J. *The First Book of Medieval Britain.* 1970

Middle Atlantic States, USA: region situated in roughly the middle of the eastern coastline of the United States and comprising the states of Delaware, Pennsylvania, Maryland, New York and New Jersey. Although the Appalachian and Adirondack Mountains are to be found in this region, it also possesses broad fertile plains supporting large-scale agriculture. Among the many rivers in the area the most important are the Hudson River in New York and the Susquehanna River, which runs primarily in Pennsylvania.

During the early colonial period, this area was settled by colonists from a variety of European nations – Swiss, Finns, Dutch, as well as the English. New York City, for example, was founded by the Dutch West Indies Company in the 1620s and remained in Dutch hands until 1664. However, the region soon became an integral part of the English colonies, and by the time of the American Revolution was a major source of supply of provisions, especially for the colonies further south. It was at Philadelphia, Pennsylvania, that the American Constitution was written, and New York City and Philadelphia served as the first capitals for the new nation. The area has, moreover, grown in significance since the early days of the republic. Although much "truck farming" is to be found in New Jersey, and though there are dairy farms and other agricultural production in the rest of this region, the Middle Atlantic states are especially noted for urbanisation and manufacturing. Thus, Pittsburgh, Pennsylvania, is a major centre for steel pro-

duction; Rochester, New York, is the site of much manufacturing of electrical goods; and many other cities and towns play vital roles in the industrial life of the United States. Overshadowing them all, however, is New York City, the hub of the region, and one of the major cities in the world. Here are concentrated the main offices of most of the major firms in the financial, commercial and communications industries. Here are also to be found such cultural centres as the Lincoln Centre for the Performing Arts, the Metropolitan Museum of Art and the Museum of Modern Art. New York is also the home of such distinguished foundations as Columbia University and New York University, the latter being among the largest private universities in the world. This region is thus in many ways central to the economy and culture of the nation.

See AMERICA for map.

Middle West, USA: area of the USA beginning at the margin of the Allegheny Plateau, stretching westwards across the Plains of the USA and ending in the dry grasslands and the "blown" areas of the Dakotas, Nebraska and Kansas. The first settlers came in the later years of the 18th century. They included many adherents of small religious sects, including the Mennonites, the Amish and the Latter Day Saints. Subsequent immigrants to the area, especially from northern Europe, reinforced this traditionally Protestant character, so much so that it is known as the "Bible Belt". The Middle West contains about a quarter of the population of the USA, and its chief cities are Chicago, the "home" of isolationism, Cincinnati, St Louis, Minneapolis and St. Paul. The region yields the greater part of the wheat, corn, cattle and dairy produce in the USA, and also a considerable share of its manufactures. In the Civil War, true to its traditions, it sided with the North against slavery. The Mid-West has always had great political importance in the country, and six out of the last eleven presidents have been Middle-Westerners. *See* AMERICA for map.

Midway, Battle of: decisive sea and air battle between US and Japanese forces, 4–6 June 1942. After the surprise attack by Japanese aircraft on the US naval base at Pearl Harbour (Hawaii) on 7 December 1941, the forces of Japan swept all before them in the Pacific and Far East. But the naval and air battle at Midway in the central Pacific resulted in their first major defeat. The attempted seizure by Japan of Midway Island ended in failure, with the loss of four Japanese aircraft carriers and 275 planes. This action restored American morale, checked the advance of the Japanese across the central Pacific, eliminated the threat to Hawaii and restored the balance of naval power.

¶ BARKER, ARTHUR J. *Midway.* 1971

Migration: the process of leaving one country or area for another, for either temporary or permanent settlement. The shiftings of peoples have been a major factor throughout human history, from prehistoric wanderings in search of food to more organised movements for religious and political motives such as, for example, the Mormon settlement in Utah, USA, or the Great Trek (1835–36) of Boer farmers from Cape Colony to the new republics of Natal, the Transvaal and the Orange Free State. There can also be migration of labour forces from rural areas to towns or from one country to another. Another type of migration need not necessarily be associated with any movement of people – a cultural migration or drift, in which ideas and artistic practices spread from one area or civilisation to another.

Milan Cathedral.

Milan: north Italian city, dating from Roman times, on the Lombardy Plain where routes through Alpine passes meet. Its cathedral (begun 1386) is one of many fine churches, one of which contains Leonardo's "The Last Supper". Milan became a duchy in 1395 and was a great Renaissance centre under the Sforza family. It was later attached successively to the crowns of Spain (1535–1713) and Austria (1713–96 and 1815–59) before being incorporated into Italy in 1861.

Miletus: Greek city on the coast of Caria in Asia Minor. It was known in Homeric times and was later seized by colonists from Athens. In its turn Miletus founded many colonies chiefly round the Black Sea, including Odessa. The birthplace of Thales and other early philosophers, it later declined into insignificance.

Mill: building for grinding grain. The word comes from Latin *molere*, to crush or grind. It was originally applied to the building in which the crushing apparatus was housed. The handmill used for grinding corn was called a quern, and consisted of two circular stones, placed one above the other. The grain was put between them and the upper one – the millstone – was rotated until the grain was crushed to form flour.

This laborious manual process survived

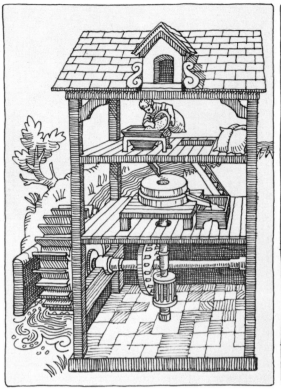

Water driven paddlewheel.

Windmill.

until people discovered other ways of turning the millstone. Wind could be used, and so could running water. So there were windmills, which caught the wind in sails fixed to a spindle connected to the millstone by rods and cogs, and watermills, each with a great external paddlewheel, turned by running water. This paddlewheel revolved the millstone in a similar way.

In medieval times milling was a profitable occupation and the miller a man of substance. The local mill was often owned by the lord of the manor or the abbot of a monastery, who charged the villagers a sum of money for its use. Sometimes ancient charters mention the right of citizens to establish a mill.

Eventually, any form of rotary processing became known as "milling", and many industrial buildings were called mills (e.g. cotton mills). In 1561 a Dutchman, Eloye Mestrel, introduced into England the milling, or scoring, of the edges of coins. This prevented unscrupulous persons from clipping silver or gold from the coins for their own use.

Milton, John (1608–74): English poet and political writer. Born in London, Milton was a precocious student. "My appetite for knowledge", he wrote, "was so voracious that from twelve years of age I hardly ever left my studies or went to bed before midnight." It was all part of his conscious preparation for becoming a great poet, and there can be no doubt that his belief in his own genius was justified. His best-known work, *Paradise Lost*, is considered one of the great epic poems of the world. He became blind in 1651, and his *Samson Agonistes*, with the blinded Samson as hero, has therefore a particular poignancy.

A supporter of Oliver Cromwell, Milton became Latin Secretary to the Council

during the Commonwealth. His prose writings, while often impractical and coloured by prejudice, include the *Areopagitica*, an appeal for freedom of thought far ahead of its time. *See colour section*
¶ MUIR, K. *John Milton.* 1955

Ming: word meaning "bright", the name adopted by the dynasty which ruled China 1368–1643. It was a period between great invasions, the Mongol and the Manchu, and a time when China deliberately chose to cut herself off, so far as possible, from the rest of the world. Such inward-looking ages are not the most favourable for artistic creation. Though many beautiful paintings, fine pottery and bronzes date from this period, they do not reach the standard of work executed under the Sung dynasty (960–1280), which preceded the Mongols. Sung works of art are outstanding for their exquisite simplicity. Ming artists and craftsmen tended to overdo the ornamentation. In so doing they lost the wonderful purity of line which distinguishes Chinese art at its best.
See also CHINA; POTTERY AND PORCELAIN.

15th century Ming ewer, decorated and with a blue underglaze.

Mining: the extraction of various natural mineral products from below the surface of the earth. This has been undertaken from at least the Neolithic period, when extensive flint mines were opened, the flints being used to make a wide variety of domestic tools. The extraction of metals and other mineral products followed. The earliest metals which were used by primitive man were obviously those which occurred at or very close to the surface. Lead and copper were mined in Britain during Roman times, and coal was used by the Romans, where it occurred close to the surface, for heating, iron working, pottery, brick and tile making, and for cremations. We do not know much about the actual mining methods used by the Romans, although a few underground galleries still exist which could be of Roman date. The Romans probably used at different periods direct slave labour and private capitalists to work such mines.

Mining continued in the centuries following the collapse of the Roman Empire, though on a smaller scale. In medieval times the mining techniques of western Europe, especially those of the Germanic states, were the most technically advanced in the world. An excellent pictorial account of the most modern usages in mining is given in Georgius Agricola's *De re metallica,* published in 1556. German miners were brought to England in Elizabethan times to open up large copper mines in the Lake District, and continental mining techniques gradually spread throughout the various branches of the English mining industry. Many of the problems which had to be faced by the miner were, of course, common to all types of mining, although the risk of an underground explosion resulting from fiery gases emerging from the mineral itself was confined to coal mining.

Mining is always carried out below the

Above: modern ore mining. Right: ancient methods of sifting ore from the De Re Metallica of Georgius Agricola: A. workman carrying broken rock in a barrow. B. First Chute. C. First Box. D. Its Handles. E. Its Bales. F. Rope. G. Beam. H. Post. I. Second Chute. K. Second Box. L. Third Chute. M. Third Box. N. First Table. O. First Sleeve. P. First Tub. Q. Second Table. R. Second Sieve. S. Second Tub. T. Third Table. V. Third Sieve. X. Third Tub. Y. Plugs.

surface, and the mineral, according to its particular physical form, is worked by opencast working (i.e. the removal of overlying strata), by shafts sunk from the surface, and by workings then extended within the mineral itself, or by inclined galleries following the line of the mineral underground. Underground water has always been a difficulty to miners. At first pumps were worked by man and beast and by various devices using wind and water. Then, in the 1710–20 period, came the first application of steam power for mining purposes.

The use of power-driven machinery for mining underground dates from the 19th century when such machines as mechanical coal cutters were invented. That century also saw the introduction of compressed air, and beginnings of the use of electricity, as motive power for mining machinery, though the pony and man's strong right arm continued as sources of power into very recent times.

The relatively small-scale mineral deposits of western Europe were rivalled, particularly from the early 19th century, by the discovery of much larger deposits in more distant parts of the world; e.g. the mineral deposits of South America were exploited on a large scale from this period. The size of these deposits, and the ease with which they were worked, overcame the disadvantage of greater distance from the manufacturing centres of western Europe. In fact, the smaller mineral deposits of many of the old-established industrial countries of western Europe ceased to be worked during the 19th century, though some countries specialised in producing certain minerals. Britain, for example, produced immense quantities of coal, which were used not only in that country but also in Europe. The North American continent found itself able to produce within its own territories most of the minerals required for large-scale industrialisation and thus was able to build its vast prosperity.

In recent years coal has been losing its position as the most important fuel, with oil and other forms of domestic heating such as electricity and gas taking its place. But mining will remain a major world industry into the foreseeable future. The vast gold-field of the Witwatersrand and the diamond pits of Kimberley, South Africa; the iron deposits of Russia and Brazil; the copper of Chile; the silver and zinc of British Columbia, Canada; the lead of Broken Hill, Australia; the tungsten, mercury and antimony of China; and the manganese, barite and cadmium of Japan, are only a few examples of the vast mining activity needed to support the modern world in war and peace.

Minoan and Mycenaean civilisations: the Bronze Age civilisations of Crete and Greece, respectively named after the legendary king Minos and the leading city in Greece, Mycenae. The chronological problems of their histories are still unsolved and the relationship between the two is far from clear. The Minoan civilisation, for example at Knossos, lasted from about 2800 to 1200 BC, while places like Mycenae and Tiryns flourished for about 400 years from 1600 BC. Knossos and Mycenae are unforgettably connected with the archaeological work of Sir Arthur Evans and Heinrich Schliemann respectively.

Crete in its heyday about 1600 BC was a peaceful place. Great palaces like those at Knossos and Phaestus were undefended. The social system was based on control by government officials. The Cretans were also seafarers, as legend states, for there is obvious evidence of extensive imports. The language they spoke has still to be discovered, but it was not Greek. By 1600 they had refined an older pictorial script to write down this language, and in this so-called "Linear A" each symbol presumably stood for a syllable. The palaces dominated life, and most of the typically Minoan works of art naturally come from them. That at Knossos will serve as an example. Covering an area of over five acres [2 hectares] it has few large rooms but a mass of storage space, and a variety of state apartments lavishly decorated with murals. Utensils and other objects in daily use were often beautifully made. The Minoans excelled in miniature art, the work on the small seals being exquisite. About 1400 BC some vast upheaval brought the golden age to an end. Possibly an earthquake or tidal wave destroyed or weakened the palaces and laid them open to Greek-speaking peoples. But the old sites were not abandoned, and the invaders adopted the Cretan writing system for their own language.

Who these Greeks were and where they came from is still a mystery. At various sites – Mycenae, Tiryns, Argos, Thebes – fortress cities seem suddenly to have sprung up. Later they were even more heavily defended, but their usual position on a hill or rock outcrop suggests a much less stable situation than in Crete. For some time these cities were artistically dependent on Crete, whatever their political position, but the rich finds at Mycenae indicate a people of a very different character. There is less fun, less dancing, more need for swords and helmets. The artistic skill was great, famous examples being the gold death-masks and inlaid dagger blades. Shortly after 1200 all these cities suddenly collapsed. Perhaps the invasion of the Dorians hastened their end, or they may have been caught up in a greater conflict over the whole of the Near East. *See colour section.*

Minorca: one of the Balearic Islands, a

detached portion of the Sierra Nevada, lying between southern France and Algeria. Because of its controlling position in the Mediterranean and its fine harbour, it was seized by the British Navy in 1708. The island was lost in 1756 owing to weakness of the British fleet, for which the nation blamed the government. The government in turn blamed the commander, Admiral John Byng, who was shot *"pour encourager les autres"*, as Voltaire said. Britain regained Minorca from the French by the Peace of Paris, 1763, but it was given to Spain under the Treaty of Amiens in 1802.

See MEDITERRANEAN for map.

Mir: the ancient village assembly or commune in old Russia. After the emancipation of the serfs in 1861, the *mir* distributed a good deal of the land and helped the poorer peasants. The *mir* formed a useful basis for the establishment of collective farms after 1917.

Mirrors: reflecting surfaces of polished metal or glass. The earliest known mirrors, apart from wet pieces of slate, were of obsidian, black volcanic glass, in use *c.* 6000 BC in Anatolia. The first metal mirrors, *c.* 3000 BC, were Egyptian – first of copper, then bronze.

Mirrors must have been regarded as of great value in the ancient world, as they were often buried with such precious objects as swords, jewellery and fine pottery. Not only was possessing a mirror a mark of distinction, it also held some religious significance. Egyptian ritual mirrors were decorated with religious scenes and inscriptions. The Greeks, Etruscans and Romans all devoted their talents to the manufacture of mirrors.

Women did not get much satisfaction from their reflections in the metallic mirrors, but in the Middle Ages the method of backing glass with thin sheets of metal was tried out extensively. A guild of glass mirror makers was in

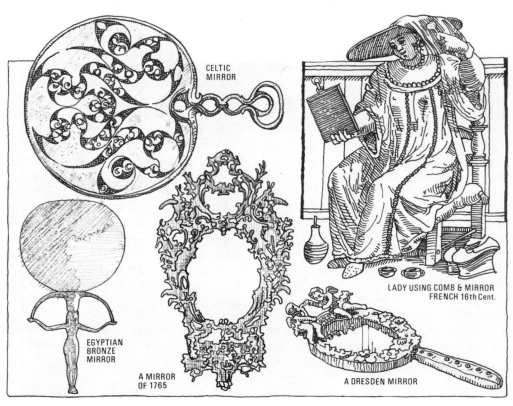

CELTIC MIRROR

EGYPTIAN BRONZE MIRROR

A MIRROR OF 1765

LADY USING COMB & MIRROR FRENCH 16th Cent.

A DRESDEN MIRROR

existence at Nuremberg, Germany, in 1373. Glass mirrors remained expensive, especially those made of Venetian glass at Murano. The Venetian method of backing glass with an amalgam of tin and mercury was introduced into England in the 17th century and was in use for over a hundred years. The chemical process of coating glass with metallic silver, known as "silvering", was discovered by Justus von Liebig in 1835.

Just as important as the reflecting power of the mirrors was the style, shape and decoration of the frames. They show some of the finest skills and artistic qualities of individual civilisations. Handles and frames of Indian mirrors were of carved ivory, Chinese mirrors had decorative settings of bronze, inlaid with gold, silver, turquoise and jade. Frames were also to become part of the decoration of a room and reflected the changing ideas in art, architecture and interior decorating styles. In Louis XIV's France, for example, mirrors were enormous, with richly carved gilt frames, and completely lined the room. One only has to think of Versailles to picture the splendour such mirrors could produce, especially at night.

Leading architects were designing mirrors for their clients in 18th century England, but this was the high peak in their design. Frames then fell out of fashion. Tomorrow's archaeologists, turning up mirrors of 20th century origin, will find them quite plain but of a brilliant reflecting power.

Missionaries: people sent abroad to spread a religious faith. The Apostles were the first missionaries, of whom St Paul was the most famous. When Christianity became established, the early Church sent missionaries to convert the heathen of Europe: Augustine to England, Patrick to Ireland and Denys to France.

The Jesuits, founded by Ignatius Loyola,

became the great missionaries of Roman Catholicism. Jesuits went out to Spanish South America and also accompanied the Armada in the hope of bringing the English back from Protestantism.

See also JESUITS; LIVINGSTONE, DAVID, etc.

Missouri Compromise: group of measures passed in the USA, 1820–21. For the first twenty years of the 19th century a precarious political balance was maintained between Northern and Southern interests by admitting "slave" and "free" territories alternately to statehood. This balance was endangered by the creation of new states out of the Louisiana Purchase (*see* separate entry) where, under the Spaniards and the French, slavery had been permitted even in the northernmost regions. In March 1820, after a bitter conflict between the Senate and the House of Representatives, Congress admitted Missouri as a slave state to be counterbalanced by Maine as a free state; but, at the same time, prohibited slavery in those regions of the Louisiana Purchase north of the line $36° 30'$. This settlement was known as the Missouri Compromise and was regarded by Southerners as being contrary to the Constitution. The Supreme Court eventually decided against the Compromise in the Dred Scott Case of 1857 (*see* separate entry).

Mogul: the Persian and Arabic form of *Mongol* (*see* separate entry), applicable to the Muslim inhabitants of west and northwest India, but used more commonly of the emperors ("Great Moguls") of the dynasty founded by Babar after the battle of Panipat, 1526, of whom Akbar (1556–1605) was the greatest. The Great Moguls held effective control of their empire continuously from Akbar's time until 1707, when Aurangzeb died. Thereafter they became puppets of native princes until the capture of Delhi by the British,

1803. The last, Bahadur Shah, was banished to Burma after the Mutiny, 1857. *See also* AKBAR; BABAR, etc.

Mohammed, Turkish, **Mahomet** (*c.* 570–632): the founder of Islam, the Muslim faith. Brought up in Mecca, he first worked with trading caravans to Syria and southern Arabia but abandoned this after his marriage (595). He became leader of a sect, at first secret, aiming at restoring the purity of the faith of Abraham. He claimed to receive, while in a trance, messages from the angel Gabriel; these were written down by his followers and formed the basis of the Koran. Preaching in public first in about 616, he offended many Meccans and was forced, in 622, to flee to Medina. From this flight, the *Hegira*, the Muslims date their calendar. Here Mohammed became dictator, broke with Judaism and declared Mecca, not Jerusalem, the holy city. Successful attacks on Meccan caravans

The Ascent of Mohammed to heaven mounted on his horse Al-burak from a Persian Ms of 1502.

brought him revenue, one such venture leading to the battle of Badr (624), where his victory enabled him to spread his influence over a wide area. In spite of a defeat in 625 at Mount Uhud, his followers increased, and in 628 Mecca surrendered to him. It now became the religious capital, and the Muslim faith compulsory for all Mohammed's followers.

Though he claimed that Islam was the confirmation of both the Jewish and the Christian scriptures, he broke with both and offered to all who came under his dominion the alternatives of conversion, destruction or tribute; the acceptance of the last provided the bulk of his revenue. Before his death (7 June 632) he was in control of the whole of Arabia, had summoned Persia and the Eastern Emperor to accept his faith and was preparing for war with Syria.

¶ WARREN, RUTH. *Muhammad, Prophet of Islam.* 1971

See also ISLAM.

Moluccas: group of islands in the Pacific between Celebes and New Guinea. The inhabitants are a mixture of Papuan, Malayan, Javanese, other races of the region and some European blood. There are extremely primitive elements, but Christianity, Islam and a higher culture generally are found where contact with other peoples has occurred, e.g. in coastal areas. The islands were a source of spices as far back as Roman times, and the group was long known as the Spice Islands.

Portuguese, Spanish and Dutch rivalry eventually resulted in Dutch control until 1942. After a period of occupation by the Japanese (1942–45) they became part of Indonesia in 1949.

Monaco: small principality on the eastern flank of southern France, bordering the Mediterranean. Monaco is also the name of its chief town occupying a peninsula which, with two other connected towns –

La Condamine and Monte Carlo surrounding the habour – is governed by a prince but under the protection of France. The headland once bore a temple used at different times by Greeks and Phoenicians and doubtless helpful to sailors identifying their position. Monaco has belonged to private families, to France, Spain, Sardinia and lastly to the family of Prince Rainier who, in 1956, married the American film star Grace Kelly.

Monastery: building housing a community of monks. Because they were designed for religious communities, monasteries tended to follow a similar general plan. The most important building was the church. On its south side was a square *garth* or garden surrounded by an arched *cloister*, in the sunniest side of which the monks could study and copy manuscripts, each man working in a little alcove known as a *carrel*. In another part of the cloister the novices were instructed, and some sections were used as offices by the cellarer, who was responsible for the monastery's domestic arrangements.

The *refectory* adjoined the cloister, and a *washing-room*, with running water, was attached to it, as the monks were obliged to wash before and after meals. The kitchen, conveniently near to the refectory, also had a water supply. Monasteries were always situated beside a stream because of this insistence on cleanliness and good drainage.

In the *warming-room* a fire was kept burning during cold weather. Above either this room or the refectory was the *dormitory*, usually approached by two flights of stairs, the day-stair leading from the monastic buildings and the night-stair by which the monks could go directly into the church for night services.

The *chapter house,* where daily meetings were held, stood close to the church. At a little distance from the main buildings

was the *infirmary*, where aged and sick monks were cared for. The abbot's house and the monastery guest-house were beside the main gateway, where stood also a small office used by the almoner to distribute food and clothing to the poor.

¶ UNSTEAD, R. J. *Monasteries.* 1970
See also ABBEYS *for* illustration; ORDERS, MILITARY; ORDERS, RELIGIOUS.

Money: medium of exchange for goods and services. R. G. Hawtrey wrote that 'Money is one of those concepts, which, like a teaspoon or an umbrella, . . . are definable primarily by the use or purpose which they serve'. Its primary function is to be the medium of exchange. Thus we receive money for the work we do or the goods we produce, and we use this to pay for the goods and services we require. This replaces a system of barter, in which goods are exchanged for other goods. Secondly, money is a unit of account. It enables us to evaluate goods, services, wages, rents, insurance contracts, etc. Thirdly, money provides a reserve of purchasing power.

All kinds of strange commodities have been used as money in different parts of the world at various times. Pastoral peoples have used cattle, and the word "pecuniary" is derived from the Latin word *pecus*, cattle. In the early days of New South Wales, rum was the medium of exchange, and cigarettes served this purpose in the black markets of Europe after World War II, while in Borneo human skulls were used as the standard of value, and pigs and palm nuts were used for the actual process of exchange. In the Western system gold is the standard of value and paper money the medium of exchange.

In highly developed countries over 90 per cent of the total value of money transactions is settled by cheque, while small transactions are usually paid for in cash. Thus the bank deposits serve as money; the cheques are merely instructions to the banks about the handling of these deposits.

¶ QUIGGIN. A. H. *The Story of Money*. 1956

Mongolia: the Mongolian People's Republic lying between China and the USSR, and Inner Mongolia, stretching along the Republic's southern border. The Living Buddha of Urga was Mongolia's titular head, with a government dominated by a local aristocracy who broke away from China after the 1911 revolution. With Russian aid a revolutionary government was set up in 1921, Urga the capital becoming Ulan Bator. Part of inner Mongolia fell under Japanese rule during Japan's Manchurian adventure in the 1930s. The revolutionary socialist leader, Choibalsan, headed the Mongolian government 1939–52. After a plebiscite in 1945 independence was recognised by China. Mongolia became a member of the United Nations in 1961. *See* CHINA for map.

Mongols: group of nomadic tribes in east-central Asia, who raided for over 2,000 years the more settled peoples,

The Mongols lay siege to a Chinese city, killing, burning, cutting down forests and overthrowing fortresses, from a manuscript in the Bibliotheque Nationale, Paris.

particularly the Chinese. They were united into a single people by Genghis Khan in the early 13th century. The empire which he established came to include nearly all Asia and Russia, omitting India and Arabia. It split up within a century but gave dynasties to China, India and Persia and contributed indirectly to the emergence of a Russian state. Though the first impact of the Mongol invasion was wholly destructive, the later Mongol rulers were in many cases enlightened administrators.

See also GENGHIS KHAN; MOGUL, etc.

Monopoly: literally, "single selling". If one person has the sole right to sell a particular article, he can charge what he likes. From Norman times onwards the English kings used the granting of monopolies to obtain money from merchants, who were then able to make huge profits. In modern times monopoly is brought about by companies engaged in the same business joining together to make one great firm. In England this is now controlled by the government through the Monopolies Commission. Some of the greatest industries, such as coal, gas, electricity and the railways, have been "nationalised", i.e. they have become government monopolies operated for the benefit of all.

In the USA the more familiar term is "Trust". Most famous of the early virtual monopolies were the Standard Oil of John D. Rockefeller and the United States Steel Corporation (1902). There were also Whiskey, Lead and Sugar Trusts, and other industrialists built empires in mining, railways and tobacco. Despite such measures as the Sherman Anti-Trust Act of 1890, there was little effective control. A more important landmark was the Clayton Anti-Trust Act of 1914, which greatly strengthened the earlier measure.

Monroe Doctrine: declaration contained in the annual message to Congress of President James Monroe (1758–1831), prompted by the threat of European powers to suppress the revolt of the Spanish-American colonies. The doctrine maintained that the American continent was no territory for future European colonisation, that there was an essentially different political system in the Americas from Europe, that the USA would regard any attempt by European powers to extend their influence in the Americas as dangerous to its peace and security, and that the USA would not interfere with existing European colonies, nor participate in purely European wars.

Montcalm, Louis, Marquis de (1712–59): French general. A soldier all his life, he distinguished himself in the wars of Polish and of Austrian Succession and in 1756 was given command of the French troops in Canada. Here he was at first outstandingly successful, capturing Forts Oswego (1756) and William Henry (1757) and defeating Abercromby's attack at Ticonderoga (1758). He did not, however, exploit his success and fell back to defend Quebec against Wolfe. For two months he repulsed all attacks but was out-

Montcalm congratulates his victorious troops after the Battle of Carellon, 1758.

flanked by the British scaling the Heights of Abraham. In the battle which followed, after behaving with conspicuous gallantry, he was mortally wounded.

Monte Cassino: ancient monastery on a mountain massif about fifty miles [80 kilometres] north of Naples. The monastery was founded by St Benedict of Nursia in 529 on the site of a temple of Apollo. Fourteen hundred years later the Germans took advantage of its almost impregnable position guarding the road northwards to delay the Allied advance in 1943. It was almost destroyed as a result but has since been rebuilt. As the first house of the Benedictine Order, Monte Cassino was the prototype of such institutions in Western Europe.

¶ MAJDALANY, FRED. *Cassino.* 1957

Montenegro: Balkan country formerly independent, incorporated in Yugoslavia after World War I. It rises from the eastern shore of the Adriatic Sea to a rocky plateau, from which it took its name meaning "Black Mountain". This difficult terrain helped its people against the Turks in the 14th and 15th centuries and against the Germans in 1941.

The seal of Simon de Montfort.

Montfort, Simon de, Earl of Leicester

(*c.* 1208–65): baronial leader in England. Born in France, Simon inherited the earldom of Leicester through his English grandmother. Provoked by favouritism to foreigners and heavy papal taxes, he led the opposition to Henry III (1216–72), whose sister he had married, and secured the concessions known as the Provisions of Oxford, which set out methods for the reorganisation and reform of the country's affairs. When Henry broke his agreement to these measures, Simon defeated him at Lewes (1264) and summoned a parliament containing town representatives for the first time. He was defeated and killed at Evesham (1265).

¶ LUCKOCK, ELIZABETH and GRUNDY, CAROLINE. *Simon de Montfort: reformer and rebel.* 1970

Montreal: Canadian city situated 1,000 miles [1,600 kilometres] up the St Lawrence river. Jacques Cartier first reconnoitred the site in the 1530s, and Catholic missionaries settled there permanently in 1642. Extensive fortifications in 1722 marked its growing defensive, trading and manufacturing importance. In 1760 de Vaudreuil effectively ceded Canada to Great Britain by surrendering Montreal. American colonists occupied the city in 1776–77. After the Lachine canal construction in 1825 it displaced Quebec as the chief port. The McGill and Catholic Universities have helped to make Montreal the educational centre of Canada, as its widely diversified industries have made it the largest city. The words of one of the early settlers, that they were planting "a grain of mustard seed destined to overshadow the land", have proved prophetic. *See* CANADA for map.

¶ COOPER, J. I. *Montreal: a brief history.* 1970

Moors (Spanish *moros*, dark): a race of people now spread widely through countries of North Africa from Egypt to Morocco, to which they give their name, and descended from the ancient Mauri with admixture of blood contributed by the various conquerors of the land: Arabs, Numidians, Phoenicians and Romans, plus some Spanish acquired through their own domination of Spain during the Saracen occupation of the peninsula between AD 710 and 1238. In the latter half of the 8th century the Moors restored the ancient Roman university of Cordova, which became their main centre of learning, and excelled in science, mathematics and philosophy. Being largely Muslims they were threatened by the upsurge of Christianity in Spain in the 11th century, but King Yusuf of the Almoravids in North Africa came to their aid and seized the whole of Andalusia, which led to the Moors' regaining control of the peninsula, with the king of Morocco as their ruler. In the first half of the 13th century, however, the Christians conquered the Muslims, who were driven into Granada, where they settled. In 1568 Philip II of Spain ordered the suppression of Moorish ways and a Christian education for all children. The Moors of Granada rebelled and many fled to Africa, the last remnants of the Muslim Moors being expelled in 1609. *See colour section*

Moral Rearmament: a 20th-century religious movement. Its founder, Frank Buchman, was a Lutheran minister in the USA who, inspired by a conference in England in 1908, returned home to devote himself to fostering, at first especially among university students, a life lived more closely under God's guidance, by strict following of moral principles and by mutual help and encouragement in spiritual matters. The movement spread outwards and reached England in 1926, where it flourished particularly in Oxford, although the name "Oxford Group" was apparently first applied later in South Africa. It met some opposition and was accused of Fascist sympathies; but it is now firmly established, though no longer conspicuously spreading, with headquarters in Los Angeles and, for Western Europe, at Caux in Switzerland.

¶ BUCKMAN, FRANK. *Remaking the World: Moral Re-Armament.* 1961; THORNTON-DUESBERY, J. *The Open Secret of Moral Re-Armament.* 1964

More, Sir Thomas (1478–1535): English scholar and statesman and Roman Catholic martyr. After studying law, he entered Parliament in 1504, and in due course his talents attracted the notice of King Henry VIII, who advanced his career until in 1529 he was appointed Lord Chancellor to succeed the fallen Wolsey. His home at Chelsea was notable both for the calm and happiness of his family life and also for the scholars and writers who were welcomed there. Of More's own writings, the *Utopia*, a description of an imaginary ideal human community, is the most famous. His strong religious principles compelled him to oppose Henry in his efforts to divorce Queen Catherine and in the king's break with the Pope, and he was executed on a charge of high treason. In 1886 the Roman Catholic Church conferred on him the title of Blessed and in 1935 that of Saint.

¶ STANLEY-WRENCH, MARGARET. *The Story of Sir Thomas More.* 1961

Morganatic: term applied to the marriage of a man or woman of royal, or occasionally of noble, birth to someone of inferior social status. This is of little account today, but in the past it could prevent the offspring of the marriage from succeeding to the nobler partner's titles or possessions. It is incorrect to apply the term to the marriage of a reigning sovereign.

Moriscos or the **Little Moors:** Spanish Muslims who accepted baptism, and their descendants, many being of the same race as the Christians but descended from converts to Islam. They were hard workers and therefore valued by the community; but, following the suppression of all Moorish ways in 1568 and the resulting rebellion, they were expelled from Spain, some of them becoming pirates on the Barbary coast and others conspiring against Spain with various enemies, especially France. It is said that the English Morris Dance is based on a dance of the Moriscos.

Mormons: religious sect, now number-

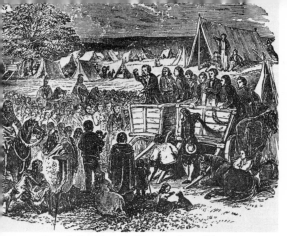

Joseph Smith preaching in the wilderness.

ing over two million followers, also known as the Latter Day Saints, owing its origins to the publication in 1830 of the *Book of Mormon*, based on a revelation claimed by Joseph Smith (1805–44; *see* separate entry). The new Church, first established at Fayette in New York State, aroused much opposition on social and religious grounds. Nevertheless, the movement spread to centres in Ohio, Missouri and Illinois, growing in numbers and influence. Violence often followed the settlers, culminating in the lynching of Smith in the jail at Carthage. The leadership of the Mormons passed to Brigham Young (1801–77; *see* separate entry), who led mass migrations to the valley of the Great Salt Lake in Utah and from 1850–57 was the governor of the new territory. The Mormon religion countenanced marriage to more than one wife at the same time (polygamy), and not till this was abolished, in 1896, was Utah admitted into the Union as the 49th State.

Temple Square, Salt Lake City, during a conference.

Morocco: the largest of the Barbary states in the north-west corner of Africa, with coastlines on the Mediterranean and Atlantic and containing the Atlas Mountains. The area was ruled by the Carthaginians and the Romans and, later, was a powerful state under a succession of Moslem rulers. The country became a French protectorate in 1912, following intense rivalry for control between France and Germany. Morocco gained independence in 1956. After a state of emergency was declared in 1965 King Hassan II (b. 1930) took over the administration. *See* MEDITERRANEAN for map.

¶ CAVANNA, BETTY. *Morocco.* 1972

Morris, William (1834–96): poet, artist, craftsman and social reformer. He held a strong belief that mechanical processes were destroying the beauty of craftsmanship, particularly in the making of household objects and the production of fine books. Some of his wallpapers may still be found in domestic use. Morris was a member of the group of artists known as the Pre-Raphaelites, formed in London in 1840.

See colour section.

¶ In WARREN, C. H. *Great Men.* Vol. 5, 1956

A mosaic in the Apse of the Basilica of S. Apollinare in Classe, Ravenna.

Mosaic: pictures and patterns made of tiny pieces of stone, glass or other substances set closely together. The word comes, not from Moses, but from the nine sister-goddesses of the arts, the Muses. Mosaic was known in ancient Mesopotamia, Greece and Rome. It was used first for floors, and later on walls and ceilings as well. It was an art which reached great heights under the Byzantine Empire, and the mosaics to be seen in the churches of Ravenna, Italy, and in St Mark's, Venice, were executed in the Byzantine tradition.

The Mayas and Aztecs of Central America used mosaic on ceremonial masks and shields and fashioned wonderful mantles out of mosaic made with feathers. *See colour section.*

¶ ROSSI, FERNANDO. *Mosaics: a survey of their history and techniques.*

Moscow: with its administrative stronghold of the Kremlin, the capital city of the USSR. The 800th anniversary of its founding was celebrated in 1947. It was a centre of resistance to Mongols and Tartars and became, in the early 14th century, the chosen base of Ivan I, grand duke of Vladimir. Ivan III (1440-1505) made it the capital of his Russian kingdom. In 1712 St Petersburg (Leningrad) replaced it as capital. Napoleon occupied Moscow for five weeks in 1812. It again became the seat of government in 1918 after the Revolution. The Germans approached within twenty miles [32 kilometres] in 1941.

See USSR for map.
See also KREMLIN.

Motion (moving) pictures also known as **movies, films, cinema pictures,** etc.: film sequence, with or without soundtrack. Properly speaking, there is no such thing as a moving picture. A great industry and art form which has had an incalculable effect on the social history of the 20th century depends ultimately on an optical illusion.

Scientists call this "persistence of vision", by which they mean the way the retina, that part of the eyeball which registers images of things seen, actually retains that image for the merest fraction of time after it has, in fact, passed from view. If, that is to say, a series of still pictures – for example, of a child running, each picture showing a slightly later development of the action than the one preceding – is viewed fast enough, the eye, by means of overlapping images, supplies the illusion of continuous movement. A reel of film consists of just such a series of still pictures. If there *is* any such thing as a moving picture it is the human eye that is its prime inventor. What the so-called inventors provided was the apparatus – the cameras, projectors, roll-film and so on – which made it possible to exploit this fact of physiology.

The development of the "movie" occurred almost simultaneously in three countries – the USA, Great Britain and France. Which deserves the chief credit is still a matter of polite patriotic contention.

In 1889 Thomas Alva Edison (1847–1931) (*see* separate entry), invented a motion picture machine which he called the Kinetoscope, a slot machine containing a film 50 feet [15.24 metres] long. Marketed commercially in 1894, it proved so popular that soon Kinetoscope Parlors were to be found all over the United States. In the same year Woodville Latham invented a rudimentary projector, the Panoptikon, which projected moving pictures on to a large screen for mass viewing. In England in 1889 William Friese-Greene patented the first of a series of motion picture cameras. Working along broadly similar lines in France were the brothers Auguste and Louis Lumière. On 23 November 1897 Queen Victoria

set the seal of royal approval on the new craze when, at Windsor Castle, she watched a film of her Diamond Jubilee procession, shot in the preceding June.

In their early days films were part of the entertainment offered at music halls. That is why the length of a reel of film was – and has remained ever since – fixed at 1,000 feet [304.8 metres], a length that took about as long to run as the average variety turn.

The film industry grew and prospered. When World War I (1914–18) broke out the United States, far removed from the battlefields, was able to draw ahead of her European competitors. Hollywood in California became the film capital of the world. The "star" system developed. Charlie Chaplin (b. 1889), Buster Keaton (1895–1966) and Mary Pickford (b. 1893) were examples of actors and actresses whose names became household words.

Colour and sound, as applied to cinematography, interested the inventors from the very beginning. Coloured film, originally coloured by hand, has gradually been improved to a point where, if it has a fault, it is that of being almost too good to be true. In 1927, with the phenomenal success of a film called *The Jazz Singer*, which was part "talkie", the motion picture industry entered a new phase.

Since then, the film industry has looked for further refinements, in particular the stereoscopic or three-dimensional image. The three-dimensional film aims at presenting moving images with a measurable dimension of depth, thus re-creating the solid world seen by binocular (two-eyed) human beings. This effect has not been achieved with complete success, although films do appear containing 3-D sequences, and several full-length 3-D films were produced in the 1950s.

Television has brought far reaching changes. An enormous proportion of the films made every year are now produced

Above left: Charlie Chaplin as he was in the days of his famous silent films. Middle: Buster Keaton in Paris with his pet monkey. Right: Mary Pickford, "America's Sweetheart" and most famous filmstar of the twenties. Right: Modern film techniques used in filming The Beast Must Die *in 1971.*

for television. The development of simple home video-tape machines (these record sound and vision very much in the same way as an ordinary tape recorder records sound) means that people will be able to record their favourite television programmes, and see them again whenever they wish. It will also be possible to hire other taped programmes from video-tape libraries. These programmes will include many famous films which once filled millions of cinema seats all over the world. Motion pictures are moving out of the cinemas into our living rooms. Sociologists are still trying to decide whether, on balance, this is good or bad. Certainly, for millions of people nowadays, moving pictures wield more influence than the printed word.

¶ ROBINSON, DAVID. *World Cinema: a short history.* 1973

Motor car, car, automobile: self-propelled passenger vehicle for use on roads. The word "automobile", more used in America than in Britain, is a hybrid of Greek and Latin. This article confines itself to the motor car, but it has, of course, much in common with the van, the coach, the omnibus and the truck in its mechanical features and in the history of its development.

Apart from wind-propulsion, the earliest motive power applied by man to a moving vehicle was steam; and indeed a steam driven car was placed on the road by Joseph Cugnot in France in 1769, some thirty-six years before the first steam locomotive ran on rails. Technical difficulties, such as the weight of the vehicle on the roads of the time and the limited range of operation, prevented its general adoption, though the steam motor car, in its later development, had reached by the 1920s quite a high level of performance, which was, however, outstripped by that of the contemporary petrol driven car. Nevertheless it still has some support, particularly in the USA, and may yet prove one of the answers to the problem of the pollution of the atmosphere by exhaust gases from petrol engines.

The first electric car was produced in 1888, and this means of propulsion has enjoyed some success, particularly for its silence and absence of exhaust, but further experiment is needed to make it suitable for general motoring use.

The motor car as we know it today is propelled by internal combustion, that is to say by the explosion of gases in the cylinders of the engine, which sets up a motion that is transmitted mechanically to the road wheels. The explosion is generally produced by an electric spark igniting vaporised petrol; the alternative of using diesel oil, exploded by compression, is less suited to motor cars than to larger commercial vehicles.

It is not easy to pinpoint the date of the appearance of the first petrol driven car, and the line between the earliest motor cars and motor tricycles is seldom clear. An experimental vehicle was exhibited in Vienna in 1873, but the honour of being responsible for the first commercially produced vehicles, in the years 1885–86, appears to lie between Carl Benz and Gottlieb Daimler.

Paul and Gottlieb Daimler in the world's first car, the 1886 Daimler.

The early motoring enthusiasts were very much shackled by legal restrictions, at a time when most people travelled the roads on or behind horses: indeed the earliest cars were often called "horseless carriages". In England, it was not until November 1896 that the last requirements were repealed of the Acts of Parliament of 1865 and 1878, that a man should walk in front of any mechanically propelled vehicle on public roads, though from 1878 he no longer had to carry a red flag. The speed limit, however, on all roads remained very low, and even after World War I it was still 20 m.p.h. for some years. The annual London to Brighton run of veteran cars commemorates the "liberation" of 1896.

The main technical problems which faced the early motorists were the means of exploding the gases in the engine cylinders and the manufacture of reliable pneumatic tyres, with which the name of John Boyd Dunlop (1840–1921) is associated. Subsequent progress in development and design can be broadly described as improvements and refinements of the original concept, such as electric lighting, four-wheel brakes, independent suspension and automatic transmission.

On the manufacturing side, the early handmade cars were, in due course, superseded by mass-produced vehicles put together on a production line. Henry Ford (1863–1947) (*see* separate entry) in the USA was a pioneer of this development with his famous "Model T".

¶ ELLACOTT, S. E. *Wheels on the Road.* 1956; ROLT, L. T. C. *Motor Cars.* 1957; THOMAS, DAVID ST. J. *The Motor Revolution.* 1961

Mountain states, The, USA: inland western region of the United States, made up of the states of Arizona, Colorado, Idaho, Montana, Nevada, New Mexico, Utah and Wyoming. In the southern reaches the dominant feature is the Great

American Desert. Although rising in the west to the Rocky Mountains, the tallest range in the United States, the land is very dry. The northern parts of the region are also fairly high, but here desert is primarily replaced with high plateaux of grasslands and vast forests. The major rivers in the area are the Missouri and Colorado.

Settlement came late to this entire region. Though many settlers passed through the desert and mountains on their way to the Pacific coast, the region remained basically in the hands of scattered tribes of American Indians until the last thirty years of the 19th century. Even after a series of Indian wars led to the opening of the area for settlement, population grew slowly. Arizona and New Mexico did not, in fact, become states until 1912, and the region remains by far the most sparsely settled part of the continental United States.

Mining, grazing and tourism provide most of the income for the region. In the north, sheep are grazed in the plains and plateaux, while in the south herds of cattle are maintained on vast areas of near-desert. In the various mountain ranges of the region, such vital minerals as molybdenum, lead, silver, copper and oil are all extracted. Tourism also is crucial. The almost untouched mountains and valleys of the north, organised into such areas as Yellowstone National Park, draw many thousands of campers and sightseers each year. In Nevada the lure of legalised gambling and elaborate stage shows have made Las Vegas an entertainment centre for the nation and provide the basic force in Nevada's economy. But this remains primarily a land of wide, thinly populated areas – the least tamed of all the land area in the continental United States.
See AMERICA for map.

Mozambique: mainly lowland malarial country on the east of the main plateau of Africa; its capital city is Lourenço Marques. From the time of its discovery in 1498 by Vasco da Gama it has been actively colonised by the Portuguese, who have made efforts to develop its economy. The tropical climate favours a variety of small-scale products. Mozambique became a centre of the slave trade till 1878. It is possible to trace historical links with this in the present conscripted labour in the sugar plantations and the exported labour to South African mines.

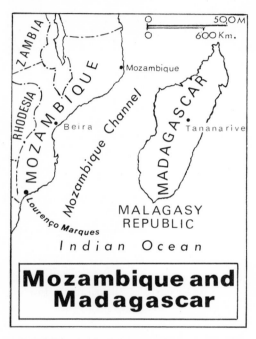

Mozambique and Madagascar

Munich: German city, capital of the *Land* of Bavaria. It originated as a Benedictine settlement (*Munichen* – home of the monks). From the 13th century until 1918 it was the home of the Wittelsbach rulers of Bavaria and grew in size and prosperity, its commercial expansion being checked only by the Thirty Years War (1618-48). The nineteenth century brought renewed and rapid expansion and it became an important centre for international exhibitions and congresses.

In the 1920s the city was the breeding-ground for extremist political groups – notably the Nazi Party – and Hitler's first mass meetings were held there.

Prime Minister Neville Chamberlain returns with the Munich Agreement of 1938.

Munich Agreement (29 September 1938): a settlement of the Czechoslovak crisis reached by France, Britain, Germany and Italy, by which the strongly fortified district of the Sudetenland was handed over to Germany. The agreement, virtually dictated by Hitler, led to the complete destruction of the Czechoslovak state by Germany in 1939.

Mural painting: painting direct on walls for decorative purposes. The art was widely practised in ancient Egypt and in many other early civilizations. In Europe the greatest surviving examples are the work of such Italian artists as Giotto, Masaccio, Fra Angelico, Andrea del Sarto and Raphael (*see* FLORENTINE ART). Among more recent examples, one of the best known in England is the Painted Hall at Greenwich, south-east London, executed by Sir James Thornhill (*c.* 1676-1734) in what is now the Royal Naval College. *See colour section.*

¶ MERRIFIELD, MARY. *The Art of Fresco Painting*, edited by A. C. Sewter. 1952

Muscovite: from Moskva or Moscow. The people of that area, and their rulers, formed the nucleus of a Russian state. Ivan III (1440-1505), grand duke of Muscovy, made himself independent of Tartar control; and Ivan IV (1530-84) was the first proclaimed Tsar of Muscovy and, in effect, the first Tsar of Russia.

Museums: buildings where natural and man-made objects from different periods of time all over the world are stored and displayed.

The word "museum" was originally the name given by the ancient Greeks to temples devoted to the Muses, the nine sister goddesses of the arts and sciences. The famous Museum of Alexandria, founded *c.* 280 BC and destroyed in 48 BC, was more like a university than a museum. There is little evidence that things were deliberately preserved for posterity during the earlier civilisations, but, with the coming of the Renaissance to Western Europe, interest in the past was awakened and people began to hunt for classical relics. Royal and noble families formed collections of antiquities and artistic treasures which were added to by succeeding generations; but they were prompted only by personal interest or pride of possession, and little attempt was made to gather objects for the benefit of others. Nevertheless the acquisitive habits of princes gave rise to many of the great European museums. These rich collections, often still housed in the palace homes of their former owners, gradually passed into state ownership as a result of social or political upheaval treasures accumulated by the Medici family can be admired today in the palaces of Florence: the famous Hermitage in Leningrad is so called because it was the retreat to which Catherine the Great invited her friends to admire the collection she started in 1765, while the Louvre, housing royal treasures, became public property during the French revolutionary period.

The 16th and 17th centuries were periods

of exploration and discovery: learned men acquired curios brought back by travellers from foreign parts, hoarding them for investigation. One such scholar collector was the naturalist John Tradescant who, with his son, built up the "Museum Tradescantianum" in London. In 1659 the younger Tradescant gave this collection to Elias Ashmole, who in turn presented it, with his own collection of coins and curios, to Oxford University. Sir Christopher Wren was commissioned to design a building to house the gifts, and the Ashmolean Museum was opened in 1683 as what seems to have been the first "public museum". The collection outgrew its first home, replaced by the present Ashmolean in 1841-8. The original building now houses a collection of scientific instruments.

So far, the collections which were to form the basis of modern museums had been miscellaneous affairs depending on the enthusiasms of their originators. During the 18th century, collecting became much more methodical and one of the foremost collectors of this period was an English doctor, Sir Hans Sloane, who gathered natural history specimens during his travels. On his death his collections were purchased by the government as the foundation of the British Museum, opened in 1759 – the first instance of public money being used to found a museum.

The Industrial Revolution contributed to a rapid development of museums in the western hemisphere, especially during the 19th century. The progress of scientific investigation and the development of technology brought in its train a thirst for knowledge and a desire for popular education. The Great Exhibition of 1851 gave impetus to museums in Britain, and the South Kensington group of national museums were constructed to house the objects of natural interest, applied and mechanical art, arranged for public exhibition at the instigation of the Prince Consort.

In the New World the first museums were established towards the end of the 18th century, and from then on nearly all of them were deliberately planned as part of the educational system. Resources were greater than in other parts of the world, and before long the USA was leading the world in the richness of collections, buildings designed to house them, the techniques applied to their preservation and display and the means adopted to make them attractively useful to the whole community. One of the most complex and exciting is the Guggenheim Museum in New York.

The Guggenheim Museum, New York, designed by Frank Lloyd Wright in 1943-46.

Modern developments have included open air museums, pioneered in Sweden, consisting of complete homes, farms, streets, etc., restored or re-erected to illustrate life in a particular region or period. In recent years increasing attention has been paid to industrial collections, representing the working lives of people and their artifacts, as well as their artistic and cultural achievements.

Today, museums are actively engaged in the life of the communities they serve, organising services for schools and children, concerts and film shows and local expeditions. They are growing closer to the original meaning of the word as homes for the muses – for history, art, music and all the branches of science which have developed since the days of Aristotle.

See also INDIVIDUAL ENTRIES.

Musical instruments: devices, made variously of metal, wood and other vegetable, mineral and animal substances, for sending out sound waves which can be received and translated by the receptive ear. While anyone can bang on a piano or twang a guitar and produce a noise, the function of musical instruments is to serve as vehicles for producing those patterns of organised sound to which we give the name of music.

The beginning of musical instruments is lost in antiquity. Probably the earliest were *percussion instruments*, those from which sound is produced by striking. The simplest of these instruments – the tom-tom of tribal Africa, the Chinese gong, the Spanish castanet, the cymbal, triangle and tambourine – can produce no melodies, no harmonics, even in the hands of the most accomplished performer. How, then, are they musical instruments at all? The answer lies in that basic ingredient of all music – rhythm.

Percussion instruments can produce rhythmic patterns of long and short beats of great dramatic quality. The beat of drums, repeated over and over again in a pattern of steadily increasing intensity, can have an almost hypnotic effect, rousing its hearers to a warlike frenzy or religious ecstasy.

Stringed instruments, from which sound is produced by vibrating a string, can be subdivided into three categories. In some, the vibration is achieved simply by plucking the string. The lyre, so often shown in representations of Apollo, the Greek god of music, is an example of an ancient stringed instrument of this type. Others are the harp (*see* separate entry), the lute and the guitar.

In a second group of stringed instruments, sound is produced by drawing a bow across strings. The bow was an oriental invention which the West adopted and greatly improved upon. As long ago as the 8th century BC the Persians possessed a boat-shaped, bowed stringed instrument called a *rubab* or *rebab*, adaptations of which are still to be found in parts of the East. From it was derived the European rebec, a stringed instrument which, in medieval religious paintings, may be seen as a component of many an angelic orchestra.

An important part of the modern orchestra is made up of the bowed, stringed instruments which form the violin family: the violin, viola, violoncello (more often nowadays abbreviated to cello) and double-bass. The ancestors of all four were six-stringed viols, which were far inferior to the instruments which superseded them. Violins made by the great Italian makers of the 17th and 18th centuries, notably Antonio Stradivari (1644–1737) and Nicolo Amati (1596–1684), both of them members of famous families of violin makers, have never been surpassed.

Strictly speaking, the third subdivision of stringed instruments, that of stringed *keyboard instruments*, requires a certain qualification. All such instruments are played by striking the keys of a keyboard, and to this extent utilise an element of percussion. In the pianoforte and clavichord, one of the piano's forerunners, percussion plays a larger part. When a clavichord key is pressed down it raises a

1. WOMAN PLAYING A HARP
2. WOMAN PLAYING A PORTATIVE ORGAN
3. MILITARY DRUMMER (FROM THREE 16th Cent WOODCUTS)

CZECH GIRAFFE PIANO 19th Cent.

18th Cent. HURDY-GURDY

OLIPHANT 14th Cent.

small, wedge-shaped piece of brass (called a "tangent") which strikes the corresponding string, setting it vibrating. In the piano, tiny hammers take the place of the tangents.

With the virginals, the spinet and the harpsichord, all three of them members of the keyboard family, we are, at one remove, back to plucking strings. Striking the keys of their keyboards activates little pieces of wood called "jacks". Quills (called *plectra* – singular, *plectrum*), which are attached to the jacks, pluck the strings.

Among stringed keyboard instruments the piano is the outstanding solo musical instrument of the Western world and one for which many composers have created some of their best works. The man who made the first instrument to which the name of pianoforte could properly be applied deserves a greater fame than posterity has accorded him. He was Bartolommeo Cristofori (1655–1731), a harpsichord maker of Padua in Italy, who made the first piano in 1709, while in the service of Prince Ferdinand de' Medici.

Not all keyboard instruments are stringed. The carillon, a complete set of bells capable of being rung by one man, and the organ, a wind instrument, both possess keyboards.

Man must have found out very early in his history that a hollow reed or stalk, or an animal's horn, plus the power of his own lungs, could produce a sound. Once he had acquired that basic knowledge the evolution of *wind instruments* was bound to follow. All wind instruments, however apparently sophisticated, are extensions of that simple pipe, that natural horn.

Among wood-winds – which, as the name implies, are wind instruments made of wood – are the flute and its smaller brothers the piccolo and the fife. The recorder, a simple wind instrument dating back to the Middle Ages and for a long time almost forgotten, has had a return to popularity in recent years. The oboe, a development of the 18th century hautbois ("high-wood") is, well played, an instrument of entrancing purity of tone. The bassoon, with its lower register, and the versatile clarinet are other wood-winds indispensable to a well-balanced orchestra.

Brass instruments were originally made of brass and are still so called even though they may be made of some different metal (just as, to make things easy, saxophones, which are made of metal, are classed as wood-winds because they have reed mouthpieces). They include horns, bugles, trumpets, tubas, trombones, cornets, saxhorns and flugelhorns.

A wind instrument of ancient pedigree is the bagpipe. Although we associate it particularly with Scotland, it arrived there only towards the close of the Middle Ages. Centuries earlier the bagpipe was known in ancient Persia, in India and China. A bronze figure, found at Richborough in Kent, of a Roman soldier playing a bagpipe suggests that the Romans may have brought the instrument to Britain.

Muslims: name given to the followers of Islam, the religion founded by Mohammed, who accept the *Koran* and undertake the five obligatory duties of reciting their creed, daily prayers, payment of alms, fasting, and pilgrimage to Mecca. There are several divisions, holding different beliefs as to who is the true successor to Mohammed as head of the whole Muslim community. The largest group are the *Sunni,* who cling to tradition and the mystical character of religion; among others are the *Shia*, who expect the return of the twelfth Imam, Mohammed al-Muntazar, who disappeared in 878, and the *Ismailis*, led by the Aga Khan. Recently "modernism" has led to changes in traditional Islam, e.g. in Muslim dress and the condition of women, who are generally allowed much greater freedom and need not, for example, wear the face-covering veil. Islam is the world's largest non-Christian religion with an estimated following, in 1968, of 475 million.

Muslim League: founded in 1906 to encourage educational and political advance among the Muslims of India, it became the principal agent in the struggle against the domination of the Hindu majority. In 1909 it secured separate Muslim constituencies under the Morley-Minto reforms. From 1916 until his death in 1947, Mahommed Ali Jinnah was its President. Though he welcomed the 1935 India Act, his fear of an India dominated by the Hindu Congress Party made him, from 1940, proclaim partition as the Muslim policy, and, more than any other influence, the League was responsible for the creation of the Muslim state of Pakistan (*see* separate entry).

Mussolini, Benito (1881–1945): Prime Minister and Dictator of Italy, frequently called *Il Duce*, the leader. The son of a blacksmith with revolutionary opinions, he early developed an insubordinate spirit, organising trade unions, promoting strikes, being sent to prison and watched by the police as a trouble-maker. Widely read and a skilful journalist, he became a powerful force in the Italian Socialist party, editing the *Avanti*, its official newspaper and, later, founding his own journal, *Il Popolo d'Italia,* which greatly influenced the workers and the younger generation.

After World War I, in which he was seriously wounded, he broke away from the Socialists and founded the Fascist political movement (*see* FASCISM). Using the symbol of authority in ancient Rome (the *fasces*), the Roman military salute of the outstretched arm, and parading in black shirts, the party staged an appeal

which won them thirty-six seats in the government (1921) and culminated the next year in the dramatic Fascist march on Rome, organised by Mussolini but not led by him (until the final stage, undramatically, in a motor-car). Awed by this show of force the king (Victor Emmanuel III, ruled 1900–46) and the government gave way and Mussolini, though theoretically remaining a monarchist, became undisputed dictator, pursuing rapid reconstruction and economic expansion at home and an aggressive foreign policy abroad. The latter made him first the ally, then the subordinate, of Hitler, and eventually brought Italy to disastrous involvement in World War II on the side of Germany. The would-be Roman emperor was executed by his own countrymen in 1945.

¶ BAYNE-JARDINE, C. *Mussolini and Italy*. 1966; ABSALOM, R. N. L. *Mussolini and the Rise of Italian Fascism*. 1969

Mutiny: the refusal of orders from, or revolt against, constituted authority, especially of men in armed forces. Though it may be revolutionary in character or the first stage in a revolutionary movement, mutiny differs from revolution in being a rising not against government but

against officers, within confined limits – ship, fleet, regiment or army.

The mutinies which have most caught public imagination have been those at sea. Perhaps the best known of all was that led by Fletcher Christian, mate of HMS *Bounty*, against Captain Bligh in 1789, when Bligh and eighteen others were cast off in an open boat in mid-Pacific and made a remarkable 4,000-mile voyage to Timor, while the mutineers established the little community on Pitcairn Island.

Two mutinies in the British Navy in 1797 are interesting in their different character. That at Spithead, led (almost certainly) by Valentine Joyce, resembled a well managed strike against intolerable conditions. Winning the sympathy of landsmen, it was fully successful, the loyalty of the mutineers never being in question, and it ended without any punishments. That at the Nore was much more bitter: "United Irishmen" and French sympathisers were among the crews, and it ended with the hanging of the ringleaders, Parker and others.

Three naval mutinies which had far-reaching effects were those of the Russian Navy at Kronstadt in 1917 – one of the early moves of the revolution – and of the Austrian Navy at Cattaro and the German at Kiel in 1918, which marked the collapse of the Central Powers in World War I.

Some mutinies on land illustrate the varied reasons prompting them. That of Dumbarton's Scottish Regiment in 1688 was a protest against the appointment of a foreign commander. The six regiments of the Pennsylvania Line who rose against General Anthony Wayne in 1781, and who might, if successful, have lost the war for the Americans, were protesting against appalling winter conditions. The very grave mutiny in the French armies in 1917, when over a million men refused orders, was due to the enormous casualties at Verdun (1916), the failure of

Nivelle's disastrous offensive, and perhaps partly to the Russian example; only Pétain's prestige and drive restored discipline in time to resist the later German offensives. The mutiny in China in 1936, when troops kidnapped General Chiang Kai-Shek and held him for several days, broke out because they wanted him to stop fighting Communists and concentrate on the Japanese in Manchuria.

For British people "The Mutiny" means the Indian rising of 1857-58. This certainly began as an army mutiny, prompted by motives which were partly social, partly religious and only indirectly political. Indian writers claim that, in spite of its limitations, it was a national movement aimed at driving foreigners out of India; and undoubtedly large numbers of civilians joined the rising, and some of the leaders wished to promote a general revolution.

Formerly the penalty for mutiny was always death. This was why escaped mutineers so often took to piracy or banditry. There was no place for them in settled society.

¶ CARDWELL, PAMELA. *The Indian Mutiny.* 1973

Mysore: state of southern India, enlarged 1953-55 to cover roughly the area in which Kanarese is spoken. Coming under the sway of the South Indian state of Vijayanagar in the 14th century, Mysore superseded that power in the 16th and, seizing Seringapatam and other territory, became prosperous under a series of able *Wadiyars* (rulers). But in the 18th century misgovernment made possible a takeover of power by Hyder Ali, whose hostility, and that of his son Tipu Sultan, towards the British led to the conquest of Mysore by Britain (1799). Responsibility for government was restored to the dynasty in 1883, and, with Indian independence in 1947, the Maharaja became Governor. *See also* INDIA.

N

Nagasaki: city on Kyushu Island and the oldest open port in Japan. In the 16th century it saw the first establishment of a Christian community in Japan. It remained open to foreign trade through two centuries of Japan's total exclusion of foreigners. Nagasaki received in 1945 the second and more powerful atomic bomb dropped on Japan. Thirty-five thousand people died, but destruction was limited by the hills which give this city its beautiful setting, damage proving less than at Hiroshima. Quickly recovering, Nagasaki soon led the world in shipbuilding output and also has steel, armaments, electrical equipment and pearl industries.

Nanking: a former capital of China, on the south bank of the Yangtze River and capital of Kiangsu province. The name means "southern capital". When the Ming emperor Chu Yüan-chang overthrew the Yüan (Mongol) dynasty in 1372, he established his capital there, building the city walls, though later Peking became the capital. Nanking was captured by the British in 1842, thus opening China to western trade. Sun Yat-sen here became president of the Chinese Republic, and in 1927 it was made the capital once more. In 1937 the Japanese captured it, surrendering it in 1945. From 1949 Peking has been China's capital.

Nansen, Fridtjof (1861-1930): Norwegian arctic explorer. Oceanographic and arctic studies led to his daring and successful venture in 1888 to cross unknown Greenland. In 1893 he sailed in the *Fram* and in three years drifted across the Arctic Ocean to Spitzbergen, whence, with one

companion, he crossed the ice along 86° 74′ N to Franz Josef Island. His work in repatriating war prisoners won him the Nobel Peace Prize in 1922. Refugee problems and Russian famine relief occupied his later years. *See colour section.*
¶ NOEL-BAKER, F. *Fridtjof Nansen.* 1958

Nantes, Edict of (1598): the order by Henry IV of France granting freedom of worship to the Protestants. Its later revocation (1685) drove many Huguenots (French Protestants) into exile, with important economic consequences both for France and for the countries that received them.

Naples: south Italian city and port. Probably founded as Neapolis ("new town") by Greek colonists *c.* 600 BC, it was captured in 328 BC by the Romans, who eagerly patronised it as a university of Greek culture (Nero's first public stage appearance was at Naples). After the fall of Rome the city changed hands many times and, having been a Habsburg possession from 1503 to 1734, became the capital of an independent Kingdom of Sicily. Thus it remained, with an interval during the Napoleonic Wars, until 1860, when it became part of the new Kingdom of Italy. Today the trade of the city flourishes but the overcrowding and poverty of many of its inhabitants is a problem yet to be solved.

Napoleon I, Napoleon Bonaparte (1769–1821): Emperor of the French 1804–15. Born in Corsica, he entered the army as an artillery officer in 1785 and was acknowledged a great general after his victories against the Austrians in northern Italy in 1796. He failed in his attempt to cut British trade routes by taking Egypt, but on his return to France in 1799 he overthrew the Directory and became First Consul. He was made Consul for life in 1802 and crowned himself Emperor in 1804. Undoubtedly an autocrat, Napoleon was also a brilliant administrator, and reforms such as his legal code (*Code Napoléon*) enshrined as state policy many ideas of the French Revolution. By 1808 a series of remarkable victories, including Austerlitz (1805), Jena (1806), Friedland (1807) and Wagram (1809) had given him control of much of Europe, but his ravenous appetite for further military conquest led to the ruinous Russian campaign (1812), in which the long winter retreat from Moscow virtually destroyed his army. Thereafter he conducted a desperate rearguard action against a circle of enemies and was forced to abdicate in 1814, when the Allies granted him the right to rule the Mediterranean island of Elba. In February 1815 he escaped, landed near Cannes, and again ruled France for the "Hundred Days", which ended in his final defeat by the British and Prussians on 18 June at Waterloo and his exile to St Helena, where he died in 1821.
See colour section.
¶ CAMMIADE, AUDREY. *Napoleon.* 1957
See also NAPOLEONIC WARS.

Napoleon and his Army during the disastrous retreat from Moscow in 1812.

Napoleon III (1808–73): Emperor of France 1852–70. Bonaparte (see previous article) was his paternal uncle. After years spent in prison or in exile, partly in England, he returned to France in 1848 on the expulsion of King Louis Philippe and was elected president of the new Republic. This he overthrew and in 1852 became emperor. His reign, known as the Second Empire, brought increased prosperity to France and saw energetic planning development in Paris; but a somewhat chequered foreign policy ended in a crushing defeat by Prussia in 1870. After a short term of imprisonment he went into exile in England, where his widow Eugénie (d. 1920) long survived him.

¶ SMITH, W. H. C. *Napoleon III*. 1972

Napoleonic Wars (1803–15): wars at the beginning of the 19th century when Napoleon I and the French armies fought two coalitions of European powers. Very few wars have been named after their leaders, and it is a measure of Napoleon Bonaparte's dominant genius that history has so labelled these struggles, just as the adjective "napoleonic" is accepted to describe someone with his qualities.

After the French Revolutionary Wars (*see* separate entry) the Peace of Amiens (1802) produced only a temporary and uneasy lull. The next year Britain declared war on France and the air was full of the threat of invasion as Napoleon massed a vast flotilla at Boulogne to cross the Channel, his overall plan involving the union of three fleets, from Toulon, Rochefort and Brest, further strengthened by the Spanish squadrons, to command the narrow intervening stretch of water. It was as near as Britain had come to successful invasion by a foreign power since the Conquest by William of Normandy more than seven centuries before.

Pitt had returned to office in 1804 and immediately set about forming a coalition to resist Napoleon. This consisted of Russia, Austria and, later, Prussia. The next five years saw the collapse and virtual annihilation of this coalition. Austria went down at Ulm and Austerlitz. ("Roll up that map," said Pitt of Europe when he heard of the latter defeat. "It will not be wanted these ten years.") Russia, too, was smashed at Austerlitz and, later, at Eylau and Friedland. Prussia was crushed at Jena in 1806, followed by Sweden the next year. Austria tried again and succumbed at Wagram in 1809. Everywhere Europe lay in ruins before the apparently irresistible French conqueror. It was more than symbolic that, after 844 years, the Holy Roman Empire was officially dissolved by his decree.

Only slowly was Napoleon proved to be less than invincible. At sea, the Battle of Trafalgar (1805) finally destroyed his dream of an invasion of England, just as, in 1798, the Battle of the Nile had prevented his conquest of the East. The story ran on, if not always with such dramatic quality, with a series of other reverses for him, the retaking of the Cape of Good Hope, the surrender of the Danish fleet at Copenhagen, the capture of Martinique, Guadeloupe, Mauritius, the forcing of the Dardanelles and the capture of the Dutch East Indies, to name but a few chapters. And in the Peninsular War (1808–14) Wellington conducted at first a defensive and then an offensive war that pinned down 200,000 French troops in Spain and finally drove them from the peninsula.

Another major reverse had already occurred in Russia when, in 1812, out of half-a-million French troops sent on the Moscow campaign only 60,000 half-starved, half-frozen and dispirited survivors straggled back over the frontier after the horrific retreat from the blazing city. In 1813 a new coalition, of Britain, Prussia, Russia, Sweden and Austria, summoned heart to defeat Napoleon at Leipzig in the Battle of the Nations (1813), and the Emperor was exiled to Elba.

The story of his escape after a few months and his last rally of the French armies to march to final defeat at Waterloo (1815) provides the last sombre scene of slaughter of the Napoleonic Wars, with up to 30,000 French troops left dead on the battlefield and the Iron Duke (Wellington) showing less than iron when he wrote: "My heart is broken... nothing except a battle lost can be half so melancholy as a battle won."

¶ LACHOUQUE, HENRY. *Napoleon's Battles: a history of his campaigns.* 1966; MORRIS, THOMAS. *The Napoleonic Wars,* edited by John Selby. 1967

Nasmyth, James (1808–90): British scientist and engineer. Although he is chiefly remembered as the inventor (1839) of the steam hammer, which revolutionised a number of processes in the production of iron and steel, he was also responsible for other inventions in the industry, including a planing machine, a steam pile-driver and hydraulic machinery, and made notable contributions to astronomy in his studies of the surface of the sun and moon.

Nassau: German duchy, now part of the state of Hesse in West Germany. The counts of Nassau adopted the title in 1160.

In 1292 Adolf I of Nassau was elected King of Germany. Nassau was created a duchy in 1806. A younger branch of the family inherited the principality of Orange in 1544 and became princes of Orange-Nassau. They included the Netherlands leaders William the Silent (1533–84), Maurice of Nassau (1567–1625) and William III (1650–1702) who became king of England in 1688. Descendants still form the Netherlands royal house and the grand-ducal house of Luxembourg.

Nasser, Colonel Gamal Abdel (1918–70): Egyptian statesman and leader in the Arab world. With Mohammed Neguib, he organised the military coup which overthrew Farouk, the last king of Egypt, in 1952 and became, first, premier (1954–56) and then president. In July 1956, without warning, he nationalised the Suez Canal Company, in which Britain was a principal shareholder, and thus gained control over the passage of ships through it. His name will also be permanently linked with building (backed by Russian finance) the Aswan High Dam, and the bitter Middle East struggle with Israel. *See also* ISRAEL.

Natal: province of South Africa. In the early 19th century the area was controlled by the Zulus under Chaka (1787–1828), a great military leader. He was succeeded by Dingaan, and in 1837 a party of Boer trekkers asked permission to settle in his land. This was given, but Dingaan later became alarmed, invited the leaders to a war dance and killed them. In 1838 they were revenged by a Boer victory at the Battle of Blood River; meanwhile the British Governor of the Cape tried to arrange peace terms. The weakness of Natal and internal unrest in South Africa, however, led England to annex Natal in 1840. It became a separate colony in 1856 and, after annexing Zululand and parts of the Transvaal, joined the Union of South Africa in 1910.

National Aeronautics and Space Administration (NASA): the controlling organisation in the USA for manned and unmanned space flights. Recently NASA has sought the co-operation of other countries, chiefly through various European ministers of technology and science, in planning future space programmes.

National Debt: the amount of money owed by a national government. Kings of England from early times had borrowed money for immediate use, to be repaid as taxes were collected, but, in 1694, a group of financiers undertook to raise £1,200,000 to lend to the government at eight per cent interest, the capital not being returnable. For this service, they became incorporated as the Bank of England, and certain government taxes were assigned to the Bank to ensure the payment of the interest, which was to be a permanent charge on the government. From this time onwards the National Debt has risen rapidly in time of war, sometimes followed by a slight reduction during the ensuing peace, and in 1974 stood at £35,839,000,000. Most nations now have a National Debt.

National Socialist German Workers' Party: German political party motivated by policies of armed aggression, anti-semitism and belief in a master race of Caucasian stock with no Jewish taint. It came into being after World War I, increased its influence in the economic crisis of 1929–30, and proved a ready vehicle for the rise of Hitler, who brought it to totalitarian power from 1933 onwards. The party disintegrated with the collapse of the Third Reich in 1945 but has since shown signs of revival.
See also HITLER, ADOLF; NAZI.

Nations, Battle of the (16–19 October 1813): also called the Battle of Leipzig, in Saxony. Encouraged by Napoleon Bonaparte's disastrous invasion of Russia (1812), the nations of Europe faced him with growing confidence and eventually defeated him with heavy losses in this battle, which, with Wellington's successes, led to the Emperor's abdication in the following year.

NATO (North Atlantic Treaty Organisation): organisation, headed by a Council of Foreign Ministers, constituted by the twelve signatories of the North Atlantic Treaty (1949) – Belgium, Canada, Denmark, France, Great Britain, Iceland, Italy, Luxembourg, the Netherlands, Norway, Portugal and the US. Greece and Turkey joined in 1952, and West Germany in 1955. The formation of NATO was promoted by President Truman of the USA as part of his policy to stop the spread of Communism by giving economic aid to underdeveloped countries. The parties to the Treaty agreed that an attack upon any one member should be considered an attack upon all. NATO forces operate under an integrated command, Supreme Headquarters of Allied Powers in Europe (SHAPE), but all retain their national identities. SHAPE was located in Paris until the late 1960s, when General Charles de Gaulle adopted an independent policy and withdrew his country from the Organisation. Amongst the generals who have commanded this "shield of the West" against the USSR and her allies were General Dwight D. Eisenhower (1950–52) and General Louis Norstad (1956–62). Each year NATO mounts a defence exercise as well as its normal observation and patrol work.

Naval Gunnery: the art and science of using the gun in a ship of war. Since the invention by the Frenchman Descharges (c. 1500) of the porthole, warships were specially built to carry guns mounted in wheeled carriages within their hulls. The muzzle-loading gun to fire cast iron cannon balls was the main armament of the sailing man-of-war from the 16th to the early 19th century. The propellant was a gunpowder cartridge ignited by match through the touch-hole. Extreme range was about one-and-a-half miles. [1·41 kilometres]. Guns were designated according to weight of shot, i.e. 6, 9, 12, 18, 24, 32 and 42 pounders. The heaviest guns were carried on the lowest gun deck. The carronade, a more powerful short range gun, was introduced into ships in 1779. The principal guns could be fired only in a fixed direction, hence the objective in naval battles was to so manoeuvre as to be able to fire a broadside.

Naval gunnery underwent great changes in the 19th century. The shell gun, firing a missile that exploded on impact, was introduced by the French, c. 1825; in 1859 the French wooden warship *La Gloire* was fitted with armour plating to withstand the new destructive shell. In 1860 the British ironclad *Warrior* was fitted with the new Armstrong rifled gun with an experimental breech opening. The largest was a 7-inch 110 pounder. Guns were now referred to by calibre (i.e. the diameter of the bore) instead of weight of shot.

In 1862 the US *Monitor* had an experimental revolving gun turret. This had far-reaching effects on future naval gunnery. In 1868 the British *Monarch* had two turrets. The year 1881 saw a satisfactory method of breech loading established.

The British *Dreadnought* of 1906 had five twin 12-inch guns in turrets. During World War I "director" control was introduced, firing all guns simultaneously and allowing for target speed, wind, roll of ship, etc. Before the end of World War II self-propelled guided missiles were introduced and are now carried in all major war vessels.

¶ WOODHOUSE, G. M. *The Battle of Navarino.* 1965

Navarino, Battle of (1827): naval engagement off south-west coast of Greece. The Turks had called on their vassal, the Pasha of Egypt, for help in resisting the Greeks' successful struggle for independence. A combined English, French and Russian fleet, under Sir Edward Codrington, was watching events, but became engaged with the Turco-Egyptian fleet and destroyed it.

Navarre: former European kingdom bordering the Bay of Biscay, now partly in French and partly in Spanish territory on either side of the Pyrenees. The kingdom was first established by the Basques in the 9th century and reached its highest power under Sancho Garcia (c. 905) and his immediate successors, including Sancho III (c. 1020) called "the Great". After 1234 the kingdom passed by marriage to a succession of French kings till, in 1516, Spanish Navarre was annexed by Ferdinand of Spain. French Navarre survived as a small separate kingdom till it was united to the French throne by Henry IV of France (reigned 1598–1610), familiarly known as Henry of Navarre.

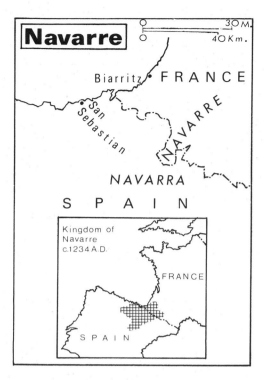

Joan (or Joanna) of Navarre was married to Henry IV of England in 1401.

Nazareth: village in Palestine where Jesus spent his early years before setting out on his ministry (*see* JESUS CHRIST). It was the home of his parents, although, at the time of his birth they had to go to Bethlehem to take part in a census. It lies about sixty miles [96·56 kilometres] north of Jerusalem, overlooking the valley of Esdraelon, and is today a notable place of pilgrimage.

Nazi: member of the *nationalsozialiet* (national socialist) party in Germany (*see* NATIONAL SOCIALIST GERMAN WORKERS' PARTY). The term became synonymous under the Hitler regime with brutal aggression, anti-Semitism and the theory of the master Nordic race. The party's symbol was the swastika.

¶ BROWNE, H. *Hitler and the Rise of Nazism.* 1969

Neanderthal man: palaeolithic type which because extinct some 50,000 years ago. The first discovery of the bones of this flint–using man were made in 1856 in the Neanderthal valley, western Germany, and remains have since been found in a number of European and Mediterranean countries. Neanderthal man had thick and curved thigh bones. The skull was large but low, with a shallow forehead and a receding chin, the whole set on a thick neck. He lived in the middle Palaeolithic period (*see* GEOLOGICAL PERIODS).

¶ QUENNELL, MARJORIE and QUENNELL, C. H. B. *Everyday Life in Prehistoric Times.* 1959; DICKINSON, ALICE. *The First Book of Stone Age Man.* 1963

Nehru, Jawaharlal (1889-1964): Indian nationalist leader, educated in England at Harrow and Cambridge. In 1920 he joined Mahatma Gandhi's nationalist movement and in the next seven years was imprisoned eight times for his leadership of resistance to British rule. The son of a president of Congress (Motilal Nehru), he became president himself in 1929 and, in 1947, the first prime minister of independent India. Though a resolute fighter for independence second only to Gandhi in prestige and influence, his resistance was directed against political domination by Britain. On the economic front, however, his early years in England made him understand the need for western industrial development to improve the general standards of Indian life, which were considerably raised under his leadership. In world affairs his policy was one of strict neutrality.

¶ LENGYEL, EMIL. *Jawaharlal Nehru.* 1970

Nelson, Horatio, Viscount Nelson

(1758–1805): British admiral and national hero. Born at Burnham Thorpe, Norfolk, on 29 September 1758, he went to sea at the age of twelve as midshipman in the *Raisonnable* under his uncle, Captain Suckling. After varied experience he was given command of the *Hinchinbroke* at the age of twenty, and was noted for being "first in every service". In 1787 he married Mrs Frances Nisbet, a widow, at Nevis in the West Indies. In *Agamemnon* in 1793 he lost an eye at Calvi. Jervis's victory off Cape St Vincent (February 1797) owed most to Nelson when, without waiting for orders, he left the British line of battle and engaged seven Spanish ships (one of them, the *Santissima Trinidad*, the largest and strongest in the world) and captured two. Knighted and promoted, Nelson lost an arm at Santa Cruz the same year. In 1798, sent to the Mediterranean to counter Napoleon's ambitions, he was elevated to the peerage after the total victory at the Battle of the Nile.

Vice-admiral under Hyde Parker at Copenhagen in 1801, and exercising his "right to be blind sometimes", he disregarded the signal to break off and

continued close action till ships and shore batteries surrendered. In 1805, after chasing the French admiral Villeneuve to the West Indies, he came ashore in England, then, after Admiral Sir Robert Calder's indecisive engagement off Finisterre, took command for the last time. "This maimed and battered little man" embarked in HMS *Victory* and won one of the most decisive battles in history over the combined fleets of France and Spain off Cape Trafalgar, 21 October 1805, falling mortally wounded about an hour and a quarter after the action had begun.

¶ BRYANT, ARTHUR. *Nelson.* 1970
See also TRAFALGAR.

Neo-Gothic: architecture and art in the revived Gothic style (*see* GOTHIC ART AND ARCHITECTURE). This revival flourished chiefly in the 19th century and particularly in the building of churches, as a reaction from the classical styles, but the line from the old to the new Gothic was never completely broken.

Neolithic (from Greek *neos*, new, and *lithos*, stone): belonging to the period of neoliths, or polished stone implements – the last period of the Stone Age. The establishment of settled communities, cultivating wheat, barley and (probably) sheep, which marked the opening of the Neolithic Age in Europe, was brought about by itinerant farmers from southwest Asia. By about 3000 BC there were large settled Neolithic communities, presumably descended from the earlier local Mesolithic (middle Stone Age) hunters and fishers. The settlements became trading centres, which in their turn enabled the arts and products of the already highly developed civilisations of Asia to become widely known among these people.

¶ QUENNELL, MARJORIE and QUENNELL, C. H. B. *Everyday Life in Prehistoric Times.* 1959; DICKINSON, ALICE. *The First Book of Stone Age Man.* 1963

Nepal: independent kingdom on the slopes of the Great Himalayas north of India. Its modern history begins with its conquest in 1768 by the Gurkha Prithvi Narayan and expansion under his successors. After war against the British, 1814–16, the present boundaries were fixed, a British envoy was accepted at Katmandu and, later, Gurkha troops served with the British Indian army.

From 1847 the country was controlled, under the king, by a hereditary prime minister, an office ending with the 1951 revolution, which attempted to introduce democratic government. The king, Mahendra, suspended the constitution in 1960, and in 1963 an indirectly elected national assembly was formed.

Nero Claudius Caesar (AD 37–68): Roman Emperor 54–68. He was the son of a Roman senator and his wife Agrippina, who later married the Emperor Claudius and persuaded him to adopt Nero. His reign was marked by violence and brutality: he caused his mother and his first wife to be murdered and was insanely jealous of any rivalry, especially in the world of music and poetry, where he delighted in performing in public. He was said to have "fiddled while Rome burned" and tried to blame the early Christians for the fire. Faced with revolt, he committed suicide.

Netherlands: kingdom of western Europe on the North Sea. The Rhine delta formed part of Charlemagne's empire (AD 800). A Duchy of Holland, later including Zeeland, was governed by dukes from 922 to 1417. Other important magnates were the dukes of Guelder and the bishops of Utrecht. Flanders and the south made progress in trade and culture, but the northern provinces were backward until the 13th and 14th centuries, when they developed fishing and carried goods to the British Isles and the Baltic, and reclaimed land for agriculture.

The Netherlands passed to the dukes of Burgundy with the death of the last duke of Holland, and then to the Habsburgs. The Emperor Charles V (1500–58) was actually born in Ghent; but his son Philip II (1527–98) was born and lived in Spain and left Margaret, duchess of Parma, as regent in the Netherlands. The Protestant Reformation had made progress in the northern Netherlands, and religious antagonism was added to resentment against Spanish troops under the duke of Alva and against the Spanish rulers, who ignored the States General, representing the councils of the seventeen Netherlands provinces, and persecuted the Protestants. The execution in 1568 of counts Egmont and Horn, who had resisted the severity of Spanish rule, started a war of independence led by William the Silent, Prince of Orange (1533–84). Don John of Austria persuaded the southern provinces to uphold Catholic orthodoxy, but the northerners, by the Declaration of Utrecht (1579), decided to fight for religious freedom and declared their independence in 1581.

William the Silent was murdered in 1584 and was succeeded as leader of a Netherlands Union by his son Maurice,

Dykes, canals and windmills, the famous symbols of the Netherlands.

stadholder or governor of five of the seven provinces of Holland, Zeeland, Utrecht, Gelderland, Overijssel, Groningen and Friesland. The defeat of the Spanish Armada in 1588 and successes by the Union on land led finally to a truce in 1609. After further war, the independent United Netherlands were recognised by the Peace of Westphalia in 1648.

The new republic was already a major European power with a growing overseas empire in the East Indies and elsewhere. It fought a series of wars, first with England, then against France. In 1688 William III, stadholder of the Netherlands, became also king of England. It was an age of great commercial and cultural activity for the Netherlands, with the Dutch East India Company successful overseas, and the Dutch school of painting at its height in the work of such painters as Rembrandt and Frans Hals (*see* separate entries). After the death of William III (1702) there was a decline, but the further wars of the Spanish Succession (1702–13) and the Austrian Succession (1741–48) strengthened loyalty to the house of Orange.

Following the French Revolution the Netherlands were overrun by the French, and in 1815 the great powers united the Netherlands, Belgium and Luxembourg in one kingdom under William I. This lasted only fifteen years. Belgium revolted in 1830 and Luxembourg also became

independent, leaving eleven provinces. In World War II the Germans occupied the Netherlands from 1940 to 1945. The Netherlands Indies achieved complete independence in 1949. In 1958 the Netherlands joined in an economic union with Belgium and Luxembourg, known as Benelux, and later entered the European Economic Community.

¶ COHN, ANGELO. *The First Book of the Netherlands.* 1963

Neutrality: the state or condition of remaining aloof from a war or controversy and assisting neither side. Thus, the federal republic of Switzerland remained neutral in both world wars, 1914–18 and 1939–45, this being one reason why the country has gained importance as the headquarters of various international organisations, including the Red Cross and the League of Nations (1920–46). It was the invasion of Belgium, whose neutrality had been guaranteed by the Great Powers, that led to Britain's declaration of war on Germany in 1914. Both world wars saw America trying to maintain a state of neutrality, till Germany's unrestricted submarine warfare forced a change of policy in 1917 and the Japanese attack on Pearl Harbour brought the same result in 1941.

New Deal: phrase used to describe the social and economic reforms of Franklin D. Roosevelt (1882–1945) between 1933 and 1939. The First New Deal (1933–35) aimed at relief and recovery from financial depression and unemployment. The Second New Deal (1935–39) was especially concerned with social security for the working population and price guarantees for small farmers.

New England: region lying to the east of the Hudson River and to the north-east of New York City. It includes the present states of Maine, New Hampshire, Vermont, Massachusetts, Rhode Island and Connecticut. It was presumably named by Captain John Smith (on his map of 1616), who discovered the rich cod fisheries off Maine. Permanent settlements began with those of the Pilgrims at Plymouth (1620), followed by the larger influx of Puritans into the Massachusetts Bay area (1630). The threat of Dutch expansion and Indian raids led to the New England Confederation (1643–84), which unified the colonists. Because New England had more extensive foreign commerce than other colonies, it was more adversely affected by the English Navigation Acts (1651–96). It was the centre of the events leading to the American Revolution, especially after 1765, and the scene of the opening engagements of the War of Independence (1775). From New England stemmed the great migration to the Northwest Territory, and prior to the Civil War the section furnished leaders for most of the social and humanitarian movements in America. It was also the leading literary and educational centre of the nation, with its well-known universities such as Harvard and Yale. In the 19th century vast numbers of immigrants from Europe changed the character of the region. The southern Irish settled in Boston and still dominate the politics of the city and its suburbs. New England remains something of a byword for social exclusiveness and moral and religious intolerance. *See colour section.*

Newfoundland: Canadian province and former British colony, situated to the north-east of the Gulf of St Lawrence in 48° North and 52° West. It is usually said that John Cabot discovered Newfoundland in 1497, though evidence of Norse settlement antedates Cabot by 500 years. Gaspar de Cortoreal's visit in 1500 quickly brought French and Portuguese to the fisheries. Sir Humphrey Gilbert in 1583

formally annexed Newfoundland for Queen Elizabeth of England. The Treaty of Utrecht, 1713, confirmed England's sovereignty. But the French claimed the fisheries on the western and southern shores and the Labrador coast, recognised as part of the colony, even after 1763, when the Treaty of Paris ended the Seven Years War.

Newfoundland had a representative assembly in 1832 and responsible government in 1855. Entry to the Canadian Confederation was unsuccessfully canvassed before the British North America Act of 1867. The economy's continuing dependence on the fisheries was the chief factor in a financial crisis in 1894. Aided by Canadian finance, the colony thereafter diversified her products into paper, timber and pulp, iron and other minerals. A referendum in 1948 resulted in Newfoundland and Labrador joining Canada as its tenth province.

New Guinea: large East Indian island north of Australia and only 100 miles [161 kilometres] from Cape York, first seen by a Portuguese sailor in 1512 and settled by several European nations later. The early inhabitants were a mixture of races, including negroid types on the west and Melanesians, resembling south-sea islanders, on the east. The Dutch colonised the west until 1963, when this territory became part of Indonesia (Irian Barat). The eastern portion is now the independent territory of Papua New Guinea.

New South Wales: oldest Australian colony, so named by Captain Cook in 1770. Sydney, the capital city, was founded on Port Jackson from the convict settlement and from free settlers. Transportation of convicts ceased in 1840. The Australian Colonies Act 1850, gave New South Wales self-government, though "squatter" sheep-farmers predominated.

Hargraves discovered gold in 1851, contributing to a population increase from 76,793 in 1837 to 503,981 in 1871. The 1855 Constitution prefaced thirty years of political, agrarian and educational advance. Despite setbacks such as a financial crisis in 1893, which forced ten banks to close, and a severe drought in 1902, the colony continued to make progress and in the period 1901-15 the area of land under cultivation was almost doubled.

Newspaper: printed publication, usually published daily or weekly, giving current news and opinion. The Romans had a kind of newspaper which was started by Julius Caesar. During the first three centuries AD orders, official notices, births, marriages and deaths and other items of interest were written on a whitewashed board and put up in a public place in Rome. These were called the *Acta Diurna* ("happenings of the day"). In the Middle Ages the great trading city of Venice had similar announcements posted up. These were called *Gazettas* after the name of the coin charged for reading them.

Modern newspapers have their origins in the handwritten newsletters sent to subscribers by professional news gatherers in various capitals such as Vienna, Augsburg, Ratisbon and Nuremberg. This was a slow process and it was not till the invention of printing that a real newspaper became possible. With a printing press, many copies could be produced in a fairly short time. The first English newspaper proper is generally considered to be *The Weekly Newes* issued in 1622. The

British government became alarmed at political and religious questions being discussed in newspapers, pamphlets and books and tried by various means to control all printing. There was great argument about "the freedom of the press", and by the time of Queen Anne (1665-1714) there were many newspapers in which politics and religion were discussed by such writers as Addison, Steele, Swift and Daniel Defoe. The first British daily newspaper the *Daily Courant* (*above*) was published in 1702. By the end of the 18th cent. news of parliament was printed in the *Morning Chronicle*, the *Morning Herald*, the *Sun* and other papers, and politicians and even the monarchy were freely criticised. During the 19th century foreign news and other new features were included and *The Times* began using steam machinery in place of printing by hand. An important factor in a vastly increased newspaper reading public was the growth of state education.

The modern newspaper contains very much more than political news. It attracts its readers by articles on sport, amusements and fashions, by cartoons and crossword puzzles, by photographs, and by advertisements. Some newspapers give away a weekly colour supplement. Producing a newspaper is now very costly indeed, and much of the cost has to come from what is paid for advertisements.

A very important part is played by provincial papers, which are able to concentrate upon the interests of particular localities much more than the great dailies. The first example in England was the *Worcester Postman*, which appeared in 1690, closely followed by the *Lincoln, Rutland and Stamford Mercury* in 1695.

The newspaper in the USA has followed much the same lines of development as in Great Britain. As early as 1619 John Pory, secretary of the Virginia Colony, was sending newsletters home to his "good and gracious lord" in London. John Campbell, postmaster at Boston, sent fairly regular news bulletins to various colonial governors in New England. These developed into the first American newspaper – *The Boston News-Letter*, which Campbell printed for the first time in April 1704. The first daily newspaper was *The Pennsylvania Packet and General Advertiser*, published in September 1784. The papers with the longest unbroken history are *The Hartford Courant*, which began life as *The Connecticut Courant* in 1764, and *The New York Evening Post*, the name of which has remained unchanged since 1801.

¶ SMITH, GEOFFREY. *News and Newspapers: the story of the British Press*. 1962; WIKERSON, MARJORIE. *News and Newspapers*. 1970

Newton, Sir Isaac (1642–1727): English mathematician and man of science. Born at Woolsthorpe, Lincolnshire, he was

educated at Grantham School and Trinity College, Cambridge, becoming Lucasian Professor of Mathematics at Cambridge (1669), Fellow of the Royal Society (1672), MP for Cambridge University (1689), Warden of the Mint (1696) and Master of the Mint (1699). He was knighted by Queen Anne (1705).

One of the greatest mathematicians, his chief discoveries were the Binomial Theorem; his Law of Gravitation, which laid the foundation of modern Dynamics; and his method of "fluxions". This last, which we now call the Differential and Integral Calculus, was almost simultaneously discovered by Leibnitz but with a better notation than Newton's. The first edition of Newton's immensely influential book *Principia mathematica* was published in 1687. His contributions to optics and the theory of light are also notable. *See also* GRAVITATION.

¶ KNIGHT, DAVID C. *Isaac Newton, mastermind of modern science*. 1963

New World: name used until the early years of the 16th century to describe the Americas. In the early years of the 16th century a mapmaker, Waldseemuller, was at work compiling a new map of the known world. He had heard of the recent voyages westwards across the Atlantic and of lands newly discovered on the far side. The New World had first been "discovered" in 1492–1504 by Christopher Columbus and his reports of inhabitants and products emphasised the contrast with the "Old World" of Spain and Portugal. Waldseemuller, however, based his map in part upon the narrative of Amerigo Vespucci, who, following Columbus, had explored much of its coast. As the New World lacked a name, Waldseemuller named it "America" after Amerigo. The New World made as great an impression on the 16th-century European mind as outer space does today with us.

New York: chief city in the United States and the centre of the most congested metropolitan area in the Western Hemisphere. Situated at the mouth of the Hudson River, New York comprises the five boroughs of Manhattan, the Bronx, Brooklyn, Staten Island and Queens. As New Amsterdam, on the tip of the island of Manhattan, in 1626 it was the capital of the Dutch colony of New Netherland and so it remained until the British seized and renamed it (after James, Duke of York, subsequently James II) in 1664. The city developed as a major commercial and shipping centre during the first half of the 18th century, and after the War of Independence it was, briefly (1789–90), the first capital of the emergent nation. The construction of the Erie Canal in 1825 enlarged New York's hinterland and it became the financial, commercial and shipping capital of the United States. The financing of vast railway networks increased the significance and power of Wall Street, where New York's bankers congregated. Before the Civil War, immigrants poured into the city from Europe, creating vast slum areas on the lower East Side. After the Civil War, migration from the South made the population of Harlem predominantly Negro. In the 20th century New York became the mecca of those seeking careers in trade, finance and the arts. The city has long been a centre of musical activity and is the headquarters of American drama (Broadway). Today the city still retains its predominance in the political and cultural life of the nation, and its experience in attempting to make city life tolerable in the 20th century is being studied by all major conurbations. New York is also the name of a state (nicknamed the "Empire State"), touching Canada in the north and the Atlantic in the south, with Albany as its capital. *See* AMERICA for map.

New Zealand: since 1907 a self-governing dominion of the British Commonwealth, comprising two large and numerous small islands in the Pacific. Though Tasman sighted the South Island mountains in 1642, our only knowledge of "Ao-te-roa", the "Long White Cloud", derives from Maori story until Cook's voyage of 1769–70. Missionaries landed in 1814, with Samuel Marsden from New South Wales (*see* separate entry), who, during a visit to London in 1807, had been presented by George III with five Spanish sheep that were the ancestors of many of the great Australian flocks. Marsden favoured the appointment of an officer to supervise the colony, but the first, James Busby, who was subordinate to New South Wales, failed to unite the Maori tribes. Edward Gibbon Wakefield (1796–1862) in 1839 organised the New Zealand Company for land purchase and settlement, stressing the danger of French annexation. The government, questioning the legality of such purchases from the chiefs and fearing Maori risings, annexed New Zealand to New South Wales in 1840. The Treaty of Waitangi, 1840, guaranteed the possession of their lands to the Maoris, with a Crown right to purchase. Wakefield's systematic settlement against official opposition encouraged colonisation, and Maori dissatisfaction smouldered until, under the governorship of Robert Fitzroy (1805–65), who had commanded the *Beagle* on Darwin's famous voyage, it broke out into the native war of 1845–48. From 1845 to 1853 a strong governor, Captain George Grey, worked for peace, held a fair balance between the races and brought about a measure of prosperity, permitting settlement in the least populated areas. In 1848 Presbyterian Scots settled at Dunedin in Otago district, and in 1850 Anglicans founded Canterbury and Christchurch. Grey gave the colony

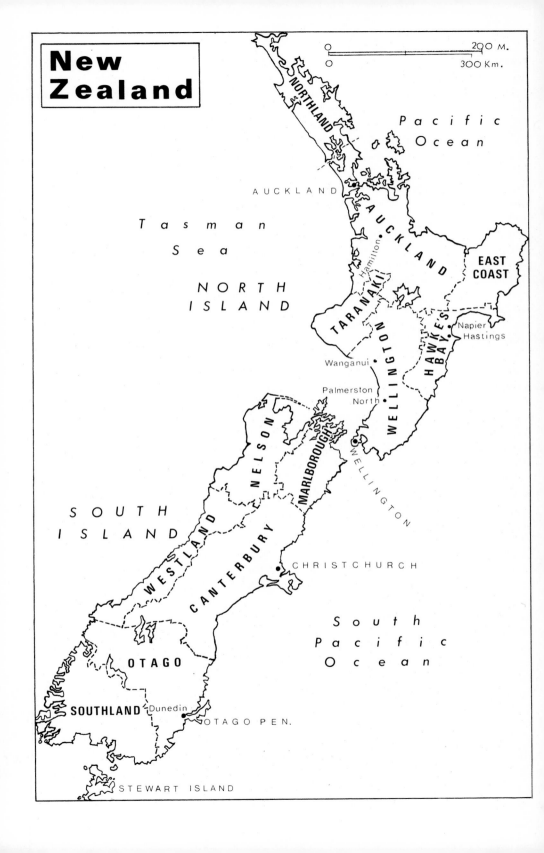

responsible government by the New Zealand Constitution Act of 1852, with provincial parliaments.

Though government purchase of land had replaced Company activities, the Maoris still felt their very existence threatened. The sending out again of Grey, the "Good Governor", for a further term of office could not prevent bitter warfare between 1860 and 1870. After the war, the Colonial Act abolished provincial parliaments and gave representation to the Maoris in the Lower House. The Native Schools Act further fostered racial partnership.

Despite the discovery of gold at Otago in 1861, New Zealand retained its essentially agricultural economy, though the Budget of 1870 encouraged railway construction and new industries to exploit resources in wool, timber and minerals. Canterbury lamb and dairy produce feature prominently in English shops.

New Zealand supported Britain magnificently in both world wars, provided forces for Korea and has joined ANZUS and SEATO. Though expanding trade with Japan, India and North America has lessened her dependence on British markets, traditional ties remain strong.

Nicholas I (1796–1855): Tsar of Russia 1825–55. Third son of Paul I, he succeeded his brother Alexander I in 1825. In contrast with Alexander, who was vaguely liberal and had played with schemes of self-government and constitutional rule in Poland and Finland, Nicholas was a sincerely convinced autocrat. He helped in suppressing popular risings in the Austrian Empire as well as in his own dominions. He extended Russian territory and power in Asia and hoped to benefit from a break-up of the Turkish Empire and to obtain Constantinople. His policy led to the Crimean War.

See also CRIMEAN WAR.

Nicholas II (1868–1918): Tsar of Russia 1894–1917. Born in 1868 he succeeded in 1894. In 1898 he issued an appeal for international peace, resulting in the first Hague peace conference of 1899. He conceded parliamentary institutions to Russia but also arbitrarily retracted concessions. His armies fought the disastrous Russo-Japanese war of 1904–05 and suffered heavy defeats in World War I. He was forced to abdicate in March 1917 and was murdered with his family in July 1918. He was the last Tsar of Russia.

Nigeria: republic of West Africa named after the Niger, one of the four great rivers of Africa. Among its many peoples the three main groups are the Hausas ruled by Emirs in the north, the Yorubas under hereditary chiefs in the south-west, and the Ibos with local councils of elders in the south-east.

Although little is known about the early history of some of the area, several considerable empires left their mark. The West African kingdom of Songhai was founded as early as the 8th century and was at its most powerful in the 15th and early 16th centuries. The powerful state of Benin continued even later, and is renowned for its sculptures in wood, bronze and ivory. (*See also* AFRICA.)

In the 16th century Portuguese, Dutch and French adventurers came from Europe, trading for palm-oil and raiding the coast for slaves. Two hundred years later the British established themselves. Between 1865 and 1885 they made treaties with the local chiefs, annexed Lagos in order to stamp out the slave trade, and finally established the Niger Coast Protectorate, combining all British trading interests in the Royal Niger Company. By 1900 treaties were made with the northern rulers, the Niger Company's rights were transferred to the Crown and Nigeria was divided into

Northern and Southern Protectorates, with the Colony of Lagos linked to the latter. In 1914 the separate Protectorates were merged into the country of Nigeria, with Lagos as the seat of government.

The first governor-general was Lord Lugard, a pioneer in the Northern Protectorate. In the period between the two world wars government was firmly established, with officers of the Colonial Service carrying administrative, professional and financial responsibilities. A network of roads and railways was extended over the whole country.

After World War II Nigeria was granted independence. The transition from British rule to a federal state was achieved happily in October 1960. Unfortunately the Nigerians proved not to be sufficiently united as a nation. In 1967 the Ibos tried to set up an independent republic, calling their land Biafra and claiming ownership of the rich oilfields in the Niger delta. Civil war broke out, and in 1970, when it ended, parts of the country were ravaged and starving. The moderate counsels of the Federal Government and the energetic relief measures taken by the Nigerian Red Cross give hope for Nigeria's future.

¶ WATSON, JANE WERNER. *Nigeria: republic of a hundred kings.* 1970

Nightingale, Florence (1820-1910): reformer of hospital nursing. After considerable study of hospitals and nursing discipline both in England and abroad, she first came into prominence in 1854 when she was invited to the Crimea to organise the nursing of the British sick and wounded sent back from the battle front. At Scutari, on the eastern shore of Bosporus, and elsewhere, she succeeded, in spite of much opposition from the military authorities, in transforming the hospitals, often working for twenty hours at a stretch, and bringing the death rate down from 42 per cent to 2 per cent in a few months. She was known as "The Lady of the Lamp". In May 1855 she visited Balaklava, where she caught Crimean fever and was desperately ill for twelve days.

She returned to England in 1856 and for more than forty years, despite frailty of body, continued her work for nursing and hospitals, her greatest achievement being the development of adequate training for nurses. Nurses trained at St Thomas's Hospital, where she founded her first establishment, are still nicknamed "Nightingales".

¶ HARMELINK, BARBARA. *Florence Nightingale, Founder of Modern Nursing.* 1972
See also CRIMEAN WAR; NURSING.

Nile: the world's longest river. It rises in Lake Victoria 3,900 feet [1188 metres] above sea level, and runs through Lake Kioga and Lake Albert, then on to Khartoum as the White Nile, being joined there by the Blue Nile, after which it is simply the Nile, finally entering the Mediterranean by a many-branched delta. Its length from the source of the White Nile is 4,053 miles [6522 kilometres].

¶ MOOREHEAD, ALAN. *The Blue Nile.* 1965; MOOREHEAD, ALAN. *The White Nile.* 1966

Nile, Battle of the, sometimes called the **Battle of Aboukir Bay,** (1 August 1798): British naval victory by which Nelson destroyed the French fleet and cut off Napoleon's army in Egypt, ensuring the failure of the French expedition.

Nineteenth Century: 1801-1900. The military dictatorship established in France by Napoleon Bonaparte (1769-1821) was an unforeseen outcome of the French Revolution. His Grand Army passed over Europe, sweeping feudal and ecclesiastical privilege away. At the same time, people in the conquered countries, resenting their subjection to France, first awoke to a sense of their own national identity. It was a realisation which was to remake the map of Europe. In 1815, after Napoleon's final defeat at the Battle of Waterloo, the great powers tried in vain to restore the old order.

The industrial revolution, in which Britain led the way, turned her in the 19th century into the wealthiest industrial nation in the world. New processes were discovered, factories were built, roads, railways and steamships were developed; the middle classes increased in numbers, power and wealth. The other side of the coin was to be found in the overcrowded slums where workers lived and their long hours of work for pitiful pay in often appalling conditions. Gradually, through the work of social reformers such as Lord Shaftesbury (1801–85), a series of Factory Acts and Mines Acts remedied some of the worst abuses. Workers began to organise themselves into trade unions. Reform Acts brought parliamentary democracy nearer reality, and in 1870 the first Education Act was passed.

Industries can only expand if raw materials are available, as well as customers to whom the finished products can be sold: hence the importance to Britain of an Empire which could supply both. But Britain did not have all her own way. Other nations which were developing their industries entered the competition for colonial lands and markets. Some of them – Belgium, Italy, Germany – were political creations of the 19th century. The rivalry which developed among the European powers for the one remaining unexploited continent has been aptly called "the scramble for Africa".

In the scramble the French spread out along the North African coast and south-ward into the Sahara. Belgium took the Congo, Italy and Germany other parts of Africa. Britain, as the major shareholder in the Suez Canal (opened 1869), controlled Egypt. She also occupied large areas in the southern half of the continent, where her differences with the Boers, settlers of Dutch origin, eventually led to the Boer War (1899–1902).

The greed for land and markets sowed the seeds of many wars. China was forced at gunpoint to grant trade and territorial concessions to the western powers. In 1853 a squadron of the US Navy anchored off Uraga, in Japan. The sight of western battleships brought Japan out of its medieval isolation into the modern world. Having decided to imitate western ways Japan became itself an aggressive imperial power, strong enough by 1904 to defeat Tsarist Russia.

Russia in the 19th century was a country where a small privileged class enjoyed a high level of culture while the great majority of the population consisted of peasants living in a state of serfdom. In 1861 Tsar Alexander II (1818–81) freed the serfs, but their material condition did not greatly improve. All reforms came to an abrupt halt in 1881 when the Tsar was assassinated. Thereafter liberal movements, however moderate, were driven underground, a state of affairs which ensured that when change came at last to Russia, as it did in 1917, it would be a violent explosion.

It is odd to reflect that the bible of the Russian Communist revolution, *Das Kapital*, was largely written in the British Museum Reading Room. It was the work of an exiled German socialist, Karl Marx (1818–83). The widespread and continuing influence of Marx's political theories makes him one of the most significant personalities of the 19th century.

Another was Charles Darwin (1809–82) whose theory of Evolution, expounded in his book *On the Origin of Species by Means of Natural Selection* (1859), shook the religious beliefs of the century. Darwin himself, as it happened, was a religious man; but people who took the Bible for literal truth attacked him.

It was during the 19th century that the United States of America emerged as a great power. Settlers poured in from Europe, some impelled by hunger, some by religious or political persecution, and others by ambition and love of adventure. Thousands of Irish people emigrated to the USA following the great Potato Famine of 1846, in which a million of their countrymen died of hunger. Towards the end of the century there occurred many brutal massacres (called *pogroms*, a Russian word meaning "destruction") of Jews living in Russia and parts of Poland. As a result Jews left Eastern Europe in large numbers, the majority going to the United States.

Ironically, the United States, the goal of the poor and oppressed, had its own problem of poverty and oppression. In the Southern states Negroes were still kept in slavery, a condition it took a civil war (1861-65) to put right. Unfortunately, Abraham Lincoln (1809-65), the American president, was assassinated soon after the close of the war, and the removal of his wise and moderating influence at a crucial time left the country with many unsolved problems.

¶ BALLARD, MARTIN. *The Age of Progress 1848–1866* (Era Histories 8). 1967; HART, ROGER. *English Life in the Nineteenth Century.* 1971

See also AMERICAN CIVIL WAR; BOER WAR; FRENCH REVOLUTION; INDUSTRIAL REVOLUTION; LINCOLN, ABRAHAM; NAPOLEON I.

Nineveh: ancient city on the River Tigris, about 500 miles [805 kilometres] from the head of the Persian Gulf and near the modern town of Mosul. It was the capital of the Assyrian Empire and was destroyed in 612 BC. The ruins were uncovered by Sir Austen Henry Layard (1817-94).

Nobel Prize Medal.

Nobel, Alfred Bernhard (1833-96): Swedish chemist and inventor. Nobel was especially interested in explosives and in 1867 he discovered the powerful explosive mixture, dynamite. From this and other inventions he became a very rich man. When he died he left most of his great fortune to provide five prizes every year for outstanding work in physics, chemistry, medicine, literature and for services in the cause of world peace. Each prize is worth about £8,000, and all prizes are open to men and women in all countries of the world. Since the awards began, many famous people (and many not so well known to the general public) of various nationalities have received a Nobel prize. The first winners, in 1901, were: W. E. Röntgen (German) for physics; J. H. van't Hoff (Dutch) for his work in stereochemistry; E. A. Von Behring (German) for his work on tetanus and diphtheria; R. F. A. Sully-Prudhomme (French) for poetry; and the peace prize was shared between H. Durant (Swiss), the founder of the Red Cross, and F. Passy (French).

¶ In LARSEN, EGON. *Men Who Shaped the Future.* 1954

Nomads: members of tribes that lead a wandering life seeking pasture for their flocks. Much early history is the story of the coming of such wandering folk into settled communities, sometimes of a different culture. Some areas of the world still demand a nomadic way of life, e.g. Lapland, where the inhabitants support themselves by herding reindeer.

Nordenskiöld, Baron Nils Adolf Eric

(1832–1901): Swedish explorer and geographer. After expeditions to the Arctic and Spitzbergen, he was the first to navigate the North-east Passage in 1878–79 in the steamship *Vega*. The results of this exploration, published 1882–87, and his book *Periplus*, 1897, contributed greatly to geographic and scientific research.

Norman Kings: the four rulers of England, 1066–1154.

1. William I (1066–87), the bastard son of Robert III, Duke of Normandy, and Arlette, a tanner's daughter, was born at Falaise in 1027. Edward the Confessor promised him the English throne, but Harold, Earl of Wessex, became king in January 1066, and William therefore invaded England, winning the Battle of Hastings (14 October 1066). He ruthlessly crushed all rebellions, strengthened the feudal system, built strong castles, e.g.

The four Norman Kings: William I, William Rufus, Henry I and Stephen.

the White Tower of London, and had the support of the Church under Archbishop Lanfranc. The Domesday Book (1086) was made largely for taxation purposes.

2. William II (1087–1100), the second son of William I, succeeded as king of England, and his elder brother Robert became Duke of Normandy, according to their father's wish. An unscrupulous, bad-tempered bully, he forced Archbishop Anselm into exile, but he was a powerful and able ruler. He was killed by an arrow in the New Forest.

3. Henry I (1100–35), the youngest and ablest of William I's sons, defeated Robert and secured Normandy. The chroniclers praised him warmly – "good man was he and there was great awe of him" – and nicknamed him the Lion of Justice.

4. Stephen (1135–54), son of William I's daughter Adela, "a mild good man", was preferred as ruler to Matilda, Henry I's daughter. "Nineteen long winters" of civil war followed, ended by the Treaty of Winchester (1153) making Matilda's son Henry successor to Stephen.

¶ DOREY, ALAN and LEON, A. *The Norman Kings.* 1964

Normandy: province of France bordering the English Channel. It took its name from the Vikings or Northmen who raided it in the 9th century. This ancestry gave the Normans a hardihood and enterprise which marked much of their history. Normandy became closely linked with the fortunes of England after Duke William conquered England in 1066. For nearly 150 years it remained intermittently in English hands and was torn by the Hundred Years War. Normandy was finally secured by France in 1450. Its unfortunate role as one of the most battle-scarred areas of Europe was revived in both world wars. The final defeat of Germany began with landings in Normandy under Eisenhower (6 June 1944).

North America: the northern part of the land mass comprising the Americas of the western hemisphere, which includes continental United States and Canada, Mexico and the countries and islands of the Caribbean area. As thus defined it is the third largest continent, occupying slightly above sixteen per cent of the earth's land area, with a population approaching 300 million. Tremendous cultural differences exist between the two major components of the continent. Canada and the United States have both experienced the colonising effects of Great Britain, and many examples of their common heritage are evident, including a common language, similar political and legal institutions, and many everyday customs. The rest of the continent received its cultural institutions from Spain and Portugal and, like the countries of South America, is primarily Latin in its culture.

The first Europeans to discover America were the Northmen, part of a population movement that took Scandinavians to Normandy, Scotland, England, Ireland and the islands to the west and north between AD 700 and 1100. They were pirates, plunderers, traders, and settlers attracted by coastal waters teeming with fish, or driven by population pressures, or by the wrath of rivals or rulers at home. The Northmen sailed by way of Iceland and Greenland and made settlements on the coast between Labrador and New England. These settlements were temporary and it was not until the nations of the Atlantic seaboard of Europe entered into an age of geographical discovery in the 15th century that attempts at permanent colonisation were made. The rise to eminence of the national states of Portugal, Spain, France, England and the United Netherlands coincided with this age of discovery.

In the tradition of militant Christianity, Europe wished to convert the non-Christians of the world. With the coming of the Reformation in the early 16th century, religious differences sharpened national rivalries as Protestants tried to outstrip the Roman Catholic Spanish and Portuguese, whose kings had divided the newly discovered areas of the world with papal approval in the Treaty of Tordesillas in 1494.

By the middle of the 16th century much of southern and north-eastern North America was known to Europeans. Sailors passed along the Atlantic coast and its main features were being accurately represented on the maps of the period. Though few penetrated inland, except perhaps up some of the great rivers, a favourable picture was given of the coastal lands from Cape Cod to Florida. Settlers were attracted by the beauty and riches of this land, but some were rudely disillusioned by disease, Indian attacks or severe winters.

Towards the end of the 16th century three areas along the Atlantic seaboard came to be settled by people of European stock. The French settled in the valley of the St Lawrence River, from the sea up to Montreal. Grain crops were grown and cattle reared, but fishing and trapping of wild, fur-bearing animals offered a means of livelihood no less important. The French also settled in the valleys of the Ohio and Mississippi Rivers, this area being known as Louisiana. The other two main settlements were by the British; the essentially Puritan colonies of New England and those of the "gentleman" adventurers (and the slaves they imported from West Africa) in the tobacco growing plantation settlements of Maryland and Virginia. There was also limited Spanish settlement in Florida and New Spain.

In the mid-18th century the total number of settlers was small. In the whole of the French-settled areas there were probably no more than 20,000 white people. The

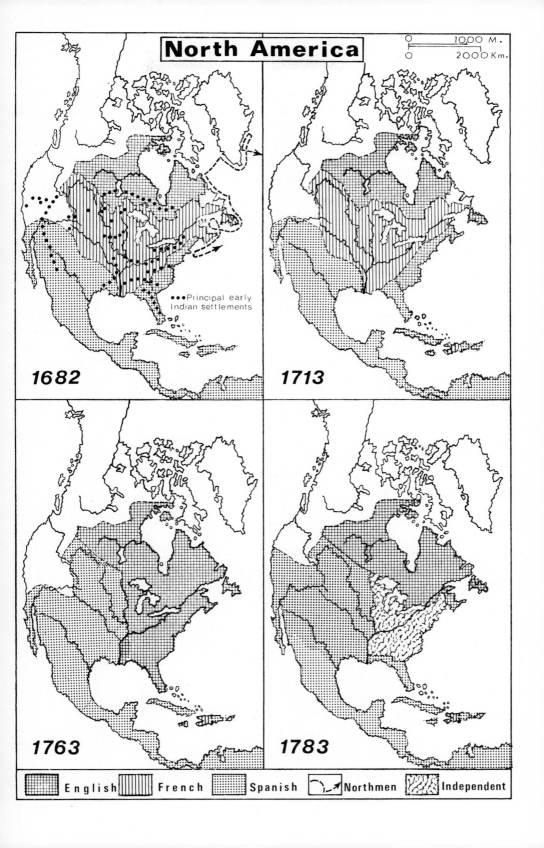

North America

1000 M.
2000 Km.

1682

●●●Principal early
Indian settlements

1713

1763

1783

English   French   Spanish   Northmen   Independent

population of the English colonies was larger, but at the same time probably did not exceed one-and-a-quarter million, including the Negro slave population. The native population of the North American continent – north, at least, of Mexico – was Indian. Their numbers were small and scattered, being probably not more than two million in total.

¶ BROWN, GEORGE W., HARMAN, ELEANOR and JEANNERET, MARSH. *The American Colonies: Canada and the USA before 1800.* 1962

For later history *see* AMERICA, DISCOVERY OF; AMERICAN COLONIES; CANADA; MEXICO; etc. For some of the early peoples of America *see* AZTECS; INDIANS, NORTH AMERICAN; MAYAN CIVILISATION.

North-East Passage: the eastern route from Europe via the Arctic Ocean to the Pacific. Though Sir Hugh Willoughby, sent by the Merchant Adventurers in 1553 to seek a north-east passage, perished, Chancellor's overland journey to Moscow led to the Muscovy Company's foundation. In 1594 the Dutchman William Barentz explored Novaya Zemlya's western coasts. In 1596 he discovered Spitzbergen and Bjornaya, wintered on Novaya Zemlya, but died before reaching home. Baron Nordenskiöld was first to complete the passage to the Bering Strait in 1878–79, and the Russian Commander Vilkitski westwards in 1913–15. Atom-powered ice-breakers have now made the North-east Passage a feasible sea lane to northern Siberia.

Northern Ireland: the six north-eastern counties of Ireland, which had their own provincial government at Stormont (Belfast) while still part of the United Kingdom. Eastern Ulster, one of the richest parts of Ireland, was settled in the 17th century by Scots and English protestants who expelled most of the catholic Irish. When, late in the 19th century, many Irishmen were demanding self-government, the descendants of these settlers feared rule by relatively poor and backward catholics. Some English Conservative politicians, resenting Irish demands for Home Rule, encouraged pro-

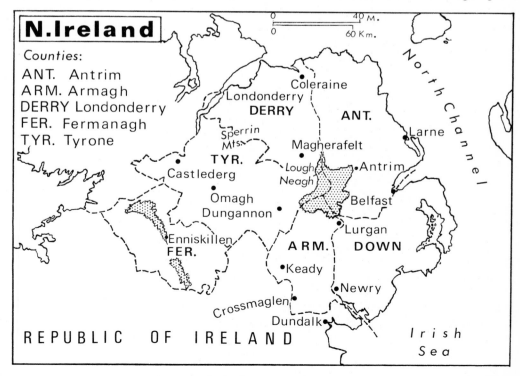

N.Ireland

Counties:
ANT. Antrim
ARM. Armagh
DERRY Londonderry
FER. Fermanagh
TYR. Tyrone

Coleraine
Londonderry
DERRY
ANT.
North Channel
Larne
Sperrin Mts.
Magherafelt
TYR.
Castlederg
Lough Neagh
Antrim
Omagh
Dungannon
Belfast
Enniskillen
Lurgan
FER.
ARM.
DOWN
Keady
Newry
Crossmaglen
Dundalk
REPUBLIC OF IRELAND
Irish Sea

testant fears. In 1886 Lord Randolph Churchill coined the slogan "Ulster will be right". When Irish self-government seemed imminent in 1912, many Ulstermen joined in a Covenant to "defeat the present conspiracy to set up a Home Rule Parliament" and preserve their United Kingdom citizenship. The leader of these Unionists was Sir Edward Carson (1854–1935), a forceful Conservative statesman of Irish protestant origin; and they recruited an armed Volunteer Force for the fray. So determined were they never to accept catholic rule that in 1920 the British Government established a separate parliament for the six counties, where most of the protestants lived. Northern Ireland has resisted all attempts at reunion with Ireland.

After disturbances in Belfast and Londonderry in August 1969, responsibility for security was given to the British Army. In April 1972, direct rule was imposed after the breakdown of talks between the British Prime Minister (Mr Edward Heath) and the Prime Minister of Northern Ireland (Mr Brian Faulkner, leader of the Unionist Party). Elections for a Northern Ireland Assembly were held in June 1973 and Mr Faulkner formed a new Executive, which took part in talks at Sunningdale (December 1973) with the British Government and the government of the Irish Republic. In May 1974, as a result of opposition to the terms of the Sunningdale Agreement, Mr Faulkner resigned and direct rule was temporarily re-imposed.

North-West Frontier (Province): the "tribal areas" of mountainous country on the north-west of western Pakistan, a separate province from 1901–55 and revived in 1970. It lies on the "pass routes" (Khyber, Malakand, etc.) to Afghanistan and neighbouring areas. The district has been, historically, in the hands of Persians,

Greeks, Sakas, Parthians, Arabs, and Turks; the last established Muslim ascendancy, though rule from Afghanistan was not effective. Sikh invasions began in 1818, and in 1849 the British annexed the area. In 1947 a referendum favoured joining Pakistan. The Afghans carried out two incursions (in 1960–61) aiming at a separate *Pathanistan*, but since 1963 they seem to have accepted the settlement.

North-West Passage: navigable route to Asia round North America. Martin Frobisher (1535?–94), sponsored by English merchants, in 1576 sailed to the Bay named after him and Baffin Island, and twice returned to the search. John Davis (1550?–1605) in 1585, 1586 and 1587 explored the Greenland coast and sailed into Baffin Bay. In 1607 Henry Hudson (d. 1611), commissioned by the Muscovy Company to find a passage via the Pole, reached the eightieth parallel. In the next decades the Dane, Jens Munk, and others sought a passage via the bay Hudson entered in 1610. In 1616 William Baffin (*c.* 1584–1622), exploring the bay named after him, discovered Lancaster Sound. The Hudson's Bay Company (1670) fostered both trade and exploration until, in the early 19th century, governments became interested. The disastrous 1845 expedition of Sir John Franklin (*see* separate entry) inspired numerous combined exploration and rescue operations. In 1850 Robert McClure (1807–73), sailing eastwards in *Investigator*, completed the passage, though largely overland, after having to abandon his ship. In 1859 Francis McClintock charted a route which the Norwegian Roald Amundsen (1872–1928) followed in navigating the passage in 1903–04. In the 1940s Larsen made the return voyage from Vancouver to Nova Scotia. In 1957 a deeper channel via Bellot Strait was discovered.
¶ NEATBY, LESLIE H. *In Quest of the North-West Passage.* 1958

Norway: kingdom in north-west Europe, with a long Atlantic seaboard. Though human life there can be traced back to 12,000 BC, Norway entered European history only when pressure of population and the rise of kings caused restless *jarls* to seek an outlet overseas. Harold Fairhair (AD 850–933) made his jarls feel the weight of his royal power, and the *vikings*, men of the *viks*, or creeks, raided abroad and presently made settlements in the Orkneys, Shetlands and Hebrides, Scotland, Ireland, Wales, northern England and the Isle of Man, and colonised Greenland, Iceland and the Faroes. At the beginning of the 11th century Norwegian vikings discovered North America.

Christianity was adopted in Norway under Olav Tryggvesson, who ruled 995–1000. In the 11th century Norway passed under the rule of Canute the Great of Denmark (*c.* 994–1035) (*see* separate entry) who invaded England and was its sole ruler from 1016 until his death. In 1066 the Norwegian king Harold Hardrada tried to conquer England. The 12th century saw civil war and much bloodshed in Norway, and the 13th century witnessed the last period of true Norwegian independence for some five hundred years. Trade and town life developed, particularly at Bergen, by intercourse with the German Hanseatic ports.

By the Union of Kalmar, 1397, Norway, Denmark and Sweden were brought under the one king; but the Swedes broke away and the union ended finally in 1523. Norway existed in obscurity under Danish domination. Through Bergen the German Reformation entered Norway and gave it a Lutheran national church.

Wars between Denmark and Sweden brought to the latter some Norwegian provinces. Royal absolutism in Denmark from 1660 gave Norway stability, and culture and literature developed. The wars of Charles XII of Sweden (1700–20) affected Norway little; and Norway was not involved in Sweden's disasters and dismemberment in 1808–09. But when the Swedes joined the last coalition against Napoleon, they obtained a transfer of Norway to Swedish rule to compensate for Sweden's loss of Finland. Norway was ceded to Sweden by the Treaty of Kiel in 1814. Norwegians objected, formed their own constitution and elected a king, but had to capitulate and accept an act of union. Under the Swedish crown Norway retained its own constitution and later even had its own flag. In 1905 the Norwegian Storting voted in favour of a dissolution of the union. Sweden conceded this, and Prince Carl of Denmark was chosen king as Haakon VII.

Norway adopted women's suffrage in 1913. The country developed a large merchant shipping industry and wood pulp industries, making great use of hydroelectric power. Labour governments have often been in office since 1935, and a welfare state began to develop with old age pensions in 1936.

In April 1940 Germany invaded Norway. Haakon VII and his cabinet escaped to London. There was strong underground resistance. Since Vidkun Quisling was unable to establish rule by Norwegian collaborators, the country was governed by *Reichskommissar* Josef Terboven. It achieved freedom once more in 1945. Norway has free trade with Sweden, Denmark, Finland and Iceland and in 1960 joined in the European Free Trade Area (EFTA). *See colour section.*

Nova Scotia: Canadian province lying between 43° and 47° N and 59°40′ and 66° 25′ W. In 1605 it was occupied by French colonists and named Acadia, but Sir William Alexander, who was given jurisdiction over the territory by James I of England, changed the name in 1621.

The Treaty of St Germain-en-Laye, 1632, restored French suzerainty. Cromwell sent occupying forces in 1654, but by the Treaty of Breda, 1677, the French returned. Nova Scotia finally became British in 1713, and in 1755 most French inhabitants withdrew. The colonists had representative government from 1758, fully responsible legislative powers in 1848, and Canadian provincial status in 1867. The capital, Halifax, was vital to Atlantic strategy in both world wars.

Nuclear power: power derived from atomic energy. The atom consists of a central nucleus surrounded by a number of negatively charged particles called electrons. The nucleus consists of positively charged particles (protons) and particles without charge (neutrons). Hydrogen, in its ordinary form, has one electron and a nucleus of one proton, and this structure becomes more and more complex as we proceed to the heavier elements, such as uranium.

Ordinary chemical reactions are associated with the outer electron structure, while atomic energy is derived from the nucleus. Energy can be released from the nucleus in two ways: (1) by fission (splitting) of the nucleus of a heavy element into two different lighter elements, or (2) by fusion of the nuclei of lighter elements. The first is the principle of the first atomic bomb, the second that of the vastly more powerful hydrogen bomb.

For producing industrial power these processes must be slowed down. This has been achieved in the fission process, and nuclear power stations use Uranium 235, subjected to a controlled bombardment of neutrons; but so far a controlled reaction of the second type has not been devised.

It has been estimated that the energy from the fission process is about 100 times that of existing coal and oil reserves; moreover, the fusion process might yield

as much as 100 million times that of those reserves.

Numerals: symbols by which numbers are represented. These came long after people had learned to count. It has been suggested that an early method of counting beyond ten was to employ two men; the first held up one finger to represent one unit and when all ten were used up the second man held up one finger to represent ten. The Mayan civilisation of Yucatan used a scale of twenty, representing numbers by a combination of dots and dashes, the dot representing one and the dash five. In the Near East vertical strokes were used (e.g. IIII for four); in the Far East they were usually horizontal, and it is possible that 2 and 3 are the result of writing cursively = and ≡. All these symbols probably represented fin-.gers, and we still use the word digit in two senses. In the same way the Roman V represented the open hand, and the X

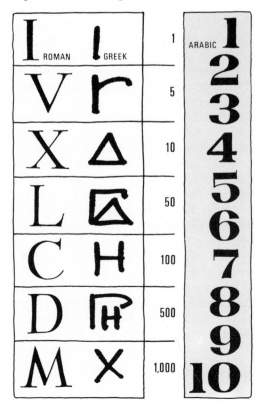

Roman	Greek		Arabic
I	ı	1	1
V	ᴦ	5	2 3
X	Δ	10	4
L	⌓	50	5 6
C	H	100	7
D	⊓ᵺ	500	8 9
M	X	1,000	10

two Vs combined. C stood for *centum* and M for *mille*.

The Greeks used the first nine letters of the alphabet for 1 to 9, the next nine letters for tens from 10 to 90, and the next nine for hundreds from 100 to 900. As their alphabet contained only twenty-four letters they reinserted two obsolete letters (*digamma* and *koppa*) and a third symbol from the Phoenician alphabet.

Our own familiar numerals seem to have developed from the Devangari numerals used in India in the 8th century, modified by the Eastern Arabs and again by the Western Arabs or Moors. The oldest known European manuscript containing our modern numerals was written in Spain in AD 976.

Nuremberg: leading manufacturing town of northern Bavaria, West Germany, medieval centre of commerce and of the German Renaissance. Among its later and less enviable claims to fame, it gave its name to the vicious Nazi anti-Semitic laws (1935) and was the setting for the trials of the leading Nazi war criminals (1945–46).

Nursing: tending the sick and injured. In ancient civilisations, nursing was done at home, by the women of the family, and was regarded as part of their duty. The word "nurse" comes from a Latin word, *nutrire*, meaning to nourish or to cherish, and has been applied to the care of the very old and the very young, as well as to the sick. Invalids were sometimes brought to temples to be healed, but there the nursing was done by male priests and slaves.

The early Christian communities appointed *deaconesses* whose principal duty was to tend the sick. After the establishment of monastic orders, their work was continued by nuns. Patients were taken to the infirmary of a religious house to be looked after, and certain orders of nuns became especially skilled in nursing. The Augustinian Sisters of the *Hotel-Dieu*, Paris, are the oldest nursing order in the world. A nun always wore a veil; this is why a modern nurse wears a white cap. A nun was addressed as "sister" – so is a senior nurse.

During the Crusades an order of knights was founded whose duty was to protect and nurse the wounded. They worked at the Hospital of St John at Jerusalem and were known as Knights Hospitallers or Knights of St John. When the Turks captured Jerusalem in 1187 the Knights of St John fled to Malta, where they built a large infirmary. Women were admitted to the order as nurses. Its badge was the Maltese cross worn today by members of the St John's Ambulance Service.

When Henry VIII closed monasteries and convents in England, some hospitals were established because homeless sick people had nowhere to go. In France Vincent de Paul, a priest, together with Mademoiselle de Gras, a wealthy Parisian lady, recruited a band of young country-women and taught them the art of nursing. They were known as Sisters of Charity, whose communities are now found all over the world.

In 1836 a German pastor, Theodor Fliedner, and his wife established near Dusseldorf a hospital where "women of good character" could be properly trained in nursing. Frau Fliedner's notes on their training became the first nursing text book. It was read with great interest by Elizabeth Fry, who visited the Fliedners' hospital. Florence Nightingale (*see* separate entry) was another visitor to the Fliedners, and was influenced by the Sisters of Charity. Through her influence, nursing in England became a real profession, with its own council, examinations and rules.

¶ EDWARDS-REES, DESIREE. *The Story of Nursing.* 1965

O

Oak: common name for trees belonging to genus *Quercus*, distributed over much of the world. To Britons and Germans the oak means strength. It is also a symbol of age. Pliny mentioned oaks in Rome older than the city itself, and there are a few trees in England probably seen by the Saxon kings. Oak timber is hard and rots slowly. For this reason it was a favourite shipbuilding timber. The Coronation Chair, made of oak by Master Walter of Durham in 1300 is still used for the coronation of every English monarch. Among oak trees famous in history are the Boscobel or Royal Oak in which Charles II of England hid after the battle of Worcester (1651), and the Charter Oak, in Hartford, Connecticut, USA, its site now marked by a memorial. In 1687 the English governor Andros came to take away the royal charter originally granted to the colony of Connecticut, since it gave the colonists too much independence. At his meeting with the officials the candles were suddenly extinguished. By the time they had been rekindled the charter had been removed from the conference table and hidden in the oak tree.

The Coronation Chair in Westminster Abbey.

Oakum: old shredded rope, usually tarred, driven into the seams (or spaces between planks) of ships by mallet and chisel to make them watertight. "Picking oakum" (i.e. untwisting old ropes) was formerly a common occupation in prisons and workhouses. The process of stopping the seams is known as caulking.

Prisoners picking oakum at Clerkenwell, 1874.

Obelisk: Egyptian stone pillar, four-sided, tapering to a pyramidal point. The Egyptians made their huge obelisks at the quarry, cutting them out on three sides and then drilling holes along the line of the fourth, into which they inserted wooden pegs. These, when made wet, swelled and split the stone. The finished obelisks were covered with hieroglyphs (*see* separate entry) and erected in temples and in towns to celebrate special events. They were also connected with sun worship. Their use spread to other early peoples, including the Canaanites, Phoenicians and Assyrians. The British Museum's "Black Obelisk" of Shalmanesar the Third shows the submission of King Jehu of Israel in the 9th century BC. A 3,000-year-old obelisk from Luxor now stands in the Place de la Concorde, Paris; in the 19th century the Egyptian government presented examples to Britain and America (*see* illustration p. 642, *and* CLEOPATRA'S NEEDLES).

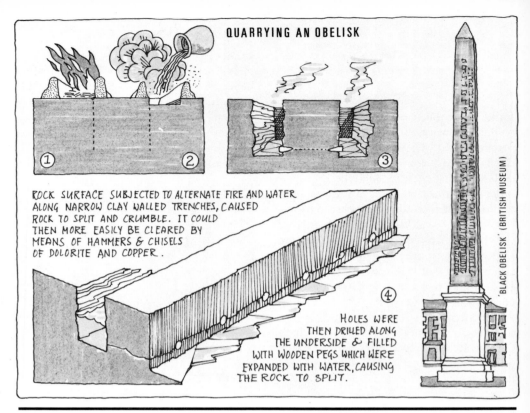

QUARRYING AN OBELISK

① ②

③

ROCK SURFACE SUBJECTED TO ALTERNATE FIRE AND WATER ALONG NARROW CLAY WALLED TRENCHES, CAUSED ROCK TO SPLIT AND CRUMBLE. IT COULD THEN MORE EASILY BE CLEARED BY MEANS OF HAMMERS & CHISELS OF DOLORITE AND COPPER.

④

HOLES WERE THEN DRILLED ALONG THE UNDERSIDE & FILLED WITH WOODEN PEGS WHICH WERE EXPANDED WITH WATER, CAUSING THE ROCK TO SPLIT.

'BLACK OBELISK' (BRITISH MUSEUM)

Oberammergau: village in Bavaria famous for its religious play. In 1633 the villagers, in gratitude for deliverance from a plague, vowed to enact every ten years the Passion and Death of Christ, appointing the cast of some 700 actors from their own members. From 1680 the basis of the ten-year interval was changed and has since been maintained, the only omissions being in 1870, 1920 and 1940 by reason of war, though a postponed performance was staged in 1922 and a 300th anniversary in 1934. The play takes eight hours and is repeated many times throughout the summer. Despite the crowds that nowadays resort to Oberammergau, the play remains a moving and unique experience. *See colour section.*

¶ SATTELMAIR, RICHARD. *Oberammergau: its environment and tradition.* 1970

Observatory: an institution where the positions, movements and physical nature of astronomical phenomena such as the sun, moon, stars and planets are observed and recorded scientifically. An essential part of this work is the accurate and regular publication of such records.

The earliest observatories, often temporary arrangements, had only rudimentary instruments. Established in temples in Mesopotamia and Egypt at the dawn of civilisation, they were principally concerned with astrological forecasts and with the computation of a calendar for religious festivals and for sowing and harvesting crops. The development of Greek mathematics, particularly geometry, from the 5th century BC and of simple angular measuring instruments such as the quadrant led to the refinement of observations and scientific astronomy. In China, government observatories were established as early as the 7th or 8th centuries BC for the regulation of the calendar. Chinese observations between the 5th and

10th centuries BC are the most reliable available for the period.

In the 7th century AD the Arab peoples conquered the Near East, inherited the work of the Greek astronomers and founded observatories at Damascus and Baghdad. In the 8th century their knowledge was transmitted to Europe as a result of the conquest of Spain in 711. Monastic and, later, university observatories were established in Europe but like their predecessors they were transitory. Ulugh-Beg, son of Tamerlane (*see* TIMUR), founded a great observatory at Samarkand about 1420, where he computed astronomical tables used by the first English Astronomer Royal, John Flamsteed, at Greenwich three centuries later.

National observatories were founded in Europe in the 17th century, in Paris by Louis XIV (1667) and in England by Charles II (1675).

Today there are great observatories throughout the world, supported by governments, universities and scientific institutions. To mention a few, Great Britain has those at Herstmonceux, Sussex, and Jodrell Bank, Cheshire, the latter housing the first steerable radio telescope. Among the most important in the USA are the Yerkes Observatory, Wisconsin, operated by the University of Chicago and using the world's largest refracting telescope; the National Radio Astronomy Observatory, Green Bank, Virginia, with its 300-foot [91·44 metres] diameter dish-type radio telescope; and the Kitt Peake National Observatory, Tucson, Arizona, which has a 480-foot [146·30 metres] long solar telescope.

Among the chief Russian observatories are those at Zelenchchukskaya in the Caucasus Mountains and Chuguyev, in the Ukraine; the first has the world's largest operational telescope and the second the largest radio telescope. Other great observatories are located at Puerto

Below, the Old Royal Observatory, Greenwich. Right, the radio-telescope at Jodrell Bank, Cheshire, England. Below right, moonlit view of the 200-inch Hale telescope dome with shutter open, at Mount Palomar, USA.

Rico, West Indies; in the Effelsberger Valley, West Germany; and in Owens Valley, California.

See also PLANETARIUM; RADIO ASTRONOMY; TELESCOPE.

Occident: the west, as distinct from the east (the Orient). The term, formerly applied to Europe, to distinguish it from Asia, is now extended to cover other parts of the world inhabited by people of European descent, including America. The word derives from Latin *occidere* (setting), referring to the sun.

Oceania: geographical area embracing the islands of the South Seas. Racially, the inhabitants fall into several distinct groups, three of them being Polynesian, Micronesian and Melanesian. Archaeological remains include the great stone figures of Easter Island (*see* separate entry), totem poles and other survivals of ancestor worship.

Oceanography: the scientific study of the oceans. Four main sciences are involved – physical, biological, chemical and geological. Man has been concerned with physical oceanography ever since he first learnt to sail the seas. He found that the course of his ship was affected by ocean currents and tidal streams. He had, however, to wait until the 19th century before scientific data concerning these ocean movements became available. The valuable scientific observations made by the British navigator Captain Cook between 1768 and 1779 proved of enormous value in determining the extent of the oceans. In 1847 the American Commander M. F. Maury published his wind and current charts. The mariner was now able to plan his ocean routes taking into account the data in Maury's charts.

The first purely oceanographic expedition was carried out by the British HMS

Challenger 1872-76. Under the direction of the Scottish naturalist Sir Wyville Thomson, the *Challenger* carried out research in every known branch of marine science and brought back samples of bottom sediments and marine life and many thousands of deep sea soundings. This information enabled the oceanographers to establish the nature and shape of much of the ocean bed. Another pioneer was Prince Albert of Monaco, who organised deep-sea expeditions between 1885 and 1915 and established the first oceanographical museum at Monaco.

In the 20th century the submarine world is explored by deep-sea submersibles. One of these, the bathyscaphe, invented by Swiss scientist Professor Auguste Piccard (1884-1962), reached the greatest known depth of seven miles in the Challenger Deep, Pacific Ocean. (*See* PICCARD, AUGUSTE and UNDERWATER EXPLORATION.)

Professor Piccard's bathyscaphe Trieste.

The enormous potential of the biological, chemical and geological aspects of oceanography can be summed up by quoting the words of Professor Piccard's son, Dr Jacques Piccard, in his introduction to *Down to the Sea: a century of oceanography* by J. R. Dean. "Fifty thousand million million tons of natural chemical products (sufficient to fill a goods train long enough to girdle the earth 1,000 million times), consisting of 2,000 million million tons of magnesium, nearly 800,000 million tons of aluminium, 30,000 million tons of iron and 15,000 million tons of copper, nearly 10,000 million tons of gold, hundreds of thousands of millions of tons of nitrates, phosphates and potassium, to say nothing of strontium, radium and uranium, and practically all the other elements too. Hundreds of thousands of square miles of floor literally carpeted with nodules of manganese and other useful metallic ores: thousands of millions of tons of plankton, continually produced and with a possible content of up to 50 per cent and more of high-quality proteins – enough to provide abundant food for many times the present population of the world. Lastly, in the form of currents, waves, tides and differences in temperature, enough calories, foot-pounds and kilowatt-hours to supply in full measure all the energy needed by man, as well as another far from unimportant item: over one million million million cubic metres of water. Such is the hereditament of the sea."

¶ DAUGHERTY, CHARLES MICHAEL. *Searchers of the Sea: pioneers in oceanography.* 1963; STEWART, HARRIS B., JR. *Deep Challenge.* 1966

O'Connell, Daniel (1775–1847): Irish statesman known as "the Liberator". O'Connell was deeply concerned at the condition of the Irish people, particularly with the subservience of the Catholic masses. He united the Irish Catholics and successfully campaigned to improve their lot. He failed, however, in the other cause of which he was a lifelong champion, the repeal of the Act of Union with Britain.

October Revolution: the second Russian revolution of 1917. Military defeat, armies and fleet near mutiny, industrial workers in revolt and an irresolute government all created a situation in Petrograd (now Leningrad) which Lenin saw as ripe for revolutionary action. The need to forestall a congress of soviets (revolutionary committees) to be held on 7 November, at which his Bolshevik party might not have had a majority, settled the date for Lenin. On the night of 6 November (24 October by the Russian calendar) infiltration of government buildings by his supporters and the absence of effective resistance put the government into the hands of Lenin, Trotsky and their followers.

¶ HINGLEY, RONALD. *The Russian Revolution,* 1970; MACK, DONALD W. *Lenin and the Russian Revolution.* 1970

Trotsky (left) and Lenin (centre) in 1917.

Octobrists: members of a moderate and constitutional political party in Russia, brought into existence to defend and secure the fulfilment of the manifesto issued by Tsar Nicholas II on 30 October 1905 granting civil rights to all and promising a *Duma* or parliament with full legislative powers.

Oder–Neisse Line: the frontier between East Germany and Poland since World War II. It follows the River Oder, then its

Oder–
Neisse
Line

tributary the Neisse, southwards from Szczecin to the Czech border. By the establishment of this frontier in 1945 Germany lost one-fifth of its prewar area, including a prosperous source of wheat and potatoes. It was intended as a temporary boundary until a freely elected government in Poland could make a permanent agreement. However, the Communists took control in both Poland and East Germany, and in 1950 they accepted the Line as a permanent frontier.

Odyssey, The: Greek narrative poem describing the adventures of Odysseus, whom we often call Ulysses from the Latin *Ulixes*. To say that the poem was composed by Homer is to repeat a tradition that ignores modern controversy over the date and authorship of the work (*see* HOMER). Like its companion Homeric poem, the *Iliad*, the *Odyssey* is divided into twenty-four books and describes the ten years' wanderings of Odysseus and his companions on their way home from the siege of Troy to the island of Ithaca, where his faithful wife Penelope awaited him.
¶ HOMER. *The Odyssey*, trans. E. V. Rieu. 1970

Oecumenical or **ecumenical:** from the Greek, an adjective meaning "embracing all the inhabitants of the earth". The word is chiefly used to describe the great councils of the Church. The earlier of these, such as the first Council of Nicaea (AD 325), truly brought together representatives of the whole Church. After the split between the Eastern and Western Churches in 1054 the term was confined to the gatherings of the Roman Church, for instance, the Council of Trent, which lasted from 1545 to 1563. In modern times an Oecumenical Movement is gathering force with the object of bringing all Christendom back into one fold.

Oersted, Hans Christian (1777–1851): Danish physicist and chemist. Oersted laid the foundation for the science of electromagnetism. In 1820 he noticed the needle of a compass wavered whenever he put it near a wire carrying an electric current. In this way he discovered the connection between magnetism and electricity which was later put to use by Faraday through his invention of the dynamo (*see* ELECTRICITY). Oersted is also credited with producing the first aluminium in 1825.

OGPU: initials of the Russian for "General Political Administration of the State"; one of the names given to the secret police of the USSR, who use espionage, arrest without trial and torture to achieve aims. Founded in 1918 (as CHEKA) to send opposers of Communist Party rule to labour camps, it was later used by Stalin to get rid of personal rivals.

O'Higgins, Bernardo (1776–1842): Chilean revolutionary leader. Son of Ambrosio O'Higgins, Irish-born viceroy of Chile and Peru, Bernardo was educated in England. He became a leader in the Chilean struggle for independence from Spanish rule and was the new republic's first president. A Chilean province was named after him.

Oilfields: areas with subterranean supplies of oil capable of being extracted for commercial use. Seepages of petroleum, together with bitumen and salt, were put to use in prehistoric times. The Chinese, for example, several centuries BC, drilled for oil, using bamboo piping. But oilfields entered modern history when Colonel Edwin Drake struck oil in 1859 after drilling at Titusville, Pennsylvania, USA. In 1861 the first cargo of American oil crossed the Atlantic to London in barrels. A hundred years later, in the 1960s, fuels from the world's oilfields provided half the world's total supply of energy. A thousand million gallons were being used each day, and the products of oilfields had become the most important single class of merchandise in world trade. The chief cause of this economic revolution was the invention of the internal combustion engine. A significant development was the application of compression ignition to larger engines in 1897 by Rudolph Diesel.

In the USA John D. Rockefeller, through his Standard Oil Company, founded in 1870, created a virtual oil monopoly by getting control of refineries, pipelines and transport. The Anglo-American Oil Company, Standard's overseas subsidiary, was organised in 1888 and soon possessed the world's largest oil fleet. In 1911, however, anti-trust legislation broke Standard Oil into more than thirty companies.

Russian petroleum output was even bigger than that of the USA, the great Baku oilfield being developed from 1874.

In the Far East drilling was begun by the Dutch in Sumatra in 1884. In Europe Rumanian oil was developed by the Germans, and in South America a big oilfield in Venezuela was opened up in 1914. Drilling was begun in Persia in 1908 by the Anglo-Persian Oil Company, which in 1914 won a long-term contract to supply the British Navy.

Oilfields had thus acquired major strategic importance to the great powers. They also had brought wealth and political importance to parts of the world which had previously been backward and little known.

After World War I there were big oil strikes at Kirkuk in Iraq and pipelines were laid to Tripoli and Haifa. This was followed by discoveries of oil in Bahrain, Saudi Arabia and Kuwait, bringing about great social and political changes in those areas of the Near East.

Governments of countries with oilfields began to contest the right of American, British, French and other foreign oil firms to make large profits from their territories. In 1938 Mexico expropriated foreign oil

Oil pipe-lines in the Agha Jari area, Iran.

Above, a member of a drilling crew waiting to receive the elevator and attach the next length of pipe. Above right, Selten Oil Field, Cyrenaica, Libya. Right, "Staflo" semi-submersible drilling platform, North Sea.

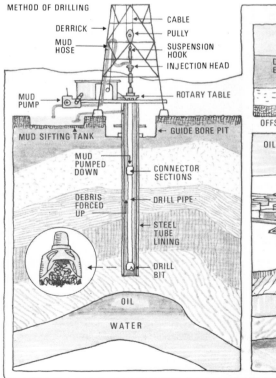

METHOD OF DRILLING

DERRICK — CABLE
— PULLY
MUD
HOSE — SUSPENSION
HOOK
— INJECTION HEAD

MUD
PUMP — ROTARY TABLE

MUD SIFTING TANK — GUIDE BORE PIT

MUD
PUMPED — CONNECTOR
DOWN SECTIONS

DEBRIS
FORCED — DRILL PIPE
UP
— STEEL
TUBE
LINING

— DRILL
BIT

OIL

WATER

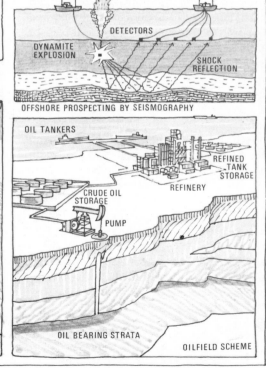

DETECTORS
DYNAMITE
EXPLOSION SHOCK
REFLECTION

OFFSHORE PROSPECTING BY SEISMOGRAPHY

OIL TANKERS

REFINED
TANK
STORAGE
CRUDE OIL
STORAGE REFINERY
PUMP

OIL BEARING STRATA

OILFIELD SCHEME

firms. In Iran, Venezuela, Saudi Arabia, Kuwait, Iraq, Bahrain and Qatar a system was adopted by which the governments got a much larger share of the profits from the oilfields in their territories.

As American and Russian petroleum was increasingly used inside those countries, and as petroleum supplies from both Near East and Far East were put in hazard at times by political disturbance, oilfields were increasingly sought elsewhere. There were new strikes of oil in North Africa, particularly in Libya in 1959, and in Nigeria. Offshore drilling for under-sea oilfields was pursued off North America, in the Persian Gulf and in the North Sea, where both oil and natural gas have been found. A big oilfield was found in Alberta, Canada, and vast new sources in Alaska.

O K (Okay): expression now common among all English-speaking peoples, meaning "I agree", "all right" or "satisfactory". It is thought it originated from a political organisation (the O K Club) formed to support Martin Van Buren (President of the USA 1837-41) in his unsuccessful campaign for re-election. O K stood for his birthplace, Old Kinderhook, New York.

Okinawa: one of the Ryukyu Islands in the Philippine Sea, approximately 900 miles [1,448 kilometres] south-west of Tokyo.

Following the crushing defeat of the Japanese navy at Leyte (23-26 October 1944) the US land and sea forces were in a position to drive north directly toward Japan itself. On 1 April 1944 the US Marine Corps and Army units landed on Okinawa. Desperate *kamikaze* (suicide plane) attacks failed to dislodge the supporting fleet, which sustained 5,000 fatalities, 368 damaged ships and 36 minor vessels lost. Using Okinawa as one of its chief bases the US mounted extensive air raids and fleet bombardments of the Japanese mainland, inflicting heavy blows at industrial targets and war plant. Preparations for the invasion of Japan, using Okinawa as the springboard for the operation, were being made when the atomic attacks on Hiroshima and Nagasaki ended the war. The Ryukyu group remained under US military control till, in 1953, the northernmost islands were returned to Japan and, in 1972, Okinawa itself.
¶ BENIS, FRANK. *Okinawa.* 1970

Olaf I (*c.* 969-1000): Norwegian king. Once a relentless Viking raider of Britain, Olaf was converted to Christianity by a hermit in the Scilly Isles. Thereafter, he ceased his marauding and attempted to convert Norway. He died fighting the Swedes and Danes and became a legendary hero to his people.

Olaf II (*c.* 995-1030): Norwegian king and patron saint. A Christian himself, he completed the conversion of Norway begun by Olaf I. His reforms provoked dissension, and he was defeated and killed by a rebel army. He became the symbol of national independence and a saint, centre of many legends.

Old Bailey: name by which the Central Criminal Court, London area, is known, from the name of the street in which the Court is situated. It is presided over by a High Court Judge and Jury. Appeals from its decisions are to the Criminal Division of the Court of Appeal and from that court to the House of Lords.

Old Guard: the crack troops of Napoleon's Imperial Guard, when this became enlarged after 1806. Service in the Guard was an honour, as only the finest troops were selected. For the Old Guard there was the added qualification of experience: at least five years service and two cam-

649

A Grenadier, one of Napoleon's Old Guard.

paigns. Napoleon deliberately limited its use in battle, keeping it in reserve for emergencies.

Today the term Old Guard is used for any section of an organisation (such as a political party) that does not want to see any change, preferring to cling to the old ways and opposing what younger members call progress.

Old master: general term covering any one of the great painters of earlier centuries, especially the European artists of the 15th to 17th centuries. It is also applied to a painting by such an artist.
See colour section.

Old North-west, The: the north-central region of the USA, bordering on the Great Lakes between the United States and Canada, and including the states of Illinois, Indiana, Ohio, Michigan and Wisconsin. The states furthest south – Illinois, Indiana and Ohio – are primarily rolling plains. Michigan and Wisconsin, although also possessing wide plains, in-

clude as well many lakes, small islands and extensive forests. The region also has some sizable rivers, especially the Ohio, which was a major factor in the growth of population and commerce.

These states, as their name implies, were formed out of the territories ceded to Britain by the French in 1763 and, after the War of Independence, acquired (1783) by the new American nation. They were organised into the Northwest Territory by legislation in 1786. Many people settled in the territory in the 1820s and 1830s. Of special importance in this movement was the development of canals to make it easier to send farm produce to the east coast. The most notable of these were the Erie Canal in New York State and the Ohio Canal system in Ohio. These, together with the Great Lakes, made settlement potentially profitable, and spurred the growth in the region. During the Civil War period, this area was a "free soil" centre (i.e. where slavery was disapproved of), and provided much of the manpower with which the Confederacy was forced back into the Union.

Agriculture is still of great importance in the region. Indiana and Illinois are leading producers of corn, wheat and soybeans; Michigan and Wisconsin specialise in dairy products; while Ohio produces large numbers of livestock. However, the region is also a major industrial area. Detroit in Michigan is the centre of the massive automobile industry; Gary, Indiana, is a major steel town; while the production of paper products is based on the forest resources of Wisconsin. Beer, iron ore and bauxite are also produced in this region. *See* AMERICA for map.

Old South, The: the south-eastern section of the United States, comprising the states of Alabama, Florida, Georgia, Mississippi and South Carolina. This region borders on both the Atlantic

Ocean and the Gulf of Mexico and is primarily an area of low plains and flat coastlands, with wide areas of swamps in Georgia and Florida. It has numerous rivers, most of them small, and, with the exception of some hills in the Appalachian range in northern Georgia, is virtually without mountains.

Although the Spanish established a number of missions in Florida, notably the settlement at St Augustine, most of the population in this region stemmed from the English settlers in South Carolina and Georgia, and from later population movements into Alabama and Georgia after the United States had become independent. Settlement in these latter two states dated from the early 1800s, when high cotton prices and the deterioration of soils in the southern states along the coast led to the expansion of the plantation system and cotton production into the fertile lands of these territories. During the period leading to the American Civil War the entire region was the centre of agitation against the Republican Party, and in favour of the protection and expansion of slavery in the United States. When secession came, it was again these states that led the way. The first capital of the Confederacy was established in Montgomery, Alabama, and much of the rhetoric and justification for the rebel cause was drawn from the writings of John Calhoun, the Senator for South Carolina.

Although efforts are being made to increase manufacturing in the region, and while there are some important cities – notably Birmingham in Alabama and Atlanta in Georgia – this is primarily a rural, agricultural region. Cotton lint, peanuts, tobacco, livestock and fruits are of primary importance. Also of growing significance is the tourist business, especially in Florida, where the mild climate and fine beaches have made a centre for recreation for retired people.

Old Testament, The: the books of the Bible covering the period before the coming of Christ, at which point the Old Testament is succeeded by the New. Books accorded a place in the Christian Bible are termed canonical, and the original canon of the Old Testament corresponds closely with that of the Jewish religion (*see* JUDAISM). After the Reformation (*see* separate entry) some Churches relegated certain books from the canon to what is called the *Apocrypha*.

The researches of modern scholarship have modified many previous ideas of dates and authorship. To the Jews the customary division of the books in question is threefold: (1) the five Books of the Law (*Pentateuch*), containing also the narrative of the early period of Jewish history, (2) the Prophets, including books of later history, and (3) the *Hagiographa* (sacred writings), such as the Psalms, which do not fit into either of the other two categories.

A translation from the original Hebrew into Greek was made at Alexandria as early as the 3rd or 2nd century BC. It is known as the *Septuagint*.

¶ GRISEWOOD, JOHN. *The Book of the Bible*. 1972
See also BIBLE; INCUNABULA.

Old Three Hundred: the original 300 American families settled in Texas in 1823 by Stephen Austin, under formal authority from the Mexican government. Stipulations were that they should be virtuous and willing to accept the Roman Catholic faith.

Old World: the Eastern Hemisphere, especially the continent of Europe, as distinct from the New World or Western Hemisphere.

Oléron, Laws of: one of the various codes of maritime law developed in the Middle Ages. The *Consolato del Mare* was used by Mediterranean ports, the Laws of Oléron by Normandy and Brittany, the Laws of the Hanse Towns by Germany, and the Laws of Wisby by ports further north. England appears to have adopted the Laws of Oléron at an early date, as they were cited in a court case in 1349 and are found in the early customs records of London, Southampton and Bristol. They deal with the duties of the Master and crew of a vessel and of the lodeman (steersman), liabilities arising between merchants and the Master, and such matters as freightage and jettison (throwing goods overboard to lighten the ship).

Oligarchy: political term meaning the rule of the few, as contrasted with aristocracy, the rule of the nobles, democracy, the rule of the people, or monarchy, the rule of a king: all display the same slight variation of the original words in Greek. In British history it is usual to speak of the Whig Oligarchy to describe the years between 1714 and 1770, when the first two Hanoverian kings, George I and II (and George III for the first ten years of his reign), allowed themselves to be dominated by parliaments managed, both at elections and in session, by a closely knit group of county families representing the Whig faction.
See also DEMOCRACY; WHIG; etc.

Olivares, Gaspar de Guzmán (1587–1645): chief minister of Philip IV of Spain. For twenty-two years (1621–43) he was responsible for controlling a vast world empire. He was blamed for Spain's repeated diplomatic failures and military defeats at the hands of the Dutch, French and Portuguese and died in disgrace.

Olympia: sanctuary in ancient Greece dedicated to the worship of Zeus and scene of the Olympic Games (*see* separate entry), held every four years in his

The Gymnasium, Olympia, as it is today.

honour. The site is in the north-west corner of the Peloponnese, and excavations have produced some outstanding relics of ancient art from its sacred buildings, as well as revealing the outlines of the stadium.

The large hall in Kensington, London, where indoor horse-shows, military tournaments, trade exhibitions and other large displays are staged, is named after ancient Olympia.

Olympiad: period of four years between successive celebrations of the Olympic Games (*see* next article). It was also used in ancient times for dating historical events, the first Olympiad starting in 776 BC and the 293rd and last in AD 393. The interval is still observed with the revived Olympic Games.

Olympic Games: athletic festival originating in ancient Greece. In the modern version a white-clad youth, the last of a series of torchbearers who have brought the flame all the way from Greece, enters the stadium. Holding his torch on high and watched by the silent crowd, he mounts the rostrum and touches his flame to the brazier. It flares into life, and the Olympic Games have begun.

It is a solemn and impressive ceremony, recalling the great Pan-Hellenic festival held every four years at Olympia in southern Greece. This was primarily a religious festival in honour of Zeus, the supreme god. In the enclosures where the Games were held stood temples. Sacrifice, prayer and hymn were the background against which the festivals were set.

To the Greeks religion implied art; and the beauty of form and athletic prowess of man ranked as high as his intellect and spirit. Poets and sculptors followed the fortunes of the Games, proclaiming to the world and posterity, in words and stone, the exploits of their heroes. The prize was symbolic – a crown of wild olive. The real triumph of the victor was the ode in which his praise was sung.

The list of Olympic victors begins in 776 BC. The great popular spectacle lasted five days. The first was taken up by examination of the competitors, all of whom were men and youths, since women were totally excluded from the Games. Then competitors and judges were sworn in to obey the rules. The morning of the second was set aside for the chariot race and other events of the hippodrome and the rest of the day for the pentathlon, a competition in the five events of running, jumping, discus and javelin throwing and wrestling. The morning of the third was devoted to the great sacrifice to Zeus. In the afternoon the contests for boys took place. The fourth day was for a programme of men's events, and the fifth was given over to feasting and celebration.

A young German athlete rehearses the lighting of the Olympic flame.

The Olympic Games reached their zenith in the 5th century BC, when victory in a major event conferred the highest distinction on the city of the victor. Later on, professionalism entered the contests, and a process of deterioration set in which led to their final suppression in the 4th century AD.

The Olympic Games of modern times resulted from the enthusiasm of Baron Pierre de Coubertin, no athlete, but a scholar who believed that Greece owed her Golden Age in part to her emphasis on physical culture. He hoped too that, on the friendly fields of amateur sport, national rivalries and political and religious differences would be forgotten. To Athens went the honour of staging the Olympic revival in 1896, with competitors from eight countries. Following the four-year cycle, the second Games were held in Paris in 1900.

Supreme control rests with the International Olympic Committee, who have ruled that every competitor must be an amateur, that women can compete, and that the highest standards of sportsmanship must be observed.

Recent Games have been staged in Rome (1960), Tokyo (1964), Mexico City (1968) and Munich (1972).

¶ GIRARDI, WOLFGANG. *Olympic Games.* 1972

Omar Khayyam (full name, Ghiath Uddin Abdul Fath Omar Ibn Ibrahim Al-Khayyam, *c.* AD 1050-1123): Persian mathematician, astronomer, philosopher and poet, born near Nishapur and employed by the Seljuk Sultan Malikshah to reform the calendar. The Persians, who judged poetry by form rather than content, regarded him as a fourth-rate poet and remembered him chiefly as an unhappy atheist and materialist and champion of Greek learning (i.e. philosophy). He is valued as a poet in England because of the free translation of his quatrains (*Rubaiyat*) published by Edward Fitzgerald (1809-83). *Rubaiyat* were epigrams designed to be read independently and were arranged alphabetically in Persian collections, but Fitzgerald arranged them to read as a coherent poem. Khayyam means "tentmaker", possibly the trade of Omar's father. Mathematicians also remember him as the author of a treatise on algebra. *See colour section.*

¶ OMAR KHAYYAM. *Rubaiyat*, trans. Edward Fitzgerald, edited W. A. Wright. 1958

Ombudsman: name (taken from Swedish) describing a kind of public watchdog called a Parliamentary Commissioner, appointed in Britain by the Parliamentary Commissioner Act, 1966, which gives greater powers of investigating citizens' complaints against bureaucratic wrongdoing than is possible by questions and letters to Ministers. So far, the jurisdiction of the Ombudsman extends only over a strictly limited field.

Omnibus: vehicle with seats for a number of passengers. The word is a Latin one, meaning "for all" and is now commonly shortened to "bus". Although we speak of an airport bus, hotel bus, etc., the term is normally applied to a public service vehicle plying on a fixed route. The modern motor bus may be either a double-decker or a single-decker.

Although hackney carriages for personal hire were used in some cities of western Europe from the 17th century, the first omnibus appeared in 1825, when an Englishman, George Shillibeer (1797-1866),

STANDARD KNIFE-BOARD GEN. OMNIBUS Cº 1859

STANDARD B-TYPE 1913

GREYHOUND 'SUPER SCENICRUISER' USA

introduced these single-decker covered vehicles, drawn by pairs of horses, on the streets of Paris and, four years later, of London also. The venture failed, but some years later the omnibus became a familiar feature of many cities. In London the bus driver and his conductor were famous for their wit and repartee in the traffic jams which occurred even then. In due course uncovered seats were added on the roof of the vehicle, reached by a steep stairway, where passengers sat back to back, which gave rise to the name "knifeboard".

Early in the 20th century the petrol engine began to replace the horse, though in the 1920s some of Tilling's steam-buses were still operating in London. Later developments included covered top decks and the use of diesel engines, while, in some places, trolley-buses were introduced to make use of the overhead wires of obsolete tramways.

Apart from urban services the bus has also made great changes in the habits of life in the country – habits which the increasing ownership of private cars is again altering.

Lower costs have caused many people to prefer coach to train for long-distance journeys, and travel organisations now offer "package tours" by which, e.g., much of Europe can be covered by coach. Interesting comparisons can be made over a period of less than a century. In England it was reckoned a great feat when, in 1888, a stage-coach was driven from London to Brighton and back, a distance of 108 miles [173·8 kilometres] at an average speed of 13·79 m.p.h. [22·19 kilometres per hour] and involving 14 changes of horse-team. In the US today, the Super Golden Eagles of the Dallas Continental Trailways, each 60-foot [18·29 metres] long and carrying more than 60 passengers, can travel at 70 m.p.h. over long distances.

¶ KAYE, DAVID. *Pocket Encyclopedia of Buses and Trolleybuses 1919-45.* 1970; *Pocket Encyclopedia of Buses and Trolleybuses since 1945.* 1968

Ontario: chief industrial and agricultural province of Canada (capital, Toronto). Following the explorations of Samuel de Champlain (1613-15), the territory was settled by French and English traders, and Jesuit missions were established to work among the Indians (*see* JESUITS). One of the saddest chapters in Jesuit history was the massacre of Fathers Brebeuf, Lalement and their companions when the Huron Indians, among whom a mission had been founded, were wiped out by the Iroquois in 1649. Apart from isolated areas, Ontario was still largely untrodden wilderness till the 19th century, when the end of the French Revolutionary and Napoleonic Wars brought opportunity for wide development. The territory had become British in 1763 and part of the province of Quebec in 1774. It achieved independence within the Dominion of Canada in 1867, when it received its present name. Ontario now dominates the international nickel market, producing half the world supply and, as well as its agricultural products, has rich resources of timber, hydroelectric power, gold, silver, copper and uranium to support its many industries.

See CANADA for map.

Open fields: arable fields without hedges. The German tribes described by Caesar and Tacitus had no permanent arable fields. A piece of land would be ploughed one year and deserted the next, while a fresh piece would be ploughed. This was "extensive" as opposed to "intensive" cultivation, where the same land was used each year. At the time of the Domesday survey (1086-87) the three-field system was in general use in England. The village was surrounded by three large fields, temporarily fenced while crops were growing but open at other times so that cattle could graze on the stubble. A three-year rotation of crops was used, one field yielding spring crops, the second winter crops, while the third lay fallow and was ploughed twice during the year. Each field was subdivided into acre or half-acre strips, and each man's holding consisted of a number of these strips scattered throughout the fields, so that the best land did not all go to one person. It has been suggested that this scattering was the result of communal ploughing.

Open shop: factory, firm or workshop where workers who are not members of a trade union are employed alongside those that are. The opposite is a closed shop, which admits only trade union members.

Opera: drama with musical setting. Opera began in Italy with the Renaissance, when Florentine aristocrats wanted to restore the Greek presentation of drama. They used mythological subjects in dramatic or poetic form with musical settings. Solo voices using natural speech were

accompanied by supporting chords. Short choruses were interspersed, moving, not like the madrigal as an interweaving of melodies, but straightforwardly in blocks of chords. Orchestras, at first, were tiny, only five instruments perhaps.

The earliest opera still surviving is *Eurydice*, by Peri, 1600. Another great landmark was *Orpheus*, 1607, by Monteverdi, who developed the style further, using a larger orchestra and establishing the Italian Aria. This led to the triumph of the solo singer with a high standard of vocal tone and musical agility.

Other great names in the early history of opera are those of Jean-Baptiste Lully (c. 1632–87), who wrote thirteen works based largely on classical themes and making considerable use of ballet; and, in England, Henry Purcell (1658?–95), who, still only in his thirties when he died, gave opera, in such works as *Dido and Aeneas*, a dramatic life it had not achieved before.

The greatest figure in 18th century opera (and for many the greatest in all operatic history) is that of Wolfgang Amadeus Mozart (1756–91), the Austrian composer who had a natural feeling for the stage and was able to convey to a remarkable degree the intense emotions of real life men and women. Two of his masterpieces are *Le Nozze di Figaro* (*The Marriage of Figaro*) and *Die Zauberflöte* (*The Magic Flute*). Another Austrian, Franz Joseph Haydn (1732–1805), though better known for other forms of composition, wrote at least fifteen operas which have recently been receiving greater attention. Beethoven's only opera was *Fidelio*, the moving story of Leonora, wife of Fer-

La Scala in Milan, Italy, is one of the world's most famous and distinguished opera houses. Above left, a scene from Rossini's highly colourful opera The Italian Girl in Algiers. *Below left,* Aïda *written by Guiseppi Verdi in 1871. It is one of his later, more strongly dramatic works.*

nando Florestan who, when her husband was a state prisoner, took the name of Fidelio and dressed as a man in order to serve as a jailer in the same prison.

The 19th century saw the cheerful, light-hearted works of the Italian Gioacchino Antonio Rossini (1792–1868), best known for *Il Barbiere di Siviglia* (*The Barber of Seville*) and, in more serious vein, *Guillaume Tell* (*William Tell*). Equally popular today are the works of Giuseppe Verdi (1813–1901), a peasant who became Italy's best-loved composer through such operas as *Rigoletto*, *Trovatore*, *La Traviata* and *Otello*. In Germany, Richard Wagner (1813–83) broke away from previous operatic conventions by seeing opera as a bringing together of all the arts – music, literature and painting – and in such tremendous works as *Tannhäuser*, *Lohengrin*, *The Ring of the Nibelungs* and *Die Meistersinger* put himself among the immortals.

The 20th century has seen a complex and diverse picture, which includes the tuneful flowing melodies of Giacomo Puccini (1858–1924) and his compatriots Leoncavallo and Mascagni; works achieved under political pressure, such as Sergey Prokofiev's *War and Peace*, the satirical operas of Kurt Weill, the advanced experimental exercises of Paul Hindemith and,

A performance of Die Miestersinger Von Nürnberg *(1862–7), one of Wagner's most popular works.*

in England, the achievements of Sir Benjamin Britten and Sir Michael Tippett, to name only a few.
See colour section.
¶ WECHSBERG, JOSEPH. *The Opera.* 1973

Opinion polls: efforts to forecast, e.g. election results, by sampling public opinion. They date from about 1935 in the United States and were associated with the names of George H. Gallup (Institute of Public Opinion), Archibald Crossley (Crossley Poll), and Elmo Roper and Paul Cherington (Fortune Survey). Conflicting results of different polls taken at the same time have cast doubt on their reliability, and they are subject to error at each stage, i.e. the selection of those interviewed, the selection of the questions, and in the recording and analysis of the answers. The first of these stages is achieved either by quota sampling, which attempts to make the small sample a copy of the entire nation according to the frequencies of age, sex, occupation, economic status, etc., or by random sampling, in which, for example, every fifth or tenth person is interviewed in a selected area.

Opium War (1839–42): a discreditable episode in 19th-century British overseas expansion. Chinese imperial authorities had protested against the import of opium into China by British traders. In 1839 a large quantity of opium was seized and destroyed. Sharp disagreement over this incident gave a pretext for hostilities from which the British gained extensive trading privileges in China. The Chinese Empire was ill equipped for resistance. The island of Chusan was captured by the British Indian fleet, along with Hong Kong and Amoy. By the treaty of Nanking, Hong Kong was thrown open to European trade, together with Amoy, Fuchow, Nanking, Canton and Ningpo. The Chinese government paid an indemnity.

Oporto: second city of Portugal, near the mouth of the River Douro. It was already a flourishing trading centre when the Romans, who called it Portus Cale, occupied it. For five centuries, from its capture by the Visigoths in 540 till its occupation by Christian forces in 1092, it suffered frequent invasion and partial destruction. Its later prosperity, though it has not been uninterrupted by European wars and internal rebellions, has been founded on the port wine trade. It also manufactures textiles, leather, pottery and various luxury goods. Among its most interesting buildings are the cathedral and the church of Sao Martinho de Cedo Feita, the latter built by the Visigoth King Theodemir to receive the relics of St Martin of Tours.

Oppenheimer, Robert (1904–67): American physicist, from 1943 to 1945 director of the Los Alamos Laboratory, New Mexico, which produced the atomic bomb used in the destruction of the Japanese cities of Hiroshima and Nagasaki (6 and 9 August 1945).

From 1946–52 he acted as Chairman of the General Advisory Committee to the US Atomic Energy Commission. In 1954, though the investigating committee declared him a "loyal citizen", and though the move was strongly opposed by many leading scientists, it was decided his communist sympathies were too strong and his government security clearance was withdrawn, thus denying him access to all secret material.
¶ In PRINGLE, PATRICK. *Great Discoverers in Modern Science.* 1955

Oracle (from Latin *orare*, to speak, to pray): the place where a deity or specially inspired priest could be consulted about the future; or the god or human agency itself. The most famous example in the ancient world was the oracle at Delphi on Mount Parnassus, Greece, consulted by, among others, Croesus and Philip of Macedon. The pronouncements of the oracle were frequently enigmatic and capable of at least two interpretations. *See also* CROESUS; DELPHI; PHILIP II.

Orange Free State: province of South Africa with a population (1970) of 1,386,202, including 276,745 whites. Originally thinly populated by Bushmen, Bechuanas and Zulus, it had known only a few European hunters and missionaries till groups of Dutch farmers from Cape Colony, ranging in search of pasture, settled with their flocks in 1834, to be quickly followed by others who took part in the Great Trek of 1835–36 (*see* separate entry). The territory was annexed in 1848 by Britain but six years later became independent as the Orange Free State. A further annexation took place in 1900 as a result of the Boer War (*see* separate entry), the name being altered to Orange River Colony, and over four million pounds was spent by the British government in repairing the ravages of war. The country was finally incorporated in the Union of South Africa in 1910.

Orange, House of: the ruling house of Holland and the founders of Dutch independence. The house takes its name from the small independent principality of Orange, now part of the department of Vaucluse, south–eastern France. William the Silent (1533–84), Prince of Orange and Stadtholder (chief magistrate) of Holland, Zeeland and Utrecht, like his ancestors, served the Habsburgs until Spanish tyranny drove him to resistance. He held his countrymen together in defeat, cutting the dykes to drive back the Spaniards. His son Maurice of Nassau (1567–1625) led the Netherlands forces to victory, and their successors further strengthened the Republic under successive Stadtholders. Marriage brought

William I,
The Silent.

William III.

William IV.

William I,
King of the
Netherlands
(1815).

close connections with England, and in 1689 William III (1650-1702), leader of the resistance to Louis XIV, and his wife Mary (1662-95) became joint rulers of England after the flight of James II. After the death of William III there were several rival claimants to the title of Prince of Orange. Eventually John William Firsco of Nassau-Dietz succeeded to the principality as William IV. In 1815 his son William VI became William I, King of the Netherlands.

Orangeman: member of an organisation, named after William III of England, Prince of Orange, formed in 1795 to uphold Protestantism in Ireland. Subsequent events have tended to concentrate the organisation's energies in the province of Ulster; but it is active throughout Northern Ireland and groups of Orangemen may also be found in many other English-speaking countries.

Orators: public speakers, particularly those who, by their eloquence and concentrated feeling, hold the attention of, move and influence their audiences.

In ancient Greece and Rome oratory was taught as a subject, much as history or mathematics is taught today. It was treated as a branch of *rhetoric*, which, in turn, may be defined as the art of using language to influence people. Budding orators were required not only to learn how to marshal their thoughts in logical order but to master an elaborate set of rules governing the grammatical construction, the rhythms and the figures of speech permissible in their orations.

The greatest orator of ancient Greece was Demosthenes (*c.* 383-322 BC), who, in a series of famous speeches known as *Philippics*, warned Athens of the threat represented by Philip of Macedon (383-336 BC) to the Athenian way of life. Stories are told of how Demosthenes, struggling to overcome a speech defect, would go down to the seashore where he would fill his mouth with pebbles and, thus handicapped, try to make himself heard above the noise of the waves. The outstanding Roman orator was Marcus Tullius Cicero (106-43 BC), who lived in the turbulent years which saw the end of the Roman Republic and was himself the victim of political murder.

In the Middle Ages many universities appointed Orators who acted as their special envoys. Oxford and Cambridge retain this ancient office in the person of Public Orators whose task it is to make speeches in the name of the university on such special occasions as the conferring of honorary degrees.

Oratory in the modern sense is not something which takes place in a vacuum. Great orations are fashioned out of great occasions, and great oratory is, therefore, a by-product of leadership, since great leaders owe much of their power to their ability to sway large numbers of people to follow their lead.

Thus, it is not surprising to find that many great orators are associated with periods of war, violence and revolution. Examples include Girolama Savonarola (1452-98), the friar who, though he did not himself preach violence, was instrumental in expelling, for a time, the ruling Medici family from Florence; Georges Jacques Danton (1759-94) and Maximilien de Robespierre (1758-94), two leading figures of the French Revolution; Charles de Gaulle (1890-1970), whose voice rallied defeated France at a later period; and Adolf Hitler (1889-1945), who exactly illustrates the point where the orator deteriorates into the demagogue, or rabble-rouser. Hitler's speeches were illogical and full of lies, but his personal magnetism led the German Reich into the horrors of World War II.

The English parliamentary system has produced many statesmen who were notable orators: Charles James Fox (1749-1806), Edmund Burke (1729-97), David Lloyd George (1863-1945) and Sir Winston Churchill (1874-1965) may be specially mentioned. In American history few could match Daniel Webster (1782-1852), the lawyer and statesman whose "clear, massive, gorgeous, overwhelming eloquence carried juries with him as well as parliaments". Religion, too, has had its orators. Savonarola has already been mentioned. A religious orator of a different kind was Peter the Hermit (died 1115), the French monk who persuaded some 20,000 people to embark on the disastrous First Crusade, from which few returned to tell the tale. John Wesley (1703-91), founder of the Methodist Church, preached more than 40,000 sermons and initiated a great religious revival. Among the 19th-century pulpit orators the English preacher Charles Haddon Spurgeon (1834-92) had an enormous following; and in our own day the phenomenal evangelistic campaigns of the American Billy Graham show that this type of eloquence can still command a vast audience in an age when political oratory is largely a thing of the past.
See also individual entries.

Ordeal, Trial by: method of trying accused persons by seeking a miraculous decision or judgment from God rather than man. The ordeal is very ancient in origin and continues today among some primitive peoples. Among its many forms have been the ordeal by boiling water, when the accused immersed his hand and arm and was adjudged innocent if the scalds had healed within a stated period of time. In Europe the ordeal by "swimming" was well known, the accused being thrown bound into water which rejected him (i.e. allowed him to rise to the surface) if guilty. If innocent he sank and was

Trial by boiling.

hauled out again. Ordeal by fire could take the form of passing through flames, carrying red-hot iron, or walking barefoot over glowing ploughshares. One queen of England, Emma, mother of Edward the Confessor, is said to have survived such an ordeal unscathed, walking on nine red-hot shares and afterwards presenting in commemoration nine manors to the Church of Winchester.

Orders of architecture: name given primarily to the three main styles of classic Greek architecture: the Doric, Ionic and Corinthian. The Romans added two further Orders, the Tuscan and the Composite, to the list. Technically, an Order, in this sense, consists of the upright column with its base and capital, together with those horizontal parts of the building – the architrave (lower part), frieze (middle part) and cornice (upper part) — which the columns support.

The Doric, the earliest to be developed, while understandably the simplest, has an unsurpassed strength and grandeur. A Doric column, which has no ornamental base, has a simple fluted shaft of, usually, twenty shallow flutes, and terminates at its upper end in a plain square slab called an abacus. The Ionic Order, with its

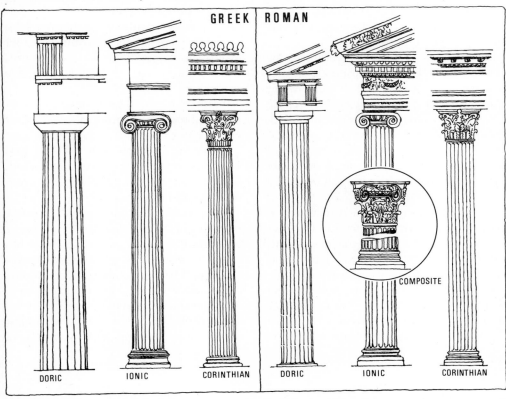

GREEK ROMAN

DORIC   IONIC   CORINTHIAN   DORIC   IONIC   CORINTHIAN

COMPOSITE

scroll capitals, which perhaps derived from the ancient Egyptian lotus motif, is more elegant than the Doric, while the last of the Greek Orders, the Corinthian, with its stylised decoration based on the leaves and calyx of the acanthus, is altogether more florid and ornate.

The Romans, who appropriated so much that was Greek, were fonder of the Corinthian style than the Greeks themselves. The Romans were imitators rather than innovators, and their Tuscan Order was based on the massive unfluted columns which were a characteristic of the architecture of the Etruscans, early inhabitants of central Italy. The Composite Order, very ornate and reserved largely for triumphal arches, combined Corinthian and Ionic decoration.

See also ATHENS; GREEK ART.

Orders, Military: organisations of knights living under various forms of monastic rule. These originated during the Crusades, when groups of knights banded together in companies having both religious and military aims. Three are especially famous.

In AD 1113 the Pope recognised the order of the Knights Hospitallers, later known as the Knights of St John. Their aims were to protect pilgrims travelling to Jerusalem and to care for the wounded. The order still survives in many countries, where its primary function is the care of the sick. In England the head of the St John's Ambulance Brigade still keeps the old title of "Grand Master".

The Knights Templar, a similar order, had a primary duty to defend holy places against the Turks. Their purpose was to be "first to attack and last to retreat", and this often led them into foolhardy situations. During the 14th century the Templars' preoccupation with worldly goods brought upon them the antagonism of King Philip IV of France and Pope

Clement V, who in 1312 disbanded the order.

The Teutonic Knights were similarly pledged to assist Crusaders and pilgrims. Later they undertook to defend Central Europe against the heathen. Their power declined during the 14th and 15th centuries. The order now survives as a small body of Dutch Protestant noblemen, whose badge is a black cross edged with white. *See also* CRUSADES.

Orders, Religious: organisations of men and women living according to rule in religious communities.

When the Roman Empire adopted Christianity as its official religion, some Christians felt that life rapidly became too easy and that only by suffering and hardship could true faith be kept alive. Such men often went to live in the desert, frequently to be near some well-known religious leader. They shared food and prayed together. The first true monastic group was formed in Egypt during the 4th century AD, by the followers of St Anthony, a hermit who lived for twenty years in a tomb. Another group, at Cappadocia, in Asia Minor, lived in caves in very uncomfortable conditions.

Members of these early religious communities had two aims – to live a life of prayer and to do without comfort of any kind, since they thought that bodily ease interfered with their devotion to God. Many neglected themselves to the point of illness and starvation.

Towards the end of the 5th century Benedict of Nursia founded a monastery on Monte Cassino, in Italy, which became a model for all monastic communities. His monks' lives were ordered by a code of conduct known as the Rule of St Benedict. It had to be kept by everyone, from the abbot to the humblest novice. The rule made it plain that a monk's first duty was prayer and the worship of God, but since a man could not pray wholeheartedly if he were underfed or ill Benedictines were allowed an adequate amount of food and rest. They wore black robes and sandals; in winter they were given woollen underclothing and fur boots.

A Benedictine's day was carefully organised. It began at midnight, when services called Lauds and Matins were held in church. He then returned to bed until seven o'clock, when he attended another service, Prime, followed by Mass. After breakfast, the monks met in the chapter house to discuss the day's business; at this meeting, any brother was permitted to voice his opinion. High Mass, the principal service, was celebrated at ten, and afterwards the monks dined in the refectory. From noon until five they worked, then attended Vespers, after which they were allowed to talk and relax. At half-past six they ate supper, re-

turning to church at seven for Compline. They then went to bed until summoned to Lauds at midnight.

During the 500 years after Benedict's death monasteries became wealthy and many monks grew lazy and fond of luxury. Reformers tried to bring back the old ideals, and new orders developed as a result of their work.

In 1084 a monk named Bruno decided to relinquish comfort for a life of hardship. With six companions he settled at a desolate place in the French mountains, named Chartreuse. Here the monks lived in deliberate austerity, doing all their own work, cultivating crops and rearing livestock. They refused to own more land and cattle than they needed, worked in silence and spent their leisure time alone. They wore plain white habits over hair shirts, and were known as Carthusians. A few branch communities were formed, but there were never many members because of the unusual strictness of this order.

Life has changed very little from the traditional pattern for these Benedictine Monks in a monastery on the Isle of Lerin, France.

Fourteen years later, twenty monks settled at Cîteaux, a swampy area near Dijon. Believing that a monastic community ought to be self-supporting, they drained the land, built their house, grew crops and reared sheep and cattle. These Cistercians were the farmers of monastic life, even shortening their services in order to attend to agriculture.

In Italy, Francis of Assisi formed an order of Friars (Brothers), who did not live in monasteries but worked amongst people. After his death his successor, Elias, reorganised the Franciscans on lines resembling a Benedictine community, although the majority still travelled about. In 1216 a friar named Dominic gathered about him in Toulouse a number of men who were prepared to explain the Bible to the ignorant. His followers were known as Dominicans. They wore white habits under black cloaks; many scholars were attracted to this order because of their interest in biblical studies, and Dominicans frequently taught in universities.

In the 12th century a Crusader named Berthold had settled on Mount Carmel with twelve others who devoted their time to prayer. The community grew, but eventually had to flee from the Saracens, reaching Europe in 1240. The majority came to England, and elected an Englishman, Simon Stock, as their General. He adopted the way of the Franciscan Friars, but the Carmelites always wore distinctive white mantles over their brown habits.

Women were admitted to this order in the 15th century. St Teresa, who was trained at the Carmelite convent of Avila, in Spain, reformed their rule, bringing back the devout self-denial of the original hermits.

See also ABBEYS; BENEDICT OF NURSIA; FRANCIS OF ASSISI; FRIARS; JESUITS; MONASTERIES; ORDERS, MILITARY; TERESA OF AVILA, etc.

Ordnance: (1) general term for heavy guns, cannon and artillery; (2) government department concerned with the maintenance of stores of weapons, munitions and other military equipment.

Ordnance Survey: government survey of Great Britain and Northern Ireland. As a result of difficulties experienced by English troops during the Jacobite rebellion of 1745, the Master-General of the Ordnance was ordered to make a survey of northern Scotland, so that accurate maps could be prepared. During the next hundred years civilian surveyors and the Royal Engineers extended this survey to the whole of the British Isles. An important feature was the preparation of detailed maps which have since been regularly revised and improved.

Oregon Question: the dispute over the western boundary between the USA and Canada, left undetermined in 1818 because the mountain chain of the area had not been explored. The British were interested in the area because of its value to the fur trade, while the Americans claimed it because their explorers had opened it up. An agreement was signed between Britain and the USA on 15 June 1846, by which the Americans acquired all the territory now comprising the states of Washington, Oregon and Idaho, while Britain obtained Vancouver Island.

Oregon Trail: the 2,000 mile [3,200 kilometres] overland route from the Missouri to the Columbia. In 1842–43 John C. Fremont (1830–90), known as "the Pathfinder", made a scientific investigation of the Oregon trail which stimulated interest in the Far West. This in turn led to a great migration to the Oregon country as "Oregon fever" spread throughout the Mid West, and resulted in an influx of settlers from Missouri,

Ohio and Kentucky. The trail, which had previously been used only by fur traders and explorers, extended from Independence (Missouri) to Astoria at the mouth of the Columbia River and became the main route for emigrants to the Far West.
¶ PARKMAN, FRANCIS W. *The Oregon Trail.* 1931

Organisation of African Unity (OAU): a movement, founded 1963 and including all independent African states, to promote African interests and maintain solidarity.

Organisation of American States (OAS): organisation, with headquarters in Washington, set up in 1948 to encourage and co-ordinate social, technical and economic co-operation among the states of the Americas, more than twenty of which are members.

Organisation of Central American States: union, formed in 1951, of Costa Rica, Guatemala, Honduras, El Salvador and Nicaragua, to promote and protect the economic, social and cultural interests of member states.

Organisation for Economic Co-operation and Development (OECD): In 1948 sixteen European nations formed an association to co-ordinate their trading and economic activities and to help administer the Marshall Plan (*see* separate entry). This was the Organisation for European Economic Co-operation (OEEC). It was replaced in 1961 by the Organisation for Economic Co-operation and Development, with wider scope and membership. This includes not only some twenty European countries as either full or associate members, but also Canada, the USA and Japan. Its aims are basically the same as those of the earlier organisation – the economic development of member countries, the expansion of world trade and aid to underdeveloped countries. Its headquarters are in Paris.

Organisation for European Economic Co-operation (OEEC): organisation set up in 1948 by sixteen European nations to co-ordinate their economic policies and to help administer the Marshall Plan (*see* separate entry). In 1961 it was replaced by the Organisation for Economic Co-operation and Development (*see* above).

Orient, The: the countries of the world lying east of Europe, especially the Far East, including China and Japan (from Latin *orientem,* to rise; i.e., the land of the rising sun). The opposite is the Occident.

Oriflamme: the ancient banner of France, meaning "gold" and "flame", carried before the king and, in time of peace, kept in the Abbey of Saint Denis. Originally plain red, the banner was later embroidered with golden flames or stars.

The Oriflamme, top left, at the Battle of Nancy.

Orléans: city on the River Loire and strategic key to central France. In AD 451 the Roman Aëtius united Romans, Gauls and Germanic tribes to repulse Attila's Huns. In October 1428 the Duke of Bedford besieged it till it was relieved by the army of the Bastard of Orléans, encouraged and guided by Joan of Arc (*see* separate entry), whose "voices" dictated the plans. She entered the city on 29 April and broke the English threat by taking the southern approaches to the bridge on 7 May. The victory was not followed up but was sufficient to encourage the crowning of Charles VII at Rheims. Orléans was a Huguenot headquarters in the Wars of Religion and was the pivot of the second phase of the Franco-Prussian War of 1870.

Orléans, Houses of: younger sons of French kings, and their descendants. Louis, Duke of Orléans, 1372-1407, was younger brother of Charles VII and governed in his name when he was insane. He was murdered by the Burgundian faction. He married Valentina Visconti and thus gave his descendants, Louis XII (1462-1515) and Francis I (1494-1547), a claim to Milan. His son, Charles of Orléans (1391-1465), was wounded and captured at Agincourt, and was a famous writer of the type of verses known as rondeaux. The family device was a porcupine. The title was revived in 1626 for Gaston, second son of Henry IV and Marie de Medici, the figurehead of the plots against Cardinal Richelieu. It was revived again for Philip (1640-1701) the younger brother of Louis XIV. His descendants were suspected of ambitions to supplant the Kings of France. Philip (1674-1723) became Regent of France 1715-22. Louis Philippe (1747-93) known as Philippe Egalité had encouraged some of the revolutionary orators, but perished in the Terror; Louis Philippe (1773-1850) became the Citizen-King of the French, 1830-48.

Orsini: family of Roman nobility of the Guelph faction, their device a bear recalling their founder, Ursus, their war-cry "Orsini for the Pope" opposed to "Colonna for the People", the cry of their Ghibelline rivals. Over many centuries they produced popes, cardinals, generals and a few poets. Celestine III (pope 1191-98) was an Orsini, so was Nicholas III (pope 1277-80) who distributed to his kinsmen principalities and castles in the Campagna from which they repeatedly threatened the citizens of Rome and later popes. On his death, two Orsini cardinals were kidnapped while their colleages elected a new pope. In 1303 the Orsini rescued Boniface VIII from the Colonna, but kept him prisoner themselves until he died. The clan was ruthlessly reduced by sword and poison of the Borgia in 1502. The last Orsini pope was Benedict XIII (pope 1724-30). Count Felice Orsini (1819-58) was guillotined for a bomb attack on Napoleon III in the cause of Italian independence. *See colour section.* *See also* GUELPHS AND GHIBELLINES.

Orthodox: (from a Greek word meaning "right in opinion") in line with traditional and accepted views, especially in faith and religion. The opposite is unorthodox, unconventional, heretical or independent.

Orthodox Eastern Church: Christian Church of eastern Europe and the lands round the eastern end of the Mediterranean. The early Christians gradually

The assassination of the Duke of Orléans.

evolved an organisation of groups of communities presided over by Patriarchs who took their titles from Alexandria, Antioch, Constantinople, Jerusalem and Rome, where the style was later changed to Pope. All enjoyed equal status, but Constantinople gained prestige as the seat of the Eastern Empire, and Rome's claim to pre-eminence through St Peter was later reinforced by Charlemagne assuming the title of Holy Roman Emperor. These rivalries were aggravated by disputes over doctrine, and the final split between Rome and Constantinople came in 1054, the other three patriarchates being, for the time, submerged in Mohammedan conquests. Attempts at reconciliation in the 13th and 15th centuries were unsuccessful.

In the later history of the Orthodox Church, the most significant event was the establishment of the Russian patriarchate in 1589, while Constantinople itself was in pagan hands: this Church still survives in the USSR though sadly harassed by the state. In the following centuries, as the

The Orthodox Cathedral of St Basil, Moscow.

Turks were driven back or became more accommodating, the old patriarchates were revived, and a number of new and smaller ones, self-governing but generally headed by archbishops, were created. The tiny patriarchate of Sinai comprises less than 150 souls.

The Oecumenical Patriarch of Constantinople is still given this traditional title as head of the general body; but this does not take away the individual independence of the other patriarchates, which is the chief bar to any reconciliation between the Eastern and Roman Churches. On the other hand, relations between the Orthodox Church and the Anglican Church are increasingly close.

¶ MEYENDORFF, J. *The Orthodox Church: its past and its role in the world today.* 1965

See also CHARLEMAGNE; OECUMENICAL; PATRIARCH; PROTESTANT; REFORMATION.

Osaka: second city of Japan, with an important trade in textiles, shipbuilding, tea, iron, glass, chemicals and sugar-refining. Its rise began in the late 15th century with the building of a temple. In 1909 a third of the city was destroyed by fire. Among its recent notable buildings is its university (1931).

Oslo: capital city of Norway. The old city was founded by the Viking, Harold Hardrada, in the 11th century, but was totally destroyed by fire in 1624. It was rebuilt on a grand scale, and its excellent harbour, landscape and Viking Museum have attracted much trade and tourism.

Ostend: Belgian sea port on the North Sea, handling considerable traffic with England and the continent of Europe. It is also the headquarters of the Belgian fishing fleet and maintains an important school of navigation. In the Middle Ages it was strongly fortified and withstood a number of sieges.

Ostia: the port of Rome, some sixteen miles [25·8 km] to the south-west, at the mouth of the River Tiber, which is not navigable to vessels of any size. Originally a naval base, its importance grew when, in the 1st century AD, it became increasingly necessary to import grain to feed the city's multitudes. The original harbour was then silting up, and a new one was built three miles to the north. The old town, however, flourished for many years and has in recent times yielded rich archaeological remains.

Ostracism: originally a system of banishment for political reasons practised in ancient Athens. The term is derived from the Greek word for the broken pieces of pottery on which the citizens scratched the name of the man whom they wished to send into exile: Many such fragments have been dug up. Ostracism was not designed as a punishment for crimes against the state, but as a kind of safety valve for relieving political pressure. A few other Greek states had similar procedures.

In modern times, we use the word to denote a community shunning (or, in Britain "sending to Coventry") persons of whose behaviour or sentiments it disapproves.

Otis, James (1725-83): Boston lawyer who was one of the early leaders of the American Revolutionary movement. In 1762 he published a pamphlet *A vindication of the conduct of the House of Representatives* which affirmed the privileges of the colonies under the British Constitution. In 1764, as a result of the Sugar Act, he published his best known writing *The rights of the British Colonies asserted* in which he raised the argument of no taxation without representation. In 1772 he became chairman of the Boston Committee of Correspondence which represented the views of the people of Boston on the question of colonial rule to the rest of the Thirteen Colonies and to the Old World. It was this committee that was instrumental in calling the First Continental Congress of 1774.

Ottawa: city selected by Queen Victoria as the capital of Canada (1858). Its original name was Chaudière, from the Indian *Asticou*, or "boiler", a reference, mentioned by Samuel de Champlain (1613), to the Ottawa river cataract with its eddying basin and its thunderous noise that could be heard "for more than two leagues". The first permanent settlement in the neighbourhood was not till 1800, and the present heart of Ottawa was once farmland, cleared in 1820. It now supports major industries in lumbering, sawmills, hydroelectricity, paper-making, and many light manufactures. Important buildings include the University (1866), the Parliament Buildings (1916), cathedrals, museums, and the Dominion Observatory.
See CANADA for map.

Otto I, called "the Great" (AD 912-73): Holy Roman Emperor (962-73) and German king (936-73). He was not only the greatest political and military leader of his time but encouraged the spread of Christianity (if only as a political instrument) and, unlettered himself, was a patron of scholarship.

Ottoman Empire: Turkish state created by Othman, a leader of ghazis – devout Muslims dedicated to Holy War and plunder. Othman's father, Ertughrul, was leader of a band of nomad refugees from Mongol-dominated Central Asia. The Seljuk Sultan gave him land near Brusa, the last Byzantine territory in Asia Minor. He could, therefore, offer hopes of plunder and conquest. Othman attracted

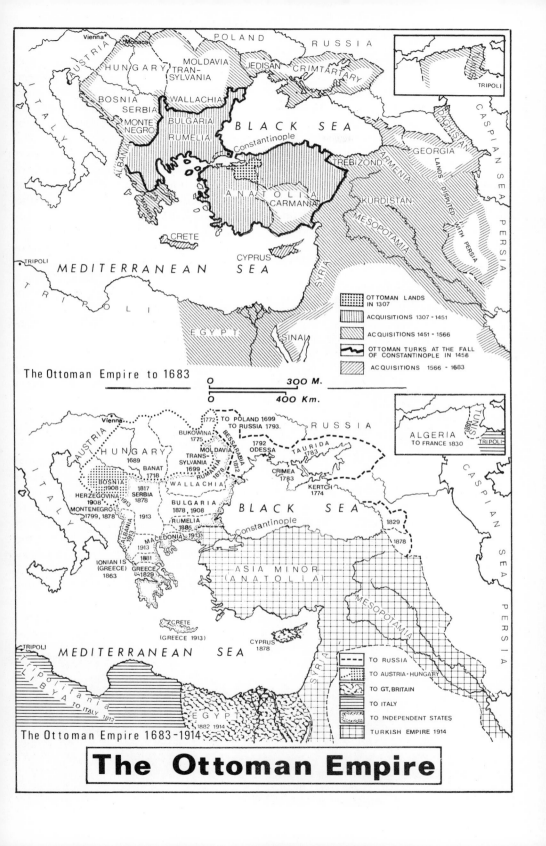

The Ottoman Empire to 1683

The Ottoman Empire to 1683

OTTOMAN LANDS IN 1307
ACQUISITIONS 1307 - 1451
ACQUISITIONS 1451 - 1566
OTTOMAN TURKS AT THE FALL OF CONSTANTINOPLE IN 1458
ACQUISITIONS 1566 - 1683

0   300 M.
0   400 Km.

The Ottoman Empire 1683-1914

TO RUSSIA
TO AUSTRIA-HUNGARY
TO GT. BRITAIN
TO ITALY
TO INDEPENDENT STATES
TURKISH EMPIRE 1914

The Ottoman Empire

a large war band and in 1307 supplanted the Seljuks. In the reigns of Orchan (1326–62) and Murad I (1362–89) the Ottoman state was developed, based on the army and the priesthood. Its forces crossed into Europe in 1361 and defeated the Bulgarians and Serbs in the late 14th century. Under Mehmet II (1451–81) the Ottomans captured Constantinople in 1453 (*see* CONSTANTINOPLE). Selim I (1512–20) took Mecca, declared himself Caliph and overthrew the Mamelukes of Egypt. Suleiman I (1520–66) defeated the Hungarians at Mohacs in 1526 and besieged

Suleiman I, the Magnificent.

Vienna in 1529, while his fleet threatened the coasts of Spain and Italy. The Habsburg family led the defence of Christendom, and after 1683 the Ottoman Empire decayed and was supplanted by the Turkey of Mustapha Kemal in 1920.

Originating from a war band rather than a race, the Ottoman Empire existed primarily for the sake of the army, and uninterrupted conquest was necessary for its survival. The Sultan himself spent every summer on campaign; provincial governors were the military commanders who contented themselves with enforcing order. The nucleus of the army was the trained, well-paid guards: sipahis (cavalry), Turks or Balkan subjects rewarded with lands, and janissaries, the "new troops" raised in 1330. Janissaries were infantry archers (later musketeers), slaves bought from the Crimean Tatars, prisoners of war, or children taken by force from Christian villages in the Balkans, brought up as Muslims, forbidden to marry, disciplined and kept loyal by good uniforms of yellow and green and by good food. Food provided the bond of unity; their badge was a wooden spoon; their ranks were "soupmaker", "head cook", "water-carrier"; they held regimental meetings round their cauldrons; if their cauldrons were captured they felt disgraced; their signal of mutiny was the overturning of their cauldrons. In 1520 there were about 10,000 sipahis and 12,000 janissaries. In addition, there were some 250,000 unpaid irregulars serving for plunder – the dreaded *bashi-bazooks*. Heavy artillery was also used.

The Sultans were absolute rulers. They

A warlike Turkish game, from a European encyclopaedia, c. 1830.

forestalled rebellion by murdering their brothers and chose their successors from the sons of their slave wives. They selected their household servants and officials from Christian slaves reared in the Palace School.

This harsh regime was tempered by the *ulema*, Muslim priests and jurists who maintained the law courts, schools and hospitals. They were chosen by the Sultan and acted as his watchdogs, being attached as religious advisers to the guilds or confraternities into which the soldiers, sailors, merchants and craftsmen were organised.

The Christian subjects were left in peace if they paid their tribute of money and children, and were allowed to practise their religion. But the Turks contributed nothing to civilisation themselves, though they used the talents of those they conquered – Persian architecture, Arabic scripts, Byzantine administrations. They remained nomads at heart, the houses even of the rich containing nothing that could not be loaded in a caravan and carried into the desert. *See colour section.*
¶ VUCINICH, WAYNE S. *The Ottoman Empire: Its Record and Legancy.* 1965

Oudenarde, Battle of (1708): victory obtained by the allied forces of Marlborough and Prince Eugène over the French during the War of the Spanish Succession (*see* separate entry). The French intended to seize Oudenarde, but, covering fifty miles [80 kilometres] in sixty-five hours and attacking before his army had finished crossing the river, Marlborough surprised and scattered their forces.

Outer Space Treaty: treaty (January 1967) inspired by the United Nations, attempting to define the aspirations and conduct of space exploration and stating that astronauts are to be looked on as "envoys of mankind". The treaty has some eighty signatories, the chief exceptions being France and Communist China. An extension of the treaty (July 1968) provides for the safety of astronauts who land in the territory of a foreign state.

Outlander: generally, a foreigner or an alien settler; particularly (*uitlander*) a British settler in the Transvaal and Orange Free State in the pre-Boer War period.

Outlawry: a primitive punishment putting an offender outside the protection of the law. In its most savage form it reduced a man to the status of a wild animal. Every man's hand was against him, and he could be killed with impunity. Later, the outlaw might be killed only if he refused to surrender or tried to escape. Otherwise the king alone had power of life and death over him.

Depending on the gravity of his offence an outlaw forfeited his goods, his lands, his civil rights, or all three. Gradually the offence, in England, lost its extreme seriousness, becoming, rather, a means of forcing accused persons to stand trial. It was used as a punishment for debt and for contempt of court. Already long obsolete, it was formally abolished in 1879.

Outlawry has gone by other names. When Lucius Cornelius Sulla (138–78 BC) was dictator of Rome he issued *proscriptions* – lists of political enemies whose property was confiscated and who were declared outlaws in the fullest sense of the term. The ancient Athenians practised *ostracism* (*see* separate entry), a relatively civilised form of outlawry by which people deemed politically dangerous might be exiled for ten (or, at a later period, five) years.

In fact, from the time when David took refuge from King Saul in the cave of Adullam, gathering about him a band of followers just as Robin Hood, the English folk-hero, did many centuries later, outlaws have often been people whose differences with authority have been political rather than criminal. Today's outlaw may be tomorrow's king.

Outremer: literally, "overseas"; the general name for the territories fought over during the Crusades, including Palestine, Cyprus, Cilicia and the Nile Delta.

Outwork: defensive structure outside the main fortifications, e.g. curtain wall, moat, ditch, earth bank.

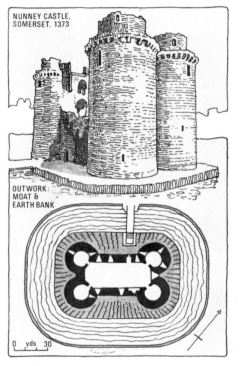

NUNNEY CASTLE, SOMERSET. 1373

OUTWORK: MOAT & EARTH BANK

0 yds 30

Ovid (Publius Ovidius Naso, 43 BC–AD 17): Roman poet. He was born at Sulmo near Rome and educated for the law, but, having private resources, devoted himself to poetry. His works, which are of outstanding quality, can be divided into three categories: (1) myths and legends of gods and men; (2) poems

Quadrille lessons at Robert Owen's Institution, New Lanark.

on the art of love and the remedies for its tortures, which incurred the displeasure of the emperor and resulted in his banishment to Tomis (less correctly, Tomi) on the Black Sea; (3) laments over his punishment and prayers for recall, which were of no avail, for he died in exile.

Owen, Robert (1771–1858): early socialist and founder of the co-operative movement in Britain. Born in humble circumstances, he prospered as a cotton manufacturer, married his employer's daughter and used his wealth for the betterment of working conditions. Visitors from all Europe came to his model settlement at New Lanark in Scotland where working hours were limited and workers had good houses and an infants' school where their children included singing and dancing among their activities. Other ventures, a

planned community, New Harmony, in America and the Grand National Consolidated Trades Union, whose members were to control industry through a system of co-operative production, were short-lived.

¶ In UNSTEAD, R. J. *Great Leaders.* 1966

Oxfam: British relief organisation, starting in 1942 as the Oxford Committee for Famine Relief and being renamed Oxfam in 1965. In 1969–70 it distributed £2,629,052 in overseas aid and relief, while its administration costs were only 2·5 per cent of its total income. It depends on voluntary contributions and the profits from its shops in many of the larger towns.

¶ JONES, MERVYN. *Two Ears of Corn: Oxfam in Action.* 1965

Oxford, England: university and industrial city on the upper reaches of the Thames, north-west of London. The beginnings of the university date from the late 12th century, but it was not until 1266 that the first college, Merton, was founded. Most of the rest had come into being by the early 17th century, though there have been later additions, particularly the women's colleges. During the Civil War the city was the Royalist headquarters (1642–46). In modern times the motor industry and others have considerably altered the character of Oxford through

such developments as the growth of suburbs to house workers, the building of trunk roads, and greatly increased traffic congestion. *See colour section.*

Oxford Movement: period of unrest within the Church of England, to which approximate dates 1838–50 may be assigned. It originated with a body of clergymen, chiefly Oxford graduates, who stood against the movement away from the Anglican ideals of the 17th century (*see* PROTESTANT) both by Parliament and by some sections of the Church itself. Since it was a recall to earlier ways, some

Cardinal Newman.

of its members in due course felt compelled to return to the Roman Church, the most notable being John Henry Newman (1801–90) who eventually became a cardinal. Henry Edward Manning (1808–92), although not prominent in the movement, was another Anglican clergyman who became a cardinal and also Archbishop of Westminster. Two other leaders, however, John Keble (1792–1866), the hymn writer, and Edward Bouverie Pusey (1800–82), an Oxford professor, remained with the English Church.

The Oxford Movement should not be confused with the Oxford Group (*see* MORAL REARMAMENT).

673

P

Pacifism: a belief in the abolition of violence and war. In peacetime most people agree with this ideal, and support efforts of organisations like UNO to achieve it. Many sympathise with individuals like Gandhi and Luther King who spoke out for non-violence. But most people would resist if attacked and fight in a conflict they thought just. Pacifists oppose all war on moral grounds and refuse normal military service. Called conscientious objectors, in Britain and the USA they must prove by argument their sincerity, or be imprisoned. Some flee abroad to avoid conscription (e.g. Americans, to escape Vietnam).

Pacific Ocean: world's largest ocean, 10,625 miles [17,000 kms] wide, covering one-third of the area of the globe. Its size, remoteness from Europe, the broad belt of equatorial calms, typhoons, the storms of Cape Horn and the reefs of the western approaches delayed its exploitation by Europeans. Chinese and Arab seamen, though well able to make ocean passages, were content with coastal trade, and the colonisation of the Pacific islands was left to peoples who never, except in Easter Island, developed a written language. The Melanesians, of Negroid type, settled the fertile volcanic islands from New Guinea to the Solomons, New Hebrides and New Caledonia. The Micronesians, of Mongoloid stock, settled the coral atolls from the Philippines – Carolines, Marshalls, Marianas. The Polynesians, of Caucasian stock, were the greatest ocean pathfinders, sailing their outriggers and double canoes 2,000 years ago to the remotest islands. Their friendliness and courteous manners endeared them to European settlers.

Europeans reached the Pacific after 1500. Antonio d'Abreu visited New Guinea from the Portuguese East Indies in 1511. Balboa saw the Pacific from a peak in Darien in 1513, and Magellan's circumnavigation (1519-22) started the Spanish search for a route to the East Indies. Miguel de Legaspi began the Spanish settlement of the Philippines in 1559, and Andres de Urdaneta, by finding the counter-trade winds back to America, made the regular Manila to Acapulco voyages possible. Spain gave half-hearted support to seekers of the Southern Continent – Terra Australis – Mendana and Torres. The discoveries of the Solomons and Torres Straits were not exploited by Spain or revealed to the world. Nor did the Dutch exploit the discoveries of Tasman or Roggeveen, who found Easter Island in 1722. British exploration, until the 1760s, was confined to the search for the North-West Passage, raids on the Isthmus of Panama and the plundering voyages of Drake, Cavendish and Anson. At the end of the Seven Years War both France and England sent frigates to probe the South Pacific, commanded by Bougainville, Byron, Carteret and Wallis. James Cook in Whitby colliers surveyed the central Pacific from the Bering Straits to the Antarctic Circle and exploded the myth of Terra Australis.

European powers were for long reluctant to annex the scattered islands of the South Pacific, and in the early 19th century the islands were exposed to the raids of ruthless whale hunters, sandalwood cutters and "blackbirders" who kidnapped islanders for slave labour in Queensland, Mexico or Peru. They aroused in the islanders a suspicion of white men that led to the murder of many of the first missionaries. The missionary societies persevered and converted the islanders from cannibalism to a Christianity which is still vigorous in many areas.

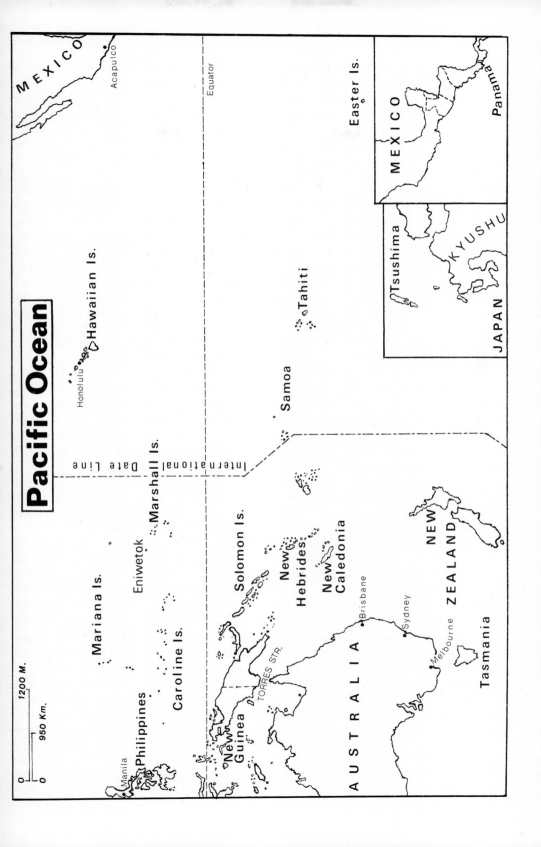

Pacific Ocean

MEXICO

Acapulco

Equator

Easter Is.

Hawaiian Is.

Honolulu

Tahiti

Samoa

International Date Line

Marshall Is.

Eniwetok

Mariana Is.

Solomon Is.

New Hebrides

New Caledonia

Brisbane

Sydney

Melbourne

NEW ZEALAND

Tasmania

AUSTRALIA

TORRES STR.

New Guinea

Caroline Is.

Philippines

Manila

1200 M.

950 Km.

0

0

MEXICO

Panama

Tsushima

KYUSHU

JAPAN

With the coming of the age of steam a new chapter began in the history of the Pacific. In 1840 the Pacific Steam Navigation Company was founded, mainly with British capital. In 1855 the Panama Railroad was built and in 1869 the Union and Central Pacific Railroad was completed, making possible for the first time the trans-continent railway journey of 1,848 miles [2,974 kilometres]. Russia became effective in the Pacific with the completion of the Trans-Siberian Railway in 1904, only to be checked by the Japanese at the naval battle of Tsushima, 1905. The USA annexed Hawaii in 1898, and took the Philippines from Spain. France took Tahiti in 1880, Chile annexed Easter Island in 1888 and Germany purchased the Caroline and Marshall Islands from Spain in 1898. Britain, for long reluctant to take responsibility for Pacific islands, occupied some for the protection of New Zealand, for naval bases or as a safeguard for missionaries and traders. The Pacific became a main arena of war with the rise of Japan, Russia and the USA. Japan, which had administered the German islands under the League of Nations, challenged American sea power at Pearl Harbour in 1941 and was defeated in the battle of the Philippines in 1944. Eniwetok atoll became the scene of tests of a thermonuclear device in 1952, and Russia and the USA now confront each other across the Pacific.

¶ HOBLEY, L. R. *Exploring the Pacific.* 1957; RABLING, HAROLD. *Pioneers of the Pacific: the story of the South Seas.* 1967

Pacific States: region forming the western boundary of the continental United States, set against the Pacific Ocean and including the states of Washington, Oregon and California. The region includes both high mountains and plateaux, and, especially in California, fertile valleys between the mountain ranges. Oregon and Washington, in particular, are mountainous regions with extensive forest cover. The principal rivers are the Columbia in Oregon and the Sacramento in California. Also of importance is Puget Sound in Washington, an extension of the Pacific Ocean and the site of much of the industry and urban development in that state.

The area that is now California was discovered in the 1540s by Juan Rodriguez Cabrillo, sailing for the King of Spain. Although Sir Francis Drake claimed the region for Queen Elizabeth I of England in 1579, the first European settlements were by the Spanish, who established a series of missions along the coast beginning in 1769. After becoming part of the newly independent Mexican nation in 1822, California was seized by the United States during the Mexican War and was ceded by Mexico by the Treaty of Guadalupe Hidalgo in 1848. Oregon and Washington, in contrast, were never part of the area of Spanish settlement, but were instead a point of contention between the United States and Britain, a dispute which was settled by treaty in 1846.

The economy of the region, like its topography, is varied. In the north, lumbering and apple growing are major industries. The Columbia River is a source of Chinook and silver salmon. California, the most populous state in the nation, is a leader in commercial fishing, agriculture and dairy products, subtropical fruits and vegetables, manufacturing and oil production. Finally, the beauty of such regions as the Grand Coulee Dam Recreation Area in the north, and such sites as Hollywood, Disneyland and the Golden Gate Bridge in California, attract many tourists each year. *See* AMERICA for map.

Paderewski, Ignace Jan (1860–1941): Polish pianist and statesman. In the 1880s he became famous as a composer and

An early photograph of Paderewski.

gifted pianist. He toured Europe and the USA for ten years, and his composition *Polish Fantasia* was very popular. He bitterly resented Russian control of Poland, and in World War I he turned from music to politics. At the 1919 Peace Conference he presented Polish claims for independence and became the country's first Prime Minister. He was respected for his moderation, although many of his countrymen thought he should have demanded more territory. In the 1920s he returned to the concert stage.

¶ In CANNING, JOHN, editor. *100 Great Modern Lives.* 1965

Padua: Italian city near the River Brenta in Venetia, 22 miles [35·40 kilometres] west of Venice. Founded in 89 BC as Patavium by the Romans, it became second in wealth only to Rome. It was sacked by Alaric but revived in the 8th century and became a free commune in 1164. Its position in the plain of Lombardy exposed it to conquest by a series of tyrants: the cruel Ezzelino de Romano, 1225–50; the

della Scala, 1338; the Visconti, 1388. Venice tried to control it by installing the native Carrara family, but when they proved treacherous Venice absorbed Padua into her Empire in 1406 and held it until 1797. Padua University, founded in 1222, flourished as Venice protected it from Papal intolerance and gave it contact with Greek scholars. It was famous for the study of law, mathematics and medicine. Vesalius and Galileo taught there, and Thomas Linacre and William Harvey (*see* separate entry) were students. The Botanic Garden was established in 1545, perhaps the first in Italy. From 1814–66 the city was ruled by Austria and then became part of United Italy.

Pakistan: former independent federal republic in southern Asia, consisting (1947–71) of West Pakistan (capital Lahore), East Pakistan (capital Dacca) and the Federated Territory of Karachi. The two main areas are separated by the territory of Northern India.

The republic was formed in 1947 as the result of the campaign of the Muslim League, led by Mohammed Ali Jinnah (1876–1948), to secure an independent Muslim state. The partition caused bitter riots in which thousands were killed and a vast cross-traffic of Hindu and Muslim refugees seeking what they felt to be their true home country.

The subsequent history has been no happier. Pakistan was at war with India from 1947–49 over the still-disputed region of Kashmir. The United Nations imposed a cease-fire, but the problem remains. In 1958 there was a military take-over of the government and Ayub Khan took the presidency, only to be ousted in 1969 by General Yahya Khan. All this internal and external turmoil took place against a background of constant food shortages and other economic difficulties. In 1970 a cyclone devastated large

677

areas of East Pakistan, causing a catastrophic loss of life and property. This natural disaster was soon followed by another, man-made and of even worse proportions. Shaikh Mujibur Rachman of East Pakistan headed a movement to found an independent new state called Bangla Desh (*see* separate entry). Yahya Khan sent in troops and put this attempt down with ruthless severity. Several million refugees crossed the border into India to add yet another problem to that country's burden.

In 1971 India invaded Pakistan, forced Yahya Khan to resign and recognised the new independent state of Bangla Desh, a move soon followed by other nations. Shaikh Mujibur Rachman was released from confinement to become Bangla Desh head of state and, in West Pakistan, Zulfikar Ali Bhutto, formerly Foreign Minister, was called to the presidency. *See* INDIA for map.

¶ FELDMAN, HERBERT. *Pakistan*. 1958

Palatinate: either of the two regions of Germany which, from the 14th century, formed an electorate (or princedom) of the Holy Roman Empire. There were originally six Electors who chose the Holy Roman Emperor. The Palatinate of the Rhine achieved supreme importance because of its strategic position controlling the trade and army routes through the middle Rhine, and because of its university at Heidelberg. In 1356 its Count Palatine, already a leading imperial adviser, became one of the electoral princes.

Commercial wealth and the electoral right involved the Palatinate in two important struggles in the 17th century. Its protestant ruler Frederick accepted the Bohemian crown in 1619 and this led to the Catholic-Protestant struggle of the Thirty Years War (*see* separate entry). Later, in 1685, France claimed the Palatin-

ate when the ruling house died out. The area was devastated by French troops when the Emperor refused and this conflict developed into the War of the Grand Alliance (*see* separate entry). After this the Palatinate declined in importance, and was gradually divided up between other German states.

Palermo: Panormus in classical times, seaport on the north coast of Sicily developed by Phoenicians and Carthaginians in a capacious bay sheltered from westerlies. It fell to Rome in 254 BC, to the Vandals in AD 440 and to Byzantium in 535. The Arabs made it capital of Sicily in 831. It reached its zenith under the Normans and Hohenstaufens between 1072 and 1266, when it was, after Constantinople, the largest and richest city of Christendom. Its cathedral of Monreale and its Palace Chapel show the fusion of Romanesque, Byzantine and Saracenic design. It was torn by the rivalry of Angevins and Aragonese and declined under Spanish domination. It was liberated by Garibaldi's patriots in 1860 and in 1946 became the seat of a parliament when Sicily was granted home rule.

Palestine: region of Asia Minor at the eastern end of the Mediterranean approximately 150 miles [240 kilometres] from north to south, between the parallels 31°30' and 33°, and stretching back from the sea, to an average depth of eighty miles [128·75 kilometres], as far as the arid eastern scarp of the Jordan valley. This famous river, rising in Mount Hermon away to the north, flows down to the Dead Sea, 1,240 feet [377·95 metres] below sea level, where, in one of the hottest and driest places in the world, its waters evaporate.

The name Palestine, said to be derived from the Philistines, is first found in the 2nd century AD and was in general use at the time of the Crusades, which were directed thither by the fact that the land was the ancient home of the Jews and contained the holy city of Jerusalem and other places dear to Christians. Now, as the modern state of Israel, it is once more the home of the Jewish race.

The area, with the inhospitable desert stretching along its eastern side, is a natural corridor through which the armies of the great empires of the ancient world would march or in which they would clash, a process which can be read as a background to the biblical account of Jewish history. In the Christian era, the Romans and their successors, the eastern emperors of Constantinople, ruled over the land until in 636 the Mohammedan conquerors took their place and, with the 200-year interlude of the "Latin" kingdom of the Crusaders, remained in possession until the collapse of Turkey at the end of World War I. The country was then entrusted to Great Britain under a mandate and the name Palestine formally revived. In 1948 it was handed over partly to the new state of Israel and partly to that of Jordan, but since then the former has occupied nearly the whole of the area.

See also ISRAEL; JERUSALEM; JORDAN; PHILISTINES.

Palestrina, Giovanni Pierluigi da (*c.* 1518–94): Italian composer of the great age of counterpoint. In counterpoint independent voice-parts, sung simultaneously, are combined to produce the kind of tonal texture later supplied by musical instruments. Palestrina's compositions are among the finest 16th-century works of this kind.

Palladio, Andrea or **Andrea di Pietro** (1508–80): Italian architect who modelled his designs, though with a freedom of invention all his own, on the buildings of ancient Rome. He designed churches and

Chiswick House, London, modelled by Lord Burlington on Palladio's Villa Rotonda, near Vicenza, Italy.

palaces and, especially, magnificent country villas which greatly influenced the work of such famous 18th-century English architects as Inigo Jones (1573–1652) and Sir John Vanbrugh (1664–1726). He gave his name to the architectural style now known as "Palladian". *See colour section.*

Palmerston, Henry John Temple, third Viscount (1784–1865): British Foreign Secretary for fourteen years and Prime Minister for ten. Intolerant of foreigners, "Pam" typified the attitudes of his time: distrust of Russia and France, sympathy for Liberal causes (e.g. in Belgium and Italy), patriotism and determination to uphold all Englishmen.

Palmyra: Solomon's Tadmor, or "city of palms", an oasis of sulphur springs at the junction of caravan routes to the Euphrates, Damascus and Petra. By 2000 BC it had been developed by Babylonians and Aramaeans and reached its zenith when Rome and Parthia confronted each other across the Syrian desert. Rome supported the local king Odenathus and his daughter Zenobia. Under them Palmyra became the greatest caravan city, of 30,000 inhabitants, a banking capital with agents on the Tigris and Danube, in Egypt, Gaul and Spain. The Palmyrenes spoke Aramaean or Greek, took their house design from Babylon, furnishings from Persia and philosophy from Greece. Their mounted archers served Rome as far away as Hadrian's Wall. Palmyra was sacked by the Emperor Aurelian in AD 273, after which it never recovered its former importance. Its ruins – the temple of Bel and the great colonnaded way – survive and were revealed to scholars by Robert Wood's *Ruins of Palmyra*, 1753.

Pan-: prefix (deriving from a Greek word meaning "all" or "completely") often applied to countries, movements and organisations aiming at unity or completeness. The following four entries are typical examples. Others are the nouns Pan-Arabism, Pan-Germanism, and the

The Ruins of Palmyra, *1753 by Robert Wood.*

adjectives Pan-Hellenic, Pan-Christian, Pan-Islamic, etc. Similarly, a *pandemic* is an epidemic affecting a whole country or a wide area of the world, e.g. the Black Death of 1347–51, which is estimated to have caused 75 million deaths. A *pandemonium* (a word coined by Milton), or state of confused uproar, means literally the abode of all demons.

Pan-Africanism: movements, especially in the 20th century, designed to promote African unity and establish black supremacy in Africa (*see*, e.g., ORGANISATION OF AFRICAN UNITY).

Pan-American Highway: the great road system running from Fairbanks, Alaska, to Buenos Aires, Argentina, with branches to all Central and South American countries. It is the longest motorable road in the world and will eventually stretch 13,859 miles [22,300 kilometres] from Alaska to southern Chile. There is at present a 450-mile [725-kilometre] gap (the "Darwin Gap") in Panama and Colombia.

Pan-Americanism: movement to promote full co-operation among all the states of the Americas (*see* ORGANISATION OF AMERICAN STATES). Pan-American Day is celebrated on 14 April. The Pan-American Union has its headquarters in Washington, DC, an organisation maintained by more than twenty North and South American countries to encourage friendly relationships.

Pan-Slavism: movement aimed at promoting the unity and independence of Slav peoples, i.e. the group of Eastern European races which includes the chief ethnic groups of the USSR, Ukrainians, Poles, Czechs, Slovaks, Serbs, Croats, Bulgars, etc. Though at its best encouraging cultural and political co-operation,

it has often been a vehicle for securing territorial expansion (e.g. by Russia) and has led to a number of wars.

Panama: republic in Central America. It covers the isthmus of the same name joining the two American continents, being some 350 miles [565 kilometres] long with an average breadth of approximately 60 miles [95 kilometres]. It is not always realised that this larger axis lies from west to east and that the Panama Canal (*see* next entry) actually runs in a south-easterly direction from the Atlantic to the Pacific Oceans.

The first contacts with Europe came when the Spaniards found the isthmus an essential link between their colonies on the two oceans, shipping their treasure from Peru to Panama and transporting it across the part of the isthmus known as Darien to Porto Bello. After the revolutions of the early 19th century, Panama was for nearly 100 years part of the state of Colombia, its neighbour to the south; but in 1902 the USA, anxious to revive the Canal project, helped to secure the independence of the Republic of Panama, in return for control of the Canal Zone, now the subject of much national emotion. The political history of the new state has been, and remains, unsteady and violent.

¶ HOWARTH, DAVID. *The Golden Isthmus.* 1966

The Panama Canal under construction.

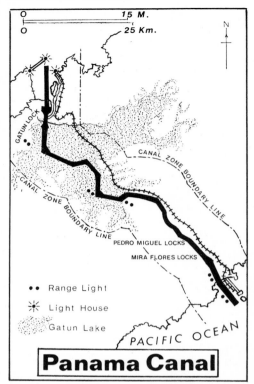

15 M.
25 Km.

•• Range Light
✷ Light House
Gatun Lake

PACIFIC OCEAN

Panama Canal

Panama Canal: passage for ocean-going vessels through the isthmus of Panama, saving the long journey round Cape Horn. The distance between deep water at either end is fifty miles [80·47 kilometres], and six massive pairs of locks are needed for crossing the central ridge. The first attempt at making a canal, by the Frenchman De Lesseps (*see* separate entry) of Suez Canal fame, ended in scandal and failure in 1889; but a fresh undertaking with the backing of the USA was successfully completed after ten years work in 1914. A project is now being examined to use atomic force to blast a fresh passage through the isthmus at sea level throughout its course.

¶ CAMERON, IAN. *Impossible Dream: the building of the Panama Canal.* 1971

Pankhurst, Emmeline (1858–1928): British suffragette leader. She worked with her husband for the passage of the Married Women's Property Act, and with her daughters Christabel and Sylvia founded the Women's Social and Political Union (1898). Their methods included interruption of political meetings, violence and hunger strikes. Several times imprisoned, once for attempting to fire Lloyd George's house, she was released in 1914 and supported the war effort. Once a Liberal, then a member of the Independent Labour Party, in 1926 she became a Conservative candidate for Parliament. She died a month before women of twenty-one obtained the vote.

¶ KAMM, JOSEPHINE. *The Story of Mrs. Pankhurst.* 1963; SNELLGROVE, L. E. *Suffragettes and Votes for Women.* 1964

See also EMANCIPATION OF WOMEN.

Pantomime: a traditional stage entertainment which includes dancing, music and spectacle devised round the core of a fairy story or folk tale. According to the particular plot, the cast includes certain characters, usually broadly comic, such as the Ugly Sisters and the Broker's Men in *Cinderella*, which have become hallowed by time.

Ancient Greek and Roman pantomimes were dumb shows. Their stylised poses

A scene from the Commedia Dell' arte, by Gillot, 18th century.

and gesticulations had more in common with ballet than with drama.

Towards the end of the 16th century a comic entertainment originating in Italy and known as the *commedia dell' arte* became popular in many European countries. France had a low-comedy entertainment of its own, popular at fairs, known as *vaudeville*. English pantomime as we know it today may be said to have developed from a combination of these two elements, with a spice of Victorian music-hall thrown in for good measure.

Paoli, Pasquale (1725–1807):

Corsican patriot. Sharing his father's exile, he trained as a cavalryman in the army of Naples. In 1755 he successfully led a Corsican rising against Genoa, and introduced reforms based on his study of Rousseau. When Genoa sold Corsica to France in 1768, he resisted French attacks but was beaten at Ponte Nuovo in 1769 and fled to London, where he was welcomed by Dr Johnson's circle. The French Revolution allowed him to resume power in Corsica in 1791, but he thwarted the Bonaparte family, was denounced by them and accepted British protection. Britain preferred to govern through Pozzo di Borgo, and Paoli retired to London, where he died.

Papacy, The:

the name given to the office held by the popes, in the same way that "the monarchy" is the name given to the office held by kings and queens. The word "pope" means father, deriving from late Latin *papa*: in earlier centuries all Christians regarded the pope as father of the Christian family, and he is still regarded in that way by Roman Catholics. The position of the pope rests on the belief that Jesus Christ came on earth to found his Church, and that before he ascended into heaven he entrusted that Church to Peter and the other disciples, but to Peter especially because he evidently took the lead amongst the disciples of Jesus and to him Jesus said, "Thou art Peter, and upon this rock I will build my church." (The name Peter comes from the Latin *petrus*, a rock.) Peter went to Rome, where he suffered martyrdom; so his successors as bishops of Rome were, from the 1st century, generally regarded as heads of the Christian Church, and they still enjoy a certain precedence among the bishops of the world, although their authority today extends only over the Roman Catholic Church. St Peter's Cathedral, at Rome, was built over the tomb of her first bishop.

In the days of the ancient Roman Empire the popes were subject, like other Christians, to persecution and martyrdom until the reign of the first Christian Emperor, Constantine (AD 307–337). But this same Constantine moved the imperial capital from Rome to the eastern city named after him, Constantinople, which left Rome subject to many centuries of war and revolutions, and the papacy itself was often in great danger. Later, in the 8th century, the Frankish kings, whose rule extended over much of what today we call France, and who had been converted to Christianity, protected the popes by giving them political rule over some territory around Rome to serve for their defence: in this way there first appeared the Papal States (*see* separate entry) over which the pope ruled as a "temporal" or *political* ruler, in contrast to his *spiritual* rule over the Christian Church as a whole; but today the pope is *political* ruler only over the city state of the Vatican at Rome.

In the Middle Ages, at least until the 13th century, the position of the popes tended to grow stronger; they settled disputes about religious doctrine, insisted on the rights of the Church against emperors and kings, or sent out missionaries to convert heathen lands, as Pope Gregory I sent Augustine to convert England in the year 597. It was in the 13th century, under Pope Innocent III, that the papacy of the Middle Ages attained to its greatest spiritual and political influence; men came to speak of the "two swords" by which they meant the "sword" of the spiritual and the "sword" of the political authority, the former wielded by the popes and the other bishops and the latter by emperors and kings; and of these two swords the more effective was often the spiritual. The pope, indeed, was often strong enough to compel even emperors and kings to obey him. Yet already the authority of the papacy was challenged. The Church centred on Constantinople (later known as the Orthodox Eastern Church) repudiated the pope's authority in the 11th century, and in the 14th century the disturbances at Rome became so serious that for a time the popes moved to Avignon in France to be under the pro-

tection of the French kings, who naturally took advantage of their position as protectors. The Protestant Reformation in England and Germany in the 16th century was largely a revolt against the papal authority, while later on, in the 18th century, even the Catholic rulers of Europe often defied the pope on matters of church discipline and dogma. The great French Revolution of 1789-99, which was partly a revolt against the Catholic Church, saw the fortunes of the papacy at their lowest ebb. The ruling pope, Pius VI, was dragged into France as a prisoner and it seemed that the life of the papacy itself was at an end.

But a new revival now took place, and the 19th and 20th centuries saw the office of the papacy renewed in strength. With the disappearance, in the 19th century, of the pope's political rule over the Papal States in central Italy, the religious authority of the popes grew stronger, playing an important part in the general religious revival which took place in that century and in the great expansion in missionary activity all over the world. In the year 1870, at a General Council of the bishops of the Catholic Church, drawn together at St Peter's Cathedral from the whole world and now known as the First Vatican Council, it was decreed that, on the (very rare) occasions when the pope defines a dogma concerning a matter of faith or a matter of morals, he speaks infallibly, that is to say he cannot be mistaken because he will be guided by the Holy Spirit. This is called the "papal infallibility", something that belongs to the office of pope rather than to a particular person, and something in which the Catholic Church has generally believed in past centuries although it only came to be defined in the 19th century.

Today, and especially since the time of "good Pope John" (1958-63) and the Second Vatican Council (1962-65), the

The Palace of the Popes, Avignon.

papacy is seen more as partner (though the leading partner) with bishops, clergy and laity in the corporate life of the Church.

See colour section.

¶ CORBETT, J. A. *The Papacy*. 1936

See also AUGUSTINE, ST; CONSTANTINE; ORTHODOX EASTERN CHURCH.

Papal States: parts of Italy at one time ruled by the pope. The pope, though bishop of Rome and spiritual head of the Catholic Church throughout the world, used also to be the political ruler of central Italy: this was called his "temporal" as contrasted with his "spiritual" power and it meant that he provided the ordinary government in that region. When he first acquired these states, in the 8th century, they extended for only a few miles around Rome: later they came to cover the whole of central Italy, including the city of Bologna, which is some 200 miles [320 kilometres] north of Rome. And, whereas at first they provided a useful protection for the papacy, they later brought so many political problems for the popes that they became a distraction and a spiritual danger. In the wars of 1860–70, by which the kingdom of Italy was united, Pope Pius IX was deprived of these states. In protest he shut himself up in the palace of the Vatican and for a time was known as "the prisoner in the Vatican"; but in 1929, by the Lateran treaty with the kingdom of Italy, Pope Pius XI recognised the new kingdom, and the king of Italy, in exchange, recognised the independence of the pope's Vatican city state, a small territory around the Vatican palace at Rome, which serves today to ensure that the pope is not the subject of any government.

¶ DEEDY, JOHN. *The Vatican*. 1970

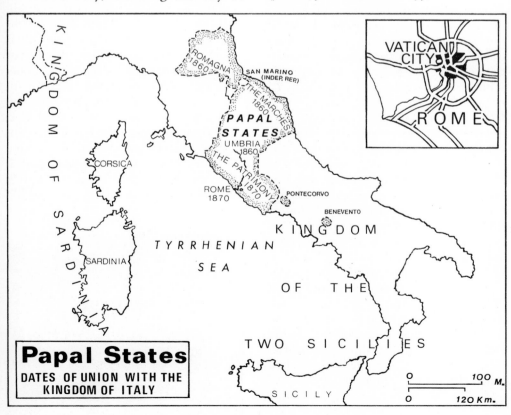

Papal States
DATES OF UNION WITH THE KINGDOM OF ITALY

Paper money: printed documents issued by a government to serve as currency. In England, the Bank Charter Act of 1844 laid down that almost the whole issue of Bank of England notes must be backed by gold. The sovereign and half-sovereign were replaced during the war of 1914–18 by Treasury notes, and the issue of these was transferred to the Bank of England in 1928. In September 1931 Great Britain abandoned the Gold Standard, and Bank of England notes became inconvertible (i.e. could not be exchanged for gold). In the USA non-convertible bank notes, the famous "greenbacks", were issued during the Civil War to the extent of $450 million. When Rutherford Hayes (president 1877–81) took office there were still about $350 million in circulation and he consented to an act of Congress (1878) making them a permanent part of the currency.

At the present time most money throughout the world is paper money, and no government promises to convert it into gold, but it remains acceptable as long as the amount in circulation is compatible with the government's true financial position.

¶ QUIGGIN, A. H. *The Story of Money.* 1956

Papua New Guinea: previously the Australian-administered territories of Papua and New Guinea, occupying East New Guinea and a number of islands. Over two million people, including a small European minority, now live on New Guinea, which is the largest island in the world. It is only 80 miles [130 kilometres] north of Australia, and its remote geographical position, combined with difficulties of coastal navigation, isolated its Melanesian inhabitants from all contact with the outside world until, in the 15th century AD, Muslim missionaries from Malaya reached the island. They called the people "Papuans" because of their curly black hair (Malay *pepuah*, frizzled).

The Portuguese named the island "New Guinea" when they discovered it in 1526. The Dutch came in the 17th century and kept control of the western half (now called West Irian) until driven out by Indonesian troops in 1962. The eastern half had been partitioned between Britain and Germany in 1884, but after 1918 Britain claimed it all for Australia. During World War II the whole island was ruled by the Japanese. Papua New Guinea achieved independence in 1974.

Papyrus: aquatic plant originating in the Nile valley. The papyrus reed can grow up to 10 feet [3 metres] tall, with a thick stem crowned by a feathery green top. As early as 3,000 BC the Egyptians knew how to make from the reeds a fabric which they used for sails, ropes and sandals, as well as for writing upon. Papyrus stems were cut into short lengths and peeled, and the inner pith sliced lengthwise into thin strips. A row of strips was arranged along a flat stone, then a second layer placed across them. The double thickness was then pounded with a wooden mallet into a solid mat. After drying, its surface was polished with a rounded stone and several sheets were pasted together to form a continuous roll. The modern word "paper" derives through Greek from this Egyptian origin.

Hieroglyphics and painting on papyrus.

Paracelsus, Philippus Aureolus (1493–1541): Swiss physician and chemist. This controversial figure attacked the foundations of ancient medicine and some of his theories foreshadowed modern medical practice. He introduced mineral baths in his treatments and added such ingredients as opium, mercury, iron, arsenic and copper sulphate to his medicines. He also wrote a book on mental diseases.

Parachute: umbrella-shaped contrivance for dropping men or supplies from a height, the fall being slowed by resistance of the air gathered in the fabric cover during the descent. The first practical demonstration, made as a useful means of escaping from fire, was from the tower of Montpellier Observatory in 1783 by Sebastian Lenormand. J. P. Blanchard (1753–1809) originated the idea of parachute drops from balloons, the possibilities being further demonstrated by André Jacques Garnerin (1770–1823), who made fre-

Garnerin's parachute.

quent descents from balloons both in France and in England. In 1797, at Monceau Park, Paris, he dropped from a height of 2,236 feet [681·53 metres]. The first parachute descent from an aeroplane was made in 1912 by Captain Albert Berry of the US Air Force. The greatest altitude (and the longest delayed parachute opening) was recorded by another US airman, Captain Joseph Kittinger, who in 1960 dropped 102,200 feet [31,151

metres], the first 84,700 [25,816] being a "free fall". The total descent was over 19 miles [30·57 kilometres], made in 13 minutes 45 seconds.

¶ DWIGGINS, DON. *Bailout: the story of parachuting and skydiving.* 1969

Paraguay: republic of central South America, between the rivers Paraguay and Parana, now inhabited by some two million people. The first Spanish settlement was made at Asunción in 1537, and this became the centre for Spanish exploration and conquest of the surrounding forests and grasslands. Here the Jesuits (see separate entry) set up forty-eight remarkable mission settlements, from which they directed the life, work and worship of thousands of natives and, by hard work and good organisation, produced cotton, tobacco and hides. Fields and cattle were common property. Unfortunately slave traders from Brazil destroyed more than half these missions, and when the King of Spain expelled all Jesuits from his empire in 1767 these prosperous communities broke up. Paraguay declared itself independent of Spain in 1811, but an attempt to extend its territory in 1865 led to a war against Argentina, Brazil and Uruguay which drastically reduced its population. Its boundaries were not finally settled until 1938 after another war (1932–35), with Bolivia. Political unrest has made steady economic progress difficult and communications remain poor. Considerable mineral resources, among them copper, iron and manganese, are largely unexploited. Exports include timber, cotton, tobacco, hides and meat.

See ENDPAPERS for map.

¶ WARREN, H. G. *Paraguay: an informal history.* 1949

Parchment: skin of calves, sheep, goats, etc., prepared for writing, or a paper made to imitate it. In former times many

documents testifying to competence in various professions were written on it, so that to "receive one's parchment" was a common expression. The name originated from the city of Pergamum (modern Bergama) in north-west Asia Minor. Since parchment was an expensive commodity it was frequently re-used in early centuries, after the original inscription had been scraped off. Such a document is termed a *palimpsest*, from Greek words for "again" and "scrape".
See also ILLUMINATED BOOKS.

Paris: capital of France, one of the most visited cities in the world, and a centuries-old leader in European art and culture.

The city's growth from what was, in the 1st century BC, a fishing village on an island in the Seine, may be attributed partly to its position at the intersection of important natural highways and trade routes, and partly to its choice by Clovis, early in the 6th century, as the capital from which he could administer his newly won territories of southern France. The present-day map shows Paris like the hub of an immense wheel with roads, railways and air routes converging on it from every point of the compass.

Among its great buildings are the Cathedral of Notre Dame, built on the site where the Romans had a temple of Jupiter; the Basilica of Saint Denis, where a succession of sixty-three abbots ruled for more than a thousand years, where the ancient banner of France was kept in time of peace and where twelve centuries of royalty were brought to rest; and the Louvre, formerly a royal palace and now the national art gallery and museum of France. More modern structures include the Eiffel Tower and the Arc de Triomphe (which Napoleon planned to celebrate the victories of his legions, but which he never saw completed). Another of Napoleon's legacies is the handsome

Looking towards the Arc de Triomphe, Place de l'Etoile, Paris.

system of boulevards or avenues, replacing, partly for security reasons, the twisting maze of medieval streets in which it was difficult to control a mob. During the Franco-Prussian War (1870-71), much damage was done by German bombardment and in the disorders that followed France's defeat; but fortunately, despite German occupation, the city emerged unscathed from World War II.

Administratively the city is divided into twenty *arrondisements* (wards or districts), each made up of four *quartiers* (quarters). Less official, but even better known, are such popular terms as "Left Bank" for the area containing the famous University (or Latin) quarter and most of the surviving medieval buildings; and "Right Bank", which is the financial and commercial nerve-centre. It must not be forgotten that, although it is over 100 miles [160 kilometres] from the sea, Paris is one of the greatest ports of France and that it is responsible for about a fifth of the country's total production.

¶ REID, ALEXANDER. *Paris*. 1965

See also BASTILLE; FRANCE; FRANCO-PRUSSIAN WAR; LOUVRE; ST DENIS; VERSAILLES.

Paris, Treaty of (1763): treaty signed after four months of negotiation to end the conflict of Britain with France and Spain in the Seven Years War (*see* separate entry). France gave up to Britain all Canada and lands east of the River Mississippi, four West Indian islands, and accepted the domination of the British East India Company in trade; to Spain, France gave Louisiana and control of the Mississippi mouth. The French had lost badly and their colonial power was virtually ended. But some Englishmen thought the treaty was not glorious enough; only difficulty in raising taxes to continue the war prevented England from demanding sterner terms.

Parliament: chief law-making body of many countries. The *Anglo-Saxon Chronicle* tells us that William the Conqueror held "very deep speech with his Witan", and the French name for this discussion or parley was *parlement*, although this name was not actually used for meetings of the great council of England until the Statue of Westminster in 1275. The Model Parliament of 1295 set the pattern of future developments. By this time, what had begun as a feudal assembly of tenants-in-chief had become an assembly of the three estates of the realm, clergy, barons, and commons. The third estate consisted of the knights of the shire and the burgesses. We first find mention of the former in a summons to a council at Oxford in 1213, which directed the sheriffs to bring with them "*quatuor discretos milites . . . ad loquendum nobiscum de negotiis regni nostri*" (four wise knights to discuss with us the business of our realm), while representatives of the boroughs were summoned for the first time in 1265 at the instigation of Simon de Montfort. On this occasion the towns received their summons directly from the Crown, and not, as in 1295, through the sheriffs of their shires. We do not know exactly when Lords and Commons began to sit as two separate houses. The historian William Stubbs thought that they did so from the Model Parliament onwards, but Frederick Maitland, professor of the laws of England at Cambridge, favoured the middle of the 14th century. The Commons sat in the Abbey Chapter House, while the Lords gathered in the painted Parliament Chamber at the south end of the palace of Westminster.

The Parliament at Westminster has been called "the mother of Parliaments", as this system has been copied in many countries. In this connection it is important to remember that the English Constitution is largely unwritten and flexible, whereas its imitators throughout the world have generally tried to base their system on a written and more rigid constitution. The constitutional struggles of the 17th century were an attempt to prevent the officers of government acting independently of Parliament and also interference by the Crown with its rights as a law-making body. The Bill of Rights 1689, and the Act of Settlement 1701, ensured the supremacy of Parliament, the responsibility of Ministers to Parliament, and the independence of judges. This type of arrangement is often referred to as The Separation of Powers; i.e. the separation of the legislative body (who make the laws) from the executive (the officials who seek to administer and enforce the laws) and the judiciary (the judges and other law officers who interpret the laws in the courts, when they have been broken or are in dispute). This was of great importance, as it inspired the French Decla-

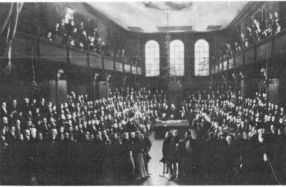

Above, seating plan for the opening of Parliament at Blackfriars, 1525, drawn by Garter King at Arms. Above right, The House of Commons, 1793. Below right, moving to address the Crown, 1833.

ration of the Rights of Man (1789) and the Constitution of the United States. Nevertheless, separation of powers does not exist in this country to the extent that it exists in the United States. The House of Lords is a part of the supreme legislature, but it is also the final Court of Appeal; the Cabinet forms the Executive, but its members are also members of either the House of Commons or House of Lords. Judges have no power to declare a statute void, although they do protect the rights of individuals against Parliament in anything less than statute. Further, a government could not remain in office without the command of a majority in the House of Commons, whereas an American President may find himself faced by a representative assembly dominated by the opposition party. This happened to President Truman in 1946 and to President Eisenhower in 1956.

Further difficulties arise in the appli-

cation of parliamentary government to federal states. Two different solutions are possible, as exemplified by the constitutions set up in Canada and Australia when they achieved Dominion status within the British Commonwealth. Australia is a genuine federation in that the states have handed over some forty topics for the consideration of the federal legislature, retaining all other powers themselves, while in Canada the reverse is the case, the provinces having definite powers of legislation on sixteen allotted subjects, while the residue of power lies with the central legislature. In the United States also the residuary power lies in the states and not with the central legislature.

Parliamentary government has met with varying success in different countries. One authority suggests that it has proved most successful in Belgium, Holland and the Scandinavian countries, where the unwritten conventions on which it depends are supported by "a basis of beliefs and traditions comparable to those that prevail in England" and by monarchies dedicated to constitutional rule. Parliamentary government in France which developed during the 19th century was intended to follow the British model, but results were disappointing, chiefly because election by proportional representation led to the creation of a large number of small parties, each incapable of forming a government by itself. Hence a government was formed by a coalition of parties, and this tended to be unstable and of short duration, and incapable of reaching a final decision on vital problems. This was seen when the system collapsed on being confronted by the Algerian problem. The arrangement later adopted (1958) was a blend of British and American elements. Similarly, the system adopted in Germany after the war of 1914-18 was on the French model, and this also collapsed and was replaced by the Nazi dictatorship. Following World War II, Germany adopted a new constitution in May 1949 which provides for parliamentary government of the British type, adapted to federalism. The president is elected for a five-year term, the Lower House is elected by universal suffrage for four years, while the Upper House consists of delegates of the *Länder* (the States of the Federation) with no fixed term of office.

It remains to discuss the power of a parliament to amend the constitution. In the United Kingdom there are no fundamental constitutional statutes, and Magna Carta or the Bill of Rights could be repealed by Parliament in the same way as any other piece of legislation, although this of course is unlikely to happen. With a written constitution, amendments to the constitution require a different legislative procedure from that used for other purposes. Thus, in the United States, the constitution can be changed only on the motion of two-thirds of each House of Congress, ratified by the legislatures of three-quarters of the states, while in Eire and Australia a referendum is used for this purpose.

¶ ALLEN, AGNES. *The Story of Our Parliament.* 1971; PRENTICE, D. M. *Your Book of Parliament.* 1967; MACKENZIE, K. R. *Parliament.* 1962

See also CONSTITUTION (AMERICAN); CONSTITUTION (BRITISH) *etc.*

Parnell, Charles Stewart (1846-91): Irish Nationalist leader. Known as the uncrowned king of Ireland, Parnell nearly obtained Irish self-government, but domestic scandal ruined his career. As an MP and head of the Home Rule Party, he used the balance of power between Liberals and Conservatives to secure land reforms for Ireland.

Pascal, Blaise (1623-62): French mathematician, scientist and religious philosopher. A precocious genius, at the age of sixteen Pascal interested Descartes in his book on geometry. Centuries ahead of his time, he worked on the problems of the vacuum, equilibrium of liquids, atmospheric pressure and the theory of probability. He also invented the first calculating machine. Because of a religious experience, he turned overnight from his former life to become a Jansenist monk. His *Provincial Letters* are literary classics that replied to Jesuit condemnation of Jansenism. *Pensées* presented his belief that only faith can free men from their tragic situation.

Pasteur, Louis (1822-95): French scientist. Pasteur discovered that bacteria spread diseases and can live almost everywhere, but can be controlled. He showed how to preserve milk, beer and foodstuffs by means of controlled heat (pasteurisation), which killed germs. In his method of vaccination, he first weakened microbes

Louis Pasteur in his laboratory.

in the laboratory, then placed them in an animal's body. The animal afterwards developed immunity to the microbe. Another great discovery was the successful treatment of rabies, for which there had previously been no remedy.

The Pasteur Institute in Paris was founded in 1888 as a world centre for the study, prevention and treatment of diseases. Here Pasteur is buried in the place where he worked on bacteriology to benefit humanity.

¶ BURTON, M. J. *Louis Pasteur: founder of microbiology.* 1964

Patagonia: region of southern Argentina. Magellan named this land "Patagonia" because he found "large footsteps" on the coast in 1520. These were made by the clumsy moccasins worn by Indians, whose descendants, though a tiny remnant, still inhabit the rocky and windswept territory which extends from 40° South latitude to the islands of Tierra del Fuego. The Spaniard Pedro Sarmiento started a settlement on the Straits of Magellan, but it was attacked by English sailors and renamed "Port Famine". Welshmen who

settled on the Chabut River in 1865 survived with Indian help, and the settlement exists today. In 1881 Patagonia was partitioned between Chile and Argentina, the boundary being the Andes.
See ENDPAPERS for map.

Pathan: generic name given to warrior Muslim tribes – Yusufzais, Khattaks, Mohmands, Afridis, Wazirs, Mashuds – on and beyond the North-West Frontier of Pakistan (formerly India). Their rising against British control in 1897 was put down by the Malakand Field Force and the Tirah expedition, both campaigns brilliantly described by Winston Churchill who accompanied them.

Patriarch: in general, the traditional founder of a tribe or family. The word, however, has a special meaning in its application to the founders of the human race up to the time of the Flood as narrated in the Old Testament. It is also the title of certain holders of the highest offices in the Orthodox Eastern Church (*see* separate entry).

Patrician: in general, an adjective denoting membership of an aristocratic or privileged class. In particular, the word is applied to a feature of the political system of Rome during the republican era (roughly five centuries from 519 BC), when the patrician class filled by right most of the chief positions in public life. *See also* PLEBEIAN.

Patrick, St (*c.* 385–461): patron saint of Ireland. Facts can be separated from legends about the apostle only by using his own writings. Reputedly born in Wales, son of a Romano-British deacon, he was captured in his youth by pirates and taken to Ireland as a slave. After escaping to France, he entered a monastery at Lérins. He was trained for the rebels entered the Tower and murdered Simon of Sudbury, the Archbishop of Canterbury, and Sir Robert Hales, the royal treasurer. For two days London was given over to mob violence, the rebels thereby forfeiting much popular sympathy. Richard again went to meet them, this time at Smithfield. Tyler's demands were now much more sweeping, his manner so threatening that the Lord Mayor and one of the King's squires killed him. Richard averted a perilous situation by courageously spurring his horse forward, shouting to the rebels: "Sirs, will you shoot your king? I will be your chief and captain, you shall have from me all that you seek."

The King did not keep his word. With Tyler's death the rebellion collapsed, and the lot of the English peasant remained much as before. *See colour section.*

¶ LINDSAY, JACK. *Nine Days' Hero: Wat Tyler.* 1964

Peel, Sir Robert (1788–1850): British politician and prime minister. When Peel died from a fall from his horse, working people wept, remembering that he had sacrificed his career and his party's interest for their welfare. He had removed the duty on imported corn, which kept up the price of bread, in opposition to his Conservative colleagues, who favoured protection. Peel was a great administrator. As Home Secretary, he had reformed the harsh penal code and created the first police force – "bobbies" and "peelers" as they were affectionately known from their founder's names. He met economic depression and a national deficit by redesigning the tariff system and reintroducing income tax.

¶ In WHITTLE, J. *Great Prime Ministers.* 1966

Peking: Chinese city of ancient origin, serving as a provincial capital under several early dynasties. Destroyed in 1215 by Genghis Khan, it was rebuilt by Kublai Khan. As Peiping it became in 1421 the capital of the Ming emperor Yung Lo who made the ground plan of the present city. Called Peking, it remained capital of the Chinese Empire. In 1900 troops of eight western nations intervened there to rescue besieged foreign nationals. Peking was capital of the Chinese Republic until

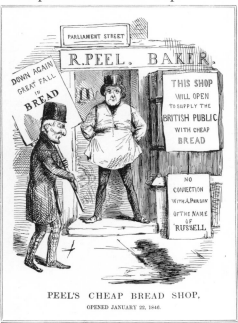

PEEL'S CHEAP BREAD SHOP,
OPENED JANUARY 22, 1846.

Above, Sir Robert Peel. Right, a political cartoon showing Peel as a baker selling cheaper bread.

The Forbidden City, Peking.

1928. Under occupation by Japan from 1927-45, it became in 1949 the capital of the Communist Chinese People's Republic. The popular Pekingese dog is an ancient breed imported from China.

Peloponnesian War (431-404 BC): struggle between Athens and her rivals for predominance in Greece. These rivals were the two leading states of the Peloponnese, the southern part of Greece joined to the northern by the narrow isthmus which took its name from Corinth, a commercial city anxious for her seaborne trade, while Sparta, her ally, was motivated chiefly by the fear that a powerful enemy might encourage her slave population (*see* HELOTS) to revolt.

On land the Peloponnesians had the advantage, and for some time an invasion of Attica, the territory of the Athenians, who took refuge inside their Long Walls (*see* PIRAEUS), was almost an annual event. At sea Athens was the more successful; but in 415 she rashly sent an expedition against certain Greek cities in Sicily which were allied to her enemies, and this ended two years later in the disaster at Syracuse (movingly described by the

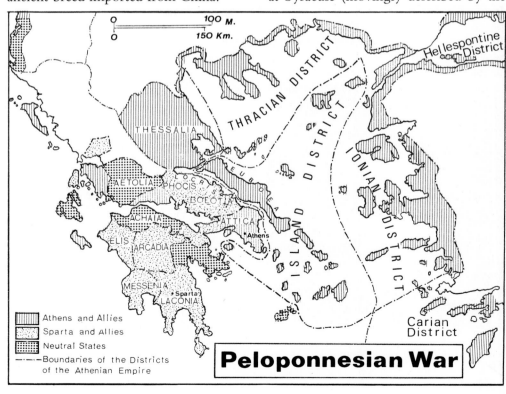

Athens and Allies
Sparta and Allies
Neutral States
—·—Boundaries of the Districts of the Athenian Empire

THESSALIA
AETOLIA LOCRIS PHOCIS BOEOTIA
ACHAIA ATTICA
ELIS ARCADIA Athens
MESSENIA Sparta
LACONIA

THRACIAN DISTRICT
Hellespontine District
EUBOEA
ISLAND DISTRICT
IONIAN DISTRICT
Carian District

0   100 M.
0   150 Km.

Peloponnesian War

historian Thucydides) when the Athenian fleet was shattered in two naval battles and the army cut to pieces on land. The war, however, dragged on for a further seven years before Athens capitulated, and her Long Walls were destroyed.

¶ THUCYDIDES. *The History of the Peloponnesian War*, trans. Rex Warner. 1962

Penang: state of Malaysia, including Penang Island and, on the mainland, Province Wellesley. The island, off the west coast of the Malay Peninsula, was almost uninhabited when it became in 1786, under the British East India Company, the first British Malayan settlement, then called Prince of Wales Island. The Sultan of Kedah finally ceded it by treaty, adding Province Wellesley on the mainland in 1800. Singapore outstripped Penang in trading activity; but with the growing demand for rubber production Penang increased in population and importance. In 1948 the island with its mainland extension became the member state of Penang in the Federation of Malaya, later Malaysia.

Penicillin: substance capable of destroying bacteria in an infected part of the body without damaging the tissues. In this it differs from antiseptics, which can cause serious injury to living matter. Penicillin was discovered by the British bacteriologist Sir Alexander Fleming (1881-1955), who was awarded the Nobel prize for medicine in 1945.

Peninsular War: war fought 1808-14 in the Iberian peninsula by Britain, Spain and Portugal against France, beginning as a defensive action and changing to an offensive which drove the French from the peninsula. It is one of the best examples in history of guerrilla tactics. The war was a permanent drain on Napoleon's resources, occupying 360,000 men in 1810

and 230,000 in 1812. In 1807 Napoleon sent Junot to occupy Portugal when her regent refused to join the Continental Blockade. In 1808 a Spanish rising against the crowning of Joseph Bonaparte allowed the Portuguese to rebel, and Sir Arthur Wellesley (later Duke of Wellington) was sent with 13,500 British and beat Junot at Vimiero. In 1809 Sir John Moore was killed extricating his force from Corunna after a raid on French communications, saving the Spaniards in the south. In 1809 Wellesley did not win at Talavera decisively enough to save Spain (only Cadiz held out) and learnt not to trust Spanish generals. In 1810 he "blooded" his Portuguese contingents in a favourable position at Busaco and preserved his Lisbon base by retiring to the Lines of Torres Vedras. In 1811 he secured the gateways into Spain by his victories at Ciudad Rodrigo and Badajoz and drove the French from Madrid by defeating Marmont at Salamanca. In 1813 he broke the French at Vittoria and drove them from the Peninsula by a series of bold outflanking marches, supplied from the Biscayan coast. The British were effectively supplied by sea, whereas the French had to live off the land. Wellington's custom, when on the defensive, of hiding his troops on the reverse side of a hill hindered the French artillery, and in the open he showed great individuality among the commanders of his day in using line regiments (i.e. men marching abreast) against the conventional columns. This gave full play to the English musketry and the redoubtable "Brown Bess" (*see* FLINTLOCK). The French, trying to subsist by plundering the peasants in a barren plateau, brought on themselves bitter reprisals from *guerilleros*. See map p. 698, *also* CONTINENTAL BLOCKADE; GUERRILLAS; TORRES VEDRAS, etc.

¶ LACEY, ROBERT, editor. *The Peninsular War* (*Jackdaw*). 1970

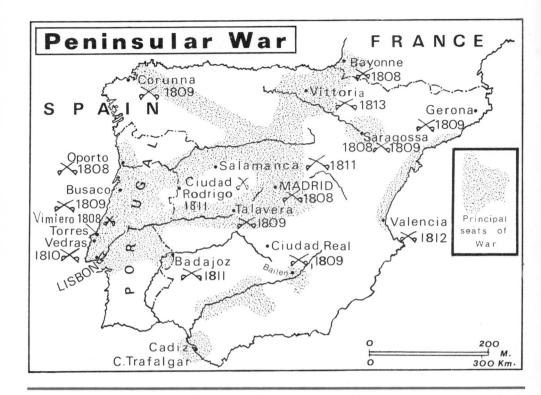

Peninsular War

FRANCE

SPAIN

PORTUGAL

Bayonne
×1808

Corunna
×1809

Vittoria
×1813

Gerona•
×1809

Saragossa
1808×1809

Oporto
×1808

•Salamanca ✗1811

Busaco•
×1809

Ciudad ✗
Rodrigo
1811

•MADRID
×1808

Vimiero 1808✗
Torres
Vedras
1810✗

•Talavera
×1809

Valencia
×1812

Principal
seats of
War

LISBON

Badajoz
×1811

Bailen

•Ciudad Real
×1809

Cadiz•
C.Trafalgar

0 _____ 200
                      M.
0 _____ 300 Km.

Penn, William (1644-1718): English
Quaker and founder of Pennsylvania.
Early in life William Penn learnt the
meaning of intolerance – he was sent
down from Oxford for his religious views.
Later, he was imprisoned three times for
similar reasons. Quakers were persecuted
by Anglicans and Puritans alike: in fact,
Penn decided he would get more sympathy from Roman Catholics.

Penn's father had influence with the
Duke of York, later James II, and was
owed money by the Crown. Penn asked
that, instead of repayment, he himself
should be allotted a territory west of the
Delaware, America. Having received a
grant from Charles II, in 1681, of a tract
of land about 300 miles by 160 [483 kilometres by 257], Penn founded a new
settlement, known as Pennsylvania
(Penn's Woods), which attracted English,
Welsh, Dutch, Scandinavians and Ger-

mans as a haven for all persecuted sects,
particularly Quakers.

Penn was the governor and drew up the
constitution, which embodied much of
his own idealism and greatly influenced
later charters, even the Constitution of
the United States.

¶ In GILLETT, N. *Men against War.* 1965

Pensions: (1) a stated allowance to a person for past services performed by himself or by some relative, or (2) a payment made to a person retired from service because of age or illness.

During the latter half of the 17th century and throughout the 18th century perpetual pensions were granted as rewards for political or military services. Thus, in Britain, the Duke of Marlborough received £4,000 and Lord Nelson £5,000 per annum. Towards the end of the 19th century there was much criticism of such perpetual pensions, and a select committee of the House of Commons was appointed to examine the question. As a result, most of these pensions were extinguished by commutation, the cost in the case of the Marlborough pension being £107,000. The Nelson pension remained until 1951, when it ceased as a result of the Trafalgar Estates Act, 1947. After the war of 1914–18 capital sums were voted to Lord Haig and others, but perpetual pensions were not created.

The second class is of much wider incidence and greater importance. Such pensions may be contributory or non-contributory, i.e. the person ultimately to receive the pension may or may not provide part of the cost by deductions from his wages during his working life. Further, such pensions may be provided by individual employers or as part of a national pensions scheme. Pension schemes of the first kind differ widely in their details, and they may be financed through an insurance company or from a specially allocated trust fund, into which the contributions of employer and employee are paid. Such a trust fund is invested in really reliable securities, and the income derived from it is used to pay the pensions as they fall due. A common division of cost between employer and employee is for the former to pay two-thirds and the latter one-third of each payment into the fund. This type of private pension scheme began on a small scale in the early years of this century, but is now widespread. In the United States, it was estimated that by 1960 about fourteen million employees of private industry were covered by about 20,000 different pension schemes.

In 1889 the German Reichstag passed a "Law of Insurance against Old Age and Infirmity", and this led to agitation in Great Britain for some form of state pension. But it was not until the Budget of 1908 that Lloyd George introduced a non-contributory pension of five shillings a week for those over the age of seventy with an income not exceeding ten shillings a week. This was replaced by a contributory scheme in the National Insurance Act of 1911, which introduced the now familiar collection of contributions from employer and employee by stamped cards. From this small beginning has arisen the present massive structure of "social security". Following the Beveridge Report (*see* separate entry), the National Insurance Act of 1946 extended the scope of compulsory insurance to cover almost everyone over school-leaving age and under pensionable age.

In the United States, President Roosevelt in 1934 called for "legislation to safeguard men, women and children against misfortune", and this led to the Social Security Act in the following year. This provided for a federal old age insurance system. In the Scandinavian countries state pensions are mainly financed by taxation. In most countries, as in Great Britain, a change in the rates of payment of pensions can be brought about only by legislation, but in a few countries (e.g. Holland) these are automatically geared to the cost of living.

Pepys, Samuel (1633–1703): English naval administrator and diarist. His diary of personal and national affairs covers the period January 1660 to May 1669. He sailed with the fleet bringing Charles II home at the Restoration, lived through the Plague of London (1665), when grass grew "all up and down Whitehall . . . and nobody but poor wretches in the street", saw the Great Fire in the next year, and heard the Dutch guns when their fleet sailed up the River Medway. Failing sight made him abandon his diary, but not before he had left an invaluable record of life and domestic incident in the 17th century. As Secretary to the Admiralty he played an important part in reforming the administration of the navy. He was also President of the Royal Society, 1684–6.

¶ In THOMAS, M. W. *Makers of Britain.* Bk. 2. 1963; MURPHY, E. *Samuel Pepys in London.* 1958

Samuel Pepys.

Pericles (*c.* 495–429 BC): leading Athenian statesman at the time of the city's greatest prosperity. Not only did he direct the external and internal affairs of the state, but he was responsible for the erection of many fine buildings, in particular the Parthenon.

¶ In ROBINSON, C., editor. *Plutarch: Ten Famous Lives.* 1963

Perry, Matthew Calbraith (1794–1858): American naval officer sent to Japan in 1853 to negotiate better treatment for American nationals and open up trade facilities. His gifts of a telegraph set and a miniature railroad convinced the Emperor and his officials of the benefits of Western civilisation, and the Treaty of Kanagawa (31 March 1854) effectively ended Japan's isolation and opened up her ports.

Persia: the ancient name of Iran (*see* separate entry) and still an official alternative name. The history of the Iranian plateau begins with the coming of invaders who spoke an Aryan language. The first wave of invaders from central Asia came about 1500 BC, many passing on into India. A second wave of these Indo-Iranians came soon after 1000 BC. Many of these Iranian tribes remained nomadic; but two of them, the Medes and Persians, adopted a more settled life, the Medes in the north in the area south of the Caspian, and the Persians south of them, towards the Persian Gulf, in the area which came to be called Persis.

The Medes, inhabiting a more fertile country, were at first dominant. In 612 BC their king Cyaxares (625–585 BC) made an alliance with Babylon, destroyed the power of Assyria and established an empire which stretched from central Asia Minor almost to the Indus. But the Persians, a hardy shepherd people, revolted under their own Achaemenid dynasty; and in 553 BC Cyrus the Great united Medes and Persians under his rule. In 539 Cyrus occupied Babylonia, and his son Cambyses conquered Egypt.

The history of Persia comes down to us as a history of kings. Of these, Darius, who reigned 521–485 BC, was the greatest. His empire stretched into north-west India, reached the Caucasus and included Thrace, the modern Bulgaria. He also

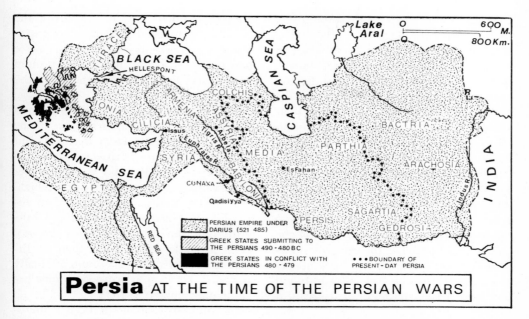

Persia AT THE TIME OF THE PERSIAN WARS

Map legend:
- PERSIAN EMPIRE UNDER DARIUS (521 485)
- GREEK STATES SUBMITTING TO THE PERSIANS 490 - 480 BC
- GREEK STATES IN CONFLICT WITH THE PERSIANS 480 - 479
- ● ● ● BOUNDARY OF PRESENT - DAY PERSIA

came into collision with the Greeks, who represented a new European kind of civilisation. Revolts of Ionian Greek colonies along the coast of Asia Minor were aided by the cities of their Greek homeland. Darius crushed the Ionian colonists but his large army was disastrously defeated, 490 BC, at Marathon by a small Athenian army. His son Xerxes, with another expedition, captured Athens but had to withdraw after a severe naval defeat at Salamis, 480 BC.

In a struggle for the Persian throne, a younger Cyrus hired an army of Greeks to fight Artaxerxes II. At Cunaxa on the Euphrates, Cyrus was killed (401 BC) but the Greeks elected new generals and fought their way back home. The Greek historian Xenophon (*see* separate entry) accompanied this expedition.

Following the tradition of Greek superiority over Persians, Alexander the Great (356–323 BC) of Macedonia (*see* separate entries) landed on the Asiatic mainland in 334, defeated the huge armies of Darius III at Issus (333) and Arbela (331). Before he died, aged thirty-two, he had con-

quered the Persian Empire and entered the Punjab. After his death Persia was ruled by the Seleucid dynasty, descended from one of Alexander's generals. The Parthian ruler Arsaces I (ruled 247-246 BC) rebelled, and in 141 BC Mithridates I established the Parthian dynasty. From the time of Phraates III (70-37 BC), Persia suffered three centuries of warfare with the Roman Empire.

A new dynasty, the Sassanids, was established by Ardashir (reigned AD 224-241). His son Shapur I captured the Roman Emperor Valerian at Edessa, AD 260, with 70,000 prisoners, including engineers and architects whom he put to good use. Chosroes II (reigned 589-628) almost destroyed the Byzantine Empire but was defeated at Nineveh in 627 by the Emperor Heraclius.

In 636 Yezdegerd III was defeated by Islamic forces at Qadisiyya and in 641 at Nihawand. With Yezdegerd's assassination in 651 the story of ancient Persia ends. *See colour section.*

¶ WATSON, JANE WERNER. *Iran: Crossroads of Caravans.* 1968

Persian Wars (499–449 BC): attempts by the Persians to conquer Greece. The trouble began when the Greek cities of Ionia, the coastal areas of Asia Minor, were in revolt, and the Persians, having crushed them, determined to punish the European Greeks for supporting their kinsmen. The first invasion in 490, during the reign of Darius, was defeated at Marathon and driven back. In 480 a much larger expedition under Xerxes crossed the Hellespont (Dardanelles) and marched into Greece with a fleet on its left flank. After overwhelming a heroic force of 300 Spartans, who perished to a man in the pass of Thermopylae, the invaders occupied Athens; but their fleet was utterly routed in the nearby bay of Salamis and the land force defeated next year at Plataea.

In the next thirty years desultory fighting eventually restored nearly all that the Greeks had lost in Ionia, and in the following century the Greeks, in their turn, overran Persia under Alexander the Great. *See also* ALEXANDER; DARDANELLES; DARIUS; MARATHON; THERMOPYLAE.

Peru: republic of western South America with a population (1965 estimate) of 11,854,000, of whom 46 per cent were Indians.

It is surprising that any people can live in the high mountains, infertile desert and inhospitable jungle of Peru; yet the republic supports this high population, and it once was the home of the remarkable Inca civilisation.

Two thousand years before the Incas came to Peru other Indian peoples learned the skills of farming and building, weaving and pottery, in the valleys of the Andes and on the coast of the Pacific. The Inca way of life was based on the knowledge of these earlier people, and the final conquests of the Incas were made in AD 1525, only a few years before the whole

Empire was destroyed by Pizarro and the Spanish Conquistadors. The native population was soon much reduced by disease and by forced labour in the Potosi silver mines, and Peru was dominated by the Spanish landowners.

Lima became the capital of the Spanish Viceroy, who ruled at first over all the territories formerly under the Inca. But in the 18th century Peru was partitioned when Quito, La Paz and Valparaiso became capitals of separate provinces which, after 1810, became the independent republics of Ecuador, Bolivia and Chile. Although the people of Peru did not fight for independence like their neighbours, Bolivar's army of volunteers finally defeated the Spanish army, and Peru became independent in 1824.

The modern republic of Peru is therefore much smaller than the Inca Empire had been, and many of the native peoples are poorer today than their ancestors were 500 years ago.

¶ PENDLE, GEORGE. *Land and People of Peru*. Black. 1966; PRESCOTT, W. H. *History of the Conquest of Peru*, edited J. F. Kirk. 1959

See also BOLIVAR; INCAS; etc.

Perugia: fortified city on a hilltop commanding the corn lands of Umbria and the Tiber valley. It was an Etruscan stronghold, which in 310 BC was taken by Rome: in Byzantine times it was one of a series of forts linking Rome and the Adriatic. In the 13th century it declared for the Guelph party and asked the help of Pope Innocent III to resist the Emperor, thereby giving later popes the pretext for claiming it. From 1350 to 1540 it maintained its independence and prospered in spite of violent internal feuds under a succession of condottieri (*see* separate entry), notably of the Baglione family. Raphael studied painting there under Pietro Perugino (1445–1523). Its university was established in 1308.

See also GUELPHS AND GHIBELLINES.

Peshawar: principal city of the north-west frontier of Pakistan, eleven miles [17·7 kilometres] from the eastern end of the Khyber Pass. Its earlier inhabitants were Indian and, at one time, under the name of Gandhara, it was a centre of Buddhism. In the 15th century it became an Afghan province and the area acquired a Pathan population (*see* PATHAN). It was a favourite residence for the Afghan rulers. It was captured by the Sikh Ranjit Singh in 1834, came under British rule in 1849 and in 1901 became capital of the North-West Frontier Province.

Pestalozzi, Johann Heinrich (1746–1827): Swiss educationalist. Pestalozzi might be lightly dubbed a glorious failure. Many of his enterprises failed because of bad management. Yet his ideas and methods produced the revolutionary concept that even the poorest child deserved education. Education, he taught, should be based on the natural development of the child, who should learn by observation and discover things for himself. At his institute, Yverdon, in Switzerland,

the curriculum included drawing, singing, physical exercises, modelling, making collections, map reading, and field studies. The centre, which housed a teacher training department, attracted educationalists, such as Froebel, from all over the world.

Pétain, Henri Philippe (1856–1951): French soldier-statesman. During World War I he won praise for his resistance to incessant German attacks at Verdun in 1916 and gained rapid promotion to lead the French army in the closing battles of 1918. He entered politics after the war and in May 1940 became Vice-Premier. This time he was convinced Germany would win and arranged an armistice. Bitterly hated for this capitulation and for his leadership of Vichy France, he was found guilty of treason in 1945 and was imprisoned for the rest of his life.

Peter I, called "the Great" (1672–1725): Tsar of Russia from 1696. Although he upheld the traditional autocratic rule which lasted in Russia, with minor con-

Peter the Great (right) and his son.

cessions, until the Revolution of 1917, Peter succeeded in many ways in bringing his country out of medievalism into the modern era. He was enormously tall and strong; simple, though sometimes coarse, in his tastes, but intelligent and firm-minded. Being interested in the way of life of Western Europe, he sent his young nobles there to study and himself spent the years 1697–98 in Holland and England, where he gave particular attention to naval architecture, himself working as a shipwright in the yard at Deptford, Kent. For this purpose he rented the nearby home of John Evelyn, the diarist, where his revels somewhat damaged the property.

He made many internal reforms and innovations, including the founding of St Petersburg (*see* LENINGRAD). At the end of his reign the Russian Empire had been increased by his conquests to stretch from the White Sea to the Caspian. He died as the result of a chill caught when he personally took part in rescuing some sailors from shipwreck.

¶ In UNSTEAD, R. J. *Some Kings and Queens.* 1962

Peter Claver, St (*c.* 1581–1654): called "the Apostle of the Negroes". He was of Spanish birth and entered the Jesuit Order (*see* JESUITS). While studying for his life's work, he was inspired to convert the heathen in the New World, to which already slaves were being shipped from Africa under unspeakable conditions. For long years he laboured among them and is said to have won some 300,000 Negroes to Christianity. He was canonised in 1881.

¶ ROSS, ANN. *Peter Claver: Saint among Slaves.* 1965

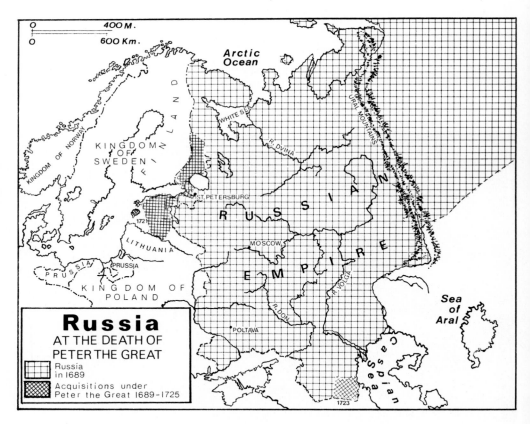

Russia
AT THE DEATH OF
PETER THE GREAT
Russia
in 1689
Acquisitions under
Peter the Great 1689-1725

Peter the Hermit (*c.* 1050–1115): one of the most forceful preachers of the First Crusade (*see* CRUSADES). He addressed himself chiefly to the common folk of his native France and led a band of them as far as Asia Minor, where they perished, though Peter himself escaped and eventually reached Jerusalem with the main body.

Peter, St (d. *c.* AD 64 or 67): the "Prince of the Apostles" and brother of Andrew, also one of the earliest to answer the call to follow Jesus. From the first he was their leader and spokesman and at times was inclined to be rash and hasty. He showed momentary cowardice when Jesus was arrested before his crucifixion; but, when their master had left the earth, he proved himself a fearless and resolute leader of the apostolic band. There is a strong tradition that in due course he came to Rome, where he met the death of a martyr under the Emperor Nero. He is said to have asked to be crucified head downwards, as unworthy to suffer in the same posture as his master. His tomb is still shown in the great church that bears his name.

It is through St Peter, whom Jesus called "the rock on which I will build my church", that the papal claim to the leadership of Christendom is principally derived.

See also PAPACY.

Petition of Right (1628): presented by parliament to Charles I (King of England 1625–49), in an attempt to prevent taxation without the consent of parliament, compulsory billeting of soldiers, marital law and arbitrary imprisonment. The king refused to allow his prerogative to be curtailed by law but could not afford to dissolve parliament. He attempted vague answers but finally consented in traditional style *"Soit droit fait comme est desiré"* (let it be done as you wish), adding later: "I have granted no new but only confirmed the ancient liberties of my subjects." Although the immediate effects were little felt he had, in fact, suffered a constitutional defeat.

Petrarch (Francesco de Petrarca, 1304–74): Italian poet and humanist. Petrarch's love poetry, especially that in praise of Laura (whose identity remains obscure), reveals him as one of the great poets of all time and master of the Italian sonnet. His style set the pattern for poetry in Europe for 250 years.

¶ WILKINS, E. H. *Life of Petrarch*. 1961

Petrie, Sir William Matthew Flinders (1853–1942): British archaeologist and Egyptologist. When Petrie arrived on the archaeological scene, he found excavating methods haphazard. Treasure hunting was the main object, finds unknown to the excavator were discarded, relative positions unnoted. Petrie's scientific system involved careful sifting, exact dating using pottery, and study of everyday objects to reveal the life of the people of the period. Thus he laid down rules followed by modern archaeologists. Petrie was first professor in Egyptology at University College, London, founded the British School of Archaeology in Egypt, and brought to light an unknown period of Egyptian civilisation.

¶ In CANNING, JOHN, editor. *100 Great Modern Lives*. 1965

Phalanx: tactical formation of Greek heavy-armed infantry. Though the word was used in earlier times, it is generally applied to the Macedonian infantry to whom Philip II (382–336 BC) and his son Alexander the Great (356–323 BC) owed much of their success in battle. In spite of being armed with pikes 13 feet [3·96 metres] long and marshalled sixteen deep, the phalanx remained comparatively mobile because of its high standard of training. Later efforts to increase its depth and to arm it with even longer weapons destroyed its effectiveness, as was proved when it confronted the Roman legion in the early 2nd century BC.

See also ALEXANDER III; PHILIP II.

Pharaoh: old title of the rulers of Egypt, just as Roman emperors were *Caesars* and Russian emperors *Tsars*. The word pharaoh means "Great House".

Egypt consisted originally of two king-doms, Upper and Lower Egypt, which were united by Narmer, the first pharaoh, approximately 3,000 years before the birth of Christ. Narmer's successors wore the Double Crown, which consisted of the tall, white linen crown of Upper Egypt, encircled by the red crown of Lower Egypt. The pharaoh also carried, on ceremonial occasions, a crook, to show that he was the shepherd of his people, and a flail, with which to punish evil-doers. A woman could be pharaoh. Queen Hatshepsut ruled in her own right for twenty years and even led her army into battle. The exact number of the pharaohs is not known, but historians divide them into family groups known as dynasties. There were probably thirty-one dynasties, beginning with Narmer and ending with Cleopatra, who killed herself in 30 BC.

The pharaohs of the early dynasties were worshipped as gods, and their subjects credited them with divine powers.

Amenhotep III enthroned. Tomb of Khaemhat.

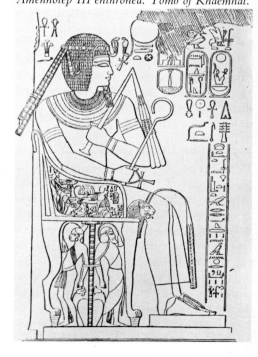

Because of this they could command absolute obedience, which was also given to the priests and visiers to whom they delegated authority. When a pharaoh died, he was buried with great splendour, and everything he could possibly need for his after-life was placed in his tomb, which was furnished like a palace. Little of this wealth remains today; it has been taken long ago by tomb robbers. An exceptional discovery was that made in 1922 of the tomb of Tutankhamen (*see* separate entry) of the 15th dynasty.
See colour section.

¶ PAYNE, ELISABETH. *All about the Pharaohs.* 1966

Pharos, The: white marble lighthouse at the entrance to the harbour at Alexandria, Egypt. Erected in the 3rd century BC, it has since disappeared. It stood on an island of the same name, which was linked by a stone causeway to the mainland, and was accounted one of the Seven Wonders of the Ancient World. The French word *phare* (lighthouse) is derived from it.
See also ALEXANDRIA; SEVEN WONDERS OF THE ANCIENT WORLD.

Phidias (*c.* 431–417 BC): Athenian sculptor of the 5th century BC. His working life coincided with the period in which Pericles (*see* separate entry) adorned Athens with building and statuary. No work from the hand of Phidias now exists: he himself worked in bronze, but he is known to have made the models (probably in clay or plaster) for the marble sculptures of the Parthenon, which have partially survived.

Philadelphia: "the City of Brotherly Love", established in 1682 by William Penn, the Quaker founder of the Commonwealth of Pennsylvania. It is situated on the north-western bank of the Delaware River, approximately 90 miles [145 kilometres] from the Atlantic Ocean. From the first the site of Philadelphia was favourable for ocean commerce; its immediate hinterland was in early days more populous and more productive than that of New York. At the time of the War of American Independence, Philadelphia, with a population of 42,000, became the capital of the Union and remained so until the foundation of the city of Washington in 1800. The city was the setting for the first Continental Congress (1774) which met in the Carpenter's Hall and later issued the Declaration of Independence (1776). It was also in this city that the Convention met in 1787 to draft the American Constitution. The 20th century has seen a great increase in population and vast industrial expansion, which proved a major factor in America's effort in both world wars. At the same time, the city's educational and cultural institutions have developed, an example being the famous Philadelphia Orchestra.

Philip II (382–336 BC): King of Macedon from 359. To the general reader of history he is greatly overshadowed by his brilliant son Alexander the Great (*see* separate entry). The latter's achievements, however, were made possible only by the fact that his father (1) unified Macedon, a state on the northern fringes of the Greek world, (2) built up the Macedonian army as a formidable fighting force (*see* PHALANX) and (3) brought the rest of Greece under Macedonian rule. Had his base not been thus secured behind him, Alexander could never have ventured into Asia. The leader of Greek resistance to Philip was Athens, where the orator Demosthenes (384–322) denounced him in speeches that are among the treasures of classical literature (*see* ORATORS).

Philip II (1527–98): King of Spain and the Two Sicilies, 1556–98. Spain under Philip was the most formidable power in the world. His empire included the

Netherlands, Portugal, parts of Italy and of the Americas as then known. One of his three marriages was to Mary, Queen of England. He was handicapped by the sheer size of his problems and his refusal to delegate responsibility. He was in conflict with France, England, the Netherlands, and, as the chief Catholic monarch, with Protestantism. Nevertheless, he had moderate success against France, won the sea battle of Lepanto (*see* separate entry) and annexed Portugal (1580). But his Armada failed against the English, and he could not tame the rebel Dutch.

¶ CUBITT, H. *Spain and the Empire of Philip II.* 1975 *See also* SPAIN.

Philippines, Republic of the: group of islands in the Far East which were ceded to the USA by Spain after the Spanish–American War of 1898. The Filipinos, led by Emilio Aguinaldo, conducted a guerrilla war against the Americans and in favour of independence from February 1899 to April 1902. It was ironic that the man whom the Americans aided in leading the struggle against the Spaniards in Manila should then turn against them. In 1902 the Philippines were given a representative assembly, but demands for full independence continued, and successive American administrations prepared various plans to give more statutory autonomy to the Filipinos. During World War II the Japanese invaded the Philippines and captured Manila in January 1942. In 1943 President Roosevelt announced that the USA would grant independence to the Filipinos as soon as the Japanese had been ejected. The Republic of the Philippines was established on 4 July 1946.

See PACIFIC OCEAN for map.

¶ AGONCILLO, TEODORO A. *A Short History of the Philippines.* 1970

Philistines: ancient race inhabiting the south-western area of what is now called Palestine, the most serious rivals encountered by the Jews (*see* separate entry) in their conquest of the Promised Land. Their principal city was Gaza, which still retains its name.

The term "philistine" is today applied to one who lacks appreciation of art, literature and music.

Philosophers: those who love and pursue wisdom, from Greek *philos*, loving, and *sophos*, wisdom or a wise man. They are people who study the most difficult subject of all – the nature of man's existence and experience in the universe.

The philosopher accepts nothing without question. His aim is to examine the appearance of things and enquire how far this corresponds to reality. Some philosophers, aware that everything exists in relation to everything else, try to uncover these relationships, to discover a pattern in the universe. This branch of philosophy is known as Metaphysics, a word derived from the Greek *metaphusica* (Latin, *metaphysica*) meaning after physics, or following on from the study of natural science. This is because in the works of the great Greek philosoper Aristotle (384–322 BC) the philosophical writings followed his lectures on physics. Another branch, ethics (from the Greek for character or disposition), concentrates on the ideas – right, wrong, justice and so on – on which we found our scale of moral values. A further branch of philosophy deals with political theory – the nature and true functions of the state and of government; and yet another with aesthetics – the appreciation of the beautiful in nature and art. Philosophers have profoundly influenced world thought and, consequently, history.

Phoenicians: a maritime nation of the ancient world. To the geographers of antiquity Phoenicia was a land at the eastern end of the Mediterranean, its boundaries corresponding broadly with those of the modern state of Lebanon; but the trading and colonising enterprise of the Phoenicians carried them into every corner of that sea as well as into the stormier waters of the Atlantic and Indian Oceans. They voyaged far along the eastern and western coasts of Africa and probably also came to Britain in search of tin from Cornwall and the Scilly Isles, though in this case they may have travelled overland. They do not appear to have penetrated the Black Sea.

Their early home is unknown, but excavations have shown them occupying the city of Byblos in the Lebanon as early as 3000 BC, and they are known to have been trading with Egypt about 1250. Later the Phoenicians of Sidon supplied some of the best ships for the invasion of Greece in 480 (*see* PERSIAN WARS).

In due course their settlements stretched along the southern shores of the Mediterranean, particularly to Carthage, traditionally founded by Queen Dido, though evidence suggests a date in the 8th century BC. It was from Carthage that the second stage of Phoenician colonisation originated, penetrating into Spain (Cadiz), southern France (Marseilles) – though these settlements are but two examples among many – and Sicily. The Phoenicians have left few remains.

¶ PHILIPS-BIRT, D. *Finding out about the Phoenicians.* 1964

Photography: science and art of producing pictures by the action of light on chemically prepared materials. The word is derived from the Greek for "light" and "writing".

Nowadays, it is necessary to keep still for only a fraction of a second to have a photograph taken, but in the mid-19th century sitters were required to remain motionless for twenty minutes, with the head clamped in position by a device with

Stone carving of a Phoenician merchant ship.

three adjustable points. Nevertheless, people in Europe and America flocked to undergo this mild form of torture.

The desire in man to represent on a flat surface the three-dimensional scenes around him began early, as we know from such prehistoric cave paintings as those at Lascaux, south-west France. Ten thousand years ago the Chaldeans and Egyptians, resting in their dark tents, were fascinated to see that sunlit objects outside, in line with a small hole in the tent's wall, formed a replica, upside down, on the opposite wall. The ancient science of optics (the formation of images by pinholes) was mentioned by Aristotle about 350 BC, and fifty years later Euclid published a treatise on optics that contained the first known construction of an image by geometric means. Neither, apparently, appreciated the full significance of this phenomenon. Nor did Leonardo da Vinci see any practical use for the *camera obscura* he described in an account, complete with drawings, published in the early 16th century.

It was Professor Barbaro in 1568 who saw in the apparatus an aid to the understanding of perspective for an artist. The *camera obscura* consisted of a darkened box or room, with a lens at one end and a flat surface at the other. If the *camera obscura* was so small that the image must be viewed from outside, a translucent screen such as ground glass was used, but if the apparatus was large enough to enter, the image was thrown, upside down, on to a white reflecting surface. An improved version of the *camera obscura*, with a complicated arrangement of lenses and mirror and, in the case of the *camera lucida*, a prism, was used by artists, famous and amateur, to secure accuracy in drawing. This apparatus was similar in principle and essentials to the modern photographic camera, but it was nearly 300 years before an effort was made to make the optical image permanent.

To reproduce an optical image by using light energy, a substance has to be used which undergoes some chemical change when subjected to light action. During the 18th century it was recognised that salts of the metal silver are very sensitive to light. Both the German J. H. Schulze, c. 1727, and the Swedish chemist Karl Scheele experimented fifty years later in this field. In 1802 Thomas Wedgwood described his process of making pictures on paper impregnated with silver nitrate and using a painting on glass as a negative. He could not, however, keep his image from darkening. John Herschel had more success in achieving permanency in a print by his use of sodium thiosulphate (hypo). He was the first to use the terms "photograph" and "photography".

All this time, experiments along different lines were being made in various countries, all with the same purpose – to "fix" the photograph permanently. In France, Niépce obtained a record of a view from his bedroom, using asphaltum coated on to metal or stone, with a full day's exposure. For a while he and the artist Daguerre were in partnership. After Niépce's death, Daguerre reverted to the use of silver salts and in 1839 announced the Daguerreotype process of making a positive image directly upon a metallic silver plate. This process became extremely popular for a few years.

It is to the Englishman Fox Talbot (1810–77) that the title "inventor of modern photography" is given. Working with a *camera obscura* and "negative" material, consisting of paper impregnated with silver chloride, he produced a number of views of Lacock Abbey. His calotype process, with subsequent improvements, has evolved into modern photographic practice.

Another experimenter, Scott Archer, invented the wet collodion plate, which

A

B

C

D

E

A. *Daguerreotype photograph, 1857.* B. *Daguerre.*
C. *William Henry Fox Talbot.* D. *Photograph
by Fox Talbot using his Colotype process, 1844.*
E. *Camera Obscura used by Sir Joshua Reynolds.*
F. *Wounded Union soldiers after the Battle of
Fredericksburg, photographed by Matthew Brady
with a stereoscopic camera, in 1863.*

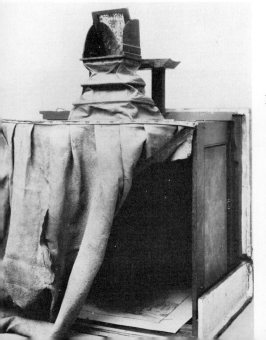

F

was used by the famous photographer Matthew Brady in his portable darkroom wagon on the battlefields of the American Civil War.

At least one woman can claim eminence in the early days of photography – Julia Margaret Cameron (1815–74), who was born in Calcutta and came to England in 1848. About 1865 she took up photography and had among her sitters Charles Darwin, Robert Browning and Lord Tennyson. Another enthusiastic early photographer was Charles Dodgson ("Lewis Carroll") the author of *Alice in Wonderland*.

George Eastman, founder of the Kodak Company of America, was responsible for the great popularity of photography as a hobby today. He marketed the first roll film, and from 1895 the home photographer could load his own film and afterwards get it developed and printed at his local chemist.

Modern developments such as high-speed shutters and automatic focusing have removed many of the difficulties of the processes of photography. Probably the camera's achievements are at their most impressive in the cinema and television studio where, rather than the carefully posed solitary sitter, vast crowds and panoramic scenes can be brought within the compass of a small screen.

¶ GERNSHEIM, HELMUT and GERNSHEIM, ALISON. *The History of Photography.* 1969

Picardy: former province of Northern France. Its chief towns are Amiens (the early capital, with a magnificent Gothic cathedral), the Channel port of Boulogne, and Abbeville, where important Palaeolithic and Bronze Age archaeological discoveries have been made.

Picasso, Pablo Ruiz (1881–1973): Spanish, one of the most influential artists of the 20th century. Most famous as a painter, he also sought expression in stone, pottery, the graphic arts and costumes for ballet. His early work is sometimes classified according to the predominating colour he used at various times, e.g. the "blue period" (1901–4) and the "rose period" (1905–7). He was one of the founders of the school of cubism, which saw familiar objects in flat geometric terms and permitted various aspects of the object to be seen simultaneously. Much of his work was dominated by horror of war and the celebration of the process of physical creation. *See colour section.*

¶ RIPLEY, E. *Picasso.* 1959

Piccard, Auguste (1884–1962): Swiss physicist who made balloon ascents into the stratosphere and developed the bathyscaphe for deep underwater exploration. In a succession of these spherical vessels he and his son Jacques progressively established new depth records from 10,335 feet [3150 metres] in September 1953 to 35,802 feet [10,912 metres] in January 1960 when, with Lieutenant D. Walsh of the US Navy, Dr Jacques Piccard took the bathyscaphe *Trieste* down into the Marianas Trench in the Pacific Ocean, the deepest part of the oceans of the world yet discovered.

¶ HONOUR, ALAN. *Ten Miles High, Two Miles Deep.* 1959

Piedmont: "foot of the mountains", fertile plain of northern Italy enclosed on three sides by alpine ranges. Ligurian Celts settled astride the mountains and were subdued by the Romans (225 BC), raided by Saracens, and overrun by Lombards and Franks. As guardian of the passes from France to Italy, Piedmont was repeatedly threatened by greater powers but retained its independence. This was due to the wariness and vigour of the House of Savoy, Burgundians from the Upper Rhone. By marriage and by obtaining titles of Imperial Vicar (12th century) and Duke (1416), by moving their capital from Chambéry to Turin (1562) and by exchanging transalpine possessions for lands in Italy, they built Piedmont into a compact state. By enlisting Habsburg aid against France they survived attacks by Francis I and, later, Louis XIV. They persecuted or tolerated the Waldensian heretics as policy dictated and maintained efficient defences. Between 1859 and 1870 Piedmont was an effective instrument in building Italian unity.

See ITALY for map.

Piero della Francesca (c. 1415–92): Italian painter from Umbria whose works include altar pieces, frescoes and portraits. His considerable gifts as a mathematician gave him a mastery of perspective, to which he added subtleties of space, light and atmosphere which mark him out as one of the greatest of Renaissance painters. *See colour section.*

Pilate, Pontius: Roman governor (procurator) of Judaea (AD 26–36), who ordered the crucifixion of Jesus under pressure from the leaders of the Jews.

Little else is known for certain about his career, but several legends have gathered round his name.

See also JESUS CHRIST.

Pilgrimage: journey undertaken from religious motives to some place reputedly sacred. During the Middle Ages a familiar figure was the wayfarer dressed in a rough grey cloak emblazoned with a red cross, wearing a broad-brimmed hat and carrying a staff, sack and gourd. He would be immediately recognisable as a pilgrim to the Holy Land, or one of the centres of pilgrimage in Europe. Possibly he would be wearing the badges of the shrines he had visited, palm leaves from Jerusalem in his hat, a cockle shell emblem from St James of Compostella in Spain, the crossed keys of St Peter from Rome, or a tiny flask from Canterbury, England, reputed to contain a drop of St Thomas Becket's blood.

Pilgrimages to a place considered sanctified by the Deity, or a holy person, are part of the cult of most religions. Every Muslim is required to visit Mecca at least once in his lifetime; devout Hindus frequently make the journey to Benares and bathe in the River Ganges; places associated with the birth, teaching and death of Buddha are the goal of Buddhists. Pilgrimages to places connected with Christ and his saints began early in Christian history. Around AD 325 the Emperor Constantine and his mother Helena erected memorial churches on the holy sites in Palestine, ushering in a great period of pilgrimages to the East. In the West, the veneration of the martyrs provided the impetus, Rome becoming the great attraction for its association with Peter and Paul. These long and often dangerous journeys were undertaken in the hope that pardon would be obtained for sins, and diseases cured. Miracles were hoped for and sometimes appeared to happen.

The medieval Church was increasingly convinced that the miraculous power of the Deity attended the bodies of saints and their relics. Santiago in Spain, Tours, Le

Puy and Chartres in France, Canterbury and Glastonbury in England, Cologne and Aix la Chapelle in southern Germany, all drew their pilgrims by the thousands. The great attraction became the acquisition of relics – objects connected with the hallowed corpse, such as wax dropped from a taper or a little dust from the grave. Soon, however, this was not enough, and the desire arose to acquire portions of the actual body, by fair means or by trickery.

Because people in the Middle Ages were acutely conscious of sin, these journeys were increasingly undertaken as expiation: in fact, a priest would often order a penitent to undertake a pilgrimage for a major sin. This led to the development of indulgences, which consisted of the remission of part of the penance, because, perhaps, the penitent returned with a relic.

In order to accommodate the increasing number of pilgrims, hospices were built along the routes, particularly on the great Alpine passes. The oldest, the Septimer, dates from 800, the Great St Bernard from the 10th century, the Simplon from the 13th century and the St Gotthard from the 14th century. There were similar refuges in the Mediterranean towns and in Jerusalem.

The hospices were run by the hospital fraternities, lay organisations working for the Church. From the most important of these, the Hospitale Hierosolymitanum, founded around 1065, arose the order of St John, earliest of the great orders of knighthood. Associations were formed to help pilgrims bound for the East. Protection was very necessary once the Holy Land was no longer held by a Christian power but had been conquered by Islam. In fact, ultimately this led to the Crusades, which in many ways were armed pilgrimages. The journey to Palestine was expensive in the 12th century as well as hazardous. Pilgrims formed themselves into unions with an elected master. Their travelling arrangements were often made through the Knights of St John and

The blessing of the sick in Rosary Square, Lourdes.

Pilgrims on their way to Canterbury.

the Knights Templar. There were even travel books – the most famous, *The Book of the Ways to Jerusalem* by John de Maundeville (*c.* 1336), was translated into several languages.

Socially the pilgrimages were important. They improved communications, increased opportunities to travel, spread ideas in art and architecture. For instance, some of France's Romanesque churches derived from St James of Compostella, Spain. In literature, they produced the *Chansons de Geste* and Chaucer's *Canterbury Tales*.

The movement was checked by the Reformation, particularly in England, but in the 16th century and again in the 19th century big revivals took place. The dedication of the church at Lourdes, France, took place in 1876, in the presence of 3,000 priests and 100,000 pilgrims. *See colour section.*

¶ ROWLING, MARJORIE. *Everyday Life of Medieval Travellers.* 1971; THOMSON, GLADYS SCOTT. *Medieval Pilgrimages.* 1962

Pilgrim Fathers: the Puritan refugees who sailed from England in the *Mayflower* (1620). In 1608 a congregation of radical Puritans fled to Leyden in Holland to escape religious persecution. They came from the area in England where York-

shire, Lincolnshire and Nottinghamshire meet, from towns such as Gainsborough and villages such as Scrooby. Though this was the beginning of the Pilgrim Fathers' journey to freedom, it was their second attempt to leave England. On the first occasion they were betrayed by the captain of the ship they had chartered, and were imprisoned in the Guildhall, Boston, in Lincolnshire. When later they reached Holland, they were extremely dissatisfied with the local people, whom they judged to be too frivolous and lacking in respect for the Puritan way of life. After long negotiations with King James I, they obtained permission to settle on English-owned land in North America. The Puritans were joined by more sympathisers – as well as by a number of adventurers – and set sail from Southampton in two ships, the *Mayflower* and the *Speedwell*. The *Speedwell* sprang a leak and had to be abandoned. The *Mayflower* put into Plymouth where the citizens who sympathised with the Pilgrims' religious views gave them a warm welcome. As they afterwards wrote, they were "courteously used by divers friends there dwelling". The Pilgrims finally sailed from Plymouth on 6 September 1620.

The Pilgrim Fathers leaving for America.

It took the *Mayflower* more than three months to cross the Atlantic, and in December 1620 the Pilgrim Fathers (as they later became known) landed at a spot which by a strange coincidence had, six years earlier, been named Plymouth by Captain John Smith. Before landing, the Pilgrims signed a simple worded Compact, which became the cornerstone of the American democratic tradition. The little colony had a very chequered career and struggled with great courage against crop failures and attacks by Red Indians. In 1691 the Plymouth colony was absorbed by the neighbouring colony of Massachusetts Bay. This new Puritan colony thrived and expanded rapidly during the next ten years, during which time another 15,000 immigrants arrived to join it. Its large numbers kept it safe against Indian attack and enabled it to absorb the smaller settlements around it. Eventually there was established a representative form of government which superseded the direct democracy of the early settlement, the population of which had barely exceeded 100 people.

¶ COWIE, LEONARD W. *The Pilgrim Fathers.* 1970; GILL, W. J. C. *The Pilgrim Fathers.* 1964

See also MAYFLOWER.

Pilsudski, Jozef (1867–1935): statesman and, with Paderewski (*see* separate entry), founder of modern Poland, in 1919. A vigorous nationalist, he led a Polish army against Russia in World War I. Afterwards, whilst trying to enlarge the new Poland into a Polish-Ukrainian Union, he was defeated by the Red Army. He believed in strong rule, and later seized power as prime minister for a time.

Piraeus, The: port of Athens, Greece, about four miles [6·5 kilometres] southwest of the city. At the height of Athenian prosperity in the 5th century BC the Piraeus was joined to Athens by two long parallel walls some 200 yards [180 metres] apart, within which the people from the countryside could take refuge from invasion (*see* PELOPONNESIAN WAR). Much enlarged, the Piraeus is still busy and prosperous.

Pirates: sea robbers. In films and fiction, pirates are often pictured as romantic figures – swarthy, black-bearded adventurers or even elegant gentlemen, with gold earrings, rapier in hand and a brace of pistols in their belts. In fact, they were more often desperate, drunken ruffians, tattered and unwashed, who had turned to piracy because of oppressive conditions at home or on board their merchant ship. They preferred a dangerous life with the chance of fabulous riches to a steady job with low pay. An undisciplined lot, they often lost their money and ships. Pirates of any nationality usually received short shrift at the hands of their captors.

Since ancient times pirates have harassed merchant ships on all the oceans of the world. Early records cite the Phoenicians, there are references to sea rovers in the Odyssey, Greek pirates were mentioned in Assyrian documents of the 8th century BC. The pirates of Cilicia destroyed a Roman fleet at Ostia, and not until the time of Augustus was the Adriatic finally cleared of marauders.

The Vikings continuously raided the coasts of Britain, Ireland and France. In North Africa the corsairs established the Barbary States: from Algiers and Tripoli, they sailed out to plunder passing ships, or landed on the Spanish coast and carried away Christians to sell as slaves. Not until the 19th century were they finally suppressed.

In Tudor times piracy flourished round the British Isles, particularly in southern Ireland, where there were safe retreats and willing receivers to buy the stolen goods

Left, the notorious pirate, Captain Henry Morgan laying siege to Port-au-Prince, 1680. Right, Ann Bonny, one of the few women pirates, convicted of piracy in Jamaica, 1720.

and grow rich on the profits. As life became more difficult in home waters, the pirates moved further afield – to the West Indies, New England, the Red Sea and Madagascar, which swarmed with pirates preying on the sea routes from Europe to India and the Indies. There, in the 1600s, they set up their own communistic state of Libertatia.

Spanish America, forbidden by Spain to trade with foreigners, eagerly bought smuggled goods at low prices from the buccaneers. As a result, the most powerful pirate fleet of all time flourished in the Caribbean. Pirate crews were reinforced by privateers (armed merchant ships licensed to attack enemy shipping in wartime) and by unemployed naval seamen, ready to take any job going, for no wages but a share of the booty. First task of a newly created pirate crew was to draw up ship's articles, and choose their flag, usually the "skull and crossbones" – the

"Jolly Roger". The commander was chosen by vote. If he was a strong character, like the famous Bartholomew Roberts, a strict disciplinarian and teetotaller, who would allow neither women nor gambling on board, then success was assured.

Piracy flourished in the Caribbean and North Africa until wiped out by the concerted efforts of British and American navies in the 1830s, but pirates were still common among the Greek islands in the 1850s, and the Chinese pirates of Taya Bay, north of Hong Kong, were active until World War II.

¶ EPSTEIN, SAMUEL and WILLIAMS, BERYL. *The Real Book of Pirates.* 1962

See also BUCCANEERS; PRIVATEERS.

Pisa: Italian port on the River Arno; one of the earliest free communes (AD 1081). It prospered greatly in the 11th and 12th centuries when its seamen with the help of the Genoese drove the Saracens

from Sardinia, Corsica and Majorca. It sent ships on the First Crusade and established factories at Acre and Constantinople. It declined in the 13th and 14th centuries because it attempted simultaneously to fight the Genoese for control of Corsica and supported the Ghibelline cause against Guelph Florence. By sacking Lucca in 1314 it drove silk weavers to Florence, by demanding tolls in 1356 it drove Florentine exporters to use Leghorn. Its trade declined, its harbour silted up. It fell to the Milanese and then in 1405 to Florentine overlordship. The Medici partially revived its trade and founded its university. Among its buildings is the famous "leaning tower" (*below*), begun in AD 1174, which is about 16 feet [4·88 metres] off the perpendicular. Modern industries include cotton and silk.
See ITALY for map.

Pitcairn Islands: British colony in the central South Pacific, administered by the governor of Fiji and consisting of the islands of Pitcairn, Henderson, Ducie and Oeno, only the first of which is inhabited (1965 population, 186). Pitcairn's place in history dates from 1789 when mutineers from HMS *Bounty*, led by Fletcher Christian, took refuge there. Most of the present inhabitants are descended from the mutineers. The *Bounty*, commanded by Captain William Bligh, was a small vessel of 215 tons purchased by the British Admiralty to carry breadfruit from the Pacific to the West Indies.
See PACIFIC OCEAN for map.

Pitt, William, first Earl of Chatham, known as "Pitt the Elder" (1708–78): British statesman and prime minister. He entered parliament in 1735. When in 1756 he took office as secretary of state, government was ineffectual, showing vagueness and indecision in the face of worldwide French aggression. Pitt breathed a new spirit into his countrymen. "I know that I can save England, and I know no other man can" expressed his unswerving confidence in himself and England's destiny. A great orator and strategist, he could inspire generals and arouse the people. His genius as war minister in the Seven Years War with France brought a succession of victories in Europe, India and Canada. His backing of Frederick the Great of Prussia against France paid dividends, leaving him free to grasp the mastery of the seas. As a result, Britain became an imperial power with worldwide commitments. Frederick the Great said of him: "England has been in labour a long time . . . but at last she has given birth to a man."
¶ PLUMB, J. H. *Chatham*. 1965

Pitt, William, known as "Pitt the Younger" (1759-1806): British statesman and prime minister, second son of Pitt the Elder. Where Chatham's genius lay in war, his son's talents were best suited to peace. The second Pitt, at twenty-four the youngest prime minister in British history, took office when England's fortunes were at their lowest ebb (1783). Her American colonies were lost, and she stood alone in Europe. Parliament was corrupt and swayed by George III's political manoeuvres. Pitt was patriotic, high principled and popular with the people. He tackled the problem of parliamentary reform, gave India good government and Ireland the Act of Union. In finance he showed his genius. Though private wealth was rapidly increasing from industry and trade, the national debt was mounting after the French and American wars. Through his budgets he established a better balance, introducing an income tax for the first time. He struggled to keep England from war with France and did much to save her when, inevitably, it came.

¶ DERRY, J. *William Pitt.* 1962

William Pitt the Younger, by Gillray.

Pittsburgh: port and industrial centre of Pennsylvania, USA. Situated at the point where the Allegheny and Monagahela Rivers form the Ohio, Pittsburgh was laid out in 1764 as a trading post and fort by John Campbell and grew rapidly until in 1816 it was one of America's largest cities. The same strategic situation that had made it the logical point for a fort to control the Upper Mississippi Valley also made it the entrepot for waves of migration to the West. Pittsburgh became a major industrial centre for the production of iron, steel and glass, and played a major role in supplying the Union armies with cannon and armour plate in the Civil War.

Pius V, St (Michele Ghisliere, 1504-72): Pope. Born of poor parents near Alessandria, he became a Dominican friar, inquisitor-general in 1551 and Pope in 1566. He combined uprightness of character and strictness of living with bigotry and harsh persecution. Rising at dawn and taking little rest, he laboured to root out heresy, repel the Turk and reform the Papal Court. He applauded Alva's executions of Flemish protestants and urged Charles IX to take no prisoners in the war against the Huguenots. He inspired the defeat of the Turkish fleet at Lepanto in 1571 (*see* separate entry). He halved the personnel and expenditure of the Papal Court. He was canonised in 1712.

Pius IX (Eugenio Mastai-Ferretti, 1792–1878): Pope, often referred to as "Pio Nono". Born at Sinigaglia, he became Bishop of Imola and, from 1846, pope for thirty-two years – the longest rule in the history of the Papacy. A man of simple piety, "warm hearted, but weak in intellect" (Metternich), he weakened his authority by relaxing censorship and freeing political prisoners, and was in 1848 cast for the role of president of a free, federal Italy. But he shrank from war with Austria and became a bitter opponent of Piedmontese attempts to absorb the Papal States. He reacted against liberalism and condemned democracy and much of modern science. To the despair of liberal Catholics he urged the declaration of Papal Infallibility by the Vatican Council, 1870.
See colour section.

Pius XII (Eugenio Pacelli, 1876–1958): Pope 1939–58. Of Roman family, after serving as cardinal secretary of state for ten years he was elected Pope in the critical year 1939, which saw the outbreak of World War II. He won respect by his ministry to the wounded in the Allied bombing of Rome, but has been criticised for failure to condemn Nazi persecution of the Jews. He was preoccupied with fear of Communism and was unwilling to imperil the Church in Germany. He became more conservative after 1950, when he proclaimed the

Pope Pius XII.

dogma of the Bodily Assumption of the Virgin Mary into heaven, condemned the theory of evolution (*see* DARWIN, CHARLES) and dissolved the worker-priest movement in France. He deepened the gulf between Catholic and non-Catholic.

Death of the Inca Atahualpa.

Pizarro, Francisco (*c.* 1475–1541): Spanish general. Pizarro was one of the most successful of the Conquistadors (*see* separate entry). In Spain he began life as an illegitimate and illiterate swineherd, yet determination drove his followers to discover and to destroy the Inca Empire of Peru. He went to America on Columbus's second voyage in 1493 and learned much from Balboa and Cortes. He began to search for a rich southern empire in 1515, but it took seventeen years before his final expedition of 183 men with twenty-five horses was ready to climb the Andes to Cajamarca, where the Inca Atahualpa was ambushed, ransomed for a roomful of gold, then killed. After the capture of Cuzco Pizarro began to build a new capital city at Lima. Unfortunately the Spaniards quarrelled among themselves. Pizarro executed a former partner, Almagro, but he was assassinated in 1541, and a new Governor was sent from Spain to rule Peru.
See colour section.

Place-names: Place-names are a code from the past which, deciphered, tells us about people who lived long ago and about physical features which time may have altered out of all recognition. They record man's hopes and fears, successes and defeats; his love of beauty and his destruction of it to serve his own ends. There was an ancient belief that every place possessed its own attendant spirit, its *genius loci*. A place-name enshrines the men and women who, by the magical act of naming, separated the human community from the anonymous wilderness.

English place-names are a roll-call of the different waves of invaders which, until 1066, swept over the country. Even if we did not know from other sources that the Romans held Britain in military subjection for nearly 400 years, we could deduce as much from their legacy of place-names incorporating *-cester, -chester* or *-caster* (Gloucester, Worcester, Lancaster, Chester and so on) all derived from the Latin *castrum*, a fort, or from *castra*, the plural form of the same word, meaning a fortified camp. These place-names were seldom entirely Roman. *Castrum* or *castra* was often added to a Celtic (i.e. early British) place-name already in existence. Thus Worcester, for example, means "the Roman fort of the tribe called Weogoran".

In the 5th and 6th centuries the Angles and the Saxons turned Britain into England. Except in the west, the British language was quite submerged in that of the conquerors. Even so, some Celtic place-names survive in the eastern half of the country, particularly the names of rivers, for which the British had a special feeling, regarding many of them as sacred. It may be that the newcomers, out of superstitious awe, forbore to tamper with these ancient names of power. Thus, for example, the Darenth (Kent) comes from a Celtic word meaning "river where the oaks are plentiful". The Thames is another river whose name, meaning, probably, and today most appropriately, "dark water", goes back to the Celts.

Some Anglo-Saxon names, like *North Folk* and *South Folk* (today's Norfolk and Suffolk), are straightforward tribal designations. The many names ending in *-ingas* and *-ingaham* (modern *-ing* and *-ingham*) denoted smaller groupings. Hameringham (Lincolnshire), for example, means "village of the dwellers on the hill".

The Anglo-Saxons became Christians during the early 7th century, but many place-names attest to their former paganism: for example, Wednesbury (Kent) from the god Woden; Tuesley (Surrey) from Tyr, the war-god; and Thundesley (Essex) from Thunor, god of thunder. Other place-names – such as Stokenchurch (Berkshire) "the church built of timber", and Halstow (Devonshire) "holy place" – advertise their conversion.

In the 9th century the Danes and other Scandinavian races began to make inroads into England. Many of them settled permanently. Place-names tell us exactly where. Those which end in *-by, -thorp(e), -beck, -dale, -car, -thwaite, -fell, -gill* and *-holme* are all of Scandinavian origin.

Last of the successful invaders were the Normans. They must have enjoyed their new possession, judging from the number of places they called *beau-* or *bel-*, "beautiful". Beaulieu (Hampshire), Bewley (one in Durham and one in Westmorland), and Bewdley (Worcestershire) all mean "beautiful place". Perhaps tastes differed in those days, since the Normans re-named Fulepet (Essex) which meant "filthy pit, or hollow", Beaumont – "beautiful hill".

The invention of English place-names did not come to an end in 1066. It still goes on, whenever a new street, new housing development or new town needs a card of identity. The Industrial Revolution spawned such names as Coalville (Leicestershire) and Ironville (Derbyshire). Another 19th-century *-ville*, Waterlooville (Hampshire), took its name from a nearby inn called *The Heroes of Waterloo*.

One of the richest treasuries of place-names is to be found in the USA. Over the centuries people have come to it from many countries, in war and peace, and – like the early English settlers who, perhaps homesick, called their new homes Boston, Cambridge, London, and so on – have re-used the names of the towns and villages they left behind in the Old World. In addition, a great many Indian place-names were taken over, with the land itself, from the original inhabitants of the American continent: names like Mississippi, "the great water", and Oklahoma, "land of the red people". Americans named many towns after their national heroes, such as Washington and Lincoln; a practice followed by the Russians when, for example, they changed Petrograd (previously St Petersburg) to Leningrad, and Nizhni Novgorod to Gorki. (With Stalingrad, named in honour of the former ruler of the USSR, the process was reversed. Today the city is called Volgograd. Thus place-names chronicle history in a nutshell.)

Other American place-names reflect the naïve optimism of the immigrants – there are sixteen places called Athens, to say nothing of Rome, Carthage, Sparta, Nineveh and Troy – and their simple religious faith. There are nine Canaans in the US and eleven Jordans. There are even two places called Sodom.

In conclusion, a few place-names from all over the world, selected at random: Peking means "the northern court"; Bolivia takes its name from the South American revolutionary leader Simon Bolívar (1783–1830); Barcelona, Spain, derives from the Carthaginian general Hamilcar Barca (*c.* 270–228 BC) who is thought to have founded the city; Hong-Kong is a contraction of Hiang-Kiang, "the place of sweet lagoons".

Plagues: pestilences, extremely infectious diseases. Throughout history, at various times, a great many people have died from plagues and they have often been regarded as divine punishments for man's wickedness.

The plagues recorded in the Book of Exodus in the Bible are in a class by themselves. The frogs, lice, boils, etc., and the killing of the firstborn were, rather, aimed at bringing home to Pharaoh the power of the Israelites' God, so that he would, as Moses demanded, "let my people go".

At a time when medical knowledge was rudimentary, almost any infectious illness of swift and high mortality might be labelled plague. Today, in medical terminology, the word is generally restricted to a bacterial disease carried, in the first instance, by the bite of a flea which makes its home on rats. People who have contracted the disease may spread it by their coughs and sneezes or other infective discharges. Plague may take one of three forms, attacking the lungs, poisoning the bloodstream, or breaking out in glandular swellings known as buboes. This last, known as bubonic plague, is actually less lethal than the first two, but since the spectacular swellings make it instantly recognisable, it is the one with the best documented history.

The first historical reference to plague dates from the time of the Roman Emperor Trajan (AD 53–117), when it was recorded as being rife in Syria, Libya and Egypt. It was from Egypt that, some 400 years later, it spread into Europe, via Constantinople, where it is said to have killed 10,000 people in a single day. In Italy so many people succumbed to it that, when Germanic invaders, the Lombards, swept down from the north, they met with little opposition and were able to establish a kingdom which lasted for over 200 years.

The terrible 14th-century visitation known as the Black Death, which killed

"Bring out your dead", the cry of the corpse collectors in London, 1665.

off perhaps half the population of Europe, had irreversible consequences. The bells that tolled the passing of so many souls tolled also the end of the Middle Ages. The feudal system could not long survive the wholesale slaughter of the human material on which it depended.

Singling out the peak plague years does not mean that the intervening ones were plague-free. For centuries the plague was one of the facts of life, though by the 17th century its virulence had much declined.

Nevertheless in 1665-6 London suffered a last dreadful outbreak in which probably at least 100,000 people died.

The Great Fire of London (1666) undoubtedly destroyed many squalid tenements where the flea-carrying rats had found congenial homes. But in fact the plague bacillus was weakening everywhere. Gradually European outbreaks ceased altogether and those in the East decreased to much smaller proportions. Modern hygiene and drainage have speeded that decline, to say nothing of such modern medicaments as sulpha drugs and streptomycin. But in exceptional conditions, when modern amenities fail, plague can still strike, as in the disaster area of East Pakistan after the cyclone havoc of November 1970.

¶ NOHL, JOHANNES. *The Black Death: a chronicle of the Plague compiled from contemporary sources.* 1961

Plains States, The (USA): In the north central region "the Great Plains" area includes the states of Iowa, Kansas, Minnesota, Missouri, Nebraska, North Dakota and South Dakota. Although actually not flat, since the plains rise from about 800 feet [244 metres] above sea level to about 4,000 feet [1219 metres] on the west among the foothills of the Rockies, this is indeed a large, uninterrupted plain. It is an area of grasslands and large farms, with no major rivers or other breaks in the landscape. Described by its first settlers as a vast "sea", its rolling hills and plains do suggest the undulating surface of the oceans.

Though parts of the region were explored by the Spanish, especially by Coronado in the 1540s, and though settlement in Minnesota began under the leadership of the American Fur Company during the 1810s, much of the region remained virtually uninhabited until the decades just before the American Civil War. In the middle of the century, the entire area, but especially Missouri, was considered the "Gateway to the West", as it was from this region that settlers venturing to California bought final provisions for their trek across the desert. Recently a gigantic arch has been erected in St Louis, Missouri, to commemorate this period in the history of the region.

This is, above all, an agricultural region. On these plains settlers, mostly from German, Irish and Scandinavian stock, established large farms devoted to the production of grains, grass and livestock. Though some coal, lead and oil are extracted, and some transport equipment is manufactured, the main feature of life in this region is the relative isolation of existence on the large farms of the plains.

Planetarium: an instrument for demonstrating the positions, relationships and movements of the sun, moon, planets, stars and other astronomical phenomena. Early planetaria had trains of gear wheels and were manually operated models of the solar system. Archimedes of Syracuse (287–212 BC), the mathematician, is recorded as having devised and used a water driven example. Later, with the invention of clockwork in medieval times, a mechanical drive could be provided.

The orrery, a table instrument, was developed in the early 18th century and named after Charles Boyle, fourth Earl of Orrery (1676–1731), for whom the first English example was devised.

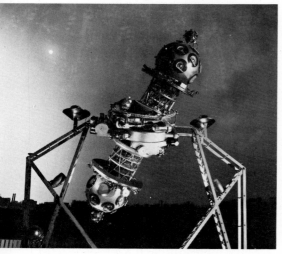

The projector, London Planetarium.

The modern instrument, which projects a representation of the heavens on to a semicircular ceiling, was invented by the German Dr Bauersfeld of the Zeiss works at Jena in 1913. The instrument operates by means of a powerful light source, electric motors, lenses and mirrors. In this way the positions and movements of heavenly bodies, not only in the present day but in the past and future, and as observed from different latitudes, can be demonstrated. The watcher can thus explore the heavens from the comfort of a chair in a warm room. Problems connected with mathematics, survey work

and navigation can be resolved and demonstrated simply.

Planetaria are used widely for educational and cultural purposes in the USA and Germany. In England the use of planetaria for educational purposes is increasing and public performances are given in the City Museum, Liverpool, and in London at The Planetarium, Baker Street, and at the National Maritime Museum, Greenwich. The world's largest planetarium, built at a cost of $1,500,000, is at Dangerfield Island on the Potomac, Washington, DC, USA.
See also OBSERVATORY.

Plantagenet, House of (1154–1399): line of English kings, here named with their dates of succession only.

The first was Henry II, son of William the Conqueror's daughter Matilda by her second marriage to Geoffrey of Anjou, called Plantagenet from his habit of wearing a sprig of broom (*planta genista*) in his cap. He succeeded Stephen in 1154 and is chiefly remembered for his strong rule and for his quarrel with Becket (*see* separate entry). To remark that his concern was as much with his lands in France as with the realm of England is to emphasise a feature, albeit with varying fortunes, of all the reigns in this line. He was succeeded in turn by two of his sons, Richard I (1189), a romantic military figure who spent very little time in England, and John (1199), one of the traditionally "bad" English kings, from whom the barons wrung Magna Carta.

Henry III succeeded his father John at the age of nine, and his reign was a long one, but he was not a satisfactory ruler. That of his son Edward I (1272) saw a revival of the prestige of the throne and the early growth of our parliamentary system. Edward II (1307) failed sadly to follow his father's path, but his son Edward III (1327) was a strong king who

The antagenets dominions in England and France

ENGLISH CHANNEL

KINGDOM OF CASTILE

Plassey, Battle of (1757): fought near a village of that name on the Hooghly river in Bengal. Here Clive, with an army of 3,200, defeated the 50,000 of the Nawab Siraj-ud-Daula, establishing thereby the dominance of the British in Bengal. Clive had previously entered into a plot to dethrone the Nawab with Mir Jafar who commanded a large section of Siraj-ud-Daula's army. Though Mir Jafar did not openly declare himself until the issue was decided, he held back the troops under his command, thus undermining the spirit of the Indians, and it was a rout rather than a battle, Clive losing 23 killed and 49 wounded, and fewer than 500 being killed in the Nawab's huge army.

¶ EDWARDS, MICHAEL. *Plassey: The Founding of an Empire.* 1969

Plastics: materials which can be made to change shape under pressure or heat. Nature abounds in such materials, some of which, such as clays and waxes, have been used from time immemorial. To-day, however, when we use the term, we generally mean the tremendous range of man-made materials (usually by-products of coal or oil) which have become all but indispensable to our industrialised society.

Plastics of this kind fall into two main categories: thermoplastic and thermo-setting. Thermoplastic resins become soft and malleable under heat (i.e. they can be shaped without being broken), but under-go no permanent change. Thermosetting resins undergo a chemical change when heated and cannot be remoulded.

Some of the first plastics to be made were produced from a combination of phenol and formaldehyde. Bakelite (named after Dr Leo Baekeland, a pioneer in this field) is an example of this kind of plastic. Other plastics resins are polyvinyl chloride (PVC), polythene, polystyrene, and various forms of cellulose.

campaigned successfully in France (*see* CRECY; POITIERS), though he sank into a sordid old age. He was a great lover of chivalric display and founded the Order of the Garter. The last of the line was his grandson Richard II (1377), son of the Black Prince, a headstrong king, unable to control his nobles. In 1399 one of these, Henry of Bolingbroke, later Henry IV and also a grandson of Edward III, over-threw him, and he was done to death.

The succession then became a matter of dispute between the houses of Lancaster and York (*see* WARS OF THE ROSES).

The last legitimate male Plantagenet had perished by 1499, but it is interesting to find the badge of the house still remembered in the reign of Elizabeth I, who had a dress embroidered with the device.

See colour section.

¶ HARVEY, JOHN. *The Plantagenets.* 1963

See also LANCASTER, HOUSE OF; YORK, HOUSE OF.

Plato (*c.* 427–348 BC): philosopher of ancient Greece, a man of aristocratic family and the disciple of Socrates, the great philosopher who was condemned to death on the accusations of the many enemies he made in his fearless pursuit of truth. Plato founded a school in the grove of Academus, just outside Athens, where mathematics, astronomy, science and philosophy were taught and ideas spread which (sometimes in distorted form) have greatly influenced Western thought. Plato's philosophy is based on two convictions – the possibility of human improvement and the supremacy of the intellect. His best-known works are in dialogue form, with his old master Socrates as the central figure. The most famous is the *Republic*, his version of an ideal state ruled by an aristocracy of intellect.

¶ In THOMAS, H. and D. L. *Great Philosophers.* 1959
See also SOCRATES.

Playing cards: cards used for indoor games and providing a history lesson in themselves, so much have they been affected by events. For six hundred years they have been known in Europe, for centuries longer in India and China. They have been used for divination, conjuring and education, as well as for gaming.

The cards, usually oblong or square, have been made in a variety of materials, but mostly of pasteboard and, nowadays, of plastic. The faces of the early European cards were hand painted, engraved or lithographed, putting them beyond any but a nobleman's purse, but after 1423 stencilling or wood block printing made them cheaper.

The earliest European pack, the *tarots*, first appeared in Italy in the early 14th century. It consisted of seventy-eight cards, including King, Queen, Knight and Varlet, together with twenty-one *atouts*, which also had pictures and titles.

Later came the fifty-two card pack we know today, with four suits, two red (Hearts and Diamonds), two black (Spades and Clubs). Each suit had three court cards, usually King, Queen and Knave, and ten spot cards.

The four suits were common to all the European packs, and represented the four estates of mankind, as known in the Middle Ages: the ruling class, the military, the commercial and the peasants. The symbols, however, varied from country to country – the Spanish signs, for instance, were cups, swords, coins and batons. Our own cards derived from the French, a great card making nation from the 15th century onwards.

Court cards down the centuries show pictures of royalty and other famous figures, sometimes, as in the French cards, with the names inscribed. Charlemagne was also Emperor in the tarot pack, and from 1480 he became the King of Hearts in the French pack. For the other Kings, the French chose David to head the Spades, Julius Caesar Diamonds, and Alexander Clubs.

During the French Revolution the emblems of royalty disappeared, the Kings became Sages, Dames (French title for the Queens) Liberties, Valets, Braves. But with the crowning of Napoleon, back came the royal insignia.

Similar republican trends were found in the American Civil War, when the packs were headed by army officers. Again, when South Africa left the Commonwealth, Kommandant, Vrou and Boer replaced the usual court cards.

The course of history can be traced in such packs as the 18th-century English "Imperial Royal Cards", with Henry VIII shown as King of Spades, Anne Boleyn as his Queen, and Cardinal Wolsey as Knave. A topical pack of 1815 portrays the Duke of Wellington as King of Spades, while the other Kings are

Blücher, Schwarzenberg and Kutusov. Their respective Queens are England, Prussia, Austria and Russia, while the Knaves represent the private soldiers of the four nations.

In World War II, a variety of pack was circulated in the Resistance Movement, with the Kings disguised as Churchill, Roosevelt, De Gaulle and Stalin.

During the 19th century the French and English packs became standardised with double-headed court cards, but individual modern cards of historic interest can still be found, with ancient Greek heroes appearing on Greek court cards and Biblical figures on those of Israel.
See colour section.

Plebeian: adjective denoting membership of the lower classes. The word is derived from the Latin *plebs*, the common folk of the city of Rome, whose political rights, particularly during the republican era (*see* PATRICIAN), were strictly limited by law.

Plebiscite: a vote of all the electors of a specific area or country to decide some important issue. The plebiscite was used by the French Republic and Napoleon to give their foreign conquests and annexations the semblance of the approval of the subjected populations. Perhaps the best known plebiscite of this century was held in the Saar in 1935, when its inhabitants voted to be reunited with Germany, thus bringing to an end the administration of this area by the League of Nations.
See also REFERENDUM.

Plimsoll line: horizontal line painted on the side of a merchant ship denoting the limit to which it may be legally loaded. It is named after the English radical parliamentarian Samuel Plimsoll (1824-98).

The frequent losses of ships at sea caused by overloading by unscrupulous owners

FREEBOARD MARKING FOR SHIPS:
A diagram of the modern markings placed on the side of merchant ships to show the levels of loading for different seasons and conditions.

Diameter of circle
1 foot (30 cm).
Length of bar
through circle 18
inches (45 cm).

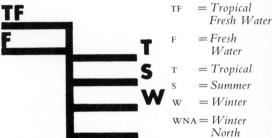

TF	= *Tropical Fresh Water*
F	= *Fresh Water*
T	= *Tropical*
S	= *Summer*
W	= *Winter*
WNA	= *Winter North Atlantic*

led Plimsoll to campaign for the introduction of a compulsory load line. After much opposition he succeeded, and the British Merchant Shipping Act of 1876 was passed bringing in the necessary legislation. In 1930 the matter was further pursued by a convention signed in London by forty nations defining the limits to which ships on international voyages may be loaded.

Plough: agricultural implement drawn by horses, oxen or tractor.

Food is the basis of life, crops are grown for food, the soil is cultivated for crops, and the plough is used for cultivation. A pointed stick can be used to scratch the soil to make a seed-bed, but such a digging-stick is not a plough. A plough pushes the soil aside as well as disturbing it. The part that does the pushing is the *breast* or *mouldboard*. This was at first a flat board; but experiments proved that a curved breast did better work, and that the shape of the curve influenced the way in which the soil was pushed to one side and turned over.

In Britain the Agricultural Improvers (*see* separate entry) were much concerned with plough design. Walter Blith, in 1641, published a book in which he described his ideas on the subject. John Arbuthnot's design was published in one of Arthur Young's volumes in 1771. James Small, calling himself "Husbandman and Artificer" (as we would say, farmer and mechanic), published his book *The Plough* in 1784. James E. Ransome, grandson of the man who founded the famous firm of Ransome, Sims and Jefferies, is recorded as lecturing on ploughs at the Royal Agricultural College in 1865.

These are but four of the many farmers and craftsmen who designed, made and used ploughs until, by the end of the 19th

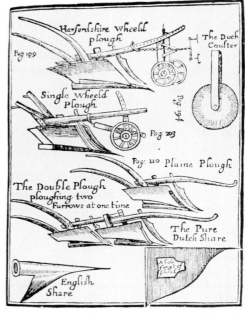

Above, 17th-century ploughs from Walter Blith's English Improver Improved, *1652. Below, 19th- and 20th-century ploughs.*

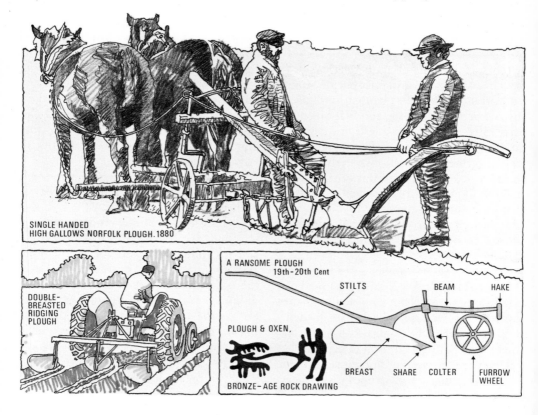

SINGLE HANDED
HIGH GALLOWS NORFOLK PLOUGH. 1880

DOUBLE-
BREASTED
RIDGING
PLOUGH

A RANSOME PLOUGH
19th-20th Cent

STILTS   BEAM   HAKE

PLOUGH & OXEN,

BREAST   SHARE   COLTER   FURROW
WHEEL

BRONZE-AGE ROCK DRAWING

century, most ploughs were being made in factories. Local requirements and manufacture resulted in a great variety of design and name, famous ones being the Hertfordshire plough, the Kent plough and the Suffolk plough, amongst others.

A plough with a single breast turns the furrow over (moves the soil aside) either to the ploughman's right or to his left, according to how the breast is fitted. If it can be changed so that when going in one direction up the field it turns it to his right, and when coming back it turns it to his left, it is called a one-way plough. Such ploughs, in the beginning, needed adjustment whenever they turned on the headland at the end of the field.

Plymouth

Plymouth (England): seaport between the Tamar and Plym estuaries, southwest Devonshire, in a capacious harbour exposed only to southerly winds. It developed on Sutton Pool in the Bronze Age and Roman times and expanded in the 13th century. Expeditions for Gascony assembled there under Edward I, wine was imported, and tin, lead, fish, hides and wool were exported. There was also a busy traffic in conveying pilgrims to the shrine of St James of Compostella in Spain. In 1254 Henry II granted a market at Sutton to the Prior of Plympton, and in 1440, after repeated French attacks showed the need for fortification, Plymouth received a charter. With the loss of Gascony in 1451 the wine trade decayed and Plymouth turned to piracy. Under Elizabeth the town flourished as the base of privateers – Huguenots, Sea-Beggars and the native Hawkins family – preying on Spanish commerce. It is also imperishably associated with the name of Sir Francis Drake and with the sailing of the Pilgrim Fathers to New England. The naval dockyard of Devonport developed after 1690, John Rennie's breakwater was built 1812-48, the Great Western Railway linked Plymouth with London in 1849.

Plymouth is also the name of at least ten places in the USA, the most celebrated being Plymouth, Massachusetts, the landing place of the Pilgrim Fathers (1620) and the first permanent settlement by Europeans in New England.

¶ BRACKEN, C. W. *History of Plymouth and Her Neighbours.* 1970

See also INDIVIDUAL ENTRIES.

Pocahontas or **Matoaka** (1595-1617): daughter of an American-Indian chief, Powhattan. According to the not entirely trustworthy account of Captain John Smith (*see* separate entry), leader of the Virginian colonists, she saved him from execution. She subsequently became a Christian and married John Rolfe, a settler, who in 1616 brought her to England where she dressed in Stuart fashion and was received at Court. She died at Gravesend, apparently on the eve of returning to America. Among her descendants through her son was the wife of President Woodrow Wilson.

See colour section.

¶ BINDER, P. and GOELL, K. *Pocahontas.* 1964

Pocket battleship: a powerful modern warship combining features of a "battleship" and a "cruiser". Battleships were designed to be the finest ships in a navy, with the most powerful guns and best armoured protection, but their high cost and international attempts to limit the power of navies led to the increased importance of the cruiser, normally of 10,000 tons standard weight and with

The Admiral Graf Spee *at the Fleet review, 1937.*

8-inch guns. Germany, however, in order to meet the Treaty of Versailles specifications, which limited size, in 1929 developed the Pocket Battleship, which was really a cruiser of 10,000 tons but with 11-inch guns and armour-plated sides and decks. In 1939 she had three, of which the commerce-raiders *Admiral Scheer* and *Graf Spee* were to become famous.

Poison gas: gas used in chemical warfare. Gas was first used effectively on 22 April 1915 by the Germans against the British and French at Ypres. It was employed throughout World War I, and in the 1930s by Italians in Abyssinia and Japanese in China.

The gas first used was chlorine, cylinders of which were opened on the German side, and the greenish-yellow cloud drifted in the breeze over allied positions. It smelt like bleach and caused a violent irritation in the lungs. Another "choking" gas, phosgene, was later fired in shells.

Mustard gas was used at Ypres in 1917. This is a pungent-smelling "blister" gas, droplets of which burn the skin after five hours. Breathing it causes bronchitis after twenty-four hours.

Nerve gas, developed in World War II, was never used for fear of retaliation. Odourless and colourless, it causes headaches, vomiting and convulsions. A droplet on the skin left untreated can kill in fifteen minutes. A less harmful but temporarily effective type, much used in quelling civil disturbances and dispersing crowds, is "tear gas", so named because of its effects as an eye irritant.

Poitiers: town on rocky promontory commanding the route from Gascony to the Loire. There Clovis and his Franks defeated the Goths in AD 507, and Charles Martel defeated the Moors in 732, the shield-wall of the Franks standing "like a rampart of ice". On 19 September 1356 John of France, with 16,000 men, out-manoeuvred the Black Prince, with 6,500. The Prince, refusing to abandon his plunder, fought off pursuit at Maupertuis, south-east of Poitiers. His men-at-arms withstood waves of French attackers, while English archers and Gascon knights attacked their flanks. King John was taken prisoner, his heir fled, but his fourth son Philip fought at his side and was rewarded with the Duchy of Burgundy, whence he and his successors plagued future French kings. Today Poitiers is a town of some 62,000 population, with important chemical and metal working industries.

Poland: republic of central Europe, bounded by the Baltic Sea, Germany, Czechoslovakia and Russia. A great imperial Polish state (Rzeczpospolita) existed in late medieval times, stretching across the central European plain from Prussia into today's Soviet Union. Through the trading city of Danzig it grew rich on the export of grain to the cities of western Europe. But the country's wealth was concentrated in the hands of the landowners. The peasants were serfs, working up to six days a week on the lord's land. For the common people life was little more than a miserable existence.

Poland's decline began in the 17th century. In a struggle for domination of north-eastern Europe Poland lost to Sweden. For over a century the two countries fought each other. Swedish soldiers brought great destruction to central Poland: grain mills were destroyed, farms left empty. A third of Poland's population fled or were killed. The strain of war weakened the government, and the introduction of the *liberum veto* (i.e. the power to veto or prevent) made matters worse. By this laws had to be voted unanimously by members of the Diet (Polish parliament). The result was that few laws were passed, let alone enforced,

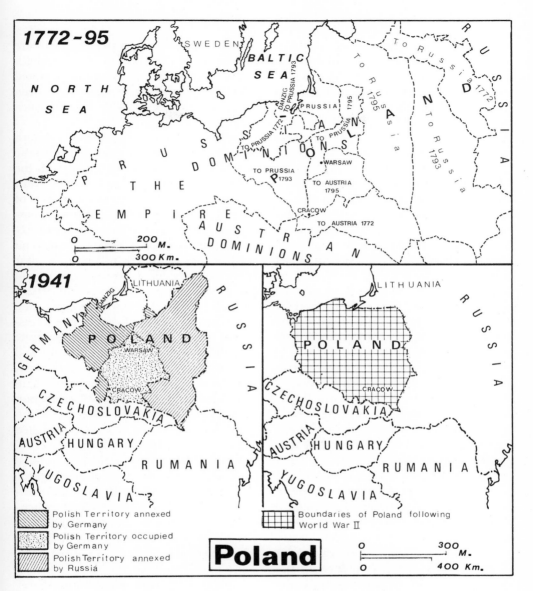

1772-95

NORTH SEA

SWEDEN

BALTIC SEA

N O R T H

S E A

TO RUSSIA 1793

TO RUSSIA 1772

R U S S I A

DANZIG TO PRUSSIA 1793

PRUSSIA 1795

TO RUSSIA 1795

TO RUSSIA 1793

TO PRUSSIA 1772

P R U S S I A

T H E

D O M I N I O N S

WARSAW

TO PRUSSIA 1793

TO AUSTRIA 1795

E M P I R E

A U S T R I A N

CRACOW

TO AUSTRIA 1772

D O M I N I O N S

0   200 M.
0   300 Km.

1941

LITHUANIA

DANZIG

GERMANY

P O L A N D

WARSAW

CRACOW

R U S S I A

CZECHOSLOVAKIA

AUSTRIA

HUNGARY

R U M A N I A

YUGOSLAVIA

LITHUANIA

P O L A N D

CRACOW

R U S S I A

CZECHOSLOVAKIA

AUSTRIA

HUNGARY

R U M A N I A

YUGOSLAVIA

Polish Territory annexed by Germany

Polish Territory occupied by Germany

Polish Territory annexed by Russia

Boundaries of Poland following World War II

Poland

0   300 M.
0   400 Km.

by the central government. Real power lay in the provinces with the landowners on their vast estates in eastern Poland. They were proud, quarrelsome and resented any interference in their local rule.

Although Sweden was defeated by Russia at Poltava in 1709, Poland was now surrounded by other hostile powers: Russia to the east, Turkey to the south, Brandenburg-Prussia and Austria to the west. Poland had no natural frontiers such as rivers or mountains. So, without an efficient central government and lacking proper defences against ambitious neighbours, the country was seized and partitioned by Russia, Austria and Prussia in three stages: 1772, 1793 and 1795.

Attempts by the Poles to resist or change this situation had little success. A revolt led by Kosciuszko in 1794 was crushed by the Russians. In 1815 a small Kingdom of Poland was re-created, but it was more of a Russian colony than a free Poland. Rebellions against harsh and foreign rule in 1830, 1846 and 1863 were failures.

Success seemed to come in the territorial settlements after World War I, when an independent Poland was established. Unfortunately the new state had two enemies. Germany resented the Polish Corridor which sliced German territory in two in order to allow Poland access to the Baltic. As well, the presence in Poland of many German-speaking peoples later gave Hitler an excuse to intervene in Polish affairs. To the east the traditional enmity with Russia was sharpened. Soviet Russia refused to accept Polish manufactures because the Poles had tried to seize land towards Kiev in the early, difficult days of Bolshevik rule. Deprived of a valuable market for her goods Poland remained poor.

In 1939 Hitler and Stalin signed a secret pact, and the German army invaded Poland and destroyed her forces. Russia and Germany then partitioned Poland between them. Britain had guaranteed Polish independence, and World War II developed from this. The Poles suffered terribly under Nazi oppression. Forced labour in concentration camps such as Auschwitz was common. Six million Polish citizens, many of them Jews, were killed during the Nazi occupation.

Poland was freed from this tyranny by Soviet forces in 1944. A premature rising of Poles in Warsaw against the Germans had been crushed, and with it was destroyed the future leadership of an independent Poland. Instead Poland came under Soviet influence. A communist government has ruled the country ever since with a frontier farther west on the Oder-Neisse line. Prosperity has slowly risen with the resumption of trade with Russia.

¶ GOLAWSKI, M. *Poland through the Ages: an outline of Polish history for young readers.* 1971

Polar expeditions: voyages to explore the areas at the northern and southern ends of the earth's axis. It should be noted that the North Pole is situated in frozen seas, while the South Pole is in the landmass of Antarctica.

North Pole. From the 16th to the early 19th centuries Polar expeditions in the Arctic regions were mainly concerned with the discovery of possible trade routes. Keen rivalry existed between the countries of northern Europe to find a northerly passage through to Cathay in order to expand their overseas interests. By the end of the 16th century it had become clear that the most likely Arctic route would be to the north-west, across the frozen wastes of Canada's northern territories. Thus began a series of expeditions to discover a North-West Passage (*see* separate entry) as a link between the Atlantic and Pacific Oceans. One of the earliest explorers was the English seaman Martin Frobisher who in 1576 caused a sensation in London by bringing back an Eskimo and a kayak (a canoe of sealskin stretched on a wooden framework).

In 1821 the British parliament offered handsome rewards for an attempt on the North Pole. Little was known of the immediate polar regions since medieval geographers supposed the existence of an Arctic ice-free sea. If this could be proved then the establishment of a northern passage by way of the Pole was a distinct possibility. In 1827 Sir Edward Parry sailed in HMS *Hecla* to a base in north-west Spitzbergen. Ice prevented further progress by sea. Parry then started off for the Pole hauling the two ship's boats on sledges. He got to within 435 miles [700 kilometres] but was forced to retire by fatigue. This was the first of many direct attempts on the North Pole by men of many nations. The North Magnetic Pole was discovered by the Englishman Sir James Clark Ross in 1831. A name in-

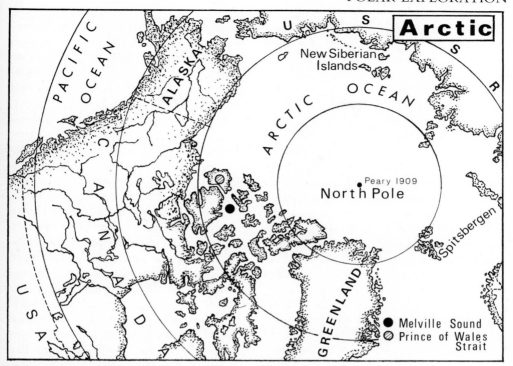

Arctic

- ● Melville Sound
- ◎ Prince of Wales Strait

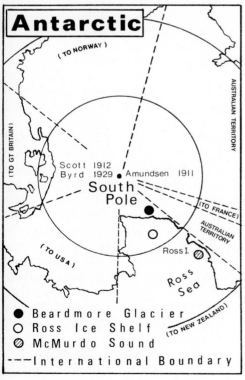

Antarctic

Scott 1912
Byrd 1929 ● Amundsen 1911
South Pole

Ross I.

- ● Beardmore Glacier
- ○ Ross Ice Shelf
- ◎ McMurdo Sound
- --- International Boundary

delibly written into the history of the North-West Passage is that of the English explorer Sir John Franklin. With his ships HMS *Erebus* and *Terror* he was trapped in the ice 1847-8. Many relief expeditions were organised but only relics were found. It was during one of these in 1850 that Captain Robert McClure in HMS *Investigator* proved the existence of the North-West Passage by sailing through the Prince of Wales Strait into Melville Sound.

By the 1850s the independent private explorer was making his appearance. The first American Arctic expeditions were sponsored by Henry Grinnell of New York. Their aim was to combine a search for Sir John Franklin with attempts to reach the Pole. The Americans Elisha Kane, Isaac Hayes and Charles Hall all made northerly discoveries in the Ellesmere Island direction. The British Arctic Expedition of 1875-6 under Sir George Nares went still further north.

733

In 1878 the Swedish A. E. Norden-skiöld in the *Vega* navigated the old North-East Passage (*see* separate entry) through to the Pacific. Further attempts on the North Pole were now made by the Norwegians Fridtjof Nansen and Otto Sverdrup. In 1893 Nansen in the specially designed *Fram* drove his ship hard into the pack ice north of the New Siberian Islands and waited for the north-west drift to carry him towards the Pole. After two years this was not achieved despite a north-west movement. Nansen then set off towards the Pole with sledges and dogs. He was forced to give up after getting within 224 miles [360.50 kilometres] – the nearest yet. The American Robert E. Peary eventually succeeded in planting the American flag on the North Geographical Pole on 16 April 1909. It was his third attempt.

South Pole. The exploration of the Antarctic presented a very different problem from that of the Arctic. The popular belief till at least the end of the 17th century was that a great fertile southern continent existed. Scientific observations made by the English navigator Captain James Cook did much to disprove this. He found no trace of the continent during his voyages in southern latitudes in the 1770s.

Early in the 19th century considerable interest in the Antarctic was aroused. British, French, German, American and Russian expeditions made important discoveries. By the end of the century the Royal Geographical Society, London, under its energetic president Sir Clements Markham, planned an expedition in which Captain Robert Falcon Scott was to explore the Ross Sea area. In 1902 Scott sailed in the *Discovery*. From Ross Island, where he wintered, sledge teams set out to explore the Ross Ice Shelf and mountainous land eastward.

In 1907 Sir Ernest Shackleton, who had accompanied Scott on the previous expedition, sailed in the *Nimrod* to carry on from where Scott had been forced to retire. Shackleton, with one party, succeeded in reaching the King Edward VII Plateau some 97 miles [156 kilometres] from the South Pole in 1909, while a second party under Professor Davis reached the position of the South Magnetic Pole.

In 1910 Captain Scott sailed in the *Terra Nova* and, arriving at Cape Evans, McMurdo Sound, in January 1911, landed ponies, dogs and two tracked vehicles. Depots were then established to the southward. After the Antarctic winter Scott, with three supporting parties, started across the Ice Shelf, up the Beardmore Glacier and across the polar plateau. He finally achieved the South Geographical Pole on foot with four men on 17 January 1912, only to find the Norwegian flag already flying there. Roald Amundsen, favouring the use of dog teams, beat Scott by little over a month, planting his flag on the Pole on 14 December 1911. Scott and his party during their homeward journey were overcome by fatigue and died in a snowed-up tent only eleven miles from one of their well-stocked depots.

Since the attainment of the two Poles on foot, mechanical transport of the 20th century began to reveal the strategic importance of the regions. Aircraft taking advantage of the shorter great circle route now fly over the North Pole. Meteorological bases are established in Greenland. The American submarine *Nautilus* achieved the first submarine crossing of the North Pole in 1958. International interest in the Antarctic mainly centres on the potentially rich mineral wealth of the region.

See colour section.

¶ BOWMAN, GERALD. *From Scott to Fuchs*. Cadet edn. 1960; KIRWAN, L. P. *The White Road*. 1959

Police: that department of the civil administration entrusted with the enforcement of law and order.

As the social units into which human beings organise themselves have become larger and more complicated, some more complex law-enforcing agency has become necessary. In Egypt, under the Ptolemies (the Macedonian kings who ruled from 304-30 BC), the police force was organised along the same lines as the army, with mounted desert patrols and detachments stationed in each of the thirty-six territorial divisions into which the country was divided. The ancient Greek city-states employed men to patrol the streets at night. Others were set the task of catching brigands. The Romans, expert organisers in many other ways, were surprisingly slow at developing a police system, a deficiency which may explain the many riots of the Roman mob. The Emperor Augustus (63 BC – AD 14) created three *cohortes urbanae* (city troops) in order to control the unruly element.

Anglo-Saxon communities were encouraged to police themselves. In Britain, citizens of each Hundred (an administrative unit, part of the shire) were held jointly responsible for a crime committed within its boundaries, unless the actual wrongdoer could be produced. This, in effect, turned everyone into an honorary policeman for, if the criminal were not forthcoming, the Hundred as a whole was penalised with a collective fine.

The London police force may be said to have had its beginning in 1285 when a statute of Watch and Ward (i.e. watch by night, ward by day) appointed watchmen to keep the peace in the City of London. Further Acts for this purpose followed in 1585, 1737 and 1777; yet still, at the end of the 18th century, England was a country infested with criminals of every kind.

A great step forward was taken in 1753 when Henry Fielding (1707-54), the famous novelist who was also a magistrate at the Bow Street police court in London, organised what was virtually the first English detective force, a small group of constables known familiarly as "Bow Street Runners" or "Robin Redbreasts" (from their scarlet waistcoats). The Bow Street Patrols, set up in 1782, were charged particularly with combating highway robbery.

Credit for the foundation of the modern British police force goes to Sir Robert Peel (1788-1850) who, as Home Secretary in 1829, persuaded parliament to agree to the formation of the Metropolitan Police. Six years later the Municipal Corporations Act set up police forces in the provinces.

In the United States, development of a police organisation followed much the same pattern as in England. The office of constable was created by many townships in the early Colonies and night-watchmen were established in the larger communities. Just as in England, the distinction appeared between "watch" by night and "ward" by day, the two forces often being of poor calibre, independently controlled and not working harmoniously together. In 1844 came a major step forward with the passing of a law in the New York State legislature for a unified "day and night police". With this lead, similar organisations soon followed in Boston, Chicago, New Orleans, Baltimore and other important cities.

Despotic or totalitarian governments use their police as tools of policy, as spies and as tormentors of their political opponents. Indeed, we have come to call such regimes "police states". Dictators, by declaring democratic opposition a crime, force it underground and turn honest men into conspirators. Louis XIV (1638-1715) established the Paris police force and used it in this way; and so, a century later, did Napoleon Bonaparte (1769-

1821), especially under the dreaded Joseph Fouché who, as minister of police, established a vast spy system. The Russian Tsars and various Communist régimes have had their Tcheka, Ogpu, NKVD, MVD – successive names for the same thing, a political police force. The Nazis' equivalents were the Gestapo and the SS.

¶ ASHLEY, BRIAN. *Law and Order.* 1971; SPEED, P. F. *Police and Prisons.* 1968

See also INDIVIDUAL ENTRIES.

Political parties (general): A political party is a group of people who have certain ideas and interests in common. It seeks power in a community to make decisions which will then become the laws of the country.

The common interests of a political party can develop from many things. A group may wish to protect its religious belief or its language from being swept away by rivals. Townspeople will find that their wish for cheap food conflicts with the countryman's desire for a high price for his produce. Those who make their living from rents paid on their property will wish for different priorities in law from those who work at a trade or profession for their living.

When one party has gained power, it may then get rid of its opponents by killing, imprisonment or exile. This has often taken place in dictatorships or one-party states. Senior army officers may use their control of military power to seize the government, but they are not properly called a political party. A fascist party argues that a regular choice of party programmes is inefficient; so it offers state-organised prosperity in exchange for a people's liberty of choice. The communist parties in soviet states refuse to allow other parties to form: they argue that these give opportunities to rivals who might be enemies of the working classes. The fairest system would allow each

group with a particular interest to have its own political party, and for all these to be represented in proportion to the votes given in an election. There would of course be many groups, and in these multi-party states politicians can discuss a problem with all opinions given a voice. But with all the talking it is very difficult to get quick decisions. Also, as one party rarely has an overall majority (that is, more than 50 per cent of the seats) it has to work with other parties to form a coalition. This easily breaks up when an important, controversial issue is discussed. So, instead of a country getting a fair government, it often gets poor, short-lived governments. Italy has had as many as seventy-three officially registered parties at one time.

In many countries a workable compromise has developed: the two-party system. Although different states give their own names to their parties, they can be roughly divided into political parties of the "right" wing and political parties of the "left" wing. Those of the right are conservatives who wish to preserve a particular society or at least allow only slow change; whilst the left are the radicals who want more or less rapid changes in support of their interests. These parties also have different ideas on how the wealth of a state should be produced and distributed. Those of the right support competition in commerce, and encourage the enterprise and judgment of individuals in the production of goods. If some people are more successful and wealthy than others, then this is the reward for their efforts. Parties of the left argue that modern economies are too complicated for individuals to control, and stress the importance of co-operation and planning by public authorities (such as nationalised industries). Any wealth produced should be shared out more equally; for instance, the highly success-

Landscape Painting: Meindert Hobbema's realistically rural *Avenue at Middelharnis* contrasts strongly with the more idealized classical setting in which Nicolas Poussin has placed his narrative painting, *Landscape with a Snake, below.*

PLATE 33

Mona Lisa, a portrait of Lisa Gherardini, the wife of Francesco del Giocondo, painted by **Leonardo da Vinci** in 1505. It has become the most famous portrait in the world and now hangs in the Louvre, Paris.

PLATE 34

The Battle of Lepanto, fought in 1571 in the Corinthian Gulf. The western forces under Don John of Austria are shown as they break through and smash the Turkish galleys, from a painting now in the National Maritime Museum, London.

The floodlit memorial to **Abraham Lincoln** in Washington DC, USA.

PLATE 35

Two of the many treasures of the **Louvre** in Paris: *above*, Giorgione's *Pastoral Concert* painted in 1510, and *below* one of Antony Van Dyck's portraits of his patron, Charles I of England, painted in 1635.

PLATE 36

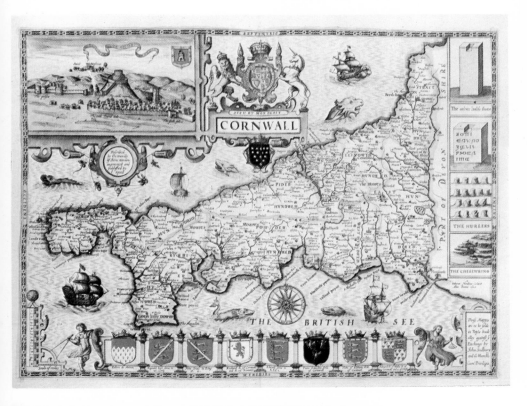

Map of Cornwall from *The Theatre of the Empire of Great Britain* drawn by John Speed in 1614.

The Pietà by **Michelangelo**, one of his most poignant and beautiful works. It is now in St Peter's, Rome.

PLATE 37

The so-called 'Mask of Agamemnon' found by Heinrich Schliemann at **Mycenae**. At the bottom of a deep shaft grave Schliemann found the preserved bodies of three princes clad in breastplates, and masks of beaten gold.

John Milton in his early twenties.

Moorish architecture at Cordova, Spain, 8th century AD.

PLATE 38

Wallpaper design by **William Morris**, 19th century.

PLATE 39

Mural painting: *above,* Christ's entrance in Jerusalem, one of Giotto's murals at Padua. *Below left,* the Painted Hall at Greenwich by Sir John Thornhill. *Below right, Portrait of America* by Diego Rivera, one of the great 20th-century Mexican masters of the art of mural painting.

PLATE 40

Above, the beauties of a **New England** 'fall' in Massachusetts. *Below left*, one of the many portraits of Napoleon I, by Jaques Louis David.

Norway: the lighthouse island of Grip, *above,* and Loen Lake *below*.

PLATE 41

'Thy staggering does thee no good, thou must on to Golgotha', a scene from the Passion Play enacted at **Oberammergau** every ten years, *above*. *Below,* two of Edmund Dulac's illustrations for *The Rubaiyat* of **Omar Khayyam**.

PLATE 42

Opera: two productions, contrasting the more traditional approach to Verdi's *Don Carlos, left,* with the experimental treatment of Peter Maxwell Davies's *Taverner, right.*

The **Orsini** family as shown in Antoniazzo Romano's painting of the meeting of Gentile Virginio Orsini and Pietro dei Medici.

PLATE 43

Ottoman Empire: *above,* the blue Mosque in Istanbul; *above right,* the interior of Hagia Sophia; *middle right,* Isnik tiles in the Topkapi Palace; and *below right,* a beautifully decorated room in the Topkapi Palace. *Below,* a manuscript showing the Tulip Festival, now in the Topkapi Library.

PLATE 44

Oxford: *above,* New College and *above right,* Merton College. *Right,* the Chiesa de San Giorgio in Venice by **Andrea Palladio**. The Villa Rotonda at Vicenza, *below,* is the supreme example of Palladian domestic architecture.

PLATE 45

The Papacy: *top,* **Pius IX** blessing the troops outside the walls of Gaeta, 1849. *Above,* the Ecumenical Council in procession through St Peter's Square, 1967. *Below,* the Venetian painter, Vittore Carpaccio, painted a scene of papal pageantry in his series 'Details from the Life of St Ursula', 16th century.

The conversion of **St Paul** from a 14th-century manuscript.

PLATE 46

Persia: *above,* a piece of brocaded twill tissue, 17th century; *left,* dervishes from an early manuscript; and *below,* stone carvings at Persepolis which have been preserved by sand dunes.

PLATE 47

Above left, Harlequin by **Pablo Picasso**. *Above right*, a painting in his Cubist style of a bather playing with a ball. *Below, The Adoration of the Magi* by **Piero della Francesca**.

PLATE 48

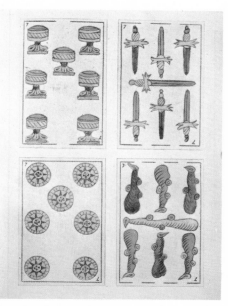

Playing cards: *left,* 15th-century French cards showing knaves known as valets. *Right,* 17th-century Spanish cards – the marks of the suits are represented by caps, swords, money and clubs.

The House of Plantagenet: *left,* 'King John hunting from a contemporary manuscript in the British Museum.

Pocahontas (Matoaka), duaghter of Powhatan, Emperor of Virginia, and wife of the Englishman, John Rolfe, painted in 1616.

PLATE 49

Polar exploration: *above*, an abandoned hut in the Antarctic; *below left, The Fram*, the specially designed ship in which **Fridtjof Nansen** explored the north polar ice pack in 1893–6. It was later used by **Roald Amundsen** in his successful expedition to the South Pole.

Pompeii: *right*, a fresco from the preserved wall of a villa.

PLATE 50

Portrait painting: *above, The Children of Charles I,* a formal royal portrait, by Antony Van Dyck, 17th century. *Below,* **Rembrandt's** portrait of his son, Titus, 17th century, and *below right,* **Francis Bacon's** character study of Isabel Rawsthorne, painted in 1968.

PLATE 51

Queen Anne Style, architecture: *above,* Clarence House, Essex, built in 1715. *Below,* the Royal Pavilion at Brighton, **Regency** architecture at its most exuberant.

PLATE 52

Rembrandt Harmenszoon van Rijn: one of his many self portraits as an old man, c. 1666.

Peter Paul Rubens: detail of his *Self Portrait with Isabella Brandt*.

PLATE 53

Romanesque: *above,* the cloisters of the 12th-century monastery of Santillana, Spain. *Below,* Notre Dame de la Grande. Poitiers, France, 12th century.

Rome: the Castel Sant' Angelo seen from the River Tiber.

PLATE 54

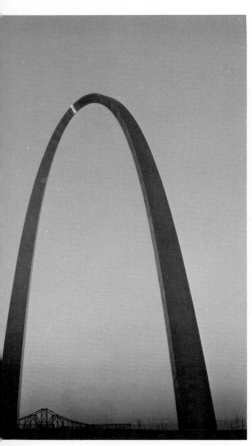

Sweden: Hällevcksstrandon on the west coast.

The Gateway Arch, St Louis, Missouri, USA, built by the Finnish architect, **Eero Saarinen**.

Below, Drottningholm Court Palace, near Stockholm, Sweden.

PLATE 55

Spain: the Mosque of Santa Maria la Blanca. *Above left,* Toledo in the Almohade style, 13th century. *Above right,* the Alcazar, Segovia, 15th century. *Below left,* a detail of *The Infanta Margherita d'Austria* by Velasquez, 17th century. *Below right,* Francesco Goya's portrait, *The Osuna Family,* 1788.

PLATE 56

Switzerland: *above left,* a view of the snow-covered town of Gstaad. *Above right,* the **Taj Mahal** at Agra, India. *Right* and *below,* two of the works of **Thomas Telford** – the aquaduct at Pont-y-Cysylltau, Wales, and the Menai Bridge.

PLATE 57

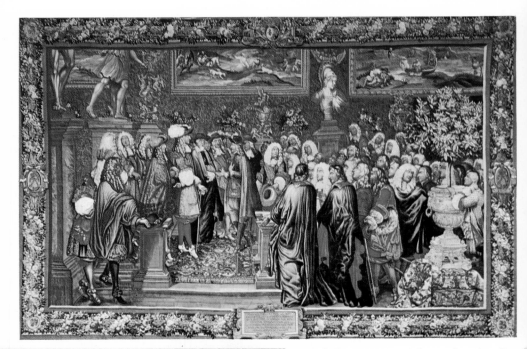

A Gobelin **tapestry,** *above,* showing Louis XIX of France receiving the Spanish Ambassador. *Left,* detail of the *Bear and Boar Hunt* tapestry, Flemish, 15th century. *Below,* Graham Sutherland's *Christ in Glory* tapestry in Coventry Cathedral.

PLATE 58

The eighteenth-century French philosopher, **Arouet de Voltaire**.

Vatican: a jewel-encrusted **cross**, part of the treasure of St Peter.

The formal gardens and facade of the palace of **Versailles**.

PLATE 59

Venice: the Grand Canal, *above left*. Examples of **Venetian Art:** *above*, Titian's portrait called *La Bella*; *left*, *The Last Supper* by Paolo Veronese; *below*, *St Mark Preaching* by Giovanni Bellini shows formal 'idealized architecture in Saint Mark's Square, contrasting with the more realistic treatment of Guaidi and Canaletto.

PLATE 60

The two great 18th-century masters of **Venetian** 'city-scape' painting were Antonio Canale, called Canaletto, and Francesco Guardi. *Above*, Guardi's painting of the **Doge** being carried through St Mark's Square by gondoliers. *Below*, Canaletto fills the harbour with gaily decorated boats during a religious festival.

PLATE 61

Diego de Silva Velasquez: *above left,* an informal portrait of his manservant, Juan de Pareja, while the painting of the Infanta Margherita, *above right,* is one of many formal studies of the Royal Family. *Below,* the Roman amphitheatre at **Verona**, Italy.

PLATE 62

Volcanoes: *above,* the eruption of Kirkjufell on the Icelandic island of Heimaey, in 1973. *Left,* the steaming crater of Mount Aso, Japan. *Below,* the eruption of Stromboli, a volcanic island off the coast of Italy.

PLATE 63

Wedgwood: *above,* white jasper bowl and covered tea-pot with green background, decorated with reliefs of domestic employment, 1786. *Below,* 'Frightened Horse plaque', in black basalt, designed by Stubbs. *Right,* black-and-white jasper vases with classical scenes, 1790.

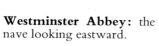

Westminster Abbey: the nave looking eastward.

PLATE 64

ful should be taxed heavily in order to provide welfare services for anyone in special need.

Thus parties of the right tend to attract property-owners, industrialists and those in jobs with great security. Parties of the left tend to attract the less well-off in a community, those skilled and unskilled manual workers whose jobs are not always secure.

Political parties, Britain: When there is an election for Parliament nowadays nearly every candidate claims to be a member of one of the three great political parties: Conservative, Labour or Liberal. This has not always been so. In the early days of parliament there were no parties. In the 13th century, when the king wanted money, he called representatives of the Church, the counties and the boroughs to meet him. Such meetings of parliament were held simply to carry out the king's wishes. As time passed, the powerful barons did not always agree with the king and by the time of Henry VIII (reigned 1509-47) there were differences about money, religion and other matters. Later, when Charles I (reigned 1625-49) claimed divine right and tried to exact taxes without the approval of Parliament at all, the members were driven to take sides for or against the king. After the Revolution of 1688, there were two main groups, or *parties*: the Tories, who supported the king, and the Whigs who wanted the king to be controlled by Parliament (*see* TORY and WHIG). But the Whigs and the Tories in the 18th century were not political parties as we know them. Both groups represented the rich and powerful: the great mass of the people had no "party" at all.

During the 19th century changes were brought about in both parties by two great statesmen: William Ewart Gladstone (1809-98) and Benjamin Disraeli (1804-81). Gladstone, who began his political life as a Tory, later became a Whig and, as its leader, changed that party into what later became known as the Liberal Party. Under Disraeli's leadership, the Tory Party became known as the Conservative Party. The Conservatives wanted to keep things as they were, while the Liberals aimed at improving the life of the mass of the people.

During the 19th century, as more people won the right to vote, they thought of themselves as either Conservatives or Liberals. When there was an election, the party with most Members of Parliament formed the government, either Conservative or Liberal. Then in 1900 a meeting was held in London of men who believed that there should be working men in parliament to speak for all working people, the largest class in the country. This was the beginning of a new party, the Labour Party. In the general election of 1906 the Liberals won a huge majority over the Conservatives, but twenty-nine Labour candidates were also elected. Although the Liberal government passed laws to improve the housing, health and education of the people and to relieve poverty and sickness in old age, it gradually lost the support of the mass of voters. Meanwhile, the Labour Party won more seats in parliament, until it took the place of the Liberal Party as the official opposition to the Conservatives. In 1924 the Labour Party, only twenty-four years old, won the general election, and its leader Ramsay MacDonald became prime minister for a short period. Since then the government has been either Conservative or Labour. The Liberals still have a small number of members of parliament, and various other minority groups, such as the Scottish National Party, occasionally win a seat, but most electors vote either for a Labour or a Conservative candidate.

The pattern of government by the strongest party numerically has occasionally been broken in times of crisis by the formation of coalitions designed to use the best abilities of all parties.

Political parties, USA: Loosely organised political parties existed in the American colonies from the latter part of the 17th century onwards. Chief among them were the Tories and Whigs, who with the coming of the American Revolution came to be known respectively as Loyalists and Patriots. Later the controversy over the Federal Constitution produced two parties, one in favour of, the other opposed to, the adoption of the Constitution. It should, however, be stressed that they were scarcely organised and disciplined in the modern sense. During this time, and for much of the early national period, real political organisations existed only in the states, and even these tended to be little more than factions springing up around some forceful and colourful personality.

National parties may be said to have come into being when Jefferson, finding himself in disagreement with the policies of George Washington's administration, resigned from the Cabinet in order to build up an organisation which would support his own ambitions for the presidency. Thus perished the hope of the Founding Fathers that all shades of opinion should be represented within the administration itself. Henceforth, competition for the presidency, as well as for other elective offices, tended to centre not on individuals but on candidates supported by rival organisations, representing the consensus of their membership. After 1832 candidates were selected by conventions of the parties. The multiplication of Federal offices (jobs) and the practice of distributing them as rewards to the party faithful – a practice which

grew up during the democratic revolt of the Jacksonian period – immeasurably increased the importance of parties. This "spoils system", indeed, gave the party system its enduring vitality. From 1789 to 1824 the Federalists, who in many cases were the original champions of the Constitution, opposed the Republicans (Jeffersonians), who were the heirs, in terms of ideas, of those who had opposed it. The Federalist party was supported principally by commercial and industrial elements, the Republicans by the agricultural elements.

Following Jefferson's election in 1800 the Federalists went downhill steadily; in 1820 they made no nomination for the Presidency. Shunning at first the title "democratic" as smacking of the French Revolution, the party of Jefferson came to be known later as the Democratic-Republican party. Toward the end of this period during the so-called "era of good feeling", which was really an era of intense personal politics, voters generally accepted the Republican label but followed various leaders: Adams, Clay, and Calhoun; Crawford, Clinton and Jackson. From 1842 to 1860 the two principal parties were the Whigs, who accepted the Federalist tradition and were supported by the same classes plus the rising manufacturing element then chiefly centred in New England, and the Democratic elements, no longer fearful of being called by that name. Fused by Jackson, these were powerfully reinforced by Western settlers and newly enfranchised labourers in the older parts of the country. Minor political groups, some of them confined to one or a few states, made their presence felt during this period, among them the Anti-Masons, Barnburners, Hunkers, Cotton Whigs, and the Know Nothing Party. By far the most successful of these were the Liberal party and its successor, the Free Soil party, out of which grew the modern Republican party – this was in fact the only instance in American history where a third party emerged to become one of the two major contenders for power. With the rise of the slavery issue, party lines were shattered; by 1856, because of this issue, the Whig party was finished and the Democratic party hopelessly split. From 1862 to the present day the two great political parties have been the Republicans and the Democrats.

Between 1860 and 1876 the major political controversies concerned war and reconstruction; subsequently issues of dispute have been mainly economic in character, though during the 1960s Civil Rights and American military involvement in South-East Asia have loomed large. Since 1862 there have been numerous "third parties". Prohibitionists nominated their first presidential candidate in 1872; Greenbackers gave expression to agrarian discontent, and they were succeeded by the Populists in the 1890s. The unrest amongst industrial workers led to the formation of the Union-Labour, Socialist Labour, Social Democratic, Socialist and Communist parties. Twice during this period the Republicans suffered heavy defections. In 1912 Theodore Roosevelt resigned his membership and formed the Progressive Party. And in 1924 Robert LaFollette led an agrarian revolt of Independent Progressives. In recent times the only major "third party" candidacies to attract a significant number of votes have been those of Strom Thurmond campaigning for "states rights" and Governor George Wallace on a "white supremacy" platform.

Poll tax: tax per head of population. Its first appearance in England was in 1377, when a groat per head was levied on clergy and laity. The poll tax of 1380 was a direct cause of Wat Tyler's rebellion in the following year. The device was intermittently used until the 18th century. Perhaps its most controversial use was in the Southern States of America, from approximately 1890 to 1920, as a means of excluding the Negro elector by requiring payment of such a tax before a vote was allowed. This device was declared illegal in both federal and state elections in 1964 and 1966.

Polo, Marco (1254-1324): Venetian traveller and author. When Marco Polo returned to Venice with his father and uncle, after twenty-five years of adventurous journeys in the mysterious East, their relatives failed to recognise the travel-stained wanderers in their outlandish garb. They laughed at Marco's wonderful stories of million-peopled cities, innumerable jewels and vast treasures, dubbing him "Messer Marco Milione". The Polos invited the doubters to a sumptuous banquet. When their guests were seated, they entered dressed in robes of crimson satin. During the meal they discarded these for crimson damask, then for velvet. Finally, Marco ripped open their old Tartar jackets and showered the guests with jewels.

Marco Polo sets out on his travels from Venice.

One of Marco's journeys, occupying four years, brought him to the court of Kublai Khan in China, where he was given an official appointment. His duties took him to Tibet, Burma, Laos, Java, Japan, even Siberia. He dictated an invaluable record of his travels and impressions to a scribe in about 1299. The original manuscript of this "Book of Marco Polo", written in rough French, is probably the one in the National Library of Paris, though more than eighty other manuscripts are known.

¶ BRETT, BERNARD. *The Travels of Marco Polo.* 1971

See also KUBLAI KHAN.

Polynesia: eastern division of Oceania (*see* separate entry). The Polynesians now inhabit the easternmost of the Pacific islands, such as Samoa and Hawaii. They were already a civilised people when they left their original homes on the Indo-Chinese coast of Asia. In the 6th century AD, using outrigger canoes and navigating by the stars, they spread rapidly east across the Pacific and south to New Zealand.

Their islands were visited by the Spanish sailor Pedro Fernandez de Quiros in the 17th century and explored thoroughly by Captain Cook in the 18th century. In 1797 the first missionaries arrived and not only converted the Polynesians to Christianity but also taught some of them to read. *See* PACIFIC OCEAN for map.

Pompeii: town in Italy on the Bay of Naples, destroyed in an eruption of Mount Vesuvius in AD 79. The same disaster overtook Herculaneum (*see* separate entry); but, whereas the latter town had retained much of the character of its Greek origin, Pompeii had been largely rebuilt by the Romans after an earthquake sixteen years before, and its remains, which have been intermittently explored since 1748, teach us much about a Roman provincial town. It served as a market for the produce of its fertile countryside, a port for Mediterranean trade and a centre for certain specialised industries. All this was buried under the lava for nearly seventeen centuries.

The letter-writer Pliny the Younger (*c.* 61–*c.* 114) has left us an account of the eruption, in which his uncle Pliny the Elder perished as the result of his own scientific curiosity.

See colour section.

¶ BRION, M. *Pompeii and Herculaneum.* 1960; TAYLOR, DUNCAN. *Pompeii and Vesuvius.* 1969

Pompey (Gnaeus Pompeius Magnus, 106–48 BC): Roman politician and general. He was born of a family of middle rank, to which the highest offices of state were normally denied; but the turbulent years of the 1st century BC, when the republican constitution was in its final decline, enabled him to use his military successes, particularly in the East, to play a dominant part in politics at home. But a rival was at hand in the person of Gaius Julius Caesar (*see* separate entry), with whom he at first collaborated. Later, however, civil war broke out between them, resulting in the defeat of Pompey (9 August 48) at Pharsalus in northern Greece. He fled to Egypt and was stabbed to death as he stepped ashore.

Pondicherry: town, seaport and district on the west coast of India south of Madras, formerly the principal French settlement in southern India. Founded by François Martin in 1674, it was taken by the Dutch in 1693, to be returned, with much improved fortifications, in 1699. It was captured by the English general Sir Eyre Coote in 1761, and given back with fortifications destroyed and a limit imposed on the size of its armed forces, in 1763. Thereafter it was occupied by the British at the outbreak of each war with France, in 1778, 1793 and 1803, to be restored on each occasion on the return of peace. Pondicherry was united with India in 1954.

"Poor whites": people at the bottom of white society in the southern USA. A relatively small group, they lived in dilapidated huts and were plagued by hookworm, pellagra, malaria and tuberculosis. The women bore the brunt of earning a livelihood while their menfolk loafed around chewing home-grown tobacco and drinking locally distilled rot-gut ("moonshine"). The poor whites, mainly illiterate, were reluctant to work for their subsistence as they thought that it would reduce them to the level of the Negroes, whom they despised. Their successors survive in diminishing numbers, but the term is not found very acceptable in modern America.

Port-of-Spain: capital of Trinidad and Tobago. One of the finest towns in the West Indies, it has two cathedrals, impressive public buildings and a safe, sheltered harbour that has made it the state's chief commercial centre.

Portrait painting: the art of painting people, especially their faces and from life. Portrait painting has always presented peculiar difficulties for the artist. On the one hand, a portrait must be a likeness, a true record of the person portrayed. On the other, when, as often happens, the portrait is specially commissioned, the intended subject wishes, not unnaturally, to be shown in the most flattering light. Only a truly great artist can reconcile these two conflicting elements with a third – the demands of his own genius. A great portrait is something more than a successful representation of a human being, whether glorified or shown, as Oliver Cromwell demanded of the painter Lely, "warts and all".

The first portrait painter known to history was Polygnotus (c. 475–447 BC), a Greek who introduced portraits into his murals on public buildings. Unfortunately none of his work, nor that of any other ancient Greek painter known to us by name, survives. Apelles (4th century BC), by reputation the greatest of them, was portrait painter to Alexander the Great (356–323 BC). By royal edict no one else was allowed to paint the great man. We can only guess, from a description that has come down to us of a portrait of Alexander holding a thunderbolt as if he were Zeus himself, that Apelles, like many court painters since, had to make concessions to his clients' vanity.

Modern portrait painting dates from the Renaissance. Medieval Christian man was taught to despise his body as a receptacle of sin, doomed to decay. Not until the 13th century did this joyless attitude begin to change. By the 15th century painters like Domenico Ghirlandaio (1449–94) in Florence, and Hugo van der Goes (c. 1440–82) in Flanders, were introducing into religious pictures portraits of the men who had commissioned them. Ghirlandaio went further, including portraits of well-known Florentines in many of his large-scale compositions.

Portrait painting proper soon came into its own. These early Renaissance portraits are among the best ever painted, full of the most delicate observation of character and, above all, honest. If anything, some of the Flemish and German painters of the period, in their search for truth, tended to go to the other extreme: their sitters cannot all have been so ugly.

Among the great Italian portrait painters may be mentioned Giovanni Bellini (c. 1430–1516), Giovanni Moroni (1520–78) and, greatest of all, Tiziano Vecelli, known as Titian (c. 1489–1576). During his long life Titian painted popes, doges, kings, dukes and duchesses with a splendid enjoyment. His portraits, while in the grand manner, are full of humanity.

To the greatest of the German portrait painters of the time, Hans Holbein (1497–1543), we owe our conception of what Henry VIII and his court looked like, reminding us that portrait painters are – or were, before photography – pictorial historians. We see the past through their eyes.

Sometimes we have to make corrections. Thus, we know from other sources that King Charles I, for all his undoubted good qualities, was not the impeccably noble monarch so often painted by Anthony Van Dyck (1594–1641). This Flemish painter settled in England and was knighted for his service.

The Spanish royal family was apparently less eager for flattery or more conscious of the deference due to genius. Diego Velasquez (1599–1660) painted the court as if it consisted of men and women no different from the common run of humanity; while, more than a hundred years later, another great Spanish painter, Francisco de Goya (1746–1828), depicted the royal family of his day almost as a collection of nincompoops.

Rembrandt van Rijn (1606–69), the Dutch painter, had, fortunately for his art if not his pocket, no such royal patronage. His incomparable portraits, full of humour, wisdom and the wounds of experience, have been called "a continous self-portrait".

England for centuries favoured foreign above native artists. Not until the 18th century did a distinctive English school of painting develop. In Thomas Gainsborough (1727–88) and Sir Joshua Reynolds (1723–92) it included two portrait painters of superb quality.

The invention of photography has undoubtedly narrowed the field for portrait painters: yet there will always be room for a view of humanity filtered through the eye and mind rather than a camera lens. Perhaps it is due to the camera taking over the task of literal presentation that for many modern artists – for example, Pablo Picasso (1881–1973) and Francis Bacon (b. 1910) – a portrait has become more a point of departure than an end in itself. *See colour section.*

See also INDIVIDUAL ENTRIES.

Port Royal: careening place on a sandy spit enclosing Kingston Harbour, Jamaica. (Careening was the tilting of a ship so that her bottom could be scraped clean of barnacles, etc.) It was developed by the British after 1655, fortified in 1656 and used by buccaneers and traders. It was partly submerged in an earthquake in 1692, survivors moving to Kingston. It was rebuilt as a dockyard in 1735 and was the base for the English Admiral Vernon's squadron, 1739–42. The harbour was capacious, but its approaches were difficult. Boats had to go seven miles [11 kilometres] for provisions and twelve [19 kilometres] for water, it was commanded from windward by the French in Hispaniola, and it was periodically scourged by hurricanes, notably in 1744.

Portugal: nation-state on the Atlantic coast of the Iberian peninsula, 350 miles [563 kilometres] from north to south and between 70 and 136 [112 and 218 kilometres] from east to west, with mountains in the north and a sandy plain in the south. Until the 12th century the history of Portugal and Spain cannot be separated. The first settlers were probably African in origin. Phoenicians, Greeks and Carthaginians came by sea to trade; Celts came by land to settle in fortified hill-villages. The Romans occupied Portugal from 206 BC to AD 409, and left roads, cities and their language. Other invaders brought the heavy wheeled plough, a law code and a form of Christianity. The Muslims invaded from Africa in 693 and, though some Visigoths held out in the northern mountains, the majority accepted Moorish rule and gained from them knowledge of seafaring, rotation of crops, grafting of fruit trees and irrigation by water-wheel.

The first step in reconquest from the Moors was taken by Alfonso of Castile-Leon (1072-1109), who gave the County of Portugal as dowry with his daughter to Henry of Burgundy. Their son Alfonso Henriques took the title of King in 1139 and was recognised as independent in 1143. By 1267 Portugal had driven out the Moors and attained her present frontiers. To encourage settlers on reconquered lands the kings granted *fueros*, or charters, to those who would establish walled towns, and any freeman could claim unoccupied land "with trumpet and royal flag". The military Order of Aviz and the Cistercian monks both played a large part in the reconquest and were granted large estates. A later king, Alfonso II (1211-23), was excommuni-

cated for trying to recover part of these estates. King Denis (1279-1325) earned the nickname "the Farmer" for his efforts to develop his kingdom. He drained swamps, developed a fleet and a system of marine insurance, founded Lisbon University (moved to Coimbra in 1537), and formed the military Order of Christ out of the disbanded Knights Templar. His French wife Isabel scattered an apronful of pine cones from Provence on the wind-swept dunes and started the royal forests.

Portuguese independence was repeatedly threatened by the growing power of Castile. In 1385 John of Castile claimed Portugal on his marriage to Beatrice, heiress of Portugal. Clergy and nobles supported him, but the merchants supported the Master of Avis, an illegitimate prince who, as John I, founded the dynasty which built the overseas empire. English archers helped him win the battle of Aljubarrota against the Castilian party. Portuguese independence was again saved when, in 1469, Isabella of Castile married Ferdinand of Aragon rather than the

Portugal: left, the Praia da Rocha, in the Algarve. Right, the Tower of Belem on the River Tagus.

elderly King of Portugal. Castile triumphed when Sebastian, King of Portugal, leading an ill-advised crusade in Morocco in 1578, lost 8,000 men and was killed himself. Philip II of Spain became King of Portugal, and from 1580 to 1640 Portugal was ruled by Spanish kings. Her empire was exposed to Dutch attacks, until the house of Braganza re-established an independent Portuguese kingdom.

The Portuguese empire in Africa, the East Indies and Brazil, built up between 1420 and 1510 with the help of Jewish and German mapmakers and Italian navigators, brought little good to Portugal. It enriched the king and freed him from dependence on the *Cortes* (parliament), but it lured the Portuguese away from agriculture into plunder of the Indies and concealed from them, for a time, the consequences of expelling the Jews and surrendering education to the Jesuits. Portugal thus began the decline which has left her with the lowest standard of living in western Europe.

Links with Flanders and England had been forged as early as the 12th century and, in the great struggles against Louis XIV, Napoleon and the Kaiser over a period of nearly 300 years, Portugal remained true to the English alliance. She lost her eastern empire to the Dutch in the 17th century, but the discovery of gold in Brazil sustained her until Brazil became independent in 1825. Though she retains her African colonies, Portugal has not restored vitality to her economy. Neither the constitutional monarchy set up in 1820 nor the democratic republic of 1910 could prevent strikes, disorder and budget deficits. In 1926 a military dictatorship was established which soon surrendered power to Dr Oliviera Salazar (1889–1970), a professor of economics, who balanced the budget and restored order by a firm but moderate dictatorship.

See SPAIN for map.

Postal history: the first mention of postal services in Europe is attributed to the Venetians in the 10th century. Early in the 14th century in Venice, well organised postal services were operated which eventually extended throughout the Venetian Empire, to Constantinople and to the Balkans. About this time, too, Omodeo Tasso from the Lombardy city of Bergamo "couriered" mails throughout Italy and into neighbouring countries. The family of Tasso became general superintendents of the posts of the Holy Roman Empire under the German emperor and, having been ennobled, added the surname of Torre to their name. Moving to Germany the family changed its name to Thurn and Taxis. This famous postal family controlled and organised the posts in nearly all of Europe for six centuries until 1867.

Postal services in Great Britain developed in a gradual and haphazard way. In order to send a letter in the 15th century it was necessary to find someone who could be trusted, usually one's own servant or a friend. Often the common carrier who went from town to town with goods, sometimes a traveller, or maybe a soldier going in the right direction, could be relied on to deliver a letter. Royal letters and letters of state were carried by the Royal Messengers who rode to all parts of the kingdom. Innkeepers along the main routes were compelled to keep ready a change of horses so that the messengers had no delay. Sir Brian Tuke in the reign of King Henry VIII was in charge of this service, with the title of Master of the Posts.

In 1635 the first attempt to establish a postal service for ordinary people was made by Thomas Witherings when a "running post", i.e. a postman on foot, was organised between cities and towns, and for the first time a system of postal rates was tabled based on mileage. The postman carried a horn to announce his arrival. On the longer journeys he rode on horseback. In 1657 the Post Office was established by an Act of Parliament, and reconfirmed on the Restoration in 1660. This important Act is known as the Post Office charter. Date stamps were first introduced in 1661 by the Postmaster General, Henry Bishopp. Private enterprise in the postal services, although forbidden, continued in many ways. The most famous of all was the venture by William Dockwra and Robert Murray, who organised the London Penny Post in 1680. This splendid service operated with hourly collections and deliveries within and around the cities of London and Westminster. Triangular shaped marks denoting ONE PENNY PAID were stamped on the letters – the first paid stamps. The government took over this private post in 1682 and maintained it on much the same lines, but less efficiently, until the end of the 18th century.

In 1711, by an Act of Queen Anne, the General Post Office established post offices in British Dominions and possessions overseas, with rates of postage tabled to and from London. Benjamin Franklin, the former postmaster of Philadelphia, was made a Deputy Postmaster General of the American Post Office – a branch of the GPO. Postal services were eventually organised and extended throughout all the North American colonies, Canada and the British West Indies. Subsequently mail services by government-subsidised packet boats and the East India Company were arranged to most places in the world, but privately owned merchant ships also played a big part in the carriage of mail overseas.

An important development was the carriage of mail by coach. The first mail coach carrying passengers and mail, attended by an armed guard, set out from Bristol to London on 2 August 1784. This

The Bristol, Bath and London coach collecting mail without halting.

was the start of a romantic period in British Post Office history, with the mail coach playing a vital part. Because of the able administration of Sir Francis Freeling, Secretary of the Post Office from 1798–1836, greatly improved postal services were now maintained throughout the kingdom. By the 1820s Penny Post Offices were functioning in nearly every city, town and village throughout the entire United Kingdom. This wonderful service enabled letters to be sent for one penny within a prescribed distance. At the same time, however, general postal rates between places were greatly increased, making it sometimes impossible for those of limited means to send a letter. Robert Wallace, MP for Greenock, attacked the Post Office in 1833 for the excessively high postage rates. His complaints and argument were followed through by a former schoolmaster, Rowland Hill, who proved that a letter could be profitably carried anywhere in the United Kingdom for less than a penny. Organised agitation and petitions for postal reforms took place during 1837–39 which ultimately resulted in a uniform postal rate of one penny per half-ounce letter coming into force on 10 January 1840. The man responsible for the clever propaganda and for much of the organi-

745

sation for these postal reforms was Henry Cole, an ardent supporter of Rowland Hill's plan. On 6 May 1840 the world's first adhesive postage stamps, the famous Penny Black and Twopenny Blue stamps – as well as pre-paid pictorial envelopes

An envelope bearing the famous "Penny Black" stamp.

and covers designed by William Mulready, RA – were available to the public.

One other reform of importance abolished the centuries-old privilege of "franking", whereby the letters of members of parliament as well as others of high rank were carried free of postage. The person's signature on the envelope or outside of the letter served as the frank (or free) mark.

With the introduction of uniform penny postage, envelopes were now popularly used for the first time; previously only those with the privilege of franking were able to use them freely, for their use automatically incurred a higher rate of postage.

Because of the new penny post, people who previously could not afford the expense of sending a letter were now able to do so. As well, greetings cards, especially Valentines, were now sent in huge quantities; in later years the Post Office had to cope with this annual flood of mail by employing extra staff.

In the same year, 1840, on 4 July Samuel Cunard started a regular line of mail steamers between Liverpool, England, and Boston, USA. This wonderful service

was responsible in later years for competition with other maritime nations, particularly the USA, for using reliable and fast steamships to carry the mail between Europe and North America. As a consequence of this, the coveted "Blue Riband" of the Atlantic came about.

The momentous postal reform giving a uniform penny post made Britain the envy of the world, so that other countries attempted to follow her example, though not all were able to offer such improved services with such greatly reduced postal rates. In the USA, where a postal system based on the British pattern had been inherited since the War of Independence, great agitation took place for postal reforms during the 1840s and 1850s. Reductions in rates came about slowly, and it was not until 1 October 1883 that a uniform two cent rate (the equivalent of a penny) was established. Certain loopholes in the US Postal Laws, however, allowed many private posts to be organised. These usually occurred where the government itself maintained no service or facilities for the carriage of mail. Consequently, in the far West many of the express companies contracted to carry the US Mail, a very well-known one being that of Wells, Fargo.

The American Overland Mail attacked by Indians on its way across the prairies, 1860.

In 1846 a series of events brought to England an American philanthropist, Elihu Burritt, known as the "learned blacksmith" because of his humble up-bringing and self-acquired education in the town of New Britain, Connecticut. This remarkable man organised a number of international movements from his offices in London and was concerned with Universal Peace, the Brotherhood of Man, and with a campaign for a cheap ocean postage which he started in 1847. His ideas for an ocean penny postage were discussed by the governments of the

London Letter Box No. 2.

United States and Great Britain. His campaign led to a reduction in the overseas postage rates and paved the way for the founding of the International Postal Union on 1 July 1875. By this Union, a uniform rate of postage was settled for all member nations. This is still in force today and is one of the most important international organisations of our time.

On 1 October 1869 the world's first post-card for a short written message was introduced by the Austrian Post Office. Great Britain followed a year later, on 1 October 1870, with a postcard rated at a halfpenny postage.

In December 1898 an Imperial Penny Post was introduced for certain countries within the British Empire. A few years later, with the collaboration of the American Postmaster General, the Hon. John Wanamaker, a Penny Post between Great Britain and the United States came about on 8 October 1908. This agreement remained in force (as the domestic rate between the two countries) until the 1950s, when it was abolished.

Experimental airmail services for special events took place in several countries during the few years before 1912, but it was not until after World War I that regular airmail services were inaugurated.

¶ JAMES, ALAN. *The Post.* 1970; MARTIN, NANCY. *The Post Office: from carrier pigeon to confravision.* 1969; ZILLIACUS, LAURIN. *From Pillar to Post.* 1956

Potemkin, Grigori Aleksandrovich (1739–91): Russian prince and statesman, adviser to Tsarina Catherine the Great. For twenty years he influenced Catherine's policies, especially in expanding the southern frontiers of Russia. Militarily he distinguished himself in wars with Turkey for control of the Crimea; as an administrator he used his great energies to improve Russian naval power (Sebastopol harbour is largely his creation); and he planned a gigantic colonisation of the south Russian steppes. He was ruthless, yet attracted many followers. In the long term his activities were too costly for the 18th-century Russian state to continue them.

Potomac, River: river draining the western slopes of the central Allegheny Mountains into the Chesapeake Bay. A freshwater river for about 300 miles [482·8 kilometres] the Potomac below Washington, DC, is a tidal estuary 125 miles [201·1 kilometres] in length and from 2 to 8 miles [3 to 12 kilometres] wide. After the founding of Maryland in 1634 the Potomac was the early passageway of the area. In the following decades this was gradually settled by Virginian colonists, and later the German and Scotch-Irish migrants crossed the Potomac and settled in the Shenandoah valley. The Potomac valley became the main pathway to the Ohio valley and was of great strategic importance in the Civil War. An Army of the Potomac was formed to protect Washington, DC, after the disastrous shattering of the North at the first battle of Bull Run. Under General George McLellan this army evolved into the best force supporting the cause of the Union.

Potsdam: East German city, 17 miles [27 kilometres] south-west of Berlin. It used to be the capital of Brandenburg and was founded by Frederick William "the Great Elector" in the late 17th century. It gradually gained a reputation as the centre of Prussian military tradition, and Frederick the Great built his palace of Sans Souci there in 1747.

Potsdam Conference: conference in July–August 1945 between Russia, the USA and Britain to decide on Germany's future after her surrender in May. The ideas and practice of Nazism were to be destroyed, and German industry was not to be used for making war weapons. To do this Germany was split into four zones, controlled by the French, British, US and Soviet armies. Stalin claimed heavy reparations from Germany to pay for the enormous war damage in Russia. This was hotly disputed, but Russia was allowed to take away industrial machinery from her zone.

748

Pottery: objects made of clay, rendered hard and durable by being subjected to fire. In some countries, in the past, pottery has been left to harden in the sun's heat; but pottery of this type does not last long and has been made only by races which have not yet learned the uses of fire for hardening their clay utensils. Porcelain is a fine, translucent form of pottery.

Pottery-making is one of the oldest of man's skills. Clay, a product of the natural decomposition of rocks, possesses, so far as pottery making is concerned, two important qualities. First, it is plastic: when moistened it can be easily kneaded or moulded. Second, as already mentioned, firing will transform the malleable clay into a hard and durable article. Pottery, while easy to break, is hard to destroy. As a consequence, archaeologists find it invaluable. A bucketful of potsherds (pottery fragments) excavated from a "dig" can tell the expert a surprising amount about the people who lived on the site many centuries ago.

The most important invention in the history of pottery making was the potter's wheel. No one person invented it, any more than one person invented the vehicular wheel. Gradually, it was found that a lump of clay, placed on a disc kept constantly rotating, could be stretched and shaped symmetrically by the potter's hands working against the centrifugal force which, unimpeded, would cause the clay to fly off the wheel.

Above, a potter operating his wheel by foot-treadle. Below left, a potter at work, showing the vase being shaped on the revolving wheel. Porcelain figure by Bustelli, c. 1770.

A further discovery was how to make pottery smooth and waterproof. This was done by means of a *glaze*, a thin coating of glass applied to the fired clay and then made permanent by a further firing. Some of the most beautiful glazed pottery ever made comes from Egypt, its glowing colours scarcely dimmed by time. Ancient Greek pottery, unsurpassed for purity of form, was varnished or polished instead of glazed, and often decorated with painted friezes of animals and human beings.

The earliest makers of porcelain were the Chinese – indeed, *china* is the name by which we now commonly call it. From *stoneware*, which is a very hard pottery but lacks delicacy and translucence, they gradually evolved a porcelain which, first known outside China in the 12th century, became the admiration of the Western world. After several earlier attempts at imitation the first successful European porcelain was produced at Meissen, near Dresden in Germany, in about 1710.

Thereafter factories for the production of porcelain were established in many countries, notably France, at Sèvres – where, at first, a porcelain known as *pâte tendre* (soft paste), a fragile, glassy material,

was used – and England, where the Bow, Chelsea, Worcester and Derby factories acquired great reputations. The English factories developed *bone china*, which incorporates burnt and ground animal bone with the china clay, and can be fired at a lower heat. Almost all English porcelain made today is of the bone china type. *See colour section.*

¶ HAGGAR, R. G. *Pottery through the Ages.* 1959
See also INDIVIDUAL ENTRIES.

Power politics: a government's policy of expanding the nation's frontiers or influence, often at the expense of smaller countries and by using threats or force; or, since important nations are often referred to as "powers", the give-and-take of international manoeuvring of a less unscrupulous sort.

Pragmatic sanction: in general, a royal decree with the force of law; in particular, the settlement (1713) laid down by Charles VI, emperor of Austria (1711–40), when he tried to safeguard the succession of his daughter Maria Theresa (empress 1740–80) to all his hereditary lands. Although upheld initially by most other European rulers, it was generally repudiated after his death.

Prague or **Praha:** capital of Czechoslovakia, on the River Vltava. Industrially important for its heavy and precision engineering, its medieval architecture and extensive Stromovka Park attract many visitors. By the 14th century Prague, then capital of Bohemia, had a university with students from all over the continent, and its position at the crossroads of east–west, north–south trade routes made it a prosperous place for craftsmen and merchants. The city has seen much controversy and fighting. Religious opponents quarrelled when Jan Hus was an heretical figure at the university, and later when Catholic fought Protestant at the Battle of the White Mountain early in the Thirty Years War. Prague was occupied many times in

the next three centuries, for it lay in the path of rival Austrian, Prussian and French armies. Czech nationalism has always been a powerful feature of Prague's history. The Nazi leader, Heydrich, was assassinated there in 1942; and in 1968 opposition to a domineering form of communism was crushed by Russian tanks.

Prehistoric: belonging or relating to the time in man's history before written records began.

Prehistoric animals: animals that lived before the age of recorded history. Discovering how ancient animals looked and behaved requires detective work. The clues are the fossils dug from the earth, petrified bones, shells, casts, even mere impressions in rock, coupled with the knowledge of living animals. Palaeontologists know that life existed 2,700 million years ago, but fossils found before the Cambrian period, about 600 million

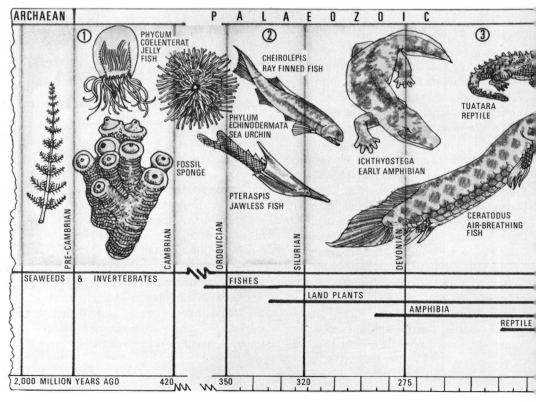

years ago, are mostly algae, simple plants.

Ancient animals ranged in size from tiny one-celled protozoa to huge awkward dinosaurs. Some looked like animals of today, others completely different. As the earth changed, animals had to change too. If they did not adapt fast enough to the new conditions they died out.

Life, it is believed, began in the ancient seas. The oldest known animal fossils, dating from the Cambrian period, were creatures without backbones, the invertebrates – trilobites, jellyfish, sponges, etc. The development of the backbone in animals, about 450 million years ago, was a major advance. The oldest of the vertebrates, the ostracoderms, resembled fish without jaws, had tiny mouths and breathed through gills. Gradually they developed jaws and, by the Devonian period, could eat other animals. Vast changes took place in the earth's structure, earthquakes shook the continents, land ranges were thrown up. One kind of fish developed lungs, so that it could breathe when the water drained away and survive in swamps. Some of these creatures grew fins resembling limbs, so that when a river dried up in a drought the fish could walk on land breathing through its lungs.

Meanwhile, land plants, mosses and ferns, had appeared, food for the newly arrived amphibians, ancestors of the present day salamanders, frogs and toads, with legs and feet instead of fins. They lived along the shores of the steaming swamps. Within the next 200 million years, all the big backboned animals, the reptiles, birds and mammals had put in an appearance. The reptiles had scaly skins that protected their bodies from drying out, so that they could live in dry places. Their eggs had shells and could therefore be safely laid on land. They grew huge and powerful, rulers of the land. The age of the dinosaurs, most spectacular of land animals, began 200 million years ago and lasted for the next 140 million years.

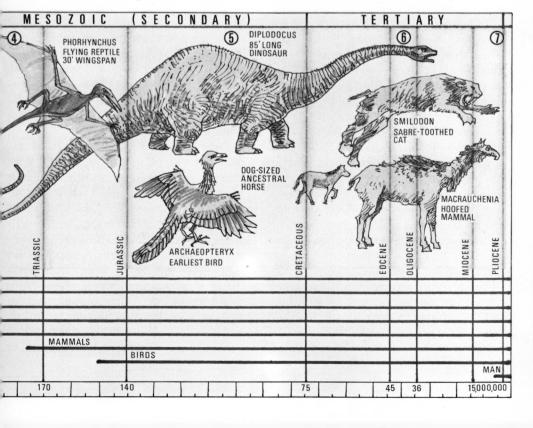

MESOZOIC (SECONDARY)　　　TERTIARY

④ PHORHYNCHUS FLYING REPTILE 30' WINGSPAN

⑤ DIPLODOCUS 85' LONG DINOSAUR

⑥

⑦

SMILODON SABRE-TOOTHED CAT

DOG-SIZED ANCESTRAL HORSE

MACRAUCHENIA HOOFED MAMMAL

ARCHAEOPTERYX EARLIEST BIRD

TRIASSIC | JURASSIC | CRETACEOUS | EOCENE | OLIGOCENE | MIOCENE | PLIOCENE

MAMMALS

BIRDS

MAN

170　140　75　45　36　15,000,000

The age of mammals, the Tertiary era, began about 65 million years ago. The surface of the earth changed considerably, mountain ranges rose, shallow oceans drained away, swamps dried up, and the climate grew colder and drier. Most reptiles could not adapt and died out, but mammals, ancestors of the modern horse, camel, cat and dog families, mice, etc., could adjust to the new conditions. Twenty million years ago, mountains began to wear down and grasslands appeared. Pigs, rhinoceros and deer roamed the plains. During the Ice Age, the Pleistocene period, prehistoric man appeared on the scene. From his drawings in caves we know he hunted bison, giant bear, long-haired mammoths, driven south by the cold.

¶ PETERSEN, KAI. *Prehistoric Life on Earth.* 1963

Prehistoric art: the art of man before he adopted a settled civilisation. That of some modern primitive tribes often shows marked similarities. Prehistoric art is essentially restricted to rock paintings and engravings, and to sculpture in stone and ivory, though more perishable media may have been lost. Prehistoric man may have thought that by painting or carving an animal he could gain magical power over it; to carve a pregnant woman was to ensure human or agricultural fertility. But some of the discoveries show a clear appreciation of line and form and an obvious delight in decoration. Prehistoric man collected interestingly shaped stones, was highly skilled in working of flints, and showed great ability in such works as "The Lady of Brassempouy" (a minute ivory head) or the horse carved on a spear-thrower from Bruniquel.

The art of prehistoric man began in the late Old Stone Age (Upper Palaeolithic), and the cultures are normally divided and dated by the geographical regions in France into which successive tribes moved.

So the Aurignacian period precedes, in order, the Upper Perigordian, the Solutrean, and the Magdalenian. These areas were all in central or south-western France, and the combined period they covered spanned a time from roughly 25,000 BC to 10,000 BC. Another great centre at this time was in northern Spain, and the whole of this general culture lasted until a change of climate altered the living patterns of the tribes. Eastern and southern Spain and the Saharan region produced a vast amount of art in the Mesolithic Age, certainly by 6000 BC, and there is a clear but unexplained link between the centres. South African prehistoric art is of about the same date, while the Australian Stone Age began about 3000 BC.

The Aurignacian period is the time of the great series of murals at Lascaux, south-western France, but the number of paintings discovered elsewhere has been considerable. At first men drew hands or abstract lines, and this led on to the great naturalistic paintings. The development of colour, browns and reds, added to the most readily available charcoal-black. The result was animal art of a very high standard, of great force and vigour. Also associated with this period are the so-called Venuses, extremely fat female figurines which have been found over a wide area of southern Europe.

In the Upper Perigordian period the development of statues of animals continued, and engravings on stone, bone or ivory appear. Sometimes these are to help rock paintings, but they are often works of art in their own right. Though the Solutrean period marked a temporary decline, the Magdalenian period shows Stone Age art at its best. The spear-thrower mentioned above dates from this time, as do other masterpieces of figurative art. Bas-reliefs in clay are found, and murals are helped by deep engraving. The great fresco of animals at Altamira in the Pyrenees belongs to this period.

The Mesolithic Age in eastern Spain shows a change to the painting of small-scale human scenes. Pictures of humans in the previous age had been very rare in rock paintings, and very rudimentary as well. In many ways these new, much more dramatic pictures resemble the contemporary works from the Sahara. There the paintings of running huntsmen (mainly in pin-man form) are joined by naturalistic and animated engravings of animals. Closely related to these are the South African murals, especially fine being a series of lifelike giraffes.

Australian Stone Age paintings are most interesting. Clearly magic had great influence here, as seen in the extraordinary wondjina figures which were thought to protect the inhabitants against tropical rains. *See colour section.*

¶ MARCUS, REBECCA B. *Prehistoric Cave Paintings.* 1970

See also CAVE ART.

Premier: from Latin *primarius*, through French *premier*, meaning first; hence, used as a noun, chief or prime minister in Great Britain and a number of other countries. The longest premiership to date was that of Antonio de Oliveira Salazar, who held office in Portugal from 1932–70. Used as an adjective, e.g. premier duke or baron, it means the holder of the oldest title of that rank. In Britain the premier duke is Norfolk (created 1483), the premier earl is Shrewsbury (created 1442) and the premier baron is De Ros (created 1264).

President: the elected head of government in many republics (e.g. USA, France and the Irish Republic) and of many educational institutions, commercial organisations, etc. Its literal meaning, from Latin *praesidere*, is one who sits over or before others.
See also AMERICAN PRESIDENTS.

Prester John: Presbyter John or John the Priest, a legendary medieval character. He was reputed to be a Christian ruler in the unknown East, located by earlier tales in central Asia, later in Ethiopia.

Pretenders: a pretender is a claimant to a throne occupied by someone else. The term is a loaded one. If you consider the claim to be well-founded, the person concerned, in your opinion, will not be a pretender at all, but the rightful ruler, deprived of his inheritance by a usurper.

Thus, James Francis Edward Stuart (1688–1766), son of the deposed King James II of England, is often called the Old Pretender, and his son, Charles Edward Stuart (1720–89), the Young Pretender. However, according to the Jacobites (who are still not extinct), their proper titles are King James III and King Charles III, respectively, since, in the view of the upholders of the Stuart dynasty, the House of Hanover had no right to the English throne. The mystery surrounding the fate of the Dauphin (1785–?95) during the French Revolution led some forty pretenders to claim to be Louis XVII, rightful King of France.

Priestley, Joseph (1733–1804): British scientist and theologian. The unusual variety of his gifts and achievements may be judged by the facts that he mastered, among other languages, Chaldee, Syriac, Arabic, French, German and Italian; became a nonconformist minister and had one of his theological works burnt by the common hangman at Dort; discovered oxygen and identified many other gases, though he had had no scientific education, and invented soda-water. In 1794 the unpopularity of his revolutionary political opinions led him to emigrate to America, where he settled in Pennsylvania.

¶ In SHEPHERD, WALTER. *Great Pioneers of Science.* 1964

Prince of Wales: Edward VII (left) was created Prince of Wales in 1841 at the age of one month and remained so for sixty years; The Duke of Windsor was a very popular Prince of Wales before his accession and abdication in 1936; and the present Prince of Wales, HRH Prince Charles.

Primitive: belonging to, or having the characteristics of, the earliest periods of civilisation (*see* e.g. ABORIGINES). Applied to a piece of art it can mean either dating from the time just before the Renaissance or a modern attempt to work in a crude or unsophisticated style.

Prince Edward Island: island in the St Lawrence River forming one of the provinces of Canada. Sighted by Cartier in 1534 and colonised by the French, it was called Isle St Jean until, after having been ceded to England in 1763, it was renamed after Edward Duke of Kent in 1808. After just over a century it joined the Canadian Confederation [1873].

Prince of Wales: title of the English heir apparent. The first native (i.e. Welsh) Prince of Wales was also the last. Llywelyn ap Gruffydd assumed the title in 1258, rallying the Welsh against the English. He was killed in battle in 1282. Two years later, Queen Eleanor, wife of Edward I, bore a son at Caernarvon. The King's heir, later Edward II, was created Prince of Wales by his father. Since then, the male heir apparent of England has almost invariably been created Prince of Wales: the title is not inherited. Since the reign of Edward II the monarch's eldest son has always been Duke of Cornwall at birth, and draws his income from the Duchy and not from the Principality of Wales.

The present Prince of Wales, Prince Charles, son of Elizabeth II, was invested at Caernarvon in 1969.

Princeton University: private university for men, Princeton, USA, founded in 1746 as the College of New Jersey, the fourth college founded in the British colonies of North America. It was inspired by the "Great Awakening" (a series of religious revivals that swept over the colonies in the early decades of the 18th century), and six of the seven original trustees were leaders of the "New Light" faction of the Presbyterian Church. In 1756 a building, known as Nassau Hall, was erected with funds raised in England and Scotland. Princeton College (as it then was) played a distinguished role in the American Revolution. One in six members of the Constitution Committee was a Princeton graduate, and James Madison of the class of 1771 was the first Princeton man to become President of the United States (1809–17). A graduate school was founded in 1877 and enhanced Princeton's academic prestige. In 1896 the College was renamed Princeton University, and in 1902 Woodrow Wilson (President of the United States 1913–21) became president of the University. To-day Princeton, though relatively small (4,000 enrolment), maintains its place of importance amongst the so-called "Ivy League" universities.

Printing: the reproduction of letters or designs upon paper or other substances by means of pressure upon the inked surface of types, blocks, or plate. By providing written information on a large scale, printing has been a major factor in the development of the modern world.

The earliest printing (originating in Asia, almost certainly China) was done with wood blocks. Ink was applied to characters or designs carved out of a flat block of wood. By pressing paper or cloth against the inked block the design was transferred. This method of reproduction was first used for making numerous copies of prayers, charms, and religious pictures. Examples of such printing survive from the 8th century, but the method may well have been in use as much as two centuries earlier. Book-printing by this method, each page in its entirety having first to be carved by hand, was, compared with our modern printing presses, a very slow process.

Movable type – whereby, instead of a whole page having to be carved and printed as a single unit, component letters or designs are made separately and can therefore be used over and over again in varying combinations – was first made in clay, in China in the 11th century. Under the Ming dynasty (1368–1644) movable type was made, successively, of wood, copper, and lead.

The West discovered printing independently. The first European books were printed from wood blocks. Credit for the European invention of movable metal type is generally given to Johann Gutenberg (c. 1398–1468) of Mainz, Germany, though some experts believe this honour rightly belongs to Lourens Janszoon Coster, or Koster (c. 1405–84) of Haarlem, in the Netherlands (see GUTENBERG BIBLE).

The first English printer learnt his craft abroad. He was William Caxton (c. 1422–91), a native of Kent who became a successful silk merchant in Bruges, in the Low Countries, where he lived for thirty-three years. Caxton was himself a man of some literary parts. In 1469 he began to make an English translation of a popular French romance of the time, and in 1474 or 1475, having set up a press in Bruges, he printed it, under the title *The Recuyell of the Historyes of Troye*. This, so far as we know, was the first printed book in English.

Caxton returned to England in 1476, setting up a press in the almonry of Westminster Abbey. There he published the first book actually to be printed in England. It was called *The Dictes or Sayengis of the philosophres* (1477). Thereafter, until his death in 1491, Caxton was indefatigable, as writer and translator as well as printer. In all he published some ninety-six works or editions of works, books ranging from the first French phrase book for the use of English visitors to France to Chaucer's *Canterbury Tales* and Malory's *Morte d'Arthur*.

For centuries afterwards Caxton books continued to be printed in much the same way as in his time. Many of these early books, employing beautifully designed typefaces, are works of art in themselves. Among printers who have left behind books of outstanding beauty may be mentioned Johann Froben (d. 1527) of Basel, Switzerland, Jean de Tournes (1504–64) of Lyons; Henri Estienne (c. 1470–1520) of Paris, his son Robert (1503–59), and other members of the Estienne family. Apart from certain improvements in the construction of printing presses – made, notably, by the Dutchman Willem Jansoon Blaeu (1571–1638) and by Charles, 3rd Earl of Stanhope (1753–1816) – printing, even with movable type, remained a slow process until the beginning of the 19th century.

The first practicable modern printing machine was invented by a German,

Friedrich König (1774–1833). In 1814 *The Times* newspaper installed two of his machines, powered by steam, and was able to print at the hitherto unheard-of rate of 1,100 sheets per hour.

Before long this achievement in turn was left far behind. A new era was at hand, improvements in printing techniques going forward with comparable improvements in the production of paper. In 1806 Henri Fourdrinier (1766–1854), a Frenchman, took out the first patent for making paper in a continuous roll. Today, newspapers are printed on continuous strips of paper more than five miles long.

Rotary presses, in which the type, first clamped, later curved, round a large cylinder, is pressed against the paper as the cylinder rotates, made their first appearance in the 1840s. Among inventors who played a significant part in the development of this type of press, which made possible a printing rate of 10,000 sheets an hour, an Englishman, Augustus

Applegarth (1789–1871), and Richard Hoe (1812–86), an American, may be specially mentioned. In 1865 another American, William Bullock (1813–67), of Philadelphia, invented the first press to print from a continuous roll of paper. The machine, after teething troubles, was a great success. Its inventor came to a sad end, killed by being caught in the driving belt of one of his machines.

The foregoing inventions were all improvements affecting only one side of printing: the actual transference of the inked pattern, whether of words, illustrations, or designs, on to paper. The other essential part of the printing process, the "setting" or "composing" of the type, was mechanised much later. Although machines to do the job mechanically were invented in the second half of the 19th century, hand typesetting persisted well into the present century.

The two principal inventions in this field were American, the Linotype and

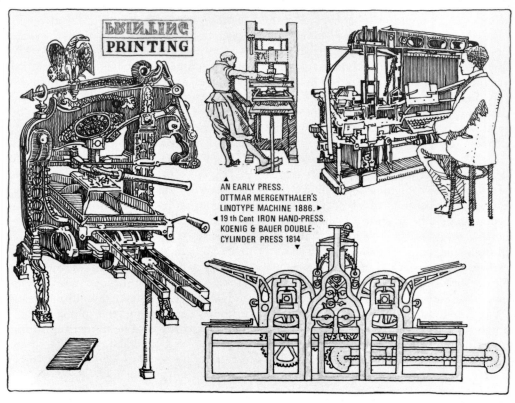

AN EARLY PRESS.
OTTMAR MERGENTHALER'S
LINOTYPE MACHINE 1886. ▶
◀ 19th Cent IRON HAND-PRESS.
KOENIG & BAUER DOUBLE-
CYLINDER PRESS 1814
▼

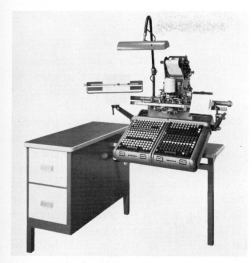

Monotype keyboard.

the Monotype, the first invented in 1886 by Ottmar Mergenthaler (1854–99), the second patented by Tolbert Lanston (1844–1913) in 1885. Both machines incorporate keyboards, rather like typewriters. When a linotype key is pressed a mould of the letter required falls into a rack. When a whole line is completed in this way, molten metal is forced into the moulds, forming a line of type which solidifies within seconds. Monotype keys punch, in a strip of paper, holes which stand for letters of the alphabet. This strip of paper is then passed through a casting machine which "reads" the holes and moves its moulds so that each presents itself in the correct order for the reception of the molten metal.

With the development of *offset lithography* the actual type no longer requires to be a three-dimensional piece of metal and this has led to the introduction of filmsetting where type is produced as an image on film for platemaking.

This book has been set on a Monophoto Filmsetter which is a later development of the Monotype Caster and presents lines of filmset characters in place of lines of hot metal type. Again it is controlled through a Keyboard, producing a punched tape which in turn activates a movable matrix case containing film negatives of the characters required. As each character is centred over a light source a photograph is made onto a roll of film within the filmsetter. After being read these "galleys" of film are made up into pages by hand.

More recently, the demand for faster typesetting, especially for newspaper and periodical work, has resulted in the development of various systems of electronic, computer assisted filmsetters. These work at much higher speeds and are operated by paper or magnetic tapes bearing coded instructions for the composing units. Page make-up instructions and corrections are punched on a separate tape and the two merged to produce a final page of film ready for printing down onto a metal printing plate.

An important development in high-speed modern printing was the introduction of *stereotyping*, a process known from the 18th century but not used to any extent until after 1850. Stereotyping is a method of copying a page of type by pressing papier-mâché against it so that the latter becomes indented with the shape of the type. If molten metal is then poured over the papier-mâché a new printing surface is formed in a fraction of the time taken if, for every duplicate required, the page in question had to be set anew. The development of a curved stereotype, which enabled rotary presses, for the first time, to print simultaneously on both sides of a strip of paper, in effect brought into being today's newspapers.

Photographic processes have further extended printing technology, making possible today's large and low-priced editions. The computer, too, has been pressed into service – as when, for example, entries in a catalogue, fed into a computer at random, have been sorted and indexed in their proper alphabetical sequence.

¶ HARLEY, E. S. and HAMPDEN, J. *Books: From Papyrus to Paperback.* 1964

Priory: religious house governed by a prior or prioress. Some large monastic houses had an abbot and a prior, the prior being the official next in seniority to the abbot. Abbeys frequently sent members of the community to found another branch of their order elsewhere; the daughter-house was known as a priory and its head as the prior. The abbot of the parent foundation made periodic visits to the priory and supervised its organisation until it became fully established.

¶ WRIGHT, GEOFFREY N. *Abbeys and Priories*. 1969
See also ABBEYS; MONASTERIES.

Prisons: places of detention. Originally they were not primarily places of punishment. Their principal function was to provide places where arrested persons could be kept in custody until trial and, if convicted, pending the carrying out of sentence. They also served as a means of persuasion for the payment of debts and fines.

To early governments the idea of keeping malefactors in prolonged confinement at the expense of the state would have made no sense whatever. From their point of view the death penalty, ex- posure in the pillory or stocks, whipping, and transportation to penal settlements overseas seemed a far neater solution to the question of what to do with convicted criminals.

Dire as such penalties were, it is arguable that they were to be preferred to the terrible squalor of the early prisons. Prisoners, convicted or not, were kept in irons, slept on filthy straw, and all but starved unless they could pay their jailers for their board. Disease was rife and many arrested persons did not survive to stand trial. At Oxford, England, in 1577, an outbreak of jail fever, as it was called, killed off 500 people, including the judge.

In western Europe, in the 16th century, the decay of the feudal system and the enclosure of agricultural land for pasture left many people homeless. In countries affected by the Reformation the dissolution of the monasteries which had provided many poor people with food and shelter added to the general misery. Governments found it hard to distinguish between such homeless wanderers and confirmed rogues and vagabonds. In

Above, the inside of Newgate in the 18th century. Above right, the treadmill at Brixton, erected 1817. Right, the centre section of Wakefield Prison. The clock tower surmounts the main entrance.

England, Holland and Germany Houses of Correction were set up where beggars and vagrants were not only deprived of their freedom but set to some useful work.

In these Houses of Correction may be seen the seeds of the modern prison. A great name in the work of humanising imprisonment is that of John Howard (1726–90). He inspected prisons in Britain and abroad and what he saw, summarised in *The State of Prisons* (1777), makes horrific reading. Slowly, improvements began to be made. The prison system set up by the Quakers of Pennsylvania, in America, made a deep impression on liberal opinion. The Quakers aimed at reforming criminals rather than merely punishing them. They tried to preserve the human dignity of the inmates of their prisons instead of degrading it. Another Quaker, Elizabeth Fry (1780–1845), an Englishwoman, also did much to improve the lot of prisoners, especially women.

Britain's loss of the American colonies closed an outlet which, in its time, had taken some 50,000 of her convicts. Between 1787 and 1867 160,000 more were transported to Australia. France, during the 19th century, established penal settlements in the Pacific and on Devil's Island (off the coast of French Guiana), a malaria-ridden hell-hole which deserved its name. The last of the French penal colonies closed down in 1950. After the loss of the American colonies some British convicts were housed, in dreadful conditions, in old warships turned into makeshift prisons. An escape from one of these hulks, as they were called, forms the nub of the plot of Charles Dickens's novel *Great Expectations*.

Many large prisons were built in the 19th century. A prison like Pentonville, London (opened 1842), which today seems so grim and forbidding, was in its time a great step forward. In 1878 prisons were transferred to state ownership under a Board of Prison Commissioners. In 1902 the first English institution designed specifically for young offenders was opened in Kent, at Borstal (from which all such institutions have subsequently taken their name). Wakefield, Yorkshire, the first "prison without bars", was opened in 1936. The 20th-century emphasis has been on a relaxation of severe restraints and on the rehabilitation of convicted persons. But the great rise in crime during recent years, coupled with some sensational escapes, has forced the prison authorities to reassess their priorities. The criminal must be deterred, restrained, and, if possible, rehabilitated; but at the same time the law-abiding community must be safeguarded.

In the USA the late 18th century and early 19th produced two very different schools of thought on prison discipline. The so-called Pennsylvanian system relied on keeping prisoners in solitary confinement in the hope that reflection and lack of contact with other vicious types would bring about reform. The Auburn system, originating in New York, preferred separate confinement at night but allowed the congregating of prisoners in the workshops and at meal-times. They were not however, allowed to talk, so that this was known as the "silent" system as contrasted with the "solitary" system. A combination of the two systems is now very common in a number of countries, with "solitary" reserved as a special punishment. Of US prisons none has attracted more notoriety than Alcatraz on a 20 acre [8 hectare] island ("Pelican" island) in San Francisco Bay. In the period 1934-62, of twenty-three men who tried to escape twelve were recaptured and eleven shot or drowned.

In addition to prisons, some countries have experimented with penal camp systems. The largest of these, in Russia, have held up to 1,500,000 prisoners at a time. It is reckoned that China has had 10 million in prison camps at some periods.

¶ SPEED, P. F. *Police and Prisons.* 1968

Privateers: armed vessels privately owned and commissioned by governments to commit hostile acts against enemy ships (*see* LETTER OF MARQUE).

Up to the 19th century privateers of many nations figured in sea warfare. Ship to ship duels were frequent, and prize money could be claimed if a captured vessel was officially condemned by a competent court. Some privateers were built on warship lines but more often they were merchantmen converted for fighting purposes. They carried no cargo and were thus able to ship large crews – necessary for sending prizes into port.

The Declaration of Paris, 1856, signed by most nations with the exception of America, Spain, Mexico and Venezuela, finally abolished privateering.

Privy Council: body which, in Britain, advises the sovereign and through which the sovereign exercises power. It has its own independent statutory duties. Until the 18th century the chief source of executive power in the state, it was gradually supplanted by the system of cabinet government and its power largely transferred to the cabinet as an inner Committee of the Privy Council. Newly created government departments have taken over much of the work of the original committees. The number of its members is usually about 300, chosen (for life) by the sovereign from eminent public men in the Commonwealth on the recommendation of the prime minister. When the sovereign is ill or abroad it is presided over by councillors of state. Usually at least four privy councillors attend, although three make a quorum;

but the whole Council meets when the sovereign announces an intention to marry, or dies.

The Privy Seal.

Privy Seal: in British history, a seal of the Crown, intermediate between the Privy Signet and the Great Seal, and employed chiefly as an authority to affix the Great Seal. The Privy Seal was abolished in 1884. The Privy Signet is one of the sovereign's seals, used in sealing private letters. The Great Seal, introduced by Edward the Confessor, is the emblem of sovereignty.

The post of Lord Privy Seal is still retained in Britain but involves only those duties which the prime minister of the day may assign to the member of the government he has nominated to fill it.

Prohibition: the ratification of the 18th Amendment to the Constitution in 1920, which ended a long campaign in the United States against the liquor traffic. The failure of brewers and distillers to curb the excessive use of intoxicants, the wild behaviours in bars and saloons and the judicious political tactics of the Anti-Saloon League (1893) led to a concerted effort to control "the demon drink". Many different motives influenced the voters as they went to the polls in the various states of the Union. The ardent reformers argued strongly that the liquor interests represented a demoralising force in American politics, that as industry became more and more mechanised employees must be sober to be safe, and that it was the taxpayer who really paid the bills for an industry which was filling the poorhouses and prisons with its victims. The amendment, originally moved by Senator Morris Sheppard of Texas, prohibited the manufacture, sale or transportation of intoxicating liquors for beverage purpose. Opponents of prohibition attacked the efforts of governmental agencies to enforce the law. They approved the banishment of the saloon, but insisted that it had been replaced by illegal "speakeasies" and night clubs. The illicit traffic in intoxicants was breeding "bootleggers", racketeers and gangsters, and, under such conditions, corruption flourished in the police forces and other enforcement agencies. Popular disgust grew over the failure of enforcement, and the Democratic National Convention of 1932 demanded the repeal of the legislation. Following the Democratic landslide election victory of November 1932 Congress accepted a further amendment to the Constitution (21st) which repealed the anti-liquor laws (22 March 1933).

Proletariat: the lowest class in modern industrial society. According to Marxist theory these are the workers who own no property and possess no capital and live by the sale of their labour to their employers.

Pronunciamento: from a Spanish word meaning, originally, a pronouncement, proclamation or manifesto. In effect, it is the Spanish equivalent of the French *coup d'état*. In the turbulent history both of Spain and her colonies of South America, proclamations stating the aims of the insurgents frequently preceded uprisings or revolutions, and the term came to be applied to the uprising itself.

Propaganda: information, often of a biased or prejudiced nature, spread in support of a cause or school of thought. The Sacred Congregation *de Propaganda Fide* (for the propagation of the faith) was founded in Rome for the education of missionary priests (1622), and the English word is taken from the Latin.

Propaganda and, to a lesser extent, advertising, are in a special class of communication because of the underlying motives. Advertisers try to arouse our longing to the point where we are willing to part with our money in order to possess the products they sell. Legislation tries to protect us from misleading advertisement for the sale of goods or services, but there is no such protection from the excesses of propaganda which deals with prejudices and emotions and is intended to incite to action. Propaganda – such, for example, as campaigns to prevent accident or disease – can be socially useful. When, however, it consists of half-truths and outright lies it is dangerous and destructive. In totalitarian countries where all the media of communication are in the hands of the state, propaganda of this kind is dinned into the population until the victims cannot distinguish false from true.

Protectorate: (1) in general, a form of government over a territory which has not been formally annexed but which, by custom, grant or treaty, is under the jurisdiction of another power; (2) particularly, the period in English history (1653–59) when the country was ruled by Oliver Cromwell and briefly by his son Richard.

Protestant: one who protests, though the term is generally applied as an adjective to the system of Christian belief and worship which had its rise in the Reformation of the early 16th century.

The originating spirit of the Reformation was Martin Luther (1483–1546) and among the contemporaries who caught his spirit were Ulrich Zwingli (1484–1531) and John Calvin (1509–64). Although simplification can only too often be misleading, the main points of their teaching may be summarised as (1) accepting the Bible as the only source of revealed truth and more important than the pronouncements of the Church (*dogma*), which in the Roman view were equally valid; (2) insisting that faith alone (*sola fides*) could secure for a Christian the hope of salvation in the world to come, though, in Calvin's view, this could be no more than hope, the ultimate decision resting in the inscrutable will of God. From this second principle it followed that salvation could not depend on the performance of good works, even if these involved stern self-denial and sustained religious exercises. Such works were, indeed, thought to have value in shaping human character (though Rome had permitted some abuses to creep in); but faith was the watchword of the Protestant creed. This had the result that sermons and teaching were regarded as more important than ceremony and ritual, some of which were held to be superfluous or even superstitious.

From these beginnings stemmed the Protestant Churches as we find them today, the Lutherans of Germany and Scandinavia, the Calvinist French Church, to which the Huguenots belonged, various other Protestant Churches in Europe and the Protestant Episcopal Church of the USA, with a membership of over 3,500,000. In the British Isles the term Protestant has never formally been accepted by the Church of England. Indeed, such is the breadth of views held within it that, while the Anglican or "High" Church (which moved less far from Rome in the first instance) would not accept it, the "Low" Churchman would be proud to do so. To the Methodists and other "dissenting" churches the title is welcome. *See also* HUGUENOTS; HUS; LUTHER; WYCLIF, etc.

Protocol: a word in the language of law and diplomacy meaning an original draft or record of proceedings in an ecclesiastical cause or, in international law, a record of preliminary negotiations. The word is also used to describe the rules of conduct and ceremony in diplomatic relationships: how dignitaries should be addressed, who precedes whom in a procession, and so on.

Provence: former province of France, occupying part of the fertile Rhone valley and the southern slopes of the Maritime Alps. The ancient capital was Avignon, famous for its bridge dating from 1177–85, the fortified papal palace where the exiled popes lived (1309–76) and the anti-popes (1378–1417), and the 13th-century cathedral of Notre Dame des Doms.

Prussia: former north German state, the largest in Germany. Its area varied considerably from the 10th century. Prussia began as a frontier land stretching across a forested and marshy plain from the River Elbe eastwards. In it feudal barons fought to keep their estates from the Slav tribes of Russia. Germanic colonists moved in from the west, but the soil was poor and standard of living low. The Hohenzollern rulers of Prussia had to be ruthless in fighting ambitious neighbours.

Two events of the 17th century changed Prussian fortunes. In 1618 Brandenberg was joined to Prussia to form a larger state. In 1640 Frederick William, "the Great Elector", became ruler. A man of great energy, he laid the foundations of

Brandenberg-Prussian power by building up the army and an efficient civil service.

In 1740 Frederick the Great used this basis to add to Prussia the rich province of Silesia, and later to seize large areas of Poland, thus linking together some of his scattered lands. But this led to a century of bitter conflict with Austria: both were rivals for supremacy in the German-speaking states of the old Holy Roman Empire. The Prussian statesman Bismarck was determined in the 1860s to end this rivalry. With a highly efficient war machine Prussia defeated Austria in seven weeks. In 1871 all the German states except Austria joined Prussia to form the German Empire. Led by the Prussian king and chancellor, the new empire inherited Prussia's military tradition and her trained soldiers, and made it a powerful new force in international affairs.

After the collapse of the Third Reich in 1945 Prussia was divided between West Germany, East Germany, Poland and the USSR. *See* GERMANY for map.

¶ MARRIOTT, *Sir* J. A. R. and ROBINSON, *Sir* C. G. *The Evolution of Prussia.* 1946

See also INDIVIDUAL ENTRIES.

Ptolemy (Claudius Ptolemaeus, 2nd century BC): mathematician and geographer. Born in Egypt, then part of the Roman empire, near Alexandria, where he spent his life, he wrote a number of scientific works, some of which survive in whole or in part. The most notable was his Geography, in eight books with an atlas of maps, which, for all its errors corrected by later discoveries, was for centuries a standard work of reference.

Ptolemy I (d. 283 BC): general of Alexander the Great (*see* separate entry) and founder of a dynasty of kings, numbering fourteen in all and known as the Ptolemies, who ruled in Egypt from 323-30 BC. Ptolemy I, called "Soter"

(saviour) built the great library of Alexandria (*see* separate entry) and wrote a reliable history of his former emperor.

Puerto Rico: fourth largest of the Caribbean islands. It was occupied by the Spaniards in 1510, and, although the natives were friendly at first, they were treated so harshly that the entire population died out, and was replaced by Negro slaves as labourers.

The island was attacked by the English in the 16th century, by the Dutch in the 17th century and by the English again in 1797, but it remained under Spanish rule until it was occupied in 1898 by the army of the USA during the Spanish–American War. Puerto Rico has remained US territory ever since.

Pulitzer, Joseph (1847–1911): American newspaper publisher. Born in Hungary, he arrived penniless in St Louis in 1865, after serving for a year in the 1st New York Lincoln Cavalry. Having worked as a reporter and qualified as a lawyer, he became a newspaper proprietor and built up an immense fortune which he used liberally in the endowment of a number of Pulitzer prizes and scholarships, awarded annually in the fields of drama, music, letters and journalism.

Punic Wars: struggle in the 3rd and 2nd centuries BC between the Romans and the Carthaginians of North Africa, whom they called *Poeni* as descendants of the Phoenicians. The clash of interests first arose in Sicily, where the Carthaginians had established themselves.

The first war (264–241 BC) saw the rise of Hamilcar as a Punic leader and a successful attempt by Rome to engage in naval warfare, where her adversary had previously excelled. It ended in the loss of Sicily and the payment by Carthage of a heavy indemnity.

After an interval in which Rome seized Corsica and Sardinia and the Carthaginians retaliated by successes in Spain, the second war (218–201 BC) saw the invasion of Italy by Hannibal and the rout of the Roman armies in several battles on their own soil. In time, however, the tide turned, and Hannibal was finally defeated at Zama in Africa by Scipio.

Carthage was no longer a great power, but certain Romans, such as Cato, continued to call for her destruction (*delenda est Carthago*). A quarrel with Massinissa, one of Rome's chief African allies, was made the pretext for the third war (149–146 BC), which resulted in Carthage being razed to the ground.

See also INDIVIDUAL ENTRIES.

Punjab: the land of the "Five Rivers" (tributaries of the Indus), and home of the Sikhs, a sect founded in the 16th century and developed into a warrior nation by Govind Singh (1675–1708). After a period of anarchy in the 18th century, the country was united by Ranjit Singh (1780–1839), who made an alliance with the British. Power later passed to the army of a military sect, the *Khalsa*, who from 1845 conducted wars against the British but were defeated notably at Sobraon (1846) and Chilianwala (1849), after which the Punjab was annexed to Britain. It was brilliantly pacified by Henry and John Lawrence (*see* separate entries). The Sikhs later formed some of the finest units of the British Indian army and did not mutiny.

The Province was diminished by the separation of the Delhi Territory (1859) and the North-West Frontier Province (1901), and in 1947 it was divided between India and Pakistan.

Puritan: a word describing all those who, in the 16th and 17th centuries, wanted to purify the Church, attacking the use of vestments and ceremonies and, finally, church government. Puritans dressed simply, often called their children by biblical names and shunned worldly pleasure and self-indulgence.

Pyongyang: ancient city of north-east Asia, now the capital of North Korea, forty miles up the Taedong River. The main settlement was founded in the early 12th century AD, but some remains date from BC. The modern city's industries include mining, mechanical engineering, textiles, chemicals, sugar and cement.

Pyramid: masonry structure with square base and triangular sides meeting at the top. Pyramidal buildings are found in a number of early civilisations. (For some examples *see* AZTECS and MAYAN CIVILISATIONS.) Probably the best known, however, are the royal burial places of ancient Egypt. During the earlier Egyptian dynasties the Pharaohs were buried in these huge tombs, the most famous of which stand near the Nile delta, at Gizeh. Of these, the largest is the colossal pyramid of Khufu, which was completed about 2600 BC. It took approximately twenty years to erect, contains over two million stone blocks each weighing over two tons [two tonnes], and its square base covers thirteen acres [five hectares].

Modern Egyptologists think that its builders were not slaves but freeborn workmen, who came to do an annual period of labour on the king's tomb. They used very primitive tools: wooden mallets and bronze knives, neither strong enough to hew granite out of the stone quarries. So they chipped shallow channels into the rock, and filled these with wood. This was soaked with water until it expanded, causing lumps of granite to break away. These were shaped into rough blocks which gangs of men hauled on tree-trunk rollers to the Nile, where barges carried the stone to the site.

To make the right-angled corners of the base, men worked in threes, using a rope twelve cubits long, each cubit marked with a knot. A man stood at the corner, holding one end of the rope, while the second man walked to a point three knots away and knelt there. Then the third man proceeded to a distance of five knots from him, knelt, and threw the rest of the rope to the first man, who pulled it tight, making a triangle. The point at which he stood was always the corner of a right angle.

After the square was pegged out it had to be levelled. The level was checked by means of a network of clay water-trenches built around the base and across it. These trenches were of equal depth, so the surface of the water they contained lay at the same height if the base were level. The level was tested by using a cord fastened to two short sticks, stretched from trench to trench like a gardener's line. Then the ground was built up until measuring rods, standing vertically beneath the line, showed an even height. But the architects at Khufu made a small error, so one corner of the pyramid is half-an-inch [13 millimetres] higher than the other three.

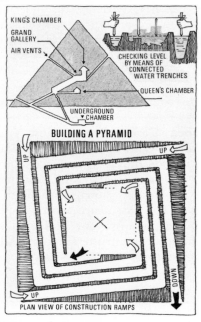

KING'S CHAMBER
GRAND GALLERY
AIR VENTS
CHECKING LEVEL BY MEANS OF CONNECTED WATER TRENCHES
QUEEN'S CHAMBER
UNDERGROUND CHAMBER

BUILDING A PYRAMID

UP
UP
×
UP
DOWN

PLAN VIEW OF CONSTRUCTION RAMPS

The granite blocks were dragged into position and hauled up ramps made to encircle the structure. Masons cut the sides smooth. The capstone is 481 feet [147 metres] above the base, and the pyramid is solid apart from the burial chambers and the galleries leading to them.

¶ EDWARDS, I. E. S. *The Pyramids of Egypt.* 1970

Pyramids, Battle of the (July 1798): victory over the Mameluke rulers of Egypt which gave Napoleon temporary control of the country. This was brought to nothing a few weeks later when Nelson's defeat of the French fleet at the Battle of the Nile isolated the Emperor's army and forced its withdrawal.

Pyrenees: the 250-mile [402 kilometres] range of mountains in south-western Europe separating France from the Iberian peninsula. Its passes have seen much of human history, the most celebrated incident being the defeat of Charlemagne at Roncesvalles in AD 778 when, returning from Spain, his rearguard was annihilated by the Moors. The tale, with Count Roland as its hero, was so enriched by minstrels and troubadours that it became the most famous story of the Middle Ages.

Pythagoras (c. 580–c. 500 BC): Greek mathematician and philosopher. Probably born at Samos, he seems to have travelled widely in Egypt and Asia

765

Minor. He eventually settled in Crotona, on the south-east coast of Italy, where he founded a fraternity having all things in common and dedicated to secrecy, self-discipline, temperance, purity, and obedience. Their system was a curious blend of morality, philosophy, and mysticism, built on a mathematical foundation. Thus their studies were numbers absolute (arithmetic), numbers applied (music), magnitudes at rest (geometry), and in motion (astronomy), these forming the *Quadrivium* of the Middle Ages. According to Plutarch, they related virtues to numbers, and believed that earth, fire, air, and water were derived respectively from hexahedron, pyramid, octahedron and icosahedron. Attributed to his school is the so-called Pythagoras's Theorem, which proves that the square on the hypotenuse (the longest side) of a right-angled triangle is equal to the sum of the squares on the other two sides.

¶ In PRINGLE, PATRICK. *101 Great Lives*. 1964

Quai d'Orsay: street in Paris from which the French Ministry of Foreign Affairs takes its name, just as the British Government is identified with Whitehall.

Quakers: members of the Society of Friends (*see* FOX, GEORGE and FRIENDS, RELIGIOUS SOCIETY OF). The name Quakers is one of a number of epithets in history given originally in mockery but later adopted as an honourable name. In this case George Fox records that "Justice Bennet, of Derby, was the first to call us Quakers, because I bade him quake and tremble at the word of the Lord" (*Journal*, 1694).

Quebec: fortress commanding the upper St Lawrence, where an expedition broke the French encirclement of the English colonies in America. Louisburg, at the entrance to the St Lawrence, was taken in 1758, but the French were able to reinforce Quebec when the ice thawed in 1759. James Cook (1728–79) piloted the expedition up-river. The campaign was successful because land and sea forces co-operated willingly. The general, the moody and brilliant James Wolfe (1727–59), and the admiral, the reserved and stolid Charles Saunder (1713–75), learned to trust each other on the voyage out. This trust survived the repulse of Wolfe's first assault on the Beauport shore, when the landing craft grounded. The passage of frigates and sloops under Charles Holmes (1711–61) into the upper river gave Wolfe the chance of making a surprise night landing above the town. Quebec surrendered on 18 September, five days after the English won the decisive engagement on the Heights of Abraham with one controlled musket-volley. Wolfe and his opponent, Montcalm (1712–59), were both killed. British command of the Atlantic ensured that it was British ships which reached the starving garrison when the ice thawed in 1760.

Quebec Act (1774): British Act of Parliament, sponsored by Lord North despite the powerful opposition of Chatham (*see* PITT, WILLIAM, the Elder) and Burke, to protect the French Canadians and secure their allegiance. It confirmed them "in their possessions, laws and rights", guaranteed freedom of worship and their own civil code of laws, with control over everything except taxation.

Quebec Conference (August 1943): meeting at Quebec during World War II of Winston Churchill, Franklin D. Roosevelt, Mackenzie King (of Canada) and Tse-ven Soong (foreign minister of China). The conference approved plans for the invasion of France and appointed Lord Louis Mountbatten supreme Allied Commander in South-East Asia.

Queen Anne style: style of English architecture, furniture design, etc., associated with the early 18th century. It produced houses of simple elegance, usually of brick, decorated in a pleasantly restrained classical manner. The furniture is characterised by the generous use of walnut wood, cabriole legs, marquetry work and graceful proportions.
See colour section.

Queen Anne's War: the American name for the War of the Spanish Succession, 1701-14, terminated by the Treaty of Utrecht. The American colonies sided with Britain against France and Spain.
See SPANISH SUCCESSION, WAR OF.

Queensland: north-eastern and second largest state of the Australian Commonwealth, with Brisbane as its capital. The Dutch reached Cape Keerweer in 1606, Abel Tasman the gulf of Carpentaria in 1644 and James Cook Bustard Bay in 1770. John Oxley discovered and surveyed the Brisbane River in 1823. The convict settlement established at Moreton Bay in 1824, on Oxley's recommendation, closed down in 1842, but aboriginal opposition tended to inhibit free settlement. Dr Leichhardt's notable discoveries, particularly of the Mackenzie and Dawson Rivers in 1844-6, and Thomas Mitchell's explorations of the Warrego and Maranoa

territories encouraged colonisation. The first immigrant ship direct from England to Moreton Bay arrived in 1848. Separatist ideas gained ground until in 1859 the whole north-east of New South Wales became the new colony of Queensland. The state, predominantly pastoral, prospered also through gold discoveries in 1848 and exports from her cotton plantations during the American Civil War. Queensland, the only Australian state unrepresented at the 1897 colonial conference, played her full part when Commonwealth replaced colonies. She retains her position as the leading cattle state, supported by dairying, mining, forestry and fisheries, though manufactures now account for two-fifths of her economy.

Quetta, locally **Shal Kot:** chief town of Baluchistan, India, standing at a height of 5,000 feet [1,524 metres] 20 miles [32 kilometres] north-west of the Bolan pass to Afghanistan. It was rented by the British from the Khan of Kalat in 1876, and became a garrison town and the southern point of the line of fortresses guarding the north-west frontier of India. On 31 May 1935 it was completely destroyed by an earthquake which killed some 20,000 people, but has been largely rebuilt and today holds the Staff College of Pakistan. It is a centre for trade with Afghanistan, Persia and much of central Asia.
See INDIA for map.

Quiberon Bay, Battle of (1759): fought near the mouth of the Loire and the crowning victory of Pitt's "Wonderful Year", 1759, where the English admiral Edward Hawke (1705-81) defeated a French squadron under Admiral Conflans in a gale on a lee shore. This vindicated the policy of close blockade by the Western Squadron. Since May, Hawke had kept his ships watching Brest, though this service was unpopular with captains and exhausting for men. By issuing fresh vegetables and sending vessels in relays to clean ship and to refresh their men in Torbay, Hawke kept his fleet fit. Conflans left Brest when a gale had driven Hawke to Torbay, but he was overtaken on 20 November at Quiberon and lost five capital ships. With Boscawen's defeat of the Toulon squadron off Lagos in August, this victory saved England from invasion and freed her navy to support the conquests of Canada and India.

Quintain: device used in the Middle Ages for knightly training. A dummy figure on a pivot was charged with lance or spear. Sometimes a weighted sandbag was attached which would swing round and strike the rider who was too slow in getting away after scoring a hit on the dummy. Such figures may still be seen in use in some annual re-enactments of medieval pageantry and pastimes, e.g. in Italy.

Vidkun Quisling.

Quisling: collaborator with an enemy power. Vidkun Quisling (1887–1945), a Norwegian, founded in Norway in 1933 the Nasjonal Samling (National Unity) party in imitation of the Nazi (National Socialist) party in Germany. At the outbreak of World War II he invited the Germans to occupy Norway and, in 1940, proclaimed himself head of the Norwegian government. From February 1942 he became the willing puppet of the Germans with whose armed support he ruled his implacably hostile countrymen who, when the Germans were defeated, arrested, tried and sentenced him to death. He was shot on 27 October 1945. The word Quisling is now a universal term of contempt for one who betrays his people into the power of a foreign despot.

Quito: capital city of Ecuador, situated over 9,000 feet [2,743 metres] high in the Andes of South America, and because of its height enjoying a mild climate even though it lies virtually on the Equator. The earliest town on this site was built by Indians who were later conquered by the Incas.

When Pizarro (*see* separate entry) captured Cuzco he ensured that Quito remained part of his territory, forestalling an expedition from Guatemala, and gradually Quito became a Spanish city with a vast cathedral and an impressive Jesuit college, both of which survived the earthquakes of 1797 and 1859.

R

Racism: fashionable contraction of *racialism*; a pernicious doctrine which holds that some races are inherently superior to others, thereby encouraging hatred of, and discrimination against, minority elements of a different racial origin from the bulk of the population. Many conquerors, from time immemorial, have enslaved those they have defeated or have treated them as second-class citizens. In its modern context racism goes further. It covers an objection to the presence of members of an alien race and, in its most virulent form – as in the Nazis' attempt to wipe out the Jews – an objection to their very existence.

¶ SNYDER, L. L. *The Idea of Racialism.* 1963

Radio: transmission and reception of messages by electromagnetic waves. An alternating current is one in which the flow of electricity starts at zero, builds to a peak in one direction and then subsides to zero; it then rises to a maximum flow in the opposite direction, after which the current again returns to zero, only to start the process all over again. One complete excursion as described is called a cycle, while the number of cycles performed in a second of time is termed the frequency. A unit of one cycle per second is a "Hertz" (Hz), named after the German physicist Heinrich Hertz (1837–94).

In 1865 a great Scottish physicist, James Clerk Maxwell (1831–79), suggested that light and heat were electromagnetic waves of incredibly high frequency which, instead of flowing along a wire conductor, were radiating through space. This was subsequently proved to be true. (To give some idea of the tremendous frequencies involved, the sensation we call heat is caused by electromagnetic oscillations at frequencies between one billion and 100 billion Hz; light wave frequencies are higher still.)

Maxwell also predicted the existence of other waves at frequencies above and below those of light and heat. We now know that above the light frequencies there are invisible waves called (in order of ascending frequency) ultraviolet rays, X-rays and gamma-rays. Those frequencies which lie below the heat waves, down to 10,000 Hz, are termed radio waves.

The existence of radio waves was confirmed by Heinrich Hertz in 1888, but no practical use was found for them until 1895–96 when the Italian Guglielmo Marconi (*see* separate entry) found that by connecting Hertz's apparatus between an elevated aerial wire and an earth connection the invisible waves would radiate for considerable distances through space. By interrupting them by means of a Morse key Marconi was able to send coded messages over several miles. This process, known as wireless telegraphy, was the earliest form of radio communication. Today, improved out of all recognition, it is still widely used and signals can be sent all over the world.

In the early 1900s various people tried to transmit speech and music by radio waves, but without much success because no means then existed of generating radio-frequency oscillations which were sufficiently pure. It was not until 1913, when it was discovered that a triode radio valve could generate oscillations of a suitable character, that radio telephony became a really practicable proposition.

Although a radio telephony system can be very complex, the basic principles are simple enough. First, a microphone is used to convert the pressure waves (sound waves) from a voice or musical instrument into electrical waves of exactly the same frequencies. The human ear can detect sounds which range in frequency from about fifteen cycles per second to about 20,000 cycles per second, so the electrical frequencies produced by the microphone are also within this range. These oscillations are fed into valve or transistor amplifiers which enlarge the signals considerably.

For various technical reasons it is not practicable to radiate these signals directly, so in another part of the transmitter special types of valves or transistors are used to generate oscillations of a much higher frequency – ones which will radiate from an aerial system. The relatively low (audio) frequencies from the microphone circuits are then superimposed in one of various possible ways on to the radio frequency waves and are in this manner carried pickaback-fashion to the aerial system and radiated as electromagnetic waves into space.

At the receiver the combined waves are picked up by an aerial system, amplified and then separated back into their original forms. The radio frequencies, having done their pickaback job, are discarded, while the audio frequency microphone signals, after further amplification, are fed to headphones or a loudspeaker. These devices re-convert the electrical oscillations into pressure waves in the air, which are interpreted by our ears as copies of the original sounds.

Although entertainment broadcasting is the most familiar form of radio, this is only one aspect of the matter. Radio telephony is very widely used in other ways. The police, for example, find it invaluable to keep their officers and squad cars in continuous touch with headquarters. Taxi drivers are directed to pick up fares by the same means, and there are a hundred and one other uses for the "walkie-talkie" type of equipment. The armed services rely heavily on radio communication. Post Office authorities throughout the world maintain huge radio stations in addition to their landline and cable services, so that it is possible to pick up a telephone receiver and speak to people in almost any land over a radio link. Such messages are not usually sent broadcast (that is, radiated in all directions) but are beamed towards their destination, a system developed by G. Marconi and C. S. Franklin in the 1920s. Again, in many countries in which the natural conditions are unsuitable for pole-and-wire communication, radio links are used instead. The signals are beamed from point to point and many simultaneous private telephone conversations can be carried on a single beam. The world's shipping and aircraft also make extensive use of radio telephony.

The most recent development is satellite communication. In this, the signals are transmitted from an earth station (such as, in Great Britain, the Post Office station at Goonhilly, Cornwall) to a satellite which has been put in orbit at just the right height (about 22,000 miles – 35,400 kilometres) for it to maintain a stationary position relative to the ground station. In the satellite a receiver picks up the ground station's transmission, amplifies it and passes it to a transmitter (also in the satellite). This re-radiates it earthward to another ground station which may be thousands of miles from the first. Provided an optical path exists between each of the ground stations and the satellite, transmission and reception can be effected. The equipment is duplicated so that signals can pass simultaneously in both directions, thus enabling normal telephone conversations to take place.

Various workers in the 19th century tried to produce television pictures but failed, largely because they lacked suitable photocells and means of amplifying signals. John Logie Baird was the first to demonstrate television pictures having movement (1926) but others soon followed. All these pioneers, however, used mechanical means of scanning (see below). In 1911 A. A. Campbell Swinton suggested the use of an all-electronic scanning system, and in the late 1920s and early 1930s such systems were developed by Zworykin (USA) and Shoenberg and his team in Britain.

In 1936 the Baird system using mechanical scanning was publicly demonstrated against the Marconi-EMI all-electronic system, and the latter was chosen to carry the world's first public high-definition television service which began in November 1936 from the BBC station at Alexandra Palace, London.

¶ DE VRIES, LEONARD. *The Book of Telecommunication.* 1962; GIBSON, D. *Radio.* 1968

See also TELEVISION.

Radio astronomy: branch of astronomy which records and interprets by means of radio apparatus electro-magnetic signals from outer space.

In 1931 Karl G. Jansky, an American electronics engineer, while working on radio communication problems, found that his radio receiver was picking up hissing and spluttering noises from outer space. It was discovered that these radiations were coming from various stars and galaxies, and from these small beginnings emerged a new branch of science called radio astronomy. The instruments used consist of specially designed aerials and highly sensitive radio receivers, the the apparatus being collectively known as a radio telescope. That at Jodrell Bank is a well-known example.

The radio signals are not generated by any form of intelligent life; they are natural radiations which occur at various wavelengths. Some of the radiations are fairly constant in strength while others, for reasons not yet properly understood, fluctuate at regular intervals. These are called "pulsars".

By careful analysis of the signals scientists have been able to discover much about the composition of stars and galaxies that could not be found by using optical telescopes, and this has enabled new theories about the origin of the universe to be formed. The radio telescope does not make the optical telescope obsolete. Each helps the other in the quest for scientific knowledge.

¶ CROWTHER, J. G. *Radioastronomy and Radar.* 1958; HYDE, F. W. *Radio Astronomy.* 1962

See also OBSERVATORY.

Railways or **railroads:** systems of pairs of steel rails laid at a fixed distance apart on a prepared road-bed, along which trains of vehicles are hauled by a locomotive. It seems to have been the iron-miners of Germany who, in the 16th century, discovered that a loaded wagon would run more easily and require less effort to draw and to guide it if the wheels ran on smooth rails rather than on a normal road surface. In these early systems, worked by humans or horses, the rails were made of wood, and when iron was first substituted (to be followed much later by steel) the cross-section of the rail assumed many different shapes. In England the term platelayer is still used for the man who looks after the track (or permanent way), thus recalling the flat metal plates with a low flange to steady the wheels, which were often used, though this made the provision of points (switches) difficult.

It was in Britain that the earliest development of modern railways took place, though the USA (where the term railroads is generally used) did not lag far behind. On Tyneside, in north-east England, the wagon-ways which conveyed coal from the pits to the quays were the scene of early experiments in haulage by steam locomotives, in which George Stephenson (1781–1848 *see* separate entry) took a leading part. These

Trevithick's Railroad, Euston Square, 1809.

trains, however, moved at little more than a walking pace. From these beginnings sprang the earliest public locomotive railway in the world, the Stockton and Darlington in Co. Durham, opened in 1825. Although it conveyed passengers, its chief purpose was the carriage of coal: indeed, anyone who was willing to pay a toll could put a horse-drawn wagon on the line, which did not lead to easy operation. The true forerunner of the modern railway was the Liverpool and Manchester, thirty miles long and opened in 1830. Here the proprietors (the railway company) had complete control of the working of their line, which carried passengers and assorted goods. In both these early railways George Stephenson was again the moving spirit.

The engineers of this period had to experiment as they went along. It took a little time to realise that the smooth iron tyre on the driving wheel of a locomotive would grip the surface on the rail, even when drawing a load up a gradient. In consequence many early lines were laid out to be as level as possible, and cable-hauled inclines were introduced as thought necessary. The stiff climb out of Euston Station (London) and the even stiffer one out of Queen Street (Glasgow) were originally tackled by this means.

As already remarked, the earliest railroads in the USA appeared almost as soon

as those in England; and here, in due course, once the eastern mountains had been crossed progress across the plains could be rapid, as the rails were pushed forward through undeveloped territory. In the older countries, by contrast, the surveyor had to find a path for his line against the resistance, sometimes amounting to physical violence, of landowners and the proprietors of canals and turnpike roads. Space does not permit a detailed account of the development of railways in different parts of the world. In Europe it gathered momentum from about 1840 onwards, often with English contractors and engineers engaged on the work. One of the early locomotive engineers in France had the good English west country name of William Buddicom.

A problem soon arose over the question of gauge (the distance between the rails), 4 feet 8½ inches [1·4 metres], chosen from that in use on Tyneside. For the Great Western Railway, however, Brunel (*see separate entry*) chose 7 feet [2·1 metres], and, though the company was soon compelled to use the standard gauge or a mixed one for most of its lines, it continued to run "broad gauge" expresses to the west country until 1892. It was also unique in laying this line with the rails on longitudinal balks of timber, in contrast to the almost universal practice of using transverse sleepers (or, as the Americans call them, ties). In Ireland, for no very apparent reason, 5 feet 3 inches [1·6 metres] was adopted. In much of Europe the gauge is close enough to our own to permit the same vehicles to run on both systems, but Spain and Portugal have 5 feet 6 inches [1·68 metres] and USSR 5 feet [1·5 metres]. In difficult country, or when traffic is light, a narrower gauge is often used, 3 feet 6 inches [1·07 metres], metre, 3 feet [0·9 metres], or even less: indeed in much of Africa some very fine locomotives work on the 3 feet 6 inches

Above, opening of Stockton and Darlington Railway, 27 September 1825. Below, locomotive race at Rainhill near Liverpool won by Stephenson's Rocket, 1829.

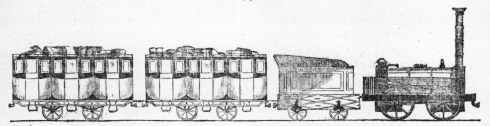

The Planet, *one of the first inside cylindered locomotives, 1833.*

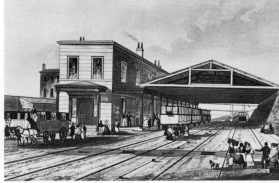

Above left, shooting buffalos on the track of the Kansas–Pacific Railroad, USA, in 1871. Below left, driving in the Golden Spike in 1869 joining the Union Pacific and Central Pacific Railroads. Above right, Liverpool Station in 1831. Below right, super modern electric commuter trains now on trial for British Rail.

[1·07 metres] lines. Australia provides a sad example of failure to foresee the time when separate systems would be linked up, there being no less than three different gauges to cause annoyance and delay.

From early days many countries kept their railways to some degree under state control. In England parliament claimed the right to decide whether or not projected lines should be approved and to enforce regulations to promote safety: although it was some years before all companies were compelled to adopt a satisfactory continuous brake for passenger trains. A proposal to nationalise the railways in 1844 was not pursued, and nationalisation was deferred until 1948.

The development of railways has made a tremendous impact on the entire way of life in many parts of the world. Whole continents, as in North America, were opened up, trade and commerce revolutionised, social habits changed. Even in warfare, as those who have studied the American Civil War (*see* separate entry) will know, strategy had to be completely revised. Nevertheless railways are now giving way to other forms of land transport which have the advantage of operating in smaller units and can convey goods and passengers more nearly "from door to door". Again, air travel can reach a far higher speed than that obtainable on the ground, though for a short journey, as between London and Manchester, accelerated rail services are bringing passenger traffic back.

In the more highly developed countries there has been, in the last few years, a large number of closures of secondary lines, but on the main routes the introduction of diesel and electric locomotives has led to notably higher speed in regular service schedules. In this, the French and Japanese have, since the end of World War II (*see* separate entry), been conspicuous pioneers, particularly where electric haulage is concerned. The future of the Railway, which in less than 150 years has played such a vital part in the lives of a large proportion of human kind, is now somewhat doubtful.

¶ FERNEYHOUGH, FRANK. *Railways.* 1970; INNES, BRIAN. *The Saga of the Railways.* 1973

Rajput: Indian warrior class, ranking second in the caste system after the Brahmin priests. Their home is northern India, notably Rajputana, where Jodhpur, Bikaner, Jaipur and Udaipur are their largest states. They are noted for pride of birth and for courage, and have always enlisted in large numbers in the army. *See also* INDIA.

Ralegh, Sir Walter (*c.* 1552–1618): English adventurer, poet and prose writer. The story, dating from the mid-17th century, that he spread his cloak over a puddle for Queen Elizabeth to walk on may well be true, as it accords so perfectly with Ralegh's personality. Dashing and quick-witted, for several years he was the Queen's favourite. In 1595 he sailed for South America, vainly seeking the legendary kingdom of El Dorado.

Ralegh was a man who made many enemies, largely because of his pride and arrogance. (John Aubrey tells us "he was damnable proud".) After Elizabeth's death he found the new king, James I, among them; was accused of treason and sentenced to death. Reprieved, he spent thirteen years in prison, obtaining his freedom by offering to return to El Dorado and bring back at least half a ton of gold. James warned that if the expedition came into conflict with the Spanish colonists his life would be forfeit. No gold was found and, while Ralegh lay ill with fever, his lieutenant burned a Spanish settlement. Ralegh returned home to die, with great courage, on the scaffold. His fortitude moved even his enemies to

Sir Walter Ralegh and his son.

admiration. Of one spectator who witnessed his trial it was reported that "whereas when he saw Ralegh first he was so moved with the common hatred that he would have gone a hundred miles to see him hanged, he would, ere he parted, have gone a thousand to save his life".

¶ TREASE, GEOFFREY. *Fortune My Foe.* 1949

Ramakrishna (1836–86): Hindu mystic in whose philosophy all religions were equally valuable as an approach to the eternal. Unlike some Hindus, he believed in active concern for others rather than withdrawal from the concerns of life.

Ramillies, Battle of (23 May 1706): the second of the Duke of Marlborough's major victories in the War of the Spanish Succession (*see* separate entry), fought between Namur and Louvain in south-western Belgium. Marlborough, commanding the allied British, Dutch and Danish forces, defeated the French under Villeroi and as a result was able to occupy most of the Netherlands.

Ramses II (*c.* 1304–*c.* 1223 BC): Egyptian Pharaoh, warrior and builder. He defeated the Hittites at the Battle of Kadesh and drove them out of Egypt. He erected many monuments and obelisks, including the temples of Abu Simbel, recently raised by the engineers above the level of the new Nile dam. Ramses was the "Ozymandias" of Shelley's poem.
See colour section.

Rangoon: capital and great port of Burma, near the mouth of the Irrawaddy. Rebuilt by Alompra, founder of the Burmese monarchy, 1753, it contained a British "factory" by 1790 and was annexed by the British in 1852 (Second Burmese War). It contains the 368 foot [112 metres] Shwe Dagôn Pagoda, covered with pure gold from base to summit.
¶ PEARN, B. R. *History of Rangoon.* 1972
See also BURMA.

Ranjit Singh (1780–1839): "The Lion of the Punjab", chief of the Sukarchakia Sikhs, whose ambition was to weld the whole of the Punjab into one Sikh empire. Seizing Lahore (1799), Amritsar (1802) and Multan (1810), by 1820 he controlled all territory between the Sutlej and the Indus. He disputed the British claim to Punjab lands south of the Sutlej, but in 1809 gave way at the Amritsar treaty. His army, trained by European officers, provided stiff opposition to the British in later Sikh wars. In 1833, when Shah Shujah of Afghanistan took refuge with him, he seized from him the Koh-i-noor diamond, now among the British crown jewels.

775

Ransom: to redeem someone from captivity, or recover possession of something which has been unlawfully detained, by paying the price demanded: also, the actual price paid or demanded.

Richard I (1157-99), King of England, on his way home from a Crusade (*see* CRUSADES), fell into the hands of the German Emperor Henry VI (reigned 1190-97), who demanded 150,000 marks as his price for the King's freedom. The ransom was paid and Richard was released after two years' imprisonment. The great Spanish author, Cervantes (1547-1616; *see* separate entry) was captured by Moorish pirates who took him to Algiers where he served in the galleys for four years until he was ransomed.

The 1970s have seen old practices put to criminal uses. In many South American countries guerrilla groups (*see* GUERRILLAS) opposed to the ruling governments have kidnapped foreign diplomats and held them to ransom against the release of political prisoners. In some cases a bargain has been struck. In others, the unfortunate captives have been murdered or else remain in captivity. In 1970 the FLQ, a French-Canadian separatist organisation, kidnapped Pierre Laporte, a member of the Quebec government, and James Cross, a British diplomat, the price demanded being the release of FLQ members held in prison. M. Laporte was found murdered: Mr Cross was eventually recovered unharmed. No prisoners were handed over, but Mr Cross's captors were allowed to leave the country.

In 1970 too, Palestine guerrillas hijacked three civil airliners and held them in the Jordanian desert, with their crews and passengers as hostages for the release of their comrades held for crimes in the countries to which the planes or the passengers belonged. The planes were blown up, but all the passengers were not freed until the countries concerned yielded to the guerrillas' demands and freed the prisoners.

Raphael (Raffaello-Sanzio, 1483-1520): Italian painter, called by his contemporaries *il divino pittore*, "the divine painter". His work is characterised by grace, gentleness and exceptional skill. Among his most famous paintings are a number of frescoes in the Papal Signature Room at the Vatican (*see* separate entry) and, in the Pope's private chapel, the Sistine Madonna. *See colour section.*
¶ RIPLEY, E. *Raphael.* 1961

Rasputin, Grigori Yefimovich (1871-1916): Russian religious leader of disreputable character. He won the favour of the Empress Alexandra, wife of Nicholas II (*see* separate entry), by his hypnotic success in checking the grave illness of her son, the heir to the throne. Rasputin used his position to influence church, government and military appointments, and became virtual ruler of the country despite the opposition of many members of the royal family and court, a group of whom conspired to assassinate him in 1916.

Hijacked airline passengers held in the Jordanian desert, 1970.

The Church of St Francis, Ravenna.

Ravenna: city of northern Italy, situated on a marshy plain six miles [9·656 kilometres] from the Adriatic coast. A thriving industrial centre, it is famous as a treasure-house of Byzantine art. Ravenna was the last capital of the Western Roman Empire and, later, the chief city of Theodoric, King of the Ostrogoths (454–526), who, despite a savage three-year-long siege to gain possession of it, brought it to a peak of splendour. It was from early Christian times the seat of an archbishop.

It is due to this admixture of political and religious importance that Ravenna possesses more than a dozen churches built between the 5th and 8th centuries when Christian art, in the opinion of many, was at its freshest and most spiritual. The many mosaics to be found in Ravenna, with their stylised, elongated figures, radiate a unique combination of stillness, strength, and deep religious devotion.
See colour section.
See also MOSAIC *for illustration, and* separate entry for BYZANTIUM; GOTHS.

Red Cross, International: worldwide organisation for the relief and prevention of human suffering. In June 1859 a young Swiss businessman, Jean Henri Dunant, seeking an interview with Napoleon III of France, entered the little Italian town of Solferino. The surrounding area had just been the scene of a battle between the Austrians, the French and the Sardinians, during the struggle for Italian independence. The town was full of wounded soldiers, and no one was doing much about them. Dunant, horrified, began to organise help. He coaxed the women of the town to nurse and to supply bandages, the children to carry water, and anyone else who happened to be there to help the wounded. After five weeks the situation improved, but Dunant left Solferino convinced that, if this were the usual aftermath of a battle, some organisation was needed to give help to all casualties, irrespective of nationality.

He published a book, *A Memory of Solferino*, recording his experience. It made a great impression in Europe. A lawyer from Geneva, Gustave Moynier, together with Dunant, established in 1863 a Permanent International Committee, the forerunner of the International Committee of the Red Cross. It was a neutral body composed of Swiss, because Switzerland was invariably a neutral country. Its aim was to assist people who became casualties of war.

In 1864 an international meeting known as the *Convention of Geneva* agreed that its member nations would allow Dunant's organisation to help all wounded soldiers. It adopted as its badge a red cross on a white ground and became known as the *Red Cross Society*. Some Islamic (*see* ISLAM) nations wished to join it: instead of a red cross, they took a red crescent as their badge, while Persia used a red lion, but their aims were identical. A war casualty was no longer an enemy, but a fellow man needing help.

As years passed more nations became members of the Geneva Convention. During two world wars the Red Cross helped the wounded, established hospitals, hospital ships and hospital trains, delivered parcels of food and clothing to prisoners of war and – most important – let their families know what had happened

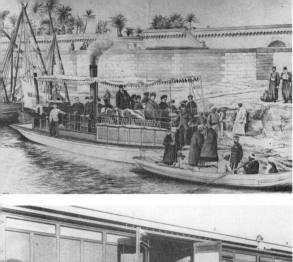

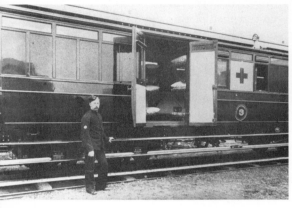

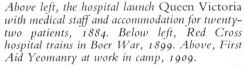

Above left, the hospital launch Queen Victoria *with medical staff and accommodation for twenty-two patients, 1884. Below left, Red Cross hospital trains in Boer War, 1899. Above, First Aid Yeomanry at work in camp, 1909.*

to them. After World War II (*see* separate entry) the Red Cross looked after refugees and helped to reunite families.

During peacetime Red Cross and Red Crescent Societies undertake relief work. The Canadian and Finnish Red Cross send medical help to Eskimo communities in the Arctic Circle. The Persian Red Lion Society specialises in mother and child welfare. Wherever disasters such as flood, hurricane or earthquake strike, Red Cross helpers are immediately at the scene. The expenses of the League of Red Cross Societies are largely met by voluntary contributions of member societies, by special grants from other international organisations and, from time to time, individual governments.

¶ PEACEY, BELINDA. *The Story of the Red Cross.* 1969; ROTHKOPF, CAROL. *Jean Henri Dunant: Father of the Red Cross.* 1971

Reformation, The: term given by historians to a period of strife and change in western Christendom which came to a head in the 16th century. It arose from a growing desire among thoughtful men to reform or remove certain beliefs and practices in the Roman Catholic Church which they felt were contrary to the truths of early Christianity. Such criticisms had been made before; but the 14th century had witnessed the scandal of the popes driven from Rome and living at Avignon in Provence (1309-77) under French protection, and this was followed by a period of forty years when rival popes held office simultaneously. The lowered reputation of the papacy was not improved by the greed and worldliness of some 15th-century popes, so that more than one of the rulers of Europe grew restless under papal claims to regulate the religious affairs of their domains. At the same time there were questionings of matters of belief, as in the teaching of John Wyclif (*c.* 1320–84) in England and Jan Hus (*c.* 1369–1415) in Bohemia.

It was, however, from Martin Luther (1483-1546) that the movement gathered full impetus. The son of a Saxon miner, Luther began by serving the Roman Catholic Church as friar, priest and university lecturer. His first protest was against "indulgences", whereby remission of punishment after death for sins committed in this life was purchased by gifts of money to the Church. Soon, however, he was challenging some of the basic principles of Catholic teaching, as when he asserted that by Faith alone could man attain salvation and not, as the Church maintained, by the practice of good works. He also denounced the papal power, with the result that some of the rulers of the German states, together with the Kings of Denmark and Sweden, reformed their Churches on his principles, thus founding the Lutheran Church which exists today.

John Calvin.

Martin Luther.

Meanwhile, a Swiss priest, Ulrich Zwingli (1484-1531), had also left the Roman Church and was preaching reform in Zurich. He gained a considerable following but was killed in a skirmish with those who opposed him.

The third great figure of the Reformation was John Calvin (1509-64). Though born in France, he exercised his greatest influence in Geneva. He does not

appear to have had direct contact with Luther, and, although he too made Faith the central theme of his message, his teaching was less humane and his conclusions were far more severe than those of the German reformer. Nevertheless, it was the doctrines of Calvin, however modified in the course of years, that had the widest influence among the Churches that sprang from the Reformation in many parts of western Europe.

In Scotland the movement, under the leadership of John Knox, who was deeply influenced by Calvinistic teaching, followed in many ways the same pattern as elsewhere. In England the course of events was different. It is true that there already existed a national tradition of resistance to the claims of the papacy, but Henry VIII's quarrel with the pope was originally on personal grounds, namely the King's desire to be divorced from Catherine of Aragon. Although he came

John Knox.

to claim the supreme headship of the English Church, dissolved the monasteries, and persecuted those of his Catholic subjects who opposed him, his own attitude to the old faith remained at his death very close to the spirit in which he had written the attack on Luther which earned him the title of *Fidei Defensor* (Defender of the Faith) twenty-six

Golden Bulla of Pope Clement VII, affixed to the Papal Bull which confirmed Henry VIII as Defender of the Faith.

years before. But reformers from the continent were already receiving a sympathetic hearing in England, especially at Cambridge University, and the reign of the boy king Edward VI that followed saw the issue of a royally approved prayer-book in the English language, largely translated from the Latin service books formerly in use. Certain Romish doctrines were at the same time formally renounced, and the removal of many church ornaments, regarded as objects of superstition, was required. But the government of the Church through archbishops and bishops was retained, and, on this and other grounds, many men in England felt that the reform of the established Church had not gone far enough. Such men formed the nucleus of the Puritans who were a divisive element in the religion and

politics of the country up to the end of the next century.

¶ COWIE, LEONARD. *The Reformation.* 1968; COWIE, LEONARD. *The Reformation of the Sixteenth Century.* 1970

See also individual entries.

Reformed Church: term applied to a body of Churches springing from the Reformation (*see* previous article). While it is sometimes used in a wider sense to embrace all Churches of such origin, it is more accurately applied to those whose beliefs and practices are founded on the teaching of John Calvin, as distinct, especially, from those which trace their history back to Martin Luther (*see* separate entry) direct and are called Lutheran. This is due to the fact that, even as early as the end of the 16th century, the Calvinistic Churches were already claiming for themselves the Latin title of *ecclesiae reformatae*.

Reformers, Religious: people who have tried to purify religion and religious institutions in accordance with what they believed to be the will of God. For centuries few people in Western Europe challenged the authority of the Church of Rome. When the Roman Empire was overrun by barbarians, the Church survived to represent civilisation, law and order, education, learning and culture. Anybody who questioned the beliefs and doctrines of the Church was accused of heresy and severely punished.

During the Middle Ages many thinking people realised the need for reform. Geoffrey Chaucer (*c.* 1340–1400) and William Langland (*c.* 1330–1400) were both critical in their writings of idle clerics who neglected their duties, or cheated people with false relics, or sold "pardons come from Rome al hoot". John Wyclif (*c.* 1320–84) believed that people should be able to read the Bible for themselves and form their own judgments, and he inspired "poor preachers", who went about preaching and teaching the scriptures in English. His adherents became known as Lollards, and their movement was one of the forces which paved the way to the Reformation. Wyclif's ideas influenced Jan Hus (John Huss, c. 1369-1415), the great Bohemian reformer and national hero, who witnessed fearlessly in his writings and his teachings for the reform of the Church and was condemned by the Council of Constance and burnt at the stake for heresy. Wyclif's ideas were also condemned by the Council of Constance: in 1415 it was ordered that his writings should be destroyed and his bones dug up and scattered, an edict which was carried out in 1428.

Some religious reformers have wished to reform the Church from within: for instance, a little group of 16th-century Christian Humanists, amongst them John Colet (1466?-1519), who taught at Oxford and later became Dean of St Paul's; St Thomas More (1478-1535), Henry VIII's personal friend, who was appointed Lord Chancellor in 1529, and Desiderius Erasmus (c. 1465-1536), a Dutch scholar who lived in England for some years and was appointed Professor of Greek and Theology at Cambridge. All these men were friends and scholars, and all believed that the Church could be reformed by a return to the ideals and the discipline of primitive Christianity. John Colet studied Greek in Italy as a young man, and, after reading the New Testament in the original, his lectures on St Paul's Epistles threw a flood of light on the life of the Early Church. He founded St Paul's School in London and encouraged the boys to learn Greek as well as the customary Latin. St Thomas More was a most lovable and charming man: he resisted Henry VIII's determination to

reform the Church to serve his own ends, and so died a martyr on the scaffold. Erasmus spent the latter part of his life in Switzerland; a man of peace, he was appalled by the violence of the Reformation which he himself had helped to create. When it was suggested to him that he had laid the egg from which the Reformation was hatched, he shook his head sadly and accused Martin Luther of hatching out "a fighting cock".

The great Protestant Reformation was brought about, not by the men of peace who had paved the way for it, but by men of iron will and determination. Even so, Martin Luther (1483-1546), the great architect of the German Reformation, did not set out deliberately to destroy the unity of the Church: he protested against the flagrant abuses which were the scandal of his time and so incurred the enmity of the authorities and the wrath of the Pope himself. The day on which he nailed his famous ninety-five theses (see INDULGENCES) to the door of the church at Wittenberg – 31 October 1517 – has been described as the birthday of the Protestant Reformation. His teachings were condemned by the Pope, who ordered his writings to be burnt, but Luther replied by publicly burning the "Bull", or papal message, which had announced the Pope's displeasure. Summoned to be tried before the Emperor at Worms, he refused to go into hiding: "I will go, though every tile in the city were a devil!" he said. At the trial he steadfastly refused to recant, though in peril of his life. "Here stand I," he declared. "I can do no other. So help me, God."

Martin Luther's courageous lead was taken up by other religious thinkers of his day: Ulrich Zwingli (1484-1531), the great Swiss reformer and admirer of Erasmus; Philip Melanchthon (1497-1560), friend of Luther but of a gentler spirit; John Calvin (1509-64), the great

French thinker and theologian, who set up a Protestant regime in Geneva which became a rigid dictatorship, but which offered shelter to Protestant refugees from other parts of Europe, including England; and John Knox (c. 1513–72), who shaped the Reformation in Scotland and became the bitter enemy of Mary Queen of Scots. The men who led the Reformation were as intolerant as they were sincere; Calvin punished those who disagreed with him, and burnt "heretics" at the stake – for instance, Michael Servetus (1511–53), who differed from other Protestants in his beliefs.

The English reformers had different problems to face. Henry VIII's seizure of power over the Church for his own ends freed England at a stroke from the power of Rome and put an end to the whole monastic system, but on the other hand it gave little indication as to what kind of Church was to survive. The great English reformers, amongst them Hugh Latimer (c. 1485–1555), Thomas Cranmer (1489–1556) and Nicholas Ridley (c. 1500–55), attacked old ways and customs and instituted new ones, only to fall from power and go courageously to their deaths at the stake when Mary Tudor restored the Roman Catholic Church during her short reign. With the establishment of her sister Elizabeth on the throne came the compromise of a "middle way" which flowered gloriously in the Anglican Church. The Catholic right wing and the Puritan or reforming "left wing" continued, and suffered persecution, until men slowly learned to tolerate one another in matters of religion.

See also REFORMATION and many of the names mentioned in this article.

Reformers, Social: people who have worked constructively to remedy social evils and injustices. Few great social reforms have occurred spontaneously. They have generally been the result of slow, pioneering work which has brought about a change of ideas and attitudes, and resulted finally in a struggle – sometimes bitter – between enlightened and reactionary forces. Sometimes the early workers are forgotten. For instance, the cause of the "climbing boys" is for ever linked with the great Earl of Shaftesbury (1801–85), but its first champion was Jonas Hanway (1712–86), better remembered as the first Englishman to use an umbrella.

In 1773 Jonas Hanway made the first protest against the use of climbing boys to sweep chimneys. At that time, master sweeps would buy unwanted children, harden their limbs with brine, and train them brutally to climb up chimneys. Many died of suffocation: others contracted diseases or were stunted or maimed. The protest spread slowly. In 1788 and again in 1794 Blake expressed it in verse: in 1837, after the first Acts restricting the practice had been passed and ignored, Dickens exposed the situation in *Oliver Twist*. Lord Shaftesbury took up the cause in 1840, and other Acts were passed in succession and again ignored. In 1863 Charles Kingsley published *The Water Babies*, and public indignation began to mount, but it took ten more years of campaigning by Lord Shaftesbury before, in 1875, a Bill was introduced which put an end to the scandal, over a hundred years after the first protest had been made.

Lord Shaftesbury also championed the child workers in the factories and the mines, continuing the protest made by such outspoken men as Richard Oastler (1789–1861) and Michael Sadler (1780–1835). The cotton spinners vowed that their industry would be ruined if restrictions were introduced, though Robert Owen (1771–1858) had demonstrated at New Lanark that it was possible to make a fortune out of cotton spinning without employing a single child under ten.

Michael Sadler.

The work of social reformers is often hampered by unimaginative people who cannot recognise the victims of social injustice as human beings like themselves. For example, Jonas Fielding described a beadle who drove some climbing boys out of church, with the comment: "What business have chimney-sweeping boys in church?" And another social reformer, Josephine Butler (1828–1905), encountered the same attitude in her work for prostitutes. "Now look at Jesus," she wrote. "He . . . never judged people as a class. He always took the man, the woman, or the child as a *person*."

It would be difficult to exaggerate the part played by men and women of letters in social reform. Dickens attacked not only the employment of climbing boys but bad housing, bad sanitation, bad schools, bad prisons, bad political and legal customs, and a bad poor law. Elizabeth Gaskell and Benjamin Disraeli exposed the social inequalities of their day in certain of their novels; Elizabeth Barrett Browning and Thomas Hood, in some of their poems; and Mrs Stowe's famous *Uncle Tom's Cabin* roused the conscience of the world against slavery. Upton Sinclair's novel, *The Jungle*, prompted an investigation by Roosevelt which resulted in the Pure-Food Legislation of 1906 and eventually swept away the scandal of the Chicago stockyards. John Galsworthy's play *Justice* was acknowledged by Winston Churchill (then Home Secretary) to have played a considerable part in the campaign for penal reform, and Brand Whitlock's novel *Turn of the Balance* (1907) influenced the same cause in the United States.

Early workers for penal reform were John Howard (1726–90) and Elizabeth Fry (1780–1845), and, in America, Dorothea Dix (1802–87), who also campaigned for the humane treatment of the insane, another reform which took generations to achieve. First in the field were the Philadelphia Quakers, who opened a hospital for the insane in 1757, and William Tuke of York (1732–1822); who founded The Retreat in 1796. Again a popular author struck a blow for reform: Wilkie Collins in *The Woman in White* (1860) and Charles Reade, in *Hard Cash* (1863), revealed the scandalous conditions in private asylums.

At one time women had no more rights than lunatics, with whom they were bracketed as persons unfit to vote. A husband might promise: "With all my

Elizabeth Fry.

worldly goods I thee endow", but in practice all his wife's property passed into his control. Mrs Millicent Garrett Fawcett (1847–1929) recorded that when her purse was stolen it was described on the charge sheet as being her husband's property. This strengthened her resolution to campaign for the right of a married woman to control her own property – from her purse to her fortune – which resulted in the Married Women's Property Act of 1870. Millicent Fawcett also worked for the Higher Education of Women and for Women's Suffrage. The cause of Women's Rights in the United States is said to have received its first impetus from the World's Anti-Slavery Convention in London in 1840, when women delegates were refused admission except as observers. Elizabeth Cady Stanton (1815–1902) and Lucretia Mott (1793–1880) resolved that "the Woman Question" must be tackled forthwith, and so followed the historic Women's Rights Convention at Seneca Falls in 1848 which launched the cause of their emancipation in the United States.

Dr Barnardo with some of his "Village" girls, Barkingside, 1890's.

Many social reformers have tackled social evils directly, by practical measures. In Britain, Doctor Thomas John Barnardo (1845–1905) founded homes for destitute children and, it is estimated, helped 250,000 during his lifetime. Octavia Hill (1838–1912), appalled by the housing conditions of the poor, and encouraged and sponsored by Ruskin, started an experiment in housing management in 1865 which proved revolutionary: she also campaigned for open spaces, and the preservation of common land, and this was to lead directly to her friendship with Canon Rawnsley and to the establishment of the National Trust in 1895. Other social reformers have tackled housing conditions indirectly, by demonstrating the possibility of creating a new kind of town – for example, Ebenezer Howard (1850–1928), who introduced the idea of a "garden city". Again, others have founded settlements in slum areas – Toynbee Hall in Whitechapel, Kingsley Hall in Bow, Hull House in Chicago (founded by Jane Addams, winner of the Nobel Peace Prize) – to serve as growing points for education and social reform. Some have influenced social reform by their revolutionary theories; for instance, William Morris (1834–96), whose crusade against ugliness in all its forms failed to check industrial development but nevertheless resulted in a revival of good craftsmanship and a more widely shared apprehension and appreciation of beauty in everyday life.

See also EMANCIPATION OF WOMEN; NEGRO; PRISONS; SLAVERY; and separate entries for HOWARD; OWEN; QUAKERS; SHAFTESBURY, EARL OF.

Refrigeration: process of producing low temperatures for long storage purposes. A mammoth found preserved in the frozen Siberian tundra had flesh good enough to feed to dogs, though it had been in cold storage for 15,000 years. After the Battle of Edgehill (1642), during the Civil War in England, the body of Sir Gervase Scroop, with sixteen severe wounds and stripped naked by plunderers, was preserved through cold and frosty weather from about 3 o'clock on Sunday afternoon till the evening of the following Tuesday, when he was discovered still alive by his son. Here, refrigeration was accidental. However, around 1000 BC the Chinese were cutting and storing ice. Until the 19th century, ice and cold cellars were the only means of preserving food. In 1831 a British ice-making process using air compression was invented: and, later, an American one using expansion of volatile fluids. The USA made the first cold air refrigerating plant: Australia developed refrigeration further in factories, ships and industrial plants.

Regency: period when, the king being under age or incapacitated, a kingdom is ruled by an administrator or a council. An example of a regency during the king's minority is that of Philip, Duke of Orleans, from 1715-23, during the childhood of Louis XV.

In 1811 King George III of Britain was judged insane. The Prince of Wales was appointed Regent, succeeding his father in 1820 as George IV. In consequence, the word is also used as an adjective to denote a style of architecture, furniture and decoration characteristic of the 1810-30 period. The Regency style flourished, though coarsening, until the first years of Victoria's reign (1837-1901). Its prime characteristic was an elegant simplicity deriving from classical forms, often softened with a touch of fantasy. John Nash's (1752-1835) terraces at Regent's Park, London, show Regency architecture at

Cumberland Terrace, Regent's Park, built by John Nash in the early 19th century.

its elegant best, while the Pavilion at Brighton (also Nash's work) shows Regency fantasy carried to an astonishing but delightful extreme.
See colour section.

Regicide: the killing of a king, or one responsible for such a killing; in England, the eighty-four men named in 1660 as responsible for the execution of Charles I (1649), among them Cromwell (*see* separate entry), Ireton, Bradshaw and Harrison; in France, men like Robespierre and Danton who had a hand in the death of Louis XVI (1793).

Regnal years: the years of a reign, dating from the king's or queen's accession. Thus, the 1st regnal year of Elizabeth I of England is from 17 November 1558 to 16 November 1559 and her 33rd regnal year is from 17 November 1590 to 16 November 1591. For historians this system is of great importance since, e.g. in English history, for many centuries no other method of dating is used in public documents, so that a mistake of one day in calculation can mean an error of a whole year in establishing a date.

Reichstag: former name of German parliament, in which in medieval times chosen members met to advise Holy Roman emperors. Bismarck re-established it as an elected group in 1867, but Catholic and socialist opponents protested that he allowed them very limited power.

First session of the new Reichstag, 27 May 1924.

After the defeat of Germany in World War I the Reichstag became the supreme law-making assembly of the Weimar Republic. Subsequently the Nazi Party gradually increased its membership of the Reichstag, and when Hitler became Chancellor in 1933 opposition to him in it was eliminated.
See also BISMARCK; HITLER; NAZIS; WORLD WARS I and II.

Reign of Terror or **The Terror:** name given to the period of the French Revolution from June 1793 to July 1794. In 1793 a ruthless political group, the Jacobins, headed by Robespierre (*see* separate entry),

Robespierre being shot in the face by a gendarme during his arrest, June 1794.

seized power and took over the Committee of Public Safety. Ruling France as a dictatorship they strove to rouse national resistance and save France from invasion. Threats by foreign armies and civil war in the west were met by a vast military conscription scheme. Food was scarce and traders who overcharged were punished. Representatives sought out thousands of royalist sympathisers, priests and opponents of Jacobin rule, who were tried before a Revolutionary Tribunal, those found guilty being publicly guillotined. Though these harsh actions preserved the revolutionary spirit in France, within a year serious quarrels split the Committee of Public Safety, and Robespierre himself was overthrown and executed. In the previous six weeks some 1,285 victims of the Terror had been guillotined.

Reims, Rheims: city in northern France on a tributary of the Aisne, called after the Gallic tribe who lived in the district in Roman times. It was the seat of a bishopric as early as the 3rd century, and Clovis the Frank was baptised there in 496 by St Remigius with oil, according to the legend, from a Holy Phial brought from heaven by a dove. In 972 the scholar Gerbert (Pope Sylvester II) was drawn to Reims, where he founded a great school of logic, music and astronomy, and introduced the abacus into northern Europe. In 1080 Bruno of Cologne developed there his ideas for the Carthusian Order of monks. Reims Cathedral, rebuilt after a fire in 1210, was the place of coronation of French kings. The sculptures there by Gaucher (worked 1247-55), graceful and vigorous, were imitated in Germany, Italy and Spain. Towards the end of the Napoleonic Wars it was captured and recaptured several times, and during the

The west front of Reims Cathedral, France.

Franco-Prussian War of 1870-71 was made the headquarters of a German governor-general. In World War I the city suffered heavy damage from enemy bombardment, the cathedral itself being severely hit. Modern industries include champagne, textiles and mechanical engineering.
See also FRANCO-PRUSSIAN, NAPOLEONIC, and WORLD WARS.

Religion, Wars of: struggles arising from attempts to impose beliefs by force and often ending by corrupting and discrediting the religions they are meant to protect. Because religious belief – unlike nationality – is a matter of choice or tradition, treachery and changing sides are hard to prevent, and therefore religious wars tend to be more bitter than dynastic wars. They are attended by massacre and assassination, and followed by exile or oppression of the defeated.

In Europe, wars of religion followed the Reformation (*see* separate entry), beginning with the war between Zurich and the Forest Cantons (1528-31) and ending with the Thirty Years War (1618-48). The term is often specifically applied to the series of Huguenot struggles for freedom of worship in France, 1562-98.

Wars of this nature may be between rival religions (Muslim and Christian) or between orthodox and reformers in the same religion (Sunni and Shia in Islam, Catholic and Protestant in Christendom). *See also* individual entries.

Rembrandt Harmenszoon van Rijn (1606–69): Dutch painter with an incomparable insight into human nature. His portraits, self-portraits, and groups such as *The Sortie of the Banning Cocq Company* (popularly known as *The Night Watch*) are among the greatest pictures ever painted. As a young man Rembrandt built a high reputation but, too original,

Old man with flowing beard *by Rembrandt.*

too uncomfortably truthful for the general taste, he outlived his popularity. In 1656 he was declared bankrupt. In contrast, in 1961 his *Aristotle Contemplating the Bust of Homer* was sold for $2,300,000, then about £821,428.
See colour section.
¶ RIPLEY, E. *Rembrandt.* 1956
See also ETCHING; PORTRAIT PAINTING.

Renaissance: rebirth; the name given in 1845 to the surge of intellectual and artistic activity which arose after 1400 in Italy and which spread in the late 16th and early 17th centuries to northern Europe after the Italian movement had been extinguished by the Inquisition. The traditional view was that a spontaneous outburst of intellectual energy revived the study of the Classics – long neglected in the Middle Ages – and led to a spirit of bold enquiry, of confidence in man's power to improve his condition by deliberate action, of frank enjoyment of worldly pleasures – conversation, physical exercise, the arts, family life. Anyone who had excelled in art or thought – Cimabue in painting, Petrarch in letters – was lifted out of the Middle Ages and explained as a "precursor" of the Renaissance. Reacting against this view, later students showed that medieval scholars grounded their physics in Aristotle (384–322 BC), their astronomy in Ptolemy, and that Gothic was more advanced than Renaissance architecture. Yet 15th-century Italians were conscious of belonging to a pioneer movement. Vasari spoke of Giotto "restoring the art of design", and Marsilio Ficino wrote: "This is an age of gold which has brought back to life the almost extinguished liberal disciplines of poetry, eloquence, painting, architecture, sculpture, music." In the other parts of Europe where arts were flourishing – the Flemish towns, South Germany, Spain – artists did not show the same dissatisfaction with the Gothic style. In the city-states of Italy there had emerged a class of wealthy merchants, educated in secular schools, well-informed by the practice of commerce, practised in public affairs in their guilds and civic councils, forced by party strife and the struggles of popes against emperors to take thought for their own survival and to regard no authority – priest or prince – as beyond attack. The ideals of the Greek city-states seemed more relevant to these men than those of knights or monks. Individually or as members of city councils, they became lavish and discerning patrons of the arts. A host of manuscript hunters, teachers of Greek, travelling lecturers on classical authors, satisfied their thirst for the works of Greece and Rome. Sculptors buried their own works and dug them up as antique discoveries. Many Renaissance scholars were devout Christians – Florentine biblical scholarship started the movement which culminated in Erasmus's New Testament and Luther's Bible – but some threw off Christian morality and provoked the reaction towards rigid orthodoxy which stifled the Renaissance in Italy after 1540. "Cicero is driving out Christ", Erasmus wrote of the Renaissance preoccupation with style. In the long run, this preoccupation killed Latin as the working language of scholars and may have diverted men from the study of science. *See colour section.*

¶ BULL, GEORGE. *The Renaissance.* 1968; BURKE, PETER. *The Renaissance.* 1964; HALE, J. R. *The Renaissance.* 1967
See also individual entries.

Reparations: money, or the equivalent in services, paid by a defeated nation in recompense for the damage and loss it has inflicted. This term first appeared after World War I, though, before then, a nation victorious in war had often levied a substantial punitive "indemnity" from its enemy.

The term has also been used for such payments as those by West Germany to Israel for Hitler's crimes against the Jews, and Israel's obligations to Arab refugees. *See* separate entries for HITLER; JEWS; WORLD WAR I.

Restoration: reinstatement to a former state or condition. Someone who has fainted may be *restored* to consciousness; a damaged oil painting may be *restored* to its original condition. Kings who have lost their thrones have sometimes, after an interval, been restored to them: e.g. Haile Selassie, Emperor of Abyssinia (Ethiopia), forced from his throne in 1936 by an Italian invasion but restored in 1941. In France in 1814 the Bourbon dynasty was restored following the enforced abdication of Napoleon I.

In English history the term Restoration specifically refers to the return in 1660 of the Stuart royal family, in the person of Charles II (1630–85), after an eleven-year

interregnum in the course of which Oliver Cromwell (1599–1658), and later, for a brief spell, his son Richard (1626–1712), assumed the title of Lord Protector. The term is also used descriptively of the years following Charles's return, e.g. in such terms as the Restoration dramatists.

¶ BRYANT, SIR ARTHUR. *Restoration England.* 1960
See also individual entries.

Revere, Paul (1735–1818): American hero of a night ride from Charleston to Lexington (18–19 April 1775) to warn the Massachusetts colonists of the coming of British troops at the outbreak of the War of American Independence (*see* separate entry). Of Huguenot descent, Revere became well known as a worker in metals and as a bell founder. Many of his bells still hang in New England churches.

¶ In *Great Lives, Great Deeds.* 1965

Rhine: chief river of western Europe, a third of its 824 miles [1,326 kilometres] being navigable. With its two tributaries, the Moselle and the Ruhr, the Rhine basin has carried much of western Europe's trade for centuries. The Romans used it as a frontier against the barbarians. Danton in 1793 proclaimed the Rhine as France's natural frontier, but German hostility has made this impossible.

¶ REES, GORONWY. *The Rhine.* 1967

Rhineland: area of West Germany, lying on both banks of the middle Rhine. Much of it is forested and hilly, but its valleys are fertile, producing famous wines. Other parts are heavily industrialised. Germany and France have fought for centuries for the control of its valuable land and river routes.

Rhodes: mountainous Greek island, the most easterly of the Aegean Sea. Archaeological remains (*see* ARCHAEOLOGY) suggest settlement as early as 2000 BC, and by the Christian era the island had reached a great height of naval and commercial prosperity, with a maritime code and standard of coinage widely recognised in the Mediterranean. One of the Seven Wonders of the World (*see* separate entry) was the statue of Helios which stood at the entrance to the harbour of Rhodes. From the 1st century BC the island ex-

perienced the rule, or misrule, of a variety of conquerors and raiders, including Romans, Saracens, Italian adventurers, Turks, Crusaders and Ottoman sultans. From 1912–47 it was controlled by Italy, after which it was ceded to Greece.

Rhodes, Cecil John (1853–1902): British statesman. Following a severe illness in 1869, he went out from England to Natal, South Africa, to recuperate, returning four years later to Oxford University. Illness again interrupted his education, but, after another spell in South Africa during which he invested in some diamond diggings in Kimberley, he eventually graduated in 1881. He then joined Barney Barnato and several other diamond diggers to form De Beers, the great diamond producers who now virtually control the market. In 1889 he was instrumental in forming the British South Africa Company, which until 1922 wielded enormous influence in the whole of southern Africa, especially Northern and Southern Rhodesia, to which he gave his name. In 1890 he became Prime Minister of Cape Colony, holding the post until the ill-fated Jameson Raid precipitated the Boer War (*see* separate entry). He died on 26 March 1902 and is buried in the Matopo Hills near Bulawayo in Rhodesia's national shrine. His Cape Town house, Groote Schuur, is now the South African Prime Minister's residence. He endowed a large number of Rhodes Scholarships at Oxford for the benefit of students from the Empire, the USA and Germany. He advocated British imperial expansion in Africa "from the Cape to Cairo". In power he was impatient of control and opposition, and for this reason failed to build up a strong team of co-workers in the worthy causes for which he laboured. But he was in many ways an enlightened administrator and is justly regarded as a principal maker of the British Empire.

Rhodesia: previously officially Southern Rhodesia, a self-governing British colony, situated in southern central Africa, with Zambia to the north and north-west, Mozambique to the north-east and east, Transvaal to the south and Botswana to the south-west. The main tribes are the Mashona and Matabele.

Between 1890 and 1923 the territory was administered by the British South Africa Company (BSA), and the Rhodesian police force is still called the BSA Police, though the company relinquished its claims to the land in 1923 except for its highly developed citrus and other estates. The principal exports are tobacco, sugar, citrus, groundnuts, gold, asbestos, copper, coal, antimony, tin and emeralds.

Rhodesia/Rwanda

An interesting chain of ancient ruins extends from the Mozambique border in the east to Botswana in the west, including Zimbabwe, Khami and other famous remains, most of which are associated with ancient mineral workings.

In 1911, after being opened up by the BSA Company, the territory was divided into north and south Rhodesia. In 1922 Southern Rhodesia rejected a proposition to join the Union of South Africa and voted for self-government, becoming a prosperous self-governing British colony, its economy thriving on tobacco. Large numbers of Africans from Nyasaland (Malawi) and Northern Rhodesia (Zambia) migrated to Southern Rhodesia, attracted by better living and working conditions, as did many British ex-servicemen, after World War II, in which a very high percentage of Rhodesian Europeans served with the British forces. In 1953 Southern Rhodesia joined with Northern Rhodesia and Nyasaland to form the Central African Federation (CAF) which showed every promise of becoming an economically sound entity. The Africans were opposed, however, feeling that federation would perpetuate white rule; and, following violent demonstrations in Nyasaland and Northern Rhodesia, CAF was dissolved, Nyasaland being granted independence as Malawi, and Northern Rhodesia as Zambia. Rhodesia immediately clamoured for independence also, but was unwilling to accept a one-man-one-vote constitution, so that Britain delayed approval. On 11 November 1965, after protracted but unsuccessful negotiations, the Rhodesian premier, Ian Smith, made a unilateral declaration of independence which is still not accepted by Britain. So far all negotiations for a settlement have foundered on British insistence that majority rule by the African population must be guaranteed within a reasonable time.

¶ HOLE, H. M. *The Making of Rhodesia.* 1967

Richelieu, Armand-Jean du Plessis de (1585-1642): cardinal, and chief minister

of Louis XIII. The third son of a Poitevin noble, he was trained for the army but accepted the family bishopric of Luçon when his brother became a monk. He worked tirelessly for the unity of France under royal authority and against the disruptive privileges of the nobles. He broke the military power of the Huguenots but preserved their freedom of worship and employed many in high office. He did not shrink from alliance with Protestant Sweden and Holland to contain the Habsburgs (*see* separate entry). He built up the French navy and mercantile marine. Frail and moody, he "lay awake at night that others might sleep in the shadow of his watching".

¶ In CANNING, JOHN, editor. *100 Great Lives.* 1953

Richmond: the name of many places in the world, two of them being the municipal borough in Surrey, England, which grew up round the royal manor and palace of Richmond, the scene of many episodes in English history; and the capital of Virginia, USA, first settled in 1609 by Captain Francis West and famous both for its part in the War of Independence and as the Confederate capital during the Civil War.

Rights, Bill of (1689): Act giving statutory force to the terms on which William III and Mary II were accepted on the throne of England. It excluded Roman Catholics from the throne, insisted that parliament should meet frequently and enjoy freedom of speech, and limited the use of arbitrary royal power, exercised by previous kings, e.g. in suspending and dispensing with laws, levying taxes without parliament's consent, and in raising an army.

Rio de Janeiro: city on the coast of Brazil, South America, discovered on 1 January 1502 by the Portuguese explorer Alphonso de Souza, who mistakenly thought that he had found the mouth of a river. Nevertheless he judged correctly that the site would become a valuable harbour. When Brazil became free of Portuguese control in 1822 Rio naturally became the capital city, but it was replaced in 1960 by a new capital, Brasilia.

Sugar Loaf Mountain, Rio de Janeiro.

Victor Emmanuel and Garibaldi meet at Teana, 1860.

Risorgimento: Italian word meaning "resurrection". In the 19th century educated Italians bitterly resented the harshness and inefficiency of the foreign governments, especially the Austrian, that ruled over them. "Risorgimento" became a rallying-cry to encourage all Italians in a national revival that would lead to unification and prosperity. In particular, the name is applied to the movements led by Mazzini, Garibaldi and Cavour, 1815–70.
¶ WOOLF, S. J. *The Italian Risorgimento.* 1969

Roads: strips of land expressly designed for the passage of men, livestock and vehicles. It is not an accident that the greatest road builders in the past have been the military powers – the Romans, the French under Napoleon, and, in the 20th century, Germany and Italy under Hitler and Mussolini. To move troops and their equipment across country quickly it is essential to have wide, straight, well-surfaced roads, with strong foundations requiring minimum maintenance.

Strong central government over a wide area, with power to command labour and employ technical experts, has always been vital for a good road system. Small or weak states rarely could afford adequate roads. Seafaring nations, like the Egyptians, the Carthaginians and the Greeks, could do with a minimum. Even Britain could manage for centuries to transport the bulk of her goods using coastal shipping and inland waterways.

The first roads probably followed trails and paths made by animals, leading from feeding grounds to watering places, and those of men, searching for food, fuel and water. As trade developed between towns and villages, early roads were built in the Near East, *c.* 3500 BC, soon after the invention of the wheel. The first known example of an empire large enough for a road system was that of the Akkadian ruler, Sargon, *c.* 2600 BC, who held sway from Babylonia to the Mediterranean. Assyria, *c.* 800 BC, also had roads, built on low embankments in the valleys, with the gradients on hills eased with cuttings.

Around 500 BC two great roads connected the Mediterranean with the top of the Persian gulf. One, beginning at Sardis, crossing the Euphrates and the Tigris, and ending at Susa, was travelled by Herodotus. After his conquest of Babylonia in 539 BC, Cyrus built a road connecting Babylon with Egypt. China exported silks, jade, etc., as far as Rome and pre-Christian Europe along caravan routes crossing Turkestan, India and Persia.

The Romans were the first great road builders: 50,000 miles [80,500 kilometres] of roads, some of them still in use, stretched across their Empire in southern and western Europe, North Africa and the Middle East. In the main these were military routes, designed to move the Roman legions and carts directly and easily. Generally the roads ran in straight lines, passing over hills rather than round them; where there were bends they were of a large radius and widened for passing. The road bed was of great strength, made by layers of broken stone bonded together with mortar. On top was a gravelled layer covered with cobbles or paving – the overall thickness varying between two and five feet [0·6 and 1·5 metres]. It is a curious fact that the British

Remains of the Roman road near Blakeney Hill, Gloucestershire, England.

had better roads under the Romans than under the Stuarts 1,200 years later, and that no one in Britain made any new hard roads till the 18th century. After the collapse of the Roman Empire, the chaotic conditions caused by the barbarian invasions led to the ruins of these fine roads. Nevertheless, some still endure; and the historian G. M. Trevelyan was able to write: "Stretches of them have been repaired and modernised, and the motor-car now shoots along the path of the legions."

Inevitably the centuries of small European kingdoms, without adequate resources and with their recurring wars, made it difficult to maintain an efficient road system. During the 12th and 13th centuries pilgrims making for the famous shrines sometimes had their routes slightly improved by feudal barons, who levied tolls and spent some of the money on the upkeep of the roads. Bishops encouraged people to give their labour to the improvement of roads as an act of piety.

By the end of the Middle Ages (*see* separate entry), despite the rise in trade and the real need for better roads, the technique of road building had greatly deteriorated. Under the medieval system in Britain it was the duty of each parish to maintain the roads within its boundaries; but, as more people travelled, trade increased, and wheeled traffic grew, the

state of the highways became deplorable and stood in the way of economic progress. Only on the other side of the world was there an adequate road system during this period – in South America, where, between 1200 and 1500, the Inca Indians built a network of 10,000 miles [16,093 kilometres] of roads to connect their cities.

Although Continental roads improved during the following centuries, in Britain it was a case of summer travel only until the late 18th century. After the authoritarian government of Oliver Cromwell (*see* separate entry), the English tended to resist any interference in local affairs by a central authority. The provision and maintenance of roads was one of the dubious privileges of local authorities, dignitaries and landowners, with the inevitable result that the main routes consisted of local roads of widely varying standards of construction and repair. The obligation on parishioners to give six days' annual labour to the roads was constantly shirked, roads often became impassable for wheeled traffic in winter, and goods had to be carried by pack animals between the new industrial centres. When the Emperor Charles VI visited England in 1703, his fifty-mile [80 kilometres] journey from London to Petworth took three days, the imperial coach overturned a dozen times, and it needed constant help from Sussex peasants to heave it out of the mud. Private enterprise, in the shape of the Turnpike Companies, which took over sections of roads, putting up gates and exacting tolls, considerably improved the situation at the end of the 18th century, as did the new techniques in road building of John McAdam (1756–1836) a century later. (*See* TURNPIKES and MCADAM.)

French roads were generally in better state than those in the rest of Europe. Strong central government, first under Louis XIV, imposed forced labour on road building. The Corps des Ponts et Chaussées was instituted, also a college for road engineers. Their studies bore fruit not only in France, but all over Europe. Standards were laid down for road construction, coach services started, toll roads opened – in fact, a new interest in road communication began. Napoleon initiated a great series of military roads radiating from Paris and others across the Alps.

Though from the 1840s railways began to divert attention from other land communications, the invention of the motor car refocused it on roads. The provision of new major highway systems has become a preoccupation of many countries.

Some examples are the modern inter-city road system of Belgium; the German *Autobahnen*, completely repaired since the devastation of World War II; the Italian *autostrade*, bidding fair to link the whole peninsula by one great highway; the newly completed Yugoslavian network, including the beautiful road running the length of the Adriatic coast; the masterpieces of highway engineering in Switzerland; the highway from Vienna to Salzburg in Austria and the *felbertauern* through the Alps; and Holland's fine system, covering the whole country. As might be expected, the USA has the greatest system in the world, with about 4 million miles [6 million km.] of graded roads. The longest motorable highway in the world will stretch, when completed, from Alaska to southern Chile, a distance of over 14,000 miles [22,500 kilometres].

¶ BODEY, HUGH. *Roads.* 1971; RUSH, PHILIP. *How Roads Have developed.* 1960

Cloverleaf complex near New York, USA.

Robespierre, Maximilien François Marie-Isidore de (1758–94): French revolutionary and leader in the "Reign of Terror" (*see* separate entry). As a lawyer in Arras in the 1780s he had gained respect for his hard work, virtuous behaviour and sympathy for the poor. During the Revolution he entered politics, becoming a powerful orator and a member of the Committee of Public Safety which saved France from defeat and civil war in 1793. His nickname "the Incorruptible", bestowed on him by his friends, is some indication of his ruthless sincerity of purpose and honesty of life; but his enemies in the Convention overthrew him in 1794 and brought him to the guillotine to which he had been instrumental in sending so many hundreds of his fellows.

Rockefeller, John Davison (1839–1937): American industrialist who, after boyhood and youth on a small farm in New York State, built up a near-monopoly of oil-refining in the USA. Reputedly a dollar "billionaire" (a billion dollars now being worth something over £400 million), he gave away some 750 million dollars in his lifetime to various medical, scientific, educational and religious funds and institutions.

Rockets: cylindrical cases of paper or metal containing an inflammable composition. They are propelled into the air by recoil action due to the high speed expulsion of gases generated by the combustion of the contents.

The origin of rockets is not known. The Chinese, Persians, Arabians and Greeks are known to have used them before the Christian era. The Chinese developed a mixture of saltpetre, sulphur and charcoal for pyrotechnic (firework) purposes and later used it for propelling arrows. By the 13th century Europe was using rockets for military purposes but with the introduction of gunpowder their use was mainly limited to display.

Early in the 19th century a new type of military rocket was introduced by the English inventor Sir William Congreve (1772–1828). Ships were specially fitted with angled firing ramps from which the Congreve rockets were fired. The 20th-century rocket was to develop into extremely formidable weapons such as the giant V1 and V2 rocket-propelled missiles used by Germany in 1944. Exceptionally powerful rocket motors have since been developed to propel ballistic missiles and moon capsules.

Pyrotechnic rockets are part of the emergency equipment carried by sea-going vessels. When a ship or boat is in distress and requires immediate assistance a rocket throwing coloured stars is fired in order to attract the attention of nearby ships or coastguards. Rockets are also used by coastal life-saving teams to fire lines to a stranded vessel and thus provide an eventual means of rescuing the crew.

The most spectacular development in rocket propulsion has taken place with the USA and USSR space programmes (*see* SPACE TRAVEL). Though the principles had been established much earlier, the first rocket launched by liquid fuel was at the hands of US inventor Robert Hutchings Goddard (1882–1945) in March 1926, when his missile travelled a distance of 184 feet [56 metres] and reached an altitude of just over 340 feet [104 metres].

V2 Rocket taking off in New Mexico, USA.

Russia's first effort came three years later. From these modest beginnings came, in less than fifty years, the mighty rockets used in space probes and moon landings. Though precise figures have not been revealed, it is estimated that the rocket which launched the Russian Proton satellites in 1966 had a thrust of at least 4 million lb [1,814,400 kilogrammes]. Saturn V, the one used for the Apollo lunar expedition of 1968 was powered by five Rocketdyne F-1 engines, each giving a 1,500,000 lb [680,400 kilogrammes] thrust. Another five engines, with a total thrust of 1,150,000 lb [521,640 kilogrammes] sent Stage II on its way, and Stage III needed an eleventh engine with a 200,000 lb [90,720 kilogrammes] thrust. The total horsepower generated was 173,800,000, the fuels used being various combinations of liquid oxygen, liquid hydrogen and kerosene. More powerful rockets have since been developed and experiments are being made with other propellents, such as caesium vapour and ion discharges.

¶ BRAUN, WERNER VON. *History of Rocketry and Space Travel.* 1967

Rodrigo or **Ruy Diaz de Bivar** (1040–99): Castilian hero known as "the Cid" or "Cid Campeador", meaning "the lord champion". He won glory fighting against the Moors but, as with many medieval heroes, such a body of legend has gathered round his name that it is now almost impossible to distinguish between truth and fiction.

¶ GOLDSTON, R. C. *The Legend of the Cid.* 1965

Roman Catholic Church: largest of the Christian Churches, with members in every land, numbering some 600 million, or about a half of all Christians. It is called Roman because its members accept the authority of the Bishop of Rome, or Pope (*see* PAPACY), and Catholic – a Greek word meaning "universal" – because it claims to be the original Church founded by Christ and continued by His disciples and their successors (the bishops) for the salvation of all mankind.

For the first thousand years of Christian history the unity of Christendom was preserved by means of General Councils of the Catholic Church (meetings of bishops and others) and the decisions of popes. But from the 11th century onwards various revolts against the authority of the popes produced a number of different churches, many of them claiming to speak and teach with the same authority as had hitherto been enjoyed by the Catholic Church. Thus, in the year 1054 a schism (separation) between the Eastern Church, centred on Constantinople, and Rome, led to the appearance of the Orthodox Churches of eastern Europe, with services, sacraments and teaching very similar to those of the Roman Catholic Church, but which denied the authority of the pope. In the 16th century, under the influence of teachers like Luther and Calvin, the Protestant churches were formed in Europe, some of them, like the Church of England, under the guidance and with the support of national governments, others, like the Baptists or Quakers, as independent sects. In the end several hundred independent Churches emerged in this way; but, although they differed greatly from each other, they were all called Protestant because they protested against the authority of the popes at Rome and the teachings of the Roman Catholic Church. They considered that the popes had grown corrupt, and were too fond of easy living and magnificent display; and they protested against elaborate ceremonies and "superstitions". Luther, in particular, claimed that faith alone was needed for salvation, and not the sacraments of the Roman Catholic Church. To these religious objections were added political objections; thus, the English kings and parliament considered that the pope had favoured the French, and the German princes claimed that he had favoured the Holy Roman Emperor, from whom they were trying to free themselves. So it came about that objections against Rome, some of them religious, some of them political, gave rise to the growth of many independent Churches, and since it was supposed that a country must have one religion only, lest its unity should be destroyed, religious toleration was seldom adopted, and the 16th and 17th centuries saw hideous and brutal religious wars that devastated most of Germany, France and the Netherlands. When at last, in the 18th century, men of different religions had learnt to live together more peacefully, and religious toleration had been widely adopted, Europe had become divided between the Roman Catholic Church and a number of Protestant Churches. Thus, the countries bordering on the Mediterranean sea – Italy, France, Spain and Portugal – were predominantly Catholic, as were also some of the countries of northern and central Europe – Poland, Hungary, Austria, southern Germany, the Rhineland, Belgium and Ireland – while the rest of Europe was mainly Protestant. The overseas dependencies of European countries followed the religion of the parent country; so that South America was Catholic and the English colonies in North America were Protestant.

There has been little change in the relative extent of the Roman Catholic Church and the Protestant Churches in the last two centuries. Excluded from most of Asia, the Roman Catholic Church, like the Protestant Churches, has spread rapidly in much of Africa and in Australia. She has also reformed herself since the days of Luther and the Reformation, first at the Council of Trent (1545–63), which dealt particularly with the abuses complained of by the reformers and set up a more rigorous system for training priests; later at the two Councils of the Vatican (1869–70 and 1962–65). But it cannot be said that the relations between the Roman Catholic Church and other Churches have been friendly, until recent years. The Roman Catholic claim to be the only true Church, founded by Christ, and the Catholic teaching that the pope, when defining matters of faith or morals, speaks infallibly, have been resented by other Christians, while the Catholic belief that the bread and wine, at Mass, become the body and blood of Christ, has been regarded by many as superstition. But since the Second Vatican Council (1962–65), summoned by Pope John XXIII, whose concern was for all mankind, there has been a marked change. That Council showed a new respect for other Christian Churches and a willingness to share with them the blame for the quarrels and persecutions of the past. It also, for the first time, encouraged *oecumenism*, which means the drawing together of all Christians in the love of their Founder and an effort to break down the barriers that still separate the Churches from each other. *See colour section.*

¶ HOARE, ROBERT J. and HEUSER, ADOLF. *Christ through the Ages, vols 1 and 2.* 1966; HUGHES, PHILIP. *A Short History of the Catholic Church.* 1967

See also individual entries.

Romanesque: European style of art and architecture of the 11th and 12th centuries, corresponding to Norman in England. It developed from a study of Roman ruins, though the 11th-century builders had not the skill of the ancient Romans and had to modify their plans accordingly. Nevertheless, Rome was the inspiration: hence the name.

Romanesque architecture is characterised by the semicircular arch. Churches with their great square towers and massive pillars give an impression of strength, fortresses of God. Sculpture, save on the west doorways of some cathedrals, was simple and formalised. Wall paintings and stained glass decorated the interiors. *See colour section.*

Romania, Roumania, or **Rumania:** republic in south-eastern Europe. Excavations by archaeologists of many ruined towns enable Romanians to trace their history back to Roman times, when their land was the prosperous province of Dacia. After the fall of Rome the noble landowners on the northern bank and near to the mouth of the Danube river faced a thousand-year battle for survival. To the north the Poles and to the west the Magyars of Hungary tried many times to seize the territory. Out of these struggles two provinces were forged, Moldavia and Wallachia, but both had to submit to the powerful Turkish Empire of the 17th century.

With the decline of Turkey, and the

Annexed by Russia in 1940

Romania

following Crimean War (*see* separate entry), the two provinces gained partial independence, and at the Congress of Berlin (1878: *see* BERLIN, CONGRESS OF) international recognition was given to the combined country of Romania. It has always been an important agricultural and timber-producing land, but in the 20th century the discovery of oil attracted the attention of Germany. In the 1930s Nazi German influence (*see* NAZIS) grew rapidly through the Iron Guard (a kind of Romanian SS). In 1940 the Romanian King, Carol II, was forced to abdicate when the Guard helped Antonescu to seize power as a dictator. But Romania suffered heavily, first in supporting Hitler's invasion of Russia, and later when the great Ploesti oilfields were severely damaged by American bombing.

After 1945 Soviet Russian influence replaced German. In 1947 a Communist People's Republican government took over. Land was shared amongst the peasants and farms collectivised. Trade also came under Soviet control, but in the 1960s Romania broke away from close Russian supervision, although remaining Communist.

Romanov: name of the last Russian ruling dynasty. Michael Romanov (1596–1645), a nobleman of Prussian descent, was elected Tsar of Russia in 1613. The Romanov male line ended in 1730 with the death of Peter II, grandson of Peter the Great (1672–1725 *see* separate entry) who had been the greatest of the Romanovs; the dynasty continued by female descent or marriage. From 1762 until the abdication of Nicholas II (*see* separate entry) in 1917, the Romanov rulers of Russia were descendants of Anne, daughter of Peter the Great.

Rome: capital city of Italy, on the River Tiber, about half-way down the western side of the peninsula and twelve miles [19 km.] from the sea. Few cities in the world have a longer history.

Its situation among low hills at the last ford over the river attracted early human settlement, but its story begins with the fable of the founding of Rome by Romulus, a descendant of Aeneas, who had escaped from the fall of Troy (in the 16th century it was fashionable to claim Trojan origin for the Britons likewise), and the traditional date for this was 753 BC, the Romans subsequently reckoning each year as the . . .th from the founding of the city. For a time the Etruscans, a neighbouring and rival tribe from the north of the Tiber, imposed a line of kings upon the city, but these were driven out at the end of the 6th century, and the period of the Republic followed, to last for the next 450 years.

The control of affairs was, to begin with, entirely in the hands of the patricians, the upper class who monopolised the senate and elected annually two chief magistrates, called consuls, one of their main duties being to command the citizen-armies in war. Over the years the plebeians, the lower classes, gradually gained some influence, so that it became at least possible for a man of humble origins but unusual ability to make his way to responsible public positions.

Meanwhile Rome was gradually extending her influence and her boundaries – often by aggressive means – throughout the rest of Italy, and this eventually brought her into conflict with other Mediterranean nations. Her struggle against the Carthaginians in the Punic Wars resulted in Spain becoming a Roman province in 201 BC and Africa in 146 BC. Over the same period she became involved in the affairs of Greece and Asia Minor, where the break-up of the empire of Alexander the Great (d. 323 BC) had in due course produced much strife and confusion: in these regions, too, new provinces were established.

By the opening of the 1st century BC Rome was almost encircling the Mediterranean (Egypt was not annexed for another seventy years), but the extent of her territories raised problems and strains with which the existing machinery of government could not cope, and political life was more and more controlled by military commanders who, with their troops behind them, could defy the authorities. The last of these, Gaius Julius Caesar (100–44 BC) had virtually made himself dictator when he was assassinated. From the civil wars which followed, his nephew Octavian (63 BC – AD 14) emerged in the year 27 BC as the first of the Roman emperors, with the title of Augustus.

The historian Edward Gibbon in his famous work *The Decline and Fall of the Roman Empire* starts his first chapter by fixing the death of the Emperor Marcus Aurelius (AD 180) as the point at which this vast organisation began, albeit with more than one period of recovery, its long period of decay. It is difficult to assign all the reasons for this. The accusations of luxury and idleness made against the Romans themselves can all too easily be exaggerated. The overriding causes seem to be that the Empire was too vast to be controlled from one centre, even by a race with a marked genius for orderly administration, and that the frontiers, which had been pushed further forward as a definite measure (the conquest of Britain from AD 43 is an example of this), could not be held against the pressures exerted on them at a time when the tribes and nations outside them were in a state of movement and restlessness. In the end these barbarians, as they were called, broke into Italy: in 410 Rome was sacked, not for the first or last time, and in 475 Romulus Augustulus, the last emperor of the west (who ironically derived his name

from the founder of Rome and the founder of the Empire) was deposed by the Gothic leader Odoacer.

In this rapid summary of the events of many centuries, Rome has been treated as the centre of wide territories, rather than as a city in itself; but the same centuries saw its development from a primitive township to one of the proudest cities in the ancient world. Only some of its main features can be mentioned here: the Capitol, which was the sacred hill at the centre, like the Acropolis at Athens, the Palatine Hill where the houses of the rulers stood (hence the word palace) and the marsh drained to establish the Forum, originally the market-place, round which the official buildings were located. To these must be added the public baths, the bridges over the Tiber, the city walls and the public water supplies. It was said of Augustus that he found Rome a city of brick and left it a city of marble, and certainly the finest of the many remains of ancient buildings which survive date from the years of the Empire, some having been ruthlessly pillaged for materials in later centuries. The Castel Sant' Angelo, originally built by the Emperor Hadrian (d. AD 138) as a mausoleum (tomb) for himself and adapted in the Middle Ages as a fortress in which popes and others at times took refuge, is still intact, while the Colosseum and the Baths of Caracalla are impressive even in their massive ruins.

From the time of the barbarian invasions until the middle of the 19th century Rome ceased to be a capital city and, as time went on, developed into one of the city-states, like Florence, Milan or Venice, which, over a long period, are a feature of Italian history. In one respect, however, there was an important difference: the growing power of the Church, which the barbarians on the whole treated with respect, and the leadership claimed by the popes, who had their dwelling in the city,

The Colosseum, Rome.

gave it a particular distinction, while in course of time the surrounding territories were claimed by or given to the papacy as its own domains. Though Charlemagne was crowned in St Peter's, Rome, in the year 800, the city was never the true capital of his empire, and in the Middle Ages it had its full share of the unrest and violence that plagued the whole of Italy. There was a time when a local family controlled elections to the papacy and in 955 chose a boy of seventeen, noted for his evil ways, as John XII. In 1089 the city was sacked by the Normans, and it was frequently torn·by internal quarrels, as when Arnold of Brescia (d. 1155) and later Cola di Rienzi (d. 1354) led popular risings against the upper class rulers. Finally things came to such a pass that the pope fled to Avignon in southern France, where he and his successors remained for much of the 14th century, and, when a return was made in 1377, there followed

a further forty years of strife and rivalries within the Church. As a result of all this, the city was by now in a sorry state of ruin and desolation: an English traveller records that he saw wolves fighting with stray dogs in the shadow of St Peter's.

The situation, however, had a brighter side. By the 15th century the Renaissance, with its delight in art and architecture, was in its early vigour, and the popes of the period, worldly and selfish as some of them were, took a leading part in encouraging the long process of restoring the city in the new styles. The rebuilding of St Peter's was taken in hand by Bramante (1444–1514) and continued by others, including Michelangelo (1475–1564), many other ancient churches were restored and new *palazzi* erected for noble families. Despite the setback of one of the most savage of all the sackings of Rome by the Emperor Charles V in 1527, the process continued. The Sistine Chapel in the Vatican was started by Sixtus V (pope 1585–90), and the restrained classical styles of the Renaissance were gradually succeeded by the Baroque, seen in the later *palazzi* and in the many fountains designed by Bernini (1597–1680) and others which still adorn the city.

During the 17th and 18th centuries Rome was comparatively peaceful and was much visited by wealthy travellers from England and other European countries; but the reign of Napoleon (Emperor of France 1804–14) saw Pope Pius VII a prisoner at Fontainebleau, near Paris, and Rome itself under French rule. On Napoleon's fall the popes regained their territories in central Italy, but lost the larger part of them, the States of the Church, in 1860 when Italy was in process of becoming one nation. Only Rome itself and the Papal State immediately surrounding it remained protected by a French garrison sent by Napoleon III which was recalled in 1870, as a result of the Franco-Prussian War. The city then became the capital of Italy, and the popes withdrew as "prisoners" inside the Vatican. In 1929 the Vatican City was declared an independent state with an area of 108 acres [44 hectares], its own postal services and its own railway station.

Rome today has a number of fine modern buildings to complement the architectural treasures of over 2,000 years. *See colour section.*

¶ JOYCE, P. W. *Concise History of Rome.* 1960 *See also* individual entries.

Theodore Roosevelt.

Roosevelt, Franklin Delano (1882–1945): 32nd president of the USA (1933–45), the first American to be elected for more than two terms of office. By a coincidence, he came to power at the same time as Adolf Hitler, the German leader whom Roosevelt's measures were to do much to defeat. The most noteworthy features of Roosevelt's presidency were

his strong lead away from isolationism, his "good neighbour" policy towards Latin America, his "New Deal" programme at home, his "Lease-Lend" support for countries fighting the Axis powers, in World War II and, eventually, his leadership of America at war after the Japanese attack on Pearl Harbour. He died a month before Germany's unconditional surrender. His wife Eleanor (1884–1962) won a great reputation in her own right as a worker for humanity and served as Chairman of the United Nations Human Rights Commission.

¶ HIEBERT, ROSELYN and ELDON, RAY. *Franklin Delano Roosevelt.* 1972 *See also* LEASE–LEND; NEW DEAL; etc.

Franklin Roosevelt.

Roosevelt, Theodore (1858–1919): 26th president of the USA (1901–09). He came into the public eye as a dashing cavalry leader in Cuba during the Spanish-American War (1898), was elected Republican vice-president in 1900 and succeeded to the White House after President McKinley's assassination. At home he attacked the power of the great business trusts and did a great deal to safeguard the country's natural resources. Abroad, he mediated successfully in the Russo-Japanese War and gained the Nobel Peace Prize in 1906.

¶ In *Canning, John*, editor. *100 Great Modern Lives.* 1965

See also individual entries.

Roses, Wars of the: wars in England carried on intermittently from 1455 to 1485, and deriving their name from the red and white emblems of the rival houses of Lancaster and York. One historian describes this period under the heading: "The Suicide of the Feudal Baronage". That there is some truth in this description may be seen from the fact that only 29 lay peers were summoned to Henry VII's first Parliament in 1485, compared with e.g. the 65 earls and barons called to Edward I's Parliament of 1295. Although forming a dynastic struggle between Lancaster and York, the Wars were largely the result of the termination in 1453 of the Hundred Years War (*see* separate entry), which had led to the formation of bands of mercenary soldiers who now found themselves unemployed, and, as Trevelyan says, "fit for any mischief".

Three periods may be discerned in these wars. Before 1459, opposition to Henry VI's advisers, notably the unpopular Duke of Somerset, was the keynote; the years 1459 to 1461 saw the struggle become a dynastic one. In 1460 Richard Duke of York (1411–60) proclaimed himself king, but two months afterwards his

THE **Wars** OF THE **Roses**

severed head, adorned with a paper crown, appeared on the walls of York. His son Edward (later Edward IV, ruled 1461–83) made good his claim to the Crown after the destruction of his enemies at Towton in 1461. Thereafter, the House of York retained the throne, although Edward's position was not really secure until he defeated the Earl of Warwick (Warwick "the Kingmaker", 1428–71) and his forces at Barnet, and followed this up by a victory over Margaret of Anjou, queen of Henry VI, at Tewkesbury in 1471. Thereafter, apart from sporadic local outbursts, England had peace for fourteen years, until the final battle was fought at Bosworth Field (1485), where Richard III was slain and Henry VII, head of the house of Lancaster, won the throne and later united the warring factions by marrying Elizabeth of York.

¶ ALLEN, KENNETH. *The Wars of the Roses.* 1973

803

Rosetta Stone: large piece of black basalt discovered during Napoleon's expedition to Egypt (*see* NAPOLEON I) bearing an inscription in Egyptian hieroglyphic script and duplicated in Greek. By translating the Greek text and matching it with the hieroglyphs the French scholar Champollion discovered the meaning of the Egyptian characters and so enabled archaeologists to decipher Egyptian writing.

¶ HONOUR, ALAN. *The Man Who Could Read Stones: Champollion and the Rosetta Stone.* 1968

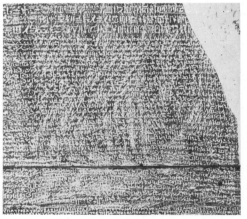

A detail of the Rosetta Stone, showing the Hieroglyphic, Demotic and Greek scripts.

Rothschild, Meyer Anselm (1743–1812): German-Jewish financier, born at Frankfurt-on-Main. Starting life as a bank clerk, he set up in business for himself and, displaying great talent in money matters, founded the great family of international bankers who dominated 19th-century European finance. Other prominent members were his son Nathan Meyer (1777–1836), who had charge of the London house, and Nathan's son Lionel (1808–79), who became the first Jewish member of the British House of Commons.

Rotterdam: second city and greatest port of the Netherlands. It rose in the 13th

century as a fishing port and place of transhipment between sea and river craft of Rhine and Meuse, beside a dam and sluice on the Rotte river, and was built on piles in drained ground. In 1572 it was one of the first towns to defy the Spaniards but was treacherously taken, and 400 of its citizens were massacred. As ships became larger and the colonial trade developed, it surpassed Dordrecht and Amsterdam as a port and became the centre of sugar refining. The German bombing of 14 May 1940 – after Holland had asked for an armistice – destroyed 30,000 homes. Reconstruction work was begun four days after the bombing and completed with vision and determination. The city's shopping centre, the Lijnbaan, with pedestrian ways, fountains, flowerbeds and sculpture, is greatly admired by town planners.

Rouen: city of northern France, on the River Seine. Today a busy manufacturing town, it was the ancient capital of Normandy. William the Conqueror died there in 1087. It was held by the English until 1204 and again between 1419 and 1449. In 1431 Joan of Arc (*see* separate entry) was burnt as a heretic in the cathedral square. The Cathedral, a magnificent structure built between the 13th and 16th centuries, was badly damaged in World War II. Its southern tower is called the Tour de Beurre (Butter Tower) because the people who contributed the money for its building were, in return, allowed to eat butter during Lent.

Rousseau, Jean-Jacques (1712–78): philosopher and writer, usually described as French though born at Geneva. He rebelled against many of the accepted ideas of his time and came to the conclusion that man in his primitive state was naturally good but had been corrupted by the progress of civilisation and by the structure of society that had developed. It was, therefore, desirable to return to the age of simplicity. These views he put forward in his main work *The Social Contract*, which had great influence on the democratic ideas which inspired the French Revolution (*see* separate entry).

Royal Society, The: leading scientific society in Great Britain. An association of "Philosophers" meeting weekly at Gresham College, London, from 1645, was granted a charter by Charles II in 1662. Since then the Society has encouraged and financed experiment, research and publication in every field of science and mathematics, and frequently advises the government. Among its presidents have been Sir Christopher Wren, Samuel Pepys and Sir Isaac Newton (*see* separate entries). The Society's published records of its activities date from 1665.
¶ ANDRADE, E. N. DA C. *A Brief History of the Royal Society*. 1960

Rubber: elastic substance formed from the juice of certain tropical trees and shrubs. Natural rubber grows in South America, Mexico and Malaya. Little is known of the early use of the product, but in AD 1500 it was mentioned by a Spanish historian. It seems possible that Columbus (*see* separate entry), on his second voyage to the West Indies, saw natives bouncing a rubber ball. In 1736 samples of rubber were sent to Europe from Peru, but no one appears to have considered it a useful commodity: it was regarded as a curiosity.

The earliest record of the export of rubber was in a Brazilian trade account of 1825. It could be made into soles for shoes, waterproof clothing and buffers to soften the impact of heavy articles, but it was not a popular material because of its tendency to become jelly-like during hot weather. A London businessman, James Hancock, set up a small factory for the manufacture of rubber articles in 1820, but it did not prosper.

An American, Charles Goodyear, was impressed by the possibilities of rubber, which was so pliable that it could be moulded into any shape. He worked at experiments to make it durable and eventually discovered the process known as *vulcanisation*. This involved mixing sulphur with raw rubber, then heating the mixture. When cooled it remained unaffected by climatic conditions.

After this the demand for rubber grew. In 1876 Sir Henry Wickham, an English biologist, brought rubber seeds from the Amazon to the Royal Botanic Gardens at Kew (London), where they were germinated in the glasshouses. The saplings, exported first to Ceylon, formed the basis of extensive plantations in Malaya and Burma. In recent years there have been considerable advances in the manufacture of synthetic rubber. Two particularly important branches of the rubber

In Ceylon rubber is still collected by tapping the rubber tree.

industry are those concerned with various types of footwear and the production of tyres for automobiles and cycles.

¶ SCHIDROWITZ, P. and DAWSON, T. R. editors. *History of the Rubber Industry.* 1953

Rubens, Sir Peter Paul (1577–1640): Flemish painter on the grand scale. Although assisted by pupils, only an artist of prodigious genius and vitality could accomplish so many enormous altar-pieces, cover so many palace walls and ceilings with fluent paintings glowing with life and colour. Rubens was also a diplomat. Sent to England, he was knighted by Charles I, who commissioned him to decorate the Banqueting Hall in Whitehall. Two of his greatest masterpieces are *The Raising of the Cross* and *The Descent from the Cross*, both in Antwerp Cathedral. *See colour section.*

¶ RIPLEY, E. *Rubens.* 1958

Ruhr: important industrial area in West Germany, with huge engineering, chemical, coal and steel production. In the peak years before 1939, 150 million tons [152,400,000 tonnes] of coal and 16 million tons [16,300,000 tonnes] of steel were produced annually. By 1914 Bochum, Dortmund and Essen had developed on the north bank of the Ruhr river, and Dusseldorf was growing just up river on the Rhine. Essen's growth was spectacular when it became the home of Alfred Krupp, whose firm soon dominated the German armament industry. A French and Belgian invasion of the Ruhr in 1923, to compel Germany to pay war reparations, met with passive resistance from the workers whose production would have helped the army of occupation. Though this resistance hindered the invaders it also caused the collapse of the German economy and destroyed the value of the currency. The Ruhr was a major target for Allied aircraft in World War II (*see* separate entry) when, from 1943 onwards, 1000-bomber raids smashed much of the industrial heart of Germany. After the war the process of recovery was amazingly rapid and the area became again the greatest industrial concentration in Europe.

Rupert, Prince (1619–82): son of Frederick V, Elector Palatine, and Elizabeth, daughter of James I of England. Coming to England in 1642, he was appointed General of the King's Horse by his uncle, Charles I, and proved a brilliant leader and strategist, the cavalry being undefeated until Marston Moor, 1644. After Naseby he was for a time estranged from Charles I, but later (1647) commanded a royalist navy until driven from the seas by Blake. In 1660 he again became Admiral and played a brilliant part in the later Dutch wars. He was the first President of the Hudson's Bay Company (*see* separate

entry). He had scientific and artistic interests and was an early expert at mezzotint engraving.

¶ KNIGHT, FRANK. *Prince of Cavaliers*. 1967

Russia: former country of eastern Europe and Asia. For post-1918 history, *see* UNION OF SOVIET SOCIALIST REPUBLICS.

For some 800 years, from 400 BC to AD 400, Greek cities flourished on the shores of the Black Sea and did much to civilise the Scythian tribes of the interior of what we now call Russia; but the westward movements of Avars, Goths and Huns wiped out these cities. Later, a few primitive Slav communities established their towns on the great rivers. Menaced by Turkish tribes and by each other, they sought the aid of the Scandinavians. In AD 862 Ruric led his Norsemen into Russia from the Baltic. They established trading cities at Novgorod and Kiev, descended the Dnieper and even attacked Constantinople. The name Russ, which applied to the energetic Scandinavians, was given to the land they now ruled.

Vladimir (980–1015), ruler of Kiev, adopted Christianity in its eastern Greek form and married a sister of the Byzantine Emperor Basil II. Religion in Russia was thus closely united with the state as in the Byzantine Empire. Kiev was destroyed in 1169 in the wars fought for the title and powers of Grand Prince. The town of Vladimir became the new Russ capital. In the 13th century Russia was overrun by the Mongolian invaders and became part of the empire of Genghis Khan. Though this empire quickly broke up, the people of the Islamic Tatar "Golden Horde" established themselves for two centuries on the lower Volga and in the southeastern steppes. The small Russian cities and princedoms survived, provided they paid tribute.

The Grand Princes of Moscow gained power by becoming the agents and tax gatherers of the Tatar Khans. The economic foundation of Moscow was agricultural rather than trading. It became the political and religious capital. From the west the Lithuanians and Poles pressed hard upon the Russians. In 1380, however, Dmitri Donskoi defeated the Tatars at Koulikovo. The Golden Horde also came under attack from Timur in the east. The Grand Princes of Moscow emerged as the heirs alike of the fallen Byzantine Emperors and of the fallen Tatar Khanate. Ivan the Great (1462–1505) took the title of Tsar or Caesar, married Sophia Palaeologos, a Byzantine princess, and adopted the imperial double eagle as his symbol.

Rus Vikings.

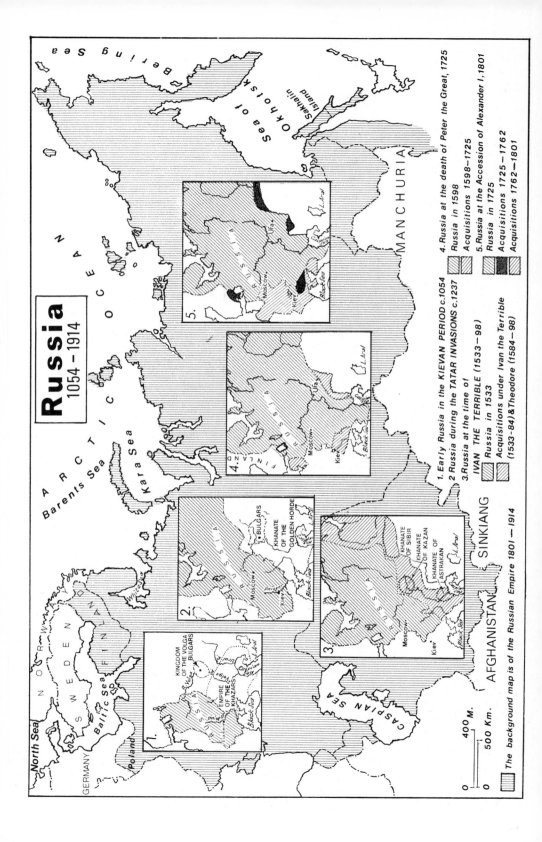

Russia
1054–1914

North Sea

GERMANY

Poland

Baltic Sea

SWEDEN

NORWAY

FINLAND

White Sea

ARCTIC OCEAN

Barents Sea

Kara Sea

Sea of Okhotsk

Bering Sea

Sakhalin Island

MANCHURIA

SINKIANG

AFGHANISTAN

CASPIAN SEA

1. Early Russia in the KIEVAN PERIOD c.1054
2. Russia during the TATAR INVASIONS c.1237
3. Russia at the time of
IVAN THE TERRIBLE (1533–98)
   Russia in 1533
   Acquisitions under Ivan the Terrible
   (1533–84) & Theodore (1584–98)

4. Russia at the death of Peter the Great, 1725
   Russia in 1598
   Acquisitions 1598–1725
5. Russia at the Accession of Alexander I, 1801
   Russia in 1725
   Acquisitions 1725–1762
   Acquisitions 1762–1801

The background map is of the Russian Empire 1801–1914

0   400 M.
0   500 Km.

1.
KINGDOM OF THE VOLGA BULGARS
Volga
EMPIRE OF THE KHAZARS
R U S S I A
Dnieper
Volga
Caspian Sea
Black Sea
L. Aral

2.
R U S S I A
BULGARS
KHANATE OF THE GOLDEN HORDE
MOSCOW
Kiev
Dnieper
Black Sea

3.
R U S S I A
KHANATE OF SIBIR
KHANATE OF KAZAN
KHANATE OF ASTRAKAN
MOSCOW
Kiev
Black Sea
L. Aral

4.
FINLAND
R U S S I A
MOSCOW
Ufa
Kiev
Black Sea
L. Aral

5.
R U S S I A
MOSCOW
Ufa
Kiev
Black Sea
L. Aral

Under the first Tsars, Russia remained backward and isolated from western Europe. In the early 17th century Russia's survival was in desperate peril, Poles and Swedes having made vast inroads. But a national army was raised, Michael Romanov was elected Tsar in 1613 by a national assembly, and the Russians ultimately drove back the Poles. Peter the Great became Tsar in 1689. He imported western methods and advisers, founded the city of St Petersburg as his capital and gave Russia military security against Swedes and Poles. His successors continued to employ German generals and ministers who carried on Peter's policy, extended Russian territory to the Black Sea, into Poland and into Asia, and maintained an alliance with Austria.

By the end of the 18th century the Russian Empire was well established as one of the great European powers, and under Alexander I (1801-25) played a great part in the defeat of the French armies of Napoleon, who invaded Russia in 1812, and in shaping the settlement of Europe after Napoleon's final defeat.

In the 19th century eastern Europe was disturbed by two developments – the break-up of the Turkish Empire and the emergence of nationalism among the many peoples of the Austrian and Turkish Empires. Russia supported Austria in suppressing nationalist revolutionary movements in 1848 and had also joined with Austria and Prussia in dividing all Poland among them. Russian governments were also eager to annex large portions of the Turkish Empire, including Constantinople, an aim which other powers, including France and Britain, wished to frustrate. From this arose the Crimean War (1854-56). Russia also expanded into Asia and caused Britain some concern for the safety of India.

Although serfdom was abolished in Russia in 1861 and many reforms were

Workers protest demonstration against provisional Government in Moscow, 1917.

made, the government of Russia was narrowly autocratic. Dissatisfied liberals, land-hungry peasants, discontented town workers, minority communities, irresponsible landowners and an inefficient administration, all in different ways threatened the structure of empire. It was further weakened by a disastrous war with Japan in 1904, by popular revolts and a shifting and irresolute policy towards experiments in parliamentary government. At last the strains of World War I broke the Russian Empire. The last Tsar, Nicholas II, abdicated in March 1917 and was later shot with his family. In November a further revolution placed power in the resolute hands of Lenin and the communists.

¶ CLARKSON, J. D. *A History of Russia from the Ninth Century.* 1965; PARES, B. *History of Russia.* 1955

See also BYZANTIUM; CRIMEAN WAR; GENGHIS KHAN; ISLAM; IVAN; LENIN; MONGOLS; MOSCOW; NICHOLAS I; NICHOLAS II; PETER I; RUSSO-JAPANESE WAR; TATAR; TSAR.

Russian authors, painters and composers: Russia has a splendid heritage of peasant songs and tales of heroes and giants, spread, centuries ago, by wandering minstrels. There is also a religious literature going back to the 11th century. Russian literature as an integral part of modern European culture dates back no further than the early 18th century, to Peter the Great (1672–1725), that most unliterary ruler who nevertheless broke down Russia's isolation from Western thought and influences.

Mikhail Lomonosov (1711–65) may be called the father of modern Russian literature, in that he was the first to use the vernacular, the everyday language of ordinary people, in his writings. Alexander Pushkin (1799–1837) is Russia's greatest poet. He was a romantic figure who died as the result of a duel at the age of thirty-seven. Mikhail Lermontov (1814–41) was another poet of great lyric gifts.

Nikolai Gogol (1809–52) ushered in the golden age of the Russian novel. Fyodor Dostoevsky (1812–81) and Leo Tolstoy (1828–1910) are among the world's greatest novelists, just as Anton Chekhov (1860–1904) is among its outstanding dramatists and short story writers.

To fulfil his function a writer must have freedom of thought and expression. This was never easy under the repressive regime of the Tsars – Lermontov and Dostoevsky, for example, were both sent into exile – and it is no easier today in the USSR. Some of Russia's greatest writers since the Revolution – for example Boris Pasternak (1890–1960) and Alexander Solzhenitsyn (b. 1918) – having had their works suppressed in the USSR, are better known in the West than in their native land.

Echoes of Russia's folk music are found in virtually all her famous composers. Prominent among 19th-century composers are Mikhail Glinka (1804–57), Alexander Dargomijsky (1813–69), Alexander Borodin (1833–87), Modeste Moussorgsky (1839–81) and Nikolai Rimsky-Korsakov (1844–1908). Peter Ilich Tchaikovsky's (1840–93) music is among the most popular classical music of the Western world.

Like the writers, Russian composers have not always found life easy. Serge Rachmaninov (1873–1943) left Russia for good in 1918. Serge Prokofiev (1891–1953) spent the years 1918–36 in France, and after his return to the Soviet Union had disagreements with the authorities. Igor Stravinsky (b. 1881), one of the great modernist composers, became first a French then, in 1945, a US citizen. Another composer in the modern idiom who has stayed in Russia, Dmitri Shostakovich (b. 1906), was in disgrace for a time because one of his compositions displeased Stalin.

Christianity spread to Russia from Constantinople, the capital of the Byzantine Empire. It is therefore Byzantine influences which are paramount in early Russian art, an art concerned entirely with religion. Icons – devotional pictures painted on wooden panels or sometimes hammered out of copper or silver – were produced in large numbers. Many of

Leo Tolstoy, 1903.

these icons are exquisite, deeply moving works of art. Experts in this field distinguish between many schools within the prevailing Byzantine idiom, each with its own characteristics.

Peter the Great brought many Western European artists to Russia: but Russian painting in modern times has not risen above the mediocre. The outstanding Russian artist of today, Marc Chagall (b. 1889), left Russia as a young man.
See also BYZANTIUM; CHRISTIANITY; PETER I.

Russian Orthodox Church: patriarchate within the Orthodox Eastern Church (*see* separate entry). Although Christianity (*see* separate entry) had been established in Russia in the 9th century and had survived the Mongol invasions (*see* MONGOLS) it was not until 1589 that the separate self-governing Russian Church was proclaimed. It still survives despite discouragement by the rulers of the USSR.

Russo-Japanese War: war of 1904-05 between Russia and Japan, caused by conflicting commercial and territorial ambitions in the Far East. With the trans-Siberian railway inefficient and incomplete, Russia was defeated in battles at the Yalu River, Nanshan, Liao-yang, Sha-ho and Mukden. The Japanese captured Port Arthur, destroyed a Russian fleet at Tsushima and overran Sakhalin. A peace very favourable to Japan was made by the Treaty of Portsmouth in 1905. This war showed grave weaknesses in Russian government and organisation, and strengthened the forces making for reform and, ultimately, for revolution. It also marked Japan's emergence as a world power.
¶ MARTIN, CHRISTOPHER. *The Russo-Japanese War.* 1967

Ruyter, Michael Adriaanszoon de (1607-76): Dutch admiral who distin-guished himself in the naval wars against England during the Commonwealth (*see* separate entry), his most noteworthy feat being to bring his fleet up the River Thames and to burn a number of ships (1667). A vivid account of him was written by Gerard Brandt, who knew him and who records that, though he was naturally healthy, "in his youth he had once been accidentally poisoned through eating bad fish" and that "this had resulted in a slight trembling in all his limbs, which lasted to the end of his life". He not only showed great skill and bravery against England, but also captured several Turkish vessels in the Mediterranean, defeated the Algerine pirates and fought for Denmark against Sweden. He was killed in a battle off Messina, Sicily, helping the Spaniards against the French. A magnificent monument to him was erected in Amsterdam.

Rwanda: central African territory, formerly part of Ruanda-Urundi, annexed by Germany in 1884 and then added to German East Africa. In 1919, after World War I (*see* separate entry), it became a Belgian Trust Territory, being administered by the Belgian Congo until 1962 when the two territories broke off and split into Ruanda and Barundi. Ruanda then became the Republic of Rwanda, with Uganda to the north, Tanzania to the east, Barundi to the south and Congo (Kinshasa) to the west.
See RHODESIA for map.

Ryswick, Peace of (1697): treaty which ended the French wars against the League of Augsburg (1686) and England (1688). France was exhausted and needed to recuperate before facing the problem of the Spanish succession. Louis XIV therefore surrendered all that he had gained since the Treaty of Nimwegen (1678), with the exception of Strasbourg, and recognised William III as king of England.

S

Saar: industrial region of Saarland, West Germany, between the Rhine and Moselle river valleys. It is rich in coal and iron. Formed in 1919 from Bavarian and Prussian territories, Saarland was administered by the League of Nations (*see* separate entry) from 1919 to 1935, when it reverted to Germany. After World War II (*see* separate entry) it formed part of the French zone and was attached to France economically, but was reunited with the German Federal Republic in 1957.

Saarinen, Eero (1910–61): Finnish-American architect, son of Eliel Saarinen, well known Finnish architect who emigrated to the United States with his family in 1923. Eero Saarinen came to the forefront of his profession with his design for the General Motors Technical Centre at Warren, Michigan (1951–55). He designed many college buildings in the USA, and also the US embassies in Oslo and London. His chapel at the Massachusetts Institute of Technology has a thin-skinned concrete dome which is of great interest to both architects and to engineers. In his best designs, such as that for the TWA (Transworld Airlines) Airport Terminal, New York, he handled concrete with an amazing lightness of touch.
See colour section.

Interior of the TWA terminal at Kennedy Airport, designed by Eero Saarinen.

Sabotage: malicious damage to property, installations, etc. Originally, an action by workmen, such as the destruction of machinery, which somehow hindered their employer, today the term has been extended to include large-scale destruction of communications and buildings by "underground" opponents of a government, and especially during a war, against an army of occupation.

Saga: ancient Norse or Icelandic prose narrative. The word derives from *segja*, "to say". Long before sagas were written down they were recited by professional story tellers. As written prose compositions they date from the Middle Ages (*see* separate entry). Some are historical, while others are a fascinating mixture of local tradition and myth. Among the most famous are the *Landnámábok*, which reached its final form in about 1220 and which contains, among other material, lives of the early kings of Norway and pedigrees of the first settlers; and, romantic rather than historical, the *Njalssaga*, the great story of Njál, a figure embodying law and justice in early Scandinavian history.

Sahara: largest desert in the world, covering approximately 3,500,000 sq miles [8,750,000 sq km] extending in the east to the Nile valley, with Chad, Niger and Mali to the south and the Atlantic coastline in the north-west. The greater part of its population consists of Arab and Berber nomads.
See AFRICA for map.
¶ WELLARD, JAMES. *The Great Sahara.* 1964

St Denis: originally a Benedictine abbey north of Paris, founded *c.* 625 and containing the shrine of the patron saint of France, of the same name, who suffered martyrdom some 350 years earlier. Many French kings are buried there.

St Helena: a remote, mountainous, volcanic island in the South Atlantic. Its capital and only town is Jamestown. It was discovered in 1502 by the Portuguese and after various changes of ownership came finally under the British Crown in 1834. The island is chiefly known as the place of the exile and death of Napoleon I (*see* separate entry). Today the farmhouse where he lived is a museum containing a collection of Napoleonic mementoes.

St James's Palace: London palace built by Henry VIII (1491–1547). After the palace of Whitehall was burnt down in 1697 the royal household moved to St James's. In 1809 most of the latter, too, was destroyed by fire. George III (1738–1820) moved to Buckingham House (later Buckingham Palace). Foreign diplomats, nevertheless, are still accredited to the Court of St James, which remains the official name of the Royal Court.

A view of St James's Palace before the Great Fire of London in 1666.

St Kitts, St Christopher: island in the Leeward group of the Lesser Antilles and the oldest British West Indian settlement (1623). French claims dated from 1624, but the Treaty of Utrecht ceded St Kitts to Britain. In 1782 Admiral Hood, though unable to prevent the island's capture by de Grasse, ejected the French from the capital, Basseterre. St Kitts was again ceded to Britain in 1783. The abolition of slavery in 1834 produced little social change. The 1956 Leeward Islands Act united St Kitts, Nevis and Anguilla, with an elected council and responsible ministers. In 1969 Anguilla broke away and claimed independence. St Kitts has so far rejected any settlement that does not end this "rebellion".

St Lawrence River: North American river flowing from Lake Ontario 700 miles [1120 kilometres] north-eastwards to the Atlantic. Jacques Cartier discovered the St Lawrence Gulf in 1534, explored the river beyond Quebec and Montreal (Mount Royal) in 1535 and 1536, and indicated the route for later explorers and traders, Chauvin (1599), Champlain at Quebec (1608), de la Salle and Duluth (1679). Louisbourg's fall in 1758, during the Seven Years War (*see* separate entry), opened the St Lawrence to British forces, thus making possible Wolfe's victory at Quebec and the seizure of Canada by Great Britain. The Great Lakes – St Lawrence – Welland Canal system, improved continuously from the 1840s, became in 1958 the St Lawrence Seaway, a combined Canadian–USA enterprise (114 miles: 184 km long) which bypassed the rapids and shoals between Lake Ontario and Montreal and opened the St Lawrence to oceangoing ships.

¶ JUDSON, C. I. *The St Lawrence Seaway.* 1966; WHITE, ANNE TERRY. *The St Lawrence: Seaway of North America.* 1962

St Peter's, Rome: principal basilica of the Roman Church. The title "major basilica" is restricted to the four great churches of the city, among which St John Lateran is, in fact, styled "the mother church of the city and the world". St Peter's, however, being in the Vatican

St Peter's Basilica, Rome.

City (*see* separate entry), is the scene and setting of the great ceremonies of the Church. The first basilica was erected by Constantine (*see* separate entry) in the early 4th century on the traditional site of St Peter's martyrdom: the present one was begun in 1506 and finished in 1614. Several architects were involved, of whom Bramante (*c.* 1444-1514) played the largest part, while Michelangelo (1475-1564; *see* separate entry) designed the dome. The basilica is 619 feet (188 m) long, the largest church in Christendom. Over 130 popes are buried there, and St Peter lies under the High Altar.

¶ LETAROUILLY, P. *Basilica of St Peter.* 1953

Saladin (Salāh-al-Din or Salāh ad-Din Yusuf, "Honour of the Faith", 1138-93): sultan of Egypt and Syria and the last and greatest of three Muslim rulers who completely altered the balance of power in the Near East in a period of fifty years. Zanghi of Mosul conquered Aleppo and Edessa, and his son Noureddin conquered Damascus and Egypt. In 1174 Saladin succeeded Noureddin, under whom he had served as a soldier. He captured Jerusalem in 1187, thus giving rise to the Third Crusade (*see* CRUSADES), organised by Frederick Barbarossa of Germany (*see* separate entry), Philip Augustus of France and Richard Coeur-de-Lion of England. This resulted only in the capture of Acre and a truce with Saladin, giving Christian pilgrims free access to the Holy Sepulchre at Jerusalem; Saladin died the following year. He was slight in stature, modest and scholarly, but a formidable leader. In an age of rough justice he is noteworthy as a chivalrous opponent and a generous conqueror. *See colour section.*

¶ WALKER, KATHRINE SORLEY. *Saladin: Sultan of the Holy Sword.* 1971

Salamis, Battle of (480 BC): naval victory of the Greeks over the Persians. In face of the overwhelming numbers of the invading Persian land army, the Athenians abandoned their city, but, through the strategy of the Athenian leader Themistocles the Persian fleet was tricked into fighting in the narrow waters of the Bay of Salamis, where its vastly superior numbers could not be used to proper advantage. The dramatist Aeschylus, who probably fought in the battle, later described the Persian king Xerxes as watching from a high cliff at the sea's edge and rending his clothes in despair as the Greeks tore the enemy fleet apart, destroying about 200 ships before the rest retreated in disorder.

¶ In ALLEN, KENNETH. *Sailors in Battle.* 1966

See also AESCHYLUS; PERSIAN WARS; THEMISTOCLES; XERXES.

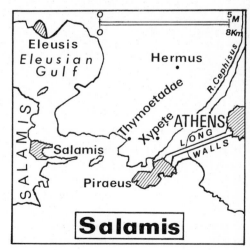

Salic Law: ancient penal code, originating with the Salian Franks though much amended and added to by such rulers as Charlemagne (*see* separate entry). The code was mainly concerned with fines for various offences; but there were some civil law enactments (i.e. concerned with the rights of private individuals rather than with criminals). The most famous of these excluded succession to land by or through females. In the 19th century it brought about the separation of Hanover from Britain when Queen Victoria came to the throne in 1837.

Salisbury, Robert Arthur Talbot Gascoyne-Cecil, third Marquis of (1830–1903): leading Conservative statesman and three times Prime Minister of England between 1886 and 1902. Like the present Marquis, he was directly descended from Elizabeth I's minister, William Cecil (*see* separate entry), whose son Robert built Hatfield House, still the family home. His foreign policy was described in 1896 as one of "splendid isolation", a peaceful imperialism based on the strength of the British Empire rather than on alliances in Europe.

Salt: name of the naturally occurring compound sodium chloride. Nowadays, salt is a cheap common commodity, but once it was so rare and valuable that it was used as money. Caesar's soldiers received part of their pay (*salarium*) in salt.

When ancient man started farming, salt became essential – meat contains a high salt content, cereals little. People living near the sea, or possessing salt mines, exported salt. Trade routes devoted to salt developed: salt from Palmyra was carried between Syria and the Persian Gulf; the Via Salaria was built from the salt works at Ostia to Rome.

Salt had a religious significance to early peoples. It was associated with sacrificial offerings, and the Hebrews rubbed salt on newborn babies to ensure good health.

Salt became symbolic of a binding agreement, not only because of its preservative qualities but because covenants and pacts were often made over a meal containing salt. To eat a man's salt was reckoned a bar to treachery or betrayal.

¶ TELFER, DOROTHY. *About Salt.* 1967

Salvation Army: international Christian organisation, originating in London in 1865 for missionary and social work, particularly among the very poor. Its founder was William Booth (1824–1912), and members of his family were prominent among its early leaders. The title, which was adopted in 1878, indicates a disciplined body organised to fight against poverty and ignorance: members wear uniform, and pride is taken in the musical proficiency of its bands. Booth himself was styled "General", and his son succeeded him, but the office became elective in 1931. Subordinate officers also have military titles, as those acquainted with Bernard Shaw's play *Major Barbara* will know. The movement flourishes in England, the USA and elsewhere in the English-speaking world.

Whitechapel Salvation Army Hostel, Britain's first Labour Exchange.

Salzburg: Austrian province and picturesque capital city beautifully sited on the banks of the River Salzach. As the birthplace of the composer Wolfgang Amadeus Mozart (1756–91) and the centre of an annual musical festival, Salzburg attracts visitors from all over the world.

Samarkand: city in the fertile loess valley of Transoxiana, West Uzbekistan, USSR; from ancient times a great trading centre on the caravan route between China and the Near East. As Maracanda, it was taken by Alexander (*see* separate entry) in 328 BC and harshly treated after his troops were twice ambushed by Sogdian tribes. It revived and was taken by the Arabs in the 8th century AD. They learnt paper-making there and transmitted it to Spain. In 1369 Timur (Tamerlane) made Samarkand his capital, enriching it with booty and captive craftsmen and scholars from India, Persia and Syria. The turquoise tiled domes of his tomb and of the great madrassehs (Muslim colleges) flank the cobbled Registan, "the noblest public square in the world". Turki princes succeeded the Timurids. The railway reached Samarkand in 1888, two years after the Russians annexed the city. Today, while not holding its former dominant position, it remains an important commercial centre, with food-processing, textile and engineering industries. *See* RUSSIA for map.
See also TIMUR.

The Shir-Dor Madrasah, Samarkand.

Samoa: archipelago of volcanic islands 2,700 miles [4,345 kilometres] east of Australia, visited by Roggeveen in 1722, de Bougainville, Lapérouse and Edwards before 1800 and von Kotzebue in 1824. Commerce soon followed the missionaries of 1830. In 1899 Britain withdrew, US interests east of 171° W were recognised, and German interests in Western Samoa. The latter, mandated to New Zealand in 1920 and a trusteeship territory from 1947, achieved independence in 1962. American Samoa has since 1951 attained universal suffrage and parliamentary institutions.

Samurai: "one who serves", a member of the class of professional warriors which rose in Japan in the 10th and 11th centuries AD when the emperors delegated power to great clan leaders. The samurai followed "the way of the horse and the bow", a code which stressed pride in pedigree and loyalty to a lord who rewarded his warriors with the lands of the defeated. In defeat, they preferred suicide to torture and dishonour. Their bows required great strength to string, and their swords were the keenest and most finely balanced ever produced. When Japan's voluntary isolation deprived them of warfare, they elaborated their chivalric code of *bushido* (literally, the doctrine of the warrior). When, after 1870, Japan began to compete with Western powers, the samurai lost their social privileges, but were the mainspring of Japanese militarism in World War II (*see* separate entry). Their swords are still greatly prized by collectors all over the world and command high prices in the salerooms. Such is the unique craft of the Japanese swordsmiths that these prized blades are still sent back to Japan for cleaning and repolishing.
¶ GIBSON, MICHAEL. *The Samurai of Japan.* 1973
See also JAPAN.

San Francisco: city of California, chief port and commercial centre of western USA. It has one of the largest natural harbours (456 square miles: 1,140 square kilometres) in the world, with its entrance spanned by the famous Golden Gate Bridge (completed 1937, 4,200 feet: [1,280 metres]). The main history of this vast centre is crammed into little more than a hundred years, from the time in 1841 when thirty families in the village of Yerba Buene, near the end of the peninsula now occupied by the city, formed the entire population.

Though the peninsula had been discovered a little earlier, the first ship to enter the Bay from the Pacific was the Spanish packet *San Carlos* in 1775. The event that transformed the small settlement was the discovery of gold at Colma, California (1849). By 1860, when the gold rush was over, San Francisco was well on the way to becoming the main port on the Pacific coast.

The havoc brought about by a number of fires and earthquakes (*see* EARTHQUAKES) has been overcome by the remarkable courage and energy of its people. The city has housed several conferences that have shaped the modern world, including that which established the United Nations Organisation (*see* separate entry) and the International Court of Justice (1945). The peace treaty between the Allies and Japan was signed there in 1951.
See AMERICA for map.

San Stefano, Treaty of (1878): treaty which ended the Russo-Turkish War of 1877-78 after the defeat of Turkey. The terms were specially favourable to Russia and included territorial gains in the Caucasus and the creation of a large Bulgaria with an Aegean Sea outlet. Fear of increased Russian power led to this treaty being severely altered at the Congress of Berlin (*see* separate entry).

Santa Fé Trail: the overland trail from western Missouri to the river port of Santa Fé in Argentina, an important trade route till the coming of the railway in the 1880s. One writer has said: "It was about eight hundred miles from Independence, Missouri, to Santa Fé, across prairie, river, creek, mountain and desert; and to travel it in fifty days was considered fast moving."

Santiago de Compostela: city of Galicia, north-west Spain. Its cathedral, dating mainly from 1078-1188, contains the shrine of St James the Greater and was one of the greatest places of pilgrimage in the Middle Ages. The special badge worn by the Compostela pilgrims was the scallop shell, mention of which occurs often in medieval pictures and literature. The road to Compostela from the Pyrenees is one of the most historic in Europe and features in the earliest guidebook for travellers known to us.

Santo Domingo: the early name of Hispaniola from 1496 when Bartholomew Columbus founded the city first called Santiago de Guzman. The western parts, occupied by the French from 1625, were called Santo Domingo (Saint Dominique after the Treaty of Ryswick, 1697; *see* separate entry) until 1804, when the Haitian Republic was established. The Dominican Republic, founded in 1844, covers the eastern half of the island. The name still exists in its capital, the oldest European town in the Americas, rebuilt as a modern city after hurricane devastation in 1931 and known as Cuidad Trujillo from 1936 to 1961 in honour of the dictator.
See also individual entries.

Saracen: name used by the later Greeks and Romans for the nomadic peoples of the Syro-Arabian desert, from whom their eastern frontiers had to be defended. During the Crusades (*see* separate entry) the word described any of the Mohammedan enemies engaged by the Christians. Later still, in the 16th century, the word was used to denote any infidel or non-Christian.

Saratoga, Battle of (1777): the first major American victory in the War of Independence when the British general Burgoyne, with about 3,500 men and near-famine conditions in his ranks, surrendered to General Gates, commanding about 16,000. The victory not only greatly heartened the rebels but had worldwide repercussions, France at once acknowledging "the Independent United States of America", closely followed by Spain and Holland.
See also AMERICAN WAR OF INDEPENDENCE.

Sarawak: a state of north-west Borneo, Indonesia, which for a century was ruled by white English Rajahs. In 1841 the Sultan of Brunei gave it to James Brooke (1803–68) when he had helped to quell a rebellion of Dyak tribes. Brooke ruled independently until 1868, when he was succeeded by his nephew, Charles Johnson Brooke, during whose reign, 1868–1917, much further territory was added. The country became a British protectorate in 1888. The third Rajah, Sir Viner Brooke, ruled until 1946 when, against opposition from native chiefs, the country became a British colony. The rule of the Brooke dynasty was enlightened: much development was undertaken and there was no public debt. In 1963 it became one of the federated states of Malaysia.

Saskatchewan: Canadian province from 1905, after responsible government from 1897, lying between Manitoba and Alberta and formed from the North-West Territories. Henry Kelsey of the Hudson's Bay Company (*see* separate entry) explored the Carrot River in 1690, and the French later built forts on the Saskatchewan River. In 1774 the oldest settlement, Cumberland House, was established, and in the 1790s Pond and Thompson explored the territory. Settle-

Indonesia/Malaysia

ment was sporadic until Canada acquired the Company's territories, established order by means of the North-West Mounted Police and encouraged railway construction. A rebellion of the Métis (half-breeds) under Louis Riel (1844–85) was shortlived, but his trial and execution for treason led to an outburst of racial feeling in Quebec and Ontario which almost brought down the government. After 1900 European settlers came into the territory in large numbers.

Saudi Arabia: kingdom formed by the union of the sultanate of Nejd with the kingdom of Hejaz under Ibn Saud in September 1932. The kingdom occupies the greater part of the Arabian peninsula, bounded by Jordan, Iraq and Kuwait to the north, by the Persian Gulf, the Trucial States and Oman to the north-east, by South Yemen to the south, and by the Red Sea to the south-west. The capital, Riyadh, is also the capital of Nejd, situated on the central plateau, whilst Mecca is the capital of the Hejaz. Other important towns are Anaida, Buraida, Medina and Taif. The population of Nejd is largely nomadic: consequently, there is little agriculture, and before the discovery of oil at Dammam the main trade was in camels and sheep; but oil in Nejd has revolutionised the whole economy of Saudi Arabia.

The Hejaz is the site of many historic events. Medina, "City of Light", is the burial place of Mohammed, who died there on 7 June AD 632. Mecca, his birthplace, contains the mosque in which is placed the sacred shrine of Islam – the Kaaba, or black stone, which Abraham is said to have received from Gabriel.

See separate entries for ISLAM; MECCA; MEDINA; MOHAMMED.

Savonarola, Girolamo (1452–98): Dominican friar who preached reform in Florence. He denounced the evils which he saw in the life of the city and of its clergy; but the severity of his language and his claim that divine inspiration placed him above human control brought

Savonarola being burned at the stake in Florence.

him into conflict with Lorenzo the Magnificent (*see* MEDICI) and Pope Alexander VI. The people of Florence turned against him, and he was hung from a cross and burned.

Saxe-Coburg-Gotha: small German duchy near Saxony in the old Holy Roman Empire (*see* separate entry). Its family gained prominence in the 19th century when Albert, the younger brother of the ruling duke, married Queen Victoria and became Prince Consort. Saxe-Coburg-Gotha became the name of the British royal house until it was changed to Windsor in 1917.

Saxon: member of a north-central German race, originally living near the mouth of the River Elbe. The first mention of the Saxons occurs about the middle of the 2nd century, when Ptolemy's *Geography* places them on the Cimbric peninsula,

which is now Holstein. From AD 286 onwards Roman historians frequently refer to them as pirates infesting the North Sea, and a naval force was maintained in the Channel and fortifications erected to protect the coasts of Gaul and Britain from their raids. In Britain the command was in the hands of an officer with the title *Comes Litoris Saxonici*, Count of the Saxon Shore. With the decline of Roman power under Honorius the Saxons not only raided the coasts of Britain but began to settle there.

Bede (*see* separate entry) says "from the Saxones . . . came the East Saxons, South Saxons and West Saxons", thus placing them in the modern Essex, Sussex and Wessex, and sharply differentiating them from the Jutes of the Isle of Wight and Kent and the Angles of East Anglia, the Midlands and the North, but recent historians have taken the view that this account overemphasises the differences

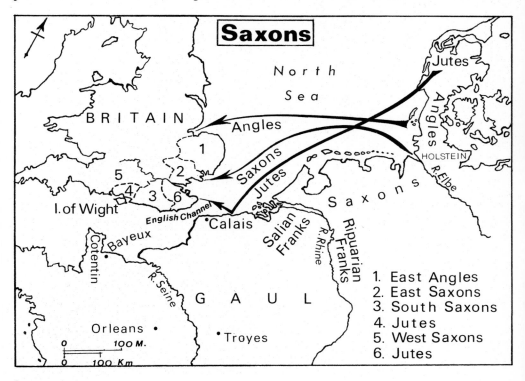

1. East Angles
2. East Saxons
3. South Saxons
4. Jutes
5. West Saxons
6. Jutes

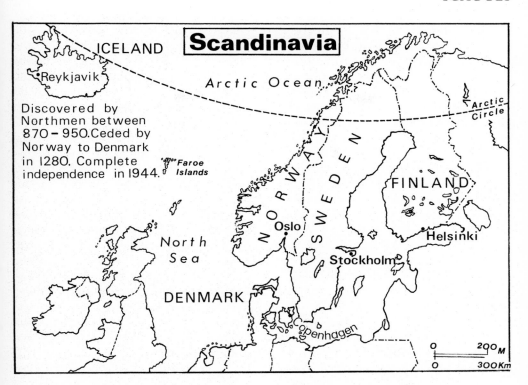

Scandinavia

ICELAND

Reykjavik

Arctic Ocean

Discovered by
Northmen between
870 – 950.Ceded by
Norway to Denmark
in 1280. Complete
independence in 1944.

Faroe
Islands

Arctic
Circle

N O R W A Y

S W E D E N

FINLAND

Oslo

North
Sea

Stockholm

Helsinki

DENMARK

Copenhagen

0   200 M

0   300 Km

between the various Germanic invaders.
Their settlements in Gaul had a less
permanent effect than in Britain. They
seized part of the north coast between the
Cotentin peninsula and the mouth of the
Seine, with Bayeux as its focal point, and
probably an area around Calais, but they
were ultimately subdued by the Franks,
and at least one authority suggests that
this diverted the stream of Saxon invaders
from Gaul to Britain.

¶ PAGE, R. I. *Life in Anglo-Saxon England.* 1970;
SELLMAN, R. R. *The Anglo-Saxons.* 1959

Scandinavia: name given to the peninsula in north-western Europe which is
divided between Norway and Sweden;
but a loose reference to "the Scandinavian
countries" is often assumed to include
Denmark as well, and sometimes Finland
and Iceland. All five countries have historic and cultural links.

¶ PROCTOR, G. L. *Ancient Scandinavia.* 1965

Schools: places where people gather in
large or small groups for education and
instruction. Although this article confines
itself to the teaching of young persons,
the word is frequently also used in an
adult context, as when military authorities establish a School of Artillery, or a
famous artist has a "school" of other
artists who base their work on his style.
Curiously enough a group of marine
mammals is also called a "school", e.g. of
whales or porpoises. Readers may be surprised to know that *scholé* is a Greek word
meaning "leisure", while the Latin word
for a school, *ludus*, means "play".

Evidence for the existence of schools
goes back to very ancient times, but, in
following the subject, two points must be
observed: the first, that, for most of the
period of past history, education was the
privilege of the upper or, at best, the
middle layers of society, although children of ability could often make their

821

way upward from below, sometimes even from the slave classes, many of the famous, or infamous, civil servants of the Roman Empire rising from such origins: the second point to remember is that much of the education of boys, and particularly of girls, was given at home or, in medieval times, in the households of patrons or relatives.

To go no further back than Greece of the 5th century BC, we lack the evidence to form a comprehensive picture of the schools themselves (which were almost exclusively for boys), but, except in Sparta (*see* separate entry), the ideal was a balanced education of mind and body and the development of an inner harmony in which music played an important part. We know, however, something about the schools attended by Roman boys, to which they went escorted by slaves to look after them in the streets and carry the wax tablets on which they wrote their lessons. These slaves were called by the Greek term *pedagogues*, which we now sometimes apply, jocularly but incorrectly, to schoolmasters. The poet Horace recalls for us the name of one such master, Orbilius, who was noted for the severity with which he flogged his pupils. The Roman schools placed great emphasis on the skills of speaking and self-expression.

The barbarian invasions of the western world brought confusion and disarray to the cause of learning, and it fell to the Church to maintain and foster what could be preserved. Bede (*c.* 673–753) in his monastery at Jarrow, in north-eastern England, was among the early upholders of the cause of learning, and the Emperor Charlemagne (742–814) urged the clergy of his dominions to improve their knowledge of Latin and encouraged the foundation of schools. He was assisted in his aims by Alcuin (753–804), an Englishman who had been headmaster of the cathedral school at York where he himself had been educated. Latin, as the language of the Church and of international diplomacy, was, from the pupils' early age, almost the exclusive study of the schools. Greek underwent an almost complete eclipse in the West until it shone forth again with the Renaissance.

Meanwhile, the growth of the feudal system saw the rise of a warrior class whose education lay in a different direction, physical prowess and the various arts of war. It is probably wrong to draw too wide and easy a distinction between such men of action and the *clerics*, as men of education, whether priests or not, came to be called. At the beginning of the period, the English king Alfred (849–899), a great patron of learning, is said to have taught himself to read when he was already a grown man, while King Henry I (1068–1135) was called "Beauclerk" because of his academic attainments. It is probable that the medieval knight, even when he lacked the elementary skills of the schoolroom, was often a ready speaker and familiar with music and poetry. Nevertheless, it was to the schools that the western nations looked for their churchmen and administrators, the functions being frequently combined in one person.

Such schools were often attached to monasteries, but the masters were generally secular priests (not members of an order) or laymen. Even before the Reformation, a movement had started to found schools by private benefaction: in England the most famous is Eton College, founded by King Henry VI in 1440. At the same time, there were certainly schools of a sort for younger children, where they made their first contact with the alphabet and other simple skills; but it is difficult to form a picture of their nature or the extent to which they existed. Another question is how far learning penetrated down the social scale. There were, of

a. Boys school from a Greek Kylix. b. 12th century scholars form a ring round their teachers, from the Canterbury Psalter. c. Flemish Village School painted by Jan Steen in the 17th century. d. Quaker school under John Bunyan's Meeting House, 18th century. e. Boys striking against corporal punishment, 1889. f. Primary school gymnastic lesson, 1973.

823

course, wide differences from century to century and country to country, but it probably went deeper than is commonly supposed.

During the Reformation the monastic schools disappeared in many countries, but those which took their place were often strongly influenced, if not directly controlled, by the various Protestant churches. In England these took the form of so-called grammar schools, some of which developed into the curiously named "public schools", the distinctive system of fee-paying schools for the middle and upper classes, often confined to resident scholars only, which still exist for boys and, of more recent origin, for girls. (The equivalent schools in the USA are more accurately called "private schools".) It was only gradually that other subjects were allowed to take their place in the curriculum beside Latin and Greek ("the classics") and mathematics. A classical education was regarded as the hallmark of an educated man until quite recent times. In 1865 John Wilkes Booth, the assassin of Abraham Lincoln, proclaimed his defiance after the deed with the words *sic semper tyrannis* ("such is ever the fate of tyrants"), and, even in the earlier part of the present century, the studies of some of the English public schools were predominantly classical.

It is from the 19th century onwards that the greatest changes in the scholastic scene have occurred. In the first place, education in an increasing number of countries has become compulsory for all children and has been more and more frequently provided at public cost, though parents are sometimes left free to patronise private schools at their own expense. Secondly, there has been a tremendous upsurge and change in the pattern of theories of education, often carrying forward the ideas of earlier pioneers such as Vittorino da Feltre (1378–1446), Com-

enius (1592–1670), Rousseau (1712–78) and Pestalozzi (1746–1827). One of the greatest educational thinkers of modern times was the American, John Dewey (1859–1952), the champion of learning through experience rather than through formal instruction.

¶ DURES, ALAN. *Schools.* 1971; MEYER, ADOLPHE E. *An Educational History of the Western World.* 1965 *See* separate entries for ALCUIN; ALFRED; BEDE; CHARLEMAGNE; LINCOLN, ABRAHAM; PESTALOZZI; PROTESTANT; REFORMATION; ROUSSEAU, etc.

Scotland: country occupying the north of Great Britain. It is, in fact, sometimes described as North Britain but, though the description is geographically correct, to those who belong by birth and ancestry the country means much more than that, since it is distinctive in structure, vegetation, climate and in the character of its inhabitants. Highlander and islander, lowlander and borderer are recognisably different even in the 20th century. Five races had settlements in the first centuries AD – Picts, Britons, Angles, Scotti and Norwegians, each with their own language and all warlike, but having to find a common allegiance. They found it in a royal line. Wars with England and the leadership of such men as Sir William Wallace and Robert the Bruce (*see* separate entries) helped to make the people one, but a spirit of individualism and independence prevailed, "for it is not Glory, it is not Riches, neither is it Honour but it is Liberty alone that we fight and contend for, which no Honest Man will lose but with his life". Such was the Declaration of Arbroath, 1320, given in a letter from the nobility, barons and commons of Scotland to Pope John XXII asking him to exhort the King of England "to suffer us to live at peace in that narrow spot of Scotland beyond which we have no habitation". Such battles as Bannock-burn (1314), when the Bruce's ragged little army broke the might of Edward II's chivalry, and Flodden Field (1514), when James IV of Scotland, less successful but equally gallant, died with about 12,000 Scots, were but two expressions of the national spirit.

This love of liberty, which made the Scottish nation, carried her people eventually far beyond "the narrow spot", to play a leading part in the colonisation of North America, India, Australia and New Zealand, and to be conspicuous in world history as warriors, traders, administrators, teachers and missionaries.

Scotland in her turn owes much to continental influence. The Court in the 11th century was "filled with southern foreigners". Norman influence was strong, and for long the royal house was "French in race and manner of life, in speech and in culture". The execution of the Roman Catholic Mary Queen of

Robert the Bruce's victory over the forces of Edward II at Bannockburn in 1314.

Scots (1587) and the triumph of Protestantism ended this "Auld Alliance". Links with England were then to be forged, and the Union of the Crowns in the person of James VI of Scotland, I of England, was achieved in 1603. The Act of Union, 1707, uniting the two kingdoms under the name Great Britain and guaranteeing the Hanoverian succession, ended years of strife. Clan risings in 1715 and 1745 on behalf of the exiled Stewarts were crushed and were followed by harsh laws which contributed to the depopulation of the Highlands. Crofts once fertile were left to the rabbit and the deer. The 18th century, however, also saw much road, canal and bridge building in Scotland, together with commercial development and the ending of the almost slavelike conditions in the coalmines and saltpits. The Reform Act of 1832 brought about much-needed voting reforms and increased the Scottish

Right, The March of the King's Forces, under the Earl of Mar, into Perth in August 1715.

representation in parliament. Today the Scottish Development Board aims at re-creating Highland industry: knitting, weaving, fishing, re-afforestation and tourism are encouraged. Aberdeen, the granite city and fishing port, Glasgow, centre of shipbuilding and industry, St Andrews, paradise of golfers, Dundee, famous for jute, marmalade and cake, Edinburgh (*see* separate entry), seat of learning, law and government, all cities with universities, give Scotland its character, *multum in parvo*, and the roll call of its great men and women in theology, medicine, exploration, engineering, literature and the arts would be difficult to parallel in any country of comparable size.

See GREAT BRITAIN for map.

¶ BROWN, P. HUME. *History of Scotland.* 1955; MACKIE, ROBERT L. *Short History of Scotland.* 1962

See also BRUCE; CARNEGIE; COVENANTERS; EDINBURGH; HADRIAN'S WALL; JACOBITES; KNOX; LIVINGSTONE; MCADAM; NASMYTH, SCOTT, SIR WALTER; SIMPSON; STEPHENSON; STUART, HOUSE OF; TELFORD; WALLACE; WATT, etc.

Scott, Robert Falcon (1868–1912): British naval officer and Antarctic explorer. He led the expedition of 1901–04 to explore the region of South Victoria Land and during a second expedition reached the South Pole, 18 January 1912. He had, however, been forestalled by one month by the Norwegian Roald Amundsen (*see* separate entry). Held back by terrible blizzards and weak from sickness and insufficient food, Scott and four companions all perished on the return journey. Scott's tent, with his records and diaries intact, was found in November 1912, only eleven miles [17 kilometres] from a food depot which might have saved him.

¶ BRIGGS, P. *Man of Antarctica.* 1959; SCOTT, CAPTAIN R. F. *Scott's Last Expedition.* Foreword by Peter Scott. 1964

See also POLAR EXPLORATION.

Scott by Sir Edwin Landseer.

Scott, Sir Walter (1771–1832): Scottish historical novelist and man of letters. The titles of some of the many biographies written of him, *The Wizard of the North*, *The Great Unknown*, *The Laird of Abbotsford*, epitomise his character, life and work. For long he remained anonymous and preferred to be so. His *Minstrelsy of the Scottish Border* and the series of *Waverley Novels* placed him in the forefront of writers of the Romantic Movement at home and abroad. Fired by his imagination, German, French and Italian literature of the period reflected his influence, and the whole world of letters was forever enriched. Among his most famous books, a number of them brought to the cinema and television screen, are *Ivanhoe*, *Kenilworth*, *Rob Roy*, *The Talisman*, *Sir Nigel* and *Quentin Durward*.

¶ In THOMAS, H. and D. L. *Famous Novelists.* 1959

Seals: stamps used to authenticate documents. The term can mean either the device which makes an impression or the impression itself. Sigillography, the study of seals, is one of the oldest hobbies in the world. It became a craze in ancient Rome, and Julius Caesar was a collector.

The art of seal engraving began around 4000 BC. A ruler could best establish his authorisation to a document in the remotest regions of his country by affixing his personal seal, without fear of forgery. People of standing had private seals for the same purpose and to mark their own property.

Sumerian "temptation" seal c. 2300 B.C.

Sumerians and Babylonians possessed them and used them for business transactions. Jars and documents were sealed with stamp or cylinder seals, made of stone and engraved with simple designs or scenes of everyday life showing the costumes, social customs and religious rites of the period. The Egyptians made scarab

Egyptian pottery seal from tomb, 18th–26th Dynasties.

and button seals of pottery, the Cretans engraved scenes such as the bull sports on pendant or bracelet seals. Chinese seals were beautifully carved on semiprecious stones, metal, wood or soapstone, the imperial examples being large, five inches by seven, others miniature, an eighth of an inch square. The Greeks engraved theirs on ivory or stone, the Persians on gems. From Roman times, the seal was often used for security, to fasten docu-

ments or chests and doors, to show they had not been illegally tampered with.

When the impression made by the die is on metal, it is called a bull. This method was used by the Eastern emperors from Justinian onwards and was later adopted by the popes. Hence, papal documents were often known as "bulls".

In England, Saxon royalty had its seals, consisting of an effigy and the inscription, Edward the Confessor originating the double seal. After the Norman Conquest, with the frequent transfer of landed property and because so few of the laity could write, the custom of sealing documents became general. At first, seals bore just an inscription identifying the owner, but, with the rise of heraldry, the upper classes used a coat of arms as well. Because forgery of a seal was more difficult than of a signature, the use of seals continued long after writing became general. King John could write, but he sealed, not signed, the Magna Carta. Where large numbers of people were parties to an agreement, dense clusters of seals are sometimes found. One early 13th-century example in the Public Record Office, London, has no less than fifty.

13th century English seal from the Public Record Office. It is in the "vesical" shape.

Signet rings were made by engraving the design on gems or metal – gold, silver, latten, brass or steel. Shapes for the clergy and for ladies were often oval or "vesical", i.e. of a shape made by two arcs of a circle, giving a point at each end. Most others were round. The impressions were formed in coloured wax, normally natural dark yellow, red or green, and applied directly on the face of the document, or appended to the deed by a parchment label or silk cord. As an added protection, counter-sealing became common, with two dies, each with its own device.

15th century Royal seal of Elizabeth I of England.

The design of the Royal Seals of England has changed with every sovereign. Monarchs and other people of rank possessed both private and official seals, which they used for different purposes. Until 1884 the Privy Seal authorised the issue of money from the Treasury. The office of Lord Privy Seal still exists in Britain.

After 1520 the combination of seal and signature became universal practice, though not until 1677 were signatures alone made legally necessary on deeds. With increased knowledge of hand-writing sealing gradually came to be a mere formality, though in Britain it is still statutory on certain documents.

See also BABYLON; JUSTINIAN; NORMAN KINGS; SAXON; SUMER.

Secession: withdrawal from an alliance, federation, political or religious organis-ation, etc. Two instances may clarify this definition. In 1733 a number of persons deserted the Established Church of Scot-land and set up a rival body known as the Secessionist Church. This remained in existence until 1847, when it became merged in the United Presbyterian Church. Perhaps the best known example gave rise to the American Civil War (*see* separate entry). In 1860–61 the Southern States individually followed South Carol-ina's example and seceded from the Union, following Abraham Lincoln's election to the Presidency (*see* LINCOLN, A.), and formed themselves into the Confederate States. Attempted secession has often led to bitter warfare. Recent examples have been the attempt (1967) of Biafra to establish a state independent of Nigeria; and the move of East Pakistan to form the government of Bangladesh, a breakaway from the federal republic of Pakistan (1971).
See also BANGLADESH; RHODESIA.

Security Council: part of the structure of the United Nations Organisation (*see* separate entry). Originally it had eleven members: five permanent (China, France, Russia, Great Britain and USA) and six elected by the General Assembly for two-year terms. Since 1965 the number of non-permanent members has been in-creased to ten.

The duty of the Council was to meet frequently to deal with emergencies which threatened world peace. But the ability to veto any decision of the Council, a power which each of the permanent members possesses, has been used over a hundred times by Russia to protect com-munist interests. With one exception, the Council has acted only in places where the Great Powers were not directly in-volved, as in the Congo or Cyprus. The exception was Korea in 1950, when a temporary Russian "walk-out" from the Council after a dispute enabled the United Nations to send a force against a communist invasion of South Korea.

Because of these difficulties, since 1950 the most important decisions of UNO have been made in the General Assembly, not in the Security Council.

Sedition: commotion and unrest in a state, likely to lead to organised rebellion, but stopping short of treason, which usually involves working with the enemy.

Segregation: literally, a separation from the flock, and hence the separation of a class of persons from the general body.

An early example of this is seen in the establishment of *ghettos*, in which Jews were compelled to live. In medieval times concentrated Jewish communities (Jewry, Juderia, etc; *see* JEWS) were found in many cities, though these were not always because of legal requirements. Later, however, the segregation was enforced. A ghetto was established in Rome in 1556, and this precedent was ultimately followed by almost all Italian cities. They were also found in Germany, where they were known as *Judengasse*. The ghettos were enclosed by walls and gates, which were locked at night. They gradually disappeared during the 19th century with the growth of more liberal opinions, though they reappeared to some extent at the time of World War II.

In the United States, following the Civil War, Washington DC and seventeen southern states established segregated school systems, under which white and black children were educated in separate schools. Transport systems were similarly segregated. Such restrictions have been much attacked since the end of World War II (*see* separate entry). In 1954 the Supreme Court ruled that segregation in schools was a denial of equality and therefore prohibited by the Fourteenth Amendment. Following this, moves towards integration met with resistance, an example being the Little Rock disturbances from 1957 to 1959. In 1955 a Negro boycott of buses in Montgomery, Alabama, was organised by Martin Luther King as a protest against segregation on buses; this was followed by a Court Order prohibiting such segregation.

In South Africa the word segregation is replaced by apartheid (*see* separate entry), but the basic idea is the same. This again involves separation of the races in public transport, banks, etc., as well as the establishment of native reserves for separate development, such as the Transkeian Territories (*see* separate entry).

Semitic: adjective denoting a group of languages found among ancient peoples of Western Asia, some of which, in a derived form, continue to this day. The word is sometimes transferred to people speaking such a language, e.g. the Jews (*see* separate entry). It comes from Shem, one of the sons of Noah.

Senate: name given to certain governing and law-making bodies, albeit differing in scope and origin. The term originates in Rome and is derived from a word meaning "elders". The Senate of the Republican era (roughly the last five centuries BC) was, despite certain political checks on its authority, effectively the power which governed the state. Although qualification for membership was earned by holding certain public offices, it was largely an aristocratic and hereditary body, which in the end lost its effectiveness when military leaders began to challenge its authority.

In more recent times, when systems of democratic government gained acceptance in the western world, and where the constitution provided for two houses of representatives, the term "senate" was sometimes given to the upper house, the members of which (senators) generally enjoyed more security of office than those of the lower house. This is the case, for instance, in France and the USA.

The word has also been adopted to denote the governing bodies of certain universities, for instance those of Cambridge and London, and is commonly so used in the USA.

Senegal: republic on the west coast of Africa between Mauritania and Guinea. Formerly a French colony, it elected in November 1958 to remain within the French Community and in 1960 attained independence as a socialist republic under its President, Léopold Senghor. The capital, Dakar, is a sophisticated city containing a large part of the European population of West Africa. It is an important industrial and trade centre and a focus of educational and research institutions. A railway runs from Dakar to Bamako on the River Niger in Mali, with branches to St Louis and Linguere. The port offers modern facilities for bunker fuelling and the export of groundnuts and phosphate ore.

¶ CROWDER, M. *Senegal.* 1962

Serbia: part of present day Yugoslavia. Its peoples, the Serbs, joined with other neighbouring Slavs (e.g. Croats and Slovenes) to form the state of Yugoslavia in 1918. The capital of Yugoslavia, Belgrade, was also the chief city of old Serbia.

A united kingdom of Serbia existed in early medieval times, but at a great battle on the Field of Blackbirds in 1389 the Turks destroyed its independence. Early in the 19th century a movement developed to free Serbs from the harsh rule of the Turks. Two rival Serbian families began a bitter contest for supremacy. At first the Karadjordjevići, who looked to Russia for support, gained the upper hand; but in 1878, when Serbian independence was once again recognised, their opponent, an Obrenovići, became its first king, with Austrian support. The rivalry became murderous when the unpopular Alexander Obrenović and his family were assassinated in 1903. Under the new dynasty Serbian ambitions rose rapidly. The cry of "Greater Serbia"

**Senegal
Sierra Leone**

**Somalia
Sudan**

G – Gambia
PG – Port. Guinea
L – Liberia
GA – Ghana
B – Burundi

T – Togo
D – Dahomey
UG – Uganda
R – Rwanda

Serbia/Slovakia

AUSTRIA – HUNGARY
Vienna• Budapest

Belgrade

ITALY

SERBIA

MONTENEGRO
ALBANIA

GREECE

1914
1918

Newly formed State
of Yugoslavia

0   200 miles

0   200 Km

GERMANY
CZECHOSLOVAKIA
AUSTRIA HUNGARY
POLAND

1918

threatened Austria, who still had many Serbs in her empire, and in 1914 Austria tried to use the Sarajevo assassinations to destroy Serbia, thus precipitating World War I (*see* separate entry).

Settlement, Act of (1701): English law establishing the Hanoverian succession to the throne. William III had no heir, and the death (1700) of the Duke of Gloucester, last surviving child of Princess Anne, left the succession open. Parliament therefore passed this Act, settling the succession on Sophia of Hanover (1630–1714) and her heirs. Sophia was the granddaughter of James I of England and the nearest Protestant heir. The Act also excluded foreigners from all offices and secured judges from arbitrary dismissal.

Sevastopol, Sebastopol: Russian Black Sea port and naval base in the Crimea, with one of the finest anchorages in Europe. In the Crimean War (*see* separate entry) it was evacuated by the Russians after an eleven-month siege which destroyed the fortifications and damaged much of the city. In World War II (*see* separate entry) it withstood another long siege (1941–2) before being taken by the Nazis. It was recaptured by the Russians in 1944.

Workers making mines in an underground factory during siege of 1942.

Seven Wonders of the World: monuments of the ancient world considered unique for their size, beauty or splendour. They have been variously listed, but, according to tradition, were described in the reign of Alexander the Great (*see* separate entry) by two Greek travellers, Antipater of Sidon and Philo of Byzantium. Only the *Pyramids of Egypt* remain today. The other Wonders were:

The Hanging Gardens of Babylon, thought to have been terraced gardens watered by an artificial irrigation system which enabled trees and flowering plants to grow in an arid country. Legend says that Nebuchadnezzar had the gardens made for his Queen.

The Mausoleum, a magnificent tomb erected for King Mausolus by his widow. Designed by Greek architects and sculptors, it stood at Halicarnassus, in Asia Minor.

The Colossus of Rhodes, a gigantic figure dedicated to the sun god Apollo, which

a. *Hanging Gardens of Babylon.*

b. *Mausoleum at Halicarnassus.*

c. *Temple of Diana at Ephesus.*

e. *Statue of Zeus at Olympia.*

d. *Colossus of Rhodes.*
f. *Pharos at Alexandria.*

stood at the entrance to the harbour of Rhodes, possibly bestriding it. After fifty years it fell in an earthquake.

The Temple of Diana at Ephesus, the city which saw the riot of silversmiths so vividly described in the Acts of the Apostles. The building was destroyed by the Goths in the 4th century AD.

The statue of Zeus at Olympia, site of the Olympic Games. The statue was of gold and ivory and was created by the Greek sculptor Phidias.

The Pharos at Alexandria, the first lighthouse. It was a stepped tower 440 feet [134 metres] high, on top of which burned a beacon which could be seen far out to sea, its brightness intensified by a mirror. The Pharos survived for over 1,000 years and was finally destroyed in the 14th century during an earthquake. An alternative is the *Palace of Cyrus*, overlaid with gold.

An attempted list of Seven Wonders of the Middle Ages gives the Colosseum of Rome, the Catacombs of Alexandria, the Great Wall of China, Stonehenge, the Leaning Tower of Pisa, the Porcelain Tower of Nankin and the Mosque of St Sophia at Constantinople.

See also EPHESUS; OLYMPIA; PYRAMID, etc.

Seven Years War (1756–63): war in which Prussia and Great Britain fought Austria, France and later Russia. Causes were the determination of Austria to regain, and Prussia to keep, Silesia, and Anglo–French colonial and mercantile rivalry. In spite of some reverses, Frederick II of Prussia (*see* separate entry) defended his country brilliantly (with victories at Rossbach and Leuthen, 1757, Zorndorf, 1758, Leignitz and Torgau, 1760), and at the Peace of Hubertsburg with Austria, 1763, Prussia emerged as a first class power. The British contribution, apart from victory at Minden, 1759, was mainly naval and colonial (battles of Lagos and Quiberon and capture of Quebec, 1759,

Wandewash, 1760), and Britain emerged by the Peace of Paris, 1763, as the principal colonial power.

¶ PARKMAN, F. *The Seven Years War.* 1968

Seventeenth century: the years 1601–1700. Perhaps the most remarkable feature of the 17th century, because it was worldwide, was the establishment of the modern states system, with more or less permanent boundaries. This occurred not only in Europe, where the treaties of Westphalia, 1648, and the Pyrenees, 1659, established national frontiers which, with comparatively minor alterations, lasted until the 20th century (though certain debatable lands changed hands from time to time); but also in the Far East where China under the Manchu dynasty, starting with Li Tzu Ch'eng in 1644, became a centralised and firmly ruled Empire, and where in Japan of the Tokugawa period, from about 1600, arbitrary centralised government under a "Shogun" was developed and the expulsion first of Christianity, after the Shimabara revolt, 1637, and then of all foreigners, left Japan a closed country.

With the establishment of boundaries came also the distinctive character and importance of various states. Brandenburg-Prussia emerged from the Thirty Years War as the most powerful state of northern Germany and moved, under the Great Elector, Frederick William I (1640–88), towards that parity with Austria

Thirty Years War: The Surrender of Breda *painted by Velasquez.*

achieved by Frederick the Great; the Austrian Habsburgs, though still powerful as Archdukes of Austria, were Holy Roman Emperors little more than in name. France, emerging from the welter of her religious wars, became, under the guidance of Henry IV, the two great Cardinals, Richelieu and Mazarin, and Louis XIV, the most powerful nation in Europe, eclipsing Spain which entered a long period of decline; the Turks, although the reforms of the Kiuprili "dynasty" of Grand Viziers from 1656 made them for a time formidable, suffered a long series of incompetent Sultans who brought about a shrinking empire; Russia, under the successors of the first Romanov, Michael (1612), gradually established itself as a European power, winning territory under Peter the Great from the Turks at the Treaty of Carlowitz, 1699, and Baltic lands from the Swedes at Nystadt, 1720. Sweden, after a period of expansion (which she had not the economic resources to support) under the Vasa kings, culminating in Gustavus Adolphus, declined from the position of a first class power, in spite of the meteoric campaigns of Charles XII (1697–1718).

The century saw also the establishment in most countries of a despotic form of government, and the decline, except in Great Britain and Holland, of representative institutions. In the East government had always been despotic, but the Manchus in China, the Shoguns in Japan and the Great Moguls in India made despotism really effective. The same can be said of the Bourbons in France where, after 1614, the States General did not meet for 175 years. And although, in Germany, the Emperor's attempt to regain effective control was finally defeated in the Thirty Years War, every one of the hundreds of individual states which made up "the Empire" was despotically ruled. Administrative reforms in Prussia and Russia only left the central authority more effectively despotic, and in countries where this was not so, such as Poland, there was anarchy. The attempt of the Stuarts to operate a despotic system in England was defeated, perhaps fundamentally because Britain's insular position had meant that kings had never needed to keep a standing army.

During the 17th century religion was displaced by economics and politics as the motive force in national and international policy. Though Spain continued during the first half of the century to support Roman Catholicism wherever it seemed to be threatened, in other countries developments which appeared to be religious in character often had fundamentally different motives. The Whigs who resisted the Catholic policy of James II were really resisting his attack on the political power they had become accustomed to, and which was the condition of their economic prosperity: they merely used the rallying cry of "No Popery!" to gain popular support. And though Louis XIV was personally a Roman Catholic he quarrelled with the Pope, and his revocation of the Edict of Nantes (1685) was as much to emphasise his personal power as to serve his religion. The Thirty Years War (1618–48) appeared to have a religious character, but, though the Emperor was backed by counter-Reformation forces, his main aim was to re-establish his imperial authority; and the treaties of Westphalia which ended the wars acknowledged the existence of Calvinism as well as Lutheranism, and in some states a practical toleration did develop. Gustavus Adolphus, "the knight-errant of Protestantism", was probably moved as much by Swedish ambition as by religion; and modern research has shown that even the stern puritans of the English revolution had an often unrealised economic motive for their resistance of the Crown.

It was a century of expanding European

Gustavius Adolphus "the knight-errant of protestantism" in 1632.

colonisation and trade, with consequent international friction which led sometimes to war, as between English and Dutch. The English and Dutch East India Companies were founded at the beginning of the century, the French somewhat later. The first permanent English colony on the North American continent, Virginia, was settled in 1607, and there were eleven more by 1700. Champlain first visited Canada and explored the St Lawrence in 1603: he was followed by a succession of French explorers, and, after 1632, the struggling "New France" became firmly established, backed by Richelieu. European traders were active all over the world, introducing new commodities such as tea and tobacco to their home countries, and beginning the "westernisation" of foreign lands which has so profoundly influenced their development.

Last, but not least important, this was the century of the "Scientific Revolution", when the freedom of thought promoted by the Renaissance began to bear fruit; when men like Galileo and Harvey, Newton and Descartes upset the centuries-old systems of thought and belief, and bodies like the English Royal Society and the French *Académie des Sciences* were investigating every branch of science and mathematics, astronomy and medicine, and were developing new systems of philosophy. In politics, economics, science, religion and philosophy, the 17th century foreshadowed the development of the modern world.

¶ CLARK, SIR GEORGE. *The Seventeenth Century.* 1947; PENNINGTON, D. H. *Seventeenth Century Europe.* 1970
See also individual entries.

Seward, William Henry (1801–72): American statesman and colleague of Abraham Lincoln (*see* separate entry). After a distinguished career as a lawyer he entered politics. In his various appointments he showed himself a humane and tolerant administrator and was one of the most powerful political opponents of slavery. Twice an unsuccessful candidate for the presidency himself, he was appointed Secretary of State by Lincoln in 1860. In Lincoln's early days, Seward, as the much more experienced public figure, strove to impose his will on the cabinet; then, coming to recognise Lincoln's personality and qualities, served him loyally and gave great service to the nation, not the least of his achievements being the purchase of Alaska from Russia in 1867.

Shackleton, Sir Ernest Henry (1874–1922): British Antarctic explorer. In 1908–09, in the *Nimrod*, he commanded an expedition that reached a point about 97 miles [156 kilometres] from the South Pole. During an attempt to cross the Antarctic continent, 1914–16, Shackleton's ship *Endurance* was crushed in the ice and abandoned. He reached uninhabited Elephant Island using boats and sledges. Shackleton, with five companions, then made an epic 800-mile [1,280 kilometres] open boat voyage to South Georgia to obtain help. He died during a fourth Antarctic expedition.

¶ ALBERT, M. H. *The Long White Road.* 1960; LANSING, ALFRED. *Shackleton's Valiant Voyage.* 1963
See also POLAR EXPLORATION.

835

Shadow Cabinet: term invented by the British Press after the parliamentary election of 1929 to describe a body of advisers selected by a Leader of the Opposition. At first there was no precise allocation of duties to its members, but the Labour Opposition between 1951 and 1964 appointed shadow Ministers, and this example has been followed by subsequent Oppositions.

Shaftesbury, Anthony Ashley Cooper, seventh Earl of (1801-85): British social reformer and philanthropist. Lord Shaftesbury was horrified at the desperate conditions in which homeless children lived in the London slums of the early 19th century. He influenced Parliament to pass laws which improved their lot and with his money founded *Shaftesbury Homes* where orphans could be trained to earn a living. He was also active in the causes of lunatics, chimney sweeps, juvenile offenders and the housing of the poor. Of particular importance were the laws he was successful in forcing through parliament limiting the hours women and children might work in factories.

¶ FANCOURT, M. ST J. *The People's Earl.* 1962

Lord Shaftesbury.

Shah Jahan, Jehan (*c.* 1592-1666): the fifth Mogul Emperor. Ruling from 1627 to 1658, when he was imprisoned by his son, he brought Mogul power to its greatest point, exerting control even over the Deccan princes. A great patron of Indian architecture, he was responsible for the Taj Mahal and the Pearl Mosque at Agra.
See also MOGUL.

Shakespeare, William (1564-1616): England's, and the world's, greatest poet and dramatist. Despite his pre-eminence, little is known for certain about him. There are even groups of people who declare that "Shakespeare's" works were written by a different person altogether, the two most popular candidates being Francis Bacon (1561-1626; *see* separate entry) and the seventeenth Earl of Oxford (1550-1604).

Leaving such controversies aside, it can be stated that Shakespeare, the son of a glover, was born at Stratford-on-Avon, a Warwickshire town which has become a shrine to his memory. In 1582 Shakespeare married Anne Hathaway, of Shottery, by whom he had three children. After his marriage he went to London where he became an actor and achieved fame as poet and dramatist. He earned enough to buy a fine house at Stratford, New Place, to which he eventually retired. He is buried in Stratford Church. His birthplace, Anne Hathaway's Cottage and New Place are among the buildings associated with him that have survived.

Shakespeare's plays fall into three main groups: the Histories (e.g. *King John, Richard II, Henry V*); the Comedies (e.g. *Much Ado About Nothing, A Midsummer Night's Dream, The Taming of the Shrew*); and the Tragedies (e.g. *Macbeth, Hamlet, King Lear*). They were written over the period approximately 1590–1613. Shakespeare also wrote several long poems and 154 sonnets. The plays were first published together in 1623 in a volume gen-

erally known as the First Folio. It is one of the most valuable books in the world and on the rare occasions when one is offered for sale it makes many thousands of pounds. Most copies are in the USA, the greatest collection being the Folger Shakespeare Library, Washington, DC.

¶ BURTON, H. M. *Shakespeare and His Plays.* 1958; HAINES, CHARLES. *William Shakespeare and His Plays.* 1971

Shanghai: China's greatest seaport, near the mouth of the Yangtze River, with an estimated total population of 9,500,000. It was little more than a small fishing town until the 1840s when, as one of the five "Treaty Ports", it was opened to foreign trade by the treaty of Nanking (1842). International settlements were established in Shanghai by Britain, France and the USA, the British and American settlements being merged in 1863 as the International Settlement. In 1896 Japan gained a concession in Shanghai, which was a scene of Sino-Japanese conflict in 1932 and 1937 (*see* separate entry). In 1943 Britain and USA restored the International Settlement to Chinese rule. Under Communist rule (*see* COMMUNISM) from 1949, foreigners were excluded but the port has remained busy and important.

Shaw, George Bernard (1856–1950): critic, novelist and playwright. Born in Dublin, he lived there until he was twenty, when he went to London to earn his living as a writer. He made little mark with his early novels but became known for his brilliant public speaking on socialism and for his criticisms of art, music and drama. When, after some years, his first plays were acted it became clear that a new and original playwright had arrived. In the course of a long life, he wrote over

fifty plays, of which perhaps *St Joan*, *Major Barbara* (*see* SALVATION ARMY), *Man and Superman*, *Back to Methuselah* and *Heartbreak House* are the best known. In all his plays he used the stage to expound his views on politics, religion, war, economics and other subjects. He was awarded the Nobel prize for literature in 1925.

¶ WARD, A. C. *Bernard Shaw*. 1951

Sheridan, Philip Henry (1831–88): American soldier and Union general in the American Civil War (*see* separate entry). His ability and daring were recognised by General Grant (*see* separate entry), who, when he was appointed lieutenant-general of the Union forces in 1864, placed Sheridan in charge of the cavalry, in which capacity he showed himself probably the best leader on the Union side. In a series of subsequent high commands he carried out a number of successful campaigns in which he showed courage combined with great tactical ability and a rare quality of leadership which made him a popular figure with his troops. One of his exploits was "Sheridan's Ride" – a 20-mile [32 kilometres] dash to meet his troops fleeing from the Confederate General Early at Cedar Creek, ending with his rallying cry, "We must face the other way!" and turning defeat into victory. It was Sheridan's decisive turning of Lee's flank in April 1865 that forced the latter's retreat to Appomattox, Virginia, where he surrendered to General Grant.

Sheriff: literally, shire reeve, the chief administrative officer of a district or county. According to the British legal historian Maitland the whole history of English justice and police might be brought under the single heading of "The Decline and Fall of the Sheriff".

For a comparatively brief period after the Norman Conquest in England the sheriff became virtual ruler of the country. He was chief accountant to the Royal Exchequer, the leader of the *posse comitatus* (a force raised to suppress riots, etc.), and the chief police, military and executive officer. The king could by writ of "Justicies" direct him to hear any plea except one relating to land. From this position of power he has descended in importance in England until today his position is a somewhat expensive and empty honour, most of the surviving legal duties being performed by an under-sheriff.

Criminal justice was largely taken out of his hands by the Assizes of Clarendon (1166) and Northampton (1196), and passed into the hands of the royal justices. Magna Carta (1215; *see* separate entry) and the rise of Justices of the Peace further reduced his power. His civil jurisdiction declined following the Statute of Gloucester, 1278. With the appointment of Lords Lieutenant in Mary's reign his military powers ceased, while his fiscal (financial) powers had long since declined with the growth of forms of taxation in which he had no part, and his attendance at the Exchequer was no longer necessary.

In Scotland the office of sheriff still retains administrative and judicial functions. The country is divided into fifteen sheriffdoms. The sheriff acts as returning officer in parliamentary elections within his area; he also is one of the judges of the Sheriff's Court, which has a wide local jurisdiction, both civil and criminal.

In the United States the office of sheriff is in most cases elective. In rural areas, acting as an agent of the state, he is the law enforcement officer, with a wide jurisdiction over most crimes and misdemeanours, but his importance is declining as law enforcement tends to become more the concern of the state or Federal authority. The formation of the sheriff's posse, so familiar in "western" films and stories, is an interesting linguistic survival of the English medieval *posse comitatus*.

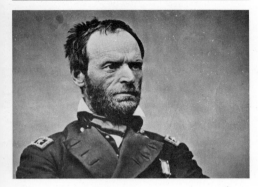

Sherman, **William Tecumseh** (1820–91): American soldier and Union general in the American Civil War (*see* separate entry). In his early years he combined soldiering with banking and the study of law. In the Civil War he rose to command first the army of Tennessee, then the military division of the Mississippi, numbering in all 100,000 men. With this force he carried out the invasion of Georgia, including the famous "March to the Sea", from Atlanta to Savannah. As a result of the campaign, a large section of the Confederate forces surrendered.

Shinto: ancient native religion of Japan, from Chinese *chin tao*, the way of the gods. Its chief features are the worship of nature, national heroes and family ancestors. It also involved belief in the divinity of the emperor, a claim renounced by the *Shinto shrine at Nikko, Japan.*

present ruler Hirohito (b. 1901) in 1946. Unlike most religions, it claims no historical founder.

Ship of the line: ship sturdy and well armed enough to take her place in a line of battle. The broadside of heavy guns, first used in the battle off Shoreham, England, in 1545, was seen by 1665 to require a line-ahead formation. Such ships ruled the sea until the days of mine and torpedo. Three-deckers of 100 guns served as flagships, but the main ships of the line were the Third Rates carrying 74

HMS Canopus, *1796, of 80 guns.*

guns on two decks. They cost some £60,000, displaced 1,400 tons [1,422 tonnes] and carried 650 men. The last of them, HMS *Defiance*, 1861, was little larger than the *Sovereign of the Seas* built for the Ship-money fleet in 1637. Though the ships were traditionally built of English oak, the shortage of home-grown timber eventually brought about a much more cosmopolitan product. In the words of R. G. Albion (*Forests and Sea Power*), "her mainmast came from the forests of Maine, her topmast from the Ukraine, her small spars from the mountains of Norway, her planking was floated down the Vistula to Dantzig, and her curved frames came from the hedgerows of Sussex".

839

Shipbuilding

Shipbuilding: the science of shipbuilding, though of immense age, is barely documented before the 16th century. The functional shape of the ship and its general outline have been known since the earliest times. The basic tools of the shipbuilder in wood, the saw, adze, chisel and drill, have been found in Egyptian tombs dating from about 2000 BC. The Viking burial ships and remains of trading vessels excavated in northern Europe provide information on ship construction of the early centuries AD. Though they had appeared earlier, towards the end of the 15th century larger vessels carrying three masts such as the Flemish carracks were becoming common. Fortunately the Renaissance artists were able to portray these vessels with considerable accuracy including details of their construction.

Shipbuilding in the 14th century.

Early in the 16th century Henry VIII (1491–1547), king of England 1509–47, built permanent dockyards at Deptford and Woolwich on the River Thames for the construction and repair of his ships. He brought in skilled craftsmen from the shipyards of Genoa and Venice and these, together with the British shipwrights, formed a technical corps well equipped to build the largest type of vessel.

One of the earliest attempts to set down on paper the form of a ship is found in *Fragments of Ancient English Shipwrightry* – preserved at the Pepysian Library, Cam-

Sovereign of the Seas.

bridge, England. It is probably the work of Mathew Baker, master shipwright, and written about 1585. The manuscript contains plans, elevations and sections of a number of ships. One of the earliest names associated with English shipbuilding is that of Pett. Phineas Pett, born in 1570, designed Charles I's great ship the *Sovereign of the Seas*, 1,522 tons [1,546 tonnes], carrying 100 guns. His son Peter supervised the building at Woolwich dockyard and launched the ship there in 1637. In America the early settlers in New England launched their first ship in 1631. By the 18th century more than a third of British merchant ships were being built in American yards.

Comprehensive textbooks on the building of ships began to appear at the end of the 17th century, and the practice of making scale models of important vessels was introduced. Draughts or plans of ships were produced by the master ship-

Shipbuilding in the 17th century.

wrights before building. The British Admiralty collection of draughts has survived almost intact from about 1700 and forms a unique record of the shape and development of warships.

During the 18th century the heavy demand for ships both for trade and war purposes led to a considerable expansion of the shipbuilding industry both in Britain and in the USA. In addition to the government dockyards, private shipyards large and small were established in rivers, estuaries and seaports. The three main requirements were a sheltered position, sufficient water for launching and easy access to the forests for timber. Some of the smaller shipyards were merely a clearing in the forest with one or more slipways running down to the water. Crude scaffolding was set up. Saw pits, kilns for steaming timbers, small furnaces for iron work, sheds for keeping the tools, pitch, tar, oakum, etc., were set up nearby.

It is not surprising that, as a result of this expansion of the industry, supplies of oak timber were becoming rapidly depleted. An example of the amount of timber required to build a 74-gun ship in 1781 is given by Henry Adams, shipbuilder, at Buckler's Hard on the Beaulieu River, Hampshire, England. His estimate was 2,000 oaks and this would deplete an area of about forty acres [sixteen hectares].

Before building, the shipwright and his assistants would go into the forest and select suitable trees for felling. These would have to include a considerable amount of naturally curved "grown" or "compass" timber from which the knees, ribs or frames could be shaped. The timber was roughly cut in the forest and transported to the shipyard. The keel was laid, usually of English elm, and the stem and sternposts scarphed (rejoined) on forward and aft. Next the floor timbers were laid across the keel and the keelson placed on top and bolted through. The frames were then set up and the ship was allowed to season "in frame" if time permitted. After this the planking was laid using oak pegs or "treenails" as fastenings. Deck beams supported by heavy wooden knees were next fitted across the ship and the decks laid and caulked. The underwater portion of the hull was "graved" with a mixture of tallow, pitch, tar and resin and the ship was ready for launching.

The effects of the Industrial Revolution soon became apparent in the shipbuilding industry. Steam paddle engines were being fitted in ships in 1812 and the screw propeller in 1838. The desperate problem of finding sufficient timber for ships was considerably resolved when iron came into general use as a substitute about 1830. The first large iron passenger vessel driven by a screw propeller was I. K. Brunel's *Great Britain* launched at Bristol, England, in 1843 and now preserved at that port.

With the added strength of iron the designers were able to increase considerably the size of ships. As a result many new shipyards sprang up on rivers and estuaries where there was access to coal and iron. In Britain the greatest concentrations were in the north of England and the lowlands of Scotland. The River Thames was an iron shipbuilding river during the 19th century but declined soon after 1900 owing to its distance from essential mineral supplies. Shipbuilding in iron required the use of heavy machinery, and large steam hammers, rolling mills, drilling and punching machines were installed in the new yards. A new and more varied labour force including platers, riveters, drillers, etc., was also required.

The substitution of steel for iron after about 1875 may be said to have abolished the limiting factor in the size of ships. As a result many shipyards adapted themselves to build vessels of the greater ton-

GALLEON

ROMAN
ROUND SHIP

LONG SHIP

CARAVEL

SLOOP

MERCHANT
CLIPPER

CARRACK

FRIGATE

SHIP OF THE LINE

CORVETTE

GALLEY

DESTROYER

ATOMIC SUBMARINE

nage. The period 1890–1914 saw an enormous expansion in the world's mercantile and naval fleets. Between 1892 and 1894 shipyards in Great Britain produced 80.8 per cent of the total gross tonnage of the world's merchant ships, but competition from shipyards in Germany, Japan, Holland and Italy soon began to be felt.

The shipbuilding industry of the 20th century is a highly competitive one. The so-called big ship era between the two World Wars produced many large passenger liners, culminating in the *Queen Elizabeth*, formerly 83,673 [85,015] and now, as a result of much modification, 82,998 tons [84,330 tonnes], and launched on the Scottish river Clyde in 1938. In July 1969 she was sold at Fort Lauderdale, Florida, with the intention of converting her to a floating hotel and convention centre. Liners have not exceeded this tonnage but oil tankers are by far the largest ships of modern times.

¶ HARDY, A. C. and TYRRELL, E. *Shipbuilding: background to a great industry.* 1964

See also individual entries.

Ships, Types of: the word "ship" in its broadest sense can be used to refer to any type of seagoing vessel propelled by sails or mechanical means. The specific definition "a three or more masted vessel with bowsprit, square rigged on all masts" is applicable only to the sailing ship.

1. *Long ships and round ships.* The countries of the Mediterranean supply us with the earliest known information about ships. The people of Crete by about 2000 BC had vessels which fell into two distinct categories. Their "long ships" with fine lines and ram bow were the fighting ships propelled by oars, while the "round ships" were the heavier type of craft built mainly for sailing. This marked difference in the fighting and trading vessels, though not apparent in Egyptian ships, can be traced through Greek and Roman vessels almost to the end of the wooden ship era. Two fine examples of long ships are the 9th-century Viking ships (*see* VIKINGS) preserved at Oslo, Norway. These are the Gokstad and Oseberg ships with their long, open, clinker-built hulls. They were double ended with high stem and stern posts and propelled by oars but a large square sail was carried in addition.

2. *Caravel.* A small vessel usually three-masted with lateen sails, the largest forward, originating in Portugal in the 15th century. One of Columbus's ships the *Nina* was a caravel, though square sails were fitted during the 1492 voyage. The *Santa Maria*, often erroneously referred to as a caravel, was a three-masted square rigged ship.

3. *Carrack.* The large 15th-century three-masted sailing vessel with a forecastle projecting far over the stem. Originating in the Mediterranean as a trading vessel it soon became known over most of Europe. The carrack usually carried large square sails on the fore and main masts and a lateen sail on the mizzen. This was to be the basic pattern for the full rigged sailing ship that was to remain the same in many essentials for nearly 400 years.

4. *Galley*. Originally a seagoing vessel propelled by oars. The descendants of the great war galleys of the Greeks and Romans with their many tiers of oars continued in the Mediterranean until the end of the 18th century. By the 15th century the biremes and triremes, etc., gave way to single decked vessels using sails in addition to oars. They were usually manned by slaves or criminals. They could be highly manoeuvrable when under oars and were the standing fighting vessels of the Mediterranean. In the Battle of Lepanto (*see* separate entry and *colour section*) in 1571 more than 200 galleys were engaged on both sides. Fighting was mainly hand to hand but in the 16th century guns began to be carried.

5. *Galleon*. This was usually a four-masted vessel built to some extent on the lines of the galley but higher out of the water and with a long beakhead extending forward. The galleon was a true man-of-war with cannon carried on decks within the ship. Spain is usually associated with the galleon but by the mid-16th century this type was to be found in most European countries. The Spaniards used their large galleons of the 17th and 18th centuries for trading with their colonies in America.

6. *Galleass*. A combination of the galleon and galley, this 16th-century war vessel was usually three- or four-masted but carried a large number of oars in addition to sails. The galleass was extensively used by Mediterranean peoples, particularly the Venetians, but it disappeared from northern Europe after about 1600.

7. *Ship of the line*. This term was applied to the larger class of sailing warship carrying not less than fifty guns. From the mid-17th century onwards the great fleets of Europe were mainly organised in line ahead for fighting purposes and only the more heavily armed ships could take their place in the "line". The modern counterpart is the all big gun battleship.

(*See* separate entry.)

8. *Frigate*. The origin of the term is uncertain but it was used in the 17th century to describe a wide variety of craft from small Mediterranean oared vessels to the great English three decker *Naseby*. It is possible that the word was originally applied to the shape rather than to a type or class of ship. The familiar frigate of the 18th century was a small, fast, three-masted vessel of twenty-four to thirty-two guns. It had two decks but guns were carried only on the upper deck. Previously the small two decker had a few guns on the lower deck but these were quite useless in rough weather. Most navies carried a number of frigates. They were used for reconnaissance work and maintained vital

signal links with the commander-in-chief afloat. They were virtually the "eyes" of the fleet and as such were greatly in demand during wartime. They were also extensively used for convoy escort work. The name still applied to such vessels until well into the steam era but lapsed during the 1880s when a very much larger version was reclassified as a "cruiser". The term was reintroduced in 1943 to describe the convoy escort vessels specifically armed against the U-boat. Frigates in large numbers are now in service in the navies of the world armed with all the sophisticated equipment for defence and attack in the nuclear age.

9. *Sloop.* There are two meanings to this word. One applies to the rig of a small single-masted vessel. The other is concerned with a class of small ship rating next below the frigate. The 18th-century sloop-of-war was a single-decked vessel carrying about eighteen guns. It was either three-masted and known as a ship-sloop or two-masted and known as a brig-sloop. Escorting convoys was one of the functions of these little vessels, which continued into the steam age as paddle and screw sloops respectively. During the two world wars convoy protection was again the main task. After 1945 the sloop was reclassified as a frigate.

10. *Cruiser.* The *Gentleman's Dictionary* of 1705 states "Cruisers are small men-of-war made use of, to and fro, in the Channel and elsewhere to secure our Merchant Ships from the enemy's small frigates and privateers. They are generally those that sail well and are therefore commonly well manned." The word cruiser, certainly used as early as the 17th century, was derived from the verb "to cruise". Any small craft, from cutters to three-masted sloops, could be termed cruisers. The modern vessel substantively classified as a cruiser appeared during the 1880s. This can be described as a self-sufficient heavily armed fighting ship of high speed and able to cruise the oceans for considerable distances without refuelling. Its main wartime function is to patrol the ocean trade routes, giving protection to the Merchant Navies.

11. *Corvette.* This was originally a French term for a small ship with upper deck armaments similar to the British ship-rigged sloop of the 18th century. Very few sailing corvettes were included in the British navy, but during the 1860s and 1870s many of the steam variety were built and the term was extended to include vessels with main deck guns. These were small-to-medium sized warships but they never figured in any fleet action. The term lapsed with the introduction of the cruiser in the 1880s. At the beginning of World War II a new type of corvette was introduced into the British navy for convoy escort work. This was the famous Flower class based on the design of a whale catcher. Numbers of these sea-worthy little craft were turned out to give anti-submarine protection to convoys. They eventually proved too small for their tasks and were superseded by the frigate.

12. *Destroyer,* originally termed torpedo-boat-destroyer. The menace of the fast torpedo carrying craft of the 1890s necessitated the building of vessels larger, faster and more powerfully armed than the craft they were to destroy. The recently invented steam turbine gave them the necessary high speed and, with their slim lines, they became the highly manoeuvrable vessel turned out in large numbers for the navies of the world. Today they are armed with guns, torpedoes and guided missiles, and can take offensive action as well as acting as main fleet and convoy escorts.

13. *Submarine.* This is a submersible warship armed with torpedoes, capable of navigating under water. Although invented towards the end of the 19th century the submarine is essentially a 20th-century vessel and now ranks as the world's most formidable warship, atomic powered and armed with Polaris missiles. (*See* separate entry.)

14. *Merchant ship*. The merchant ship, designed for cargo and passenger-carrying purposes, developed on much the same lines as the warship until the 19th century. By about 1840 the need for speed brought about a change and a much finer type of hull was designed. This was the birth of the clipper ship (*see* separate entry). The introduction of steam power at about the same time saw the evolution of the screw-propelled merchant ship.

15. *Aircraft carrier*. With the greatly increased use of aircraft in modern warfare has come the development of warships with specially constructed decks to carry them for operational purposes. In 1914 the British Government fitted a tramp steamer, renamed the *Ark Royal*, with a flying-off deck and two cranes to hoist seaplanes on board. From such small beginnings have come such giants as the atomic powered USS *Enterprise*, of 85,350 tons [86,720 tonnes] and a complement of 100 aircraft using a $4\frac{1}{2}$ acre [1 hectare] flight deck; and the even larger USS *Eisenhower* approved in the 1969-70 Defence budget.

¶ LANDSTROM, BJORN. *The Ship*. 1961

Shorthand: method of speedy writing by substituting contractions or arbitrary signs for letters, words, syllables and sounds. It is also known as stenography.

The ancient Greeks appear to have had a shorthand system as early as the 4th century BC, but the first one of which we have accurate knowledge is that devised by Marcus Tullius Tiro, a friend of Cicero (*c.* 60 BC). Plutarch tells us that the speeches made in the Roman Senate at the time of the Cataline conspiracy were recorded verbatim by various *notarii* using this system.

Modern shorthand originated in England with the publication in 1588 of Bright's *Characterie: an Arte of Shorte, Swifte and Secrete Writing by Character*. This was followed in 1602 by *The Arte of Stenographie* by John Willis. This had a complete alphabet, but also used dots placed near the consonants to represent vowels. Thomas Shelton some thirty years later used signs to denote two or more consonants, such as ng, sh, th. Perhaps the best claim to fame of Shelton's system is that it was used by Samuel Pepys (*see* separate entry) in his *Diary* (1659-69), which remained undeciphered until 1825.

These systems were orthographic or alphabetic. The idea of a phonetic system came later, in the second half of the 18th century. One of the best known systems appeared in 1837, when Isaac Pitman (1813-97) published his *Stenographic Sound Hand*. This uses straight lines and simple curves to represent consonants, while vowels are represented by a dot or a dash, the position of which indicates the particular vowel. On this system, not all strokes are of even thickness, as opposed to "light-line" systems, where no shading or thickening of the characters is used. Perhaps the best known of these is the Gregg system, widely used in the United States.

See also HANDWRITING.

Siberia: part of the USSR east of the Urals and north of the central Asian republics. Once the Tatar Khanate of Sibir, it passed gradually under Russian rule from the 16th century. Military, civil and penal settlements were made in the 18th and 19th centuries. A trans-Siberian railway was constructed 1891-1900. Siberia was the scene of fighting after World War I, anti-Soviet Russian forces under Admiral Kolchak being supported by a Czechoslovak Legion and by an American, British, French and Japanese expeditionary force in Eastern Siberia. Kolchak was defeated and shot in 1920 and his allies withdrew. Though its resources are not yet fully known or

The main street of Salikhard, Siberia, centre of reindeer breeding.

developed Siberia plays an important part in the economy of the USSR and is rich in coal, iron and other minerals, with the western lowlands producing oil and gas.

Sicily: island off south-western Italy, now an autonomous area of Italy. Settlement is recorded before 1000 BC, and the island afterwards became a prosperous Greek colony (9th – 5th centuries BC) with Syracuse as the most important town. Its subsequent troubled history included occupation by Carthaginians, Romans (for whom it was a main source of corn supplies), Vandals, Saracens and Normans. In 1282, following the islanders' revolt (known as the Sicilian Vespers) against Charles Duke of Anjou, a Frenchman who was their ruler at the time, Sicily was temporarily joined to Aragon whose king, Pedro III, had come to its help. After a later long period of domination by Spain, a more settled time began in 1860 when Garibaldi (*see* separate entry) united Sicily to the kingdom of Italy. The complexity of Sicilian history is increased by the existence for a long period of the Kingdom of the Two Sicilies, a state made up of the island and the southern portion of Italy.
See ITALY for map.
See also MAFIA.

Sidney, Sir Philip (1554–86): English poet, diplomat and soldier, remembered above all as the soul of honour and chivalry. His best known works are *Astrophel and Stella*, the *Defence of Poesie*, and *Arcadia*. In 1586 he joined an expedition sent to help the Netherlands in their fight against Spain. In an attack on Zutphen Sidney who, recklessly but characteristically, had taken off his leg-armour so as to put himself on equal terms with a friend who wore none, was wounded in the leg. Offered some water, he handed it instead to a dying soldier with the famous words: "Thy necessity is yet greater than mine." Sidney died of his wounds twenty-six days later.
¶ In UNSTEAD, R. J. *Discoverers and Adventurers.* 1965

Sieges: operations, often protracted, to reduce fortified positions by starvation and bombardment. They began as soon as man fortified his settlements. The very early siege of Troy showed many characteristics of siege warfare – the failure to take the city by storm at the start; the besiegers wearying and falling out; the defenders sallying to the Greeks' ships; the attempt to terrorise the citizens by dragging the body of Hector before the walls; the final capture of the city by stratagem (the wooden horse). The great sieges have been of positions so vital that they must be held at all costs: capital cities – Constantinople in 1453, Vienna in 1683; river-crossings – Orleans in 1428; naval bases – Gibraltar in 1782, Sebastopol in 1854-55, Port Arthur in 1904. Often sieges, not battles, have been the decisive events: Charles V abdicated partly because he failed to take Metz in 1553; the Dutch revolt might have collapsed had Leyden fallen in 1574; "Peace lies within the walls of Maastricht", said Marshal de Saxe and, when he took it, France gained their terms at Aix-la-Chapelle in 1748.

847

When fortifications are stronger than missile weapons, or when generals are reluctant to risk battle, sieges dominate warfare. In the First Crusade, the great events were the capture of Antioch by the help of a traitor in 1098, and of Jerusalem, by siege-towers, in 1099. By 1400 artillery was dominating fortification, notably the guns of the Bureau brothers who blasted the English out of France; but by 1520 engineers had developed improved fortresses with guns mounted in bastions to cover every wall-face, and with water-filled ditches proof against mining. The Dutch revolt of 1572–1647 was decided by sieges: towns secure behind water defences commanded the water routes by which alone siege guns could be moved, and neither the Duke of Alva nor Maurice of Nassau liked open warfare. The greater generals of Louis XIV's time, Turenne and Marlborough, preferred open warfare but could rarely find an opponent prepared to

meet them. More typical of the age was Sebastian de Vauban, the greatest exponent of siege warfare both in attack and defence. In the 18th century roads and guns improved, and the great generals avoided sieges: Frederick the Great would not defend even his capital and relied on keeping his field army intact; Napoleon struck at his enemies' field armies; Tsar Alexander refused to be trapped in Moscow. Since 1860 artillery has grown in destructive power, and the bomber and missile have appeared, but some areas are so vital that they must still be defended.

Sieges make great demands on the morale of attacker and defender. Months of watching and digging test the determination of the attacker: Richelieu at la Rochelle in 1628 and Wolfe at Quebec in 1759 stood this test. Troops who took walls by storm expected the reward of pillage, and the laws of war allowed it. Defenders, encumbered by women and children, eating rats and boiled harness,

Roman assault towers being rolled into position.

threatened by epidemic or massacre, need firm leadership, and great leaders have emerged under siege. La Valette inspired the knights of Malta to repel the Turks in 1565; Adrian van der Werff shamed the citizens of Leyden by offering his right arm for their sustenance; Baden-Powell mobilised the boys of Mafeking (in the Boer War) to bear a part in its defence.

¶ BELFIELD, E. M. G. *Sieges*. 1967; JEFFREYS, STEVEN. *A Medieval Siege*. 1973

See also CONSTANTINOPLE; CHARLES V; CRUSADES; FREDERICK THE GREAT; NAPOLEON I; RICHELIEU.

Siege weapons: devices for breaking down the defences of besieged towns and fortresses. Siege weapons of great variety and ingenuity were in use in warfare from early times for demolishing walls and for throwing heavy stones, flaming projectiles and other missiles into enemy strongholds. The earliest and simplest was the battering ram, either manhandled or slung from a heavy protective framework.

Siege engines dating from Roman and Greek times included the catapult, balista, trebuchet and spring engine, each with individual mechanical principles. The catapult for throwing small stones developed into the perrier or petrary, which consisted of a heavy beam, one end being secured in a huge skein of twisted horsehair or sinew which acted as a powerful hinge when the beam was pulled backwards. On release a stone weighing forty to sixty pounds [18 to 27 kilogrammes] was projected from a cup at its extremity.

The balista was really a large cross-bow mounted on a massive wheeled frame. Its mechanism was set by a windlass and it projected four- to six-foot javelins [1.2 to 1.8 metres] a distance of about 450 yards [410 metres]. A variation of this was the arcubalista which incorporated two separate arms fixed in two wound-up skeins of hair or sinew.

The trebuchet was invented in the 12th century, its principal component being an arm up to 50 feet [15m] in length with a sling at one end pivoted about an axis and having a heavy counterpoise at the other end. This could project stones weighing up to 300 pounds [136kg] a distance of 300 yards [274m].

The spring engine, which was probably the least effective of these machines, had a flexible arm so arranged as to strike a bolt or javelin forwards with great violence. Medieval armies were accompanied by special siege trains, bringing along most of the necessary equipment. Some, however, such as scaling ladders and movable wooden towers, were often knocked up on the spot from whatever timber was available. With the development of artillery (*see* separate entry) the use of these primitive devices declined.

Siena: hilltop walled city commanding the road from Tuscany to Rome. Founded by the Etruscans (*see* ETRURIA) in the 13th century it vied with Florence and Pisa as a trading centre for cloth, spices and banking. It was ruled by a bishop until 1186 when Frederick Barbarossa (*see* separate entry) granted municipal rights. It supported the Ghibelline faction, and in 1261 it defeated the Florentines at Montaperto after the protecting shadow of the Virgin Mary had been seen on its walls. Painting in Byzantine style and Gothic architecture flourished there. St Catherine of Siena

The Market Square, Siena.

(1347–80) nursed victims of the Black Death and persuaded the popes to return to Rome in 1377. Weakened by feuds of nobles and townsmen, it surrendered to Charles V in 1555 and was ceded by Spain to the Medici Dukes of Tuscany in 1557 (*see* MEDICI, FAMILY OF). The Palio, the traditional barebacked horse race between the ten wards of the city, is still held annually for the honour of gaining the silk banner.

Sierra Leone: independent state on west African coast, bounded to the north-west to north-east by Guinea, to the south-east by Liberia and to the south-west by its Atlantic coastline. Sierra Leone was so called by the Portuguese navigator Pedro de Sintra (1462) either because the background mountains bore a rough resemblance in shape to a lion or because of the menacing roar of thunder-storms along the mountain ridge. At the time of de Sintra's exploration the area was inhabited by African peoples such as the Temne. The first settlements from outside, apart from early trading posts, were designed by philanthropists seeking to provide a home for runaway slaves and Negroes discharged from the US army and navy after the American War of Independence (*see* separate entry). In 1792 1,100 Negroes were brought from Nova Scotia, and the population was further increased when slavery was declared illegal by the British parliament. Frequent changes in governorship (17 changes in 22 years) made steady development difficult, but ultimately an industrious and self-reliant community was built out of the poor material dumped by outside agencies. Freetown, the present capital, provides the best harbour on the west coast of Africa, and exports include iron ore, diamonds, bauxite, palm kernels, coffee and cocoa. In 1961 Sierra Leone became an independent state within the Commonwealth and the one-hundredth member of UNO.
See AFRICA for map.

Signalling: the sending of orders or intelligence by prearranged signs – visual or aural – quickly and over long distances. It is so vital in warfare that it is of great antiquity. It probably developed first in the clear air and wide plains of Asia. A shield flashing in the sun told the Persians at Marathon (490 BC) that Athens was empty of troops. Aeschylus wrote that the news of the fall of Troy reached Greece by fire signal, but this story may originate from the line of signal stations across the Aegean built by the Persian Mardonius in 479 BC. When Alexander sent a patrol to scale the Sogdian Rock (328 BC) with rope and tent-peg, he learnt of their success by the waving of white flags. In Roman times Polybius (204–122 BC) described a method of signalling by flag or torch which could transmit an alphabetical code. In Britain Hadrian's Wall was linked to York by a line of signal stations, and remains of six round bases at one of these suggest that an elaborate code with six columns of smoke was used. Trajan's column shows a signal tower with haycocks and bundles of faggots at hand.

Europeans were very slow to develop signalling systems: they were outclassed by the Africans with their tom-toms and the Red Indians with their smoke signals.

Semaphore arms are suggested by Vegetius (4th century AD). It was not till the 17th century that they were demonstrated to the Royal Society by Robert Hooke (1635–1703), and it was 1799 before a line of frames with six shutters relayed messages from Portsmouth and the Nore to the Admiralty. The tactical use of signals in land battles developed even more slowly. Dust or gunsmoke made visual signals unreliable, and the din

Samuel F. B. Morse.

breathless messages were often misunderstood. The Mongols, operating in small mobile detachments, used bells and gongs to communicate, but among Europeans no effective land communications were established until the introduction of telegraphy. Invented by Samuel Morse (1791-1872) it was used in the Crimea and the Indian Mutiny, when the mutineers cursed it as "the wire that strangled us". Visual signals by Morse Code were used by the British in Abyssinia in 1867. By 1904 the Admiralty could send messages by wireless to Gibraltar.

Signalling has played a bigger part in sea warfare. Distances and visibility are greater, despatch vessels less reliable than gallopers, the ships' masts are a ready-made signal frame and there is greater scope for concerted manoeuvre after

of battle drowned the drum and, at times, even the trumpet. Most commanders agreed with Wellington: "I was always on the spot. I saw everything, and did everything myself." Verbal messages carried by galloper were used, though their

The International Code of Signalling, adopted for general use in 1934, and used by all nations at sea.

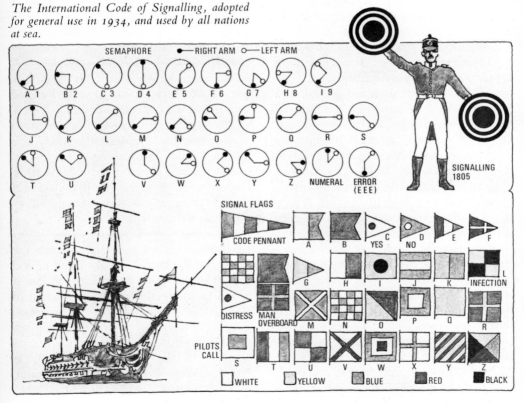

battle is joined. At Salamis (480 BC) a red cloak on an oar signalled the wheel and advance of the Greek fleet on the Persians. The Byzantine Emperor Leo VI (AD 866-912) wrote that an admiral should use a banner or streamer in a conspicuous position to convey his orders and that all officers should be practised in interpreting the signals. In England King John first demanded the salute at sea in 1201, and the Black Book of Admiralty (1378) listed two signals – for sighting an enemy and for summoning captains to a Council. The Spanish developed a slightly more elaborate code in 1430, using flags by day and lights by night, but there was little progress till the late 17th century, when large professional navies developed. In the Anglo-Dutch wars Robert Blake devised twenty-five signals based on five prominent parts of a ship's rigging. Fighting Instructions prescribing the main movements of a battle fleet required a set of prearranged signals, and in 1172-3 James Duke of York produced what were perhaps the first printed codes. These were supplemented by Additional Signals issued by individual admirals. Edward Vernon added a signal for "engage the enemy more closely" and stationed frigates to relay signals to the battle line. By 1746 commanders could make 144 signals with sixteen flags; by 1780, 330 with fifty. Thereafter progress was rapid, Admirals Howe and Kempenfelt and Sir Home Popham, by using fewer flags in hoists of three or four, made 1,000 words available. Nelson admitted that his victories depended on these codes, but they had their dangers, for mistakes were easily made: on one occasion Kempenfelt's own ship signalled for "weekly accounts" when "form line" was meant. Codes could be compromised: Popham's code was captured by the French in the frigate *Redbridge* fifteen months before Trafalgar. Fortunately the French betrayed their knowledge of it by using it to lure a ship into Toulon. Thereafter code books were bound in lead for easy sinking. The development of wireless made communications at sea easy, but wireless silence is still needed to elude the enemy, and the Admiralty is sometimes tempted to radio tactical decisions which would be better taken on the spot.

Reference was made at the beginning of this article to a shield flashing in the sun. This could be reckoned an early example of the heliograph, an apparatus designed to send signals by reflecting sunlight from a movable mirror. Its invention is attributed to Sir Henry Christopher Mance (1840-1926), who developed it during his work with the Persian Gulf Telegraph department of the Indian Government. As recently as World War II the equipment was issued to some British troops when an invasion by Hitler seemed imminent.

¶ DOWNING, J. G. *The Story of Signalling.* 1967
See also TELECOMMUNICATIONS.

Sikh: a breakaway sect from Hinduism (*see* separate entry), centred in the Punjab. Originally the disciples of Nanak (1469-1538), they were turned by Muslim persecution into a military theocracy, the *Khalsa*, which provided the finest of all Indian fighting forces. All true Sikhs took the surname of Singh (the Lion). Their greatest chieftain was Ranjit Singh (1780-1839; *see* separate entry).

Sikh Wars: wars in India between the Sikhs and the British. A disturbed period in the Punjab after the death of Ranjit Singh (*see* separate entry) culminated in 1845 in a Sikh invasion of British territory. The Sikhs were defeated, in spite of magnificent fighting and of some incompetence in the British command, at Mudki, Ferozeshah, Aliwal and Sobraon, and peace was made (1846), the Sikhs losing Kashmir and territory east of the Sutlej, and accepting a British Resident and garrison at Lahore. In spite of enlightened control by Henry Lawrence, unrest flared again into fighting in 1848. Lord Gough fought a costly action at Chilianwala, and finally won a decisive victory at Gujrat (1849), after which the Sikhs surrendered. The Governor General, Dalhousie, then annexed the Punjab, which was settled under Henry and John Lawrence (*see* separate entries). *See* INDIA for map.

Silver: precious metal capable of being shaped and drawn out without breaking. In ancient times silver was associated with the moon goddess because of its pale gleam. In the Acts of the Apostles a lively account is given of a riot of the silversmiths of Ephesus, who, since they sold silver images to travellers visiting the temple of Diana, feared that they would lose their livelihood if Christianity spread.

Silver ornaments were made long before St Paul's day: the metal has been found in tombs dating back to 4000 BC, and the Code of Menes, reputedly the first Pharaoh, 3500 BC, laid down that "one measure of gold equals in value two-and-a-half measures of silver". Silver was known in Crete, where inlaid silver daggers have been found and one silver cup almost 4,000 years old. The Egyptians knew how to do silver inlay work, and silver vases have been discovered in Etruscan tombs in northern Italy. Phoenician traders sometimes carried silver bowls. The Greeks had mines at Laurium in 1000 BC, and Greek silversmiths were much employed by the Romans, though the latter imported most of their supplies of the metal from Spain. The early Christians used silver for making church vessels, a tradition still widely followed in altar furnishings and communion plate. The discovery of America brought vast new sources of supply. It has been calculated that between the years 1493 and 1520 the average annual world production of silver was 1,511,000 ounces [42,836,000 grammes] of fine silver. By 1545-60 this figure had risen to 10,018,000 ounces [284,005,290 grammes].

The addition of lead made silver easier to work, but this gave dishonest smiths an opportunity to add too much of the baser metal, so silver articles were examined by officials who marked them to certify their value. In England these marks, known as assay or hallmarks, were first used in Edward I's reign. They are invaluable in establishing the dates of silver. Early silver articles, especially by famous makers, command prices far in excess of the value of the metal. In 1965, £45,000 was paid in London for a soup tureen, cover and stand made in 1758 for the Empress of Russia. In 1968, also in London, a pair of 1686 silver tankards was sold for £56,000.

The world's largest silver mines are now in British Columbia, Canada, and New South Wales, Australia.

¶ TAYLOR, GERALD. *Silver through the Ages.* 1964
See also CHRISTIANITY; PHARAOH; PHOENICIANS.

Simpson, Sir James Young (1811-70): Scottish physician. Simpson was certain that chloroform, first prepared by German chemists in 1831, would prove a successful anaesthetic, but he did not know how much of it could safely be given to a patient. To find out, he administered it to himself in varying quantities and in 1847 published the result of his experiments, which greatly aided the development of painless surgery. He also made important contributions to the knowledge of obstetrics (childbirth).

Singapore: independent republic on a small island at the tip of the Malay Peninsula. Sir Stamford Raffles chose and

annexed it in 1819 as the site of a new British stronghold under the East India Company. In 1826 Singapore was joined with Penang and Malacca to form the Straits Settlements and became, in 1832, their seat of government. In 1867 the Straits Settlements became a crown colony. Trade rapidly expanded in rubber and tin from Malaya and with the Netherlands Indies. In 1922 Singapore became the main British defence base in the Far East. It fell to the Japanese in 1942 but was liberated in 1945. It became independent in 1957, but joined the Federation of Malaya in 1963. It became independent again in 1965, remaining a member of the British Commonwealth (*see* separate entry).
See SARAWAK for map.

Sinn Féin: name (meaning "we ourselves" or "ourselves alone") of an Irish political movement established in 1905. It asserted the right to complete political and economic independence, to be brought about by self-initiated action and not by legislation or negotiation in Britain. After an unsuccessful rising in 1916, Sinn Féin candidates were overwhelmingly successful in southern Ireland in the 1918 general election and met in Dublin as *Dáil Éireann* to form the nucleus of an independent Irish government, which came into effect in 1921, with the six counties of Northern Ireland remaining outside the new Free State. Today the movement survives as a comparatively small extremist group which represents politically the outlawed Irish Republican Army (*see* separate entry).

Sino–Japanese Wars: The first major conflict between Japan and China occurred in 1894-95 and was a battle for supremacy in Korea. By the treaty of Shimonoseki (1895) China acknowledged Korean independence and ceded territory to Japan together with an indemnity and large commercial concessions. China's incapacity in this war encouraged the movements of revolt which ended the Manchu empire in 1912. In the 1920s further conflicts occurred in Manchuria. In 1931 Japan seized Mukden and in 1932 established the new state of Manchukuo. Open war began in 1937. Rapid Japanese advances captured most ports and cities as far west as Hankow, but after the first two years there was stalemate till 1944 and the onset of Japanese defeat in World War II. Meanwhile guerrillas had taken over wide territories behind the Japanese lines and Communists took control of the government of China in 1948.

Sixteenth century: the years 1501-1600. Though it would be absurd to confine the historical development of the 16th century within exact dates, it has a flavour and character of its own, particularly in Europe. Here it was the era which saw the abandonment of the medieval ideal of a united Christendom and the creation of completely independent sovereign states, not all practising the same brand of Christianity. Spain was dominant; the work of Ferdinand of Aragon (1479-1516) and his wife Isabella of Castile (1474-1504) in creating a nation from at least five independent states, and the magnificent army trained by "the Great Captain", Gonsalvo de Cordoba, led to a climax of Spanish power under Charles I (1516-56), who became Holy Roman Emperor Charles V in 1519; and signs of decline were not evident until towards the end of Philip II's reign (1556-98). France fought its first recognisably national war when Charles VIII (1483-98) led his troops into Italy in 1494. In England, after a long period of civil disturbances, Henry VII founded a lasting dynasty in 1485, and Henry VIII emphasised national sovereignty by taking control of the Church (and its finances) and by sweeping Wales into the national system of administration.

In Germany and Italy, certainly, moves towards national cohesiveness were either defeated, as was Charles V's attempt to exert imperial control, or non-existent, as in Italy, which formed the battle ground of the great powers, Spain, France and the Empire. But the general feature was the development of strong monarchies and recognisably national states, such as that created by the Vasa dynasty in Sweden. Portugal, with largely extra-European interests, although she was absorbed by Spain in 1580, followed the same course under the remarkable line of Avis kings, of whom the most powerful was John III (1521–57). The whole process is typified by four young monarchs who came to the throne early in the century: Charles I of Spain (1516–56) (Emperor from 1519), Francis I of France (1515–47), Henry VIII of England (1509–47) and Suleiman I, "the Magnificent", of Turkey (1520–66), under whom the Ottoman Empire reached its greatest point. Further east, though conditions were different, there are indications of the same kind of movement, with the establishment of the Mogul dynasty in India by Babar (1526–30) and Akbar (1556–1605), and with the work of the Ming dynasty in China, which prepared the ground for the centralisation of the Manchus in the next century.

In the West it was the century of the Reformation and of religious discord. Luther's revolt in 1517, followed by those of Zwingli at Zurich and Calvin at Geneva, caused a final rupture in the fabric of western Christendom. The adoption of the new doctrines by half the princes of Europe, for political and economic as well as for religious reasons, and the attempt of "Counter Reformation" forces to win them back to Roman Catholicism, led to a long period of religious struggles, both within individual states – as in France for most of the second half of the century – and internationally. Charles V failed to recapture Germany as a whole for the old faith, largely, perhaps, because his political enemies, notably Francis I and his ally (from 1530) Suleiman, never allowed him uninterrupted time to do so; Philip II's attack on Elizabeth of England had the nature of a crusade, and its failure helped to confirm the peculiarly national form of Protestantism in the Church of England; and, although the revolt of the Netherlands against Spain, lasting roughly from 1567 to 1609, was prompted by political and economic grievances, before its end it had the character of a struggle between Catholics and Calvinists. There grew out of the religious struggle also a radical reform of the Roman Catholic Church, the creation of new Orders, notably the Jesuits, and the final definition of Catholic doctrine at the Council of Trent (the Tridentine Decrees, 1563). The religious turmoil led also to a remarkable period of theological scholarship, of which Luther's vernacular Bible (which almost standardised the German language), Erasmus's Greek New Testament, and the Spanish Polyglot Bible were the first fruits.

The century witnessed the first great period of European expansion. In 1487 Bartholomew Diaz had rounded the Cape of Good Hope and ten years later Vasco da Gama reached India by that route: Columbus, in an attempt to find a westward route to Cathay, had discovered new lands across the Atlantic in 1492. Eastwards, the Portuguese were the first in the field by the new route, ousting the Arabs from their monopoly of trade in the Indian Ocean and, with remarkable speed, establishing trading stations in India, Malacca, China and Japan. West-

The Spaniards subduing Mexico.

wards, the Spaniards took the lead, Cortés discovering and subduing Mexico, Pizarro, with a ridiculously small but ruthlessly efficient company, conquering the Incas of Peru. Following the Treaty of Tordesillas (*see* separate entry) both Spaniards and Portuguese claimed a monopoly of the areas in which they operated. The objective of the Spaniards was at first the Far East, but the three ships which crossed the Pacific in 1527 found the Portuguese too strongly entrenched there, and Spain was comforted by the discovery in her central American colonies of immensely rich silver and gold deposits, which were to play a powerful part in the price rise which began to afflict Europe. In the second half of the century the Spanish monopoly was challenged by English seamen, notably John Hawkins, who opened the slave trade from Africa, and Francis Drake, and the mounting Anglo-Spanish friction which resulted was one cause of the war in the latter part of the century. Cathay and the Spice Islands (Moluccas) remained a powerful lure and were responsible for the many attempts to find a north-west or a north-east passage to the Far East, and for the century's most notable geographical discoveries. The Far East experienced the coming not only of traders but of missionaries too. The Jesuits reached China and Japan, Xavier landing in the latter in 1549, and they were for some time in charge of the Chinese Bureau of Astronomy, though they were expelled from Japan in 1587.

The outward-looking adventurousness of the century was reflected in a vigorous literature, served and encouraged by the new art of printing.
See colour section.

¶ HILLERBRAND, H. J. *Men and Ideas in the Sixteenth Century.* 1969; KOENIGSBERGER, H. G. and MOSS, GEORGE. *Europe in the Sixteenth Century.* 1968

See also individual entries.

Skyscraper: any very tall narrow building, usually with many storeys, a term originating in the USA which pioneered this form of architecture. The term was also used in the sailing navy to describe the topmost sails, above the fore, main and mizzen royals. Among the best known skyscrapers are the Chrysler Building, New York (1929–30, 1,046 feet [318 metres]), and the Empire State Building, New York (1929–30, 1,250 feet [381 metres]). The new Port of New York Authority's World Trade Centre (1966–72) is a twin-towered building of 110 storeys, 1,353 ft [412 metres] high. Others of even greater height are planned for Chicago.

The New York skyline.

Slavery: a condition involving the entire subjection of one set of human beings to another. A slave belongs to his master, earns no wages and has no rights as a citizen.

Slavery dates back to very early times. Primitive warriors killed their captives, but, as the first civilisations grew up, conquered people were enslaved. Many of the great civilisations of the past depended on slavery. Slaves could be captives from a conquered nation, or people who had been born into slavery, or debtors unable to pay their debts, or children sold into slavery by their parents or other relations (the story of Joseph and his Brethren in the Old Testament is an example of this) or the victims of pirates or slave-raiders. St Patrick, for instance, first went to Ireland as the victim of pirates who sold him for a slave.

The last trace of slavery, in its modified form of serfdom (attachment to the land of an overlord), disappeared from England during the 16th century. Englishmen could, however, still be sold into slavery overseas by their own countrymen – e.g. Royalist prisoners by Cromwell and West-Countrymen after the Monmouth rebellion. Scottish and Irish prisoners suffered a similar fate after the Jacobite risings. African slaves introduced into England by travellers were at first regarded as the property of their masters, but in 1772 the Lord Chief Justice decreed that slavery did not exist in the British Isles and that as soon as a slave set foot on British soil he was free. This judgment was given in a case supported by Granville Sharp (1735–1832), an indefatigable campaigner against slavery.

The iniquitous slave trade across the Atlantic was begun by Spain and Portugal. One of the first Englishmen to pursue this traffic was Sir John Hawkins (1532–95), in 1562. In 1620 a Dutch ship offered African slaves for sale to the tobacco planters of Jamestown, Virginia, and thus slavery was introduced into the English colonies on the mainland of America. In the ensuing years millions of Africans (for instance, 2,130,000 between 1680 and 1786 alone) were transported to the West Indies and the mainland in hideous and inhuman conditions, many of them dying on the way. The trade became firmly entrenched and prosperous. In England the principal ports involved were London, Bristol, Liverpool

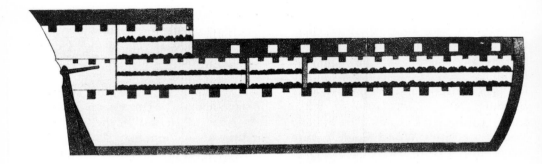

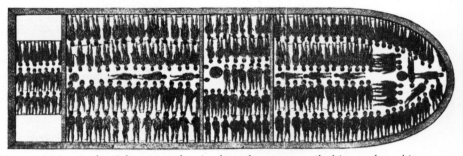

Diagrammatic print by Ackermann, showing how slaves were packed into a slave ship.

and Lancaster; between them they were responsible for over 50 per cent of this infamous traffic. Subsidiary industries grew up, giving many people a vested interest in the trade: shackles, handcuffs and chains were manufactured and sold, and the farmers round Bristol found a new and profitable crop in horse-beans, which provided a diet sufficient to keep a slave alive.

The first organised protest against slavery was that of the Germantown (Pennsylvania) Quakers in 1688. This protest was continued by many of their co-religionists, notably by John Woolman (1720–72) and Anthony Benezet (1713–84). The writings of Anthony Benezet inspired Thomas Clarkson (1760–1846), the great English leader in the early campaign against slavery, to devote his life to the cause: he in his turn inspired William Wilberforce (1759–1833), member of parliament for Yorkshire and friend of William Pitt. When, eventually, Wilber-

force, for reasons of health, had to play a less active part in the fight against slavery, he looked "for some member of parliament who . . . would be an eligible leader in this holy enterprise" and enlisted Thomas Fowell Buxton (1786–1845), later to be known as "Buxton the Liberator".

Denmark was the first European country to prohibit the slave trade. Shortly afterwards, in 1807, it was abolished throughout Great Britain and her dominions by Act of Parliament, largely owing to the untiring efforts of the Society for the Abolition of the Slave Trade, formed in 1787 under the chairmanship of Granville Sharp.

The campaign to abolish slavery itself was continued by the British and Foreign Anti-Slavery Society, founded in 1823. In 1833 a Bill was introduced to free the slaves and compensate their owners. The dying Wilberforce said: "Thank God that I have lived to witness a day when

England is willing to give twenty million sterling for the abolition of slavery." The emancipation of the slaves throughout the British Empire took place at midnight on 31 July 1834. A scheme for an interim period of Negro apprenticeship was so badly misused by the planters in the West Indies that it was brought to an end summarily, largely owing to the work of Joseph Sturge (1793-1859) who himself went out to the West Indies to collect the necessary evidence.

Slavery seemed firmly entrenched in the southern states of the United States of America, in spite of the declared views of many leading American statesmen. "I tremble for my country when I reflect that God is just", wrote Thomas Jefferson (1743-1825). The earlier efforts of the Quakers had cleared their Society of slave-owning. Some of them, including the poet Whittier (1807-92), played an active part in the vigorous anti-slavery movement, led by William Lloyd Garrison (1805-79), but others favoured a more gradual approach. Women were active in the campaign, including Lucretia Mott (1793-1880) and Harriet Beecher Stowe (1811-96), author of *Uncle Tom's Cabin*. The abolitionists met with unreasoning hostility from those who did not share their views: their meetings were mobbed and their homes threatened, and in

Slave auction at Charleston, South Carolina, in 1856.

Philadelphia their newly built centre, the Pennsylvania Hall, was set on fire and destroyed. The British abolitionists rallied to the support of their American colleagues, and in 1840 a World's Anti-Slavery Convention was held in London.

The feeling between the Northern states and the great slave-owning states of the South on this issue became so acute that the anti-slavery movement was held to be one of the main causes of the American Civil War, which broke out in 1860 when the Southern states attempted to secede. The Northern victory in 1865 preserved the Union, and the emancipation of the slaves immediately followed.

Slavery has now been abolished in nearly all parts of the world, and where it still lingers, openly or in a disguised form, it continues to be the active concern of the still-existing Anti-Slavery Society and of the United Nations.

¶ GRATUS, JACK. *The Great White Lie.* 1973; LANGDON-DAVIES, JOHN, editor. *The Slave Trade and its Abolition* (Jackdaw). 1965; WHITE, JOHN and WILLETT, RALPH. *Slavery in the American South.* 1970

See also AMERICAN CIVIL WAR; CROMWELL; HAWKINS; JEFFERSON; PITT, WILLIAM, the Younger; QUAKERS; TOUSSAINT L'OUVERTURE; WILBERFORCE.

Slave state: in the USA, any one of the fifteen states south of the Mason–Dixon line (i.e. the boundary line between Maryland and Pennsylvania) in which slavery was legal before the American Civil War (*see* separate entry). They formed the bulk of the Confederated States which broke away from the Union.

Slovakia: an area of central Europe inhabited by Slovaks, a Slav people. It is mostly mountainous, but part of it lies in the fertile Danube valley. It has never formed a separate country. After its peasant peoples were overrun by the Magyars in the 10th century, it formed part of Hungary and, later, the Austro-Hungarian Empire. In 1919, after the collapse of this empire in World War I (*see* separate entry), Slovakia became the eastern section of the new state of Czechoslovakia. Some Slovak leaders have resented being governed from Prague in the west but have never succeeded in breaking away to form a separate state. *See* SERBIA for map.

Smith, Adam (1723-90): Scottish political economist. He is best remembered for his book *The Wealth of Nations* (1776), which condemned monopolies and too much state control, and supported free trade, competition and private enterprise. His work exercised great influence both in Great Britain and the USA, and laid the foundations of the modern science of political economy.
¶ PIKE, E. R. *Adam Smith*. 1965

Smith, Ian Douglas (b. 1919): Rhodesian political leader. Educated at Selukwe School, the Chaplin School, Gwelo, and Rhodes University, Grahamstown, South Africa, he served with distinction in the RAF 1941-46; then, while farming, he became interested in politics, being elected to the Southern Rhodesia legislative assembly in 1948 and serving as an MP in the Federal Parliament from 1953 to 1961, when he resigned from the United Federal Party to assist in founding the so-called Rhodesian Front which proved successful in the 1962 elections. In 1964 he was appointed Premier, and minister for external affairs and defence. On 11 November 1965, after protracted negotiations with Britain on independence had broken down, he made a unilateral declaration of independence. *See also* RHODESIA.

Smith, Captain John (1580-1631): soldier and colonist, the effective founder of Virginia, where he voyaged in 1607 as one of a company of 120 settlers. The truth of the most famous story about him, that he was taken prisoner by Indians and rescued by the princess Pocahontas (*see* separate entry), has never been satisfactorily proved. Smith was president of the new colony in 1608-09 and afterwards published the first account of it – *A True Relation of such Occurrences and Accidents of Note as hath happened in Virginia since the first planting of that Colony* (1608). Smith's 1612 map of Virginia was so accurate that it was still in use in the 19th century.
¶ GILL, W. J. C. *Captain John Smith and Virginia*. 1968; SYME, RONALD. *John Smith of Virginia*. 1954

Smith, Joseph (1805-44): American founder of the Mormons (*see* separate entry), or the Church of Jesus Christ of Latter-Day Saints. Smith claimed to have found, in 1827, guided by a vision, a series of golden plates, covered with hieroglyphics of Egyptian character, which he translated and issued in 1830 as *The Book of Mormon* (the name of the mythical author of the original writings) which is accepted by Mormons as one of the scriptures, divinely inspired, along with the Old and New Testaments.
See also MORMONS.

Smuts, Jan Christiaan (1870-1950): South African soldier and statesman. After graduating at Stellenbosch University, he came to England and gained a double first in law at Cambridge and afterwards practised as a lawyer in his home country. During the Anglo-Boer War (1899-1902) he served as a Boer commando leader but later, as Colonial Secretary in the Transvaal, worked with the British to heal the rift between the two countries. In World War I he commanded the Allied forces in East Africa, and in World War II, despite opposition in the

Jan Christiaan Smuts.

South African Parliament, led his country into the struggle against Germany and was promoted Field-Marshal. A dedicated internationalist, he helped to start the League of Nations, supported the development of the British Commonwealth and, in 1945, assisted in drafting the UNO Charter and himself led the South African delegation. In 1948 he was defeated by the Nationalist Party under Doctor Malan. He was a keen botanist and President of the British Association in 1931.

¶ In GILLETT, N. *Men Against War.* 1965
See also BRITISH COMMONWEALTH; LEAGUE OF NATIONS; WORLD WARS I AND II.

Socialism: political theory which teaches that land, business, industry, transport and the means of production should not be owned by individual people or groups of people but by all the people of a country. Socialism is different from communism, with which it is often confused, in that it aims to bring about the change by democratic methods and not by revolution.

The idea of common ownership was known to the ancient Greeks, the Romans and to the early Christians. There have always been those who asked, why are the few rich and the many poor? For many hundreds of years it was believed by most people that there was no answer to this question. There had always been rich and poor and there always would be. In the 19th century a number of writers, of whom the most famous is Karl Marx (1818-83), explained that the poor were poor because they did not own any land or other property and had to sell their labour in order to live. They sold their labour to those who did own the property, or "capital". If all capital was owned by all of the people, there need not be any more rich and poor, it was thought. Communists said that the only way to do this was by revolution: socialists thought it could be done through parliament when a majority of the people voted for a socialist party.

Socialism spread rapidly through many countries of Europe in the 20th century but made very little headway in the USA. In Great Britain, many workers' organisations such as the trade unions, co-operative societies and the Christian Socialists supported the Labour Party which was formed at the beginning of the century. By 1924 the Labour Party had most seats in parliament and formed a government which remained in office for a short time. After World War II the Labour Party won a great victory in the general election of 1945. It then began the move towards socialism by taking the great industries of coal mining and the railways from their private owners and making them the property of the nation. This was called nationalisation. The owners received compensation, and the change was brought about by peaceful means. Since that time, the government has changed several times, with Labour winning in 1964 and 1966 but losing to the Conservatives in 1970. The Conservative Party is opposed to socialism and therefore to nationalisation, and when it is in power it puts a brake on what the Labour

Party has tried to do to bring about common ownership.

As in England, socialism spread after World War I in Belgium, France, Germany and Scandinavia, where the Social Democratic parties have been particularly successful. The Labour Party has held power in Australia and New Zealand for long spells but Canada, like her neighbour USA, has developed no strong socialist party.

¶ MACKENZIE, NORMAN. *Socialism*. 1966

See also CAPITALISM; COMMUNISM; CO-OPERATIVE SOCIETIES; DEMOCRACY; MARX, KARL; TRADE UNIONS; WORLD WARS I AND II.

Social security: the provision of a minimum income for a family when its normal sources of income are cut off or reduced, health services, retirement benefits, etc. In 1935 the United States passed the Social Security Act as part of the New Deal (see separate entry). This measure, financed mainly from a tax upon employers of eight or more persons, provided for unemployment and old age. In England the term first became familiar following the Beveridge Report, which was followed by the enactment of the National Insurance Act 1946, the National Health Service Act 1946, and the National Assistance Act 1948.

See also PENSIONS.

Societies, Secret: organisations whose rules, ritual and, sometimes, purposes are communicated only to their members who, on invitation, take vows never to disclose the organisation's secrets. Many primitive communities have secret societies restricted to the adult males in the community. At puberty a boy is introduced into the confraternity in a ritual which usually includes some test or ordeal. In the Poro, a secret society found among tribal groups in West Africa, the initiate is scarred and circumcised and acts out a ritual which symbolises his death as a child and rebirth as an adult who must share responsibility for the tribe's well-being. Secret societies of this kind are the repositories of tribal wisdom, morals and religion. Myth and magic, the two ways in which primitive peoples try to explain and control the forces of nature, are an important part of the secrets which must be guarded under threat of dire penalty if the oath be broken.

In ancient civilisations there were many secret religious cults, or "mysteries", as they were called, whose members, by following the prescribed ritual, felt themselves assured of immortality. At Eleusis, in Greece, Demeter, the "corn mother", was the presiding deity. Ancient Egypt had its secret cults of Serapis – a combination of god and sacred bull – and the goddess Isis. From Persia came the cult of the sun god Mithras, who was supposed to have a sacred bull from whose flanks sprang corn and vines. Initiates were bathed in the blood of a dying bull, and then sat down to a sacred feast of bread and wine.

Many secret societies had purposes both religious and political. The Assassins, members of a dissident Muslim sect, settled in the mountain fortress of Alamut, in Persia, and terrorised the surrounding lands, using secret murder as a weapon of policy. The young men selected to do the murders were first drugged with hashish (hence the word *assassin*). The power of the Assassins was broken in 1256 when the Mongols captured Alamut.

The Thugs, or Phansigars, an Indian secret society, combined religion with murder and robbery. Before being robbed, travellers were strangled with a twisted waistcloth as sacrifices to Kali, the Hindu goddess of destruction. The Rosicrucians, the Brotherhood of the Rosy Cross, founded in Germany in the

16th century, were members of a mystical secret society which appears to have combined elements of alchemy, the Hebrew mystical book the *Cabala*, and the Hermetic Books (actually written in the 3rd century AD but believed by the Rosicrucians to contain the key to the ancient Egyptian mastery of the spiritual and physical universe). Interest in the Rosicrucians revived in the 19th century. In 1915 H. Spencer Lewis, a New York advertising man, founded the Ancient Mystical Order Rosae Crucis. Its headquarters are in California. Another secret society of American origin is the Church of Scientology, founded by L. Ron Hubbard. Its methods, which involve a certain mental and psychological "processing" (its own word) of its initiates, have evoked much adverse criticism in countries as far apart as Australia and Great Britain.

Though there are between five and six million Freemasons the society still endeavours to remain secret. There are passwords and ceremonials and oaths of secrecy. The movement, which makes great use of words and symbols associated with building (God is the "Great Architect"), may have grown out of the medieval stone-masons' guilds. The earliest Freemasons' lodge was founded in London in 1717. The aims of freemasonry are wholly benevolent—to help fellow masons and their dependents, to dispense charity, to encourage brotherhood generally. Freemasons are required to believe in God, to be loyal to the state and never to discuss either religion or politics at their meetings.

Many secret societies grew out of political oppression. At the end of the 18th century some 20,000 Irish Catholics joined the United Irishmen, a secret society which, in 1798, unsuccessfully attempted a rebellion against their English rulers. The Fenian Brotherhood was

The symbols of 18th century Freemasons' lodges surround the portrait of their founder, Sir Richard Steele.

founded in 1848, after the miseries of the Potato Famine. In 1916 a third Irish group, The Citizen Army, dedicated to driving the English out of Ireland failed in its Easter rebellion in Dublin. Other politically motivated secret societies include the Boxers or *I Ho Chuan* ("Fists of Righteousness"), directed against foreign aggression in China; the Carbonari (the "charcoal burners"), prominent in the struggle for Italian national unity; and the anarchists or nihilists (Latin *nihil*, "nothing") who held that *all* national states should be overthrown. Like the Assassins of old they made rulers their target, killing, among others, the Russian Czar Alexander II (1881) and King Umberto of Italy (1900).

The notorious secret society called the Mafia (Arabic, "place of refuge") also began as a movement against injustice. Romans, Arabs, Normans, Spaniards successively oppressed the Sicilians, many of whom took to the hills rather than become the serfs of an invader. The modern Mafia, while enjoining great loyalty and brotherliness between members, frequently perpetrates murder and barbarous acts of revenge on outsiders and on members who transgress its code. Today it, rather than the legal government, is the real ruler of Sicily. Between 1922 and 1928 the Fascists did much to suppress the society. Ironically, it was the Allies who put the Mafia back in charge when, in 1943, during World War II, they accepted Mafia help during the landings in Sicily. Sicilian immigrants took the Mafia to America, where it has become a criminal conspiracy with international ramifications. Nowadays the vast profits from illicit activities are often channelled into legal enterprises, and former *mafiosi* become, at least outwardly, respectable business men.

The Ku-Klux Klan, a secret society founded out of a sense of grievance, became a vicious instrument of racial big-

A member of the Ku Klux Klan holds a burning cross, 1923.

otry. After the American Civil War (1861–64) the North did not treat the defeated Southern States gently, and the Klan first operated as a guerrilla movement against the corrupt Northerners who were profiting from their humiliation. Then, with its white hoods and sheets it began to terrorise Negroes, to stop them from exercising their newly acquired right to vote. The Klan's history is a hateful record of whippings, tarring-and-featherings and murders. Its ignorant, bigoted members were against Roman Catholics and Jews as well as Negroes. Officially, the Klan disbanded in 1947; but that its influence still casts a baleful shadow over the South is shown by the murder of Civil Rights workers and of the Negro leader Martin Luther King (1929–68).

¶ DARAUL, A. *Secret Societies.* 1966
See also AMERICAN CIVIL WAR; ASSASSINATIONS; FENIANS; KU-KLUX KLAN; JEWS; MAFIA; MONGOLS; MUSLIMS.

Socrates (469–399 BC): Athenian philosopher, of whose personal life little is known. For his philosophical teaching we are wholly indebted to the writings of Plato (*see* separate entry), who shows that his method of seeking the truth was through questions and answers among small groups of friends, in which he usually took the lead. When he was eventually accused of spreading harmful ideas among the youth of Athens, he declined to go into exile and drank the poison offered to him, as described in Plato's *Phaedo*.

¶ MASON, C. *Socrates: The Man Who Dared To Ask.* 1963

Solomon (*c.* 986–*c.* 932 BC): king of the Israelites, succeeding his father David *c.* 972. He built the national Temple (*see* separate entry) and was renowned for his influence over the neighbouring kingdoms, and for his wealth and his wisdom, which, we are told, caused the legendary Queen of Sheba to pay him a visit.

Solomon Islands: Melanesian archipelago in the western Pacific, named by de Mendana in 1568, but not rediscovered until 1767 by Carteret. The Solomons, a British sphere of influence from 1886 and a protectorate by treaty with Germany in 1893, were mandated to Australia in 1920, becoming trusteeship territories in 1947. *See* PACIFIC OCEAN for map.

Somalia or **Somali Republic:** republic occupying the coastline of the north-east horn of Africa, from the Gulf of Aden past Cape Gardafni to the Kenyan border. The Somali are a proud and turbulent race of Hamitic origin, traditionally nomads tending herds of cattle, ponies, sheep and camels and owing no allegiance to their Arab neighbours in the hinterland of Aden. The rockbound coast was uninviting to traders or explorers, and

European contact came only late in the 19th century when Britain, France and Italy established protectorates. The small French protectorate based on the port of Djibouti remains constitutionally attached to France.

The former destructive tribal jealousies have recently merged into common political consciousness. The British Somaliland Protectorate, administered since 1905 by the Colonial Office, and the former Italian Colony, latterly a United Nations Trust Territory (*see* separate entry for UN), merged on 1 July 1960 in an independent Somali Democratic Republic with its capital at Mogadishu (Mogadiscio). In 1969 power passed to a Revolutionary Council with General Mohammed Siyad as Chairman.

Bananas from the Italian-owned estates form the staple export. The possible discovery of oil and other minerals could lessen the present dependence on foreign aid.

See AFRICA for map.

Sorbonne: part of the University of Paris, a college founded by a priest, Robert de Sorbon (1201–74). It became a famous theological centre and attained a European reputation. In 1792 it was suppressed as an independent foundation, and in 1808 was formally made part of the university. It now houses the faculties of letters and science. In 1968 it was the scene of serious riots, led by militants who openly proclaimed their intention of using the universities as bases from which to overthrow the capitalist system.

Soto, Hernando de (1496–1542): Spanish soldier and explorer. He accompanied Pizarro (*see* separate entry) when in 1532 he led the Spanish expedition to conquer the Incas of Peru. De Soto afterwards returned to Mexico and was created Governor of Florida, but his own search for the fabulous cities of Cibola failed, and he died in 1542 on the banks of the River Mississippi.

South Africa, Republic of: republic occupying the southern part of the continent of Africa, with the Atlantic washing its south-western shores, and the Indian Ocean to the south and south-east. South West Africa, an ex-German colony, now administered by South Africa under a League of Nations mandate, lies to the north-west; Botswana to the north; Rhodesia, Mozambique and Swaziland to the north-east with Lesotho, a small mountainous enclave lying on the western side of the massive Drakensberg range. South Africa consists of four provinces: Cape of Good Hope (or Cape Province), Transvaal, Orange Free State (OFS) and Natal. The administrative capital is Pretoria, Transvaal; the legislative capital, Cape Town, Cape Province.

The country has great natural wealth in minerals, its principal exports being gold, diamonds, copper, tin, silver, asbestos, wool, wines and spirits, fresh and canned fruit, and canned fish.

The Cape of Good Hope was first reported by Bartholomew Diaz in 1487, and in 1652 Jan van Riebeeck established a "Tavern of the Seas" at Cape Town as a staging post for the Dutch East India Company. At that time the only inhabitants of what is now South Africa appeared to be the nomadic Bushmen and Hottentots. It was in the 18th century, when the venturesome Dutch Voortrekkers were pushing northwards, that equally adventurous Bantu tribes were moving south from central and east Africa, and inevitable clashes followed, during which the indigenous nomads were squeezed out, fleeing to the Kalahari regions, which still support a fair number of Bushmen who have adapted themselves so well to desert conditions that they have no wish to live elsewhere. There was an influx of French Huguenots in 1688, following the revoking of the Edict of Nantes, and these brought new skills and arts to the country. The British occupied the Cape in 1795, staying for eight years before returning control to the Batavian republic. In 1820 five thousand British settlers landed and settled in what later became the eastern Cape and south Natal. This followed the cession of the Cape to Britain by the Dutch in 1814 and began a period of dissatisfaction on the part of the Boers which led to the Great Trek of 1837, when some 10,000 of them trekked north in a great convoy of covered wagons, each drawn by the traditional span of sixteen oxen, in order to escape from the hated British rule and to found the new republics of Natal, the Orange Free State and Transvaal. For courage and hardihood this epic exodus was on a parallel with the opening up of the Wild West in America. Clashes with the Bantu became frequent, and in 1838 there was a massacre of the Boers by the Zulus at Weenen which was avenged on 16 December that same year at the battle of Blood River, where the Zulus were heavily defeated, and the Boers finally won control of the country.

While the Boers were establishing themselves on the farms of South Africa, the British settlers were developing the mining resources of the country, its businesses and communications. In 1871 Cape Colony was granted self-government, and the Transvaal republic was proclaimed in 1880, arranging a sort of union with the Orange Free State in 1897 as a first step towards a united South Africa. In 1899 the Boers invaded Natal, and this was the beginning of the Boer War, which was finally ended in May 1902 by the Peace of Vereeniging. The Transvaal and Free State were then annexed to the British Empire along with Cape Colony and Natal which the British already held, and

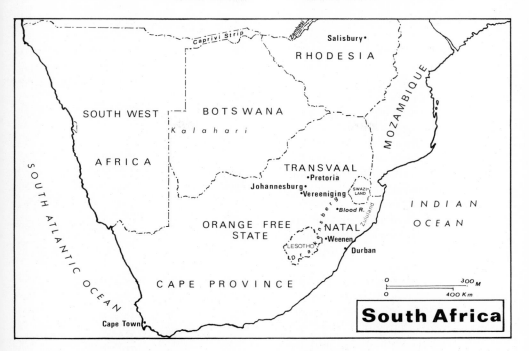

South Africa

the Union of South Africa came into being with the passing of the South Africa Act by Britain in 1909. World War I revealed great differences of opinion between Boer and British, but eventually South Africa was led into the war by Botha and Smuts on the British side, and defeated the Germans in South West Africa, Smuts becoming an international statesman and one of the great figures in World War II. On 4 September 1939 Smuts became Prime Minister, defeating Hertzog on the neutrality issue, remaining in office until he was defeated in turn by Malan who led a coalition of Afrikaner and Nationalist parties. This was the government that initiated the policy of apartheid, or separate development, and Malan began the direction of the country towards independence as an independent republic and to leaving the British Commonwealth on 31 May 1961.

¶ KIEWIET, C. W. DE. *A History of South Africa.* 1966
See also APARTHEID; BOERS; CAPE OF GOOD HOPE; GREAT TREK; HERTZOG; ORANGE FREE STATE; SMUTS, J. C.; TRANSVAAL; VORSTER; ZULU, etc.

South America: fourth largest continent, constituting nearly one-sixth of the total land surface of our planet. It is so remote from most historical centres of population that its people have always been on the edge of events in world history, and have not yet played a full part in the affairs of the world. In the 20th century the ten republics of South America were little affected by the world wars which so devastated other parts of the globe.

Altogether over 160 million people live in South America. Although some parts of the continent have fertile soil for farming, and parts of Chile and Venezuela are rich in mineral resources, most of the people are very poor. The tropical forests of the Amazon and the mountain blocks of the Andes and the Brazilian Highlands have made trade or travel very difficult. As an English historian wrote 100 years ago: "The mountains are too high to scale, the rivers are too wide to bridge. The progress of agriculture is stopped by impassable forests, and the harvests are destroyed by innumerable insects." Much of the Pacific coast is barren desert, while

867

most of southern Patagonia is unfit for human habitation. The main centres of population, therefore, are the tropical highlands of Peru, Brazil and Colombia.

The first civilised inhabitants of the American continent lived in these same highlands. The Incas (*see* separate entry) of Peru used a system of irrigated fields in the Andes valleys which supported life in many cities as the Inca Empire expanded. The Chibchas of Colombia grew maize and potatoes on their high plateau. Most of the other native peoples lived as hunters and food gatherers spread out thinly over the rest of the continent.

In the 16th century this pattern of life was abruptly shaken by the arrival of Spanish and Portuguese ships, carrying explorers who demanded gold, then bringing soldiers with horses and muskets, followed by settlers with sheep and cattle. The old empires were destroyed and a new way of life developed.

Different types of people came to live in South America. The Spaniards in the 16th and 17th centuries intermarried with the natives to produce a large "Mestizo" population, while at the same time the native population was cut by European diseases to half its previous size. The Spanish government passed laws in 1542 to prevent the natives from being treated as slave labour, but many died working in the Spanish silver mines at Potosi. Meanwhile the Portuguese brought Negro slaves from Africa to cultivate a new crop, sugar cane. Other Negroes were employed as household servants, and in Brazil a population of mixed race also developed. By 1600 there were in South America many new cities with fine cathedrals and universities. Ports grew on the Atlantic and Pacific coasts. Precious shipments of silver went regularly to Spain, while the "Manila Galleon" sailed annually across the Pacific Ocean to Acapulco. The Spanish language was used

everywhere, except in Brazil, and the Catholic faith was practised by natives and settlers alike.

In fact life had not changed so completely as may appear. The Spaniards did not create one united empire, but left the continent to be administered in provinces or even smaller units. The cities did not all flourish: the ports were often sleepy collections of wooden huts. Not all natives were easily subdued: the Araucanians of Chile refused to surrender to the Spaniards, and warfare was prolonged. The Spaniards abandoned their first settlement on the Rio de la Plata when (in spite of its name) it failed to produce gold. The horses they left behind there were tamed and ridden by the native gauchos of the pampas. The Inca peoples were not completely subdued either. They continued to fight from mountain retreats for the next 200 years.

The Spaniards and Portuguese were not the only Europeans to be drawn to South

America. French sailors were among the first to explore the coast of Brazil and to collect the red-coloured dyewood which gave Brazil its name. The English were particularly attracted to the forests surrounding the Orinoco, where they hoped to find the kingdom of the fabulous Eldorado. Sir Walter Ralegh (*see* separate entry) explored this coast in 1595, noting with interest Trinidad's lakes of pitch. The Dutch, during their 17th-century conflict with Spain, captured many of the Brazilian coastal sugar plantations, but these were regained by Portugal after 1644. The Dutch then concentrated on developing trade with all peoples in North and South America, disregarding any colonial rules which forbade such commerce. The Dutch also began settlements on the same coast of Guiana which had attracted Ralegh. The British and the French, too, claimed territory there.

Nevertheless Spain and Portugal together dominated South America for 300 years. At the end of the 18th century British colonies in North America fought to obtain independence, and the French Revolution began to spread ideas of equality as well as those of freedom. So when Spain was invaded by Napoleon (*see* NAPOLEON I), American leaders like Bolivar (*see* separate entry) and San Martin began to liberate South America, decisively defeating the Spanish forces in 1824. The result was not a United States of South America, but a continent divided into ten republics, often hostile to each other and still bound to sell their cash crops to Europe. Each republic was free to rule itself, but every experiment in democracy seemed to lead to dictatorship. Too often the history of South America has been one of unsuccessful wars, civil strife and boundary disputes; of rebellions, military coups and political instability, of dictatorships and oppression by privileged groups; of poverty, depressions and economic crises. Few areas have escaped this pattern of events. But much ground has been gained. Membership of the United Nations Organisation has helped bring the various republics into the main stream of world history. *See also* ENDPAPERS for map.

Southampton: port and county borough in Hampshire, with one of the finest harbours in Britain, 79 miles [127 kilometres] south-west of London. Remains of Saxon (*see* separate entry) and Roman settlements are plentiful, and it was a royal borough before 1086. It has a long history as a flourishing port and in the 13th century was the second wine port in the country. Though there was later some decline, prosperity returned in the 19th century with the opening of the rail link to London and the provision of extensive pier and harbour facilities. It is now the chief port for express transatlantic passenger services.

South Arabia, Federation of: British-protected federation situated at the southern end of the Arabian peninsula, with Saudi Arabia and the Yemen to the north. The federation, which co-ordinates education, defence, medical services and the exploitation of natural resources, was formed in 1959 by the states of Audhali, Aulagi, Baihan, Dhala, Fadhli and Yafa, which were joined in 1963 by Aden and several other small emirates. The federation suffered much interference from terrorists and political agents, which resulted in the suspension of the constitution in 1965. The federation is now incorporated in the Peoples Republic of South Yemen. *See* SAUDI ARABIA for map.

South Australia: state in south-central Australia, with Adelaide the capital. The coast, surveyed by Tasman (*see* separate entry) in 1644, was charted by Flinders in

1802. Following explorations of the Murray River after 1828, an English colony was proposed, and was founded in 1836 with Adelaide as the capital. Poor resources, difficulties between governors and commissioners and shortage of settlers resulted in South Australia becoming a crown colony in 1842. Copper discoveries in the 1840s helped the economy, but gold strikes in the state of Victoria in 1851 affected trade and drew away population. In 1856 responsible government was achieved, and from 1863 the colony took over responsibility for the Northern Territory. In the 1860s drought and the inability of many squatters to purchase their holdings caused much land to be abandoned. Oversettlement in the 1870s exhausted the soil and competition from Queensland made farming hazardous. Iron deposits on the Spencer Gulf assisted manufactures, though agriculture, mainly wheat-growing, still lagged behind the economy generally. In 1901 it became one of the states forming the Commonwealth of Australia and conditions gradually improved. Since World War I (*see* separate entry) moderate labour and liberal country party governments have done much to stabilise the economy.
See also AUSTRALIA, and for map.

South Central, USA: region, including the states of Arkansas, Louisiana, Oklahoma and Texas, bordering on the Gulf of Mexico, Mexico, the Old South and the Old Northwest. It is really two regions, separated by the Mississippi River. To the east of the river are Arkansas and Louisiana, to the west Oklahoma and Texas. Arkansas is a land of low, rugged hills, picturesque valleys and substantial forests of hardwood and pine trees. Louisiana has some low hills in the north, but its southern areas, bordering on the Gulf of Mexico, are mainly coastal marshes, creeks and tributaries. Especially important in southern Louisiana is the Mississippi River Delta, formed by silt carried down by the river. The Delta, ever growing, is at present one-third of the total area of the state. On the western side of the river, Oklahoma and Texas are part of a relatively flat rolling plain and are largely given over to grasslands.

Much of this region was explored by the Spanish and the French in the 16th and 17th centuries. Spanish settlements were concentrated to the west of the Mississippi, while a large French colony grew up in the Louisiana Territory. Picturesque streets, houses, and other survivals from this period can still be found in parts of New Orleans, the major city of Louisiana. The territory east of the river, as well as parts of Oklahoma, were bought by the United States in 1803 as part of the Louisiana Purchase (*see* separate entry). Texas remained part of first the Spanish Empire and then of Mexico until 1836, when a rebellion, led by Americans who had settled in the region, succeeded in establishing an independent Texas nation. This was in turn annexed to the United States in 1845. During the American Civil War (*see* separate entry), this entire region joined the Old South in secession.

South-East Asia Treaty Organisation (SEATO): established by the Manila Pact of 1954 as a collective security device in that area and as a Pacific version of NATO (*see* separate entry). Not as strongly constituted as NATO, it provided for no joint force or command. Member states were to act together if any one of them should be attacked. The Organisation's council consisted of the foreign ministers of the member countries, Australia, France, New Zealand, Pakistan, the Philippines, Thailand, the United Kingdom and USA. All except France had participated in the Colombo Plan of 1950 to promote economic welfare.

Southern Pacific Railroad: part of the first transcontinental railway link between the Atlantic and Pacific seaboards of the USA. This was achieved in 1869, when the Union Pacific, pushing west from Omaha, Nebraska, met the Central Pacific, later incorporated into the larger system of the Southern Pacific, coming out eastward from Somerset, California.

South West Africa: territory, administered as part of South Africa, facing the Atlantic Ocean between Angola, Botswana and the Cape Province of the Republic of South Africa. It was a German colony from 1884 until World War I (*see* separate entry), and from 1920 was administered by South Africa under a League of Nations mandate. In 1945 the United Nations (*see* separate entry) established a Trusteeship Council with the duty of encouraging the economic, social and educational development of all the former mandated territories, the responsibility to include visits of inspection.

The Union of South Africa declared that it would continue to administer South West Africa in a responsible manner, but could not accept the Trusteeship Council, or visits of inspection. Appeal to the International Court of Justice has failed to settle the problem.

A semi-permanent bushman's hut.

The land includes part of the Kalahari Desert, which is separated from the coastal plain by a high plateau. The diminutive Bushmen in this area are the last remnant of the primitive nomad hunters who once swarmed across southern Africa. The Ovambo tribe constitute half the population. Since 1968 they have advanced to self-government by an elected Legislative Council; the remaining tribes are governed by South Africa. Two-thirds of the children are at school.

The main wealth of the territory is derived from fishing, cattle and minerals. *See* AFRICA for map.

Space travel: travel in the regions outside the earth's atmosphere. For years men have dreamt of travelling through space, but have known that in order to do so the pull of earth's gravity must be overcome by the development of propulsion units of immense speed and power. For years, too, rockets have been considered the only possible source of such power and in 1944, when the German Wernher von Braun (b. 1912) developed the V2, capable of rising to a height of 60 miles [96 kilometres], post-war space research became a reality. It was then realised that a space vehicle composed of several stages, each falling away in due course in order to increase the speed of the nose capsule, was within the bounds of possibility.

Although von Braun was recruited by the USA after the war, it was the Russians who launched the first satellites in orbit: *Sputnik 1* in October 1957 and *Sputnik 2* in November, with a dog aboard. The American *Explorer 1* and *Vanguard 1* were launched early in 1958, and later that year the National Aeronautics and Space Agency (NASA) was organised. The Russians still led, and in April 1961 Yuri Gagarin (1934–68) became the first man to orbit the earth. A month later America's first space man Alan Shephard (b. 1923) made a fifteen-minute sub-orbital flight to a height of sixteen miles [25 km]. In August 1961 Major Titov (b. 1935) became the second man in orbit and in February 1962 the American John Glenn (b. 1921) became the third, orbiting the earth three times in *Friendship 7*.

Space travel has not been confined solely to moon probes, and in March 1962 an orbiting solar observatory was launched by the Americans followed by *Ariel 1*, an international satellite designed to collect data about the upper atmosphere, and in July 1962 by *Telstar*, a communications satellite. In December 1962, after a sixteen-week journey, *Mariner 2* sent back scientific data from a distance of only 21,594 miles [34,751 km] away from the planet Venus, and in November 1964 *Mariner 4* was launched towards Mars. In April 1965 *Early Bird*, the world's first commercial communications satellite, was launched into service above the Atlantic. Meanwhile, manned space flight had been taken a stage further by Gordon Cooper's (b. 1927) thirty-four-hour 22 orbit flight in May 1963 and the following month by Russia's Valentina Tereskhova (b. 1937), the first and, so far, only woman in space, who orbited the earth forty-eight times in *Vostock 6*.

In October 1964 the Soviet *Voskhod* took three men into space – the first multi-seater space craft – and another "first" was Leonov's (b. 1934) first walk in space, lasting ten minutes, in March 1965, the same month that two American astronauts became the first men to steer their craft from one orbital path to another. In June 1964 Edward White (b. 1930) walked for twenty-two minutes in space and in December two *Gemini* space craft made a rendezvous, coming to within a foot [31 centimetres] of each other.

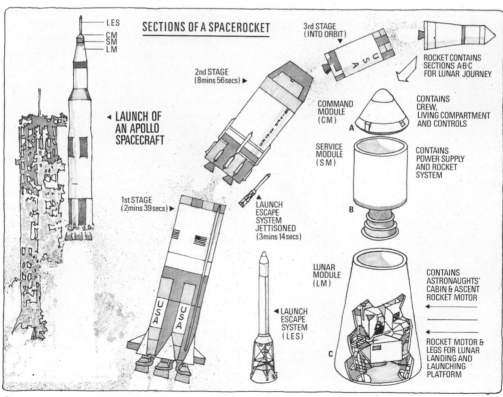

LES
CM
SM
LM

SECTIONS OF A SPACEROCKET

3rd STAGE (INTO ORBIT)

ROCKET CONTAINS SECTIONS A·B·C FOR LUNAR JOURNEY

2nd STAGE (8mins 56secs) ▶

◀ LAUNCH OF AN APOLLO SPACECRAFT

COMMAND MODULE (CM)

CONTAINS CREW, LIVING COMPARTMENT AND CONTROLS

A

SERVICE MODULE (SM)

CONTAINS POWER SUPPLY AND ROCKET SYSTEM

1st STAGE (2mins 39secs) ▶

LAUNCH ESCAPE SYSTEM JETTISONED (3mins 14secs)

B

USA USA

LUNAR MODULE (LM)

CONTAINS ASTRONAUGHTS' CABIN & ASCENT ROCKET MOTOR

◀ LAUNCH ESCAPE SYSTEM (LES)

C

ROCKET MOTOR & LEGS FOR LUNAR LANDING AND LAUNCHING PLATFORM

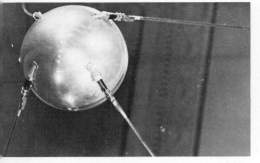

The first Soviet sputnik, 1957.

Yuri Gagarin became the first man to orbit the earth in 1961.

Apollo 8 blasts off from Cape Kennedy on 21 December, 1968.

US astronaut, Edwin Aldrin, walks on the moon, 16 July, 1969.

The first landing on the moon had been made in July 1964 by the American *Ranger 7* with a planned crash landing after sending back valuable photographs; and the first soft landing was made by the Russian *Lunar 9* in February 1966. In 1966 the Russians put an artificial satellite, the first of five, into orbit around the moon, and the American *Surveyor 1* soft landed, sending back TV pictures of the surface.

In January 1967 occurred the first known space tragedy when three American astronauts were killed by fire on the launching pad at Cape Kennedy, followed three months later by Vladimir Komarov's death when the braking parachute on *Soyuz 1* failed to open.

The first unmanned space link was in October 1967 when two Soviet satellites linked and separated automatically. In September 1968 the Soviet *Zond 5* was the first craft to go round the moon and return to earth. Meanwhile the Americans were testing out new space craft designed to take men to the moon, and *Apollo 7* made a ten-day space journey in October 1968. Then in December 1968 came a great leap forward into the unknown when Borman (b. 1928), Lovell (b. 1928) and Anders (b. 1933) made the first manned flight to leave the influence of earth's gravity, when they flew ten orbits round the moon, each lasting two hours, in their *Apollo 8* space craft powered by the giant *Saturn 5* rocket. For the first time ever, human beings came under the gravitational influence of another planet and for the listeners in the control room at Houston, Texas, there were tense moments when the astronauts were out of radio communication as they passed round the far side of the moon.

For the first time men saw the moon's surface at close range, including the rear part which never faces the earth; and short range photographs were obtained.

The dress rehearsal for a moon landing came in May 1969 when *Apollo 10* orbited the moon thirty-one times and the command module, detached from the main space craft, descended to within nine miles [14 kilometres] of the moon's surface. Then on Sunday, 20 July 1969, at 9.17 p.m. (BST) the lunar module *Eagle* of *Apollo 11* touched down on the moon's surface whilst the command vehicle *Columbia* continued in orbit under Collins (b. 1930). For the final descent Aldrin (b. 1930) had to take over manual control of the module in order to avoid the enormous boulders littering the Sea of Tranquillity. The next morning at 3.52 a.m. Armstrong (b. 1930) took man's first step on the moon whilst his colleague televised him. Both men gathered rock samples from the surface and left mementos of their visit, including a plaque inscribed "Here man from the planet Earth first set foot upon the Moon, July 1969 AD. We came in peace for all mankind."

Though subsequent moon voyages have not, naturally enough, entirely recaptured the high drama of that first landing, each one has been marked by great technical advances and new discoveries, made possible for example, by a "moon car" in which the astronauts have been able to travel considerable distances.

¶ BRAUN, WERNER VON. *History of Rocketry and Space Travel.* 1967

Spain: state (sometimes defined as a kingdom without a sovereign) of southwestern Europe. The country entered history in the 3rd century BC as part of the empire of Carthage, conquered and organised by Hamilcar Barca, father of Hannibal. The Romans also had interests in Spain. While Hannibal campaigned in Italy, the Roman general P. Cornelius Scipio drove the Carthaginians out of Spain, crossed into Africa in 204 BC and decisively defeated Hannibal at Zama. From that time the independent and turbulent people of Spain came under Roman rule. They were not rapidly conquered, but by the first century of the Christian era a great part of the peninsula was permanently Romanised. City life was well established and the language, fashions and culture of Rome prevailed. The agriculture, minerals and manufactures of Spain contributed to the economic stability of the Roman Empire. Two of the early Roman emperors, Trajan (98–117) and his successor Hadrian (117–138), though not related, were both of Spanish birth.

With the Empire's decline, Spain suffered severely. When the Rhine frontier broke in 405, the Sueves, Alans and Vandals pillaged Gaul for three years and then entered Spain. Later Spain was ruled by the Visigoths. Efforts by the eastern Emperor Justinian (483–565) failed to restore more than the seacoast to Roman rule. A Visigothic Christian kingdom lasted in Spain till the early 8th century. Then the militant expansion of Islam in North Africa reached the Straits of Gibraltar, and in 711 the Muslim army of Tariq won a decisive victory over the Visigoths on the Guadalete. By 713 all Spain, except the country of the Basques and a few other small northern areas, was under Muslim rule.

The history of Spain during several centuries was thus largely concerned with war to the death between the proud and fanatical representatives of two rival civilisations, the Christian and the Islamic. Islam was too divided by theological and dynastic issues to endure as an empire, and Spain, under the highly civilised Umayyad Chalifate of Cordova, was largely cut off from the eastern sources of Muslim

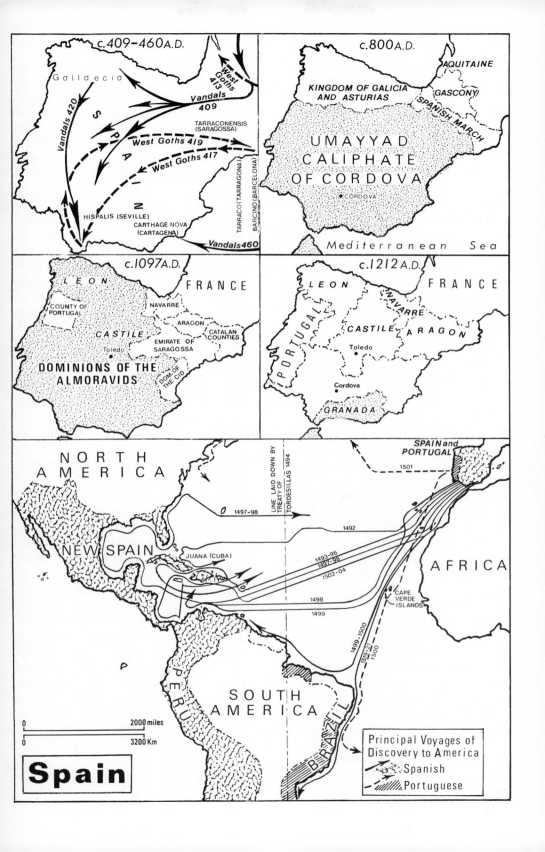

c.409–460 A.D.

Gallaecia

West Goths 413

Vandals 409

Vandals 420

S P A

TARRACONENSIS (SARAGOSSA)

West Goths 419

West Goths 417

TARRACO (TARRAGONA)

BARCINO (BARCELONA)

I N

HISPALIS (SEVILLE)

CARTHAGE NOVA (CARTAGENA)

Vandals 460

c.800 A.D.

AQUITAINE

KINGDOM OF GALICIA AND ASTURIAS

GASCONY

SPANISH MARCH

UMAYYAD CALIPHATE OF CORDOVA

CORDOVA

Mediterranean Sea

c.1097 A.D.

LEON

FRANCE

COUNTY OF PORTUGAL

NAVARRE

ARAGON

CATALAN COUNTIES

CASTILE

EMIRATE OF SARAGOSSA

Toledo

DOM. OF THE CID

DOMINIONS OF THE ALMORAVIDS

c.1212 A.D.

LEON

FRANCE

NAVARRE

PORTUGAL

CASTILE

ARAGON

Toledo

Cordova

GRANADA

NORTH AMERICA

LINE LAID DOWN BY TREATY OF TORDESILLAS 1494

SPAIN and PORTUGAL

1501

1497-98

1492

NEW SPAIN

JUANA (CUBA)

1493-96

1497-98

1502-04

AFRICA

1498

1499

CAPE VERDE ISLANDS

1499-1500

1500

1500

1502-21

PERU

SOUTH AMERICA

BRAZIL

0   2000 miles

0   3200 Km

Spain

Principal Voyages of Discovery to America
Spanish
Portuguese

power. Small Christian states kept alive in the north. While the Umayyad dominions broke into many small states, the Christians co-operated rather more. Alfonso VI (1073-1109) united Castile and Leon and conquered Toledo in 1085. This advance from the north continued until the battle of Las Novas de Tolosa in 1212 confined Islamic rule to Granada. Then for two centuries the Spanish Christian kingdoms competed with one another and were torn apart by turbulent nobles. Castile alone had a frontier with Granada. Unity came only after Ferdinand, the heir of Aragon, married Isabella, the heiress of Castile, in 1569. Granada had been conquered in 1492. War with France gave Ferdinand the opportunity to seize all Navarre south of the Pyrenees. Portugal still preserved its separate existence. The Spanish Inquisition harshly imposed religious uniformity upon Jews, Muslims or any others out of step with Catholic orthodoxy.

Thus united, Spain, at the close of the 15th century, was on the threshold of a great imperial destiny. The notion was already in circulation that the wealth of the Indies might be reached by sailing west instead of using the eastern land routes. In 1492 the Pope Alexander VI, himself a Spaniard, issued bulls awarding to Spain and Portugal all lands and islands already discovered or hereafter to be discovered "in the west, towards the Indies or the Ocean seas". With the voyage of Christopher Colombus in that year, the new world was opened to European conquest. The Pope's ruling of 1492 was quickly followed by the Treaty of Tordesillas in 1494 which assigned to Portugal everything east of a line drawn down the Atlantic 370 miles [595 kilometres] west of the Cape Verde Islands and everything west of it to Spain. This enabled the Portuguese to claim Brazil; but the rest of the new world, the extent of which was still unknown, was thrown open to exploration and exploitation by Spain. In the years that followed Spanish *conquistadores*, with tiny forces but superior arms and tactics, added vast territories to a great Spanish American empire, Cortés in Mexico, Pizarro in Peru, and many more. Fleets carried gold and the produce of "the Indies" to Spain. This brought Spain into sharp competition with other naval powers omitted from the Pope's award.

In Europe, also, Spain went through great change. Not only did Spanish conquests extend to Sicily, Naples and parts of Italy, but several dynastic marriages united the Spanish crown with the rulership of other European lands, including the huge Habsburg dominions. Charles V (Holy Roman Emperor 1519-58) became the ruler of Spain, Austria, Hungary, Bohemia, parts of Germany, the Netherlands, Milan, Naples, Sicily, Sardinia, Mexico, Central America, Venezuela, Peru, Bolivia, western Chile, Argentina and Paraguay, and his empire was extending into California and Florida. There was at the same time a notable flowering of literature and art in Spain.

The peak of power reached under Charles V was not wholly maintained under Philip II (reigned 1556-98) and a steady decline set in. Though Philip did not succeed to the whole of the Habsburg dominions, his empire, still huge and cumbersome, invited hostility in too many quarters and came into collision with formidable opponents in England, France and, particularly, the Netherlands on which Spain tried to impose its religious orthodoxy. Concentration solely on military and administrative tasks and dependence on gold from overseas and on colonial slavery caused decline of productivity and economic life in Spain.

Spain remained a major European power through the 17th and 18th centuries, but a declining and unfortunate one. By the close of the 18th century the overseas empire was breaking up, and Spain itself became a battleground for France and Britain in the Napoleonic War of the early 19th century. The Spanish American lands achieved their independence.

Spain was not involved in either of the World Wars of the 20th century. A democratic republic was established in 1931 but was overthrown by an army mutiny led by General Francisco Franco, who, after a savage civil war (1936–39), established a dictatorship. In the 1960s Spain experienced a great industrial expansion. A frequent cause of friction with Britain, leading to frontier restrictions, has been Spain's repeated claims to Gibraltar. *See colour section.*

¶ VILAR, P. *Spain: A Brief History.* 1967

Spanish–American War (1898): war fought by the USA and Cuban revolutionaries to free Cuba from Spanish control. Spain was quickly defeated (in the four months of the war America lost only twenty men) and by the Treaty of Paris Spain gave up the Philippines, Guam and Porto Rico to the USA, and Cuba came under temporary military occupation by US forces.

Spanish Civil War (1936–39): struggle between Fascist and republican forces in Spain. The policies of a right-wing government (1933–35) precipitated revolt in Catalonia and Asturias. In February 1936 a left-wing government came into power with a strong majority. In July General Francisco Franco (*see* separate entry) led a mutiny of the army, moving into Spain from Morocco. A savage civil war followed, in which Germans and Italians participated on the rebel side and Russia and Mexico aided the government. An ill-equipped and largely untrained anti-Fascist International Brigade was formed of foreign volunteers. In June 1937 Bilbao fell to the rebels, Barcelona in January 1939 and Madrid in March 1939, after a siege of twenty-eight months. It was a struggle that embittered Spanish life for years after the war had ended; and one that led to the passionate involvement of many people from other countries who saw the clash for what it was, a cynical curtain-raiser by powerful aggressor nations for the conflict that followed.

¶ PURCELL, HUGH. *The Spanish Civil War.* 1973

Spanish Succession, War of (1701–14): war between England, the Netherlands and certain German states against Spain, France, Portugal and other allies. It arose because Louis XIV of France accepted the will of the last Spanish Habsburg, Charles II (1661–1700; *see* HABSBURG, HOUSE OF), and broke the Partition Treaty by which interested powers had agreed on the fate of Spain. Charles left the Spanish Empire to Louis's grandson, Philip, and, if he refused it, to the Austrian Archduke Charles. Louis made war inevitable by moving French troops into the Spanish Netherlands and into the Dutch forts there. The Grand Alliance of Austria, England and Holland, formed in 1701 by William III, was sustained by the victories of Marlborough and Eugène in Flanders and Italy, and of Peterborough in Spain. The terms of the Peace of Utrecht, 1713, confirmed Louis's remark that the war was about trade. Though Holland gained nothing after exhausting efforts, England gained Gibraltar, Minorca, Newfoundland and Nova Scotia, the Asiento (*see* separate entry) allowing trade with the Spanish Indies, and trading rights in Portugal. Philip retained Spain, but Austria was compensated with the Spanish Netherlands and Naples. Savoy and Prussia were expanded as checks on French power. The Catalans, who had assisted the allies against Philip, were abandoned to his vengeance.

The Great Sphinx of Giza.

Sparta: state in the centre of the Peloponnese, the southern peninsula of Greece. Sparta was also the name of the capital and the whole territory was often called Lacedaemon. The Spartans came as invaders from the north, and, though they subdued the people whom they found in possession, they were always on guard against internal revolt and attack from surrounding states. This resulted in a highly organised society, with military efficiency and physical endurance as primary aims. The rigorous training to which boys – and girls too – were subjected has become proverbial, and the word Spartan is applied to any situation of austerity or discomfort.

The armies of Sparta were held in awe by the rest of Greece, where Athens was her traditional enemy. By the early 1st century BC Sparta was absorbed into the Roman Empire.

¶ FORREST, W. G. *A History of Sparta 950–192.* 1968 *See also* ATHENS; HELOT; PELOPONNESIAN WAR; THERMOPYLAE.

Sphinx: type of monument originating in Egypt and spreading, in a variety of forms, throughout the ancient world. In Egypt, the leonine body represented the sun god, while the human head was a likeness of the Pharaoh. The great Sphinx of Giza was erected by Chepheren, builder of the second pyramid. Its huge head was battered by Turkish artillery, and until 1816 most of its body lay under drifted sand. When this was cleared away a ruined temple was discovered between the paws, and an inscription relating how, centuries before, Tuthmosis IV had also caused the sand to be removed, having been told to do so in a dream.

In Greek mythology the Sphinx was a female monster who inhabited a rock near Thebes and hurled from its top all passers-by who could not answer the riddle: "What walks on four legs in the morning, on two at noon, and on three in the evening?" Oedipus (whose story is used by the dramatist Sophocles), son of Laius, king of Thebes, solved the riddle as describing man in infancy, in his prime and in old age.

Spies: or secret agents, people paid by others, usually to secure information, especially naval, military, aeronautical and scientific from other countries. They have also been employed internally by governments against their political opponents. Thus, in the 16th century agents were used extensively, especially by Lord Burleigh and Sir Francis Walsingham, ministers of Elizabeth I of England. Walsingham at one time had thirteen agents in France, seven in the Low Countries, five in Italy, six in Spain, nine in Germany and three in Turkey; such men were usually business agents reporting on the state of the markets as well as being in government service.

Modern times have seen a tremendous increase in the scale of international espionage, both in war and peace, and the activities of secret agents have been greatly helped by the clever inventions that science has brought to their aid in the shape of special cameras, a wide range of ingenious microphones and other "bugging" devices, telephone tapping techniques, etc.

Since 1945, when World War II ended, there have been a number of notorious cases. In 1950 Karl Fuchs, a brilliant German-born nuclear physicist working at Harwell, England, believed that all scientific information should be shared internationally and passed vital atomic secrets to the Soviet Union. In 1951 Guy Burgess, who had worked for British Intelligence, and Donald Maclean, of the Foreign Office, were about to be arrested for acting as Russian agents when they escaped to the Soviet Union after being warned by the so-called "third man", Harold Philby, who had been a Communist since 1934 and a Soviet agent since 1956. Philby also was given political asylum in Russia. In 1961 George Blake was given the heaviest sentence ever passed in Britain, of 42 years imprisonment, for espionage on behalf of the Soviet Union, though he escaped after five years. In 1962 Oleg Penovsky, a Russian senior military intelligence officer who had passed vital information to the Western powers, was arrested and shot; and Greville Wynne, his contact with British Intelligence, was kidnapped in Budapest and imprisoned in Russia. He has since been released.

In 1969 Russia had about 250,000 secret agents – more than the number employed by all the Western powers together. The financial estimate for maintaining the British Secret Service in the same year was £10·5 million.

In the USA the main responsibility for espionage and counter-intelligence work is in the hands of the Central Intelligence Agency. There, too, the post-1945 period and the long "cold war" with the Soviet Union, has produced a number of espionage cases that made headlines all over the world. Shortly after the Fuchs affair in Britain had created such disquiet, five Americans were arrested and put on trial for acting as Soviet agents in the United States. All were found guilty and two,

Julius and Ethel Rosenberg, were executed. In 1950 Alger Hiss, a high official in the Department of State, was sentenced to five years' imprisonment for conveying secret documents to a Russian courier as far back as 1937 and 1938. Another sensational case was that of Francis Gary Powers, an airman in the employ of the Central Intelligence Agency who was shot down while taking high altitude photographs over Russia in 1960. He was sentenced to ten years' imprisonment but was later exchanged for a Soviet spy captured in the United States.

Spoils system: system ("to the victor belong the spoils") by which the offices and privileges formerly belonging to a defeated political party are taken over by its victorious opponents when they come to power. While such a system is, within varying limits, an inevitable part of changing political fortunes, it is particularly associated with the USA where, e.g., not only politicians but also trusted government servants have been stripped of office.

Sports and athletics: Although there is evidence of organised sports and athletics in very early times, such as wrestling among the Sumerians (*see* SUMER) in Mesopotamia 5,000 years ago, it is among the ancient Greeks that athletics seem first to have become a major part of social life. The word itself comes from Greek *athlon*, a prize.

Certain basic forms of sport have developed in widely separated parts of the world. Contests between man and man, or between teams, have been organised in many forms, but basically as a kind of fight, with or without weapons. The imposition of rules also came very early, to prevent sporting contests from leading to real fighting. The rules were not always such as we have now. The ancient Greek athlete who, realising that he could not himself win the race, tripped up another runner in order to ensure that his friend would win, was praised and admired.

In Homer's *Iliad* there is an account of games being held as part of the ceremonies at a funeral. The religious and social importance of games was particularly expressed in the Olympic games (*see* separate entry), established in 776 BC and held every four years. The ancient Greeks also looked for all-round accomplishment and not only for specialisation in one sport. A characteristic institution among them was the *pentathlon* or fivefold contest in ability in running, long jumping, throwing the javelin, throwing the discus and wrestling.

Women were excluded from the Olympic games even as spectators, but athletic ability was not regarded as unwomanly. Girls engaged in athletics, particularly among the Spartans, and there still exists an attractive statue of a mini-skirted Spartan girl running. At Argos women held their own games in honour of Hera, who was peculiarly the goddess of complete and fulfilled womanhood.

The word gymnastics also comes from Greek, from *gymnos* meaning naked. From 720 BC no clothing at all was worn at the Olympic games by competitors; but Greek girls normally wore some clothing at their games.

It may be noted that the Olympic games of 624 BC included horse-racing, a sport at least 3,000 years old. The earliest known horse race in Britain was held in about AD 210, during the Roman occupation.

As early as the 5th century BC the distinction between amateurs and professionals began to emerge, the ancient Greek professionals being slaves. This led on to the practices of Roman times, when gladiators (Latin *gladius*, a sword) fought for the entertainment of spectators. Gladiatorial shows were an institution borrowed by the Romans from the Etruscans, an older Italian civilisation. The first recorded Roman gladiatorial event was at funeral games held in 264 BC.

Generally the Romans were interested in games as a spectacle rather than as expressions of healthy living. At Rome itself they were largely professional performances provided by the state, appealing increasingly to a brutal and degrading interest in scenes of violence, cruelty and slaughter. Gladiators fought to the death, with each other and with animals. Bull fighting was a Roman practice which still survives in Spain and elsewhere. Yet there was as well much display of ordinary athletic speed and skill at the Roman public games, races, particularly with horses and chariots, being popular. The Roman games also had political as well as social importance, for they provided an occasion when a large crowd could show approval or disapproval towards its rulers.

After the decline of the Roman Empire, and through the Middle Ages of European history (*see* separate entry), war and the struggle for existence occupied so much of human life that sport and athletics were not separated from training for war or from hunting. From archery practice or contests with staves among the humbler people to the jousting and similar exercises of their knightly masters and rulers, nearly every exercise of skill or stamina seemed to be directed to training for attack or defence.

Yet the human impulse to pursue sport for enjoyment and for healthy exercise kept emerging. In 1365 Edward III of England felt it necessary to prohibit the playing of football because it interfered with military training.

More civilised, stable and leisurely ways of life produced an increasing readiness among the wealthy and aristocratic classes to pursue sport and athletics as a rec-

SPORTS: *Above, Roman gladiatorial combat. Above right, tennis as played in the 17th century. Right, cricket in the 18th century. Below, Victorian ladies archery tournament held in Regent's Park, 1894.*

Show jumping.

Skiing.

reational outlet. In addition, the renaissance of classical learning in the 15th and 16th centuries encouraged imitation of the ancient Greeks in many fields, including their cultivation of athletics. Various ball games were popular. Henry VIII of England was fond of tennis, then a form of handball played against a wall, which had indeed been popular from the 14th century; and Mary Queen of Scots took an interest in golf, a game which was being played at St Andrews about 1552.

From the middle of the 18th century various sports were taken up at English public schools. Football began to take its modern form; and at Rugby in 1823 the game took on its alternative form, which allowed the ball to be carried as well as kicked.

For track running, the first meeting on modern lines in Britain was held in 1817.

In many European countries in the 19th century, athletic meetings were held in association with nationalist political movements. This occurred in Germany and among the Czechs and Magyars and to some extent in Ireland.

In the later decades of the 19th century a golden age of sport and athletics began. Settled life and increasing prosperity and leisure in the more technically and politically advanced countries gave opportunity for far wider participation in sports. Improved travel facilities and communications caused the forms of sport which were once confined to particular countries to become known throughout the world.

From now on sports were adopted by people living far away from the physical or social conditions which had given rise to them. Mountaineering and winter sports were taken up by people living in countries where there was little or no natural ice or snow and possibly no mountains, but travelling abroad to pursue these interests. Japanese forms of wrestling, e.g. *jujitsu* and *judo*, were taken up by people in countries far from Japan. French Canadians adapted an Indian game and called it lacrosse because the netted stick used in playing it resembled a bishop's crozier. In athletics, forms of skill previously confined to particular places became more general. Pole vaulting achieved status as a recognised form of athletics. Above all, nearly every sport that had hitherto been confined to men was now pursued also by women. Under the stimulation of variety, new forms of old games were invented, lawn tennis coming into being in 1873, while ice hockey was invented in 1875.

The wider interest in athletics led to the setting up of organisations to standardise the rules of various games, to regulate matches and competitions and to encourage interest in them. An English Amateur Athletic Association was founded in 1880, and similar associations were established in many other countries. To enable these associations to work together, adopting similar standards and holding international track meetings and competitions, an International Amateur Athletic Federation was set up in Sweden in 1913. Already, in 1896, the Olympic games had been restored in modern form. Similar national and international bodies were established to organise and regulate a wide variety of games and sports, such as football, swimming, skating, cycling, horse riding, lawn tennis, boxing, etc.

An acute problem facing some of these bodies was that of defining amateur and professional status. The paid player could give his whole time to training and practice and could treat his sport as a full-time occupation, gaining thus a great advantage over amateurs, who pursued the sport as a spare time amusement. But, with growing competition, bigger prizes and the growth of national and institutional support for various sports, many so-called amateurs came to be in reality paid professionals, though they managed to gain their financial support in ways which were not strictly direct payments for competing in sport. Scholarships or specially created employments in which no work had to be done, and similar devices, enabled supposed amateurs to be paid to give their whole time to competitive sport.

The greater organisation and standardisation of sport by the many national and international associations did not remove all the varieties simultaneously existing in the various games. Thus, for example, in football the two main types remained – those played with feet only, as controlled in Britain by the Football Association and familiarly known as "soccer", and those in which the ball is handled – and there remained also much variety inside the two types (see FOOTBALL).

In the late 19th century, and more particularly in the 20th, technology entered sport. This vastly changed the older instruments of sport, making them better adapted to their purpose, and it also introduced new ones like the modern trampoline in gymnastics. Footballers in older times kicked a ball filled by the inflated bladder of an animal; today they kick a highly sophisticated industrial product; and so it is in many other forms of sport, where there are better rackets, better hulls and rigging for yachts, and so on. Technological advance also brought into being completely new types of sport involving powered machines, such as motor cycles or speed boats for racing, or activities such as water skiing behind power boats or motor-paced pedal cycling. Technology also created the airborne sports such as gliding and parachuting, and the underwater forms of sport and recreation.

Technology transformed sport in another way, through scientific study of the human body, giving an entirely new understanding of what is required in the training of an athlete, while a wide variety of devices, from the stop watch to the electrocardiograph, have made it possible to measure much more accurately both the performance of the athlete and the physical resources on which he or she can venture to make demands. At the close of the 1920s the Finnish long-distance runner, Paavo Nurmi, made history by measuring his performance, not by what the other competitors were doing, but by calculations based on reading a stop watch which he carried in his hand. Calculations and research into what is physiologically possible produced performances which would at one time have been thought impossible. The early 1960s saw a hundred yards [91 metres] run in ten seconds and a mile [1·6 kilometres] in four minutes.

By the mid-20th century sport and athletics had become a major aspect of educational and social life in nearly every country. Many established ministries of sport as part of their governments.

¶ MOSS, PHILIP. *Sports and Pastimes through the Ages.* 1962

Sri Lanka: formerly Ceylon, an island off the southern tip of India, producing tea, rubber and rice. A republican constitution was adopted in 1972. Sri Lanka continues to be in the Commonwealth. Population in 1972: 12,747,755.

Stalin, Joseph (Joseph Vissarionovich Dzhugashvili, 1879-1953): Russian dictator whose adopted name means "man of steel". After studying for the priesthood and being expelled from his seminary, he joined the Bolshevik wing of the Communists, organising a bank robbery in Tiflis in 1907, and over 1,000 other raids, to provide funds for the party. In 1922 he became powerful as general secretary of the Communist party and

after Lenin's death in 1924 became virtual ruler of the USSR. In 1928 he inaugurated the first five year plan for industrialisation and collective farming. The "second revolution" in Russia was achieved by ruthless "re-education" of the people, involving forced labour, the seizure of land, the corruption of the law courts, the extermination of all rivals, the suppression of free opinion in the arts and literature and all the other machinery of the police state. Graphic pictures of the terror of life under Stalin may be found in such books as Arthur Koestler's *Darkness at Noon*, Alexander Solzhenitsyn's *One Day in the Life of Denisovitch* and Boris Pasternak's *Dr Zhivago*.

In August 1939, though he and Hitler were completely opposed on many points, Stalin signed the Russo-German pact. If this was a drastic shock to the Western powers, so, in June 1941, was the German onslaught on Russia to Stalin. Thereafter it may be considered that Stalin showed at his best, as a patriotic war leader, uniting his vast country, ordering that "the enemy must not be left . . . a single pound of grain or gallon of fuel". They must be "hounded and annihilated

at every step". He subsequently took part in the Allied Conferences at Tehran (1943), Yalta (1945) and Potsdam (1945).

Three years after his death in 1953 his methods, particularly the "personality cult" which demanded pictures and statues of himself all over Russia, were officially condemned by his successors. History will be slow to pronounce a final valid verdict on the leader who, "capricious, irritable and brutal" (in Khrushchev's words) achieved great things for Russia at such a price of human life and happiness.

¶ LIVERSIDGE, DOUGLAS. *Joseph Stalin*. 1970; ROBERTS, ELIZABETH MAUCHLINE. *Stalin, Man of Steel*. 1968

Stalingrad, now **Volgograd:** Russian city on the lower Volga, once called Tsaritsyn, on the River Tsaritsa. Joseph Stalin (*see* separate entry) took a leading part in its defence in the revolution of 1917, and in 1925 it was renamed Stalingrad in his honour. It saw rapid and extensive industrial development under Soviet rule. In World War II (*see* separate entry) the Germans tried to cut the River Volga here (August 1942–February 1943), but Stalingrad was stubbornly defended and the Germans were driven out in January 1943 with losses estimated at 330,000. The city was rebuilt and, in 1961, renamed Volgograd.

¶ JUKES, G. *Stalingrad*. 1969; SAMMIS, E. R. *Last Stand at Stalingrad*. 1966

Stamp Act (1765): British Act of Parliament that was one of the immediate causes of the War of American Independence. By it, customs duties were charged on imports into the colonies, and it forecast "certain stamp duties" as a basis for further legislation. The act aroused the famous cry, echoed by Pitt in Britain, "No taxation without representation", and the Stamp Act was repealed in March

1766, along with some of the most ob-
jectionable customs duties.

¶ DICKINSON, ALICE. *The Stamp Act.* 1971

See also AMERICAN WAR OF INDEPENDENCE;
PITT, WILLIAM, THE ELDER.

Standish, Miles (1584–1656): one of the
original Pilgrim Fathers who sailed from
Leyden to America in the *Mayflower*
(1620, *see* separate entries). He settled at
New Plymouth and became military captain of the colony, largely contributing to
its success by his skilful exploits against
the Indians. Standish House, built by the
son of Miles Standish in 1666, still stands
in Duxbury, Massachusetts.

Stanley in Africa, 1878.

Stanley, Sir Henry Morton (1841–
1904): British explorer. He was born in
North Wales but moved to New Orleans
in 1856. After travelling widely in the
West Indies, Spain and Italy during
1863–64, in 1867 he joined the staff of the
New York Herald, continuing his travels
as a special correspondent. He achieved
world fame by seeking and finding the
missing Scottish explorer David Livingstone (*see* separate entry) at Ujiji on Lake
Tanganyika in 1871.

¶ HALL-QUEST, O. *With Stanley in Africa.* 1962

Star Chamber: building in Westminster,
England, used for meetings of the King's

Council from Edward III's time, and
developing into a court of royal justice
dealing with riots, maintenance, libel, etc.
Strengthened by Henry VII, it dealt
effectively with overpowerful subjects.
Used by the Stuarts to support arbitrary
royal power, it became hated and was
abolished by the Long Parliament in
1640. The court was so called because of
the building's ceiling, decorated with
golden stars.

Stars and Bars: the original flag of the
Confederate States (*see* separate entry) of
the USA. It consisted of three wide bars,
red, white and red, with, in the upper
left-hand corner, seven stars on a blue
field, representing the seven states (South
Carolina, Mississippi, Florida, Alabama,
Louisiana, Georgia and Texas) that broke
away from the Union in 1861.

Stars and Stripes: the national flag of the USA, consisting of thirteen alternating red and white stripes (*see* THIRTEEN COLONIES) and, in the top left-hand corner, fifty white stars on a blue field – one star for every state. The flag (with the crosses of St George and St Andrew instead of the stars) was first raised by George Washington (*see* separate entry) in 1776.

Star-spangled Banner, The: poetical name for the USA flag, from the famous poem, officially adopted in 1931 as the national anthem, written in 1814 by Francis Scott Key (1779–1843). The original manuscript is in the possession of the Maryland Historical Society, Baltimore. The refrain (with slight variation from verse to verse) runs:

> And the star-spangled banner in triumph shall wave
> O'er the land of the free and the home of the brave.

Statue of Liberty: the bronze figure of a woman lifting a torch on Liberty Island, New York Harbour, the proper name being "Liberty Enlightening the World". Designed by F. A. Bartholdi, the statue was the gift of the French people and was dedicated in 1886. The statue itself weighs 225 tons [240 tonnes] and is 151 feet [46 metres] high, though, on its pedestal, from sea level to the tip of the torch is 330 feet [100 metres].

The Statue of Liberty in New York Harbour.

Steam: vapour produced by raising water to boiling point. In civilisation it has a number of uses, but this article is confined to considering steam as a source of mechanical energy, which will be discussed from a historical rather than a technical standpoint.

Steam engines as we know them today (and the term includes many types besides railway engines, which are properly called locomotives) work on principles derived from the power of steam to expand. The earliest engines of the Industrial Revolution, however, worked by the condensing of steam in a cylinder, causing a vacuum and producing a power stroke. This type of engine was developed by Thomas Newcomen (1663–1729) and greatly improved by James Watt (1736–1819, *see* separate entry). These engines worked slowly and had limited application, being largely used for draining mines.

It seems that Watt appreciated the possibilities of using a cylinder or cylinders into which steam was admitted alternately at either end to act directly on a piston; but he was probably discouraged by the extremely low steam pressure – considerably less than ten pounds per square inch (p.s.i.) [0·7 kilogrammes per square centimetre] which was all that the boilers of his time could safely produce. It is difficult to trace clearly the first stages of the development of the non-condensing high pressure engine: the name of the Cornishman Richard Trevithick (1771–1833) and in America, Oliver Evans (1755–1819) may be mentioned, but records are scanty. From these beginnings, however, was derived the steam engine which revolutionised industry – and indeed life itself – in almost every part of the world during the 19th century. It provided power for factories, it changed the railways from local horse-drawn affairs to a vast network in many countries and a thin lifeline in others, and

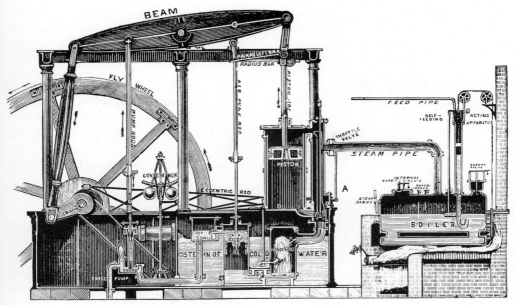

The Watt double-acting steam engine.

it enabled ships of increasing tonnage to cross the oceans in a fraction of the time required under sail.

The action of steam on a piston in a cylinder remained the basic principle of all types until the turbine was developed in the 1880s by Charles Parsons (1854–1931). Here motion is produced by steam acting on a number of vanes arranged round a shaft. Turbines, which are capable of a high rate of revolution, are particularly suitable for ships' engines and for driving electric generators.

The first necessity for any type of steam engine is a suitable and sufficient supply of steam. As the 19th century advanced improvements in the art of boiler-making, especially after the use of steel was adopted, enabled increasingly higher pressures to be used. For the locomotive trials at Rainhill, Liverpool (1829), a pressure of 50 p.s.i. [3·5 kg p.s.cm] was specified (and a leaking boiler on one of the competitors was plugged with oatmeal until the feed-pump was clogged with porridge); but, by the middle of the century, although in the meanwhile boiler explosions were fairly frequent, 150 p.s.i. [10·5 kg p.s.cm] was being used. Except for occasional experiments, locomotive boilers have never exceeded 250 p.s.i. [17·6 kg p.s.cm], though steamships have used up to twice this pressure, while in industry a lower one has generaly sufficed.

Steam, however, has its drawbacks. It is "inefficient" in the sense that a considerable proportion of the energy produced in the form of heat by the burning of fuel (coal or oil) to raise steam is lost in the process of converting this into motive power. Moreover, a locomotive or a ship has to carry its fuel with it: a locomotive also carries water to replenish its boiler, while a ship needs space for apparatus to make sea-water usable. Lastly, the maintenance of boilers, particularly those burning coal, requires the frequent clearance of ash and clinker from tubes and fireboxes. For this purpose the fire must be allowed to die, and it takes some time to raise steam again. In contrast, a diesel or electric engine can stand idle for a long time and then be started merely by pressing a switch. For these reasons, steam as a source of mechanical energy is in many fields being abandoned in favour of internal combustion or electric power.

¶ HART, I. B. *James Watt and the History of Steam Power.* 1961

Steel: any one of numerous alloys of iron and carbon (the latter in the general range of 0·1 to 1·5 per cent), often combined with other metals, such as nickel, chromium and manganese, according to the special physical properties required for the job in hand. As compared with iron, steel has a higher tensile strength, with consequent saving in weight, and greater hardness.

In ancient times, long after iron was in general use, bronze or brass was often preferred for armour or weapons, but in the Middle Ages steel came into favour, the sword blades produced at Damascus (Syria) and Toledo (Spain) being especially prized.

As long as wood remained the fuel for smelting, even though a primitive blast-furnace was invented, little technical progress was made, until, in the early 18th century, the use of coke was introduced and higher temperatures could be applied. In 1740 Benjamin Huntsman (1704–76) discovered a process of making cast steel which revolutionised the cutlery industry and showed the way to the development of machine tools.

In 1856 Sir Henry Bessemer (1813–98; *see* separate entry) invented the "converter": this blew hot air through the molten metal to remove impurities and produced a "mild" steel, which immediately had many engineering applications throughout the world. On railways, for instance, the use of steel instead of iron for rails and wheel-tyres led to greater safety and economy: boilers of all sorts could be made to withstand higher steam pressures: ships' hulls could be made of steel and warships armoured. The Forth Bridge, Scotland (1889), was the first large bridge to be built of this material.

An event of domestic importance was the development of "stainless steel" for cutlery, etc., following the discovery in 1912 that steel containing 12 per cent chromium is virtually rustless. Another important modern discovery was that of tungsten, a particularly hard element now much used for tipping cutting tools and for electric lamp filaments. The technique known as "continuous casting" has recently speeded up steel-making by cutting out some of the chief steps in the long-established conventional processes.

¶ FISHER, DOUGLAS. *Steel: From the Iron Age to the Space Age.* 1968

Stephenson, George (1781–1848) and **Robert** (1803–59): father and son, early British railway engineers. George is rightly regarded as the "Father of Railways". A self-educated man from Northumberland, he used his early experience of transport in the coalfield to lay out and construct the Stockton and Darlington Railway (opened 1825) and the Liverpool and Manchester (1830), continuing thereafter to assist the development of railways and of the coal and iron industries in Derbyshire. Robert, though perhaps less famous in common estimation, became, thanks to his early co-operation with his father and a better

The Bessemer "converter", 1856.

education, an engineer of wider scope and impressive achievements both in England and abroad.

¶ ROLT, L. T. C. *George and Robert Stephenson.* 1935; WILLIAMSON, J. A. *George and Robert Stephenson.* 1958

Stockholm: capital, chief port and industrial centre of Sweden. Sometimes called "the Queen of the Baltic" or "the Venice of the North" from the beauty of its setting, it began as a fortress and a trading post in the 13th century on an island linking Lake Mälaren with the Baltic. Stockholm spread till it occupied a large cluster of islands and peninsulas and became the capital in the 17th century. It supports a variety of industries including iron and steel, engineering, textiles, chemicals, petrol refining and printing. There are also highly important educational and medical foundations.
See colour section.

Stone Age: period in all human cultures when man used stone tools. Stone survives though humans become dust, so prehistorians learn about early man from his tool-making techniques. The Stone Age began when man first used flint chopping tools, about 700,000 years ago, and ended when he discovered how to make bronze.

The Palaeolithic (Greek *palaios*, ancient, and *lithos*, stone) period roughly corresponds to the Ice Age, finishing about 8000 BC. People lived nomadic lives, sheltering in caves, the men hunting and fishing, the women gathering wild fruits and vegetables. They learnt how to make fires, to flake blades from flints for harpoons and spears. Ritual, centred on hunting magic and fertility cults, was served by artistic schools producing animal paintings, engravings and carvings. When the ice retreated, forest replaced tundra, and the great herds, man's food, disappeared. Mesolithic (i.e. Middle Stone

Stone Age pierced axes found in Germany.

Age) man had to change his way of life and devise new tools. He set tiny flints in shafts as arrows for the hunt. While women collected shellfish, he went fishing and fowling in canoes, which he made with his new wood cutting tools, and built huts for shelter.

The Neolithic (New Stone Age; *see* separate entry) period was revolutionary. The foundations of civilisation were laid in lands from the Nile Valley to the Indus. Animals were domesticated, crops planted, food stored, wealth accumulated. People stopped wandering, lived in settlements and built houses of brick or stone. They ground and polished their tools and began potting and weaving. Religion centred on agricultural life, good crops depending on weather, so that earth, rain and sun were thought of as gods.

¶ DICKINSON, ALICE. *First Book of Stone Age Man.* 1965; QUENNELL, MARJORIE and C. H. B. *Everyday Life in Prehistoric Times.* 1959

Stonehenge: remains of a very ancient arrangement of large stones, set in concentric circles, on Salisbury Plain, England, probably erected between 1800 and 1400 BC. It seems to have been a place of great religious significance and was probably an observatory. Some of the stones appear to have been brought from South Wales, and despite a variety of attempted

Stonehenge, on Salisbury Plain.

explanations, it is a mystery how the men of the time could handle such massive weights.

¶ ATKINSON, J. R. C. *What is Stonehenge?* 1962; BRANLEY, FRANKLYN. *The Mystery of Stonehenge.* 1972

See also AVEBURY.

Stowe, Harriet Elizabeth Beecher (1811–96): popular American writer. Her best known book *Uncle Tom's Cabin* made her world-famous and powerfully influenced public opinion against slavery. Translated into many languages, it is still read, though considered out of tune with modern thought on race relations. Mrs Stowe was honoured by Queen Victoria and admired by many famous writers of her day, including Tolstoy and Dickens.

Strasbourg: main city of Alsace, eastern France, situated on a tributary of the Rhine. Originating as a Celtic settlement, it became the headquarters of the Roman eighth legion against the barbarians to the east. It became part of the German kingdom in the 10th century and was given the status of a free imperial city. It was annexed by Louis XIV in 1681. Among its notable buildings is the magnificent cathedral with a famous astronomical clock built in 1574 and restarted after a considerable overhaul in 1843. Another claim to fame was the city's association with the work of the printer Gutenberg (*see* GUTENBERG BIBLE; PRINTING). In 1949

Strasbourg was chosen as the official meeting place for the Council of Europe.

Strategy: literally, the art of the general or commander-in-chief, though strategic decisions can be taken by a group, e.g. a council of war. In contrast, tactics are concerned with the actual manoeuvring of troops or ships in contact with the enemy and are therefore the job of subordinate commanders.

Strikes: the refusal of workers, acting together, to go on working unless the employer grants them some improvement such as more pay or shorter hours. When this happens, both sides suffer. The workers get no pay from their employer while they are on strike, and the employer himself has no goods to sell and so loses his profits. Sooner or later, one side or the other gives in. Sometimes there is an agreement in which both sides yield a little with the workers accepting less than they asked for and the employer granting more than he wanted to. The opposite of a strike is a lock-out, that is, the employer offers no work to his workers unless they accept new terms. When a strike is ordered by the trade union concerned, it is called "official": other strikes, not supported by the trade union, or in defiance of it, are called "unofficial".

Millions of working days are lost every year through strikes. In 1926 coal miners in Britain struck against the coal owners' demand for them to take lower wages and to work longer hours. The position of the miners grew desperate, and the Trades Union Congress (*see* TRADE UNIONS) called a General Strike in sympathy. All trade unionists in the great industries struck, and a very serious situation arose. Over three million workers were on strike, and the major public services, such as the railways, came to a halt. There were no newspapers, but the government

Strikers in the streets of London during the 1926 General Strike.

issued a special paper called *The British Gazette* and took control of the radio. After ten days of great anxiety, the General Strike collapsed after a loss of 14,500,000 working days. The workers went back to work, and the miners were left to continue their strike alone.

The British government was so alarmed by the General Strike that in 1927 it made a new law, the Trades Disputes and Trade Unions Act, which made sympathetic strikes illegal, but this was repealed by the Labour government in 1946. In recent years there have been many strikes, both official and unofficial, and the concern of the TUC and of the government has been to bring both sides in a dispute together for a settlement. Not much progress has been made. In 1970 over 12 million working days were lost through strikes. The weapon of the strike is now recognised by professional workers such as teachers and doctors as well as by most industrial workers. Legislation affecting the conduct of strikes was introduced by the Conservative government in 1971.

Strikes are not confined to Great Britain: they happen in most advanced industrial democratic countries where "the right to strike" is recognised. In totalitarian states the trade unions are controlled by the government, and strikes are not permitted.

Organised strikes became fairly common in the USA in the 1830s and 1840s, and in 1834 President Jackson (*see* separate entry) used the army to break a strike of Irish labourers building a canal in Maryland. Massive strikes, sometimes involving the use of federal troops and state militia and serious loss of life, have occurred on the railroads, and in the steel, automobile and mining industries. In 1947 the Taft-Hartley Act introduced important new strike legislation, prohibiting the "closed shop" and providing a "cooling off" period of sixty days.

The world's longest strike, involving barbers' assistants in Copenhagen, Denmark, has lasted for thirty-three years.

¶ COOTS, R. J. *The General Strike.* 1964

Stuart, Stewart, or **Steuart, House of:** the royal dynasty which ruled Scotland 1371–1603 and, from 1603–88, Scotland and England combined. The ancestors of the Stuarts came from Brittany. King David I (reigned 1124–53) made one of the family, Walter, seneschal, or steward, of Scotland; and from this hereditary office came the family name. Another Walter married Marjory, daughter of Robert the Bruce. In 1371 their son, as Robert II, became the first Stuart king of Scotland. For centuries England and Scotland were enemies. In one of the few peaceful intervals James IV of Scotland (reigned 1488–1513) married Margaret, daughter of Henry VII. It was this marriage which gave the Stuarts a claim to the English throne. When, in 1603, Queen Elizabeth of England died unmarried, James VI, son of the ill-fated Mary Queen of Scots, became, in addition, King James I of England.

Stuart rule was interrupted from 1649–60. Disputes with Parliament led to civil war, the beheading of the King, Charles I, in 1649 and the establishment of a Commonwealth under Oliver Cromwell. In 1660 the Stuarts were restored, but in 1688 the dynasty came to an end when James II, who had become converted to Roman Catholicism (*see* separate entry), was forced to abdicate.

Two rebellions, in 1715 and 1745 respectively, the first led by James II's son James, the second by the latter's son Charles Edward (Bonnie Prince Charlie), were equally unsuccessful. Stuart supporters, called Jacobites, are still not extinct – though few would go so far as to wish to see the Duke of Bavaria, present head of the House of Stuart, on the throne of England.

¶ TREVELYAN, G. M. *England under the Stuarts.* 1904 *See also* COMMONWEALTH; CROMWELL; JACOBITES.

THE HOUSE OF STUART: *Above (left to right), Mary Queen of Scots, James I, Charles I. Below (left to right), Charles II, James II, James Francis Edward, the Pretender.*

Submarines: vessels so designed that they can be submerged and navigated when under water. As an instrument of war they can be traced back to the 18th century. Manually operated submersibles were produced by the Americans David Bushnell (1742–1824) and Robert Fulton (1766–1815). The *Nautilus*, built by Fulton in 1800, was designed to blow up enemy

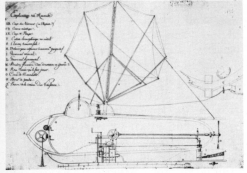

Section of Fulton's submarine Nautilus, *1798.*

ships at anchor by planting bombs under their hulls. In 1863 the American Confederate Navy built the *Davids*, semi-submersibles with long projecting spars on which torpedoes were attached. They also produced a "torpedo diving boat" driven with a steam engine in 1865.

The USA's *Holland* of 1898 marked the beginning of the modern submarine era. Armed with guns and torpedoes the craft was driven on the surface by a petrol engine and, when submerged, by an electric motor powered from a battery. Horizontal rudders, or hydroplanes, and ballast tanks served by compressed air, controlled the diving and surfacing.

The first submarine circumnavigation was achieved in 1960 (24 February–25 April) by the US nuclear submarine *Triton* (Captain Edward Latimer Beach). Fittingly enough, the voyage was named "Operation Magellan", in tribute to the first surface sea voyage round the world made by Ferdinand Magellan in his flagship *Vittoria* four and a half centuries before.

Sudan: republic in north-east Africa, having 400 miles [644 kilometres] of Red Sea coastline in the north-east, common boundaries with Ethiopia in the east, Kenya, Uganda and Congo Republic in the south, with the Central African Republic and Chad in the west, Libya north-west and Egypt to the north. Formerly it formed the eastern section of an enormous indeterminate belt known as the Belad es Sudan of Negritia, extending across Africa south of the Sahara, now split up by various agreements and treaties between the Sudan, Chad, Niger, Mali and Senegal and other West African states. The capital is Khartoum, at the confluence of the Blue and White Niles. There is extensive cultivation of the area between the White Nile and Atbara lying to the south-east of Khartoum, thanks to dams and irrigation schemes. The main products are cotton, which is the chief export, millet (the staple food), gum arabic, ebony, papyrus, groundnuts and dates. Cattle and sheep are also reared for the Egyptian market.

Between 1500 and 1200 BC North Sudan, or Kush, was part of the Egyptian empire but existed as an independent kingdom from 750 BC to AD 350. Between 350 and the 7th century the history of Kush is obscure, though some time in the 7th century Muslim invaders replaced Christianity by the Islamic faith. South Sudan, cut off from the north by extensive marshlands, remained primitive until the 19th century, when Mohamet Ali conquered the Sudan in 1801, beginning a period of misrule which General Gordon, as governor-general, tried to put right on his appointment in 1877; but the revolt of the Mahdi led in 1885 to the fall of Khartoum and the death of Gordon, and the Mahdi's successor, the Khalifa, proved to be an even more ruthless ruler. In 1896 General (later Earl) Kitchener started military moves designed to end the regime, which was finally destroyed by the battles of Atbara and Omdurman, and the death at Gedid of the Khalifa.

In 1899 Britain and Egypt began a condominium (joint) form of rule of the Sudan, the country being known as the Anglo-Egyptian Sudan until 1956, when it became an independent state and joined the Arab League. Since then the North and South Sudan have found it difficult to maintain harmony. *See* AFRICA for map. *See* separate entries for CHRISTIANITY; GORDON; ISLAM; MUSLIMS.

Suez Canal: waterway joining the Mediterranean with the Red Sea and thus allowing oceangoing vessels to reach the East without sailing round Africa. From Port Said, at the Mediterranean end, the canal runs for 101 miles [163 kilometres] through Egyptian territory. The construction of the canal was undertaken by the Frenchman de Lesseps (*see* separate entry), work starting in 1859 and being completed ten years later. In 1875 the major share in the capital of the canal company was purchased by Britain from the bankrupt Khedive (viceroy) of Egypt. In 1956 the Egyptians nationalised the canal, and in 1967 it was put out of action by the war with Israel. In March 1975 Egypt promised its reopening within six months, to all nations except Israel.

¶ BURCHELL, S. C. *Building the Suez Canal.* 1967; HIRSCHFELD, B. *The Vital Link: the Story of the Suez Canal.* 1968

Sugar: sweet crystalline substance extracted from a variety of plants, especially sugar cane and beet. Sugar cane originated in New Guinea, India and China. Honey was for centuries the only sweetener known in Europe, but in 325 BC Alexander the Great's (*see* separate entry) soldiers ate, in India, "honey not made by bees", and this was the boiled juice of the sugar cane, known in modern India as *jaggery*.

By AD 500 there was a flourishing sugar industry in the Tigris-Euphrates valley. Arab traders carried the sugar to Europe where the trade was continued by Venetian merchants.

In 1420 the Portuguese colonised Madeira and established sugar plantations there. In 1516 the Spanish government started a sugar industry in Cuba. This was unsuccessful, but other attempts in Mexico and Peru, where Cortés and Pizarro had introduced the cane, flourished. In 1641 Colonel Holdip started a sugar factory on the island of Barbados. The Dutch and French encouraged the growth and processing of sugar in the West Indies, much of which eventually came under British rule.

Sugar played an important part in the origins of the American Revolution against Britain. The Sugar Act of 1764, instigated by British West Indies sugar planters with influence in London, strove to prevent the colonists buying molasses (a treacle obtained during sugar refining) from French, Spanish and other foreign islands by imposing an import tax of threepence per gallon. The loss of French and Spanish currency was a strong factor in the "no taxation without representation" cry.

Sugar can also be made from sugar beet, a root vegetable which was eaten in Roman times. In 1912 a beet processing factory was established in Norfolk, England, but people did not like beet sugar, although it was used widely in Holland. During the economic difficulties of the 1930s housewives started to buy it because it was cheaper than cane sugar. Its use increased during World War II, when shipping space was scarce. Nowadays, about one-third of the sugar used in Britain, which is one of the highest consumers in the world per head of population, is beet sugar.

Suleiman I, called **"the Magnificent"** (1494-1566): Ottoman Sultan who succeeded to the throne in 1520. He attacked the Christian states, capturing Belgrade in 1521 and driving the Knights of St John from Rhodes in 1522. Defeating the Hungarians at Mohacs, 1526, he was checked only outside Vienna in 1532. His fleets ruled the Mediterranean Sea. For his period he was an enlightened ruler, drafting many new laws, encouraging the arts and planning fine buildings.
See also OTTOMAN EMPIRE.

Sully, Maximilien de Béthune, Duc de (1560-1641): French statesman. His devoted service assisted Henry of Navarre (Henry IV) to the French throne in 1594. As superintendent of finance, he reformed the fiscal system and became in effect sole minister of France. After Henry's assassination in 1610, Sully surrendered many offices, but was appointed a marshal of France in 1634. His *Mémoires* provide a valuable picture of the times.

Sumatra: Indonesian island south-west of Malaya and west of Borneo, a Hindu kingdom from AD 600 to the 11th century, after which Islamic influences predominated. The Portuguese traded in spices from 1509 but were expelled by the Dutch before 1600. Except during the Napoleonic Wars and the Japanese occupation in World War II, the Dutch East India Company and the Dutch Indies Government ruled until 1950, when Sumatra became three provinces of the Indonesian Republic.
See INDONESIA, MALAYA for map.

Sumer: ancient region of southern Mesopotamia. The farmers of Sumer lived on the fertile soil of the Euphrates valley and used the river water to irrigate their crops. Ur was their most famous city, dating from about 4000 BC, and the later Babylonian civilisation (*see* BABYLON) adopted the Sumerian religion and their "cuneiform" system of writing on clay tablets.
¶ CARRINGTON, R. *Ancient Sumer.* 1960
See also ALPHABETS.

Sumter, Fort: fort on an artificial island in Charleston harbour, South Carolina, where Confederate troops fired the first shots of the American Civil War (12 April 1861 *see* separate entry) when provisions were being brought to the Federal force which had occupied the fort.

Sun Yat-sen (1866-1925): Chinese republican leader, more familiarly known in China as Sun Wen. A medical doctor by training (he was the first graduate of the new medical school at Hongkong), he turned to politics in 1893 and soon became involved in revolutionary plots against the Manchu regime. As a result he spent some years in exile, where he worked to bring about revolution and the establishment of a democratic government in China based on the three principles of nationalism, democracy and social welfare. When the revolution took place, ending 2000 years of Imperial rule, Dr Sun Yat-sen returned in 1912 to head the new government, a position which he soon resigned in favour of the younger Yuan Shih K'ai. He held various other offices but was always more effective as a propagandist and theorist than as an administrator.

As organiser of the Kuomintang (*see* separate entry) and inspirer of the revolution, he has fairly been called the Father of the Chinese Republic.
¶ BUCK, PEARL. *The Man Who Changed China.* 1955

Supreme Soviet: the highest legislative authority in the USSR. It has two chambers with equal legislative rights, elected for four years – the Soviet of the Union, consisting of one deputy for every 300,000 citizens of the USSR, and the Soviet of the Nationalities, elected on a regional basis from the various component republics and other areas. Each has over 750 members. The Supreme Soviet elects the Presidium, the supreme authority while the Soviet is not sitting. "Soviet" is the Russian word for "council".

Surinam: formerly Dutch Guiana, on the north coast of South America, an overseas part of the Netherlands since 1922. The first permanent settlement was made by the Englishman Lord Willoughby of Parham in 1650. In 1667 Surinam was exchanged for New Amsterdam, now New York, though twice again, 1799–1802 and 1804–15, it came into British hands. Slave rebellions were common in the 18th century. In the late 1800s Indian and Japanese labourers were imported to ease plantation problems.

Sutton Hoo: site of East Anglian ship burial. This Suffolk (England) burial mound contained a large boat and burial deposit of great richness, belonging to a 7th-century East Anglian king. The custom of ship burial shows links with Sweden, as does the workmanship on the gold buckle, clasps, purse frame, etc.

¶ BRUCE-MITFORD, R. L. S. *The Sutton Hoo Ship Burial.* 1968; GREEN, CHARLES. *Sutton Hoo: the excavation of a royal ship burial.* 1969

Hinged gold clasp decorated with garnets, glass and filligree, from the Sutton Hoo Treasure.

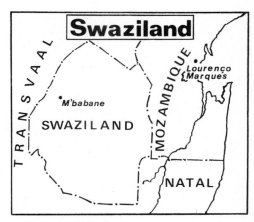

Swaziland: British Protected State, which became self-governing on 25 April 1967, having previously been the smallest of the three High Commission Territories in southern Africa. The main exports are iron ore, sugar, asbestos, wood pulp, cotton, rice, wattle bark and pineapples. Swaziland's chief trade outlet is via Lourenço Marques in Mozambique.

Sweden: kingdom of north-western Europe, forming the larger part of the Scandinavian peninsula. It is difficult to establish accurately the early story of the country, because of the absence of reliable written records. The only evidence comes from surviving runes, legends and sagas, and from many archaeological excavations. It is clear that the Swedish Vikings moved eastwards to the rivers of Russia, and as far as Byzantium. Although they were warlike, they established trading routes. Christianity spread very slowly among the pagan Swedes, who were the scourge of northern Christendom until the 12th century.

After the decline of Viking power, Sweden was rather an isolated country, one of the marchlands on the edge of northern Europe. Its kings were weak, and real power lay with a highly privileged aristocracy of nobles and bishops. In an effort to regain past glories they united with Norway and Denmark by the Union of Kalmar in 1397. But this attempt to make a powerful, single nation of Scandinavia failed. A Danish king who tried to curb the importance of the nobility stirred up a revolt. Led by Gustavus Vasa, a two-year struggle ended in Swedish independence in 1523 and a new royal house of Vasa. At the same time a quarrel with the Papacy led to the acceptance in Sweden of Protestantism. As in England, the monasteries were plundered and their lands sold to the nobility.

On these foundations Sweden became a great European nation with a northern empire. In the 17th century Gustavus Adolphus, "the Lion of the North", built up his power against the Catholic Emperor of Austria by spectacular military leadership. Gustavus's intelligence, courage and statesmanship made him one of the great figures of modern history. He was killed at the battle of Lützen in 1632.

Sweden failed to hold its empire against the increasing power of Prussia and Russia. It had neither the money nor the population to stand the strain of long warfare with ambitious neighbours. Though reduced in military status the Swedes looked for and found a new role to play, gaining an international reputation in the arts. August Strindberg (1849–1912) was a genius of literature and the theatre. In the new art form, the cinema film, Ingmar Bergman (b. 1918) has established an international reputation and the country has produced a number of famous film stars. In the social field, too, the world found Sweden in the forefront of progress. Since 1842 education has been compulsory and free, and early in the 20th century her housing schemes became models for other European countries. The millionaire Alfred Nobel increased Sweden's reputation abroad when he established the various Nobel Prizes.

Politically also Sweden has adopted a new role, that of neutrality, preserving it through both World Wars, though much relief work was undertaken in the devastated countries. As a member of UNO Sweden's troops became vital in disputes in which they had no political interest. The country gave the United Nations one of its greatest Directors-General, Dag Hammarskjöld. *See colour section.*

¶ MERRICK, HELEN HYNSON. *First Book of Sweden.* 1971

See also BYZANTIUM; CHRISTIANITY; HAMMARSKJÖLD, DAG; NOBEL, ALFRED; PROTESTANTS; VIKINGS.

Switzerland: republic of west central Europe, formed by a confederation of twenty-two cantons (or administrative areas). The Swiss people are descendants of Teutonic tribes which moved westward as the Roman Empire declined, though they did not at first form any kind of united area. First they came under the dominion of Charlemagne. Later the western section became part of the Kingdom of Burgundy, whilst the rest split into small areas with their own rulers. In the 13th century the House of Habsburg extended its control over part of the east.

Because of the dominance of foreigners the Swiss within their various valley regions spoke French, Italian or German. But in spite of this multiplicity of languages there was a general wish for self-rule, preferably in their own localities. For 200 years a struggle for power took place. From small beginnings, in which three forest cantons defeated the Austrians (1315), a combination of most of the Swiss groups developed. In 1499 this Confederation at last achieved independence when it defeated Charles the Bold of Burgundy and the Emperor Maximilian I.

Over the years the Swiss created a tradition of local self-government. Each

897

Switzerland

canton had its own laws and it was not until 1942 that a national criminal code was drawn up. Even today some parts have "open-air democracy" in which, once a year, the men of an area meet to make some particular laws. Again, only since 1970 have women been allowed to vote. When Napoleon conquered Switzerland and tried to impose a single central government, he failed. In 1815 Switzerland not only regained its independence, but also had its neutrality permanently guaranteed by the big powers of the day. Keeping this independence and neutrality has been both a rewarding and a difficult task. In the 1920s Geneva became the headquarters of the League of Nations with its peace-keeping and humanitarian work; in World War II she found her neutrality extremely hazardous, being surrounded by the German and Italian Axis governments.

Internally one of Switzerland's most serious problems has been religion. Since the Reformation different cantons have been Catholic and Protestant rivals. In the 16th century the country became the centre of international Protestantism. John Calvin established his Church in Geneva and created a model which was followed by groups throughout the world, including Presbyterians in Scotland and the Huguenots in France. Catholic opposition was bitter, and a series of savage conflicts as late as the 19th century showed how prolonged the struggle was.

Switzerland has only a small population and few natural resources. It has relied for its prosperity on the tourist industry and on the specialist talents of a wide variety of people. To the centuries-old craftsmanship of clock- and watch-making they have added optical instruments, banking facilities, medical centres, Pestalozzi schools and the Nestlé milk industry. *See colour section.*

¶ EPSTEIN, SAM and BERYL. *First Book of Switzerland.* 1965
See also LEAGUE OF NATIONS; MAXIMILIAN I; NAPOLEON I; ROMAN CATHOLIC CHURCH; WORLD WAR II.

Sydney: capital city of New South Wales, Australia. Cook sighted the harbour in 1770. In 1788 Captain Phillip established a penal colony, named after Thomas Townshend, first Viscount Sydney, the Home Secretary, on Sydney Cove in preference to Botany Bay, the first choice. The cessation of the transportation of convicts from Britain in 1840 encouraged free settlement. Sydney has developed into the commercial and industrial capital of Australia, with a population increasing from 3,000 in 1815 to two-and-a-half million in the metropolitan area today. Outstanding features are the magnificent single-span arch Port Jackson Bridge (1932), the universities of Sydney (1850) and New South Wales (1949), and the famous cricket ground, the scene of many notable England v. Australia Test Matches.
See AUSTRALIA for map.
¶ KENNEDY, BRIAN. *Sydney.* 1970

Syria: republic of western Asia, stretching along the eastern shore of the Mediterranean and to the River Euphrates. Ruled successively by Egyptians, Babylonians, Hittites, Assyrians and Persians, Syria was deeply influenced by Greek civilisation. It fell under Roman influence in the 1st century BC and was under Roman and Byzantine domination until, by AD 640, it had passed permanently under Muslim rule. Damascus until 750 was the capital of the Umayyad dynasty (and indeed of the Muslim world) but declined with the rise of Baghdad. A cultural and literary flowering in the 10th and early 11th centuries ended with conquest by the Seljuk Turks.

The Christian Crusaders introduced Christian communities into some towns, but Damascus remained Muslim, and the Crusaders lost Acre in 1291, their last stronghold. Already in the 1250s the Mongol invasions had ruined Syria. Ruled for a century by the Mamelukes, the province then spent four centuries under the rule of the Ottoman empire.

During the 18th and 19th centuries, France became the patron of Catholic Christians in Syria, and Russia of the Orthodox. With the break-up of the Turkish empire, Syria came under the control of France, who acquired a mandate in 1930. Full Syrian independence was conceded only in 1945, after World War II.

An active member of the Arab League, Syria suffered a setback with the establishment of Israel. The Syrian Baath party combined socialism with the ideal of Arab unity. In 1958 Syria joined with Egypt to form the United Arab Republic but withdrew from it in 1961. In 1967 the country's spring army exercises, involving the shelling of Israeli settlements, flared into the full-scale Middle East War.

See SAUDI ARABIA for map.

See also BYZANTINE EMPIRE; CRUSADES; MONGOLS; MUSLIMS; OTTOMAN EMPIRE; WORLD WARS I and II.

Tacitus, Publius Cornelius (*c.* AD 55– *c.* 118): Roman historian. His major works, of which portions are now lost, give an account of the times of the early Roman emperors. Among his shorter books is a life of his father-in-law Agricola (*see* separate entry), describing his military successes in Britain.

Tactics: the art of manoeuvring armed forces in contact with the enemy; the army corporal studies minor tactics, the formation commander and his staff decide major tactics. Tactics depend on thorough training, quick information about enemy movements, an eye for ground, an understanding of the role of each weapon. There is usually a timelag between the introduction of a new weapon by one or two farseeing enthusiasts and the development of suitable tactics. Liddell-Hart wrote that the early battles of World War II were "lost on the steps of the Cavalry Club". He turned to history – the infiltration tactics of the Mongols (*see* separate entry) – to work out the implications of the tank and the lorry.
See also STRATEGY.

Taft, William Howard (1857–1930: 27th president (1909–13) of the USA and chief justice of the Supreme Court (1921–30). He continued the policy of Theodore Roosevelt (*see* separate entry) in promoting his country's financial and commercial interests in Latin America and successfully enforced the laws against the great oil and tobacco trusts, which were broken up.

Taft–Hartley Act (1947): law passed by the US Congress (*see* separate entry) in an effort to control industrial strikes. Among its other provisions, it required sixty days' notice to be given of the ending of a wages contract, and enabled the government to obtain from the courts a legal injunction delaying for eighty days any strike which could be considered harmful to the country's wellbeing or security.

Tagore, Sir Rabindranath (1861–1941): Indian poet, novelist, educationist, social reformer, preacher and mystic, who won the Nobel Prize for literature in 1913. In over 150 books, on immensely varied subjects, he stressed spiritual as against material values. He founded the unconventional Santiniketan School (where weather dictated the daily timetable) in 1900, and Viswabharati University in 1921.

Taiping Rebellion (1850–65): a major rising against the Manchu dynasty in China, begun in 1850 among a Christian sect in Kwangsi and Kwangtung provinces. Its leader was Hung Hsiu-ch'uan, who tried to impose a sort of puritanical Christian socialism. Advancing northwards and down the Yangtze, the rebels captured Nanking in 1853, but their fortunes fluctuated with a changing leadership. When their army approached Shanghai, they were opposed by European and Chinese forces and began to lose ground, Nanking finally falling in 1864. The Chinese emperor was assisted in his military recovery by the British General Gordon (*see* separate entry).

Taj Mahal: built at Agra, 1632–50, by the Indian Emperor Shah Jehan as a tomb for his favourite wife Mumtaz-i-Mahal. Designed by Ustad Isa, of white marble with a dome rising to 210 feet [64 metres], it is the finest example of Mogul architecture and one of the most beautiful buildings in the world. *See colour section.*

Talking machines: devices which record and play back the human voice and other sounds. The first step towards such a device was taken in 1857, when Leon Scott constructed his "phonautograph", which recorded on the smoked surface of a rotating cylinder the movements of a vibrating diaphragm. This, however, was not capable of reproducing the sounds recorded. In 1877 Thomas Edison invented the "phonograph", which was capable of playing back a record formed on a surface of tinfoil wrapped round a cylinder. The familiar disc record was invented by Emile Berliner, who started to manufacture his "gramophone" in 1894. This was further developed by Eldridge Johnson, who devised a spring-driven motor. The variations in the record track were lateral, not vertical as in the case of the "hill-and-dale" indentations of the Edison cylinder. Johnson and Berliner formed the Victor Talking Machine Company in 1901. Thus far all development had been in the United States, but, in England, the Gramophone Company was formed in 1898, and adopted the familiar "His Master's Voice" trade mark in the following year. In the late 1940s the American Columbia Company produced what was called the Microgroove recording, now familiarly known as LP or long-playing. This was made possible by speed reduction, finer grooves on the disc and a much finer stylus. In the 1950s further advances came with stereo (stereophonic) recordings which diffuse the concentrated sound produced by a single loudspeaker.

The tape recorder, in its modern form, appeared in the 1920s. An early form, invented by Valdemar Poulsen of Denmark, using a wire of magnetised steel, was shown at the Paris Exhibition of 1900. The application of these ideas to the requirements of a modern business office has led to a variety of dictating machines, using wax cylinders, plastic discs, wire and coated tape, the earliest of these being Edison's Ediphone.

It only remains to mention the telephone, invented and patented in the United States by Alexander Graham Bell (*see* separate entry) in 1876. His original electromagnetic transmitter served also as a receiver, the instrument being presented alternately to the mouth and the ear. This was improved by Edison's invention of the variable-contact carbon transmitter. In England the first telephone exchange was opened in London in 1879 with only eight subscribers. By 1968 it was estimated that in Great Britain there was one telephone to every 4·5 members of the population, more than in any other European country, but still behind Japan and the United States, the latter with one telephone to every two persons (1968).

¶ CHEW, V. K. *Talking Machines, 1877–1914: some aspects of the early history of the gramophone.* 1968

See also TELECOMMUNICATIONS.

Talleyrand-Perigord, Charles Maurice de (1754-1838): French diplomat, usually known as Talleyrand. He was an aristocrat and a man of extraordinary adaptability. Under Louis XVI he was Bishop of Autun, but the French Revolution (*see* separate entry) saw him president of the National Assembly and later

foreign minister, an office which he continued to hold under Napoleon, who made him a prince. On the latter's fall, Talleyrand took a leading part in the recall of the Bourbon king and showed brilliant skill in the negotiations over the reconstruction of Europe. When the Bourbons gave way (1830) to Louis Philippe, he was appointed French ambassador in London.

Tallies, talley sticks: wooden sticks for recording hours of work, payments, etc. In the more complicated examples, notches of increasing width to represent units, tens, hundreds, etc., were cut. The stick was then cut down the middle and the two parties to a monetary transaction each kept one half as evidence of the account, matching them together again when necessary. Tallies were probably introduced into England by the foreign merchants attending fairs and markets, and were recognised by the Law Merchant, while still disapproved by the Common Law. In 1292 we read of a barrister's disgusted remark: "We do not think he ought to be answered on a bit of wood like that, without writing."

Once established, they became the recognised form of receipt for payments into the Royal Treasury until 1826. In 1834 nearly all the ancient tallies were burned in the furnaces which heated the House of Lords. The usual tally was about 9 inches [22·8 cm] long, but the Bank of

13th century exchequer tallies, showing the names of those who had paid and the nature of the account. The notches represent the sums paid, with pounds above and pence below.

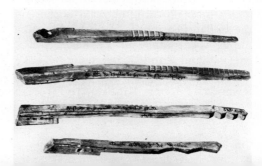

England (*see* separate entry) still preserves a giant specimen over 8 feet [*c.* 2·5 metres] long. Tallies, from the French *taille*, notch, were also put to simpler uses such as keeping the score (itself a Saxon word for notch) in the game of cricket. A free-scoring batsman is still sometimes described as being "in good nick".

Talmud: Jewish religious book (compiled in Babylonia and put into writing from the 2nd to 6th century of the Christian era) giving guidance on the conduct of spiritual life. It embodies the teaching of many centuries and has from time to time been revised.

¶ COHEN, A. *Everyman's Talmud.* 1949
See also JEWS.

Tammany, Tammany Hall: political organisation founded in New York after the War of American Independence and named after an Indian chief noted for his wisdom and love of liberty. At first Tammany represented the interests of the middle classes against the land-owning aristocrats. Later it became a corrupt organisation, with great influence over the Democratic party, organising gangs in furtherance of its political ends and dishonestly acquiring funds, sometimes for private gain for its members. It regained a measure of respectability but since 1930 has declined in power. Its old headquarters, Tammany Hall on 14th Street, occupied since 1868, was sold in 1927 and a new building erected.

Tanganyika: now major part of United Republic of Tanzania, bounded in the north by Kenya and Uganda, the east by its 500-mile [800 kilometres] coastline on the Indian Ocean, the south by Moçambique, the south-west by Lake Nyasa, Malawi and Zambia, the west by Lake Tanganyika and Zaire, Barundi and Rwanda. Mount Kilimanjaro (19,340 feet: 5,894 metres – the highest point in Africa) and Mount Meru (14,970 feet: 4,562 metres) rise from the Tanganyika section of the central African plateau, whilst the famous Serengeti National Game Park covers 6,000 square miles [15,500 square kilometres] of the Arusha, Mara and Mwanza districts.

Arab traders probably arrived in Tanganyika in the 16th century and later opened up a slave route from Ujiji on Lake Tanganyika to the Indian Ocean coast. British exploration began with Burton's expedition in 1856, he being followed by Speke, Livingstone and Stanley; but in 1884 Karl Peters established a German protectorate by signing treaties with local chiefs. Revolts which occurred in 1889 and 1905 were ruthlessly crushed. Following World War I Tanganyika was placed by the League of Nations under British mandate, and a legislative council was set up in 1926. After World War II Tanganyika became a United Nations trusteeship territory, still under Britain's wing, then in 1961 was granted independence within the Commonwealth, with Dr Julius Nyerere as its first president. In 1964 it united with Zanzibar to form what is now Tanzania. *See also* BRITISH COMMONWEALTH; LEAGUE OF NATIONS; LIVINGSTONE, D.; STANLEY, H. M.; UNITED NATIONS; WORLD WARS I and II.

Tannenberg (Grunwald)**, Battle of** (1410)**:** climax of a struggle for control of an area between the rivers Vistula and Nemen in eastern Europe. The Order of Teutonic Knights (*see* ORDERS, MILITARY) had been extending its power eastwards and setting up small German settlements. This so alarmed two of the strong states of the area, Poland and Lithuania, that they sent a joint army under Jagiello against the Order. The Knights attacked but failed to break the ranks of the Poles, who

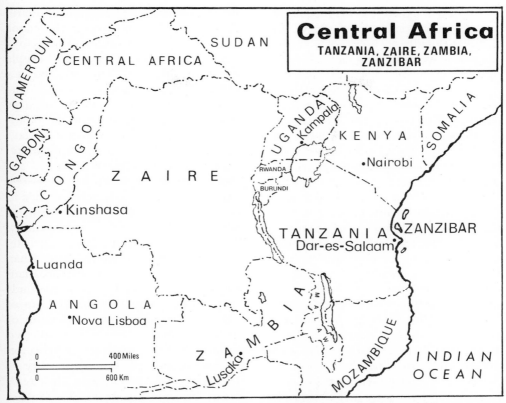

Central Africa
TANZANIA, ZAIRE, ZAMBIA, ZANZIBAR

won an overwhelming victory. From this defeat the Teutonic Knights never recovered, whereas Poland emerged as a great power.

Tanzania, United Republic of: East African republic composed of Tanganyika and Zanzibar, which became united in April 1964 following army mutinies earlier in that year. In October the name Tanzania was applied officially, Dr Nyerere being president, the First Vice President Sheikh Abeid Amani Karume, and the Second Vice President the Hon. R. M. Kawawa.

Coffee, cotton, oilseeds, sisal and cloves (Zanzibar) are grown for export, and diamonds, gold, lead and mica are mined.

¶ KIMAMBO, I. N. and TEMU, A. J., editors. *History of Tanzania.* 1971

See also TANGANYIKA.

Tapestry: cloth woven with patterns or pictures; in late medieval and early renaissance times it was used in great houses as a wall covering to give colour and warmth. The earliest known examples are Egyptian, dating from the 2nd century BC.

From the 15th to the 17th century Arras, in the Netherlands (*see* separate entry), was the chief centre for tapestry making – indeed, tapestry was frequently referred to as *arras*. Two people played an important part in its manufacture, the artist and the weaver. The weaver worked from the artist's design copied on to the warp threads of his loom. He filled it in with different colours, using many bobbins; sometimes gold and silver threads highlighted the design. One such tapestry may be seen in Angers castle, western France. It was made in 1377 for the Duke of Anjou, designed by Hannequin de Bruges and woven by the master weaver Nicholas Botaille.

Tapestry weaving was an important industry in medieval France and was protected by the many trade guilds involved in its manufacture. But during the Hundred Years War the industry declined and was not revived until the 17th century, when the Gobelins factory was founded in order to produce tapestries for Louis XIV's palaces.

Not much tapestry was made in England. During Elizabeth I's reign William Sheldon, a Warwickshire man, started a factory to give employment to people in his neighbourhood. His chief weaver, Richard Hyckes, went to the Netherlands to learn the art.

A fine example of modern tapestry, "Christ in Glory", hangs in the new Coventry Cathedral, England. This is among the largest single pieces ever woven, measuring nearly 75 feet by 38 feet [22·8 × 11·5 metres]. It preserves the ancient roles of artist and weaver, the designer being the well-known painter Graham Sutherland (b. 1903) and the weavers Pinton Frères of Felletin, France. *See colour section.*

See also TEXTILES; WEAVING.

Tartars, Tatars: Turkish-speaking Bulgar tribes, which spread out from the Sea of Azov area in the 7th and 8th centuries. In the 13th century they formed the spearhead of the Mongol conquest of Russia; with other tribes they made up the Golden Horde, dominating southern Russia for two centuries. The Kipchak princedom or khanate of Kazan fell under Russian rule in 1552. Other tribes had broken away to form the Mishars and the Kazimov Tartars, settling on the River Oka. The Tartars continued to be a distinct people through Russian history, speaking their own Turkic language and

mostly following the religion of Islam. Under the Russian empire the name Tartar was applied rather loosely to a variety of Turkic or Muslim people within the empire. There are about 4·5 million Tartars in modern Russia. "Tartar" has passed into the English language to describe a person of particularly difficult temper; and to "catch a Tartar" means to come into conflict with someone who is more than one's match.

Tartary, Tatary: early name applied to a large area of southern Russia, formerly ruled by the Mongols (*see* separate entry). Previously occupied by a Bulgar khanate, it was the area in which Batu Khan founded the Golden Horde, the barbarians who overran eastern Europe in the mid-13th century. This was the khanate of Kipchak, the westernmost extension of the Mongol empire, which for nearly two centuries had an important influence on eastern Europe and the early history of Russia. In 1430, however, the khanate of Kazan broke away from the Golden Horde and was finally broken up by Ivan the Terrible in 1552. Tartaria is now an autonomous state of the USSR.

¶ PARKER, E. H. *A Thousand Years of the Tartars.* 1969

Tasman, Abel Janszoon (*c.* 1603–59): Dutch navigator, sent in 1634 by the Dutch East India Company (*see* separate entry) to explore in the Pacific. In 1639, in search of certain "islands of gold and silver", he penetrated to the north-east of Japan and, between 1642 and 1644, discovered Van Diemen's Land (Tasmania), New Zealand, Tonga and Fiji, and explored the Gulf of Carpentaria.

¶ SHARP, ANDREW. *The Voyages of Abel Janzoon Tasman.* 1968

Tasmania: formerly Van Diemen's Land, discovered by Abel Tasman in

1642, the smallest Australian state, lying on latitude 42° S and longitude 146° E, to the south of the mainland, with Hobart the capital. Du Fresne visited it in 1772, Furneaux in 1773, Cook in 1777. Captain Bligh called on his way to Pitcairn, and Bass and Flinders charted its coasts in 1798. Governor King of New South Wales (*see* separate entry) sent the earliest settlers, convicts, in 1803. Progress, especially under Governor William Sorrell after 1817, came with the establishment of sheep-breeding with merino rams in 1820, and of the Bank of Van Diemen's Land in 1823. The Aborigines (*see* separate entry), settled in reservations on Flinders Island in 1840, are now extinct. When the transportation of convicts from Britain to Australia generally ceased, Tasmania continued to receive "recidivists" (re-convicted criminals) till 1853.

The island, a separate colony from 1825, achieved self-government in 1856. Frozen fruit was first shipped to England in 1877. Discoveries of tin, copper and gold in the 1870s and 1880s, and the construction of railways, assisted the economy, though the Bank of Van Diemen's Land failed in 1891. Tasmania became part of the Commonwealth of Australia in 1901, and at times since then has needed considerable economic help from Canberra.

¶ WEST, JOHN. *History of Tasmania.* 1972
See AUSTRALIA for map.

Taxation: compulsory contributions to the support of local or central government. Under the feudal system the lord lived on the proceeds of his own demesne and the dues exacted from his tenants. The king, as the apex of the system, likewise derived his income from the feudal dues exacted from his tenants-in-chief. In England it was not until the 12th century that a new expedient was tried, when a tax of a fractional part of the value of every man's movables (i.e. goods, furniture, etc.) was granted for a crusade (*see* CRUSADES). This was known as the Saladin Tithe (1188). Later this was applied to secular purposes, the fraction ultimately becoming fixed as a fifteenth for counties and a tenth for towns. We learn of the early means of assessing this tax as follows: "If anyone in the opinion of his neighbours give less than he ought, let four or six lawful men be chosen from the parish to state on oath the amount which he ought to have stated, and then he must make good the deficit." From about 1334 onwards the grant of a fifteenth and tenth seems to have meant a grant of about £39,000, and, if more than this was required, parliament would grant several fifteenths and tenths.

The poll tax (tax payable per "poll" or head of population) introduced under Richard II proved unpopular, though it was resorted to intermittently until the 18th century.

Indirect taxation was derived from customs duties, and a London merchant of Charles I's reign complained that "in no part of the world are traders so screwed and wrung as in England". A calculation made in 1756 estimated that the average artisan paid £1 5s 1d, and the average labourer 15s 10d in taxes each year, and the taxable items included beer, salt, sugar, leather, soap, candles, drugs, tobacco, and windows. In England there are many reminders of the last imposition in the shape of windows filled in or left blind to avoid payment of the tax.

Income tax (*see* separate entry), now a major source of revenue for modern states, was a 19th-century development. Recent examples of new types of taxation in Britain are a *capital gains* tax, levied on the profit made on an asset between its purchase and sale, and a *value added* tax levied as a percentage of value added at each stage of production.

Adam Smith (*see* separate entry) in his *Wealth of Nations* (1776) laid down four guiding rules for taxation. These were: (1) equality – subjects should support the state according to their ability; (2) certainty, not arbitrariness; (3) convenience of payment; (4) economy of collection. Since then, at least three different schools of thought have emerged. These may be summarised as follows: that taxation should be designed purely to raise the revenue required by the expenditure to be met; that it should be used as an instrument to promote social justice; and that it should be used as a part of general economic policy to promote stability. In practice, much of modern taxation arises from a combination of these principles.

Resistance to taxation has been a powerful motive for many great events. A few examples must suffice. Magna Carta (1215) and the Bill of Rights (1689), although now rightly regarded as landmarks in England's constitutional history, were much more the result of a dislike for arbitrary taxation than of any lofty constitutional principles. Again, in the 18th century, the principle of "no taxation without representation" played a large part in the events which led up to the War of American Independence. The French Revolution was also to a large extent caused by a chaotic and inequitable system of taxation.

See separate entries for AMERICAN INDEPENDENCE, WAR OF; BILL OF RIGHTS; FRENCH REVOLUTION; MAGNA CARTA.

Taxi, Cab: car carrying passengers for a fee, either agreed upon beforehand or measured by a taximeter fitted inside. The origin of the word is uncertain, but one interesting suggestion connects it with the ancient German family of Thurn und Taxis who won from the Emperor Maximilian I the right to carry imperial messages.

Tea: dried and processed leaves of a shrub used for making a beverage, or the beverage itself. Tea-drinking appears to have been a general custom in China in the 7th century AD. Tea was introduced into Europe by the Dutch East India Company and at the beginning of the 17th century could be bought in England at £10 a pound. In 1660 Pepys mentioned in his diary that he "did send for a cup of tee, a China drink, of which I had never drunk before".

A London merchant, Thomas Garraway, sold tea, and in 1668 the British East India Company sent one hundred pounds of it to London. Charles II's Queen, Catherine of Braganza, enjoyed it, and so tea became popular in court circles. It continued to be expensive, however, and smugglers frequently brought it into the country. In 1777 Parson Woodforde paid 10s 6d to a smuggler for a pound of tea.

In Victorian times a cheaper tea was imported from India which, although cultivation began there as late as 1836, is now the largest producer in the world. Among other producing countries are Japan, Ceylon, East Africa, Argentina, Paraguay and Rhodesia.

¶ BRAMAH, EDWARD. *Tea and Coffee: Three Hundred Years of Tradition.* 1972; JONES, TREVOR. *Tea.* 1958

See also EAST INDIA COMPANIES.

Technocracy: government by technicians. The word first appeared in the United States in 1932 to denote the views of certain engineers, scientists and sociologists, who held that economic control of the social system should be vested in scientists and engineers rather than in politicians, whom they thought to be incapable of understanding modern conditions.

Tehran Conference (1943): four-day November meeting in Persia at which

Roosevelt and Churchill, representing USA and Britain, and Stalin, the Soviet leader, were present. They discussed the World War II situation and worked out detailed plans to defeat Germany and Italy. The scale and timing of carefully co-ordinated attacks from the south, east and west were agreed.

Tel Aviv: largest town in Israel, on the Mediterranean coast, north of and adjoining Jaffa which, by Tel Aviv's phenomenal growth since its founding by Zionists (*see* ZIONISM) in 1909 as the first all-Jewish community, has now been absorbed into the larger town. It is Israel's main business centre and also boasts outstanding cultural developments – universities, museums, art galleries, theatres and orchestras. *See* ISRAEL for map.

¶ KALIR, M. *et al*, editors. *Tel Aviv's Fifty Years.* 1967

Telecommunications: the sending of signals or messages over a long distance (Greek *tele* = far off) by telegraph, telephone etc.

We shall probably never know who first thought of an electric telegraph. Someone who signed himself "C.M." wrote to the *Scots Magazine* in 1756, suggesting that pith balls, attracted or repelled by electric charges, might be used for remote signalling purposes, but the idea does not seem to have been pursued at the time.

Ten years later the invention of the electric battery made it possible to generate a steady current of electricity, and this in turn made possible a really practical electric telegraph. Thereafter many systems were tried, but proved too expensive because twenty-six wires were required between points – one for each letter of the alphabet. At last, however, the English-

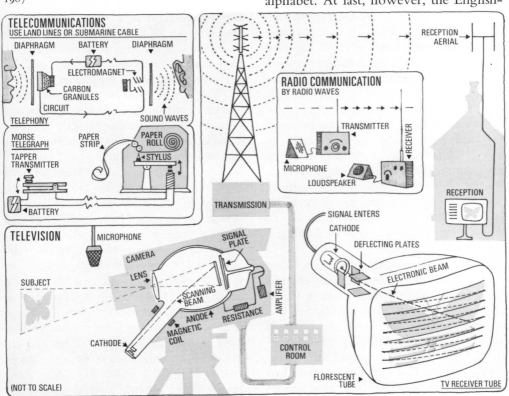

TELECOMMUNICATIONS
USE LAND LINES OR SUBMARINE CABLE
DIAPHRAGM   BATTERY   DIAPHRAGM
ELECTROMAGNET
CARBON GRANULES
CIRCUIT
TELEPHONY   SOUND WAVES
MORSE TELEGRAPH   PAPER STRIP   PAPER ROLL
TAPPER TRANSMITTER   STYLUS
BATTERY

RADIO COMMUNICATION
BY RADIO WAVES
TRANSMITTER
MICROPHONE   RECEIVER
LOUDSPEAKER

RECEPTION AERIAL

RECEPTION

TRANSMISSION

SIGNAL ENTERS
CATHODE
DEFLECTING PLATES
ELECTRONIC BEAM

TELEVISION   MICROPHONE
CAMERA
LENS
SUBJECT
SCANNING BEAM
ANODE   RESISTANCE
MAGNETIC COIL
CATHODE
SIGNAL PLATE
AMPLIFIER
CONTROL ROOM
FLORESCENT TUBE
(NOT TO SCALE)   TV RECEIVER TUBE

men William Fothergill Cooke and Charles Wheatstone managed in 1837 to reduce the number of wires to five, and later both they and Samuel Morse in the USA found means of telegraphing messages over a single wire. The electric telegraph had arrived. In 1845 a Telegraph Company was formed in England and the use of the new telegraphic system spread from city to city and ultimately even to the smallest village. In the USA Samuel Morse, after failing to sell his system to the Government for $10,000 (the Postmaster General having been "uncertain that the revenues could be made equal to the expenditures"), found private backers, and in 1844 a scheme was launched to erect a telegraph line between New York, Baltimore and Washington. Within little more than six years fifty other companies were using Morse's patents in the US.

The next step was to lay cables under the sea to foreign countries. This was tremendously difficult, but by 1851 the first successful cable was in operation between England and France. By 1866, after two unsuccessful attempts, a submarine cable was laid between Newfoundland and what is now Eire. A direct cable between England and India was completed in 1873. The world's longest submarine telephone cable is the Commonwealth Pacific Cable inaugurated in December 1963 and running more than 9,000 miles [14,500 kilometres] from Australia to Canada via Auckland, New Zealand, and the Hawaiian Islands.

By an extraordinary coincidence, on 14 February 1876 two inventors entered the Patents Office at Washington, USA, and registered patents for an electric telephone. One was Alexander Graham Bell (*see* separate entry), a Scot living in the USA, and the other was Elisha Gray, an American. Bell's apparatus proved to be the better, and this, improved out of all recognition, is still in use today. The Bell Telephone Company (to which the inventor gave his name) is now the largest in the world.

The first telephone exchange in London was installed in 1879 and served eight subscribers. As more and more people began to use the telephone, exchanges grew in size and employed large numbers of operators whose task it was to connect one subscriber to another. Over the years, however, the Post Office has introduced automatic exchanges, whereby the action of selecting numbers on the dial of the home telephone activates electromechanical switches at the exchange and connects the caller's telephone to the one he has dialled. At first it was possible to dial only local numbers but now the STD (Subscriber Trunk Dialling) system permits a great number of places throughout the world to be dialled direct. Even the electro-mechanical switching described is going out of date, and the automatic exchanges of the near future will be all-electronic in operation, with the switching accomplished by transistors.

In 1969 there were only two sovereign countries without telephones, Bhutan and Nauru. At one end of the scale was Pitcairn Island with fifteen telephones and at the other the USA with 103,752,000.

Over the years vast improvements have been made in telegraphy and telephony, largely in the amount of information which can be passed over a single line and in the reduction of errors in the messages. Many developments have been brought about by the use of electronic devices such as the thermionic valve and the transistor. These, used in conjunction with the coaxial cable (again, a device originally developed for radio work), now permit a great number of telegraphic or telephonic messages to be sent simultaneously over a single line. The most recent development, now in its experimental stage, is to enclose a radio type of wave in a hollow pipe called a waveguide and to superimpose the signals on this. By such means it is anticipated that ultimately about 200,000 (or possibly more) simultaneous two-way telephone conversations may be carried in one single pipe. Even more complex systems, using special forms of light wave trapped in a pipe, are being considered, and theoretically these could carry far more messages. It is certainly a far cry from the days when twenty-six wires were needed to convey one telegraphic message, or even from the first Bell telephone, when only one conversation could be effected on a single line.

For a number of other methods of communication *see* SIGNALLING.

¶ DE VRIES, LEONARD. *The Book of Telecommunications.* 1962
See also RADIO; TELEVISION.

Tel-el-Amarna: site of the capital city of Akhnaten, the "heretic" pharaoh, and now a small village on the right bank of the River Nile. When he established the worship of Aten, the power of the sun, Akhnaten determined to build a new city free from the influence of the ancient gods of Egypt. He named it *Akhetaten*, meaning "Aten is satisfied", and encouraged architects, painters and sculptors to make it as beautiful as possible, in honour of the god.

After Akhnaten's death the priests of the old gods regained their power. The court returned to Thebes and the new city was deserted. *See colour section.*
See also AKHNATEN; PHARAOHS.

Telescope: optical device for studying distant objects. This instrument seems to have originated in Holland about 1608. At least three different persons have been credited with its invention, but the traditional story is that Hans Lippershey, a spectacle maker, while holding two lenses, one at a short distance behind the other, happened to direct them towards the steeple of a neighbouring church and was astonished to find that the steeple appeared to be nearer. He afterwards fitted the lenses at opposite ends of a tube and thus constructed the first telescope. He does not appear to have thought of using it as an astronomical instrument, but in 1609 news of it reached Galileo, who constructed several telescopes having a convex objective and a concave eyepiece. This form is still found in the modern opera glass, as it gives an erect image. The largest of his telescopes was little more than an inch [26 mm] in diameter, but the astronomical discoveries he made with it included the mountains of the Moon, the phases of Venus, the satellites of Jupiter, the starry background of the Milky Way and the shapes of spots on the Sun.

In 1611, in his *Dioptrice*, Kepler recommended the use of a convex eyepiece, and the development of this, which is the modern type of refracting telescope, is due to Christiaan Huyghens, who, on 28 November 1659, used it to make the first drawing of Mars.

The reflecting telescope was invented by Newton, who presented one to the Royal Society in London in 1671. In this type the eyepiece is situated in the curved wall of the tube. In 1672 Cassegrain invented a reflecting telescope in which the eyepiece is at the end of the tube. Early instruments had their reflectors wrongly shaped. The shape which gives the best results is a paraboloid or revolution, and this was introduced by Hadley in 1723. Towards the end of the 18th century William Herschel began to make really large instruments of this type. In 1781 he discovered the planet Uranus, using a reflector of aperture 6½ inches [166 mm]. In 1789 he completed an instrument of aperture 4 feet [1·2 m]. Modern instruments of this type include those at Mount Wilson and Mount Palomar, California, of diameters 100 and 200 inches [2,560 and 5,120 mm], respectively. Early reflectors were made of a copper–tin alloy, which soon tarnished and required repolishing, but were later made of glass coated with a thin film of silver. About 1930 a process was devised for making reflectors of glass covered with aluminium; mirrors of this type may last up to ten years without renewal.

Newton developed the reflecting telescope because in the early refracting types the image became distorted as the light passed through the lens, causing a chaotic mixture of colours. This defect was put right by an Englishman, Chester Moor Hall, who constructed the first achromatic telescope in 1733. This was further developed by John Dolland. The object glass of such an instrument is made of two different kinds of glass, a convex lens of crown glass combined with a concave lens of flint glass. Refracting telescopes have so far been made with apertures up to 40 inches [1,020 mm], including the 62-foot [19 metres] long example at the Yerkes Observatory, USA, the largest of this type in the world.

An important recent development has been the radio telescope for studying radio signals of cosmic origin (see RADIO ASTRONOMY). The largest in the world is at Chuguyev, USSR, covering an area of just over 37 acres [15 hectares].

¶ KING, H. C. History of the Telescope. 1955
See also GALILEO; HUYGHENS; KEPLER; NEWTON; ROYAL SOCIETY.

Television: transmission and reception of visual images by electromagnetic waves. The "eye" of a television camera is a device called a camera tube. In one type of tube the image of a scene is focused on a flat plate which consists of a mosaic composed of millions of little specks of a photo–electric substance – that is, material which alters its electrical characteristics in accordance with the amount of light falling on it. The effect of the image falling on this mosaic is to produce a pattern of electric charges on a glass target plate which is mounted close to it. This pattern is an electrical image of the scene being televised.

From the far end of the tube an electron beam is made to sweep or scan the target methodically in a series of lines, one below the other, so that the beam makes contact with each charged point in turn. This neutralises the charge at that point and in doing so decreases the number of electrons in that portion of the beam. Thus a white part of the scene will cause a relatively large charge on the target plate which in turn will, in being neutralised, rob the beam of a considerable number of electrons at that instant.

The electron beam is made to bounce back from the target plate, but, whereas before impact with the target there was constant density of electrons in the beam, the return beam shows a variation of electron numbers along its length; in other words, a variation in current. This, after passing through a special amplifier in the camera tube, emerges as a train of electrical signals, each variation in which represents the amount of light reflected from one point of the televised scene.

These video signals, as they are called, are amplified still more and then superimposed on to a radio frequency carrier wave for radiation throughout the service area of the station.

In the home receiver the picture is displayed on a cathode ray tube. The glass screen is the end wall of the tube and is coated on its inner surface with phosphors which have the property of emitting white light when bombarded with electrons. The greater the bombardment, the brighter the light.

At the back of the tube an electron gun is mounted. This shoots a beam of electrons toward the phosphor coating, which produces a bright spot at its point of impact. The beam, however, is caused to scan rapidly to and fro across the screen in exactly the same way as the target plate is swept in the camera tube and precisely in step with it. (Special signals are transmitted to keep the receiver scanning in step with that occurring in the camera tube.)

In the receiver, the video signals are separated from the carrier and after amplification are used to control the strength of the cathode ray tube electron beam. When a white point on the studio scene is being transmitted, the video signal will be correspondingly strong and so the receiver's electron beam will also be strong, producing a brilliant white spot on the screen. A black point will produce no video signal and consequently the receiver's electron beam will be cut off, producing no glow in the phosphor. All variations of light between the maximum and minimum reflected from the studio scene will be reproduced in terms of black-and-white on the receiver screen.

Although only one spot at a time is being illuminated on the receiver screen, the electron beam traverses the screen at such a fast rate that the eye is deceived into seeing the rapid sequence of spots as a complete picture. When one complete scan is completed the whole process begins again and another picture is built up. Again, the eye is deceived, because the pictures follow one another so rapidly that we get the illusion of seeing one picture which has movement in it.

Colour television makes use of the fact that three coloured lights (usually red, green and blue) can be combined in suitable proportions to produce most other colours, including white. The colour camera contains three camera tubes (sometimes four) one of which is masked by a red filter, one by a green and one by a blue. Thus the video signals from these tubes represent, respectively, the red, green and blue content of the televised scene as three separate signals. A very complex process is used to superimpose these signals on to a radio frequency carrier for transmission to the home receiver.

At the receiver the cathode ray tube contains three electron guns, one for dealing with each colour signal. This time the screen is composed of millions of phosphor dots in groups of three. On impact by an electron beam, one dot emits red light, another green and a third blue.

As before, the video signals, on arrival at the receiver, are separated from the carrier. Each is fed to its appropriate gun and is used to control the strength of its beam. It is so arranged that each gun can illuminate only those phosphor dots which correspond to its colour control signal – that is, the red signal gun can only illuminate red phosphor dots, and so on. Thus, as with the black-and-white process, a strong video signal from a red part of the transmitted picture will cause a bright red spot to appear on the receiver screen at the right point, and similarly with green and blue portions. As the phosphor dots are microscopic and extremely close together, the eye blends the colours to form pinks, browns, yellows and so on, according to the proportions of brightness of the red, green and blue dots.

The sound to accompany the television programmes is produced in the same way as has been described in the earlier section on radio and is transmitted as part of the overall television carrier wave. Colour transmissions are so arranged that the owner of a black-and-white set will receive the colour picture in black-and-white.

¶ ROBERTS, FREDERICK. *Television.* 1964

See also RADIO; TELECOMMUNICATIONS.

Telford, Thomas (1757–1834): civil engineer of Scottish birth. At a time when the Industrial Revolution was demanding better transport for its raw materials and finished products, he was responsible for the improvement of many roads and harbours, particularly in Scotland, and the development of canals in Great Britain, railways being still in the future. He constructed the Caledonian canal from sea to sea through the highlands of Scotland to take sea-going ships of the size then in general use, and the similar Gotha canal from the Baltic to the North Sea for the Swedes. The suspension bridge carrying the road over the Menai Straits, between the Isle of Anglesey and the Welsh mainland, is another monument to his skill. He was also responsible

for the Conway Bridge, for the Ponteysulte aqueduct near Llangollen (one of the finest examples of the canal age) and for St Katherine's Docks, London.

See colour section.

¶ MEYNELL, LAURENCE. *Thomas Telford.* 1957

The temple as it appeared in 33 AD.

Temple of Jerusalem: for 1,000 years the religious centre of the Jews. The first Temple was built by King Solomon (ruled *c.* 970–*c.* 933 BC) and destroyed by the Babylonians in 586. The second was started in 520 and was enlarged and beautified by Herod the Great (ruled 37–4 BC). This was the Temple known to Jesus, who foretold its total destruction, which took place in AD 70, when the city was reduced to ruins by the Romans. A Muslim shrine now occupies the site.

See also BABYLON; HEROD; JESUS CHRIST; MUSLIMS; SOLOMON.

Tène, La: Iron Age (*see* separate entry) culture flourishing in Europe from the 5th to the 1st century BC. La Tène culture took its name from a settlement on Lake Neuchâtel, Switzerland, containing many iron weapons decorated with tendril ornamentation. The same motif, the S shape, producing continuous waves and spirals, was found in Celtic art, and helped in identifying the far-ranging movements of Celtic tribes over Germany, France, Switzerland, Hungary, Britain and Ireland.

Left: La Tène carving on iron showing s-shaped motif. Above: Pierced metal work chariot piece from the Somme-Bionne Burial, France.

La Tène culture was first developed by the Celtic peoples in the Middle Rhine region and the Marne area of France, where a wine-drinking warrior aristocracy traded with the Mediterranean wine regions, especially Greece and Etruria (*see* separate entry). This led to the introduction of the Etruscan two-wheel chariot, and the flowering of a magnificent decorative art. In the rich Celtic barrows were found gold and silver ware, shields, jewellery, mirrors and pottery, ornamented with the flowering arabesques of the new style.

Tennessee Valley Authority: founded in 1933 as part of F. D. Roosevelt's (*see* separate entry) New Deal economic programme; a central agency of the US government for controlling and developing the resources of the Tennessee valley states – Tennessee, Alabama, Georgia, Kentucky, Mississippi, North Carolina and Virginia. Its responsibilities include flood control, electric power, afforestation, navigation and fisheries. The venture has been called "the greatest development in large-scale social planning in the United States" and over a period raised the income level of the inhabitants by 75 per cent compared with a general increase in the country of 56 per cent.

Teresa of Avila, St (1515–82): Spanish nun and reformer. Teresa became a Carmelite nun at the age of twenty-one. The Order had originally been very austere, but the rule had become more lax. She determined to restore its strictness and began her reforms while Prioress of the convent of St Joseph, Avila.

Her ideas were unpopular, but she was a woman whose strong personality and great intelligence attracted likeminded nuns. She was witty and lively and wrote several books. Much of her correspondence has been preserved.

Teutonic: adjective associated with north German peoples. Originally they were Teutons, a tribe who migrated from the North Sea coast to central Europe before being defeated by the Romans. Later the name was given to all Germans, and particularly to a famous group of Knights formed during the Crusades.

Textiles: woven fabrics or fibres suitable for weaving. Primitive man used hides for clothing and warmth, but animal skins were stiff, hot and uncomfortable to wear. It was found that natural fibres – silk, wool, linen and cotton – could be spun into thread and woven into cloth on a wooden frame known as a loom. The spinning and weaving processes did not involve physical strength so in tribal communities were usually done by the women.

The Chinese are thought to have woven silk cloth as early as the second millennium BC. Linen was used in Egypt 5,000 years before the Christian era, cotton in India and Persia about 3000 BC and woollen cloth in Scandinavia and Switzerland during the Bronze Age. In South America cloth woven from llama wool was worn in the year AD 1000 and probably earlier.

The first woven cloths were made very simply, by darning thread wound on a shuttle under and over other threads stretched on the loom. Some looms stood upright, others were horizontal. The finished cloth was usually left in its original colour, although sometimes people tinted it with vegetable dyes.

About 200 BC the Chinese invented a method of weaving patterns into silk, and patterned material dating from the 4th century AD has been found in Egyptian tombs. Patterned silk from Byzantium and Damascus (*see* separate entry) was introduced into Europe in the 7th century, when it was carried by caravans of traders across Asia to Constantinople. For the first time Europeans began to consider silkworm rearing and the manufacture of silk; the Norman conquerors of Sicily established silk workshops there. Silk was also made in southern France.

Northern Europe was more concerned with woollen cloth. Wool from England was exported to the Netherlands to be made up into cloth by the skilful Flemish weavers. Later, English weavers learned to make cloth. Many of the medieval guilds were connected with spinning and weaving, and women usually did the spinning – hence the term "spinster".

In the 16th century there was a great vogue for Persian silks woven with lifelike pictures of flowers, birds and animals. These were copied in Italy and used as wall hangings. The Netherlands were famed for woven table linen and special sets were designed for wealthy buyers. Henry VIII possessed tablecloths made to his order by Belgian weavers.

Cotton was introduced to Europe from India during the 17th century. England, France and Holland had all established

Persian brocade in coloured silk on yellow satin ground, 16th century.

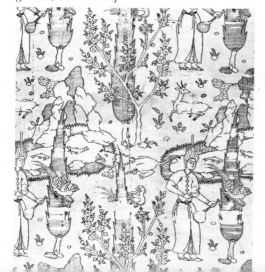

American roller-printed cotton, 1835–40.

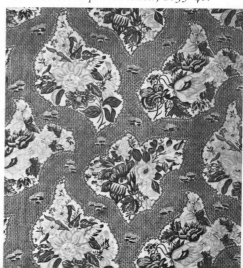

trading companies in India and many textures and varieties of cotton were among their exports. By 1710 colonists in the southern part of North America had discovered that the climate was suitable for the cultivation of the cotton plant. The soft, fluffy heads – cotton wool – were picked by slaves, baled and sent across the Atlantic to be spun and woven into cloth, just as English wool had been shipped to the Netherlands 600 years before. In England this spinning and weaving was done in the homes of villagers, frequently in Lancashire.

Some silk cloth was made in England, but it was very expensive. For years there has been a flourishing silk industry in France. During the religious wars of the 16th century many of the weavers fled and some settled in Spitalfields, London, which became the centre of a small silk industry.

The 18th century in England saw that phenomenon known as the Industrial Revolution (*see* separate entry). Once it

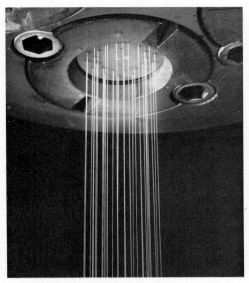

Spinning 100 denier nylon in Courtaulds modern factory.

was discovered that machinery could be worked by water power, or later by steam, far more efficiently than by manpower, all kinds of inventions appeared, some more successful than others. Many

Immediately after spinning, viscose rayon yarn is strengthened by a process of stretching it while immersed in hot water.

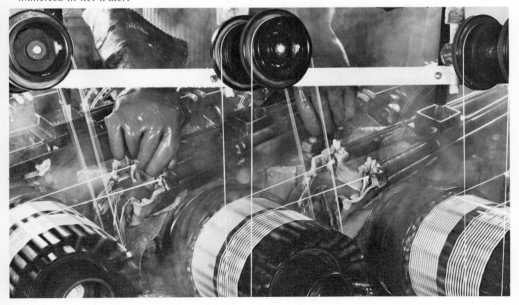

affected textiles. Kay's *flying shuttle*, Arkwright's (*see* separate entry) *spinning jenny* and Crompton's *mule* all made it possible to produce large quantities of cloth in factories far more quickly and cheaply than by a hand loom at home. These inventions could also be applied to wool, and northern England became a centre for cheap cloth, cotton in Lancashire and wool in Yorkshire. There was also a considerable textile industry in Derbyshire, Nottinghamshire and Leicestershire. Factory owners made fortunes, and until the end of World War I (*see* separate entry) England was the world centre for the manufacture of cotton and woollen goods, a position later rivalled by Japan.

It was cheaper to print patterns on to cloth than to weave the design into the fabric. The Egyptians had known how to do this in very early times, but the process was not introduced into Europe until the 12th century AD. In the 17th century the Italians began to print patterns on cotton imported from India, and the idea spread. A large block was made, usually from wood, and a design cut into it. This was impregnated with dye and stamped by hand on to a roll of material, forming a repeating pattern. The great disadvantage was that when the fabric was washed the colours blurred, but chemists discovered ways of fixing them.

Colour printing by hand was a slow process. In 1783 Thomas Bell, an Englishman, invented a method by which the design could be engraved on rollers and the length of cotton passed mechanically between them. By 1820 *roller printing* was in general use in Lancashire. In 1856 a chemist named Perkins experimented with *aniline dyes*. The colours were harsher than those of vegetable dyes, but, because they were more durable, manufacturers used them. By the close of the 19th century Lancashire mills were turning out quantities of cotton cloth in coarse colours. William Morris (*see* separate entry), an artist and writer, tried to improve standards, urging a return to handprinting textiles with vegetable dyes.

Man-made fibres are of two kinds: *regenerated* types such as rayon, made from natural fibrous materials dissolved and then forced through fine holes before solidifying; and *synthetic* types produced by submitting chemical compounds to polymerisation, i.e. a chemical reaction in which two or more molecules react to form larger molecules until a long chain of identical units results.

During World War I *artificial silk* was invented – a fibre made by a chemical process. It was cheap to produce but had many disadvantages. Garments made from it tended to lose their shape easily. But scientists continued to experiment with man-made fibres and in 1935 the first *nylon* of serious commercial interest was produced. The world's first factory began production in 1940 in the USA. Nylon fabrics are more successful than artificial silk, but they lack the warmth and flexibility of cloth made from natural fibres. The term "nylon" covers a whole range of fibres. *See colour section.*

¶ PAGE, C. E. *Textiles*. 1965; *Textiles* (Macdonald's Junior Reference Library). 1969

See also COTTON; DYEING; LOOM; TAPESTRY; WEAVING; WOOL.

Thailand, Siam: kingdom in south-east Asia. The earliest kingdom of Siam was set up in the 13th century, with its capital at Ayutthaya. The Siamese expanded and several times occupied Angkor, capital of Cambodia. Hindu influence became strong and the king of Siam was hailed as divine. The Portuguese, Dutch, English and French made some contacts with Siam in the 16th and early 17th centuries. Ayutthaya was destroyed by the Burmese in 1767 and Bangkok presently became the capital. Rama IV (reigned 1851–68) established diplomatic relations with the western powers and he and his successor introduced many western innovations. Siam's security depended on a balance between Britain and France. The period 1893–1909 was one of lengthy negotiations (involving various boundary revisions, ceding of territories, treaties, etc.) between Siam, France and England, eventually resulting in greater stability for Siam and freedom to concentrate on internal reforms and trade expansion. In the 1930s Japan took over some of France's influence. From 1935 the dominant figure in Siam was Field Marshal Pibul Songgram, at first defence minister and then prime minister (1938–44), through World War II and a period of Japanese dominance. In power again from 1947, Pibul Songgram experimented with several forms of constitution. Finally out of office in 1957, he was succeeded by other army chiefs. The name of the kingdom became Thailand in 1949. It joined the United Nations in 1946 and SEATO in 1954. With frontier disputes and guerrilla activities within Thailand, fears of Chinese communist infiltration threw the Thai government into dependence on aid from the USA. Thai troops entered the war in South Vietnam in 1967.

See ENDPAPERS for map.

¶ WATSON, JANE WERNER. *Thailand: Rice Bowl of Asia.* 1968

See also SEATO; UNITED NATIONS.

Thanksgiving Day: the last Thursday in November, set aside annually in the USA for commemorating the good harvest of the Pilgrim Fathers (1621; *see* separate entry) and as a general thanksgiving for God's mercies. Thanksgiving days were celebrated in the 17th century in a number of the early colonies and the practice continued spasmodically till President Lincoln (*see* separate entry), in 1864, appointed the last Thursday in November, each president since following the example by annual proclamation.

Thebes: ancient city of Upper Egypt, on the River Nile. During the 18th dynasty of pharaohs, and for a brief period of two centuries before them, Thebes was the chief city of Egypt.

Ahmose I, who drove out the Hyksos (*see* separate entry) about 1,500 years before the Christian era, came from Thebes, so he and his descendants made it their capital. They attributed their rise to power to *Amon*, the local deity, and caused him to be ranked with the greatest gods of Egypt. Eventually the Theban priests became so powerful that they virtually ruled the kingdom.

Thebes was the religious as well as the secular capital of the country. The government was carried on from there, great temples were built to honour Amon, and in Western Thebes the pharaohs were buried in concealed rock tombs in the Valley of Kings. Later, the countryside round Thebes was the scene of the earliest experiments in Christian monasticism. The city itself was destroyed by an earthquake in 27 BC. The ancient site is now occupied by the villages of Luxor and Karnak.

The great temple at Karnak, itself a ruin, stands on the site of the ancient city of Thebes.

Thebes (now Thiva) was also the name of the chief city of Boeotia, which for a time in the 4th century BC occupied a leading position among the states of Greece.

Themistocles (*c.* 525–*c.* 460 BC): Athenian statesman. He laid the foundations of the naval power of Athens, which crushed the Persian fleet at Salamis in 480 and which later secured her supremacy in Greek waters for many years. After Salamis, however, his intense suspicion of Sparta led him to intrigue with the Persians of Ionia, and he died in exile.
¶ In *Plutarch. Ten Famous Lives*, edited C. ROBINSON. 1963
See also SALAMIS, etc.

Thermometer: instrument for measuring temperature. The familiar type of thermometer, using alcohol as the liquid, seems to have been brought into use by the Grand Duke Ferdinand II of Tuscany as early as 1654. The liquid is inserted in a tube with a very small bore and expands or contracts with variations in temperature. In 1714 Fahrenheit (*see* separate entry) invented the mercury-in-glass thermometer and his scale of temperature. In 1730 the French physicist de Réaumur invented a scale of temperature in which the freezing point of water is $0°$ and boiling point $80°$. The international centigrade scale was originally proposed by the Swedish astronomer Celsius (1701–44). A mercury thermometer cannot be used for temperatures below $-40°C$, because of the freezing of the mercury. Mercury has a normal boiling point of $357°C$, but the range of a mercury thermometer can be increased to about $570°C$ by filling the upper part of the stem with an inert gas. Alcohol thermometers can be used down to about $-110°C$ and are useful for meteorological work. In order to measure higher temperatures various forms of gas

thermometer were evolved in the 19th century.

Thermopylae: name of a narrow pass in north-western Greece between the mountains and the sea. Here, in 480 BC, the invading Persian army was held up by Leonidas with a small force of 300 Spartans. The enemy, using a mountain path, surrounded them, and they were annihilated. *See also* PERSIAN WARS.

Third Reich (1933–45): official name which the Nazi Party gave to its rule in Germany from January 1933. Reich means "empire". The first had been the Holy Roman Empire, the second Bismarck's Empire (*see* BISMARCK, OTTO) which collapsed in 1918. The term "Third Reich" appeared in Germany in the mid-1920s and was quickly accepted by politicians, who looked back with regret at former glories. The Third Reich, officially proclaimed early in 1934, ended with Germany's defeat in 1945.
See also NAZI; WORLD WAR II.

Thirteen Colonies, The: the early American colonies which afterwards formed the United States of America. These may be considered in three groups, those of Virginia, New York and New England.

The *Virginia* group owes its name to Sir Walter Ralegh, who named an unsuccessful settlement, abandoned in 1586, after Elizabeth I of England, the "Virgin Queen". The first permanent English settlement came on the James River in 1607, when the three ships *Sarah Constant*, *Godspeed* and *Discovery* arrived with a company of 105 colonists. *Maryland*, originally a part of Virginia, was named after Charles I's queen, Henrietta Maria. It became a separate colony under royal charter in 1632. *North* and *South Carolina* originated in the Carolinas, named by

French settlers in honour of Charles IX of France. The name was bestowed afresh by Charles II of England, who granted the settlements to eight different groups of proprietors. The arrangement proved unworkable and the colonists reorganised themselves into two governments. *Georgia*, originally part of the Carolinas, was founded in 1732 by Colonel James Oglethorpe as a refuge for debtors and Protestant dissenters from English prisons.

New England colonies were first named by Captain John Smith, who made one of two unsuccessful attempts to establish a settlement in the area. In 1620 the Pilgrim Fathers founded a permanent colony and new settlements developed at *New Hampshire* (1622), *Massachusetts* (1628), *Rhode Island* (1631) and *Connecticut* (1633).

The New York group consisted of *New York, New Jersey, Pennsylvania* and *Delaware*. New Amsterdam, which began as a trading station of the Dutch West India Company, was granted to James, Duke of York, by Charles II of England in 1664 and renamed New York, and the district between the Hudson and Delaware Rivers became New Jersey. Pennsylvania (named after William Penn, though he was strongly opposed to the idea) was purchased by Penn from Charles II and founded as a Quaker colony in 1682. Delaware, also ceded to Penn and originally attached to Pennsylvania, became a separate state in 1776, having the distinction of being the first state of the USA.

In chronological order of becoming states of the Union, from 1787 to 1790, the list is Delaware, Pennsylvania, New Jersey, Georgia, Connecticut, Massachusetts, Maryland, South Carolina, New Hampshire, Virginia, New York, North Carolina and Rhode Island.

¶ BROWN, GEORGE W., HARMAN, ELEANOR and JEANNERET, MARSH. *The American Colonies: Canada and the U.S.A. before 1800.* 1962

See also INDIVIDUAL ENTRIES.

Thirteenth century: the years 1201–1300. One historian says that "as we cross the threshold of the 13th century the dream of world dominion, which had died with an Emperor, springs to life again in the policy of a Pope". This refers to Innocent III, who became Pope in 1198 at the early age of thirty-seven. His reign marks the summit of the temporal power of the Papacy. He excommunicated the Emperor Otto IV, placed England and France under an interdict, secured from the rulers of England, Aragon and Portugal the surrender of their countries as fiefs of the Holy See, and imposed the rule of the Western Church on Constantinople. All this was done in only eighteen years.

This century saw the age of eastern imperialism, with the ruthless Mongol hordes of Genghis Khan sweeping over North China and vast territories in Asia and Asia Minor and threatening, as Attila the Hun had previously threatened, to flood over Europe and submerge western civilisation. The West was so preoccupied with its internal quarrels that it did not appreciate its peril until it was almost too late. In fact, it was an accident of history rather than any dramatic concerted policy by its ill-organised opponents that the overwhelming threat from the East receded, not to return, a pale imitation, till the "Yellow Peril" movement of the 19th century.

In Europe one of the outstanding figures was the Holy Roman Emperor, Frederick II (1194-1250), "the World's Wonder", a complex and brilliant ruler whose achievements included the leadership of the Sixth Crusade, in the course of which he set the crown of Jerusalem on his head, and the establishment of a Court at Palermo where Christian, Jewish and Muslim scholars rubbed shoulders in academic harmony.

As in every century, institutions, dynasties, modes and movements changed, died, were born. The Latin Empire, set up after the Fourth Crusade and based on Constantinople, fell to pieces after a brief and inglorious existence of half a century. The Hohenstaufen line of kings and emperors, which had included Frederick I ("Barbarossa") and Frederick II, ended with the decapitation of Conrad IV in 1268.

This period saw also the foundation of the Franciscan and Dominican orders of friars in 1208 and 1215, respectively. During the century their influence spread all over Europe, and even beyond it, bringing with it a religious revival. Mention should be made, too, of ecclesiastical architecture, in which notable progress was made during the century. There was a movement away from the heavy building of the Norman period to a lighter style, typified in England by the Angel Choir of Lincoln, and the Cathedrals of

Salisbury and Wells, while in France the same style was executed on an even grander scale, of which Amiens Cathedral is a good example. In the field of education, the earliest European university, Naples, was founded in 1224, and in England University College and Merton College at Oxford and Peterhouse College at Cambridge had their foundations.

In England the century is one of vast importance for its constitutional developments – developments which were to prove of incalculable significance in later world history. In 1215 we have Magna Carta, about which many different opinions have been expressed, ranging from those which regard it as "the palladium of English liberties" to the view of it as nothing more than an attempt at feudal reaction by a few barons acting with entirely selfish motives. The legal historian Maitland says of Edward I

(1239-1307): "In Edward's day, all becomes definite – there is the Parliament of the three estates, there is the King's Council, there are the well-known Courts of law." By this time the *Curia Regis* (the King's Court) had definitely split up into separate parts of clearly differentiated functions. The Exchequer had appeared in the previous century, but we now have also the Court of King's Bench, which followed the king on his travels, and the Court of Common Pleas, which decided suits between subject and subject not amounting to a breach of the peace; Magna Carta established that it should meet "in some certain place", i.e. at Westminster. By the time of the Model Parliament of 1295 the foundations of the modern Parliament had been laid, that "Mother of Parliaments", in John Bright's felicitous phrase, that in after centuries was to nurture so many offspring all over the world. *See colour section.*

¶ DUGGAN, ALFRED. *Growing Up in the Thirteenth Century.* 1962; POWICKE, SIR M. *The Thirteenth Century, 1216–1307.* 1962

See also INDIVIDUAL ENTRIES.

Thirty Years War: political and religious struggle over the years 1618-48. The struggle, consisting really of a series of wars, was caused fundamentally by the growth of Calvinism (the strictly Protestant religion which spread throughout France and Switzerland during the sixteenth century and which was unrecognised by the Religious Peace of Augsburg, 1555), by continuing Protestant seizure of Church property, by the increasing strength of the Counter-Reformation, and by the crystallisation of the opposing forces into the Calvinist Union, under Christian of Anhalt, and the Catholic League, under Maximilian of Bavaria. The occasion was the revolt of Bohemian nobles against their elected king, Ferdinand of Styria, and his replacement by the Calvinist Frederick, Elector Palatine, which seriously unbalanced the body of Electors, to Catholic disadvantage. (For Calvinism, *see* REFORMATION.)

The first (Bohemian) war, 1618-24, saw Mansfeld, a soldier of fortune leading a Protestant army, defeated in the Palatinate, Christian defeated at White Hill, outside Prague, and the departure of Frederick (the "Winter King"), now dispossessed of all his lands, to the Netherlands.

Protestant fears roused by this Catholic success brought about an alliance of the Northern Protestant Union with Denmark and England, an apparently formidable league which fought imperial forces, led by the Holy Roman Emperor Ferdinand III, in the second (Danish) war, 1625-29. The Emperor was saved by the army created by Wallenstein, which defeated Mansfeld at Dessau and the Danes at Lutter, and was not checked until the siege of Stralsund, after which peace was made at Lübeck.

The victorious Emperor then issued the Edict of Restitution, ordering the return of all Church lands "secularised" since 1552. This offended Wallenstein, who was dismissed and disbanded his army, leaving the Emperor militarily weak just as the Swedish King, Gustavus Adolphus (*see* separate entry), began his incursion into Germany, supported later (1631, Treaty of Barwalde) by France. The third (Swedish) war which followed saw the terrible sack of Magdeburg by Imperial troops (1629), Gustavus's victories at Breitenfeld and Lechfeld and his victorious march to the Rhineland and then to Bavaria. The Emperor then recalled Wallenstein, who met Gustavus on the field of Lützen where, though the Swedes had the advantage, their king was killed (1632). The war continued but the Swedes were overwhelmingly defeated at Nordlingen, 1634, and peace was made the following year at Prague.

It was to France's interest to continue the war, though first results were poor. The tide really turned with the defeat of the Spaniards by the brilliant young Duc d'Enghien (later "the great Condé") at Rocroi, 1643. The Spanish general the Count of Fuentes, over eighty years old and crippled with gout, calmly and gallantly met his end in the chair from which he had been directing the battle in the midst of his choicest troops. Later campaigns wore down the Emperor, and peace was at last made (Treaties of Westphalia) granting recognition to Calvinism, substantial territorial gains to France, Sweden and Brandenburg, and independence to Holland and Switzerland.

¶ STEINBERG, S. H. *The Thirty Years War*. 1966; WEDGWOOD, C. V. *The Thirty Years War*. 1938

See also SEVENTEENTH CENTURY.

Thomas Aquinas, St (*c.* 1225–74): teacher whose writings have profoundly influenced the Church. He was born in southern Italy of noble family and became a Dominican. He pursued his early studies chiefly at the university of Paris, with an interlude at Cologne, but his last years brought him back to Italy, though his body rests at Toulouse (France). One theme of his message, in his *Summa Theologica*, the most famous of his many works, was an attempt to reconcile the principles of Christian belief with a philosophical explanation of the operations of the human intellect, and for this purpose he drew largely on the teaching of the Greek philosopher Aristotle (384–322 BC). His friends called him "The Angelic Doctor": his enemies, "The Dumb Ox of Cologne".

¶ PITTINGER, NORMAN. *St. Thomas Aquinas: the Angelic Doctor*. 1969

Tibet: a country of high tableland and mountains, bordered by China, Pakistan, India and Nepal. Its considerable military power up to the 10th century was altered to spiritual influence with the development of government by Buddhist priests, headed by the Dalai Lama (supposedly reincarnated after each death since 1494).

In the 18th century the Chinese established control and closed the country to Europeans for over a century. But in 1903–04 a British expedition under Sir Francis Younghusband forced a treaty on the Tibetans, and in 1911 the revolution in China enabled Tibet to throw the Chinese out. Thereafter relations with Britain improved, Tibet even offering 1,000 troops to fight in World War I (*see* separate entry), inviting a British representative to Lhasa in 1920 and allowing expeditions to climb Mount Everest (*see* separate entry).

Tibetan independence was again destroyed in 1950 by a Chinese invasion which drove out the Dalai Lama and imposed complete military and administrative control.

See ENDPAPERS for map.

¶ RICHARDSON, H. E. *Tibet and Its History*. 1962

Tigris, River: river of Mesopotamia, flowing south-east for more than 1,000 miles [1,600 kilometres] from Turkey until it joins the River Euphrates. Two great cities have been built on the Tigris: Nineveh, the capital of the Assyrians, was destroyed in 612 BC, but Baghdad became a centre of Arab and Persian culture after AD 762, and is now capital of Iraq. *See* MESOPOTAMIA for map.

¶ MEADE, G. E. *Tigris and Euphrates*. 1963

See also BAGHDAD; EUPHRATES; MESOPOTAMIA; NINEVEH.

Timbuktu, Timbuctoo: isolated town in Mali, West Africa, on the fringe of the Sahara, 9 miles [14·5 kilometres] north of a navigable stretch of the River Niger at Kabara. In the Middle Ages (*see* separate

entry) it was an important junction of caravan trade routes from Algeria and Morocco to the south and from the 14th to the 16th century was a centre of Islamic trade and culture (*see* ISLAM). Captured by the French in 1895 and fortified, it was demilitarised in 1923 but remained under French rule until 1960 when Mali became an independent state.
See AFRICA for map.

Timur, Tamerlane (*c.* 1336–1405): Tartar conqueror who was born near Samarkand and threw himself into tribal politics. By 1369 he had made himself the sole ruler of Turkestan and set out on a series of conquests. His forces reached the Caspian Sea, subdued most of Persia and defeated the Golden Horde (*see* TARTARS). In 1398 he invaded India and sacked Delhi, defeated the Turks in 1402 and, when he died in 1405, was preparing to invade China. Though his immense energy and resounding victories created a legend and shook every country bordering on Turkestan, he did not found a lasting empire.

Tithe: tax, originally a tenth of agricultural produce, etc., almost universal in the ancient world from Greece to China. Samuel warned the children of Israel, who wanted a king, "he will take the tenth of your seed and your oliveyards . . . the tenth of your sheep". The term later became attached exclusively to religious dues, and the laws of Charlemagne (*see* separate entry) made tithes compulsory for the maintenance of the clergy.

In England payment in early days was in goods and livestock. The historian G. M. Trevelyan says "the tenth sucking-pig went to the parson's table; the tenth sheaf was carried off to his tithe barn".

The Tithe Commutation Act, 1836, substituted a tithe rent charge for payment in kind: an Act of 1891 made the landowner, not the occupier, responsible for its payment; and in 1936 an Act was passed for the extinction of tithes.

Titian, Tiziano Vecelli (*c.* 1480–1576): Venetian painter. A superb colourist, for luminosity, subtle gradations of tone, and richness of texture Titian achieved paintings that are unsurpassed. A man of the world, his paintings are sensuous rather than spiritual. He lived a long, successful life, the friend of popes and princes. He was one of the earliest painters to recognise landscape as a subject for painting in its own right, not a mere background detail. *See colour section.*
¶ RIPLEY, E. *Titian.* 1962

Tito, Josip Broz (b. 1892): Yugoslav marshal and statesman, president of the federal people's republic of Yugoslavia since 1953. He emerged as leader of the guerilla resistance against German occupation forces 1941–45 and, with liberation, became head of state. He established a communist republic but has showed remarkable individuality and courage in successfully resisting domination by the USSR, preferring to maintain a neutral foreign policy.
¶ ARCHER, J. *Red Rebel: Tito of Yugoslavia.* 1969

Tobacco: dried and cured leaves of a plant of American origin (probably from Spanish *tobaco*, the native name for a pipe). The North American Indians smoked tobacco both in pipes and rolled into cigars. It was introduced into Europe by Spanish explorers, one of whom presented tobacco plants to Philip II (*see* separate entry) in 1558. Jean Nicot, a Frenchman, gave some tobacco to Catherine de' Medici, who is said to have enjoyed it. The word "nicotine" comes from Nicot's surname. Tobacco was known in England in Elizabeth I's reign, when Ralegh (*see* separate entry) probably popularised its use at court. James I detested it and attacked it in *A Counter Blaste to Tobacco*, published in 1604. Portuguese sailors took tobacco to Africa. When Livingstone (*see* separate entry) explored central Africa he found that the natives smoked and that a warrior's pipe was often buried with him.

In modern times the most popular form of smoking has become the cigarette (or "paper cigar"), reputedly first smoked in Britain by the artist George Richmond (1809-96), the oldest actual example being one made *c.* 1885 and preserved in a New York collection. It was calculated that in 1967 528,000 million cigarettes were smoked in the USA alone. The 1968 figure for the United Kingdom was 2,980 cigarettes for each adult. Recently very considerable evidence has been produced to show a direct connection between cigarette-smoking and certain respiratory diseases, including lung cancer, and intensive advertising and instructional anti-smoking campaigns have been conducted, with unfortunately small results.

Togo: republic lying between Ghana and Dahomey in West Africa, with a seaboard of thirty-five miles [56·3 kilometres] on the Gulf of Guinea. It was part of the German Colony of Togoland from 1884 until World War I (*see* separate entry) and from 1920 was administered by France under a League of Nations mandate.

It became an independent republic within the French Community in November 1958 and attained full independence in 1960. The economy is mainly agricultural, the principal exports being cocoa, coffee, copra, cotton and palm kernels. The production of phosphates by a Franco-American consortium provides one-third of the export revenue.
See AFRICA for map.

Tokyo: capital of Japan, the world's most populous city, passing the ten

million mark in 1962 – the first urban area in history to do so. In 1590 the village of Edo was made a provincial capital and grew into a substantial city. In 1868 Edo became the imperial capital of Japan and its name was altered to Tokyo. Earthquake and fires destroyed the city in 1923, but it was resolutely rebuilt. Heavy bombing during World War II (*see* separate entry) again destroyed much of the city, but a new influx of population from lost overseas territories, industrialisation and a high birthrate has caused acute problems of urban organisation and planning.
See JAPAN for map.
¶ KIRKUP, J. *Tokyo.* 1966

Toledo: city on rock in a bend of the Tagus, Spain. In AD 453 it became capital of the Visigoths. Betrayed to the Moors in 712, it became a centre of sword-making and weaving. Its recapture by Alfonzo VI of Castile in 1085 was the first success in the Christian reconquest of Spain. It then became the meeting place of Muslim, Jewish and Christian scholars, where Gerard of Cremona (1114–87) translated Arabic texts of Greek medical and geographical works. It early became an important Church centre, and, in another sphere of activity, geographers used it as their prime meridian. In 1519 it was the centre of the Castilian rising against Charles V (*see* separate entry). In 1936 a small garrison of Falangists (members of the Spanish fascist movement which triumphed during the Spanish Civil War) survived a bitter siege of seventy days in the Alcazar, its citadel.
See colour section.
See also SPAIN.

Tolpuddle Martyrs: name given to the six agricultural labourers of the village of Tolpuddle in Dorset, England, who in 1834 were tried and convicted of

A vast public demonstration in April 1834, in protest against the deportation of the Tolpuddle Martyrs.

administering an unlawful oath in the course of setting up a Friendly Society of Agricultural Workers. They were tried at Dorchester and sent for seven years' transportation. In 1836, in response to public outcry, they were given a free pardon and in 1838 returned to England. The sum of £1,300 had been collected to provide them with farms and five settled in Essex, whilst one remained at Tolpuddle.

The threat of this type of legal action discouraged the formation of all trade unions for some time.

¶ In LARSEN, EGON. *Men Who Fought for Freedom.* 1958

See also TRADE UNIONS.

Tonga: autonomous kingdom in the western Pacific, formed of a group of islands discovered by Tasman in 1643, though earlier sighted by Le Maire and Schouten. Wallis visited Tonga in 1767 and later Cook, who named them the Friendly Islands. Wesleyan missionaries (*see* WESLEY, JOHN) landed in 1826. This period saw continuing dynastic and civil strife until in 1845 Taufa'ahua Tupou defeated rival claimants. Converted to Christianity in 1831, he and his wife took the names of George and Salote (Charlotte). By the time of his death in 1893 Tonga had been transformed from a group of cannibal islands – in 1806 only one sailor from a British ship survived the

cooking pots – into a Christian state with a postal system, legal code, constitution and developing parliamentary government. In 1900 Tonga became by treaty, revised in 1958, a British protected state. George II was succeeded in 1918 by Salote, who reigned for forty-seven years, the world's tallest queen of the world's smallest kingdom, and who, during her visit to England for Queen Elizabeth II's coronation, became a popular figure with the British public.

See PACIFIC OCEAN for map.

Tordesillas, Treaty of (1494): treaty implementing a ruling given by Pope Alexander VI as to the territorial rights of Spain and Portugal in the New World, of which little was then known. Everything east of a line drawn down the Atlantic 370 miles west of the Cape Verde Islands was assigned to Portugal, the rest to Spain.

GREENLAND

NORTH AMERICA

LINE OF DEMARCATION 1494

SPAIN

Atlantic

AFRICA

Ocean

SOUTH AMERICA

0   2000 Miles
0   3200 Km

TREATY OF **Tordesillas**

This enabled Portugal in due course to claim Brazil. The settlement was quite unacceptable to other maritime powers such as France and England and, later, the Netherlands, who were not participants. Religious bitterness entered the situation when Protestant England and the Netherlands became Spain's main competitors.

Toronto: city on the site originally called York and chosen in 1793 by Lord Dorchester as the capital of Upper Canada. It suffered greatly at the hands of American troops who captured it in 1813. Self-governing from 1817, York achieved city status in 1834 as Toronto, the Huron Indian word for "meeting place", important for Indians, French, Americans and British alike. Ontario, again separated from Quebec in 1867, took Toronto as its capital. The University was founded in 1827 and the Medical School houses the Banting and Best Institute, named after the discoverers of insulin.

Torpedo: self-propelled submarine missile carrying an explosive head which is detonated on impact, so named after the torpedo or cramp fish, capable of emitting electric shocks.

Original torpedoes were submarine mines towed or carried into action by small craft or submarines. The prototype of the modern self-propelled torpedo was invented by the Austrian, Captain Luppis. He and an English engineer, Robert Whitehead, produced the cigar-shaped Whitehead torpedo at Fiume on the

A blunt-nosed torpedo being hauled aboard ship during a training exercise.

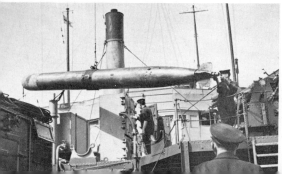

Adriatic in 1864. By 1875 special torpedo boats were being built to carry this new weapon, and by 1900 it was fitted in most major war vessels.

The early torpedoes had a propeller driven by a compressed air engine. Horizontal rudders controlled the depth and a gyroscope held it to its course. The warhead containing dynamite had a pistol detonator in the nose. The modern version is blunt nosed, is powered by heated gases and can be "homed" on to its target.

Torquemada, Tomás de (1420–98): Spanish inquisitor. A Dominican, he became confessor to Queen Isabella and her husband Ferdinand. Obsessed with an urge to suppress heresy, Torquemada persuaded Ferdinand and Isabella to restore the Inquisition in Spain in 1478 and to pursue the conquest of Moorish Granada, completed in 1492. He became sole Inquisitor General in the Spanish dominions in 1483 and with fanatical zeal pursued a reign of terror against Jews, Moors, or Christians who deviated from orthodoxy in any form. Over 2,000 of his victims were condemned to death by burning and thousands more were expelled from the country.
See also INQUISITION.

Torres Vedras: two parallel lines of defence, built by Wellington (*see* separate entry) across the Lisbon peninsula 1809–10 (*see* PENINSULAR WAR). Dams, ditches and stone walls were constructed to join natural barriers, such as steep hillsides and rivers. The land in front was levelled for miles. Behind these lines British troops were supplied by sea, thus preventing the French from gaining total control of Portugal.

Tory: word of Irish origin, originally applied about 1680 to the English political party which stood for loyalty to the throne and devotion to the Anglican Church. The party was thus thrown into some confusion when James II tried to restore the Roman Catholic religion (*see* separate entry) in England and so had no part in the invitation sent by the Whigs – the rival party (*see* separate entry) – to William III. The name has survived in British politics and is still applied to the Conservative party.

¶ KEBBEL, T. E. *History of Toryism: from the accession of Mr. Pitt to power in 1783 to the death of Lord Beaconsfield in 1881.* 1972

Toussaint L'Ouverture, Pierre Dominique (1743–1803): Negro guerilla leader and liberator of Haiti. Born a slave, he taught himself to read and made himself leader of the slave revolt against the French. From 1791 he displayed outstanding skill in defeating attempts to crush the rebellion, and became ruler of Haiti in 1801. Finally, Napoleon (*see* separate entry), incensed by Toussaint's assumption of governing powers, sent a French expeditionary force which effectively compelled his surrender. He died in prison in France the year before Haiti achieved independence.

¶ BENTLEY, J. D. *Touissant l'Ouverture of the West Indies.* 1969

See also HAITI.

Tower of London: complex of historical buildings in the City of London, on the north bank of the Thames. Today it is a combined museum and barracks. In its time it has been fortress, palace and prison. The chief building, the White Tower, or Keep, is Norman. The Crown Jewels are kept in the Wakefield Tower.

Many famous people were executed in the Tower, a number of them buried in the Tower chapel of St Peter ad Vincula. Queen Anne Boleyn (1507–36) and James, Duke of Monmouth (1649–85) are both buried there.

The Tower is looked after by the Yeomen Warders of the Guard, popularly called Beefeaters, who wear Tudor dress. A long-established legend has it that when the ravens leave the Tower of London the British royal line will come to an end.

¶ DOBBING, DOUGLAS S. *Tower of London.* 1970; SHUTTLESWORTH, DOROTHY. *The Tower of London.* 1972

Townshend, Charles, 2nd Viscount, "Turnip Townshend" (1674–1738): politician and agricultural improver. Although brought up in the Tory tradition, he attached himself to the Whigs (*see* separate entry) and married a sister of Robert Walpole. But he was of too independent a spirit to succeed in party politics and eventually quarrelled with his brother-in-law, who said, "The firm must be Walpole and Townshend, not Townshend and Walpole". In 1830 he retired to his Norfolk estates, where he demonstrated that the fertility of his land was improved by applying marl and made notable advances in the cultivation of root crops, particularly turnips.

See also AGRICULTURAL IMPROVERS; WALPOLE, SIR ROBERT.

Townshend, Charles, second son of 3rd Viscount (1725–67): British statesman, responsible for the Townshend Acts (1767) which, through their imposition of taxes on such commodities as glass, lead, paper and tea, aroused the bitter opposition from the American colonists that formed a prime cause of the War of American Independence (*see* separate entry). Townshend was a distinguished orator but his career was marred by lack of judgment and principle.

Trade marks: distinctive marks or names, affixed to articles, indicating the

TWO 18th Cent
TRADE CUTS
BY BEWICK

ARMOURER'S
MARK

ASSOCIATED
ADHESIVES

MOTHERCARE

McKELLAR
WATT
(sausages)

CRAFTOR
SHOE
REPAIRS

SWAN GARAGES

OSMOND TURNER

SOME FAMILIAR TRADE MARKS

928

manufacturer or owner of the commercial rights. The practice of trade marking has been traced among Syrian glass manufacturers in the 1st century BC. Samian ware, made in Etruscan factories (*see* ETRURIA) in the 1st century AD, was commonly stamped with the pottery owner's name. Bronze domestic articles were frequently marked in similar fashion. Around 1285 Italian sheet paper makers began to use watermarks. Then in 14th-century England it was ruled that wherever possible manufacturers should have their name imprinted on an article produced, as a safeguard against fraud, to maintain high standards of quality and to enforce guild monopolies. In Germany and Austria, hammersmiths had to stamp their marks on armour, swords and cutlery, and similar regulations were made for goldsmiths and silversmiths in England, France and Italy. During the Middle Ages these were proprietary rather than trade marks, and enabled authorities, especially guilds, to control trade.

Trade marks, in the sense that every maker had an individual stamp, began in the 18th century. They had publicity value and helped the retailer to identify the object for re-ordering. Laws to protect the rights of the trade mark owner were developed during the 18th century, and by the first years of the 19th century traders were being restrained from fraudulently passing off their goods as those of another, thus laying the foundation on which later law could be built. As trade became increasingly competitive in the second half of the 19th century, businessmen demanded more legislative action, statutes were enacted, and far more branded goods became registered. At present, in Britain, registered trade marks hold good for seven years and are thereafter renewable indefinitely for periods of fourteen years.

Trade routes: established ways followed by merchants and traders. The Middle East provides the earliest history of goods transported by land and water, between the civilisations of the Tigris–Euphrates and the Nile, eastwards to Southern Arabia, between Egypt and Crete, from Ophir up the Red Sea, and by Phoenicians island-hopping along the African coast to Spain. Carthage, Cadiz, Marseilles, originally trading posts, became independent city-states, as did Greek Tarentum and Syracuse. Trading expansion eastwards followed Alexander's conquests.

Though the Romans are not considered a commercial people, the *pax Romana* (Roman peace) provided the security essential for trade. Roman traders ranged from Britain to the Hellespont, and outside the confines of empire beyond the Rhine, Danube and North Africa. Perfumes, spices, gems, silks from India, Arabia and China arrived through Mediterranean ports and Red Sea depots, whence hundreds of ships sailed annually with wares in exchange. After the fall of Rome and the rise of Islam the Ottoman kingdoms controlled the caravan routes, with Bagdad, Damascus, Cairo and North African and Spanish cities the important entrepôts (i.e. centres importing and re-exporting commodities). After AD 1000 European trade generally revived, and the Crusades intensified the process. Venice and Genoa established factories on the Black Sea. In the mid-13th century Capuchin friars followed the trade routes through Central Asia taken later by Marco Polo. Genghis Khan (d. 1227) and Kublai Khan (1259–94) encouraged foreigners to establish trading posts. By the 14th century routes ran from China via Turkestan, the Caspian and the Volga to Novgorod, or via Azov to the Crimea, through Persia and the Black Sea to Constantinople, and from Mesopotamia to Syria. India had outlets by the Red Sea to Egypt, by the

Persian Gulf to Aleppo and Syria, or over the Khyber Pass to Persia. Mediterranean routes led to northern Italian cities, to Spain through Barcelona, into France through Marseilles and the Rhone, and over the Alps to Germany. Great trading associations, the Hanseatic, Swabian and Rhenish Leagues, distributed commodities to northern Europe and Russia through a network of markets, with reciprocal trade in local products.

The demand for new trade routes was one of the reasons for the work of Prince Henry the Navigator from 1418. Turkish intrusions into Europe, even before the capture of Constantinople (1453) and Egypt (1517), threatened the old routes. Columbus strongly believed in a shorter westward route and Vasco da Gama's voyage proved the practicability of a sea route to India. Thereafter shippers preferred the direct Cape of Good Hope route which, though perilous, was less subject to raids from pirates and avoided the inconvenience of transhipment (the transfer of goods from one vessel to another). The Portuguese regularly despatched trading fleets from 1501 and the capture of Malacca by their forces (1511) finally assured their freedom of action. By 1580, starting from Mozambique, routes ran via Socotra to Ormuz, via Goa, Bombay, northwards to Bassein, eastwards to Colombo, Sumatra, Java and the Moluccas, and from Malacca to Macao. With respective spheres of influence decided, Spain could organise its routes from the Philippines to Acapulco and from the Americas home. Consequently Mediterranean ports declined in importance, though Spanish gold and silver stimulated European trade generally. The Portuguese lost much of their trade to the Dutch in the 1600s, and the Spaniards endured growing English competition. The Treaty of Utrecht, 1713, opened Spanish colonies to Britain and established her as the chief slave-trading nation.

All trade routes shared one common feature, their attraction for pirates. In ancient Rome Pompey was honoured for suppressing African pirates: in the 14th century Simone Bocanegra, Doge of Venice, restored her prosperity in the same way. Barbary corsairs from North Africa were a threat throughout the centuries, attacking Mediterranean commerce, and even entering the English Channel. Later, Chinese pirate junks and Arab dhows were equally troublesome. Spain suffered more than most from piracy, both the English and the Dutch on several occasions capturing her treasure fleets. Drake's circumnavigation (1578–80) and Anson's (1740–44) combined privateering with attacking Spain's colonies and commerce. West Indian pirates from Jamaica and Tortuga were attracted only by prospects of loot.

The Seven Years War confirmed Britain's commercial ascendancy, which continued even after the American War of Independence, with ever expanding traffic in textiles, slaves, tobacco, sugar and machinery, until British traders were found on all the world's routes. After the coming of steam, the sailing ship, especially the clipper, was still employed bringing tea and wool from China and Australia. After the Suez Canal opened in 1869, these fine ships declined but continued for a time sailing the Cape Horn and African routes. By the 1880s refrigeration ships were sailing from New Zealand, and steam had ousted sail on passenger routes. The Suez Canal reduced the voyage from London to Bombay to eighteen days. The Panama Canal, opened to shipping in 1914, shortened the Liverpool to San Francisco voyage by 5,666 miles [9,118 kilometres] and brought the latter 7,873 miles [12,608 kilometres] nearer New York. The interwar years were the heyday of the passenger liner, with American, British, French and Italians competing for the Atlantic Blue Riband, and regular sailings of luxury liners the world over.

Simultaneously, trans-Atlantic, trans-Pacific and transcontinental air routes were developing, though economic difficulties limited expansion. Since World War II almost every country has its air lines, and trade routes have been greatly affected, both favourably and adversely. 1957 saw North Atlantic air passengers as numerous as those by ship. Bulk carriers and supertankers still sail the oceans, but by 1971 only the liners *La France* and *Queen Elizabeth II* were operating weekly services and winter schedules were drastically reduced. Now 250,000 passengers fly the Atlantic annually and vast consignments of valuable and perishable goods are carried on world air routes. On land nations construct vast motorway networks. Russian and American ventures into space bring ever nearer the possibility of interstellar flights from space platforms, and, for future generations, the establishment of interplanetary trade routes, pioneered by men as hardy and adventurous in spirit as those whose pack-horses and caravans threaded their way through the mountains and deserts of Europe and Asia in the Middle Ages.

See ENDPAPERS for map.

¶ DUCHE, J. *The Great Trade Routes.* 1969
See also INDIVIDUAL ENTRIES.

Trade unions: organisations of workers formed mainly to bargain with employers on wages and conditions of work. The modern trade union does many other things for its members, but wages, or the price they can get for their work, are still its chief concern. In Britain in the 18th century craftsmen began to band together to resist the attempts of their masters to buy their skills for as little as possible. The Industrial Revolution (*see* separate entry) brought vast numbers of workers together in great factories, and unions grew quickly in many trades. The employers called these early unions "combinations" and did all they could to stop them. A number of Acts of Parliament were passed to prevent such combinations. Some union leaders were imprisoned, and their unions broke up, but new ones were formed in their place. At last, in 1824, the Combination Acts were repealed and the right of workers to form unions was recognised. But other ways were found of making it difficult to form unions. In 1834 six labourers were charged with "administering unlawful oaths" when starting a union. They were found guilty and were transported to Australia with other convicts. This was the famous case of the "Tolpuddle Martyrs" (*see* separate entry). It caused such anger that after two years the men were pardoned.

In spite of all difficulties the trade unions continued to grow in strength. In addition to their main concern with pay and hours of work the unions offered help in times of unemployment and sickness and built up funds from their members' contributions to help them with strike pay when their wages were cut off. There were many ups and downs for the unions as trade was good or bad. When it was good, there was plenty of work and the unions prospered: when it was bad, there was much unemployment, members fell away and the unions were weakened. By the end of World War I (1918) the number of trade unionists in Britain had doubled, but in the slump that followed the war they had a severe setback. The General Strike of 1926 (*see* STRIKES) was a failure, and as a result fresh restrictions were put upon the unions by an Act of Parliament which was not repealed until 1946.

Unions for workers in skilled trades and crafts were followed by general unions, mainly for unskilled workers of many different industries. Such unions as the Transport and General Workers Union

and the National Union of General and Municipal Workers are today among the largest. More recently unions have been formed among professional workers such as doctors, teachers and civil servants, and among entertainers such as actors and professional footballers.

As unions grew during the 19th century, trades councils were formed in most industrial areas. The trades council was made up of representatives from the branches of the different unions in the area. From these local bodies of trade unionists came the idea of a national body, the *Trades Union Congress* which was formed in 1868. The TUC is made up of delegates from all the trade unions affiliated to it who meet for four days every year. A General Council is elected to deal with day-to-day affairs.

Nearly all trade unionists in Britain are now represented at the TUC which has grown from about one million members in 1874 to about 9 million in 1970. Today the TUC has great influence as representing the great majority of organised workers of the nation and its General Secretary is a national figure. When there is a dispute between unions, the General Council may be asked to give a ruling. Although every union is independent, the advice of the General Council is often accepted. When there is a dispute between a union and the employers, the General Council tries to bring about a settlement and to avoid strike action if possible. The General Council has regular meetings with the national body representing employers, the Confederation of British Industry, and it keeps in touch with certain government departments.

The TUC links up with trade unionists abroad through the International Confederation of Free Trade Unions. It is also a member of the International Labour Organisation to which over one hundred countries belong. The ILO is specially concerned with social justice and peace among nations. In countries which have some form of dictatorship the trade unions are not independent: they are controlled by the state and have no "right to strike".

In the United States of America, the first attempts by workers to form unions were fiercely resisted by the employers, as in Britain. After the Civil War (1861–65; see separate entry) when industry developed rapidly, trade unions were formed in the major industries, and, in spite of even more violent opposition from the employers, the unions came together on a national basis in the *American Federation of Labor*. This happened in 1886, only eighteen years after the foundation of the TUC in England. The early years of the AFL were marked by violent clashes between unions and employers, who were often backed by the government. Two railway strikes, in 1877 and 1886, were both ended by the government using the army against the strikers. As American industry prospered, both the AFL and the employers made a move towards settling disputes on a national basis by agreement and arbitration. One of the most active men in the AFL was the leader of the United Mine Workers, John L. Lewis. After World War I he grew dissatisfied with the AFL because it favoured skilled workers. The rapid development of mass production had led to the employment of many unskilled and semiskilled workers. Lewis said that the AFL should include all workers, both skilled and unskilled. In 1935 he left .the AFL and organised the *Congress of Industrial Organisations*. This was made up of his own union, the United Mine Workers, and a number of other unions in steel, glass, rubber and car manufacture. The CIO became a very powerful body and, for the next twenty years, the AFL and the CIO existed side by side. Even in 1955, when the two came together again, a number of unions stayed outside the Federation as independent unions. Thus, trade unions in the USA have grown in a different way from the English unions. They have also had more restrictions placed on them by government action, e.g. by the Taft–Hartley Act of 1947.

See also INDIVIDUAL ENTRIES.

Trafalgar, Battle of: naval battle fought on 21 October 1805 off Cadiz, Spain, between Nelson's fleet of 27 British ships of the line and Villeneuve's 33 French and Spanish. It ended the three-year blockade of French squadrons – in Brest by Cornwallis, in Toulon by Nelson. Napoleon ordered these squadrons to escape and concentrate with Spanish ships in the West Indies, then to clear the Channel for his *Grande Armée* to invade England. On 30 March Villeneuve eluded Nelson's open blockade of Toulon and reached the West Indies, but, when the Brest squadron failed to break out, he sailed to Cadiz. On 1 September Napoleon struck his camp at Boulogne, marched to the Danube and ordered Villeneuve to carry troops to Naples. When Villeneuve sailed, Nelson's watchful frigates kept contact and warned the main fleet. The battle, fought in light airs and a swell, was won by British seamanship and gunnery, perfected in the months of blockading. It was bloody and decisive, in contrast to the 18th-century actions fought by the book of Fighting Instructions. A lieutenant wrote, "We scrambled into action as best we could, each man to catch his bird" – a fair resumé of "the Nelson touch", which was to strike at the enemy centre and rear before their van could turn and engage, and to trust each captain to engage closely without orders. Nelson was killed by musket shot, but 19 enemy ships were taken, all but four being lost in the gale which followed the battle.

¶ LANGDON-DAVIES, JOHN. *The Battle of Trafalgar* (Jackdaw). 1963; WARNER, OLIVER. *Trafalgar*. 1959

See also NAPOLEON I; NELSON.

Tramways: systems of public transport by means of cars (trams), sometimes with one or two trailers attached, running on rails laid in the streets. The term "tramway", however, is sometimes applied to minor railways, while the origin of the word "tram" is obscure. Moreover, many tramways, especially in the USA and Europe, run or formerly ran for part of their route on their own tracks across open country. In the USA the word for tram was "street-car", but this is one of the parts of the world from which this form of transport has almost disappeared. In England, where many urban corporations once had their tramway system, that at Blackpool (Lancashire) was the first, as it is now the last, to operate and seems likely to do so for some time. There is a tramway museum at Crich in Derbyshire. In Western Europe, however, as also in India and elsewhere, tramways are still extensively used.

Horse-drawn tram c. 1900.

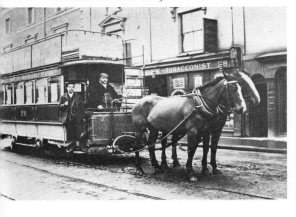

The earliest trams, drawn by horses, were introduced in New York in 1832, in Paris in 1853 and in London in 1861. In the 1880s a system of cable operation was widely adopted, but by 1900 the use of electricity became general, current being supplied to the vehicles by means of overhead wires. In the early years of the century trams were to be found in many parts of the world, including such remote countries as China and the Sudan.

The disadvantage which has since led to the widespread disappearance of many tramway systems is the lack of manoeuvr-

Traffic jam at the Elephant and Castle, London, in 1922.

ability of the vehicles in narrow streets with heavy traffic. In some cases tramcars have been superseded by trolley-buses, running on rubber-tyred wheels and steered by the driver, but deriving electric power from the existing overhead system, suitably modified. These, though more manoeuvrable, still have their drawbacks and, as they become worn out, are seldom replaced.

¶ JOYCE, J. *Tramway Heyday*. 1964; JOYCE, J. *Tramways of the World*. 1965

Transkeian Territories: African reserve in Cape Province, in the south-east of the Republic of South Africa. The area, of some 16,500 square miles [42,700 sq km], was set aside in 1963 as a partly self-governing reserve for 1·5 million Xhosa-speaking people. The legislature consisted of 4 paramount chiefs, 60 other chiefs and 45 elected members. Voting and taxation extended to Xhosa speakers outside the territory. All laws were subject to review by the South African government. Courts had no power over criminal cases or those involving white people. An area of agriculturally poor land without resources of value, the Transkei has been financially dependent on the South African government.

Transport: the carrying of people, equipment and goods. From ancient times to the 19th century, transport overland was based on the strength of human or animal muscles and on road conditions. Sea transport depended on the oarsman and the vagaries of the wind. Man himself was the first beast of burden, sometimes with a light yoke slung across his shoulders to carry his belongings. He was able to make life easier for himself by such devices as placing his load on a framework of boughs which he dragged behind him. Around 6000 BC he learnt to tame animals. In warm countries oxen, donkeys and camels were trained to pull or carry his loads: in the north, dogs, in south-west Asia, horses.

The sledge was the earliest vehicle, made first of hide or tree bark and then, in Sumerian times, of wood with a boxlike contraption on top – ancestor of the four-wheel wagon. The slide car was another

The "travois", used by the Sioux Indians.

means of transport in ancient times. Two poles were tied to one or two animals at one end, with the other end, carrying the load, dragging behind. This type, known as a "travois", was formerly much in use among the North American Indians.

The wheel was one of man's greatest inventions, made around 3000 BC. The first wheels evolved from logs used as rollers to move heavily laden sledges. Rough discs of wood were cut from tree trunks and fastened to each end of a small roller. It is believed that the Sumerians were the first to use wheeled vehicles, and that the nomads of the Central Asiatic steppes were first in putting on roof covers.

Assyrian chariot.

Around 2000 BC the Egyptians were using chariots with spoked wheels. Assyrians, Babylonians and Greeks all used chariots to speed a messenger or launch an attack; so did the Celts (*see* separate entry), the most skilful cartwrights of ancient times. Roman emperors travelled their splendid roads with great pomp. Though they were probably exceptional in their craze for display, Heliogabalus is recorded as journeying in a gem-studded carriage, Nero with a thousand vehicles. One imperial carriage, ancestor of the motor car, is said to have had slaves hidden in its structure, propelling the vehicle with their hands and feet.

Logs were man's first water transport – first just one to ferry him across a stream, then several lashed together for a raft. Using a stone axe he hollowed out a log for a canoe which he could paddle against the current. Later, for a lighter craft, he stretched bark over a wooden frame. At the same time as the invention of the wheel, boats and ships developed, propelled by oars and sails. Fifty centuries ago the Egyptians were sailing on the River Nile in a craft made of planks fastened to a wooden frame.

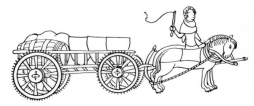

A medieval cart pulled by horses wearing horse collars. Cart wheels and horses' shoes were spiked because of the mud.

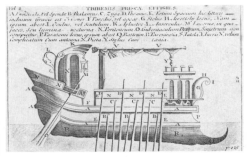

Plan of a Greek trireme.

Soon ships were venturing out into the sea in search of trade. The Phoenicians (*see* separate entry) sailed along the Mediterranean shores using galleys with rows of oars. Their sturdy trading ships began to sail further westward, to Malta and Spain, planting trading stations as they explored. Greater speed was wanted for warships, so boat builders produced first the light bireme, then the heavier trireme, with three rows of oars requiring as many as two hundred slaves, a single sail suspended from the mast and an iron-shod ram at the prow. Greeks and Romans used them for war and the establishment and maintenance of their colonies. Even larger vessels were developed, from quadriremes (four banks of oars) and quinqueremes (five banks) up to a reputed fifteen-banked ship. Roman merchantmen, 180 feet long [64·9 m] and carrying up to 700 passengers, transported armies and equipment to Carthage and Gaul.

After the fall of the Roman Empire the road systems in Europe deteriorated badly. Wagons and carts were still used

but were so uncomfortable that only the poor used them. The noblemen and well-to-do, even women, preferred to go on horseback or by litter. Packhorses were used to transport goods. During the early Middle Ages (*see* separate entry), modern harnessing methods, long known in China, enabled the horse to draw heavier loads, and as a result more freight and passenger transport went by road, though in addition to dust, mud and potholes there was the danger from bandits.

The first carriage with suspension of its body by chains and ropes appeared in Europe during the 15th century, for royalty and the aristocracy; later, the stage coach, suspended on iron or wooden supports, came into general use.

Queen Elizabeth I's coach, from a drawing done in 1572.

The main transport developments of the Middle Ages were on water. The magnetic compass, long known by Chinese and Mediterranean navigators, came into general use, while ships became larger and more seaworthy. Although we hear of a three-masted Saracen ship being sunk by Richard I as early as 1191, the earliest known dated portrayal of such a vessel is on a seal of 1466. It was certainly not till the 15th century that the three-master became common in European waters and, with its greater wind-power and man-œuvrability, made longer voyages possible. Columbus voyaged to America (1492), other explorers sailed around Africa and across to India. In 1522 Magellan (*see* separate entry) completed the first voyage round the world.

The 18th century saw the development of the steam engine, but its first applications were to pumps and industrial machinery. It was some time before it was adapted to the propulsion of locomotives and ships. John Fitch of America constructed a steamboat in 1787, with the steam engine operating a set of paddles on either side of the boat, and in 1839 John Ericsson, a Swedish engineer, invented the screw propeller, more efficient than paddle wheels.

Although steam locomotives had been in use on mineral railways since soon after the turn of the century, the first public railway in Britain using this form of traction for some of its traffic was opened in 1825. This was the Stockton

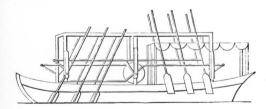

Above: Outline of Fitch's first paddleboat. Below: Fitch's second steamboat.

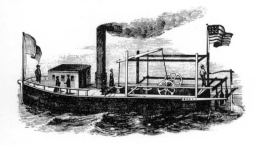

and Darlington Railway, but the Liverpool and Manchester (1830) was in a truer sense the forerunner of the modern railway systems since from the first it used only locomotive power. At much the same time as the latter the first railway in the USA began operation. Steam railways made it possible to open up vast areas of the continents, with a cheap, fast and powerful means of transport. In recent years diesel and electric locomotives have almost entirely replaced those driven by steam.

Travelling by motor car in 1908.

For local transport the tram or street-car, at first drawn by horses or by cable, but later driven by electricity, enjoyed considerable popularity during the later 19th and early 20th century, but it has now given way to the motor bus and this in its turn is threatened by the private motor car (*see* separate entry), which gives a man and his family their own personal means of transport. Tremendous strides have been made in air travel since the Wright Brothers in 1903 made their historic flight. The comparatively new word "aeronaut" (literally, one who sails in the air) is already giving place to "astronaut" (one who sails to the stars).

¶ RIDLEY, ANTHONY. *An Illustrated History of Transport.* 1969

See also AVIATION; RAILWAYS; ROADS; SHIPS; SPACE TRAVEL; STEAM; TRAMWAYS.

Transportation: removal of convicts to penal settlements abroad. James I of England despatched "dissolute persons" to Virginia and his grandson Charles II commuted the death penalty to transportation. Legalised in 1719, transportation flourished after Australia was annexed. The visits of the reformer Elizabeth Fry (1780-1845) to 106 ships carrying 12,000 convicts indicate its scale. New South Wales (Botany Bay; *see* separate entry) took convicts from 1788, including the "Tolpuddle Martyrs" (*see* separate entry). In 1840 Tasmania expanded existing settlements to take in hardened criminals from the mainland. Transportation from Britain ended by 1868. France used Guinea from 1763, and New Caledonia, Guiana and Devil's Island until 1950. In a less familiar sense, transportation may be held to include the removal of political "undesirables". The salt mines of Siberia have served the rulers of modern Russia in the same way as they did the imperial Tsars.

Trans-Siberian Railway: constructed by Russia (1891-1900) to link her own European system with her possessions in the Far East. The length from Chelyabinsk in the Urals to Vladivostok in the Pacific was 4,627 miles [7,446 kilometres]. It was a single line with passing places, and Lake Baikal was crossed by a train-ferry equipped as an ice-breaker. It proved quite inadequate for the military requirements of the Russo-Japanese war of 1904-05 (*see* separate entry). Under Soviet rule the line has been largely doubled (i.e. double-tracked), the lake has been by-passed, and electrification is in progress.

Transvaal: province of the Republic of South Africa. The capital is Pretoria, other main towns being Johannesburg, Germiston, Springs and Benoni, which are situated on the Witwatersrand, where most of the older gold mines are located and where 50 per cent of the Republic's engineering and metal industries are concentrated. The mineral wealth is great and varied. Platinum, chrome, manganese, asbestos, magnetite, diamonds, corundum, beryl, antimony and vermiculite are produced in addition to gold, and granite and marble are quarried. A new opencast copper mine which is now being developed is likely to become the biggest in the world. In the low veld of the East Transvaal and the Magaliesberg district citrus and other subtropical fruits are grown in considerable quantities.

The republic was first established by the Boers who crossed the River Vaal in the course of the Great Trek (*see* separate entry) and in 1836-38 defeated the Matabele tribes, who had earlier driven out the Bantu, Hottentots and Bushmen.

In 1852, after the Sand River Convention had declared the Transvaal an independent republic, the situation became so confused by disputes, in which Marthinus Pretorius and Paul Kruger (*see* separate entry) figured prominently, that in 1877 the Transvaal was annexed by Britain. In 1883 Kruger was elected president, being re-elected in 1886; but, following defeat in the Boer War, Kruger fled to Europe. The Transvaal became part of the Union of South Africa in 1910 and, later, one of the four provinces of the Republic of South Africa. *See* AFRICA for map.

Trieste: port in the north-eastern corner of the Adriatic, sheltered by the peninsula of Istria. The victim of disputes between the patriarchs of Aquilaea and Venice, jealous of its seaport, it accepted the protection of Duke Leopold of Austria in 1382. In 1719 Austria attempted to develop it as an Imperial Free Port and base of her Levant Company. Napoleon annexed it in 1809, but Austria recovered it in 1815, and it became the terminal of the Austrian Lloyd service to the Levant from 1840 to 1860, and later of the Lloyd Triestino Line. Italy demanded and obtained it in 1919 as the price of her joining Britain and France in 1915. In 1945 Yugoslavia hoped to gain it, but the western powers occupied it, and it was awarded to Italy in 1954, though the Yugoslav frontier runs close to it.

Trinidad and Tobago: West Indian islands off Venezuela, originally inhabited by Arawak and Carib Indians. Columbus (*see* separate entry) discovered Trinidad in 1498, but established no settlement. Despite Spanish searches for gold and occasional Dutch and French visits, progress in this Spanish colony was slight. Cocoa was cultivated before 1700, but the economy revived only with the admission of Catholic foreigners in 1783 and French emigrés from Haiti and Domingo during the Revolution. Finally ceded to Britain by the Treaty of Amiens, 1802, Trinidad became a crown colony with legislative and executive councils. Amalgamation with Tobago came in 1888. Elective government from 1924, adult suffrage in 1946, and responsible self-government in 1950, led to independence, with membership of the Commonwealth and United Nations in 1962, after Trinidad's withdrawal from the West Indian Federation. Government is through a legislature, with Prime Minister, Senate and House of Representatives. The economy, formerly dependent on sugar and cocoa, now includes asphalt, rum, fertilisers, oil and coffee.
See ENDPAPERS for map.

Triple Alliances: agreements made by three states for mutual support against their enemies. Of those known to historians by this title, the following are the most important: (1) the pact made in 1668 between England, Holland and Sweden to check French aggression in the Spanish Netherlands which was, however, made largely ineffective by the secret dealings of Charles II with the French king; (2) the alliance between Great Britain, France and Holland made in 1717 to uphold the terms of the Treaty of Utrecht, which next year became quadruple when Austria joined in; (3) the inclusion of Italy (1882) in the existing alliance between Austria and Germany against the possibility of war with France or Russia. By the eve of World War I (*see* separate entry) this was confronted by the Triple Entente, as it was called, between England, France and Russia. Italy eventually entered the war on the latter side.

Trojan War: struggle between Greece and Troy, lasting for ten years and ending in the capture and destruction of Troy. The legend of the war was told by the Greek poets, especially Homer, and the later Greeks believed absolutely in the historical truth of the story. Helen, the wife of the Spartan king, had been

The legendary Trojan Horse.

abducted by Paris, son of the king of Troy. To regain her, a Greek fleet under Agamemnon attacked Troy and eventually took it by means of a wooden horse concealed in which some Greeks were able to get inside the walls and open the gates. The poets recounted many isolated episodes, like the arrival of the Amazons, or the death of Patroclus and the vengeance of Achilles.

For many centuries these stories were regarded as myths, but the German archaeologist (see ARCHAEOLOGY) Heinrich Schliemann in 1871 excavated Hissarlik, the traditional site of Troy, and discovered a complex series of remains. He and others have been able to distinguish nine or ten different cities on the same spot, and one of them bears clear evidence of destruction by fire. This city, known as Troy VIIa, appears to date from the early 12th century BC, which tallies well with the traditional date for the fall of Troy in 1184. So Troy, we may assume, existed and was destroyed. Evidence is still lacking about the historical truth of the details told in the story. A reasonable guess is that Troy, situated a short distance from the entrance to the Hellespont (Dardanelles) on the Asian side, imposed a control on those straits and that the Greeks fought to remove it.

¶ HOMER. *Iliad*, translated by E. V. RIEU. 1969

Tromp, Maarten Harpertszoon (1597–1653): lieutenant-admiral of Holland in the First Dutch War between England and Holland. Born at Brielle, he went to sea at the age of eight, was present at a Dutch victory over the Spanish in Gibraltar Bay, saw his father killed by an English privateer, and survived capture by her and, later, by Tangier pirates. He was dismissed his ship in 1629 for criticising the decay of the Dutch fleet, but, recalled in 1639, he destroyed a great Spanish fleet at the Downs under the eyes of the English fleet. His brush with Blake's fleet in 1652 started the First Dutch War. A Bible-reading Calvinist (see REFORMATION), painstaking and level-headed, he developed signalling, gunnery and the tactics of the line. With inferior ships and equipment, he protected Dutch convoys up and down the Channel. He was killed off Scheveningen in July 1653 breaking the English blockade. He was "the only admiral under whom all others were content to serve – the adored of the seamen". His second son, Cornelius, also became a distinguished naval commander.

See also BLAKE, ROBERT.

Trotsky, Leon, Lev Davidovich Bronstein (1879–1940): Russian revolutionary. He joined the Bolsheviks only in 1917 but took a prominent part in the Russian revolution, becoming people's commissar for foreign affairs. As commissar for war he showed enormous energy and brilliant organising capacity, building up the Red Army and ensuring victory in the civil war. An advocate of world revolution rather than of socialism in any one country, he was ousted by Stalin from positions of power after Lenin's death, forced into exile in 1932 and murdered in Mexico in 1940. He was the founder of a worldwide tradition and philosophy of communist activism.

See also BOLSHEVIKS; LENIN; etc.

Troubadours: minstrel poets of Provence, in the south of France, in the 12th–14th centuries. The name comes from a word in the old Provençal language (the *langue d'oc*) meaning "to find" or "to invent". The troubadours, many of whom were of noble birth, travelled from castle to castle. Their poems, sometimes recited to a musical accompaniment, were most often about some aspect of love. Another group of minstrel-poets, known as *trouvères*,

Truman, Harry S. (1884–1973): 33rd president of the USA (1945–53). A Democrat and vice-president to Franklin Roosevelt, he came to the White House on the latter's death in 1945, "a farm boy from Missouri . . . too small for Roosevelt's shoes". Against all expectation and prediction, he was elected to a second term in 1948, his simplicity and moral courage appealing to a great mass of American citizens. He took the decision to drop the first atomic bomb on Japan (1945), produced the Truman Doctrine for aiding foreign countries to resist the spread of Communism and introduced the domestic programme of reform known as the Fair Deal. He was also a promoter of the North Atlantic Treaty Organisation (NATO).

See also AMERICAN PRESIDENTS; ATOMIC BOMB; ROOSEVELT, F. D.; NATO.

flourished in northern France. In Germany a group known as *minnesingers* (literally "love singers") flourished *c.* 1150–1350.

Troy: ancient city in modern Turkey, a short distance from the entrance to the Dardanelles. *See* TROJAN WAR.

Trucial States, Trucial Oman, Trucial Coast: seven independent Arab sheikhdoms on the south coast of the Persian Gulf, between Cape Masandam and Qatar, with Saudi Arabia to the south. In 1885 Britain renewed and extended an earlier anti-slavery and anti-piracy treaty by concluding the "Perpetual Maritime Truce" with the seven states. Oil, first produced in 1962, provides through concession payments an ever-expanding source of revenue. Britain has contributed greatly to educational institutions, providing finance, teaching better methods of agriculture and giving technical instruction in various trades, etc., through the Trucial States Development Scheme.

Tsar, Tzar, Czar: title of the former emperors of Russia, deriving from Latin *Caesar* and sharing its origin with the German and Austrian title *Kaiser*. The last of the Tsars was Nicholas II (*see* separate entry), murdered with his family at Ekaterinburg by his revolutionary captors on 16 July 1918.

See also IVAN; NICHOLAS I and II; PETER I; RUSSIA etc.

Tudor, House of: dynasty ruling in England from 1485 to 1603. Welsh genealogists trace the Tudor line to Ednyfed Vychan, a 13th-century steward of Prince Llewellyn, but it was Owen Tudor who, two centuries later, introduced royal blood into the family. In about 1428 he won the favour of the dowager Queen Catherine, widow of Henry V; and, whether or not they were married, they produced five children. Their son Edmund, Earl of Richmond, added another royal, if questionably legitimate, strain when he married Margaret Beaufort in 1455, and it is not surprising that their son Henry, when he assumed the crown after his victory over Richard III at Bosworth, did not stress his claim as hereditary. He made it real by his victory, by parliamentary sanction, by uniting Yorkist with Lancastrian claims when he married Elizabeth of York, and by his success in defeating all pretenders.

As king (1485-1509), Henry VII established a secure dynasty. Dealing firmly with over-mighty subjects, encouraging trade, avoiding expensive foreign commitments and husbanding his resources with great financial skill, he was able to leave to his son an uncontested title and a considerable sum in the treasury.

There are few periods of history from which the personalities of rulers emerge so sharply (if not always accurately) defined and so firmly impressed on the fickle memory of posterity.

Probably the rising art of the portrait painter has much to do with this. Michel Sittow's portrait of Henry VII in the National Gallery, London, shows, in the words of a former director, "a fascinating face but not a sympathetic one; the thin lips in a line that borders on the smirk, the almost sharp nose and the bead-bright eyes calculating under the utterly untrustworthy angle of the eyelids. He has the air, in his little niche, with the Golden Fleece round his neck, of a far too wordly saint, a mean St Money-Bags." The legend of the shrewd, skinflint king has endured almost unchallenged; but the documentary records show that, though he was certainly a careful housekeeper, he was often a lavish spender, not only on personal adornment and gifts to his family, but on his table, on sports and festivities, on the encouragement and patronage of scholars.

Henry VIII, his son and successor, has come down to us as a personality chiefly

The Tudors: Above: Henry VII and Edward VI. Below: Henry VIII, Mary I, and Elizabeth I.

through the master-brush of Holbein (*see* separate entry), "one hand on hip, one hand on the dagger, the shoulders wide, the legs straddled like those of Atlas, but to bear his own weight, his own Church, his own kingdom" (David Piper: *The English Face*). It is said that, long after Henry was dead, people still shivered when they saw that picture, doubtless remembering the slow corroding transition from the auburn-haired, athletic prince described in the despatches of the Venetian ambassador, to the ruthless tyrant of later years, his rotting legs unable to support his vast bulk.

Succeeding to the throne at nine years of age and living only another six years, the boy-king Edward VI passes as a pathetic shadow, though he was an accomplished linguist and scholar as well as musician.

To his half-sister, Mary, history has been less than just. Nature did not endow her generously. She was small of stature, thin and shortsighted; though another Venetian ambassador reported that "her eyes are so piercing as to command not only respect but awe from those on whom she casts them". There is plenty of evidence that she was spirited and courageous. Humble children were apprenticed and educated at her expense and she visited the poor in their homes that she might learn how they lived. She was not without mercy, forgiving conspiracies against her and freeing political prisoners. But in religion she was narrow and steadfast to the point of bigotry, and she was insensible to the tide of national feeling that steadily turned against her. It is probably true that she was the only one of the Tudors who executed from principle and not because it was expedient. But the fires of Smithfield dimmed all else; and Charles Dickens unfortunately spoke truly when he said: "As Bloody Queen Mary she will ever be remembered with horror and detestation."

It was left to the last of the Tudors, Elizabeth I, to attain a stature that probably no monarch in English history has been accorded before or since. She was shrewish, vain, vacillating and of no marked beauty, especially in her later years. She could swear at her courtiers, lecture an arrogant ambassador in Latin and aim a kick at another. She could reprimand the Dean of St Paul's in the middle of a sermon. But she could smile, too. Her godson Sir John Harington recorded that "when she smiled it was pure sunshine, that everyone did choose to bask in if they could: but anon came a storm from a sudden gathering of clouds, and the thunder fell in wondrous manner on all alike". Therein lay much of her strength and her power of command – the pure sunshine, the sudden intimidating gathering of clouds. Add to that the mastery of the English tongue that could rise to the heights of the speech at Tilbury and the last "Golden Speech" to her parliament in 1601. "Though God hath raised me high, yet this I account the glory of my crown, that I have reigned with your loves." That this was true was the greatest accomplishment of the greatest of the Tudors.

¶ WINCHESTER, B. *Tudor Family Portrait.* 1955

Tuileries: former palace in Paris on the banks of the Seine, incorporated in the 17th century into the nearby palace of the Louvre by joining the two with a long building called the Grande Galerie. In 1871, in riots following France's defeat in the Franco-Prussian War (*see* separate entry), the Tuileries were burnt down and never rebuilt.

Tull, Jethro (1674-1741): English farmer and agricultural writer who, out of his own practical experience, invented implements, notably seed drills, which brought about a great advance in agricultural methods. His *Horse-hoeing Husbandry, or an Essay on the Principles of Tillage and Vegetation* was published in 1733. *See also* AGRICULTURAL IMPROVERS.

Tunisia: republic of North Africa, with a Mediterranean coastline between Algeria and Libya. The people are mainly Arabs and Berbers. The capital is Tunis. Other towns (some of which figured prominently in the North African campaigns of World War II; *see* separate entry) are Sfax, Bizerta, Sousse, Gabes and Kairouan. The main exports are olive oil, phosphates, grain and wine, with recent oil strikes now being developed.

In the 2nd century BC Tunisia became the original part of the Roman province of Africa, but fell to the Vandals (*see* separate entry) in AD 439, and was later absorbed into the Byzantine empire in 533, conquered by the Arabs in 698 after a fifty years war of attrition, and converted to Islam (*see* separate entry). Nine hundred stormy years followed with Berber rule predominating in spite of Bedouin and Norman attempts to gain control. In 1575 the North African empire of Turkey spread to Tunisia, and in the 17th century a Turkish Bey founded a dynasty that persisted for three centuries. In the 19th century Britain, France and Italy competed for influence, but Britain dropped out, and the French, by force of arms, obtained the Bey's recognition of Tunisia as a French Protectorate in 1883, the territory achieving independence again in 1956 and becoming a republic on 25 July 1957. President Habib Bourgiba was confirmed as head of state by subsequent elections in 1959, 1964 and 1969. *See* MEDITERRANEAN for map.

¶ SYLVESTER, A. *Tunisia*. 1969

Tunnels: man-made passages beneath the surface of the earth. This article does not include natural caverns or mine-workings or the tunnel-tombs of ancient kings.

A tunnel several thousand years old, beneath the River Euphrates, has been discovered in Mesopotamia. In the 6th century BC one nearly a mile [1·6 km] long was constructed to provide a water supply in the Greek island of Samos. The Romans drove one of 3·5 miles [5·6 kilometres], and 400 feet [122 metres] down at its deepest point, to drain Lake Fucino in Italy. Early methods of tunnelling were slow and laborious. A short tunnel completed in 1681 to carry the Canal du Midi in southern France for 500 feet [152 m] underground was regarded as a notable achievement. Later and longer canal tunnels in England were generally made low and narrow, so that the bargemen could lie on the deck on each side and "leg" the vessel along.

It was with the coming of railways that the problems of tunnelling were really faced. To penetrate rock, the pick wielded by hand gave way in due course to blasting and to the compressed-air drill. In soft ground the difficulty was to prevent the collapse of the roof, and most tunnels had to be bricklined as the work went forward. This delicate operation was made easier by the use of a "shield", a ring of iron, or later steel, at the working face. This was first used in England in making the short but costly Wapping Tunnel for pedestrians under the Thames, completed by Marc Isambard Brunel (*see* separate entry) in 1843. The shield had a

Railway through the Thames Tunnel at Wapping shown in 1870.

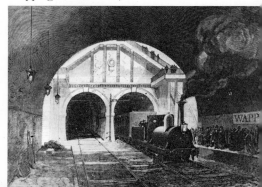

later development in the construction of underground railways in London and elsewhere, when a continuous metal tube was built up behind it, thus producing, in effect, the longest railway tunnels in the world. One of the "tube" railways under London is over 17 miles [27 km] long. A hazard often met by engineers was the unsuspected presence of underground water, as in the Severn Tunnel (1873–86) and earlier in that at Kilsby in Northamptonshire (1838). Two further problems, in the days of steam locomotives, were ventilation (usually met by vertical shafts leading up to the surface) and surveying (which was brought to such perfection that the workings of a long tunnel started from both ends could meet with dead accuracy deep below the earth).

Only a few of the many long railway tunnels in the world can here be mentioned. Those beneath the Alps are among the most famous, that under Mont Cenis (1871) being the earliest and the Simplon (12·3 miles [19·7 km]) the longest.

Road tunnels of any length are products of the motoring age and face the problem of ventilation in an acute form. In spite of this, an Alpine tunnel under Mont Blanc (7·3 miles [11·7 km]) was opened in 1965. Under water the solution is more difficult; the first Mersey Tunnel, Liverpool (2·6 miles [4·2 km]), has ventilators at the ends only, and any traffic hold-up means that all engines must be switched off: a second tunnel has recently been completed. For the proposed Channel Tunnel (approximately 25 miles [40 km]) intermediate ventilator shafts would endanger shipping, and it seems that it would be necessary to carry motor vehicles through on the trucks of an electric railway. The short, double-decked Yerba Buena Island Tunnel at San Francisco, USA, is remarkable for its great width (76 feet [23 m]) and height (58 feet [17·7 m]). It is used by 35 million vehicles a year.

Tunnels to convey water present considerably less difficulty – the Delaware Tunnel in the USA (1945) is 85 miles [137 km] long – but the ease with which the natural course of streams and rivers can be diverted in mountainous country is being increasingly recognised.

¶ JAMES, ALAN. *Tunnels.* 1972; WYNYARD, J. *Tunnels and Bridges.* 1964

Turin: city and industrial centre of Piedmont, northern Italy, with extensive trade in mechanical engineering, chemicals, textiles, food processing, leather, etc. Its history goes back to pre-Roman times, and from 1861–65 it was the capital of Italy. Its notable buildings and institutions include its university (1404), cathedral (15th-century), fine palaces, libraries, and several museums internationally famous for Renaissance Art and Egyptian collections.

Turkestan: a name formerly applied to a large area of central Asia. We now speak of Russian Turkestan, Afghan Turkestan and Chinese Turkestan. This area was once peopled by speakers of an Iranian language with trading cities such as Samarkand. It was influenced by the Greeks in the 4th century BC and by the Chinese from the 1st century AD, and was overrun from the 6th century by Turkic tribes who adopted Islam (*see* separate entry), introduced in the 8th century. A Mongol population (*see* MONGOLS) was added in the 13th century. The three modern states divided the area effectively from the later 19th century onwards.

Turkey: republic in western Asia and south–eastern Europe. The ancient Asia Minor was peopled by Hittites in the second millennium BC. It later saw Phrygian invasions, a kingdom of Lydia, settlements of Greeks and the rise and fall of Homer's Troy. The Persians conquered it during the 6th and 5th centuries BC and Alexander the Great in 334 BC. It later became part of the Roman and Byzantine empires. The Seljuk Turks arrived from the deserts of Turkestan in the 10th century AD, and by 1050 had conquered Afghanistan and central Persia. In the 11th century they increasingly controlled Asia Minor. In 1071 the Byzantines were defeated and a Seljuk Sultanate of Rum or Rome was established. Appeals from the Byzantine empire brought in the Crusaders who set up the empire of Trebizond (1204-1461). In the 13th century the Mongol invasion broke the Turks into many small states, but Osman (1259-1326) drew them together, and by the end of the 14th century the Ottoman empire extended from the Euphrates to the plain of Hungary. Constantinople was taken in 1453. The Ottoman empire reached its peak in mid-16th century under Suleiman I (1520-66). Decline set in, with two centuries of ineffective rulers. In 1740 the French won privileges within the Turkish empire and the Russians also gained ground. Outlying provinces in the Balkans and elsewhere became independent in the 19th century. The empire ended in 1908 and a republic was established. Turkey was westernised under Kemal Ataturk (1880-1938). Neutral in World War II, Turkey subsequently accepted extensive American aid.

¶ PRICE, M. P. *History of Turkey.* 1961

See also ATATURK, KEMAL; BALKANS; BYZANTINE EMPIRE; CONSTANTINOPLE; CRUSADES; MONGOLS; OTTOMAN EMPIRE.

Turnpikes: barriers preventing entry to roads and bridges until a toll is paid. Tollgates were much the same thing. From being the name of a type of gate, the term "turnpike" soon became applied to the road itself.

Under the late Stuarts, the state of British roads was holding back commercial expansion, as well as being a national disgrace. Previously, an unfair burden of road repair had been laid, not on the actual users of the roads, but on the parishes, whose labourers had to give several days' unpaid labour each year to their maintenance. In Queen Anne's reign, the system of turnpike roads was introduced to provide for the great in-

crease in wheeled traffic. First the management of the turnpikes was given to local justices of peace; later special Turnpike Trusts were established by parliament.

The trusts were composed of local landowners and dignitaries, noblemen and farmers. They were empowered to construct and maintain certain stretches of road, erecting gates and collecting tolls from particular classes of traffic. The tolls were adjusted on sliding scales, taking account of weight (the principal roads had weighing machines), number of horses and width of wheels. Animals "on the hoof" and even flocks of geese and turkeys paid toll, though foot passengers were exempt.

The first turnpike gates had tapered counterbalanced bars, and swung across the road on upright posts. At each one stood a toll house. Rights for toll collecting were farmed out and much defrauding of the trusts went on, so profits were not large. By 1840 there were 22,000 miles [35,200 kilometres] of good roads in Britain. There are still a few survivals of the turnpike or toll-gate system in Britain, but most have now disappeared.

The establishment of turnpikes also played an important part in the rise of inland urban centres in the USA. Maryland and Virginia were pioneers in this method of financing road development. The 62-mile [100 km] stretch of road between Philadelphia and Lancaster, laid down as a stone highway covered with gravel (1792–94), is still known as the Lancaster Pike.

Tutankhamun (ruled 1352–43 BC): Egyptian king of the 18th dynasty. This pharaoh succeeded his father-in-law, Akhnaten, "the heretic" (*see* separate entry) and, after a short reign, died when only about 19 years of age. His tomb in the Valley of Kings was discovered by the archaeologist Howard Carter in 1922, almost untouched by tomb robbers. The treasure which it contained demonstrates the splendour of a pharaoh's burial.
See colour section.

¶ STREATFEILD, NOEL. *The Boy Pharaoh, Tutankhamen*. 1972

See also JEWELLERY; PHARAOH.

Twelfth century: the years 1101–1200. So far as England is concerned, the hundred years which began with the accession of Henry I to the throne are of great importance in that they saw the growth of a nation. A writer of the early 12th century describes William the Conqueror as "Rex Norm-Anglorum" (king of the Anglo-Normans), and the English kings for much of the period address their subjects in their writs as "French and English". But, shortly after the close of the century, Magna Carta described John simply as "Rex Angliae" (king of the English). This development is inseparably linked with the foundation of strong central government. The *Curia Regis* (King's Court) began to appear as the supreme central court whose business was the government of the country in all its branches. The *Dialogus de Scaccario* (1117) gives an interesting account of the Exchequer side of its work. In the administration of justice the Assize system was developed, and visitations by itinerant justices, only occasional under Henry I (reigned 1100–35), became regular under Henry II (reigned 1154–89), who first divided the country into circuits.

In the rest of Europe as a whole the picture is very different. In France the monarchy was relatively weak since, though Henry II of England was theoretically a vassal of Louis VII in respect of his French possessions, the English king, through his acquisitions from his parents and his wife, controlled a much greater area of France than Louis himself. In some areas, as in Italy, towns and city-states,

The building of a church in the 12th century, based on a manuscript in the Bibliothèque Nationale, Paris.

unrestrained by strong central government, were often at war with one another. H. A. L. Fisher wrote: "If Florence took one side in a quarrel, it was sufficient for Pisa, Siena and Genoa to take the other; if Milan entered into an alliance with other cities, it would not at least be with Cremona and Pavia."

Much of the century was taken up by a prolonged struggle between the Empire and the Papacy, the air being thick with quarrels, renunciations, repudiations, interdicts and all the weapons of Church and State in conflict, including the setting up of half-a-dozen anti-popes. The century saw, incidentally, the election of the only Englishman in the long history of the Papacy – Adrian IV (Nicholas Breakspear) in 1154.

In some other directions, religion enjoyed a more constructive period. The century witnessed the early years of the Cistercian Order, which was to grow to greatness under St Bernard and St Stephen Harding. The Abbey of Clairvaux was founded in 1115. The Carmelites were established in 1150, and Gilbert of Sempringham, the only Englishman to found an Order (the Gilbertines), received his abbot's staff from St Bernard. Soon after 1180 Francesco Bernadone was born in Assisi (Francis of Assisi), later to renounce riches and found the Franciscan Order.

There were more militant foundations, though a number of these, too, were vowed to the service of religion. The Knights Templars, who adopted the rule of the Benedictines, were established for the protection of pilgrims and the defence of the Holy Sepulchre. The Knights of St John of Jerusalem (the Hospitallers or Knights Hospitallers) fulfilled the same function. It is recorded in 1112 that their monastery or Hospital could accommodate 2,000 guests as well as caring for the sick. In 1190, at the siege of Acre, was founded the third great religious-military Order – that of the Teutonic Knights or

Knights of the Virgin Mary, who took the vow of poverty, chastity and obedience and concerned themselves especially with German pilgrims.

The Second and Third Crusades followed their courses, achieving much empty glory but slight success. The Second (1147–49), led by Conrad III of Germany and Louis VII of France, produced an ineffective siege of Damascus. The Third (1189–93), renowned in history for its two chief protagonists, Richard I of England and Saladin (Salah-al-Din), resulted only in the capture of Acre and a truce with the Saracens.

The Norman invasion of England in the 11th century has always demanded and received much textbook space. Less well known, but in its different way equally remarkable, was the Norman conquest of southern Italy and, in 1130, the establishment of the kingdom of Sicily. There was this great difference: in England Norman power was built on union with the conquered people, whereas in Sicily it sought to preserve a sharp distinction between rulers and ruled. This was a matter of shrewd policy dictated by circumstances. In England, as we have seen, the English were becoming one nation. In Sicily and Italy the Normans ruled many different peoples, and could best hold them in peace and prosperity by allying themselves exclusively with none.

The 11th century had seen a partial break up of the Byzantine Empire with the loss of most of Asia Minor and the revolt of various tribes. Under the Comnenus dynasty, which ruled 1057–59 and 1081–1185, some recovery was made. But the end was in sight for the vast political and economic structure that since 395 had stood as a bastion between western Europe and the barbarians and had preserved so much of Roman and Greek culture. Within a few years of the close of the 12th century Constantinople was sacked by the Crusaders and the Empire gradually broke up into independent states. It was to stage another partial and temporary recovery, but the old prestige and power were not to be regained.

Farther east, in China, one of the country's greatest periods of culture and artistic achievement, under the Sung dynasty, was also approaching its end. The borders of the empire were being threatened or occupied by outlying tribes and the mighty shadow of Genghis Khan, born in about 1162, was soon to fall over the empire.

To return to Europe and to the pursuits of peace, the century is remarkable for the growth of towns all over the continent and, with the towns, the development of organised trade and commerce. A notable factor in this development were the various craft guilds, formed not only to watch over the interests of their members but to insist on proper standards of craftsmanship. Towns began to join together, if only in loose federations, to protect their common trading interests – a movement especially prominent in Germany and the Baltic. The most important group was soon to develop into the Hanseatic League whose headquarters, Lubeck, was founded in 1143, and which, at the height of its power, included over seventy towns which stretched, in the words of Professor Day of Harvard, "from Thorn and Krakow on the east to the towns of Zuider Zee on the west, and from Wisby and Reval in the north to Gottingen in the south."

On the sea, too, with the ever-growing number of merchant ships going about their business, it became necessary to organise and control codes of conduct. From the end of the 12th century (though they are probably based on even earlier codes) have survived the famous Judgments or Laws of Oléron, named after a small island off the coast of France, which was a centre of the wine trade and a rendezvous for shipping.

Finally, the century witnessed a revival of learning in Europe. The University of Bologna became renowned as a Law School, while Peter Abelard made Paris famous as a centre of thought, although the University of Paris itself dates from some time between 1150 and 1170, some years after Abelard's death in 1142. It was from Paris that the University of Oxford is traditionally said to have received its earliest scholars. In 1133 the theologian Robert Pullen came from Paris to lecture there, by the mid-1160s it was apparently a fully equipped university, and a hundred years later was second only to Paris. Thus the scene was set for men who were soon to dominate and change the thought of Europe, among them Roger Bacon (c. 1215–94) and John Wyclif (c. 1320–84).
¶ BROOKE, C. *The Twelfth Century Renaissance.* 1970

See also INDIVIDUAL ENTRIES.

Twentieth century: the years from 1901 onwards. The century has been one of major warfare, with the maintenance of peace by the old method of a balance of power between rival nations demonstrated as a precarious and outmoded device.

In most countries at the beginning of the century small ruling classes controlled the power and wealth of the community. They seemed mainly interested in seeking international prestige. It was a European-dominated world, and Great Britain with her vast empire, her industrial wealth and sea power had enjoyed an impressive lead for many years. In the rest of the world few countries other than the USA and Japan had the qualities of a world power.

Slowly this pattern changed. Tension over colonies, national boundaries, trade and prestige resulted in World War I. Old and powerful monarchies, among them the German and Austrian empires, collapsed in defeat. The Tsarist regime in Russia disintegrated, and the crumbling Turkish empire was finally destroyed. New forces appeared. Lenin and the Bolsheviks seized and kept power in Russia with ruthless efficiency. Dictators with histrionic appeal to the masses, such as Mussolini and Hitler, came to power. The Japanese set out to become masters of Eastern Asia. Hopes that 1914–18 was the "war to end all wars" faded with the renewed tension which culminated in 1939 in the outbreak of World War II. During this period it became increasingly clear that requirements for world power status had changed. Now huge manpower and natural resources had to be combined with high technical skill. By 1945 only two countries, the USA and Soviet Russia, possessed these in sufficiently vast quantities.

They differed widely in their ideas on politics (control by the Communist Party in Russia compared with free speech and elections in the USA) and economics (Soviet state control of production and distribution compared with American insistence on the advantages of free enterprise and the incentive of profit). These differences generated an atmosphere of yet more fear and tension, nicknamed the Cold War. Hostile alliances like NATO and the Warsaw Pact were created, and a third world war has nearly resulted from a series of crises as far apart as Berlin and Korea, Cuba and Suez.

Apart from China, in whose spectacular modernisation since the Communist victory of 1949 both the USA and Russia see future danger, no individual nation can rival these two super-powers. However, two groups of countries might equal them in power and influence. First, the British Commonwealth of Nations which gave determined and constant resistance to Nazi and Japanese aggression in World

War II; though since 1945 the Commonwealth link has been weakened because of a deliberate policy of granting independence and because of some unhappy disputes between members over questions of race and colour. Secondly, there is the European Economic Community, which was formed in 1957 to counterbalance the giant industrial power of the USA. Again, disputes over sovereignty rights of members and whether Britain should join have prevented the Common Market from acting with a sufficiently powerful and united voice in world affairs. After a strong parliamentary battle, whose echoes continue, the necessary legislation to enable Britain's accession to this Community with effect from 1 January 1973, was passed in 1972.

Although there has been so much war and threat of war, disarmament conferences have had little success; yet two world organisations have made an effort to negotiate over difficulties rather than fight. The League of Nations, created in 1919, was the great hope of the post-World War I generation, but it failed through the absence of the USA and Soviet Russia and its lack of a "police" force. The United Nations Organisation of 1945 has been more efficient, both in its social work against poverty and disease and in its efforts to prevent crises in places like the Congo and Suez developing into wider conflicts. But UN meetings at its New York headquarters have often been used by the USA and Russia as propaganda platforms in seeking support from the uncommitted nations of the "Third World".

This Third World of underdeveloped nations has grown rapidly since the 1940s, as more and more colonial territories have gained independence. These have provided one of the biggest problems of the 20th century, particularly because of poverty and the gulf between the rich and poor peoples of the world. While the North American continent, Japan and Europe have become wealthier, many countries of South America, Africa and southern Asia have faced the tremendous difficulties of low food production, little money for industry and, worst of all, a high population growth. Religious teaching and a long tradition of large families prevent many people from accepting modern ideas of birth control.

Scientific developments of the century have given the wealthier nations a great advantage. The "second industrial revolution" in oil and steel, electricity and chemicals, was well under way in 1901; but since World War II yet a third industrial revolution could be said to have developed: Nuclear power offers enormous possibilities, though its peacetime uses have been overshadowed by the fear created since the first atom bomb exploded at Hiroshima. Computers are showing important calculating and information storage possibilities. The space exploration programmes of the USA and Russia have extended the frontier of man's knowledge far beyond the earth, as well as providing superb practical results like worldwide satellite television. Associated with these developments have been some significant changes in the scale of agricultural and industrial organisation. High crop yields and huge numbers of machines and manufactures have resulted from the adoption of mass production techniques.

The century has seen dramatic progress in the conquest of disease: cholera and plague disappeared from Europe as the principles of immunisation became known, whilst antibiotics like penicillin have largely conquered tuberculosis. Ideas on diet, and particularly the discovery of the importance of vitamins, have had a great effect on diseases like rickets and scurvy which spring from not eating the right kind of food. The effects have not all been beneficial. Control of diseases like malaria have cut the death rate so quickly that the resulting population explosion raises serious doubt whether all peoples in future can be properly fed, housed and employed. The world population in 1901 numbered 1,600 million; by 1960 it had almost doubled. It could easily double again by the end of the century unless birth control methods, which have spread through many advanced countries, gain more general acceptance.

Achievements in communication have been revolutionary. The internal combustion engine was already known in 1901, but since then the car has grown to be the most important means of personal transport in industrialised countries. The Wright brothers' first controlled, heavier-than-air flight in 1903 began a development that enabled distant parts of the globe to be reached with ease and speed. Marconi's and Baird's successes with radio and television introduced millions to a powerful medium of information, propaganda and entertainment.

Ease of communication has shown people how others live, and given an impetus to the worldwide desire for equal rights. Throughout the century this has been seen in many ways. First, socialists have demanded voting rights and state welfare schemes for everyone in an effort to improve the way ordinary people live and work. Secondly, possession of material things such as cars and radios has become an important demand by the peoples of the Third World. Thirdly, there have been universal and powerful movements to end discrimination on grounds of religion, race and sex. Jews have fought for and won a new state, Israel, where victims of persecution in Russia, Germany and elsewhere could find safety; black peoples have conducted a long and bitter struggle for civil rights in the USA

and against the apartheid ideas of South African governments; in many countries women have won the right to vote and to compete freely in many professions hitherto regarded as the special province of men.

The provision of educational opportunities for large numbers of children instead of the select few has led to a tremendous rise in world literacy. Books for the mass of ordinary people as well as the highly educated are sold in millions, and the "paperback" revolution in publishing is spreading across the continents. Huge sales of books for leisure reading, as well as for acquiring information, are recorded. New forms of entertainment, too, have been directed at the mass market. The century has seen the decline of the western theatre and music hall in favour of filmed tragedy and comedy, which can be seen on large cinema screens throughout the world, or on the small television set in a home.

Personal achievement has always been a feature of man's life. The 20th century's contribution in this field has been varied. Everest has been climbed, the Poles reached, and innumerable height, depth and speed records surpassed. Many thousands choose sport in striving for distinction. "Barriers" such as the four-minute mile have been broken, while the peak of amateur sporting attainment has become a gold medal in the Olympic Games. But the real appeal in terms of mass support is exercised by professional "stars" of football and baseball teams. Here excellence can be highly paid as well, and other sports such as tennis and golf have organised themselves similarly.

From these achievements it would seem that the main characteristic of the 20th century has been a rapid rise in the standards of living for the common man. This has certainly been so in countries where the speed of technological change has given people many extra hours of leisure and the money to enjoy life, rather than spend it in the drudgery which was the lot of the masses in previous centuries.

But this progress, though impressive, cannot conceal the problems facing the next generations. Poverty still exists on a massive scale. Poor countries have few doctors and teachers to improve their standards of health and education. Disasters such as the great San Francisco and Tokyo earthquakes of 1906 and 1923, and the Bengal floods of 1970, show that man has not yet succeeded in forecasting and adapting to nature's behaviour. Even the rich countries have created new problems: the loneliness of people living in big cities; the rising pollution menace that threatens the sea, the air and the landscape; the increasing scarcity of certain resources; the destruction of valuable agricultural land by the relentless growth of towns and industries; a traffic casualty rate of thousands a day on the world's highways.

¶ TREASE, GEOFFREY. *This Is Your Century.* 1965; UNSTEAD, R. J. *Britain in the Twentieth Century.* 1966

See also INDIVIDUAL ENTRIES.

Typewriter: machine with a keyboard and inked ribbon for producing printed characters in substitution for handwriting. The typewriter seems to have been first thought of by an English engineer, Henry Mill, who, in 1714, took out a patent for "an Artificial Machine . . . whereby all Writing whatever may be Engrossed in Paper or Parchment so Neat and Exact as not to be distinguished from Print", but no details of its construction are known. In 1829 William Austin Burt of Detroit took out a patent for his "typographer", not unlike a modern toy typewriter, with all the type mounted on one semicircular frame, which was turned by hand till the required letter was in position, then pressed on to the paper by a lever.

The first typewriter to be produced on a commercial scale came on the market in the United States in 1874, and Mark Twain is said to have been the first author ever to submit a typescript to a publisher. Early typewriters printed in capital letters only, but the familiar shift key mechanism appeared on the Remington Model 2 in 1878. This was followed, a few years later, by the first machine to provide visible typing. The early machines printed on the underside of the cylinder, which had to be raised in order to see what had been printed. These were followed by models which printed downwards on top of the cylinder, and later by those of the modern type which print on the front of the cylinder.

Early typewriters were large and heavy, but portable models began to appear about 1909. The latest development is the electric typewriter, which made its appearance about 1920.

Tyranny: Greek word meaning absolute rule, not necessarily by a single man. Athens, for a brief period, endured Thirty Tyrants. Many of these tyrants were enlightened rulers and patrons of art and literature; but others displayed harshness and brutality, characteristics which are generally attached to the idea of tyranny.

Tyre: city and seaport of the Phoenicians at the eastern end of the Mediterranean. In ancient times it carried on a prosperous maritime trade, as did its neighbour Sidon. In the mountains behind the coast grew the famous Cedars of Lebanon, which were used in the building of the Temple of Jerusalem (*see* separate entry): very few of these trees survive today in their former habitat. Jesus visited the area in the course of His ministry. Tyre was a stronghold of the Crusaders (1124–1291; *see* CRUSADES). The city survives today as Sur, one of the smaller ports of the republic of Lebanon.

U

Uganda: former British protectorate in East Africa adjoining Sudan in the north, Kenya in the east, with Tanzania and Lake Victoria in the south and Rwanda in the south-west. The eastern halves of Lakes Albert and Edward form part of its western boundary with Zaire. The main exports are coffee, cotton, copper and tea. Physical features include high mountains, with the peaks of the Ruwenzori range (the "Mountains of the Moon") rising over 16,700 feet [5,089 m], great lakes, and vast forests infinitely diverse in character and vegetation owing to the country's widely varied altitude. There is a great variety of flora and fauna.

At a very early period, probably three to four thousand years ago, the inhabitants came under the influence of Egyptian civilisation, manifested in such crafts as pottery and metalwork and brought in by Hamitic invaders. Afterwards powerful Negro kingdoms grew up, Bunyoro, Busoga, Ankole and, especially, Buganda. The first European to enter the territory was the British explorer John Speke, in 1862, and Anglican missionaries followed in the 1870s. Britain proclaimed a protectorate over Uganda, 1894–96, and British administration continued until the country was given independence within the Commonwealth in October 1962, becoming a republic five years later, with Dr A. Milton Obote as president. His successor, General Amin, caused a crisis in 1972 by the ruthless expulsion from the country of many thousands of Ugandan Asians, most of whom were received into Britain.
See AFRICA for map.

Ukraine: eastern European constituent republic of the USSR. From Neolithic times Ukrainian people dwelt in the Dnieper and Dniester valleys. There the city of Kiev arose. The Mongol invasion in the 13th century destroyed Ukrainian cohesion. A shortlived Ukrainian Cossack state emerged in 1648 under Russian protection, while from 1690 western Ukraine was under Poland and later Austria. In 1917 a Ukrainian republic was formed but passed under Russian rule. It became a battleground in World War II. After the war Galicia, the western Ukraine, was reunited to Russian Ukraine and the country became a member of the United Nations in 1945.
See USSR for map.
See also COSSACKS; MONGOLS; NEOLITHIC; UNITED NATIONS; WORLD WAR II.

Ulster: northern province of Ireland. After the Ice Age (*see* separate entry) it was through Ulster that man entered Ireland about 6000 BC, and the province is rich in remains of prehistoric peoples. At the beginning of the Christian era a kingdom of Ulster extended as far south and west as the Boyne and Shannon but soon shrank. Christianity spread through Ireland from Ulster in the 5th century. The rugged coastline and impenetrable terrain repelled invaders, and Ulster was not finally brought under English rule till the early 17th century. An English and Scottish Protestant population was introduced. Heavily industrialised in the 19th and 20th centuries, Ulster resisted Irish secession from the United Kingdom and, in 1921, six Ulster counties were given a subordinate government within the United Kingdom as Northern Ireland, with Belfast as capital. Ulster is now generally used as another name for Northern Ireland. The mixture of religions and the activities of revolutionary and republican elements have combined to make the province a centre of frequent unrest that has not stopped short of bloodshed, terrorist bombing and sectarian assassinations. So acute did this near-anarchy become that in 1972 Stormont, the Northern Ireland parliament, was suspended and direct rule from Westminster substituted.

See also IRELAND; IRISH REPUBLICAN ARMY; NORTHERN IRELAND; PROTESTANT.

Underwater exploration: the study of wrecks, submerged towns and harbours and other offshore sites. The archaeologist on land has learned to familiarise himself with every kind of environment, but confronted with the world beneath the sea he is a comparative newcomer. Nevertheless, underwater exploration with the aid of modern diving techniques is a fast developing science.

The examination of offshore sites is usually carried out after a diver has chanced to bring up something of interest.

The Mediterranean, for instance, has certain points off the coast where the seabed is littered with pottery, anchors and other forms of ancient debris. The number and nature of such objects would indicate that the site was once an anchorage for vessels seeking shelter. The excavation of submerged harbours is basically an extension of land archaeology and requires teams of professional draughtsmen, photographers, etc., in addition to the divers.

The ancient wreck is perhaps the most challenging of all tasks facing the underwater explorer. Probably the first archaeological venture in this field was started in the 15th century. Two large Roman pleasure barges were traditionally thought to have been sunk in Lake Nemi, southeast of Rome. In 1446 the wrecks were located. A raft built of barrels was moored over one of them and ropes were taken down by swimmers and

Divers photographed 50 feet below the surface of the Mediterranean, plotting the position of the wreck of a Greek trading ship, sunk near Syracuse in Sicily about 800 BC.

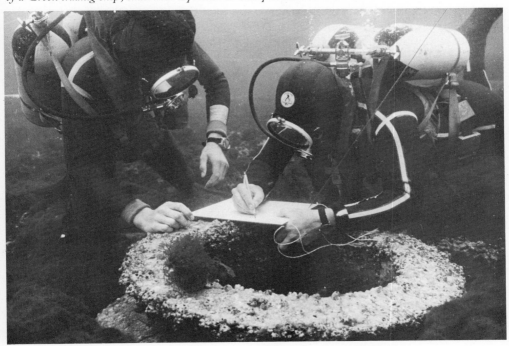

fastened to the wreck. Efforts to float it and pull it ashore failed. In 1535 an early form of diving suit was tried. It had a wooden helmet with a crystal plate in the front which enabled the diver to observe the wrecks. Measurements were taken and samples of the wood brought to the surface. In 1827 a diving bell was submerged close by the wrecks and many fine fragments of marble, mosaics, etc., were recovered. At the same time a barge was constructed, but elaborate equipment to raise one of the wrecks failed once again. In 1895 an amateur diver brought up bronze lion and wolf heads and many more pieces of mosaics, etc. Finally, in 1928–29, the lake was drained and exposed two giant barges of 234 feet [71 metres] and 239 feet [72 metres], respectively, both richly decorated. The hulls were well preserved and proved an invaluable guide to Roman ship construction methods. Unfortunately both barges were burnt during the German occupation in 1944. The long story of the Nemi ships, with the exception of the last unhappy chapter, serves to illustrate some of the attempts at raising and preserving ships and underwater objects over a period of 500 years.

Another successful operation in rescuing ancient ships by the drainage method was carried out in Denmark. In 1962 the remains of five 900-year-old Viking ships (see VIKINGS) were discovered in Roskilde Fiord. The water was shallow enough for a large sheet steel cofferdam to be built to enclose the entire site. The water was then pumped out, and the remains of the boats were revealed. The timbers were then cleaned, carefully recorded, photographed and finally removed. A chemical hardening process followed, and the boats were then reconstructed and put on display in a museum nearby.

The seabed of the Mediterranean provides almost unlimited scope for the underwater explorer. The remains of hundreds of ancient Greek and Roman trading vessels together with their cargoes lie submerged close by the coasts and reefs. In 1900 sponge-divers off Antikythera, on the south coast of Greece, accidentally located a considerable quantity of partially buried bronze and marble figures. These were subsequently found to be part of the cargo of a Roman trading vessel of the 1st century BC. A salvage expedition was organised and sponge-divers wearing diving suits and helmets succeeded in bringing up a considerable number of valuable treasures. In 1907 another Roman vessel of about the same age was discovered by sponge-divers off Mahdia, Tunisia. This was carrying priceless Greek works of art. Similar methods were employed in bringing up much of this cargo. In both the above instances the divers, wearing cumbersome equipment, had a difficult and dangerous task. Their periods under water were severely limited: there were no attempts to excavate the hulls and no photographs, drawings or records were made. The two discoveries were, however, regarded as marking the beginning of modern underwater archaeology in the Mediterranean.

Little more of note happened in the Mediterranean until about 1948. The wartime inventions of the aqualung and swimfins now made it possible for the amateur as well as the professional diver to explore the seabed with a freedom hitherto unknown. The French Commander Cousteau and his associates were soon to popularise this new form of "free diving". Many new wrecks were located, mostly dating from the 1st and 2nd centuries BC. In all cases they were trading vessels carrying cargoes of liquids contained in amphorae. With the new equipment now available divers were able to salvage these in great numbers. They were also able to carry out detailed studies

The Wasa: *Above: Grinning lion heads which decorated the gun port lids of the warship* Wasa. *Below: The* Wasa *raised out of the water on a concrete pontoon and held in an aluminium "cage". Above right: The lower gun deck after excavation. Below right: Coins being sifted.*

of the remains of the ships, and photographs were taken with underwater cameras. With the resulting information divers were able to make scale drawings.

Hunting for sunken treasure is mainly confined to the Caribbean area. Between the 16th and early 18th centuries the great Spanish treasure fleets carrying precious metals for the monetary systems of Europe made regular sailings from South America to Spain. The hazards of the sea, and to a lesser extent enemy action, were responsible for a number of sinkings in the Caribbean and off the coast of Florida. Twentieth-century divers have located many of these and have reaped a rich harvest of treasure.

In northern European waters some of the sunken ships of the 1588 Spanish Armada (*see* ARMADA) have been found. The so-called treasure galleon sunk off Tobermory, Isle of Mull, Scotland, has so far yielded little of its riches, but divers have recovered some of the iron cannon.

Owing to the absence of the destructive teredo worm in the Baltic some remarkably well preserved wrecks have been found in Scandinavian waters. Most famous is the great Swedish sixty-four-gun ship *Wasa*, sunk in Stockholm harbour in 1628. Her hull was raised in 1961 and is now being chemically treated and dried so that restoration may be carried out.

¶ COGGINS, JACK. *Hydrospace: Frontier beneath the Sea.* 1967; COOK, J. GORDON. *Exploring under the Sea.* 1964
See also ARCHAEOLOGY.

UNESCO (United Nations Educational, Scientific and Cultural Organisation): a specialised agency of UNO (*see* UNITED NATIONS ORGANISATION) with headquarters in Paris. It came into operation late in 1946 to help peace by supporting close cooperation between nations in education, the arts and science. It works through project committees which investigate problems such as the use of drugs, the effect of television on children, and women's rights; through publications which try to reduce racial hatred and ignorance; and through money grants for travel and study.

¶ LAVES, WALTER H. C. and THOMSON, C. A. *Unesco: Purpose, Progress, Prospects.* 1958

Union Jack: national flag of the United Kingdom. In 1606 the English national flag was combined with the Scottish flag. The red cross of St George on a white ground, device of the king of England at least as early as the 13th century, and the diagonal white St Andrew's cross on a blue ground, recorded in the 14th century, formed the Union flag.

After the union of England and Scotland, difficulties arose over the bearing of the national flags at sea, and in 1606 King James I ordered the use of the new flag instead, the two crosses to be "joined together according to a form made by our Heralds". The details of the design have not survived; but we know it was not popular with the Scots, who rarely used it till the Act of Union in 1707. In 1800 the union with Ireland took place and the red saltire cross which was the badge of the Order of St Patrick was combined with the Union flag of England and Scotland.

A jack is any flag flown from the jack staff in the bows of a warship. Strictly speaking, this is the correct usage of the term Union jack, though the term is now used indiscriminately for the national flag, wherever displayed.

Union of Soviet Socialist Republics (USSR): federal republic in eastern Europe and northern and central Asia. By 1917 the Russian empire was disintegrating. Its armies were breaking up on World War I fighting fronts. The Tsar had been forced to abdicate. The old ruling class was incapacitated by war casualties and disunity. Food and all commodities were short.

Administration was breaking down under the provisional government of Alexander Kerensky. The Bolshevik wing of the revolutionary movement, led by Lenin, gained control in Petrograd through workers' soviets and on 7 November 1917 the government was seized by the Bolsheviks.

To stop German invasion, the treaty of Brest-Litovsk was signed by Russia and the Central Powers on 3 March 1918 depriving Russia of 62 million people, a quarter of its territory, a third of its food-producing land and half of its industries. There followed a desperate struggle for existence against foreign intervention and counter-revolutionary forces. The new Red Army finally triumphed and the rulers of Russia had to face the problems of a ruined land and a starving people.

Lenin died in 1924, to be succeeded soon by Stalin, who gained an autocratic control over Russia. He set about economic reorganisation, introducing the first five-year plan in 1928. The aims were the development of heavy industry, the mobilisation of all resources and the establishment of collective farms. Stalin reorganised rural and industrial society without regard to the human material he used, meeting resistance with slaughter. Russian life in the 1930s was bleak and dangerous, as Stalin sought to strengthen his personal position by "purges" and mass executions. The country was organised in separate republics but all dominated by the one central policy.

In 1939 a Russo-German pact embodied Stalin's hope that Germany and the western powers would ruin one another in war, while the USSR remained a spectator. In 1941, however, Germany invaded the USSR. Victory over Germany cost over 20 million lives, but the treaty of Brest-Litovsk was avenged, and the Russian style of revolution spread into a wide area of eastern Europe.

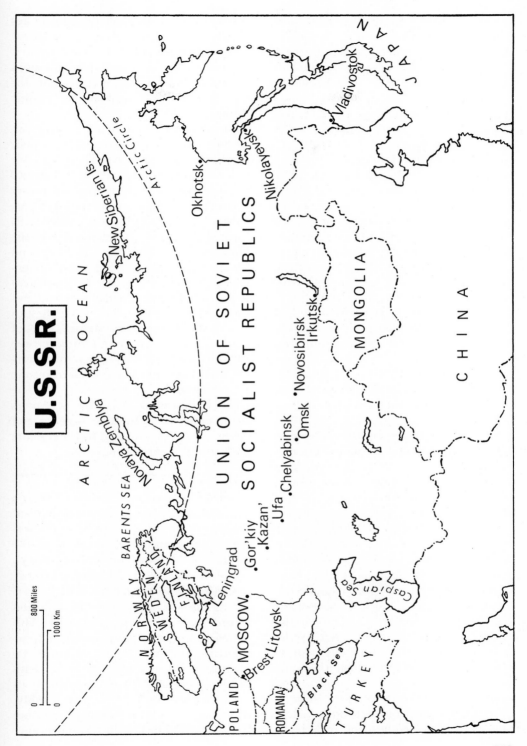

After World War II the USA was regarded as the chief rival of the USSR, and a "cold war" developed between the two, emerging in many episodes, including the Korean War. Russia quickly followed the USA in developing fission and fusion bombs and sophisticated rocket devices, putting the first space traveller into earth orbit in 1957. NATO was confronted by the Warsaw Pact.

Stalin died in 1953, lifting a cloud of fear, and at the twentieth communist party congress in 1956 his record of personal rule and terrorism was condemned. Among his successors, Nikita Khrushchev (1958–64) did something to reduce the "cold war" atmosphere. The identification of communism with Russian interests led to clashes with communists in other countries, including Warsaw Pact governments, and there has been grave tension with communist China.

¶ ARAGON, L. *History of USSR.* 1964
See also BOLSHEVIKS; LENIN; NATO; RUSSIA; STALIN; WARSAW PACT; WORLD WARS I and II.

United Kingdom Atomic Energy Authority (UKAEA): body responsible for atomic research and development in the United Kingdom. At the end of World War II (*see* separate entry) it became clear that the possibilities of atomic energy must be explored, and the British government established research centres at Harwell, Berkshire, and Risley, Lancashire. In 1953 a start was made on the construction of a nuclear reactor at Calder Hall, Cumberland. In 1954 the Atomic Energy Authority Act established UKAEA, which took over atomic research and development on 1 August 1954.

The Research Group at Harwell conducts fundamental research into nuclear physics, and its equipment includes a million-volt electron microscope for research into radiation damage, while investigation into radioactive isotopes is carried on at Wantage. The Weapons Group at Aldermaston is responsible for the further development of atomic weapons.

The groups responsible for Production, Development and Engineering have their headquarters at Risley. These provide specialist advice to electricity boards and overseas customers anxious to build reactors and are also responsible for UKAEA's own atomic power plants at Calder Hall; Chapel Cross, Dumfriesshire; Windscale, Cumberland; Winfrith, Dorset; and Dounreay, Caithness. These produce electricity, which is sold to the electricity boards and fed into the national grid, but their primary purpose is research into atomic fuel and reactor systems. These, of course, are not the only atomic power stations: the Central Electricity Generating Board operates a further seven atomic power stations.

The Radiochemical Centre at Amersham prepares radioactive isotopes and other substances produced by the reactors for medical and scientific use.

United Nations Organisation (UNO): international organisation of independent states founded at the end of World War II (*see* separate entry) as successor to the League of Nations (*see* separate entry). A conference of the "United Nations" (the Allies who fought the Axis Powers during the war) met in San Francisco and signed the Charter in June 1945. This aimed to maintain peace and to support human rights throughout the world. To do this an organisation was set up with headquarters in New York, where its debating chamber, the General Assembly, meets annually, and in which each member has one vote. The Organisation has other councils and agencies, such as the Food and Agriculture Organisation, the International Atomic Energy Agency, the International Civil Aviation Organisation and the International Monetary Fund. Its chief judicial body is the International Court of Justice.

¶ SAVAGE, KATHERINE. *The Story of the United Nations.* 1969

See also INTERNATIONAL LAW; HAGUE, THE; YALTA CONFERENCE.

United Provinces: name given to the seven northern provinces of the Netherlands (Holland, Zeeland, Utrecht, Gelderland, Overijssel, Groningen and Friesland) who declared their independence in 1581.

United States of America: federal republic in North America. Much of the history of the USA is distributed through this work in nearly a hundred separate entries, as well as in biographies and other articles where the country's story is interwoven with other events and destinies. By way of introduction, there are at least three considerations that are sufficiently obvious to citizens of the US but are not so well understood outside it.

The first, and major, point is the comparative shortness of the period into which the history of the USA is packed. The most significant part of the history of North America is crammed into a period of less than 500 years. The historian C. F. Strong has written: "In the 1940s it became possible to fly across the Atlantic in ten hours. Christopher Columbus first crossed that ocean 450 years before, and it took him ten weeks to do it. What happened on the other side of the Atlantic between those two dates constitutes one of the most romantic and exciting stories in the history of the world."

The second consideration is that, while there are citizens of America, there is no

American race: even the original Indians only now enjoy full citizenship. In 1790 the total population was about three million, of whom more than 2,700,000 were British. It has been estimated that in the period 1820-1967 the USA received over 44 million immigrants, so that, today, "the Americans . . . are not merely a people of many races: they are proud of it".

The third, and least important, is that films and television programmes, in giving a portrait of America to the rest of the world, have exercised an influence out of all proportion and have provided a completely unbalanced one. Thus, to a great many people, the USA is almost entirely peopled with gangsters, corrupt politicians, tough cops, cowboys, strident musicians and of course glamorous film stars. The truth is otherwise.

Below are suggested some of the main divisions into which the story falls and some of the entries through which the theme may be pursued. There is rarely, of course, any sharp division. For example, the settlement of the various states was still proceeding in the 19th century, long after the War of Independence, and the 49th and 50th states, Alaska and Hawaii, were not added till 1959.

The first obvious historical phase is that of discovery, the first occasions when, confronting the eyes of Scandinavian, Spanish, French, Dutch, Italian, English seamen, the vast continent of North America loomed out of the haze, stretching – although they did not imagine its magnitude – some 2,800 miles [4,506 km] from the Atlantic to the Pacific and nearly 1,600 miles [2,575 km] from north to south, a size possible to grasp only in terms of comparisons, i.e. that the present state of Texas is three times the size of Great Britain; and that the smallest state, Rhode Island, is nearly 130 times bigger than England's largest county, Yorkshire.

Next came the long struggle for permanent settlement, the early failures and disappointments; the first harvest of the Pilgrim Fathers, still celebrated in Thanksgiving Day; the grants of vast tracts of land to private individuals and companies; the struggle with the Indians, the Dutch and the French and the beginnings of the long, ugly story of slavery.

A rising sense of nationhood, combined with a lack of understanding and foresight on the part of the British government, led, first to argument and friction, then, when no other choice seemed open to the colonists, to the War of Independence. Many leading colonists, George Washington among them, did not visualise and did not want independence of the Crown. But once the train of events had been set firmly in motion there was no turning back. The final phase came, not with the Treaty of Paris in 1783 but thirty years later in the needless and shortlived War of 1812, after which America finally turned her eyes away from Europe. "It is our true policy to steer clear of permanent alliance with any portion of the foreign world," George Washington wrote in 1796 in his "Farewell Address to the People of the United States"; and five years later Thomas Jefferson expressed the same sentiment: "Peace, commerce, and honest friendship with all nations – entangling alliances with none." The 1812 war turned this theory into hard fact and a practice that was to continue for over a century.

When Jefferson, in two of his 1787 letters to friends, said "a little rebellion now and then is a good thing" and "the tree of liberty must be refreshed from time to time with the blood of patriots", he could have visualised nothing so tragic and wasteful as the events of 1861–65, when North and South were locked in a civil war which left the country poorer by 620,000 men out of three million engaged

in fighting – a higher proportion than in World Wars I and II (*see* separate entries).

Interrupted by these periods of strife, but all the time continuing, and accelerating in times of peace, was a vast build-up of commerce and industry, the foundation of great business empires, the opening up of the interior, the driving of roads and railways, the growth of cities, a wealth of invention and educational progress.

Finally, a picture might emerge of the USA, its policies, vicissitudes and achievements in the 20th century including the massive development of the automobile industry and, in another element, the aeroplane; the reluctant emergence from the isolationism proclaimed by Washington and Jefferson; the vast scale of help given to new and emerging countries; on the one hand work for peace and security and, on the other, conflict at home and abroad both social and military; and, capturing above all else public imagination and interest throughout the world, man's first steps in space.

See AMERICA entries for map.

¶ HILL, C. P. *History of the United States.* 1966; SOMERVELL, D. C. *History of the United States.* 1955

See also INDIVIDUAL ENTRIES.

Universities: communities of teachers and students to which the following features normally apply: (1) the university is a corporate body governed by a charter or constitution granted by the state, or in earlier times by the Church; (2) the students are seeking to graduate, that is to say, to be awarded degrees; (3) there are a number of faculties in which different subjects are studied; (4) selected students who have graduated may pursue further studies leading to higher degrees, while the teachers themselves often give part of their time to research. Entry to a university normally depends on a candidate having reached a certain educational standard, and competition is often severe.

In earlier times this was not always the case: John Donne (1573–1621), later Dean of St Paul's, was admitted to Oxford at the age of eleven.

In Roman times, while there were no universities in the modern sense, young men used to resort to Athens, Rhodes and Alexandria to study philosophy and rhetoric (the art of speaking). The pattern, however, which we know today, and which is followed in most parts of the world, gradually developed in western Europe during the Middle Ages. It follows from this that the Church, for long the sole upholder and protector of learning, took a leading part. The seeds were usually first sown when a small band of students gathered in a town or city to attend the lectures of some teacher, and this attracted other similar groups to the same place. In time the community thus formed would achieve enough stability and reputation to apply, often to the local bishop, sometimes to higher authority, for a charter. One of the chief objects of this was to gain protection from townspeople, who often regarded the newcomers with suspicion and jealousy. The word university itself was originally applied to a guild or company of students banded together for welfare and safety. At Vercelli, an Italian community which had a brief existence in the 13th century, there were four universities for young men who came from England, Germany, Italy and Provence.

The earliest chartered university was at Salerno in southern Italy, already famed for many years before its formal incorporation in the first half of the 12th century as a centre of medical studies. It was followed not long after by Bologna, 300 miles [483 km] to the north, where civil and canon (Church) law were particularly studied. The most renowned of all, however, was the University of Paris, the origins of which can be traced to the early 12th century, though its incorporation was by a "brief" of Pope Innocent III dated 1211. It was probably here that degrees were first instituted, that of Master of Arts regarded as a licence to teach, that of Bachelor of Arts being, as it were, a stage in apprenticeship.

From this point there was a steady growth of fresh foundations throughout western Europe: Seville (1242) in Spain, which helped to bring the learning of Christendom into contact with that of the Arabic world, Heidelberg (1386) in Germany, where in later centuries so many universities sprang up, the Polish Cracow (1364) in the east, the Swedish Uppsala (1477) in the north.

In England, Oxford is said to have been started about 1133 by a migration from Paris, but the choice of this particular place suggests that a nucleus may have existed there already. Here, too, strife with the inhabitants was bitter, and a particularly violent riot in 1209 drove the students away, some of them, it is said, going off to form the early beginnings of Cambridge. Five years later, however, Oxford received the protection of papal recognition. In these first two English universities there soon grew up the feature of a number of separate colleges, each to a large extent controlling its own affairs, but preparing its students for degrees conferred by the central body. Merton College (1274) was the earliest of such colleges at Oxford, Peterhouse (1284) at Cambridge. Though Oliver Cromwell (*see* separate entry) proposed a northern university at Durham, this was not achieved until 1832. London (1835) was the first to admit students who did not belong to the Church of England, a requirement abolished in the older universities from 1854 onwards. Scotland's three oldest foundations, St Andrews, Glasgow and Aberdeen, date from the 15th century and Edinburgh from 1582. Trinity College, Dublin

(1591), a protestant stronghold in a Catholic country, was for over 300 years the only university in Ireland. From the middle of the 19th century there have been in England, Scotland, Wales and Ireland over twenty additions to the list, nearly half of them since World War II.

In the USA the old foundations of Harvard (1636, reputedly the wealthiest university in the world), William and Mary (1693) and Yale (1701) enjoy a very high reputation. Other famous universities include Princeton, New Jersey (1746), called by President Woodrow Wilson 'a seminary of statesmen'; Columbia, New York City (1754), another very wealthy institution; and Chicago (1890), which is especially well known for its work in education, social sciences and atomic physics. The first separate college of high standing and adequate endowment for women in the US was Vassar, New York (1865), though degrees were being granted to women thirty years earlier. Some of the greatest libraries in the world are housed in American universities, a good example being the collections at Texas.

Universities are now a feature of nearly every country in the world. Great universities established in the British Commonwealth include McGill, Toronto and Laval in Canada; Sydney and Melbourne in Australia; and others in South Africa and India. The largest purpose-built university structure is probably the MV. Lomonosov State University, south of Moscow, 32 storeys high and containing 40,000 rooms.

Returning to Great Britain, another significant development should be mentioned. In 1969 a new type of university received its charter – the Open University or 'University of the Air', providing degree courses largely through the medium of radio and television programmes. *See also* INDIVIDUAL ENTRIES.

Upanishads: a series of prose commentaries on the Vedic hymns, the earliest dating probably from about 500 BC, which form one of the most remarkable sections of ancient Sanskrit literature. They had much influence in developing Hindu beliefs (*see* HINDUISM), particularly in *Brahman*, the all-embracing spirit, *Karma*, the importance of "works" and *Yoga*, personal discipline.

Uruguay: republic on the south-east coast of South America. The territory contains rich grasslands which are good for cattle, so that possession has frequently been a matter of dispute. It was colonised first by the Portuguese, coming south from Brazil in 1680; but in the early 18th century the Spaniards of Argentina founded a rival centre at Montevideo, and in 1777 this became the capital city of a Spanish Uruguay.

Uruguay, like all the other Spanish territories in South America, became a free republic early in the 19th century (1814), but it was too small to defend itself easily from the rival claims of Brazil and Argentina, and there was conflict over its boundaries until 1853, when a treaty was made. With a total population of about three million, Uruguay is still the smallest of all the South American republics.
See also SOUTH AMERICA.

Utopia: an ideal but impracticable social or political system; originally, an imaginative work published in 1516 by Sir Thomas More (*see* separate entry). The title, from the Greek, means "Nowhere", and the book describes an ideal community living according to the laws of nature. This gave scope for implied criticism of the abuses of the times. Samuel Butler (1835–1902) in his *Erewhon* and *Erewhon Revisited* presents a fantasy on similar lines.

V

Vaccination: inoculation with a virus to secure immunity from smallpox or other disease. Edward Jenner (1749-1823), a doctor in Gloucestershire, England (*see* separate entry), studied smallpox and reached the conclusion that no one had it twice and that people whose work brought them into contact with cattle were never infected, although they frequently suffered from a similar, milder illness known as "cowpox". Certain that cowpox protected the body from smallpox, Jenner deliberately infected patients with it, then exposed them to smallpox. They remained immune. Jenner's method of infection by cowpox was termed vaccination, from the Latin *vacca*, a cow.

Vagrancy: wandering, with no fixed home and often no work. In order to live vagrants may do odd jobs but sometimes beg or steal. Because of this, vagrancy in many parts of the world is an offence against the law.

In the Middle Ages (*see* separate entry) vagrants in England often found food and a night's shelter at one of the many monasteries throughout the country. After the monasteries were destroyed in the time of Henry VIII (1491-1547) this help was not available, and the growing numbers of vagrants became a serious problem, with a great increase in begging and robbery. Towns and villages were besieged by large numbers of these "rogues and vagabonds". From the time of Queen Elizabeth I (1533-1603) many laws were passed to control vagrancy but the problem was not solved. Between the various wars, disbanded soldiers with no trade took to the roads, and, as the army of vagrants grew, the punishments became more severe and hanging was frequent.

Today, in countries with a well developed welfare organisation, vagrancy is no longer a serious problem. In less advanced communities the difficulties remain and, indeed, there are still places where vagrancy is an accepted profession rather than an economic misfortune.

Valletta, Valetta: capital and chief port of the island of Malta on the north-east coast, with a fine strongly fortified harbour. In the 16th century it was the headquarters of the Knights of Malta (formerly the Knights Hospitallers or Knights of St John of Jerusalem) and many evidences of their occupation survive, including the lodging of the grand master, armour, and tapestries. Under British occupation, Valletta became an important naval and military base. Its continued use, either by Britain or NATO forces, has become a matter for dispute with the Maltese government.
See also MALTA.

Valois, House of: French dynasty of kings (1328-1589). Valois is part of France, just south of Paris, formerly owned by a younger branch of the powerful medieval Capetian kings. The Valois first became the ruling house in the person of Philip VI (ruled 1328-50). Some later rulers, such as Francis I, were very able, but many were weak monarchs who lost France much prestige during the Hundred Years War and the Wars of Religion. The House died out with Henry III (ruled 1574-89), to be succeeded by the Bourbon Henry IV.
See also INDIVIDUAL ENTRIES.

Valparaiso: South American city (named by the Spaniard Juan de Saavedra after his birthplace in Spain) founded in 1536 on a fine sheltered bay on the Pacific coast. In spite of two disastrous earthquakes, its inhabitants have made it the commercial capital of Chile. Many Scots, Irish, French and Germans live there, attracted by its pleasant climate. Its greatest hero is Bernardo O'Higgins (*see* separate entry).

Vandals: an east Germanic people who invaded Gaul with other peoples in AD 406, passed on into Spain in 409, and then, in 429, into North Africa. Establishing a kingdom with capital at Carthage, they cut Rome off from vital grain supplies. Unlike other Germanic peoples they were implacably hostile to Rome and, having built a navy, sacked the city in 455. They occupied Sicily and Sardinia. Few in numbers, their kingdom lasted only a century, until North Africa was reconquered by the Byzantine Empire. Their destructive energy gave "vandal" and "vandalism", as words of sinister meaning, to the language of later nations.

Varanasi, Banaras, Benares: important commercial centre in north-eastern India, on the River Ganges. The City of Benares (Kasi) was once a Buddhist centre (*see* BUDDHA), containing in the 7th century at least thirty Buddhist monasteries. Now the most sacred city of Hinduism, it has over 1,500 Hindu temples, of which the "Golden Temple" is the most sacred. The Moslem Mosque of Aurangzeb is spectacular. The city attracts annually a million pilgrims who carry out ceremonial bathing in the Ganges.

Vatican and **Vatican City:** The palace of the Vatican, at Rome, is the residence of the popes, or bishops of Rome, the supreme heads of the Roman Catholic Church (*see* separate entry) throughout the world; it also contains one of the finest collections of pictures and manuscripts in the world. The palace, and its grounds, are situated within a part of Rome that is called the Vatican City. Although this city is not much more than a hundred acres [40 hectares] in size and has little more than a thousand inhabitants, it is an independent state, in its own right, and not a part of Italy. An independent papal state has existed since the 8th century, and at one time extended right across central Italy. But when the Italian peninsula was unified in the 19th century and the modern Italian state was formed, the Pope's lands were taken from him (1860-70). It was only in 1929 that a treaty was made between Italy and the Vatican setting up the Vatican City State. The importance of this state to the Pope is that, as head of the World Church, he should not be subjected to pressure from any particular country, and he should be free to receive the ambassadors of all foreign powers. The value of this independence to the Pope was made especially clear in World War 11 (*see* separate entry), when Italy was overrun first by the Germans and then by the Western Allies, but the neutrality of the Vatican City was respected by both sides.
See colour section.

Vedas: collections of hymns and rituals, developed in the upper Indus region, which form the earliest scriptures of the Aryans in India. The most important, possibly the earliest, work in any Indo-European language, is the *Rig-Veda*, compiled between *c.* 2000 and 1000 BC. The hymns are addressed to the chief Vedic deities, such as Agni the fire god and the divine warrior Indra.

Velasquez, Diego Rodriguez de Silva y (1599-1660): Spanish painter. Born in Seville, Velasquez became court painter to Philip IV of Spain, but he was no mere flatterer of royalty. High-born or lowly, his subjects were painted with equal honesty and unrivalled realism. Visits to Italy, particularly Venice, where he could study the works of the Venetian painters (*see* next entry), tempered his early, rather austere, style with colour and warmth. Yet it is not really correct to speak of Velasquez as influenced by the Italian painters. He made his own rules and remained in a class by himself. In 1970 his portrait of his servant Juan de Pareja changed hands for £2,310,000 at auction in London and is now in the USA. *See colour section.*

¶ In THOMAS, H. and D. L. *Great Painters.* 1959

Venetian art: the school of painting, sculpture and architecture associated with the city and republic of Venice. Splendour and colour, warmth and a sensuous delight in the beauties of the material world – these, the prime characteristics of Venetian art, are what might be expected of the artists of a city whose face, as it were, was turned to the East rather than to the rest of Italy; a city into whose busy harbour came the rich fabrics of the Orient, carpets and jewelled metalwork, perfumes and spices. By a miraculous chance Venice produced a succession of painters of genius who, in their works, captured the spirit of this inimitable city.

Not that the Venetian artists were without spiritual values: closely linked culturally with the Byzantine Empire (*see* separate entry), the works of its earlier painters, notably Giovanni Bellini (*c.* 1430–1516), are full of that noble and moving religious feeling which is so much part of Byzantine art. Bellini, however, one of the earliest great painters to use oils, moved far beyond the static decorativeness of Byzantine art. His figures are full of movement, his landscapes luminously alive. Giorgione (1477–1501), one of the greatest painters of all time, who may have been Bellini's pupil, allowed the landscape, in a sense, to take over the picture instead of being mere background. In Titian (Tiziano Vecelli, *c.* 1480–1576) Venice found an artist who in the course of his long life produced a number of magnificent works which sum up the civilisation of his native city-state. Tintoretto (Jacopo Robusti, 1518–94), a follower of Titian, was a vigorous painter and splendid colourist, though not the equal of his master. Paul Veronese (Paolo Caliari, 1528–88), born in Verona as his nickname indicates, did his best work in Venice and is usually classed with the Venetian School. He painted many very large paintings which, if they lack deep feeling or insight into human nature, give a wonderful impression of magnificence. Jacopo Sansovino (Tatti, 1477–1579) was a second-rate sculptor but a first-rate architect who enriched Venice with many splendid buildings, richly carved and decorated. Andrea Palladio (1518–80), an architect of more austere taste, looked for his inspiration in ancient Roman models. His *I quattro libri dell' architettura*, The Four Books of Architecture (1570), an English translation of which was published by the architect Inigo Jones (1573–1652), had a great influence on English architecture.

In decay, her glories fading, Venice in the 18th century still could boast three great artists. Giovanni Battista Tiepolo (1692–1769) was a decorative painter of tremendous facility. Antonio Canale, or Canaletto, (1697–1768) painted sparkling views of his native city (and of London, which he visited). The works of Canaletto's pupil Francesco Guardi (1712–93), while often very like those of his master, are more impressionistic, sometimes self-consciously picturesque.

Paintings by the great Venetian masters are to be found in the major art galleries of the world. But much of their work – altarpieces, murals, painted ceilings – remains in the Venetian churches and buildings for which it was originally designed, making Venice one of the treasure houses of the world.

See colour section.

See also PALLADIO; TITIAN; VENICE.

Venezuela: republic of northern South America, in the tropical region of South America that lies north of the Amazon basin. The native peoples of the mountains, the Sierra Nevada de Merida, are tough and have always dominated the low-landers on the coastal plain and on the delta of the River Orinoco.

This coast was discovered by Columbus on his third voyage to America in 1498. A year later Ojeda, accompanied by Amerigo Vespucci, named the land Venezuela, meaning "little Venice". Pearl fishing from the Margarita Islands provided some quick profits, but few Spaniards settled in the small towns which were created along the coast. In the 17th century English and Dutch sailors raided the coastal towns, but Venezuela remained a Spanish province until in 1811 Simon Bolívar began the rebellions which eventually freed all of South America.

Like most republics in South America, Venezuela has suffered from prolonged boundary disputes with all her neighbours and from repeated internal disorder. Over fifty revolutions were attempted in the 19th century, ten of them successful. The exploitation of the vast oil reserves near Lake Maracaibo has brought revenue to the government since 1920 but has not greatly enriched the people themselves. *See also* BOLIVAR; COLUMBUS; SOUTH AMERICA; VESPUCCI.

Venice: Italian city built on a number of small islands – little more than mudbanks – within a lagoon at the head of the Adriatic Sea. It would be hard, on the face of it, to choose a less suitable location for a city. Traditionally, it was founded (*c.* 452 AD) as a refuge by families fleeing from Attila, the "Scourge of God", and his terrible Huns.

Despite the fact that its "streets" were waterways and that its buildings had to be raised on piles for want of firm founda-

A "street" in Venice.

tions, the city grew, and grew rich, for Venice lay on important trade routes by land and sea. It became an independent city-state, famous for its magnificence. The Church of St Mark, its principal sacred building, is one of the most richly decorated edifices in the world. Venetian traders travelling to the East were required, by law, to bring back something beautiful for its adornment.

Recognising that the city owed its prosperity to the sea, every Ascension Day the *Doge*, the head of state, went out in a ship and threw a valuable ring into the Adriatic, to symbolise the "marriage" of Venice and the sea. With the discovery of America, however, and of routes round the Cape of Good Hope, the pattern of trade shifted and the fortunes of Venice declined. In 1797 it was occupied by Napoleon I (*see* separate entry) and, on his downfall, handed over to Austria. In 1866 it became part of the kingdom of Italy.

Today (population 364,000) it is a great tourist centre. Its centuries-old glassworks are still famous and there is heavy industry on the mainland. Built on mud, Venice is gradually sinking into the sea. Plans are afoot to construct a system of locks and dams to preserve this unique island city. *See colour section.*

See also DOGES OF VENICE; VENETIAN ART.

Verona: fortified city of north-eastern Italy, on the River Adige. Its long history begins with settlement by a variety of early peoples, including the Ligurians, Gauls (*see* GAUL) and Etruscans (*see* ETRURIA) and later development as a Roman colony. Its notable buildings include a Roman amphitheatre, second only to the Coliseum in size; a 7th-century church, renowned for its fine vestry and choir; a Romanesque cathedral (12th–16th centuries); and the ancient fortress of Castelvecchio now housing a famous art collection. To the sentimental tourist with Shakespeare's tragedy of *Romeo and Juliet* in mind, the house and tomb of Juliet are a major attraction. Among its industries are paper manufacture, food processing and fertilisers. *See colour section.*

Versailles: French town near Paris, famous as the site of one of the largest and most ornate palaces in the world, a memorial to the vanity and ambition of King Louis XIV (reigned 1643–1715), who ordered its building. The palace is so vast, so ornamented with sculpture, paintings and gilded furnishings, that it is hard to conceive of anyone actually living there; and indeed, the letters and journals of Louis's courtiers are full of references to the discomforts of life at court. The gardens, planned by André le Nôtre (1613–1700), are, with their statuary, ornamental urns and fountains, beautiful in a very formal way. The town has given its name to a number of treaties, most recently the Treaty of Versailles (28 June 1919) at the end of World War I. *See colour section.*

Versailles, Treaty of (28 June 1919): treaty usually considered as securing the settlement of Europe at the end of World War I (*see* separate entry), because its opening sections proposed the formation of the League of Nations (*see* separate entry). But as other treaties were signed later with defeated powers, the Treaty of Versailles should properly be named for the German settlement only. The terms were imposed on Germany despite protests that they should have been negotiated on the basis of President Wilson's Fourteen Points (*see* separate entry).

Germany surrendered all her colonies and some territories on her frontier, such as Alsace-Lorraine to France and Schlesvig to Denmark; also, by giving part of eastern Prussia to Poland, Germany was partitioned by the Polish Corridor. Controversial areas such as Danzig and the Saar were to be placed under the League of Nations, and the Rhineland was demilitarised. German military forces were severely limited. She was forced to accept responsibility for the war, the cost of which was to be worked out later by a Reparations committee.

Versailles also gave its name to the Peace of Versailles (3 September 1783) which recognised the independence of the United States.

Vespucci, Amerigo (1454–1512): Italian merchant and navigator who made three voyages to the New World 1497–1512, in the service of Spain and Portugal. It seems likely that he explored the northeast coast of South America, but his own accounts of his expeditions are conflicting and unreliable. A German cartographer, Martin Waldseemüller, first suggested in 1507 that the newly discovered continent should be called America "because Americus discovered it", but the consensus of opinion is that Vespucci has little claim as the pioneer discoverer.

¶ POHL, F. J. *Amerigo Vespucci, Pilot Major.* 1967

Vesuvius: Italian volcano, 5 miles [8 km] south-east of Naples. Early man saw Vesuvius erupt and Roman legends attribute the disturbances to warring amongst the gods. Dormant for hundreds of years, Vesuvius erupted in AD 79, destroying Pompeii and Herculaneum and, incident-

Vesuvius erupting in 1767.

ally, causing the death of the Roman writer Pliny the Elder, whose scientific curiosity was greater than his prudence. In 472, ashes were blown as far as Constantinople. In 1631 18,000 people in surrounding villages were killed by lava and boiling water.

See also VOLCANO.

Victoria: state of the Australian Commonwealth in the south-east of the continent. Though originally part of New South Wales (*see* separate entry), no serious attempts at penal settlement were made. Small-scale free settlement began at Port Phillip in 1814. Edward Henty's party from Tasmania established a station at Portland Bay in 1834 for farming and whaling, in unpromising conditions, but other parties in 1835 founded what was to become the capital city, Melbourne. Reports on this area by Major Thomas Mitchell (later knighted) and settlement schemes attracted immigrants from Britain and farmers from New South Wales, and the population increased rapidly. Hume's explorations, 1824-25, and Mitchell's more extensive researches, 1831-46, opened up districts suitable for

further settlement and farming, which flourished with English demands for wool. In 1847 Melbourne, named after the British prime minister (just as the state was named after the British Queen), was raised to the status of a city. In 1851 Victoria separated from New South Wales and formed another colony, with a lieutenant-governor. Responsible constitutional government was achieved in 1855. Victoria early introduced adult voting rights, and equal elective rights for women in 1908.

Gold was discovered at Ballarat in the 1850s. Agriculture, primarily grazing, has extended to dairying, fruit and wine. The chief industries are food processing, textiles, chemicals, farm machinery, iron and steel. The 1937 Kiewa project provides readily available hydroelectric power.

Vienna: capital of Austria on the River Danube, and until 1916 the hub of the great Austrian empire. Vienna was founded by the Celts in pre-Roman times. In the Middle Ages its importance as a trading centre grew slowly, but after 1278 the population increased rapidly because of the city's selection by the Habsburg family (*see* separate entry) as the Imperial capital. Since then Vienna's history has been largely the history of central Europe. It was the focal point of resistance to the Turks and was twice unsuccessfully besieged by them (1529 and 1683). Habsburg leadership of the Catholic cause for three centuries made Vienna a symbolic centre and many churches were constructed in the Baroque style. Its art museums hold collections of the great masters, and strong musical and cultural traditions, built up in the 18th and 19th centuries, continue. Of great popular appeal is the *Spanische Reitschule*, the only school of horsemanship in the world to maintain the methods and traditions of the Classic Riding School. As well as giving regular

Classic horsemanship displayed by one of the White Horses of Vienna.

displays for most of the year, the White Horses of Vienna are famous in many other countries.

Vienna, Congress of: conference of European powers, 2 October 1814 – 23 March 1815. The fall of Napoleon left the disposition of his empire to the principal allies, Russia, Prussia, Austria and Great Britain, and the Congress was held, in an atmosphere of gaiety and magnificence, mainly to ratify the decisions of these four. However, owing to the ineffectiveness of certain of the delegates and the astuteness of the French minister, Talleyrand, animosity arose almost immediately between the allies. Talleyrand's admittance to the counsels of the "four" and the diplomacy of the British delegate, Castlereagh, and of the Austrian chairman of the Congress, Metternich, secured temporary harmony despite the rival claims of the different countries, and a settlement was concluded in June 1815. Among its results, involving much give and take among the powers, France was deprived of all her imperial

conquests and Britain gained many colonies, including Cape Colony and Malta. *See* separate entries for METTERNICH; NAPOLEON I; TALLEYRAND–PERIGORD.

Vietnam: region along the southern and eastern coasts of Indo-China. The territory was inhabited by Indonesian tribes which mingled with Thai people who arrived about the 6th century BC and with Mongol people (*see* separate entry) between the 5th and 3rd centuries BC. By the 10th century AD a new distinctive people had come into being on the Red River delta. Ruled first by China, Vietnam, consisting of Tonkin and north Annam, gained independence in the 10th century and expanded southwards, at last reaching Cochin China and the Mekong delta. From the 17th century trading posts were established by western powers. In the 19th century the French became the predominant power and undertook the conquest of Vietnam, establishing the colony of Cochin China in 1867 and protectorates over Annam and Tonkin by 1884. Economic development in French Indo-China was pursued intensively only from the close of the 19th century, rice, rubber and anthracite being main exports. Under French rule a new Vietnamese middle class emerged. After World War I (*see* separate entry) national Vietnamese resistance to French rule increased. Following harsh suppression of uprisings in 1930, nationalist leadership passed to the communists, led by Ho Chi Minh (*see* separate entry). Under Japanese rule (1941–45) during World War II (*see* separate entry), a league of independence, Vietminh, dominated by communists, was formed and, on Japanese withdrawal, proclaimed an independent republic. Chinese forces occupied North Vietnam, and British forces were in the south. France tried to negotiate with the Vietminh for a "free state within the French Union". In Hanoi the Vietminh attacked

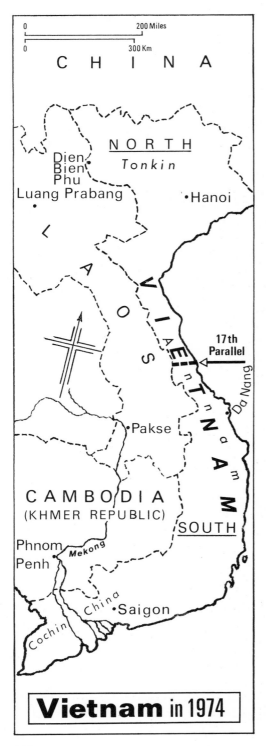

Vietnam in 1974

the French (1946). France tried to rally southern nationalists against Vietminh, but years of struggle led to French disaster at Dien Bien Phu. An international Geneva convention on Indo-China in 1954 arranged an armistice and partitioned Vietnam at the seventeenth parallel of latitude.

Vietnam, Democratic Republic of North Vietnam: republic of south-eastern Asia. After the partition of Vietnam in 1954 a communist government was free to consolidate its position, with Hanoi as its capital and Ho Chi Minh (*see* separate entry) as its leader. Sweeping agrarian and other economic reforms won widespread popular support, and extensive aid was provided by other communist countries. Giving active support on a large scale to substantial guerrilla elements in South Vietnam which were inspired by profound economic discontents there, the Hanoi government became involved in warfare with the South Vietnamese government and its US allies. Using supply routes through Laos and Cambodia and possessing an outstanding military commander in General Vo Nguyen Giap, North Vietnam, in spite of heavy casualties, retained a military initiative through the later 1960s. Peace talks with South Vietnam and the USA were begun in Paris in 1968 and dragged on for four years. The treaty eventually signed has been indifferently observed, and intermittent fighting, particularly in Cambodia, has continued.

Vietnam, Republic of South Vietnam: republic of south-eastern Asia. After the partition of Vietnam (1954) the Emperor Bao Dai, last representative of the Nguyen imperial dynasty which had ruled 1802–1945, was deposed in 1955 by Ngo Dinh Diem, and a republic with a strongly presidential type of constitution was established with capital at Saigon. Diem was overthrown in 1963, and governments dominated by military men followed. The government was heavily dependent on military and economic aid from the USA. The countryside was overrun by insurgent (Vietcong) guerrillas aided by North Vietnam. Only huge US forces preserved the Saigon government. Unpopularity of the war and absence of decisive results have led to increasing US withdrawal and replacement of US personnel by South Vietnamese. South Vietnam invaded Cambodia in 1970 and Laos in 1971 to cut supply routes from North Vietnam, with only limited success.

Vikings: Scandinavian warriors and sea-raiders who ravaged the coasts of Europe in the 8th–10th centuries and penetrated to Iceland, Greenland, the Baltic and Constantinople. They sacked Paris in 845 and 860 and, as the Northmen or Norse-men, gave their name to Normandy. In England they were known as Danes (i.e. men from Denmark), eventually occupying the throne and establishing an empire under Canute or Cnut. It seems probable that expeditions also reached the coasts of North America about the year 1000. Fierce fighters and magnificent sailors, they were among the most remarkable of early voyagers and colonisers. Though ruthless and with a reputation for faithlessness, their courage was supreme and, given the opportunity, they showed talent for peaceful government.

See map, page 284.

¶ GIBSON, MICHAEL. *The Vikings.* 1972; HENRY, BERNARD. *Vikings and Norsemen.* 1971

See also CANUTE; ERIC THE RED; LEIF ERICSON; SHIPBUILDING; etc.

Virgil, Vergil, Publius Vergilius Maro (70–19 BC): Roman poet born near Mantua. His fame rests on three works, all written in the hexameter metre, or lines

of six metrical feet: (1) the *Ecologues* or rustic idylls, (2) the *Georgics*, four books dealing with the farmer's life and occupations, and (3) the supreme achievement of the *Aeneid*, describing the adventures of Aeneas, fleeing with his companions from Troy and founding in Italy the future Roman nation.

¶ In CANNING, JOHN, editor. *100 Great Lives*. 1953

VJ Day: day of popular celebrations by the allied peoples of the United Nations to mark the Victory of their forces over Japanese imperialism in 1945. The Japanese government surrendered officially on 14 August, and worldwide festivities over the next twenty-four hours signified the end of World War II (*see* separate entry).

Vladivostok: large seaport in the far east of the USSR, on the Sea of Japan, founded in 1860. It was occupied by the Japanese 1918–22 and, during the first two years of this period, was the base of the anti-Soviet leader Admiral Kolchak. It is the eastern terminus of the trans-Siberian railway and the air line from Moscow, and has major shipbuilding, food-processing and oil-refining industries. *See also* DOCKS; USSR.

Volcano: rift in earth's crust through which subterranean material is ejected. The word derives from the name of the island of Vulcanus, near Sicily, so called by the Romans, because they believed it to be the forge of Vulcan, their god of fire and blacksmith of the gods. The mountain seemed to be burning inside like a blacksmith's forge. Vulcanus, or Vulcano as it is called today, has been built, like all volcanoes, of molten material from the inside of the earth, pushed up through cracks in a weak part of the earth's crust. Sometimes, on reaching the earth's surface, it has spilt over as lava and tremen-dous explosions of gases have flung out cinders and ash.

Probably no part of the earth's surface has not been at some time the site of volcanic activity. Regions such as the British Isles, not thought of as volcanic, have, in the distant past, experienced violent and prolonged activity. Crater Lake, Oregon, USA, was created 6,000 years ago by a tremendous eruption; Mount Ararat, where the Bible relates that Noah's Ark came to rest, is an extinct volcano. Some archaeologists believe that the great civilisation of Minoan Crete was destroyed as a result of the Bronze Age eruption of Thera, seventy-five miles away, accompanied by devastating tidal waves and ash fall-out.

The eruption of Etna in Sicily, in 475 BC, was described by Pindar and Aeschylus – one of many in historic times, though

Mont Pelée's great plug of hardened lava.

the most catastrophic was in 1669, when the nearby city of Catania was practically destroyed. Although Strabo, the Greek geographer, had recognised Vesuvius as volcanic, the mountain had been quiescent for a long period before its destruction of Pompeii in AD 79. There was a lake at its centre when rebellious gladiators took refuge there 150 years before.

A fifth of the population was killed when Skaptarjökul, Iceland, erupted in 1783. More violent still was the Krakatoa eruption in 1883, when two-thirds of the island in the Sunda Strait was blown away. Tidal waves caused the deaths of 36,000 on the coasts of Java and Sumatra, atmospheric waves travelled three times round the earth, a blanket of ash shrouded shipping a thousand miles away, and a pall of darkness spread for 150 miles around. For three years the dust from the eruption produced wonderful sunsets, particularly in Great Britain.

Mont Pelée, in Martinique, one of the islands of the West Indies, though long dormant, erupted again in 1902. An avalanche of red-hot lava and clouds of hot gas swept down the mountain on to the inhabitants of St Pierre, only one of whom, a prisoner in the jail, escaped.

Although there have been thousands of volcanoes in the world, only about five hundred have been active in recorded history. Most are situated in the "Ring of Fire", round the edges of the Pacific Ocean – the Philippines contain ninety-eight, Japan thirty-three, Alaska thirty-five. Other areas are the Andes, West Indies, and the Mediterranean. Most are near the coast, and it is possible that eruptions are caused by seeping water contacting subterranean molten matter near a weakness in the earth's crust.
See colour section.

¶ HIRST, W. *Volcanoes.* 1971; FURNEAUX, RUPERT. *Volcano.* 1974

See also VESUVIUS.

Voltaire, François-Marie Arouet de (1694–1778): French philosopher, historian and man of letters. Voltaire was a great mocker, merciless in exposing prejudice, pretentiousness and superstition: as a result he made many enemies. During an enforced stay in England (1726–29) its relative freedom compared with that of France greatly impressed him. In 1833 his *Lettres philosophiques sur les Anglais,* praising England, was burnt by the French authorities, and Voltaire was forced to leave Paris again to avoid arrest.

A strangely contradictory personality – greedy and generous, unscrupulous towards his enemies while hating injustice – Voltaire was a puller-down rather than a builder-up. He proffered no blueprint for a new society. Yet in such masterly satires as *Candide* his witty pen, probing the weaknesses of a corrupt system, helped to pave the way for the French Revolution.
See colour section.
See also EIGHTEENTH CENTURY; FRENCH REVOLUTION.

Vorster, Balthazar Johannes (b. 1915): South African prime minister. Elected Nationalist MP for Nigel in 1953, he became deputy minister of education in 1958, minister of justice in 1961 and prime minister in 1966 after the assassination of Dr Verwoerd. He has been an influential member of the Ossewabrandwag, a society pledged to perpetuate the language and traditions of Afrikaner Voortrekkers (*see* GREAT TREK).
See also SOUTH AFRICA, REPUBLIC OF.

Vulgate: Latin version of the Bible (*editio vulgata*) compiled in the 4th century by St Jerome. There had been earlier versions, but the Vulgate has been the most widely used in the Western Church for nearly 1,600 years.

975

W

Wagner Act (1935): law passed by the US Congress (*see* CONGRESS, AMERICAN) giving employees the right to organise trade unions and to make collective bargains, i.e. agreements affecting all the workers in one union or group of unions. The Act also set up the National Labour Relations Board (NLRB) to investigate labour disputes, prevent unfair practices and protect the rights given to employees.

Waitangi, Treaty of (6 February 1840): treaty between Britain and Maori chiefs of New Zealand. Gibbon Wakefield in 1839 organised the New Zealand Company for land purchase and settlement. The government, questioning the legality of such purchases from the Maori chiefs, sent a naval officer, Captain Hobson, to negotiate and in 1840 annexed New Zealand to New South Wales (*see* separate entry). The chiefs acknowledged British sovereignty, without perhaps fully understanding its implications. The tribes were guaranteed possession of their lands, subject to crown right of purchase. The Treaty did not prove the hoped-for "happy solution of the coloured-race difficulty". Continuing settlement in new areas and expropriations drove the Maoris to rebellion in 1845–48 and 1860–72. They proved themselves skilful and extremely courageous guerrilla fighters, but were eventually worn down and conciliated by such measures as special representation in Parliament.
See also GUERRILLAS; MAORI.

Wales: principality, situated in the southwest of Great Britain and flanked on three sides by the sea. Its land boundary with England runs from the estuary of the River Dee to the Bristol Channel. Wales

is a rugged country with more than 60 per cent of its total acreage over 500 feet [152 m] above sea level. The highest mountain is Snowdon, 3,560 feet [1,084 m].

The Cambrian Mountains form the heartland of Wales. Further south are the Brecon Beacons, the Black Mountains and the Carmarthenshire Fans. Round this rocky core is a lowland area of varying width which is the most productive part of the country. Here, and in the deeply grooved river valleys, lives the majority of the Welsh people.

Wales has a damp mild climate. As much as 150 inches [3,810 mm] of rain a year falls on the higher mountains, and most of Wales gets at least 40 inches [1,020 mm] annually. There are, however, no great extremes of temperature.

Much of the land is infertile – bare rock, or moorland good only for rough grazing. Some oats and barley are grown on the coastal plain and along the river valleys but most of the land available for agriculture is grassland, used for raising cattle and for dairy-farming. Where the countryside is not scarred by industrial development it is among the most beautiful in the British Isles.

The wealth of Wales comes not from its soil but from the minerals that lie beneath

Some of the most beautiful of Welsh scenery, looking east towards Mt. Snowdon.

it – tin, ironstone, lead, copper, slate, a little gold (plans are afoot to prospect anew for this) and, above all, coal. The great coalfields of Glamorgan and Monmouthshire produce nearly all Britain's anthracite coal and much of its steam coal. The steel industry of this area, of which Rhondda (population 98,000) and Merthyr Tydfil (population 57,000) are the two largest towns, produces almost all Britain's tinplate and a large proportion of its sheet steel. During the depression years of the late 1920s and 1930s Wales suffered greatly from unemployment. Great efforts have since been made to diversify the country's industrial output, thus making it less vulnerable to trade recessions. Factories have been established for the manufacture of many types of goods, including plastics, clothing, synthetic fibres, and electronic equipment. The chief cities of Wales are its ports: Cardiff, Swansea and Newport.

Though Wales was conquered by King Edward I (reigned 1271–1307) in 1283, and united with England by Act of Parliament in 1536, the Welsh have retained a strong sense of national identity. The descendants of early Celtic settlers, forced back into the mountains of the west by successive waves of Roman, Saxon and Norman invaders, they still display many Celtic characteristics both of physique and temperament – on the short side, stocky, dark-haired and long skulled; more emotional than the phlegmatic English and with a great love of music. The Welsh language, spoken by some 26 per cent of the population, is taught in all Welsh schools. Of recent years a militant group, *Plaid Cymru*, has perpetrated acts of violence against government property in its efforts to secure the independence of Wales from England. Many other Welshmen, less extreme, would like to achieve a greater measure of home rule for their country. *See* GREAT BRITAIN for map.

Wallace, Sir William (*c.* 1272–1305): Scottish patriot. Although only a knight of low degree, he won renown for the part he played in fighting for his country's independence. Victory over the English at Stirling Bridge in 1297 gave him authority, but a second invasion brought crushing defeat for the Scots at the Battle of Falkirk followed by the subjugation of Scotland and Wallace's capture and execution. Standing trial in Westminster Hall, accused of treachery, Wallace declared: "To Edward of England I cannot be a traitor, for he never was my Sovereign, he never received my homage, and while life remains within this frame he never shall."
¶ In GRICE, F. *Rebels and Fugitives.* 1963

Walpole, Sir Robert, 1st Earl of Orford (1674–1745): English Whig politician. He entered parliament in 1700 and first held office in 1708. When the Tories (*see* TORY) gained power in 1712, his enemies drove him from parliament and, for a time, secured his imprisonment. In 1714, however, on the succession of George I, he returned to public life and soon became first lord of the treasury and chancellor. He resigned in 1717 but was recalled in 1720 as the only man who could save the situation after the financial disaster of the South Sea Bubble. He held office for the next twenty-one years and helped to ensure both peace and prosperity for the country. Although the position of prime minister was not yet recognised, his leadership foreshadowed the cabinet system (*see* separate entry).

Walsingham, Sir Francis (*c.* 1530–90): English secretary of state from 1573. A supporter of the policy of alliance with France, he urged the necessity of war against Spain and active help for Protestants abroad. As ambassador to France 1570–73, he was responsible for the

Treaty of Blois (1572). Expert at counter-espionage, he raised the English intelligence service to a high pitch of efficiency and was responsible for disclosing many plots, notably Babington's, which led to the execution of Mary Queen of Scots.

War of 1812: war between America and Britain caused mainly by disputes on the high seas, the blockading of American ports, and the alleged support by Britain of the Indians in their struggle for survival. Congress declared war in June 1812 and fought what has been called a second War of Independence, and one conducted with great bitterness. The war marked the beginning of a new era in American history, with the American people finally turning away from Europe and setting out to shape their own destiny. One visible legacy today is the White House (*see* separate entry). In 1814 the British burned the President's official residence, and it was painted white to cover the marks of the fire.

Warsaw, Warszawa: capital of Poland since 1596. In 1795, at the third partition of Poland, Warsaw fell to Prussia, but in 1807 Napoleon created a separate independent Grand Duchy of Warsaw. Under Russian rule this independence was partly preserved but ended in revolt in 1830–31. After World War I, Warsaw became capital of a new Poland. Under German occupation in World War II the Jews of Warsaw were "liquidated", their "ghetto" (or special quarter) being virtually destroyed. In 1944 there was a rising in which, given no aid by the Russians, Warsaw and its patriots were destroyed by the Germans and 600,000 people perished. After 1945 the city was rebuilt and repopulated.
See WORLD WAR I for map.
See also JEWS; NAPOLEON I; WORLD WARS I and II.

Warsaw Pact: a defence pact established by the Warsaw Treaty of 14 May 1955 by the USSR with Albania, Bulgaria, Czechoslovakia, East Germany, Hungary, Poland and Romania, as a counterweight to NATO (*see* separate entry). Warsaw Pact forces intervened to influence events in Poland and Hungary in 1956 and Czechoslovakia in 1968.

Washington: (1) state of the extreme north-west of the USA, washed by the Pacific; capital Olympia, chief city Seattle. (2) capital of the USA, on the other side of the continent, over 2,000 miles [3,218 km] distant. It occupies almost all the seventy square miles [180 sq km] of the District of Columbia and is designated Washington DC, distinguishing it from the Pacific state, abbreviated Wash.

The original plan of the capital was drawn up by Major Pierre L'Enfant, under the supervision of George Washington himself (*see* next entry), and has been largely preserved, the Government making a praiseworthy effort, in the early 1900s, to clear away some of the 19th-century excrescences that had obscured the fine vistas and viewpoints. The most impressive stretch is the Mall, running from the Lincoln Memorial on the Potomac River north-east to Capitol Hill. The Mall forms the axis around or near which are found most of the great public buildings including the Capitol (modelled on St Peter's, Rome), where the Senate and House of Representatives meet, the Supreme Court buildings, the Library of Congress and the White House (*see* separate entry).

Washington, George (1732–99): first president of the USA (1789–97). Coming from a land- and slave-owning family in Virginia, his early education came more from outdoor occupations and practical pursuits than from books, though he taught himself a good deal of mathematics and became an expert surveyor. In 1753 he was commissioned in the army and spent several years fighting against the French and Indians. After his marriage in 1759 he gave up his military career and devoted himself to his estates. As one of the wealthiest tobacco planters, he showed himself a very efficient and hardworking employer, caring for his slaves and employing a doctor for the sick. He was one of the chief leaders of the opposition to British colonial policy and, when the War of American Independence broke out, became commander in chief of the so-called Continental army. With only small forces at his disposal, he had to rely on patience, devotion and courage, rather than any dramatic display of military genius, which he probably never possessed. Even after he took the supreme command, he did not anticipate, and did not want, independence of Britain. It was only when he realised that there was no longer any choice that he changed his mind and, after the struggle was over, accepted the presidency.

As president he showed himself cautious and methodical, trying to stand aloof from party politics. In the words of Professor Nevins "he believed the head of the nation should be no man's guest. He returned no calls and shook hands with no one, acknowledging salutations by a formal bow." He strove to strengthen the central government and, in the wider affairs of the world, to preserve a strict neutrality.

He resisted pressure to serve for a third term and retired in 1797 to his estates at Mount Vernon (named after the British admiral Edward Vernon). When he died in December 1799, a resolution in the House of Representatives described him as "first in war, first in peace, and first in the hearts of his countrymen". When the news reached Europe, the armies of Napoleon I (*see* separate entry) and the British fleet both paid him tribute.

¶ COY, HAROLD. *Real Book of George Washington.* 1963

See also AMERICAN PRESIDENTS.

Waterloo, Battle of (18 June 1815): scene of the final defeat of Napoleon I, near the Belgian village of Waterloo, by the Fourth Coalition forces under Wellington and Blücher. Faced with continued opposition to his rule in France after his escape from Elba, Napoleon moved his army quickly. He crossed the Belgian frontier intending to strike the Prussians at Ligny and the British at Quatre Bras, before they could link up and before help came from Russia and Austria in the east.

Napoleon had the advantage of mobility and numbers (about 72,000 against 68,000), but he made several miscalculations. He relied on Marshal Ney to defeat the British, but Ney moved too slowly, allowing Wellington to retreat and choose a good defensive position at Waterloo. Napoleon's own defeat of the Prussians at Ligny was not followed up properly, and they later regrouped to move in decisively on the crucial battle being fought at Waterloo between Napoleon and Wellington. Repeated French cavalry charges broke against well-trained British infantry "squares". After eight hours heavy fighting Wellington, now supported by the Prussians, moved against the tired and dispirited French army, which disintegrated, leaving up to 40,000 casualties. It is reckoned one of the decisive battles of history and is the source of many anecdotes and quotations, not least Wellington's words in a letter written almost immediately after his return from the field: "Believe me, nothing except a battle lost can be half so melancholy as a battle won."

See also INDIVIDUAL ENTRIES.

Watermarks: identifying marks in sheets of paper. Although the Chinese were the first paper-makers, they did not use watermarks. Paper manufacturing methods from the East reached Europe in the mid-12th century, and around 1285 emblems and designs began to be pressed into paper during its manufacture in Italy.

Early watermarks were simple in design, consisting mainly of maker's initials, stars, crosses and circles; then heraldic devices appeared and ecclesiastical or biblical symbols, such as the paschal lamb, the Holy Grail and the cardinal's hat. The more complicated designs served at first to identify products of individual mills, but later they often became technical terms to describe various types and sizes of paper. Thus the "post horn" watermark, the origins of which can be traced back to the horn that Roland blew in the pass of Roncesvalles, gave its name to post paper; and foolscap came from the watermark of a jester with cap and bells, used by an Elizabethan paper-maker in England. In the late 17th century many marks bearing royal arms or arms of cities occurred in England and Germany.

Paper was made by placing rag pulp in shallow trays with a base of interwoven wires. The long wires, set close together, were the "wire lines". The cross-wires were more widely spaced and known as "chain lines". Their impressions are visible in all hand-made paper when held up to the light and are in themselves a form of watermark. The special devices described above were additional wire designs interwoven with the rest in the bottom of the tray. Watermarked paper is often used for documents, bank-notes, etc., to prevent counterfeiting. The occurrence of watermarks is characteristic of hand-made paper. In the machine-made product, a

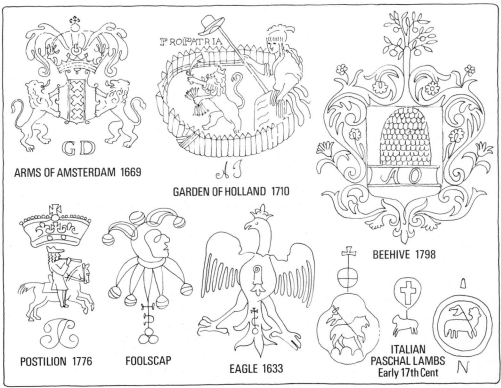

ARMS OF AMSTERDAM 1669

GARDEN OF HOLLAND 1710

BEEHIVE 1798

POSTILION 1776　　FOOLSCAP

EAGLE 1633

ITALIAN PASCHAL LAMBS Early 17th Cent

circular rubber form can be used to roll symbols over the surface of the wet paper, but these do not have the clarity and beauty of the other type.

Watt, James (1736-1819): developer of the steam engine, born at Greenock, Scotland. The engines of his time worked on the principle developed by Thomas Newcomen (1663-1729), whereby steam was admitted into a vertical cylinder and then condensed, the resulting vacuum forcing a piston down the cylinder and producing a power-stroke. In operation they were very wasteful of steam, and their use was largely confined to pumping water from mines. By applying scientific principles Watt used a separate condenser, which greatly improved performance. In partnership with Matthew Boulton (1728-1809; *see* separate entry) at the Soho factory, Birmingham, and enjoying the protection of a patent, he produced large numbers of his type of engine, devising detailed improvements and new methods of transmitting motion which made them adaptable for many uses.

¶ WEBB, ROBERT N. *James Watt.* 1972
See also STEAM.

Wayne, Anthony (1745-96): American general. He distinguished himself in the War of American Independence, combining military skill, stubbornness and great personal daring. His exploit in personally leading the charge over the walls of the British fort at Stony Point, New York, (July 1779) earned him the popular nickname of "Mad Anthony".
See also AMERICAN WAR OF INDEPENDENCE.

Weaving: process of interlacing threads to make a fabric. Strands are stretched longitudinally on a simple frame and other threads passed in and out of them. The frame is called a *loom*, the threads stretched on it the *warp* and the transverse ones the *weft*. The earliest looms were probably two separate rods between which the warp threads were stretched: the weft thread was wound on a shuttle and the weaving was pushed up into position with a flat piece of wood.

Prehistoric people are likely to have made textiles by weaving grasses, but once a method was discovered of spinning wool, flax or silk into thread, the woven material would be more useful and durable. Egyptian and Greek weavers seem to have made long, narrow strips of cloth on small looms. Later people discovered how to make wider material. Large, strong looms were made of wood, and on these the finished cloth could be pulled back and rolled as it was completed. The warp threads were passed through a perforated strip of wood – the *heddle* – which could be lifted up and down, making it easier to pass the shuttle carrying the weft from side to side. A pattern could be woven into the fabric by using coloured threads.

Civilised man required many different textures of cloth. In cold climates wool was used for weaving, in hot lands linen and cotton. The Chinese appear to have been the first people to weave on a large scale. They used silk and, although their looms were big, they were light because the threads were so fine. Chinese merchants traded in silk, and it is on record

Chinese loosely-woven silk, 6–8th century AD.

Weavers using handlooms in the Netherlands, 17th century.

that a party of them set out in AD 97 to sell silk in Rome. When they reached the eastern Mediterranean they turned back because they thought they could never cross the sea. The Romans wove both wool and linen. In AD 369 an Imperial decree restricted weaving with gold and silver threads to specialist workshops.

In western Europe people made woollen cloth on heavy handlooms. The people of the Netherlands were particularly skilled weavers and imported wool from England. The English learned how to weave, but for many years preferred imported cloth. The first loom to be mechanically driven was set up in Danzig in 1661. It was said to be capable of weaving cloth without human aid. The authorities, afraid of unemployment among the weavers, destroyed it and had the inventor put to death.

The same fear of unemployment was displayed in other countries. In England,

when Dr Cartwright invented a power loom which he established at Doncaster in 1786, rioters damaged the machinery and burned the factory; but eventually it was realised that mechanical weaving would result in more trade, so that power looms came to be accepted.

By 1825 there were about 75,000 power looms in Britain in addition to 250,000 hand looms.

In France an important type known as the Jacquard loom, fitted with a device for weaving figured fabrics, was invented by Joseph-Marie Jacquard (1752-1834). In 1860 an electric loom was set up in London, devised by Bonelli of Turin. The invention of automatic processes has made it possible for hundreds of looms to be supervised by one weaver. However, the fundamental principle of weaving is the same as it was many thousands of years ago.

See also LOOM; TEXTILES.

Webster, Daniel (1782-1852): American statesman. He combined the practice of law and politics and was elected, first to the House of Representatives, then to the Senate (1827), becoming secretary of state in 1841. His chief fame was as a superb orator. The English clergyman and wit Sydney Smith described him as "a steam engine in trousers"; and, after one of his speeches in Congress (*see* separate entry), another member said: "Mr Webster, I think you had better die now, and rest your fame on that speech."

Webster, Noah (1758-1843): American dictionary maker. His *Compendious Dictionary of the English Language* (1806) and *American Dictionary of the English Language* (1828) are comparable to Doctor Johnson's achievement in England (1755) and have far exceeded it in the number of later revisions and reprints.
See also DICTIONARIES.

Wedgwood, Josiah (1730-95): English pottery manufacturer. Born in Burslem, Josiah Wedgwood established a pottery in 1759. He copied Greek designs and in 1769 opened a new pottery which he named *Etruria*, after the district of Italy, now called Tuscany, where a remarkable type of native pottery, possibly derived from Greek models, had been produced in ancient times. The Etruria pottery produced black basalt vases, decorated plaques like cameos, and a wide range of domestic ware with a new standard of artistic merit. *See colour section.*
¶ ARCHER, STUART M. *Josiah Wedgwood and the Potteries.* 1974

See also ETRURIA.

Wellington, Arthur Wellesley, 1st Duke of (1769-1852): British soldier and politician, popularly known as the "Iron Duke". The fourth son of an Irish peer, he entered the British army in 1785. His service in India (1796-1803) first showed his great military qualities, but his outstanding achievement was the successful conduct of the Peninsular War (1809-14) in Spain and Portugal which drove the French out of the Iberian peninsula. For this he was created a duke. When in 1815 Napoleon made a bid to restore his fortunes, it was Wellington who withstood him at Waterloo and, when the Prussians came up, drove him from the field.

Many years of political life now awaited him. He was prime minister 1828-30, and for some time his resistance to change brought him unpopularity; but this was soon forgotten by the nation in its affectionate recognition of one of the greatest men in British history.
¶ WARD, S. G. P. *Wellington.* 1963
See also INDIVIDUAL ENTRIES.

Wesley, John (1703-91): English divine and founder of Methodism, the fifteenth child of Samuel Wesley, rector of Epworth in Lincolnshire. For a time he followed an orthodox university and Church career, being ordained an Anglican priest, preaching in many churches round Oxford and periodically acting as his father's curate. In his early years he enjoyed company, dancing, walking and field sports and was a good swimmer. Around him and his brother Charles in Oxford gathered a small group of serious minded students known as the "Holy Club" who began to follow a stricter rule of life and received the nickname of "Methodists".

In 1735 John and Charles went on a missionary journey to Georgia and founded a religious society at Savannah. His dictatorial methods made him many enemies in America and he left Georgia in 1737. Back in England he appointed lay preachers, founded Methodist chapels (the first at Bristol in 1739) and established a great reputation as a field preacher, riding the length and breadth of the country on yearly journeys which have been called "the most amazing record of human exertion ever penned by man". He regularly travelled some 5,000 miles a year, preaching fifteen sermons a week, often to hostile audiences, his rule being always to look a mob in the face. As a social reformer he was far in advance of his time and, apart from his preaching, his twenty-three collections of hymns and his prose works continued to exercise a powerful influence long after his death. *See also* METHODISM.

Western Australia: largest Australian state, all the territory west of 129° East longitude, with Perth the capital. A plaque in the Amsterdam Museum records the visit in 1616 of Dirk Hartog. Tasman navigated the north-west coast in 1644, William Dampier visited King Sound in 1688, Vancouver took possession of the south-west in 1791, and King explored the north coast 1818–22. Convicts from New South Wales (*see* separate entries) in 1827 settled on King George's Sound under Captain Stirling. In 1829 Captain Fremantle (later knighted) founded the west coast Swan River settlement, the real beginnings of colonisation. In 1850 the colony, in order to secure more settlers and workers, sought the admission of convicts, and transportation continued until 1868, when the protests of other colonies could no longer be disregarded. Between the 1830s and the 1890s Grey, Gregory, the Forrests, Giles, Warburton and Lindsay explored the interior. Western Australia achieved responsible government in 1890. In the 1880s and 1890s gold discoveries at Kimberley and Kalgoorlie made mining the main industry. The state still produces seven-tenths of Australian gold, and is rich in minerals, among them tin, asbestos and silver. After World War I (*see* separate entry) wheat production expanded, with stock-raising and dairying in the south-west. Programmes of education and welfare have assisted the survival of the Aborigines (*see* separate entry), who chiefly follow pastoral and domestic occupations.
See AUSTRALIA for map.

West Indies, Federation of the: confederation of certain Caribbean islands within the British Commonwealth (1958–62). In the years after World War II (*see* separate entry) serious consideration was given to the best method of leading colonial peoples towards self-government and independence. In the West Indies the Caribbean Commission, created during World War II by the United States, France, the Netherlands and Great Britain, advised on political and other problems. Previously British West Indian islands had shown little interest in each others' political affairs. Cricket appeared the only common point of contact. The war ended, Britain cultivated the idea of federation of her West Indian colonies as the way of advancement towards independence. The Colonial Development and Welfare Act of 1940 was doing something to ease the widespread distresses of prewar years and to promote the social and economic development of the West Indies; but economic and population difficulties persisted. The physical nature of the West Indies, an archipelago stretching in a curve north-westwards from the coast of Venezuela to Florida, was itself daunting. Constitutional progress for so many separated units seemed impossible, and federation became official British policy.
Numerous conferences resulted in agreement in 1956 to establish the Federation of the West Indies. The Order in Council was signed on 31 July 1957, Lord Hailes, first Governor-General, arrived in Trinidad in January 1958, and

Princess Margaret inaugurated the first Parliament of the West Indies at Red House, Port of Spain, on 23 April.

Following serious differences of opinion among the members of the Federation on such matters as economic control and representation in the federal parliament, Jamaica left the Federation, to be followed soon after by Trinidad and Tobago. The Federation of the West Indies ended on the date planned for Independence Day, 31 May 1962.

See also INDIVIDUAL ENTRIES.

Westminster Abbey: great church, in Westminster, London, dedicated to St Peter. Built on what was once a marshy islet, it stands on a site where, traditionally, a church has stood since the 2nd century. In 1085 Edward the Confessor founded a new church and in 1245 Henry III began a vast rebuilding which was the beginning of the Abbey as we know it today, and developed later into one of the finest examples of Perpendicular style of Gothic to be found in the country. Over the centuries additions and alterations took place: cloisters and monastic buildings were erected for the Benedictine monks (1300-1400); the nave and aisles were rebuilt (1340-1483); in 1502 Henry VII laid the first stone of the exquisite chapel which bears his name.

Except for Edward V every English monarch since William I (reigned 1066-87) has been crowned in Westminster Abbey. Some of them are buried there, as well as many of the nation's greatest men and the Unknown Warrior, symbol of the nation's dead of World Wars I and II (*see* separate entries). The building must not be confused with Westminster Cathedral, built 1895-1910, the seat of the Roman Catholic Archbishop of Westminster. *See colour section.*

¶ LOXTON, HOWARD, editor. *Westminster Abbey* (Jackdaw). 1967

Whaling: the pursuit and killing of whales, immense marine mammals, of which there are many species, measuring up to 120 feet [36 m] and weighing as much as 200 tons [200 tonnes].

Whales were being caught by Norwegians as early as AD 890. The Basques from northern Spain established a whaling industry during the 11th century. The two main commodities obtainable from the whale – oil for lighting and making candles, and baleen (whalebone) – were much in demand. Other byproducts are ambergris, used in the manufacture of perfume, and spermaceti, an ingredient in a number of cosmetics and textile finishes. The Arctic whaling industry was started by the English and Dutch in 1611 and 1614, respectively, and the Germans, Danes and French followed in the next century. The enormous slaughter of the Greenland whale resulted in its near-extinction by about 1860.

In 1712 the Americans from New Bedford started hunting the sperm whale in the Atlantic. This creature, which frequents the warmer waters, is the toothed variety and has no baleen. It yields large quantities of sperm oil, so well suited as a lamp oil. The whaler *Amelia* was the first British ship to hunt the sperm whale in the Pacific, in 1789.

The early whalemen hunted in open boats. The whales were captured by the hand harpoon and finally killed with a spear. Flensing (the stripping away of the skin or blubber) was carried out at the

shore establishments or alongside the mother ship. In 1868 the Norwegian Svend Foyn perfected the gun harpoon with explosive head. This led to an expansion of the industry in which the Norwegians played a leading part.

The 20th-century whale factory ship with fast catcher ships to hunt the rorqual whale in the Antarctic has established the present industry. Whale oil is processed for margarine and soap and the flesh and bones for fertiliser. An International Whaling Commission was founded in 1946 to save the whale from extinction.

¶ REINFELD, FRED. *Real Book of Whales and Whaling.* 1963

Whig: political term in Britain, of Scottish origin and applied from about 1680 to a member of the country party, which, in opposition to the Tories (*see* TORY), stood for the moneyed and trading interest and mistrusted the policies of the Crown. The Whigs were responsible for inviting William III to England in 1688. They continued as a recognised political party until about 1850, when the term Liberals began to be applied to those who inherited their traditions.

White House, The: the official residence of the president of the USA, in Washington, DC. It is the oldest public building in Washington, designed in 1792 by James Hoban, and is esteemed for its architectural simplicity and purity of line, as well as for its many historical associations. (For its name, *see* WAR OF 1812.) As with Downing Street in Britain (*see* separate entry), the term White House is often used to mean the government itself.

Whitney, Eli (1765-1825): American inventor. In 1783 he invented a machine for separating cotton lint from its seeds. Many law suits followed when Whitney tried to protect his invention by taking

out a patent, or sole right to manufacture. He turned his attention to the manufacture of fire-arms and obtained many government contracts.

Whittle, Sir Frank (b. 1907): British engineer and inventor of the modern jet aircraft engine. Until 1948 he served with the Royal Air Force as apprentice, cadet, flying officer, instructor, test pilot, etc., reaching the rank of Air Commodore. The first flight of a Gloucester jet-propelled aeroplane with a Whittle engine took place in May 1941. Numerous international awards and decorations have been bestowed on the inventor.

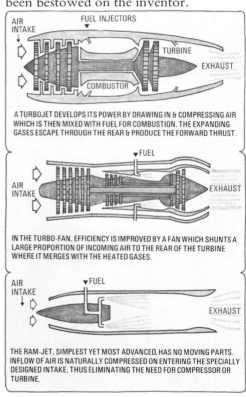

A TURBOJET DEVELOPS ITS POWER BY DRAWING IN & COMPRESSING AIR WHICH IS THEN MIXED WITH FUEL FOR COMBUSTION. THE EXPANDING GASES ESCAPE THROUGH THE REAR & PRODUCE THE FORWARD THRUST.

IN THE TURBO-FAN, EFFICIENCY IS IMPROVED BY A FAN WHICH SHUNTS A LARGE PROPORTION OF INCOMING AIR TO THE REAR OF THE TURBINE WHERE IT MERGES WITH THE HEATED GASES.

THE RAM-JET, SIMPLEST YET MOST ADVANCED, HAS NO MOVING PARTS. INFLOW OF AIR IS NATURALLY COMPRESSED ON ENTERING THE SPECIALLY DESIGNED INTAKE, THUS ELIMINATING THE NEED FOR COMPRESSOR OR TURBINE.

¶ In EVANS, I. O. *Inventors of the World.* 1962

Wilberforce, William (1759-1833): leader of the anti-slavery movement in Britain. Born of an old Yorkshire family, he became Member of Parliament for

Hull at the age of twenty-one. With the support of the younger Pitt he more than once persuaded the House of Commons to pass resolutions against the slave trade (*see* SLAVERY), but he had to wait until 1807 to see an Act passed prohibiting the trade as far as British subjects and British territories were concerned. He continued his untiring labours in the cause, the Emancipation Act, freeing all slaves in British possessions, becoming law in the year of his death.

¶ LAWSON, A. and D. *The Man Who Freed the Slaves.* 1962

Wilhelm I (1797–1888): king of Prussia from 1861 and emperor of the newly formed German Empire from 1871. He believed in strong government and the existence of a large Prussian army. He appointed Bismarck (*see* separate entry) as his minister-president in 1862 and in him found a man of character and ability whose ideas were similar to his own.

Wilhelm II, known as **"The Kaiser"** (1859–1941): emperor of Germany from 1888 to 1918. He believed in vigorous personal direction of government to increase Germany's world prestige. But he had little political skill and antagonised many European states. Though not entirely to blame for starting World War I (*see* separate entry), he fled into exile in Holland in 1918 rather than stand trial on the charge of so doing.

Wilkes, Charles (1798–1877): American explorer who, in 1840, first reported the existence of an Antarctic continent. As a US naval officer during the American Civil War (1861–64; *see* separate entry) he stopped a British ship, the *Trent,* and removed two Confederate envoys who were aboard. This violation of neutrality nearly led to war with England.

Wilkes, John (1727–97): English politician, champion of parliamentary reform. In the course of a turbulent career he was imprisoned in the Tower, expelled from the House of Commons, and declared an outlaw. He was four times returned as member for Middlesex, but the elections were disallowed, leading to great popular agitation under the banner, "Wilkes and Liberty!" In 1782 Wilkes was allowed to take his seat in parliament.

Wilson, Thomas Woodrow (1856–1924): 28th president of the USA (1913–21). After endeavouring to pursue a policy of neutrality in World War I, he reluctantly agreed to the declaration of war on Germany in 1917. In January 1918 he enunciated the famous "Fourteen Points" (*see* separate entry), as a basis for a peace settlement, helped to set up the League of Nations, and was awarded the Nobel Peace Prize in 1920.

¶ In CANNING, JOHN, editor. *100 Great Modern Lives.* 1965

Winchester: cathedral city 64 miles [103 km] west-south-west of London on the River Itchen. The Roman invaders of AD 43 found the site occupied by the Belgae, a tribe which had come over from Gaul about a century earlier. Under the name of *Venta Belgarum,* it was one of the most flourishing towns of Roman Britain. Later the kings of Wessex, the Anglo-Saxon kingdom in south and west England, including Alfred the Great, made it their capital: caskets said to contain the bones of several of them can still be seen in the cathedral. During Norman times the city continued to prosper, and the royal treasury was located there. There also grew up a considerable Jewish settlement still commemorated in the name Jewry Street. From the 12th century decline set in, and later recovery never restored Winchester to its former importance.

The present cathedral dates from the 11th century and is the longest in England. Among medieval buildings still in use are the College, founded by William of Wykeham in 1378, and the hospital (almshouse) of St Cross. Among the important events witnessed by the city were the marriage of Mary I of England and Philip of Spain (1554) and the trial of Sir Walter Ralegh (1603), the court having been convened there because of an outbreak of plague in London.

See separate entries for ALFRED THE GREAT; JEWS; PHILIP OF SPAIN; RALEGH, SIR WALTER.

Windsor, House of: English royal house. King George V, second son of Edward VII, came to the throne in 1910. He was a grandson of Queen Victoria, whose husband, Prince Albert, had been a member of the German family of Saxe-Coburg-Gotha. Many German princes were related to this family, so that in 1917, during World War I, King George was advised to change his name and by royal proclamation took the surname of Windsor for himself and his descendants.

George V became an extremely popular monarch. Because he and Queen Mary travelled extensively both at home and abroad, they were known to their subjects in a way that Queen Victoria and King Edward VII had never been.

When George V died in 1936, his eldest son became king. Edward VIII reigned for less than a year and was never crowned.

He had been a popular Prince of Wales, but, not prepared to conform to the will of his ministers in some matters, broke with them completely over the question of his proposed marriage to Mrs Wallis Simpson, a twice-divorced American. He abdicated, married Mrs Simpson and was given the title of Duke of Windsor, being succeeded by his brother, George VI, who was king during World War II and the troubled years that followed it. His daughter, Elizabeth II, became Queen after his sudden death in 1952. She and her husband, Prince Philip, have four children, the eldest of whom is Charles, Prince of Wales.

Witchcraft: the practice of magic, usually understood to be "black" (i.e. malevolent) as distinct from the "white" or beneficent variety. Magic, in world history, occupies a unique place, somewhere between science and religion. Primitive peoples, unable to comprehend the natural forces governing the universe, looked for an explanation elsewhere; in gods and goddesses, each charged with dominion over some particular aspect of nature, and in certain human beings who, by invoking supernatural powers, were themselves enabled to exercise control over nature and events.

In developing civilisations witchcraft was early seen as a kind of heresy, a threat to organised religion. The Book of Exodus (22:18) enjoins "Thou shalt not suffer a witch to live". Educated people in ancient Greece deplored the use of magic. Nevertheless, there are many references to it in Greek myths. Medea, the witch who helped the hero Jason obtain the Golden Fleece, later restored Jason's father to youth by boiling him in a stew of magic herbs. The goddess Hecate was the protectress of all witches.

The ancient Romans passed laws punishing witches. The idea of witchcraft which emerged in Europe in the Middle Ages (*see* separate entries) was a combination of myth, folk-beliefs, and the early Christian belief in the power of Satan and his devils. The typical witch was seen as a woman (while male witches, or warlocks, were thought to exist, the profession was considered primarily a female preserve) who could assume animal form, had a familiar – a demon in animal guise who was her helper and guide – and could fly through the air, with or without a broomstick. By spells, waxen images and the evil eye she could bring harm and death; she ate little children, called up storms, and raised the dead, she celebrated obscene witches' sabbaths with the Devil, when a travesty of the Christian mass was performed.

From the 13th century on, with the establishment of the Inquisition (*see* separate entry), the ecclesiastical tribunal concerned with the rooting out of heresy, the persecution of witches greatly increased. In 1484 Pope Innocent III issued

Matthew Hopkins, Witch Finder Generall, surrounded by the symbols of his trade.

a bull against witchcraft, as a result of which thousands of so-called witches were put to death. Between 1580 and 1595 900 died in Lorraine alone. The persecution was by no means an exclusively Roman Catholic activity. Many witches were persecuted in the American colonies, the trials at Salem, New England, being particularly notorious. In England between 1645 and 1647 Matthew Hopkins (d. 1647), known as the Witch-Finder, procured the hanging of some hundred persons in East Anglia.

¶ HART, ROGER. *Witchcraft.* 1971

Witte, Count Sergei Yulievich (1849–1915): Russian statesman, responsible as minister of communications for a rapid expansion of Russian railways (especially the Trans-Siberian), and as finance minister for doubling imperial revenues. He was plenipotentiary at the Portsmouth (USA) treaty which ended the Russo-Japanese war (1905; *see* separate entry), and largely responsible for the constitutional reforms introduced into Russia at that time.

Wolsey, Thomas (*c.* 1475–1530): English statesman. As Cardinal, Lord Chancellor to Henry VIII, Archbishop of York, holder of many other benefices and papal legate, he was virtual ruler of England 1511–29. He strengthened the monarchy by concentrating justice under the Crown, but his expensive foreign policy, successful until 1518, failed after his alliance (1521) with Charles V (*see* separate entry) in a bid for the papacy. He joined with France in 1528, hoping to free the Pope from imperial control and secure papal sanction for Henry's divorce from Catherine of Aragon; but his policy collapsed with France's defeat in 1529. Wolsey was dismissed and died at Leicester on his way to answer charges of high treason.

Wool: fine soft hair forming the fleece of many animals, particularly the sheep. Woollen fibres are easy to spin and weave, and in cold climates woollen cloth is warm and comfortable to wear. In Britain, sheep were reared long before the Roman occupation and cloth was made from their wool. The Romans established a centre for making woollen cloth to keep their soldiers in Britain supplied with clothing.

The climate and low grassy hills made Britain an excellent place for sheep to flourish, and the quality of British wool was renowned. Although the Saxons (*see* separate entry) encouraged their women-folk to spin, very little weaving was done in Britain. Raw wool and spun thread were exported to the Netherlands for weaving and the finished cloth shipped back to Britain. But William the Conqueror encouraged Flemish weavers to come to Britain, and by the end of the 11th century there were settlements of them at Carlisle and in Pembrokeshire. Henry II encouraged weaving by giving official patronage to a fair, held annually in St Bartholomew's churchyard in London, for the sale of woollen cloth.

The woollen merchants of London were granted the sole right to export raw wool. Edward III forbade this, insisting that all the wool produced in Britain must be woven by British cloth-weavers. This led to wool smuggling on a large scale, and the act proved impossible to enforce. The unrestricted export of wool was not permitted until Elizabeth I's reign. Evidence of the wealth of the wool merchants can be seen in the magnificent churches built and paid for by money made from the sale of wool. Later efforts were again made to control the sale of wool, and it was not until the cotton industry of Lancashire became so profitable after the Industrial Revolution that all restrictions on the sale of raw wool were finally lifted.

There was a woollen industry in Spain, where the Moors had introduced Merino sheep with their fine, silky hair. Merino sheep were later introduced into Australia, and cloth made from their wool was manufactured at Botany Bay – hence the name "botany" for light woollen fabric. With the growth of the trade in frozen meat other breeds of sheep were introduced into Australia and New Zealand. They were sometimes crossed with merinos and produced a heavier wool. Nowadays, little weaving is done in Australia or New Zealand, but a great deal of raw wool is exported.

See also WEAVING.

World War I (1914–18): Simply known as the "Great War" at the time, the term "world war" was given only after the Armistice. The spark was the assassination on 28 June 1914 at Sarajevo of the heir to the Austrian throne by a Serb – a member of the "Black Hand" secret society whose aim was the unification of all Slav peoples of south-eastern Europe under their own government. Austria and Serbia were quarrelling over power in the Balkans, and a month later Austrian troops invaded Serbia. The conflict might have been restricted to that area had it not been for twenty-five years of rising international tension.

Germany had ambitions of becoming a world power, and this caused mistrust in

1914, Archduke Franz Ferdinand and his wife at Sarajevo shortly before the assassination.

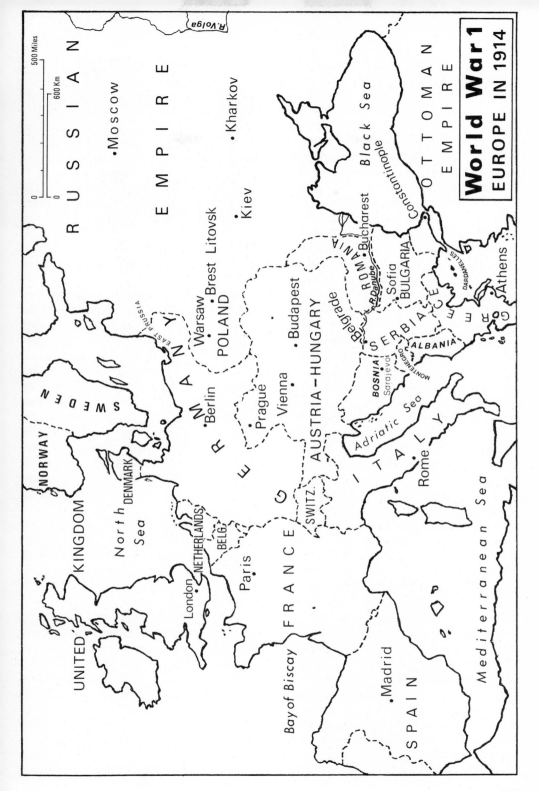

World War 1
EUROPE IN 1914

R.Volga

500 Miles
600 Km

R U S S I A N   E M P I R E

•Moscow

•Kharkov

•Kiev

•Brest Litovsk

Warsaw•   POLAND

Black Sea

Constantinople

OTTOMAN   EMPIRE

DARDANELLES

•Bucharest

R O M A N I A

R.Danube

Sofia•   BULGARIA

•Athens

G R E E C E

ALBANIA

MONTENEGRO

BOSNIA   Sarajevo•

S E R B I A

Belgrade•

Budapest•

AUSTRIA–HUNGARY

Adriatic Sea

Vienna•

Prague•

G E R M A N Y

EAST PRUSSIA

Berlin•

SWEDEN

NORWAY

DENMARK

North Sea

NETHERLANDS

BELG.

London•

Paris•

F R A N C E

SWITZ.

I T A L Y

Rome•

Bay of Biscay

Mediterranean Sea

•Madrid

S P A I N

UNITED KINGDOM

the other states. Rival "camps" had developed: a close Austro-German alliance, supported halfheartedly by Italy, faced Franco-Russian co-operation. Britain, fearful of German naval and colonial intentions, was drawn closer to France. The extension of the war from the Balkans in 1914 became inevitable. Russian support for Serbia was well known, but her speed of mobilisation was slow. So, working to a tight timetable known as the Schlieffen Plan, a German army aimed a swift hammer-blow through Belgium to destroy France, Russia's ally. This should have left Germany free to face Russia in the east.

The invasion was in direct breach of an 1839 treaty, signed by Germany among others, guaranteeing Belgian neutrality. It was the contemptuous ignoring of this "scrap of paper" that brought Britain into the war. Stalemate was to replace dreams of a speedy victory by both sides, and for three years French and British armies matched the Germans. Efforts by one side to dislodge the other from extensive trench systems failed, partly because of the balance of numbers and war machinery, and partly because of the High Commands' unimaginative use of frontal assaults. Massive attempts, involving millions of men, to achieve a breakthrough at Ypres (1915 and 1917), the Somme and Verdun (1916) were halted either by mud or by superior defensive machine guns.

The German effort in the Balkans and against Russia was more successful. The threat that Russia might be forced out of the war led the British into the disastrous Gallipoli campaign of 1915, in an effort to bring aid into Russia by the Black Sea route. Russian military resistance crumbled, and in 1917 revolution destroyed first the Tsarist government and then the country's will to fight. A Soviet Russian government accepted a ruthless peace giving Germany huge areas from

Soldiers in the trenches at the Somme, 1916.

the Baltic through Poland to the Ukraine and Caucasus.

But these gains were to have little lasting importance. The appearance of tanks (first used by the British in September 1916) introduced new strategic possibilities. Following a rash German naval decision to sink neutral ships supplying Britain and France, the USA entered the war and in 1918 the enormous American power in men and machines ended the stalemate in France. This, coupled with shortages of food and mutinies in Germany itself, led to the Armistice, in which the Germans not only had to submit to a peace settlement but also give up her gains in the east.

In 1914 men had rather lightheartedly gone to war in support of their nation's glory and prestige. By 1918 eleven million had died, and the horror and waste of it all were clear to many.

¶ HOARE, ROBERT J. *World War One.* 1973; SCOTT-DANIELL, DAVID. *World War I.* 1965

See also BALKANS; BELGIUM; CONVOY SYSTEM; DARDANELLES; TSAR; VERSAILLES, TREATY OF; etc.

World War II (1939-45): war fought to limit the ambitions of Hitler's Germany in Europe and of Imperial Japan in East Asia and the Pacific. At first there were two separate conflicts, which merged into a world war in 1941, when the British

Commonwealth and USA were involved in both theatres of war.

The European war began in 1939, when Britain and France tried to stop Hitler's gradual extension of German territorial power. Throughout the 1930s both countries were worried at the rise of Italian, German and Spanish dictatorships, but feared that the only alternative was the spread of Soviet communism. Only after Hitler's destruction of Czech independence in March 1939 and his invasion of Poland in September, in spite of British and French diplomatic opposition, did they feel they must act.

The Asian conflict began in 1937 with a Japanese invasion of China. Japan's growing population and shortage of land increased her need for raw materials and markets for her manufactures. She had already moved into Manchuria six years before and now she wanted total control of China. A quarrel with the USA developed and, when American oil to Japan was cut off in 1941, Japan attacked US naval power at Pearl Harbour and launched a campaign to seize all southeast Asia's riches in oil, food and metals.

Both German and Japanese military forces gained spectacular successes. The European continent as far east as the suburbs of Moscow and the Caucasian oilfields came under German control, as well as North Africa as far as the Nile delta. The Japanese conquests extended to the Indian frontier and over the Pacific islands to just north of Australia and west of Hawaii. Yet both aggressors took on an impossible task. Their ruthless and sometimes atrocious treatment of the peoples they conquered ended any hope of a quick and acceptable peace, and secret resistance movements engaged in guerrilla warfare against Germany's and Japan's "New Order". The tremendous resources and determination of their four main enemies, the USA, the Soviet

Street fighting in Stalingrad, 1942.

Union, the British Commonwealth and China, meant that in a prolonged war they had little hope of victory, despite the earlier conquests.

The seeds of German defeat were already clear in the failure to win control of air and sea power in the Battles of Britain and the Atlantic, but the turning point came in 1942–43. At Stalingrad and El Alamein the German military advance was checked, whilst the Japanese were halted at Midway and Guadalcanal in the Pacific and at Imphal in India. There followed a gradual, three-year destruction of their power. Hitler's "Fortress Europe" was invaded, first through Italy and Normandy by Commonwealth–American armies, and then from the east by Soviet forces. As the Russians fought their way into Berlin Hitler committed suicide and Germany surrendered unconditionally. The Japanese, too, lost control of the sea to the Americans, who forced them out of key islands such as Saipan and Okinawa. In the climax of the struggle in 1945 the Americans faced the desperation of the Japanese "Kamikaze" suicide pilots. In August two atomic bombs were dropped on Hiroshima and Nagasaki and the Japanese government immediately surrendered.

There were over 30 million deaths in World War II. Some people were killed in battle, others in air raids; but more

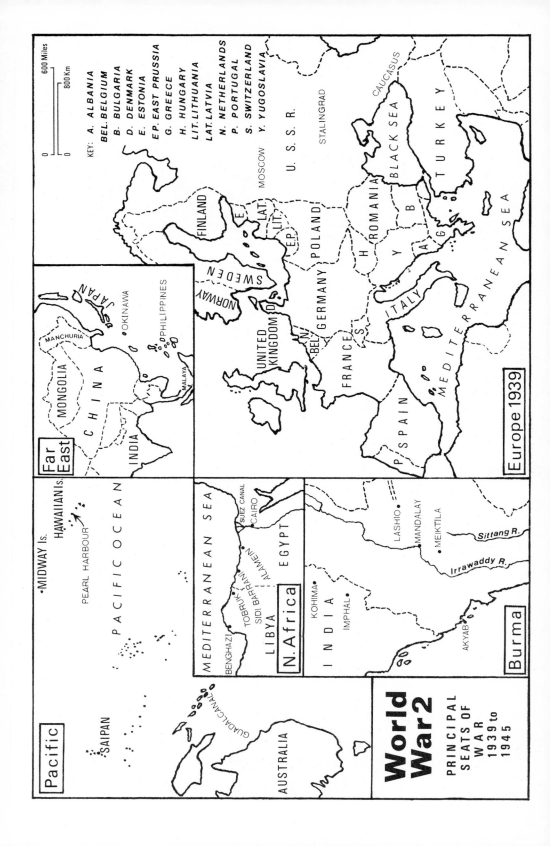

were victims of Japanese and German persecution. Prisoners-of-war in the Far East were ill-treated, whilst in Europe millions of Jewish and Slav civilians died in concentration camps such as Auschwitz. The war had been successfully fought to end this type of tyranny but had created many new problems. Widespread destruction by bombing added the homeless to the already vast number of refugees. There were renewed fears of communism, with the Russians intent on imposing their own rule on areas they had freed from German control. Overshadowing all was the destructive power of the atomic bomb.

¶ HOARE, ROBERT J. *World War Two.* 1973; SCOTT-DANIELL, DAVID. *World War II.* 1966

See also ALAMEIN, BATTLE OF; ATLANTIC CHARTER; AXIS; BATTLE OF BRITAIN; EISENHOWER, DWIGHT DAVID; HITLER, ADOLF; LEASE-LEND BILL; MIDWAY, BATTLE OF; MUSSOLINI, BENITO; NAZI; PAPEN, FRANZ VON; PEARL HARBOUR; YALTA CONFERENCE.

Wren, Sir Christopher (1632–1723): one of England's greatest architects. He was also sufficiently skilled in mathematics and astronomy to have been elected professor of astronomy at Oxford. The Great Fire of London (1666) provided

St Paul's Cathedral by Christopher Wren.

Wren with his great opportunity. Earlier, Charles II had asked him to prepare a plan for the restoration of old St Paul's. As a result of the fire Wren designed a new St Paul's and fifty-one parish churches in addition. Unfortunately for London, his splendid scheme for a comprehensive replanning of the entire city was not adopted. Other buildings designed by Wren include the Royal Exchange and Greenwich Hospital. A famous inscription over the interior of the north door in St Paul's is attributed to Wren's son: *Si monumentum requiris, circumspice* (If you would see his monument, look around).

¶ GOULD, HEYWOOD. *Sir Christopher Wren.* 1972

Wright, Frank Lloyd (1869–1959): American architect who was one of the first to use architectural features – wide windows, open-plan interiors, etc. – which have become extensively adopted in modern design. Among his best-known buildings are the Imperial Hotel, Tokyo, and the Guggenheim Museum, New York, as well as private houses which seem to have grown out of the landscape, so much are they in sympathy with it.

¶ In CANNING, JOHN, editor. *100 Great Modern Lives.* 1965

See also INTERNATIONAL STYLE.

Shop front in San Francisco by Frank Lloyd Wright.

Wright, Orville (1871–1948) and **Wilbur** (1867–1912): American aircraft engineers (brothers) who built the first stable and controllable heavier-than-air machine. Beginning with a modest bicycle repair business, they developed a passionate interest in mechanical flight and brought their experiments to a successful conclusion on 17 December 1903 when, at Kitty Hawk, North Carolina, a machine powered by a four-cylinder petrol motor of 12 horsepower made four free flights, the longest of 59 seconds, the maximum speed 30 miles [48 km] per hour, the greatest height 852 feet [260 metres]. The original machine is in the Science Museum, London.

¶ GLINES, CARROLL V. *The Wright Brothers.* 1970
See also AVIATION.

Wyclif or **Wycliffe, John** (*c.* 1320–84): English philosopher, theologian and religious reformer who sought to purge the Church of those who held office for private enrichment rather than the glory of God. With his band of 'poor priests" he preached a Christianity that ordinary people could understand. He published many learned works in Latin, but his chief service to literature was the first English translation of the Bible, to which he contributed probably the whole of the New Testament as well as part of the Old.

¶ STACEY, JOHN. *John Wyclif and Reform.* 1964

X

Xenophon (*c.* 430–*c.* 354 BC): Athenian soldier and author. In the confused state of the times he lent his services on occasions to the Spartans (*see* SPARTA) and to Cyrus, who claimed the Persian throne. His best known work, the *Anabasis*, describes the latter's expedition into Asia with an army of Greek mercenaries, of whom Xenophon was one. He also wrote on philosophy, history and country pursuits.

Xerxes I, called **"the Great"** (*c.* 519–*c.* 465 BC): King of Persia 485–465 BC. He attempted to revenge his father's failure to subdue Greece, but his large fleet was destroyed at Salamis (480) and his vast army defeated at Plataea in the following year (*see* PERSIAN WARS).

X-ray: At the end of the 19th century a German scientist, Wilhelm Roentgen, was engaged in experiments with electricity. He discovered that if an electric current were passed through a black tube containing certain gases a very powerful greenish glow resulted. This glowing light, or radiation, could be used in photography. It could illuminate the body, showing what was inside it, but would not pass through metal. Roentgen did not know what this radiation was, so he named it the "X" ray. Doctors soon realised that it could be used to photograph the interior of the body, revealing diseased bones and other internal malformations. The technique of making X-ray photographs is known as radiography.

The first precise x-ray photograph of a man's hand, made by Wilhelm Roentgen in 1907.

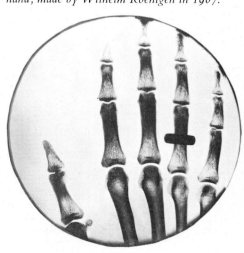

Y

Yale University: the third oldest university in the USA, situated in New Haven, Connecticut. Founded in 1701 it was named, in 1718, after Elihu Yale (1649–1721), son of one of the first settlers in New Haven. Elihu Yale became the governor of the East India Company's (*see* separate entry) settlement in Madras and made a fortune in the Indian trade. Through his generosity the university was able to expand greatly from its modest beginnings. Together with Harvard (at Cambridge, Mass.) and Princeton (NJ), Yale today occupies a position of high prestige and scholarly esteem.

Yalta Conference (4–11 February 1945): meeting at Yalta, in the Crimea, between Stalin (USSR), F. D. Roosevelt (USA) and Churchill (Britain) to discuss the final defeat of Germany and the problems which would follow that country's surrender. This was to be unconditional and Germany would then be split into four zones for occupation by US, British, French and Russian forces, with headquarters in Berlin. Arrangements to destroy German military power for ever would be made at a future conference. Some details of the new United Nations Organisation were agreed, including the power of veto in the Security Council. The "Big Three" renewed their resolve to create "a world order under law, dedicated to . . . the general wellbeing of all mankind". Ironically, the conference marked the end of much of the wartime unity, since there were serious disagreements with Stalin over such things as the proposed all-communist Polish government and the drawing of the Oder–Neisse Line.

See also INDIVIDUAL ENTRIES.

Yangtze Kiang: the most important river (3,340 miles; 5,374 km long) in China, passing through the cities of Ipin, Chungking, Wan-hsien, Ichang, Kiangling, Wu-ch'ang, Hankow, Wuhu and Nanking. The great port of Shanghai is near its mouth.

¶ SPENCER, CORNELIA. *The Yangtze, China's River Highway.* 1966

Yankees: among its various meanings, any citizen of the USA; earlier, a native of one of the northern states or a soldier in the Union forces in the American Civil War (*see* separate entry), as opposed to those of the Confederate states. The origin of the word is doubtful.

Yemen: republic of south-western Arabia. The area had a highly developed civilisation as early as the 8th century BC. The Romans took possession at the end of the 1st century AD, and later the Abyssinians. Judaism and Christianity were established in the 4th century. Under Persian and Islamic rule, Yemen had its own dynasty from the 11th century. Turkey occupied it in 1538 and

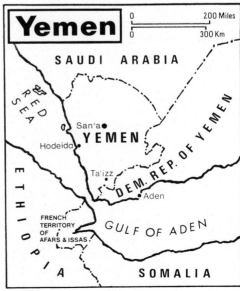

1849. When it was invaded by Saudi Arabia in 1934, Yemen was supported by Britain. Becoming a member of the United Nations in 1947 and a republic in 1962, Yemen has been the scene of conflict between Saudi Arabia and the United Arab Republic.

Yiddish: the language of about six million Jews. It developed from the 12th century AD, based mainly on German (jüdisch = jewish), but about 10 per cent of its vocabulary comes from Hebrew and another 10 per cent from Slav languages. A literature developed from the 16th century and includes many modern novels. *See also* JEWS; JUDAISM.

Yokohama: Japan's chief seaport and second largest city, adjoining Tokyo. It was only a fishing village when the American Commodore Perry landed there in 1854, opening Japan to the western world. Destroyed by earthquake and fire in 1923 and heavily bombed in World War II, it is now a major industrial city, with extensive shipyards and manufactures in steel, chemicals, motor cars and mechanical engineering.

York, England: cathedral city on the River Ouse, 194 miles [312 km] north-north-west of London. Here the Romans in AD 71 founded Eboracum, a military station for the Ninth Legion, and here in 306 Constantine (*see* separate entry) was proclaimed Roman emperor. In 625 Paulinus was consecrated the first Archbishop of York. The medieval city enjoyed great commercial prosperity: its walls, two-and-a-half miles [4 km] in circumference, still largely survive. The present minster (cathedral), one of the finest in Europe, dates from the 13th century. By Tudor times (*see* TUDOR, HOUSE OF) trade was declining, but York played an important part in the English

Civil War of 1642-49, and still retains some of the characteristics of England's "northern capital".

York, House of: royal house which occupied the English throne from 1461 to 1485. It traced its ancestry from Edward III. Edward IV was the son of Richard, the grandson of Edmund, fifth son of Edward III and of Anne, great-granddaughter of Lionel, third son of Edward III. The rival House of Lancaster descended from John of Gaunt, fourth son of Edward III.

Edward IV has been described as "the first English Prince of the Renaissance type" (*see* RENAISSANCE). Unlike the Lancastrians, Edward was rich. A new kind of extortion, benevolences or forced loans, yielded large sums of money, which enabled him to "live of his own" without recourse to taxes voted by parliament, which met only once between 1475 and 1483.

On Edward's death in 1483, his rightful heir, Edward V, was displaced by his uncle, Richard III, about whom historians have little good to say, although the parliament of 1484 did some useful work. The dynastic history of the House of York ended with the marriage of Henry VII to Elizabeth of York, thus uniting the houses of Lancaster and York. The badge of the House was the white rose.
See also LANCASTER, HOUSE OF.

Yorktown: small town of south-eastern Virginia, USA, founded in 1691 as a port of entry for York County. In 1781 it was the scene of the surrender of the British forces under General Cornwallis at the end of the American War of Independence (*see* separate entry). Yorktown is now the centre of a national historical park containing original and reconstructed buildings, remains of the War of Independence earthworks, guns, etc.

Eager Klondike gold prospectors pitch their tents along the ledge below the treacherous icy trail over the Chilkoot Pass in the Canadian Rockies.

Young, Brigham (1801–77): American Mormon leader who headed the migration to Utah in 1847 and founded Salt Lake City. *See also* MORMONS.

Young Turks: early 20th-century revolutionary/political movement in the Turkish empire. After a rising in Macedonia in 1908 the reformers obtained power in 1909 under Enver Bey, deposing the Sultan. A surviving member of the movement was Kemal Ataturk (1880–1938), who modernised Turkey after World War I.
See also ATATURK; WORLD WAR I.

Yukon: territory in north-west Canada, constituted a separate political entity in 1898, and sending one member of parliament to Ottawa. The 1897–98 Klondyke gold rush temporarily inflated the population. Mining remains important, along-side furs, forestry and fishing. The Yukon River, first explored by Schwatka in 1883 and navigable in summer from Whitehorse, the capital, to the Bering Sea, formerly provided the chief means of transport. The construction and strategic importance of the Alaskan Highway, the railway from Whitehorse to Alaska, air transport, the oil pipeline to Norman Wells and oil potential, have combined to improve the Yukon's economy and attract population.

Z

Zaire, The Republic of: central African republic, formerly Belgian Congo, bounded in the north and north-west by the Central African Republic and Republic of the Congo; north-east by the Sudan; east by Uganda, Rwandi Burundi and Tanzania; south-east by Zambia; south-west by Angola. The total area is 904,990 square miles [2,343,915 square kilometres], and its population in 1970 was 21,637,000.

The central tableland has an average altitude of 3,000 feet [914 metres] and is largely wooded savannah, with forest country in the river valleys. A great forest region stretches from Lake Albert to the mouth of the Aruwimi River, and is inhabited by the Pygmies. Agriculture is underdeveloped, but rubber, teak, ebony, mahogany, cotton, coffee, rice, tobacco, caoutchouc and oil palms are grown. There are rich deposits of copper, cobalt, iron, zinc, uranium and radium in Katanga, gold at Ruwe, Kilo and the Mboga district, and diamonds in the Kasai district.

Cameron's expedition of 1875 led to the formation of the *Association Internationale Africaine*, under the personal auspices of Leopold II of Belgium, which was given its status in 1885 by the treaty of Berlin. Its original object was to suppress slavery and civilise Africa, but before any real progress could be made war broke out between Belgium and the Arabs under Tippoo Tib. The postwar economy, based on a system of concessions for development and the exploitation of natural resources, led to abuses, and the territory was formally annexed by Belgium in 1908, administered by a Governor General representing the King. As a result of Congolese pressure and world opinion it became the independent Democratic Republic of the Congo in June 1960, renamed the Republic of Zaire in October 1971. The country has suffered much civil strife and civilian massacre, with spasmodic intervention by UN forces, Belgian paratroopers and foreign mercenaries, but achieved some measure of stability under General Mobutu, President and Prime Minister since 1965.

See CENTRAL AFRICA for map.

Zambia: republic, formerly Northern Rhodesia, bounded in the north by Zaire and Tanzania, in the south by the Zambesi, which forms its boundary with Rhodesia, and the Caprivi Strip, and in the east by Angola. The chief exports are copper, cobalt, vanadium, zinc, lead and tobacco, with copper predominating so greatly that the economy is dependent on it. The greater part of the country lies 4,000 feet [1,220 m] or more above sea level, which tempers what would otherwise be a tropical climate. It is watered by great rivers, among them the Zambesi which thunders a mile wide over the 360-foot [110 m] Victoria Falls, near Livingstone, spreads into Lake Kariba, then shoots through the great sluices of the Kariba Dam on its way to Mozambique.

The country has a very long history and important prehistoric settlements have been discovered. The Bantu people, who now form the majority of the population, invaded from the 17th century onwards, to be followed by Arab, Zulu and Basuto tribes. Portuguese expeditions in the 18th and early 19th centuries led to a great deal of slave traffic. Livingstone explored the territory in the 1850s and discovered the Victoria Falls. Later the British South Africa Company (1889–1900) virtually took over control. The British Crown assumed administration in 1924, following unification of the country as Northern Rhodesia.

Northern Rhodesia, with Southern Rhodesia and Nyasaland, formed the experimental Central African Federation in August 1954. This broke up in 1963, however, and on 24 October 1964 Northern Rhodesia became the independent Republic of Zambia, with Dr Kenneth Kaunda as head of state.

Zanzibar: former British protectorate, now part of the United Republic of Tanzania, comprising the islands of Zanzibar, Pemba, Lamu, Manda, Patta and Siu. The principal town is Zanzibar. The islands supply most of the world's cloves and clove oil.

The islands probably served South Arabian traders as a staging and trading post for many centuries, and were also visited by traders from the east coast of India. In the 10th century the population appears to have been Muslim, and by the end of the 15th century each island was ruled by a chief of mixed African and Asiatic blood. At the beginning of the 16th century the Portuguese dominated the islands but were deposed by the Arabs in 1698. In 1829 the Sultan of Oman moved his capital from Muscat to Zanzibar, and when he died in 1856 his son Majid became Sultan of Zanzibar, which, following a dispute, was thereafter judged to be independent of Oman. In 1888 Sultan Khalifa granted the lease of a large part of his territory to Germany, but when Count von Caprivi was the German Foreign Minister, 1890–93, he withdrew Germany's claim to Zanzibar and negotiated a deal with Britain in which Zanzibar was exchanged for Heligoland and the Caprivi Strip (a long narrow wedge of land between Zambia and Botswana). Zanzibar was a British protectorate until 1964, when it became part of Tanzania. See CENTRAL AFRICA for map.

Zeppelin: type of cigar-shaped airship developed by the German inventor Count Ferdinand von Zeppelin (1838–1917). His first airship (1900), wrecked on landing, remained in the air for 20 minutes. From this modest beginning these dirigibles progressed till they were used in bombing raids in World War I (see separate entry) and, later, on transatlantic voyages. See also AIRSHIP.

Zionism: political movement begun in 1897 by Theodor Herzl (see separate entry) to secure a national home for Jews in Palestine, an objective achieved in 1948 with the establishment of the republic of Israel. Zionism takes its name from the hill in Jerusalem on which the ancient palace of King David and, later, the Temple, were built. See also ISRAEL, JEWS.

Zulus: a proud Bantu tribe whose ancestors probably migrated from East Africa, settling in Natal in South Africa, where, under their chief Chaka, they terrorised a large area, conquering other Nguni Bantu tribes and forming themselves into a great warrior nation. Chaka was killed by his brother Dingaan in 1829. The Zulus were as great a threat to the Dutch farmer settlers (Boers; see separate entry) as the Red Indians were to the settlers of the western states of America, and in 1838 the Boers fought a pitched battle against them, defeating them heavily at Blood River. Dingaan was succeeded by Umhanda and Cetewayo, and in 1887 Zululand was annexed by the British, who brought peace to the region. Early in the 19th century a rebellious regiment of Zulus under Mzilikazi fought its way north and settled in the western half of Rhodesia, where they founded the Matabele nation.

Zurich: largest city and administrative canton in Switzerland, on Lake Zurich in the upper Rhine valley. Following even earlier settlements it was founded as a Roman customs station called Turiam, and has always been an important trading and craft area. During the Reformation Zurich, like Geneva, became a refuge for people fleeing Catholic persecution. In recent years it has gained newspaper prominence as an influential banking and financial centre ("the gnomes of Zurich").

Index

Balboa, Vasco de (1475–1517), 196, 547, 674
Baldwin Bras-de-Fer, Count (1058–1118), 315
Bali, 222, 455. *Map 456*
Balkan War (1912), 78
Balkans, **76–7**, 262, *77*
ballads, **78**
balloons, **78–9**, *78*
ballott, **79**
Baltic Provinces, 286
Baltimore, George Calvert, 1st Baron (*c.* 1580–1632), 21
Bancroft, George (1800–91), 415
Banda, Dr Hastings (b. 1905), 549
Bangladesh, **79**, 678. *Map 449*
Bank Charter Act (1844), 79, 80, 686
Bank of England, **79**
banks, **79–80**
Banks, Sir Joseph (1740–1820), 110
banner, **81**
Bannockburn, Battle of (1314), 35, 45, 120, 825, *825*
Banting, Sir Frederick (1891–1941), 574
Bantu tribes, 866, 938, 1000
Baptists, **81**
Barbados, 119
barbarians, 9, **81–2**, 291, 370. *Map 82*
barber-surgeons, **82–3**, *83*
Barcid family, 148–9
Barentz, William (d. 1597), 636
Barnard, Christian, 575
Barnardo, Dr Thomas (1845–1905), 784, *784*
Barnet, Battle of (1471), 87
Baron, **83**
Baronet, **83**
Baroque, **83**, 268, 970. Plate 7
Barry, Sir Charles (1795–1860), 190
Barwalde, Treaty of (1631), 921
Basic English, 519
Basil, St (AD 330–79), 171
Basle, Council of (1431–49), 208
Basques, 352
Basra, 512
Bass, George (1771–1803), 62, 905
Bastille, **83–4**, 337
baths and bathing, **84–5**, *84*
Batista, General Zaldivar y (1901–73), 152, 382
battering-ram, **85**
Battle of Britain (1940), **85**, 87. *Map 86*
battles, decisive, **85–7**
Batu Khan (d. 1255), 506
Baudouin, King of the Belgians (1951–   ), 3
Bavaria, 67, **87**, 607. *Map 66*
Bayard, Pierre du Terrail (*c.* 1474–1524), **87**, 170
Bayeux Tapestry, 42, **87–8**, 243, *88*. Plate 7
Bazaine, François (1811–88), 334
Beaker people, 68
Beard, Charles A. (1874–1948), 415
Beaufort family, 515
Beaufort, Margaret, Countess of Richmond (1433–1509), **88**, 941–2, *88*
Bechuanaland Protectorate, *see* **Botswana**
Bechuanas, 658
Becket, St Thomas (1118–70), **88**, 153, 204, 724; shrine, 155, 164, 713
Beckett, Samuel (1906–   ), 252
Becquerel, Henri (1852–1908), 60
Bede, the Venerable (AD 673–735), 16, 28, **88–9**, 96, 130, 174, 380, 822
Beethoven, Ludwig von (1770–1827), 656

Bedford, Francis Russell, 5th Duke of (1765–1802), 10
Bedouin, 31, 944
Behaim, Martin (15th cent.), 555
Behaine, Pigneau de (18th cent.), 455
Behring, Emil von (1854–1917), 632
Belgae, **89**, 119
Belgium, 89, 315–16, 446, 623, 1000. *Map 292*
Belisarius (*c.* AD 494–565), 82, **89**, 502
Bell, Alexander Graham (1847–1922), **89**, 900, 908, *89*
Bell, Patrick (1801–69), 11
Bell, Thomas (1792–1880), 207, 916
Bellini, Giovanni, (*c.* 1430–1516), 516, 741, 967
Benedict III, Pope (1724–30), 666
Benedict Biscop (*c.* AD 628–89), **89**
Benedict of Nursia, St (AD 480–550), 1–2, **90**, 340, 599, 662
Benedictines, 90, 528, 662–3, 948
benefit of clergy, **90**
Benelux, 89, **90**, 623
Beneš, Eduard (1884–1948), 219
benevolences, **90**
Benezet, Anthony (1713–84), 858
Bengal, 448, 450. *Map 449*
Bengali language, 518
Ben-Gurion, David (b. 1886), 475
Benin, **90–1**, 629, *90*
Bentham, Jeremy (1748–1832), 464
Bentinck, Lord William Cavendish (1774–1839), 451
Benz, Carl (1844–1929), 606
Bérain, Jean (1638–1711), 343–4
Berbers, 944
Bergen, 394. *Map 394*
Bering Strait, 19, 335, 636
Berlin, **91–2**, 360. *Map 358*
Berlin Wall, 92, 361
Berlin, Congress of (1878), **92**, 262, 500, 799
Berlin, Congress of (1884), 8
Berlin Decree (1806), 101, 200
Bernadette, St (1844–79), 541
Bernadotte, Count Folke (1895–1948), 476
Bernard, St, 948
Bernard of Clairvaux, St (*c.* 1090–1153), **92**
Bernini, Giovanni Lorenzo (1598–1680), 84, 268
Berwick, Battle of (1333), 383
Bessarabia, *Map 77*
Bessemer, Sir Henry (1813–98), **92**, 888, *92*
Bethlehem, **93**, 217
Bethlehem, USA, **93**
Beveridge Report, **93**, 699, 862
Beveridge, Sir William (1879–1963), 93, 403
Bhutan, 908. *Map 449*
Bhutto, Zulfikar, Ali, 678
Biafra, 300, 630
Bible, **93–5**, 106, 135, 262, 276, 493, 855, *94*, 447; English Bible (1539), 210; genealogies, 353; Gutenberg Bible, **384**, 447; translations, 284, 328, 384; Vulgate, 384, 490
Bihar, 448, 450. *Map 449*
Bill, Parliamentary, **96**
billeting, **96**
biography, **96–7**, *97*
Birkhoff, George (1884–1944), 374
Bismarck, Prince Otto von (1815–98), **97–8**, 105, 333, 360, 443, 763, 918, *98*
Black Death (1347–51), **98–9**, 279, 328, 402, 587,

681, 694, 722-3
Black Hole of Calcutta (1756), **99**, 181
Blackmore, R. D. (1825-1900), 304
Blaeu, Willem (1571-1638), 555, 755
Blake, Admiral Robert (1599-1657), **99-100**, 806, 940, *99*
Blake, William (1757-1827), 287, 782
Blanchard, J. P. (1753-1809), 78, 687
Blenheim, Battle of (1704), 87, **100**, 175, *100*
Blériot, Louis (1872-1936), 69
Bligh, Captain William (1753-1817), 613, 905
Blith, Walter (17th cent.), 11, 728
blockade, **100-01**, 230, 767, 930, 940
Blois, Treaty of (1572), 978
Blood River, Battle of (1838), 375, 618, 866
Bloodless *or* Glorious Revolution (1688-9), **101-2**, 500
Bloody Assize (1685), 500
Blücher, Gebhard Leberecht von, Prince of Wahlstadt (1742-1819), 979
Boboadillo, 121
Boccaccio (1313-75), 328
Boccanegra, Simone, Doge of Venice (1339-44), 930
Bodley, Sir Thomas (1543-1616), 529
Boeotia, 377, 918. *Maps 376, 696*
Boer War (1899-1902), 194, 411, 510, 631
Boers, **102**, 589
Bohemia, **102-3**, 218-19, 564, 921. *Maps 66, 421*
Bohemian War (1618-24), 921
Bohemund, Lord of Otranto (*c.* 1050-1111), 215
Bohr, Niels (1885-1962), 60
Boleyn, Anne (*c.* 1507-36), 389
Bolingbroke, *see* Henry IV, King of England
Bolívar, Simon (1783-1830), **103**, 265, 521, 722, 968, *103*
Bolivia, 103, 702
Bologna, 685, 693
Bolsheviks, **103**, 525, 940, 958
Bolyai, Farkas (1775-1856), 356
Bombay, **103**. *Map 449*
Bonaparte family, **103-5**, 683, *104*
Boniface VIII, Pope (1295-1303), 186, 331, 666
Book of Common Prayer, **105**
books and the book trade, **105-7**
Boone, Daniel (1734-1820), **107**, 453, *107*
Booth, John Wilkes (1839-65), 25, 533
Booth, William (1824-1912), 815
Border States (USA), **107-8**. *Map 23*
Borders (Scotland), **108**
Borgia family, **108-9**, 286, 544, *109*
Borneo, 455. *Map 456*
Borodino, Battle of (1812), 85
Borromini (1599-1667), 83
Bosch, Hieronymus (*c.* 1450-1516), 316. Plate 16
Bosnia, *Maps 77, 991*; Bosnia-Herzogovina, 500-1
Boston, USA, **109-10**, 624, *110*; "Boston Tea-Party", 4, 24, 109
Boswell, James (1740-95), 97, 497
Bosworth Field, Battle of (1485), 98, **110**, 308, 803, 942
Botany Bay, 61, **110-11**, 938. *Maps 63, 64, 110*
Botswana, **111**, 119. *Maps 7, 791*
Botticelli, Sandro (1445-1510), 308, 320. Plate 19
Bougainville, Comte Louis de (1729-1811), 177, 674, 816
Boulle, André-Charles (1642-1732), 343, *344*
Boulton, Matthew (1728-1809), **111**, 981

Bourbon, House of, **111-12**, 120, 789, 901
Bourguiba, Habib, President of Tunisia, 944
Boussingault, Jean (1802-87), 11
Bouts, Dirk (*c.* 1415-75), 316
Bow Street Runners, **112**
Boyars, **112**
boycott, **112**
Boycott, Charles Cunningham (1832-97), 112
Boyle, Charles, 4th Earl of Orrery (1676-1731), 724
Boyne, Battle of the (1690), **112**, 472
Bradley, James (1693-1762), 57
Brady, Matthew (1823-96), 712, *711*
Braganza, House of, 744
Brahe, Tycho (1546-1601), 57, 371, 504
Brahmins, **112**, 122
Bramante, Donato (*c.* 1444-1514), 814
Brandenburg, 922. *Maps 66, 358, 421*
Brandt, Willy (b. 1913), 360
Braque, Georges (1882-1923), 516
Brasilia, 114, 467, 466, 792
brass, **112-14**, *113*
Braun, Werner von (b. 1912), 871
Brazil, **114**, 237, 744, 868-9. *Maps 868, endpapers*
Brecht, Berthold (b. 1898), 252
Breda, Declaration of (1660), **114**
Breda, Treaty of (1667), **114-15**
Breitenfeld, Battle of (1631), 384
Bremen, 395
Brendan, St (AD 484-578), 471
Brescia, Battle of (1796), 338
Brest-Litovsk, Treaty of (1918), 958
Brétigny, Treaty of (1360), 434
Bretton Woods Conference (1944), 505
Breuer, Marcel (b. 1902), *466*
brewing, **115**, *115*
Brian Boru (AD 941-1014), 471
Briand, Aristide (1862-1932), 503
bribery, **115-16**
bridges, **116-17**, *117*
Bridges, Robert Seymour (1844-1930), 392
Bridgnorth, Battle of (AD 895), 16
Brigantes, 386
Briggs, Henry (1561-1630), 38, 132
Bright, John (1811-89), 921
Bristol, **117-18**, 121, 459
Britain: political parties, **737-8**; Roman occupation, 386
Britannia, 371
British Columbia, 136, 139. *Maps 137, 138*
British Commonwealth of Nations, **118-19**, 374
British Empire, 277-8, 374
British Merchant Shipping Act (1876), 727
Britons, **119**
Brittany, **119-20**, 159, 330, 371
Britten, Sir Benjamin (b. 1913), 657
Broken Hill, Australia, 65. *Maps 63, 64*
Bronze Age, 8, 514
Brown, Arthur (1886-1948), 70
Brown, Capability *or* Lancelot Brown (1716-83), 350
Brown, John (1800-59), 396-7, 525
Browne, Robert (1550?-1633), 195
Bruce, Gen. Charles Granville (1866-1939), 293
Bruce, Robert the (1274-1329), 45, **120**, *120*
Breughel family (1525-1638), 316
Bruges, 394
Brunel, Isambard Kingdom (1806-59), 117, **120-21**, 374

Brunel, Marc Isambard (1769-1849), **120-21**, *944*
Brunelleschi, Filippo (1377-1446), 319
Brunswick, 394. *Map 394*
Brutus, Marcus Junius (85-42 BC), 61, 130
buccaneers, **121**, 281, *121*
Buchman, Frank (1878-1961), 601
Buckingham, 2nd Duke of (1454-83), 129
Buckingham Palace, **121-2**
Buddha, Siddharta Guatama (563-483 BC), **122**, 428, *122*
Buddhism, 122, 428, 448, 512, 520; Burma, 126; Chan, 122; India, 52; Japan, 486-7; Korea, 509; Zen, 122. Plate 4
budget, **123**
buffalo, **123-4**, *124*
Bulgaria, 817. *Map 77*
Bulgars, 76, 126-7, 904. *Map 127*
Bull, Papal, **124**, 827
Bull Run, Battle of (1861), 482
Bullock, William (1813-67), 756
Bunche, Ralph Johnson (b. 1904), **124**
Bunker Hill, Battle of (1775), **124**
Bunyan, John (1628-88), **124-5**
burgher, **125**
Burghers of Calais, **125**, *125*
Burgoyne, General John (1723-92), 24, 818
Burgundians, 125, 330
Burgundy, **125**, 315. *Map 358*
Burgundy, House of, 622
Burke, Edmund (1729-97), **125-6**, 399, 660
Burleigh, *see* Cecil
Burma, **126**, 775. *Maps 449, endpapers*
Burr, Aaron (1756-1836), 389, *388*
Burt, William Austin, 953
Burton, Sir Richard (1821-90), 902
Burundi. *Map 7*
Busby, James, 627
Bushmen, 658, 866, 938
Bushnell, David (1742-1824), 893
Busia, Dr Kofi, 362
Butler, Samuel (1835-1902), 964
Butler, Josephine (1828-1905), 783
Buxar, Battle of (1764), 541
Buxton, Thomas Fowell (1786-1845), 858
Byblos, 709
Byng, Admiral John (1704-57), 594
Byrd, Admiral Richard (1888-1957), 70
Byron, George Gordon, Lord (1788-1824), 225, 283, 378, 388
Byzantine Empire, 126-8, 153, 331, 442, 544, 946; Crusades, 215-17, 291; war with Bulgaria (977-1019), 76. *Map 127. Plate 8*
Byzantium, 126, **128**, 171, 198, 243, 914. *Map 376*

Cabal (1667-73), **129**
cabinet, **129**
cables, 908
Cabot, John (d. 1498), 19, 117, 136, 237, 433, 624
Cabot, Sebastian (1476-1557), 136, 237, 433, 578
Cabral, Pedro (1467-1520), 237, 347
Cabrillo, Juan Rodrigues (d. 1543), 676
Cadiz, 39, **129**, *129*
Caedmon, St (7th cent.), **130**
Caesar, Gaius Julius (100-44 BC), **130**, 133, *130*. *See also* Julian calendar
Cairo, **130**, 475
Calah, 54. *Map 55*
Calais, **130-31**, 308, 435; Peace of (1360), 331

calculating machines, **131-2**, *132*
Calder, Admiral Sir Robert, 621
calendar, **132-4**
Calhoun, John Caldwell (1728-1850), **134**, 651, 738
Calicut, 347
California, USA, 582, 676. *Maps 22, 23*
Californian Gold Rush (1847), 180, 366, *366*
Caligula, Gaius Caesar, Roman Emperor (AD 37-41), 411, 426
Caliph, Calif, Khalif, **134**
Calixtus II, Pope (1119-24), 423
Calles, Plutarco (1877-1945), 583
Calvin, John (Jean Cauvin, 1509-64), 9, **134**, 172, 353, 762, 779, 781, *779*
Calvinism, 921
Camblan, Battle of, 47
Cambodia (Khmer Republic), 49, **135**, 455, 519, 972-3. *Maps 454, 972. Plate 4*
Cambrian Age, 257
Cambridge University, 963
Cambyses II, King of Persia (529-522 BC), 226, 700
Camden, William (1551-1623), 174
Cameron, Julia Margaret (1815-74), 712
Cameroon, *Map 7*
Campo Formio, Peace of (1797), 338
Canaan, Canaanites, **135**, 493-4. *Maps 135, 494*
Canada, 119, **135-40**, 374, 690; arctic exploration, 335; Durham Report (1839), 255; exploration, 520; settlement, 634; 49th Parallel (1846), 136, 139. *Maps 137-8*
Canadian National Railway, **140**
Canadian Pacific Railway, **140**, *140*
Canaletto (1697-1768), 967. Plate 61
canals, **140-41**, 650, 912, 945, *141*
candle, **141-2**
Cannae, Battle of (216 BC), **142**, 149, 157, 392
Canning, Stratford (Viscount Stratford de Redcliffe, 1786-1880), 211
Cano, Juan Sebastian del (c. 1460-1526), 177
Canova, Antonio (1757-1822), 484
Canterbury, England, 40, **142**; Cathedral, 88, 153, 232, 267, 268, *154*
Canterbury, Archbishops of, **142-4**, *143*
Cantii, 119
Canute *or* Cnut (c. 994-1035), **144**, 230, 638, 973, *144*
Cape Cod, **144**
Cape Horn, **144**
Cape Kennedy, **144**, *145*
Cape of Good Hope, **145**
Cape Sagrés, **145**
Cape St Vincent, Battle of (1797), **145**, 621
Capet Dynasty, 111, **145-6**, 162, 331
Capet, Hugues, comte de Paris (c. AD 940-96), 145
capital punishment, **146**, *146*
capitalism, **147**
Cappadocia, 662. *Map 55*
Caprivi Strip, 1000
Carbonari, **147**
Carcemish, 522
Cardigan, 7th Earl of (1797-1868), 428
Carib Indians, 939
Carlowitz, Treaty of (1699), 834
Carlyle, Thomas (1795-1881), 304, 416
Carmania, *Map 669*
Carmelite Order, 340, 664, 913, 948
Carnegie, Andrew (1835-1919), **147-8**, 529, *147*
Carnot, General Lazare (1753-1823), 338
Carnot, Nicholas (1796-1832), 356

Condé, Prince Louis de Bourbon (1621–86), 46, 922
condottieri, **194**, 702
Confederated States, **194-5**
Confucianism, 390, 509
Confucius (550–480 BC), 166, **195**, *195*
Congo, Belgian, 8, 527. *See also* **Zaire**
Congo (Brazzaville), *Map 7*
Congo (early history), 6
Congo, Republic of the, **195**. *Map 7*
Congregationalists, **195**
Congress, US, 129, **195-6**, *196*
Congreve, Sir William (1772–1828), 796
Connecticut, USA, 919. *Map 23*
Conolly, John (1794–1866), 574
Conquistadors, **196-7**, 702. *Plate 11*
Conrad III, Holy Roman Emperor (1138–52), 216, 419, 920, 949
Conrad IV, Holy Roman Emperor (1250–54), 420, 920
Conradin of Hohenstaufen (d. 1268), 420
conscientious objectors, **197**
conscription, **197**
constable, **197**
Constable, John (1776–1837), 516, *517*
Constance, Councils of (1414–18), 207, 435, 781
Constantine I, the Great, Emperor (AD 306–37), 126, 170, **197-8**, 207, 214, 291, 683, 713, *197*; Donation of Constantine, 422
Constantine II, Emperor (337), 429
Constantine Palaeologus, Emperor (1448–53), 126, 583
Constantine, King of Greece (b. 1940), 378
Constantinople, **198**, 667, 722; conquered by Turks (1453), 126, 128, 306, 475, 527, 583, 946; plundered by Crusaders, 216, 583
Constitution, British, **198-9**
Constitution US, **199**, 385; Constitutional Convention (1787), 389; Fourteenth Amendment (1866), **327**; Fifteenth Amendment (1870), **306**; Nineteenth Amendment (1919), 276-7
Constitutional Act, Canada (1791), 136
consul, **199-200**
Conti family, 112
Continental Congress (1774), 707
continental system, **200**
convoy system, **200-1**, *200*
Cook, Captain James (1728–79), 61, 163, 177–8, **201-2**, 309, 400, 539, 624, *201*; Australia, 767; Botany Bay, 110; as navigator, 644, 674, 734; Pacific voyages, 740; Tasmania, 905
Cooke, William Fothergill (1806–79), 908
Coolgardie, Australia, 65. *Maps 63, 64*
Coolidge, Calvin, US President (1925–29), **202**, 395. *Plate 3*
co-operative societies, **202**
Coote, Sir Eyre (1726–83), 436, 740
Copenhagen, Battle of (1801), 339, 621
Copernicus, Nicolaus (1473–1543), 57, **202**, 346, 407, *202*
Coptic Church, 287
Copyright Act (1709), 106
Coral Sea, Battle of the (1942), **202**. *Map 202*
Corday, Charlotte (1768–93), 556
Cordoba *or* Cordova, 475, 600
Corfu *or* Corcyra, 469. *Maps 376, 468*
Corinth, Corinthians, 375–8, 469, 696. *Maps 376, 696*

Corinthian Order, 661–2, *661*
Corn Laws, Repeal of the (1846), 336
Corneille, Pierre (1606–84), 250
Cornwall: Celts, 280; china clay, 258
Cornwallis, Charles, 1st Marquess, General (1738–1805), 24, 261, 450, 933, 998
Coronado, Francisco Vasquez de (*c.* 1500–54), 124, 196, **203**, 723
coronation, **203-5**; British coronation reglia, 204, 234, *205*. *Plate 31*
Corrupt Practices Act (1883), 115
Corsica, 288, 304, 683. *Map 685*
Cort, Henry (1740–1800), 469
Cortés, Hernán (1485–1547), 196, **205**, 206, 237, 329, 381, 424, 856
Corunna, Battle of (1809), 697. *Map 698*
Cossacks, **205**, 506, 954, *205*
Coster *or* Koster, Lourens Janszoon (*c.* 1405–84), 755
cotton, cotton industry, **206**-7, 914-15, *206*
Coubertin, Pierre de (1863–1937), 653
Councils of the Church, **207-8**, 684. *Plate 46*
court, **208-9**, 947
courts, international, 209-10
Cousteau, Jacques-Ives, 239, 956
Covenanters, **210**
Coventry Cathedral, 647, 904, *467*
Coverdale, Miles (1488–1568), 95
Cracow, 963
Cranmer, Thomas (1489–1556), 95, **210**, 782, *210*
Crassus, Marcus Licinius (115–53 BC), 130, 313
Crécy, Battle of (1346), 35, 47, **210-11**, 267, 328, 331, 383, 435, *211*
Cressent, Charles (1685–1768), 345
Crete (Minoan), 257, 375, 379, 593, 974
Crimean War (1853–56), 75, **211-12**, 262, 347, 367, 630, 809, *75*, *212*
criminal investigation, **212-13**
Crimtartary, *Map 669*
Cripps, Sir Stafford (1889–1952), 451
Cristofori, Bartolemmeo (1655–1731), 611
Croatia, 500–1; Croats, 999
Croesus, King of Lydia (560–547 BC), 53, 79, **213**, 366, 658
Crompton, Samuel (1753–1827), 206, 459, 916; mule, *458*
Cromwell, Oliver (1599–1685), 46, 172, 191, **213**, 590, 786, 789, *213*; Ireland, 471; Jews, 495
Cromwell, Richard (1626–1712), 191, 789
Cromwell, Thomas, Earl of Essex (1485?–1540), **214**, *214*
cross, **214-15**, *215*. *Plate 59*
Crusades, 130, **215-17**, 490, 587, 946, *586*; 1st (1096–99), 354, 365–6, 456; 2nd (1147–49), 949; 3rd (1189–93), 336, 949; 4th, 243, 583. *Map 216*. *Plate 10*
Crystal Palace, 298, *298*
Cuba, 194, **217**, 400; 1959 revolution, 193, 217, 382; missile crisis (1961), 101. *Map, see endpapers*
Cuchulainn, 471
Culloden, Battle of (1746), 484
Cunard Line, 746
Cunaxa, Battle of (401 BC), 701. *Map 701*
cuneiform writing, 8, 17, 72, 419
curfew, **217-18**
Curia Regis, 294
Curie, Marie (1867–1934), 574
Curie, Pierre (1859–1906), 574
Custer, General (1839–76), 454

customs, excise, **218**
customs union (*zollverein*), 359
Cuthbert, St (d. AD 687), 254
Cuzco, **218**
Cyaxares, King of Media (625–585 BC), 700
Cyprus, 119, **218**. *Map 576*
Cypselids, 375
Cyril, St (9th cent.), 76
Cyrillic alphabet, 17, 76, 500
Cyrus I, the Great, King of Persia (d. 529 BC), 53, 73, 213, 375, 581, 700
Cyrus II, King of Persia (d. 401 BC), 701
Czechoslovakia, 29, 102–3, **218-20**, 279, 608, 860, *219*. *Map 831*

Dacia, **220**, 798. *Maps 82, 798*
Dagobert, King of the Franks (AD 628–39), 581
Daguerre, Louis (1789–1851), 710, *711*
Dahomey, *Map 7*
Daimler, Gottlieb (1834–1900), 606, *606*
Dalai Lama, 922
Dalhousie, 11th Earl of (1801–74), 451
Dallas, Texas, 503
Damascus, **220**, 914
Damasus I, Pope (AD 366–84), 95
Dampier, William (1652–1715), 61, 121, 984
dams, 65, **220-21**, 617, *221*
Danby's Case, 442
dance, **222-3**. Plate 12
Dandolo, Enrico (1192–1205), 243
Danelaw, 280
Danes, 16, 144, 280, 973. *See also* Denmark
Danish War (1625–29), 921
Dante *or* Durante Alighieri (1265–1321), **224**, 283, 318, 328
Danton, George Jacques (1759–94), 338, 660, 786
Danzig *or* Gdansk, **224**, 969. *Map 224*
Darby ironmasters, 460
Dardanelles, 176, **225**, 616, 940. *Map 225*
Dark Ages, 9, 306
Darien scheme, **225-6**. *Map 226*
Darius I, King of Persia (521–485 BC), 140, 204, **226**, 375, 448
Darius III, King of Persia (4th cent. BC), 33, 701
Darwin, Australia, 65. *Maps 63, 64*
Darwin, Charles Robert (1809–82), 226, 631–2. Plate 11
Dauphin, **226**
David, Jacques Louis (1748–1825), 278
David, King of Israel (1038–97 BC), 490, 494
David I, King of Scotland (1124–53), 892
Davis, Jefferson (1808–89), 194–5, **226-7**, *227*
Davis, John (*c.* 1550–1605), 237, 637
Davy, Humphry (1778–1829), 26, 574
Dawes Act (1887), 454–5
Dayaks, 550
Dead Sea scrolls, **227**, 325, *227*
Deccan, **227-8**, 448
Decebalus, 220
Declaration of Independence (1776), 4, 24, **228**, 334, 488
Decorated style, 368
Defoe, Daniel (*c.* 1660–1731), 499, 625
Degas, Edgar (1834–1917), 444. Plate 29
Delaware, 21, 919. *Maps 22, 23*
De La Warr, Lord (1577–1618), 485
Delft (Dutch pottery), 257–8
Delhi, **228-9**, 448, 451, *229*. *Map 449*

Delian League, **229**, 376. *Map 376*
Delphi, 658. *Map 376*
Demetrius Poliocetes (3rd cent. BC), 377
democracy, **229**, 290
Democritus (*c.* 460 BC), 59
Demosthenes (*c.* 383–322 BC), 59, 659–60
Denis, King pf Portugal (1279–1325), 743
Denmark, 6, **229-30**, 380, 384, 438; Danish invasions of England, 16, 144, 280. *Map 821*
dentristry, **230-1**, *231*
Denys, St, 595
depressions, trade, **231**
Desbarres, Joseph (1722–1824), 556
Descartes, René (1596–1650), 356, 691, 835
Dettingen, Battle of (1743), 67. *Map 66*
de Valera, Eamon (b. 1882), 472, 473, *473*
Devil's Island, 938
Dewey, John (1859–1952), **231**, 824
Dewey, Melvil (1851–1931), **231**
Diaghilev, Serge (1872–1929), 223
dialling, **231-3**, *233*
diamonds, **233-4**
Diaz, Bartholemew (d. 1500), 145, 236, 367, 855, 866
Diaz, Porfirio (1830–1915), 583
Dickens, Charles (1812–70), 417, 782
dictionary, **234**, 983
Dido, Queen of Carthage, 709
Dien Bien Phu, 972. *Map 972*
Diesel, Rudolf (1858–1913), **234**, 647
Dingaan (19th cent.), 375, 618, 1001
dinosaurs, **235**, *235*
Diocletian, Gaius Aurelius Valerius, Roman Emperor (AD 284–305), 356, 561
Diophantes (3rd cent. AD), 16
diplomacy, **235**
diplomatic immunity, **235**
directories, 235, **337-8**
disarmament, **235**
Discovery, Age of, 91, **236-7**. *Map, see endpapers*
Disraeli, Benjamin, 1st Earl of Beaconsfield (1804–81), **237**, 262, 460, 737, *237*
District of Columbia, **238**
divers, **238-9**, 955–7, *238*
Divine Right, **239**, 737
divining, **239**
Dix, Dorothea (1802–87), 574, 783
Dnieper River, 506, 954
docks, **240-1**, *240*
dockyards, **241-2**, 840
Doges of Venice, **242-3**, 968, *242*. Plate 61
Dodgson, Charles (Lewis Carroll, 1832–98), 712
dogs, famous, **243-4**, *244*
Dolci, Carlo (b. 1925), 546
dole, **244**
Dollond, John (1706–61), 910
dolls, **244-6**, *245*
Dolmetsch family, 397
Domesday Book (1087), 37, 160, **246**, 633, 655
Dominica, 119
Dominican Order, Dominicans, 664, 922, 926
Dominican Republic, **247**, 387, 414, 817
Domitian, Titus Flavius, Roman Emperor (AD 81–96), 220
Donatello (1386–1466), 319, 587
Donne, John (1573–1621), 963
Doppler, Christian (1803–53), 57
Dorians, 375, 593

Doric order, 661–2, *661*
Dostoevsky, Fyodor (1812–81), 810
Dover, Secret Treaty of (1670), 129
Downing Street, **247**, *246*
Doyle, Sir Arthur Conan (1859–1930), 99
drachma, **247**
dragon, **247–8**, *247*, *248*
dragoon, **248**
Drake, Sir Francis (*c*. 1543–96), **248–9**, 676, 729, 856, *248*; Cadiz, 39, 129; circumnavigation, 177, 930. *Map, see endpapers*
drama, **249–52**, 382, *250*, *251*
Dravidians, 52, **252**, 448
Dred Scott Decision (1857), **252**, 595
Druids, 570, 693
Dubček, Alexander (b. 1921), 220
duels, **252–4**, *253*, *388*
Dumas, Alexandre (1802–70), 417–18
Dunant, Jean Henri (1828–1910), 632, 777
Duncan, Isadora (1878–1927), 223
Dunkirk or Dunquerque, **254**, 338, *253*
Dunlop, John Boyd (1840–1921), 606
Dunois, Jean d' Orléans, comte de (1403–68), 435
Dürer, Albrecht (1471–1528), **254**, 282, 286–7, 308, *254*, *281*, *287*
Durham, England, **254–5**, *255*
Durham, John George Lambton, 1st Earl (1792–1840), 255
Durham Report (1839), 136, **255**
Dutch West Indies Company, 588. *See also* **East India Company, Dutch**; **Holland**; **Netherlands**
dwarfs, **255–6**, *256*. Plate 13
dyeing, **256**, *256*

Eadmer (1060–1124), 174
Earhart, Amelia (1898–1937), 70
earth, age of, **257**
earthenware, **257–8**, *257*, *258*. Plate 13
earthquakes, **258–60**, 953, *259*
earthworks, **260**, *260–1*
East India Company, 181, **261**, 436, 448–50, 550, 906; Council, 399
East India Company, Dutch, **261**, 367, 455, 623
Easter Island, 261–2, 674, 676, *262*. *Map 675*
Eastern Question, **262**
Eastman, George (1854–1932), 712
Ecbatana, *Map 15*
eclipses, 201, **262–3**, *263*
economics, **263–5**
Ecuador, **265**, 702. *Map, see endpapers*
Ecumenical or Oecumenical Councils, *see* Councils of the Church
Edgehill, Battle of (1642), 399, 785
Edinburgh, **265–6**, *266*
Edington, Battle of (AD 878), 16
Edison, Thomas Alva (1847–1931), **266**, 276, 442, 607, 900, *266*
Edmund, Earl of Richmond (d. 1456), 941
Edmund Ironside, King of England (d. 1016), 144
Education Acts (1870), 631
Edward the Black Prince (1330–76), 211, **276**, 493, *267*. Plate 3
Edward the Confessor, King of England (1042–66), 161, 164, 409, 633, 641, 985
Edward I, King of England (1272–1307), 150, 724, 729, 754, 920–1
Edward II, King of England (1307–27), 724, 754

Edward II, King of England (1327–77), 130, 164, 331, 357, 383, 514, 724–5
Edward IV, King of England (1461–83), 803, 998
Edward V, King of England (1483), 985, 998
Edward VI, King of England (1547–53), 190, 389, 392, 943
Edward VII, King of England (1901–10), 282, 484, 558, *754*
Edward VIII, King of England (abdicated 1936), 3, 203, 988, *754*
Edward, King of Wessex (AD 901–25), 16
EEC, *see* European Common Market
effigy, **267–8**, *267*, *268*
EFTA (European Free Trade Association), **269**, 337, 638
Eglinton tournament (1839), 499, *499*
Egypt, *now* United Arab Republic, 130, 206–7, **269–70**, 338. *Map 269*
Egypt, ancient, 187, 269–70, 349, 377–8, 481, *270*; astronomy, 56; calendar, 133–4; hieroglyphics, 411–12, 518; housing, 430; land reclamation, 515; language, 33; Jews, 493–4; medicine, 26, 428; mummies, 267, *268*; pottery, 257; pyramids, 764; transport, 936. Plates 14, 31
Eiffel Tower, 12, 298, *298*
eighteenth century, **271–3**, *273*. Plates 56, 59
Einhard, 162
Einstein, Albert (1879–1955), 263, **273**, 356, 371, *273*
Eire, 472. *See also* Irish Republic
Eisenhower, General Dwight David, US President (1953–61), **273**, 619, 690, *177*. Plate 3
Ekaterinburg, 941
El Alamein, 993
Elam, Elamites, 72. *Map 55*
Elba, 288, 434, 615, 979
El Dorado, **274**, 774, 869
electoral systems, **274–5**
electricity, **275–6**, *275*
Elgin Marbles, 301, 379, *379*
Eliot, T. S. (1888–1965), 252
Elizabeth I, Queen of England (1558–1603), 39, 158–9, 172, 230, 493, 943, *942*
Elizabeth II, Queen of England (1952–   ), 988
Elizabeth of York, wife of Henry VII (d. 1502), 268, *268*
El Retiro, Treaty of (1750), 54
emancipation of women, **276–7**, *277*
emeralds, **277**. Plate 15
Emmanuel I, King of Portugal (1495–1521), 236, 347
empire, **277**. Plates 1, 11, 41
Empire style, **278**, *278*. Plate 15
Ems telegram, 105
enamel work, **278**. Plate 15
enclosures, **279**, 328
Engels, Friedrich (1820–95), 192, 463, 562
England, 28, **279–80**, 371, 435. *Maps 372, 373*. Plate 31; kings of, *see* **Hanover**, **Plantagenet**, **Stuart**, **Tudor**, *etc*.
Enlightenment, Age of, 271
English Channel, **280**
English kings, *see* **Hanover**, **Norman**, **Plantagenet**, **Stuart**, **Tudor**, **Windsor**
English language, **280–81**
English Navigation Acts (1651–96), 624
engraving, **281–2**, *281*
Eniwetok, 676. *Map 675*
Entente Cordiale (1904), **282**

Florence, 224, **318-19**, 477-8, *477*. Plates 18, 19

Florentine art, **319-20**. Plates 18, 19, 34, 37, 40

Florey, Howard (1898-1968), 574

Florida, 650-51. *Maps 22, 23*

Fokine, Michael (1888-1943), 223

Folger, Henry Clay (1857-1930), 529

font, **321**, *321*

Fontainebleau, **321**

Fontainebleau Decree (1810), 200

Fontenoy, Battle of (1745), 67. *Map 66*

food preservation, **321-2**

fool, **322**, *322*

football, **322-3**

Ford, Henry (1863-1947), **323**, 606, *323*

Foreign Legion, **324**

forgery, **324-5**. Plate 17

forging (of metals), **325-6**, *326*

Formosa, 487, 512. *Map 167*

Forrest, General Nathan Bedford (1821-77), 511

Fort Knox, 367

Fort Sumter, 20. *Map 23*

forum, **326**

fossils, **326-7**, *327*

Fouché, Joseph (1758-1820), 736

Fourdrinier, Henri (1766-1854), 756

Fourteen Points, **327**, 969, 987

Fourteenth Amendment, **327**

fourteenth century, **327-9**. Plates 5, 11, 15, 18, 40

Fox, Charles James (1749-1806), 254, **329**, 399, 660, *329*

Fox, George (1624-91), **329-30**, 340, 766, *330*

France, **330-32**. *Map 292*; African colonies, 481; Canadian colonies, 21, 136, 520, 634; electoral system, 275; Reign of Terror (1793-94), 483, **786-7**; Republic, 332; rule in Italy, 477-8; Second Empire, 104; Second Republic, 104; taxation, 446; wars with Britain, 373-4. Plates 11, 20-21, 29, 36, 54, 59. *See also* **Bonaparte, Bourbon, Capet, Valois**

Francis I, King of France (1515-47), 149, 306, **332**, 526, 666, 855, 966, *332*. Plate 20

Francis Joseph I, Emperor of Austria (1848-1916), **332**, 565, *332*

Francis of Assisi, St (*c.* 1181-1226), **332-3**, 338-40, 664, *333*

Francis Borgia, St (1510-72), 491

Francis I, Duke of Lorraine (1745-65), 385

Francis Xavier, St (1506-52), **333**, 486, 491

Franciscan Order, 948

Franco, General Francisco (b. 1892), 111, 129, **333**, 877

Franco-Prussian War (1870-71), 105, **333-4**, 360, 414, 666, 688. *Map 334*

Frankfurt, Treaty of (1871), 334

Franklin, Benjamin (1706-90), 275, **334-5**, 745, *335*

Franklin, Sir John (1786-1847), **335**, 637, 733

Franks, 303, **335**, 352, 357, 585; Ripuarian, 330, 335; Salian, 330, 335, 815

Franz Ferdinand, Archduke (d. 1914), 332, 501, *990*

Fraunhoffer, Joseph von (1787-1826), 57

Frederick I Barbarossa, Holy Roman Emperor (1155-90), 216, **335-6**, 419, 423, 849, 920

Frederick I, Holy Roman Emperor (1220-50), 217, 381, 420, 423, 463, 919-20

Frederick William, the Great Elector (1640-88), 359, 748, 762, 833, 921

Frederick I, King of Prussia (1701-13), 420

Frederick William I, King of Prussia (1713-40), 336

Frederick II, the Great, King of Prussia (1740-86), 67, 157, 271, **336**, 359, 557, 748, 763, 833, *336*

Freemasons, 863, *863*

free trade, **336-7**

Fremont, John C. (1830-90), 664

French Indo-China, 971

French language, 518

French Revolution (1789-9), 271-2, 276, 299, 331, **337-8**, 906; calendar, 134; Committee of Public Safety, 189; Directory, 235. *See also* **Reign of Terror**

French Revolutionary Wars (1792-1802), 331, **338-9**

fresco painting, **339**. Plates 14, 20, 50

Freud, Sigmund (1856-1939), **339**, 501, 575, *339*

friars, **339-40**, 664, 920, *340*

Friedland, Battle of (1807), 615, 616

Friendly Societies, **340**

Friends, Religious Society of, 330, 329, **340-1**, *330, 341*. *See also* **Quakers**

Froben, Johann (d. 1527), 755

Frobisher, Sir Martin (*c.* 1535-94), 237, 387, 637, 732

Froebel, Friedrich (1782-1852), 703

Froissart, Jean (1337-*c.* 1410), 125, 175, 211, **341-2**, *342*

frontier, **342**

Froude, J. A. (1818-94), 415

Fry, Elizabeth (1780-1845), 341, 640, 759, 783, 938, *783*

Fugger, Family of, **342-3**

Fujiwara family, 486

Fuller, Thomas (1608-61), 97

Fulton, Robert (1766-1815), 893

Furneaux, Tobias (1735-81), 177, 210, 905

fur, **343**

furniture designers, **343-5**, *344*

Gaberones, 111

Gabon, *Map 7*

Gadsden Purchase, *Map 22*

Gaelic, 470; Gaelic alphabet, 18

Gagarin, Yuri (1934-68), 871, *873*

Gainsborough, Thomas (1727-88), 273, 742

Gaiseric, *see* **Genseric**

Galatians, 53, 81

Galicia, 954

Galilee, 411

Galileo *or* Galileo Galilei (1564-1642), 57, **346**, 371, 677, 835, 909, *346*

galleon, **346**, *347*, *842*

galley, **346-7**, *347*, *842*

Gallipoli, **347**. *Map 225*

Galton, Sir Francis (1822-1911), 289, 310

Gama, Vasco da (1460-1524), **347-8**, 367, 607, 855, 930; voyage to Calicut (1497), 206, 236, 308. *Map, see endpapers*

Gambia, 119. *Map 7*

Gandhara, 703

Gandhi, Mohandas Karamchand (1869-1948), 178, **348**, 451, 621, *348*

Gandhi, Mrs Shrimati Indira, 452

Ganges River, 49, **348**, 713

gangsters, **348-9**

gardens, **349-51**, *350-1*. Plate 23

Gardiner, S. R. (1829-1902), 416

Garfield, James A., US President (1881), 25

Garibaldi, Giuseppe (1807-82), **351**, 479, 567, 678, *793*

Garnerin, A. J. (1770-1823), 78-9, 687, *687*

Garrison, William Lloyd (1805-79), 859
gas, **351-2**
Gascony, **352**, 729
Gaul, Gauls, 53, 330, **352**, 355, 969. *Map 82*
Gaulle, General Charles de (1890-1970), 16, 324, **352-3**, 619, 660, *352*
Gaza Strip, **353**
Geeraerts, Marcus (1561-1635), 316
Gelasius, Pope (AD 494), 356
genealogy, **353**
Geneva, **353-4**. *Map 898*
Geneva Conventions (1864, 1968, 1929), 19, **354**, 77
Genghis Khan (*c.* 1162-1227), 52, 166, **354**, 469, 505, 598, 695, 919, 929, 949, *354. Map 50*
Genoa, **354-5**, 477, 683, *479*
Genseric *or* Gaiseric (*c.* 395-477), 82, 149, **355**
geological periods, **355-6**
geometry, **356**
George I, King of England (1714-27), 393
George II, King of England (1727-60), 393
George III, King of England (1760-1820), 121, 329, 393, 398, 484, 785
George IV, King of England (Prince Regent 1811-20, King 1820-30), 36, 329, 785. Plate 24
George V, King of Hanover (1851-78), 393
George V, King of England (1910-36), **394-5**, 988
George VI, King of England (1936-52), 988
George, St, 248, **356-7**, 371, *357*
Georgia, USA, 21, 258, 650-51, 835, 919. *Map 22*
Georgia, USSR, **357**
Gerald of Wales (1146-1223), 174
Gerard of Cremona (1114-87), 924
German Confederation, 66
German Empire (1871-1918), 161, 277
Germania, *Map 82*
Germanic tribes, 291, 305, 335
Germany, **357-60**, 446; army, 324; colonies, 924; Christianity, 330; duels, 253-4; language, 518; National Socialism, 618; navy, 200. *Map 358-9*
Germany, Federal Republic of West Germany, 91, **361**, 388, 691
Germany, German Democratic Republic, 91, **361**
Gettysburg, **361**, 525; Gettysburg Address, 533
Gettysburg, Battle of (1863), 361. Plate 2
Ghana, 119, **361-2**. *Map 7*
Ghaznavid Dynasty, 469
Ghirlandaio, Domenico (1449-94), 741
Gibbon, Edward (1737-94), 416
Gibraltar, **362**
Gilbert, Sir Humphrey (*c.* 1539-83), 387, 624
Gilbertine Order, 948
Gilgamesh, Epic of, 72
Giorgione (1477-1501), 967. Plate 36
Giotto (1266-1337), 319, 328, 587, 608, 788, *333*. Plates 18, 40
gipsies, **362-3**, *363*
Girl Guides, **363**
Girondins, 338
gladiator, **363-4**, *364*
Gladstone, William Ewart (1809-98), **364**, 737, *364*
glass, **364-5**, *365*. Plate 21
Glencoe, 304
Ghika, Mikhail (1804-57), 810
Glorious First of June, 101, **365**
Goa, 333, 451, 491. *Map 449*
Gobelins, 904. Plate 58
Goddard, John (1724-85), 345

Goddard, Robert Hutchings (1882-1945), 796
Godfrey of Bouillon (1060-1100), 215, **365-6**
Godwin-Austen, Mount, 413
Godwine, Earl (d. 1053), 144
Goes, Hugo van der (*c.* 1440-82), 741
Goethe, Johann Wolfgang von (1749-1832), 273, 336, 420
Gogol, Nikolai (1809-52), 810
gold, 65, **336-7**, 970, 984, *139*, *366*
Gold Coast, *see* **Ghana**
Gold Standard, 686
Golden Horde, 807, 904, 923. *Map 50*
Golden Legend (*c.* 1275), 356
Gonzaga family, 255
Good Hope, Cape of, **367**
Goodyear, Charles (1800-60), 805
Gordon, Charles Henry, General (1833-85), **367**, 505, 893, 900, *367*
Gothic art and architecture, 328, **367-9**, 788, *369*. Plate 21
Goths, 129, 367, **370**. *Maps 82, 127*
Goya, Francisco de (1746-1828), 273, 287, 742, *287*. Plate 56
Gozzoli, Benozzo (1421-75), 320
Granada, Spain, 600
Grand Alliance, 175, 678
Grand Canal, China, **370**
Grand Remonstrance (1641), 96
Granicus, Battle of the (334 BC), 14. *Map 15*
Grant, General Ulysses Simpson (1822-85), 20, **370**, 496, 525, 838, *370*. Plate 3
Graves, Robert (b. 1895), 418
gravitation, **371**
Graziani, Field Marshal (1882-1955), 530
Great Britain and Northern Ireland, **371-4**. *Maps 372, 373*
Great Eastern, **374**, *374*
Great Exhibition (1851), 14, 609
Great Trek (1835), **374-5**, 589, 938
Greathead, James Henry (1844-96), 530
Greece, ancient, 264, **375-8**; arms and armour, 42, 44; astronomy, 56; calendar, 133-34; city-states, 290; coinage, 247; colonies, 443; gravestones, 267; housing, 431; medicine, 26, 571-2; pottery, 257; schools, 822. *Map 376*
Greece, modern, 78, **378**, 382
Greek alphabet, 17
Greek art, **378-80**, 516, *379*. Plate 22
Greek fire, 128, 198, 383
Greek language (ancient), 5, 17, 518
Greek War of Independence (1821-30), 262, 378
Greenland, 284, **380**, 614
Greenwich Mean Time (GMT), **380**, 539
Greenwich, Royal Observatory, 163-4, *643*
Gregory I, the Great, St Gregory, Pope (590-604), 16, 60, 142, **380**, 684
Gregory VII, Pope (1073-85), **380-1**, 422-3, 468
Gregory IX, Pope (1227-41), 463
Gregory XIII, Pope (1572-85), 133 (Gregorian Calendar)
Grenada, 119
Grenville, Sir Richard (*c.* 1541-91), **381**, *381*
Gropius, Walter (1883-1969), 465, *466*
Grote, George (1794-1871), 416
Grotius, Hugo (1583-1645), 464
Guadalcanal, 993. *Map 994*
Guadeloupe, 616
Guadeloupe Hidalgo, Treaty of (1848), 582, 676

Henry VI, King of England (1422–61), 515, 822

Henry VII, King of England (1485–1509), 110, 308, 515, 942, 985, 998, *241*

Henry VIII, King of England (1509–47), 286, 493, 942–3. Plate 20; dissolution of the monasteries, 2, 255, 429; divorces, 210, 214, 601, 779; as Head of Church, 172; meeting with Francis I, 306; portrait, 420, 742

Henry II, King of France (1547–59), 331, 571

Henry III, King of France (1574–89), 383, 966

Henry IV of Navarre, King of France (1589–1610), 111, 112, 331, 434, 571, 615, 619, 834

Henry the Navigator, Prince of Portugal (1394–1460), 145, 236, **409**, 534, 930

Hepplewhite, George (d. 1786), 345, *344*

Heraclius, last Roman Emperor (AD 610–41), 126–7, 701

heraldry, **409–10**. Plate 25. *See also* **Armorial bearings**

Herculaneum, 34, **410**, 740, 970, *410*

heresy, **410**

Hereward the Wake (11th cent. AD), 78, 382

Herod Agrippa I (d. AD 42), 411

Herod Agrippa II (d. AD 100), 411

Herod Antipas (21 BC–AD 39), 411

Herod the Great, King of Judaea (37–4 BC), **410–11**, 490, 491, 912. Plate 4

Herodias (d. *c.* AD 39), 411

Herodotus (*c.* 485–425 BC), 206, 262, 291, **411**, 514, 569

Herschel, Sir John (1792–1871), 710

Herschel, Sir William (1738–1822), 57, 909

Hertz, Heinrich (1837–94), 769

Hertzog, James Barry Munnik (1866–1942), **411**

Herzl, Theodor (1860–1904), **411**, 495, 1001

Hesiod (8th cent. BC), **411**, 575

hieroglyphics, 8, 17, 34, **411–12**, 518, *18*

highwaymen, **412**, *412*

hijacking, 776, *776*

Hill, Octavia (1838–1912), 784

Hill, Sir Rowland (1795–1879), **412–3**, 745–6

Hillary, Sir Edmund (b. 1919), 294

Hilliard, Nicholas (*c.* 1547–1619), 493

Himalayas, 293, **413**, *413*. Map *449*

Himera, Battle of (480 BC), 148

Hindenburg, Paul von (1847–1934), **413–4**

Hindu Kush, 14, 54, 512. *Map 15*

Hinduism, 112, 348, **414**, 447–8, 451, 966, *414*

Hipparchus, 232, 407

Hippias (4th cent. BC), 58

Hippocrates (*c.* 460–377 BC), 401, 548, 571–2

Hiroshima, 60, 614, 658, 951, 993

Hispaniola, 387, **414**, 817

historians, American, **414–5**

historians, British, **415–6**

historical novelists, **416–8**

Hitler, Adolf (1889–1945), **418**, 524, 993; Austrian *anschluss*, 28, 66, *418*; Battle of Britain, 85; Jugoslavia, 501; as orator, 660; rise to power, 91, 360, 786

Hittites, 53, 73, **419**, 775, 945; Hittite language, 33

Hobbema, Meindert (1638–1709), 516. Plate 33

Ho Chi Minh (1890–1969), **419**, 971, 972, *419*

Hogarth, William (1697–1764), **419**, *419*. Plate 26

Hohenfriedberg, Battle of (1745), 67. *Map 66*

Hohenlinden, Battle of (1800), 338

Hohenstaufen Dynasty, 5, 335, 357, 381, **419–20**, 423, 678, 920

Hohenzollern Dynasty, 359–60, **420**

Holbein, Hans (1497–1543), 232, **420**, 742. Plate 26

Holinshed, Raphael (1515–80), 131, 174, 415

Holkham, *see* **Leicester**

Holland, 6, 114, 261, 316, 338, **420**, 515. *See also* **Netherlands**

Hollywood, 604

Holmes, Charles (1711–61), 766

Holstein, *Map 358*

Holy Alliance, **420**

Holy Land (Palestine), 291

Holy Roman Empire (800–1806), 162, 278, 291, 357, 381, **420–3**, 585. *Maps 66, 421*

Home Rule, **423**, 636–7

Homer (*c.* 8th–7th cent. BC), 262, 283, 379, **423–4**, *423*

Honan, **424**

Honduras, **424**. *Map, see endpapers*

Hong Kong, **424**, 487, *424*. *Map 425*

Hood, Samuel, Viscount (1724–1816), 338, 813

Hooke, Robert (1635–1703), 850

Hoover, Herbert Clarke, US President (1929–33), **425**. Plate 3

Horace (Quintus Horatius Flaccus, 65–8 BC), 61, 408, **425**

Horatius Cocles (6th cent. BC), 116

horn-book, **425**, *425*

horses, famous, **426–8**, *427*

hospitals, **428–9**

hostage, **429**

Hottentots, **430**, 866, 938

Houphouet-Boigny, Félix (b. 1905), 481

hour-glass, **430**, *430*

housing, **430–3**, *431*

Housing Act (1851), 403

Howard, Catherine (d. 1542), 389

Howard of Effingham, Charles, Baron (1536–1624), 39

Houston, **433**

Howard, Ebenezer (1850–1928), 784

Howard, John (1726–90), **433**, 759, 783

Howe, Admiral Earl (1726–99), 101, 365

Hsia Dynasty (2205–1766 BC), 166

Hsüan, Emperor of China (74–48 BC), 390

Hubertusberg, Peace of (1763), 336, 849

Hudson, Henry (*c.* 1570–1611), 136, 237, **433**, 637

Hudson's Bay Company, 136, 164, 343, **433–4**, 806, 818. *Map 138*

Huggins, Sir William (1824–1910), 58

Hugo, Victor (1802–85), 417

Huguenots, **434**, 615, 729, 787, 866

Hulagu the Mongol (13th cent.), 73, 74

Hume, David (1711–76), 416

Hun, **434**

Hunan, **434**

Hundred Days, 104, **434**

Hundred Years War (1337–1453), 175, 210, 307, 328, 331, **434–5**

Hungary, **435**; 1956 revolt, 324, 435. *Maps 77, 292*

Huns, 49, 76, 81, 156, 330, 335. *Map 82*

Hunt, John, Baron (b. 1910), 294

Hunter, John (1728–93), 574

Huntsman, Benjamin (1704–76), 888

Hunyadi Dynasty, 547

Hus, Jan, *or* John Huss (*c.* 1369–1415), 102, 172, 207, 307, **435**, 778, 781

Huygens, Christiaan (1629–95), **435–6**, 570, 584, 909, *436*

Hydaspes, Battle of the (326 BC), 14. *Map 15*

Jamaica, 119, **484-5**, 985, *485. Map, see* endpapers

James, Duke of Monmouth (1649-85), 927

James I, King of England (1603-25), 95, 239, 371, 482, 774, 825, *892*

James II, King of England (1685-88), 143, 286, 483, 627, 927; Bloodless Revolution, 101-2, 112, 500

James IV, King of Scotland (1488-1513), 892

James, Jesse Woodrow (1847-82), 412

James of Compostela, St, 155, 713, 729, 817. *See also* **Santiago di Compostela**

Jameson Raid (1895), 790

Jamestown, USA, 21, 107, **485**, *485*

janissaries *or* janizaries, **485**, 670, *485*

Jansenism, 691

Jansky, Karl G. (1905-50), 771

Japan, **486-8**, 833, 924, *487, 488*; annexation of Korea (1910), 509; archery, 35; bridge-building, 116-7; Christianity, 333, 491, 561, 833; drama, 250; earthquakes, 259; occupation of Indonesia (WWII), 455; occupation of Vietnam (WWII), 971; titles, 83. *Map 486.* Plates 30, 63

Japanese art and architecture, 481, 488

Java, 455, 475, **488**. *Maps 456, 818*

Jay Treaty (1794), 209

Jefferson, Thomas (1743-1826), 25, 228, 282, **488-9**, 540, 738, 859, 962, *489*. Plate 3

Jeffreys, George, Judge (1648-89), 500

Jeffries, Dr (1744-1819), 78

Jehangir, *see* **Jahangir**

Jellicoe, Admiral John (1859-1935), 502

Jemappes, Battle of (1792), 337-8

Jena, Battle of (1806), 615, 616

Jenkinson, Anthony (d. 1611), **489**

Jenkins' Ear, War of (1739-41), 444, **489**

Jenner, Edward (1749-1823), **489-90**, 574, 965, *490*

Jericho, 34, **490**

Jerome, St (Eusebius Hieronymus, 347-420), 95, **490**, *281*

Jerusalem, 476, **490-1**, 494-95, 667, 714; Crusades, 215-7, 814; Temple, 953, *953. Maps 475, 494*

Jervis, Admiral Sir John (1735-1823), 145, 621

Jesuits, **491**

Jesus Christ, 93, 410, 411, **491**. Plate 27

jet propulsion, 70, 986, *986*

jewellery, **492-3**, *492*. Plate 31

Jews, 227, 418, **493-5**, 499, 769, 829; captivity in Babylon, 73; in Poland, 732, 978. *Map 494. See also* Zionism

Jewish calendar, 133

jingoism, **495**

Jinnah, Mohammed Ali (1876-1948), **495**, 612, 677

Joan of Arc *or* Jeanne D'Arc, St (1412-31), 307, 330, 435, **495-6**, 666, *308, 496*

Joanna of Navarre (d. 1437), 268, 620

Jodrell Bank, 643, 771, *643*

Johannesburg, 366-7. *Map 867*

John of Australia, Don (1547-78), **496**, 527, 622

John the Baptist, St, 411

John, King of Bohemia (d. 1346), 102

John Damascene, St (d. AD 749), 301

John, King of England (1199-1216), 164, 305, 429, 547, 724, 947

John of Gaunt, Duke of Lancaster (1340-99), 409, 514-5, 998, *515*

John I, King of Portugal (1383-1433), 743

John II, King of Portugal (1481-95), 145, 496

John III, King of Portugal (1521-57), 855

John XII, Pope (AD 955-963), 801

John XXII, Pope (1316-34), 824

John XXIII, Pope (1958-63), 208, 684

John III Sobieski, King of Poland (1674-96), 217

Johnson, Amy (1903-41), 70

Johnson, Andrew (1808-75), 443, **496-7**

Johnson, Lyndon B., US President (1963-69), 26. Plate 3

Johnson, Dr Samuel (1709-84), 107, 234, *497*, 506, 683, 983. Plate 32

Joinville, Jean (1224-1317), 175

Jones, Inigo (1573-1652), 432, 483, **497**, 680, 967, *497*

Jones, John Paul (1747-92), **497-8**

Jordan, 490, **498**. *Map 476*. Plate 32

Jordanian Arabs, 476, 498

joust, **498-9**, *499*

Juan Fernandez Islands, **499**. *Map 675*

Juarez, Beinto (1806-72), 583

Judah, 73, 493-4, 499. *Map 135*

Judaea, 493, 495. *Map 135*

Judaism, **499**

judge, **499-500**

Jugoslavia, **500-1**, 830, 923. *Map 830*

Julian Calendar, 133-4

Juliana, Queen of the Netherlands (b. 1909), 3

Julius II, Pope (1503-13), 583

Julius Caesar, Gaius (100-44 BC), 61, 116, 220, 269, 291, 330, 800

Jung, Carl Gustav (1875-1961), **501**, 575, *501*

juries, **502**

Justinian I, Emperor (AD 527-65), 81, 126, 198, 370, 402, **502**, *502*. Plate 8

Jutes, 28, 82, 280, **502**, 820. *Map 820*

Jutland, 81. *Map 82*

Jutland, Battle of (1916), **502**

Kaaba *or* Ka'bah, **503**

Kaanbaligh (Peking), *Map 51*

Kabul, **503**, 505

Kadar, Janos (b. 1912), 435

Kadesh, Battle of (1291 *or* 1299 BC), 775

Kaffir, **503**

Kalgoorlie, Australia, 65, 984. *Maps 63, 64*

Kalmar, Union of (1397), 638, 897

Kamehameha Dynasty, 400

Kanagawa, Treaty of (1854), 700

Kanchinjunga, Mount, 413

K'ang Hsi (1654-1722), **503**

Kansas, USA, 723. *Map 23*

Kant, Immanuel (1724-1804), 336

Kao-tsu, Emperor of China (202-195 BC), 390

Karakorum, 413. *Map 51*

Kariba Dam, 221, 1001, *221*

Kashmir, 452, **503**, 677

Katanga, 1001. *Map 791*

Kaunda, Kenneth, President of Zambia, 444, 1001

Kay, John (1704-78), 206, 459, **503**

Kazan, 481, 904

Keaton, Buster (1895-1966), 604, *605*

Keble, John (1792-1866), 437, 673

Kellogg-Briand Pact (1928), **503**

Kelly, Ned (1854-80), 412, *412*

Kelvin, William Thomson, Baron (1824-1907), 59

Kennedy, John F., US President (1961-63), 25-6, 144, 342, 489, **503-4**, *504*. Plate 3

Leignitz, Battle of (1757), 833
Leipzig, Battle of, *see* **Nations, Battle of the**
Leipzig fair, 297
Lemass, Sean (b. 1899), 472
L'Enfant, Major Pierre (1754–1925), 978
Lenin (Vladimir Ilyich Ulyanov, 1870–1924), 192, 463, **525–6**, 645, 809, 940, 958, *526*, *645*
Leningrad, 525, **526**
Leo VI, Byzantine Emperor (AD 866–912), 852
Leo III, Pope (AD 795–816), 162, 357, 422, 585
Leonardo da Vinci (1452–1519), 320, 339, 441, **526**, 541, 583, 710, *308*, *526*; aviation, 68. Plates 20, 34
Leonidas (d. 480 BC), 918
Leopold II, King of the Belgians (1865–1909), 8, 443, **527**
Leopold III, King of the Belgians (1934–51), 3
Leopold I, Emperor (1658–1705), 393
Lepanto, Battle of (1571), 160, 496, **527**, 577, 708, 719. Plate 35
lepers, leprosy, 429
Lesotho, 119. *Map 7*
Lesseps, Ferdinand Vicomte de (1805–94), 141, **527**, 682, *527*
Letter of marque, **527**
Leucippus (*c.* 440 BC), 59
Leuctra, Battle of (371 BC), 377
Leuthen, Battle of (1757), 833
Levant, 354, **527**; Levant Company, 189, 938
Lewis, John L. (1880–1969), 933
Lermontov, Mikhail (1814–41), 810
lexicographers, 517, 518
Leyte, Battle of (1944), 649
Lhasa, Tibet, 922
Liberal Party, 364, 737
Liberia, **527–8**. *Map 7*
libraries, **528–9**, *528*, *529*
Libya, **529–30**. *Map 7*
Lieber, Francis (1800–72), 381
Liebig, Justus von (1813–73), 595
lifeboats, **530–1**, *531*
lighthouses, lightships, **531–2**, *532*
Ligurian Republic, 338; Ligurians, 969
Lilburne, John (1614?–57), 106
Lilienthal, Otto (1848–96), 68, *68*
Lima, Peru, **532**
Lincoln, Abraham, US President (1861–65), 165, 370, 496, 525, **532–3**, *20*, *533*. Plates 3, 35; assassination, 25, 632; biography, 97; election, 20, 194; Gettysburg address, 361; Thanksgiving, 917
Lindbergh, Charles (b. 1902), 70
Linear B, 33
Lingard, John (1771–1851), 415
lingua franca, **533**
Linnaeus, Carolus (Carl Linné, 1707–78), **533**
Lippershey, Hans (17th cent.), 909
Lisbon, Portugal, 258, **533–4**, *534*
Lister, Joseph, 1st Baron Lister (1827–1912), **534**
Liston, Robert (1794–1847), 26
Lithuania, **535**. *Map 534*
Little Big Horn, Battle of (1876), 454
Liverpool, England, **535**, 925
Livingstone, David (1813–73), 6, 8, 11, **535**, 550, 885, 902, 924, 535
Livy (Titus Livius, 59 BC–AD 17), 61, **535**
Lloyd George, David, 1st Earl Lloyd George (1863–1945), **536**, 660, 699, *536*

Lloyd's of London, **536**, *536*
Locke, John (1632–1704), **537**
Lollard, 307, **537**, 781
Lombard cities, 335–36; Lombards, 82, 370, 422, **537**. *Maps 127*, *358*
Lombardy, 338, 479
Lombe, John (1693?–1722), 295
Lombe, Sir Thomas (1685–1739), 295
Lomonosov, Mikhail (1711–65), 273, 810
London, **537–8**; London Bridge, **538**, *538*; Great Fire (1666), 313, 432, 700, 723, 995; London University, 963
longitude, 397, **539**, *539*
loom, **539–40**, *540*
Lorraine, **540**
Louis V, King of France (AD 986–87), 145
Louis VII, King of France (1137–80), 216, 306, 949
Louis VIII, King of France (1223–26), 174
Louis IX (St Louis), King of France (1226–70), 175, 217, 331
Louis XII (1462–1515), 666
Louis XIII, King of France (1610–43), 136, 434, 567
Louis XIV, King of France (1643–1715), 111, 234, 271, 331, 343, 735, 969
Louis XV, King of France (1715–74), 331, 345, 785
Louis XVI, King of France (1774–93), 145, 190, 331, 337, 483, *272*, *335*; Louis XVI style, 325
Louis XVIII, King of France (1814–48), 111
Louis Philippe, King of France (1830–48), 111, 324, 616, 666, 901
Louis Philippe *or* Philippe Egalité (1747–93), 666
Louis, Duke of Orléans (1372–1407), 666
Louisiana, USA, 520, 689, 870. *Map 23*
Louisiana Purchase (1803), 489, **540–1**, 595. *Map 22*
Lourdes, **541**, 715, *714*
Louvre, **541**, *541*. Plates 34, 36
Low Countries, Pays-Bas, **541**. *Map 541*
Lübeck, 388, 394–5, 949. *Map 394*
Lucknow, **541**
Luddites, 207
Lully, Jean-Baptiste (*c.* 1632–87), 656
Lunéville, Peace of (1801), 339
Lusignan, Guy de, King of Jerusalem (1186–92), 216
Luther, Martin (1483–1546), 172, 456, **541–2**, 762, 779, 781, 855, *779*
Lutyens, Sir Edwin (1869–1944), 229, 351
Lützen, Battle of (1632), 384, 897, 921
Luxembourg, **542**, 617, *542*
Lydia, Lydians, 53, 263, 282, 375, 945. *Map 55*

McAdam, John Loudon (1756–1836), 460, **543**, 794
McCarthy, Senator Joseph (1909–57), 543, *543*
McCarthyism, **543**
Macaulay, Thomas Babington, Baron (1800–59), 116, 125, 415, 444, 497
Maccabees (Hasmonaean family), 494
McClintock, Francis (1819–1907), 335, 637
McClure, Robert (1807–73), 637, 733
Macdonald, Ramsay (1866–1937), 737
Macedon, **543**
Macedonia, 291, 544. *Maps 15, 77, 376, 543.* Macedonian army, 706; Macedonian language, 500; Macedonians, 127

McGill University, Canada, 529, 600
Machiavelli, Niccolo (1469-1527), 109, 194, **544**, *544*
Machu Picchu, **544**, *544*
McIntire, Samuel (1757-1811), 345, *344*
Mackenzie, Sir Alexander (1763-1820), 136
McKinley, William, US President (1897-1901), 25, **544**. Plate 3
Madagascar, *see* **Malagasy Republic**
Madeira, 409, 443, **545**, 894. *Map 545*
Madison, James, US President (1809-17), **545**, 754. Plate 3
Madras (Fort St George), 67, 181, **545**
Madrid, **545**, 837
Maecenas, Gaius Cilnius (*c.* 70-8 BC), 61
Mafia, 349, **546**, 864
Magdeburg, Battle of (1629), 921
Magellan, Ferdinand (*c.* 1480-1521), 177, 237, **546-7**, 674, *178*. *Map, see endpapers*
Magna Carta (Great Charter, 1215), 164, 198, 305, **547**, 827, 920-1
Magnesia, 275
magnetism, 275
Magonid family, 149
Magyars, 435, **547**, 859
Maharaja, Maharajah, **547**, *547*
Mahdi, the (Mohammed Ahmed, 1844-85), 367
Mahomet, *see* **Mohammed**
Mahrattas, Marathas, **547**, *547*
Maiden Castle, 260, *260-1*
Maillart, Robert (1872-1940), **547-8**, *548*
Maine, USA, *Maps 22, 23*
Mainz (Mentz), 446-7, **548**
Maitland, F. W. (1850-1906), 416
Malagasy Republic (Madagascar), 548. *Maps 7, 565, 607*
malaria, **548**
Malawi (Nyasaland), 119, **549**, 791. *Maps 7, 791*
Malaya, 475, 487, 854; Malay language, 518
Malaysia, 119, 455, **549-50**, 697. *Maps 549, 818*
Malcolm II, King of Scotland (1005-34), 144
Mali (French Sudan), 6, **550**. *Map 7*
Mallory, George Leigh (1886-1924), 293
Malplaquet, Battle of (1709), 175, **550**
Malta, 119, **550-1**. *Map 576*
Mamelukes, 31, 130, 153
mammoths, **551**, *551*
Mamun, Caliph (*c.* 786-833), 74
Mance, Sir Henry Christopher (1840-1926), 852
Manchester, **551**, *551*
Manchu Dynasty (1644-1912), 168, 272, 509, 833, 855, 900
Manchukuo, 552, 854. *Map 552*
Manchuria, 487, **551-2**, 854. *Map 552*
mandarin, **552**
mandates, **552-3**
Mandeville, Sir John (14th cent.), **553**
Manet, Edouard (1823-83), 444. Plate 29
Manila, 708. *Map 675*
Manitoba, 136. *Map 138*
Mannerheim, General (1867-1951), 311
Manning, Cardinal Henry (1808-92), 673
Manson, Patrick (1844-1922), 574
Mantegna, Andrea (1431-1506), 553
Mantua, 338, **553**, *553*
Manuel, King of Portugal (1495-1521), 546
Manutius, Aldus (1449-1515), 106
Manzikert, Battle of (1071), 53, 128. *Map 127*

Manzoni, Alessandro (1785-1873), 418
Maori, 353, **553-4**, 627-29, 976
Mao Tse-tung (b. 1893), 165, 168-9, 192, 512, **554**, *554*
map, **554-6**, *555*. Plate 37
Maquis, **556**
Marat, Jean Paul (1743-93), **556**, *556*
Marathon, Battle of (490 BC), 87, 226, 290, 375, **557**, 701. *Map 376*
Marconi, Guglielmo (1874-1937), **557**, 769-70
Marcus Aurelius, Roman Emperor (AD 161-180), 800
Marengo, Battle of (1800), 338, 428, **557**
Margaret of Parma, Regent of the Netherlands (1559-67), 622
Maria Theresa (1717-80), 385, **557**
Marie Antoinette (1755-93), 184, 190, 337, 493, **557**, *557*
Maria Feodorovna (1847-1928), **557-8**, *558*
Mariana Islands, *Map 675*
Marines, **558-9**
marionettes, **559-60**, *559*
Maritza, Battle of the (1371), 76
Mark Antony *or* Marcus Antonius (*c.* 82-32 BC), 61, 220, 269
Marlborough, Duke of, *see* **Churchill**
Marlowe, Christopher (1564-93), **560**
Marne river, **560**
Marrakesh, Marrakech, **560**
Marsden, Samuel (1765-1838), 627
Marseillaise, **560**
Marseilles, **560**
Marshall, George C. (1880-1959), 561
Marshall Islands, 676. *Map 675*
Marshall, John (1755-1835), 414, **560-1**
Marshall Plan, **561**, 665
Marston Moor, Battle of (1644), 243, 806
Martello towers, 183, 280
Martial (*c.* AD 80), 105
Martinique, **561**, 616, 975
martyrs, **561-2**, *561*
Marx, Karl (1818-83), 147, 192, 463, 525, **562**, 631, *562*. *See also* **Economics**, **Imperialism**, **Socialism**
Marxism, 53
Mary, Queen of Scots (1542-87), 39, 159, 825, 892, 978, *892*
Mary I (Mary Tudor), Queen of England (1553-58), 131, 204, 210, 708, 943, 988, *942*
Mary II, Queen of England (1689-94), 365, 390, 483, 659
Maryland, USA, 21, 919. *Maps 22, 23*
Masaccio (*c.* 1401-28), 319, 516, 608
Masaryk, Jan (1886-1948), 219, **562**
Mason-Dixon Line, **562-3**. *Map 563*
Massachusetts, USA, 21, 919. *Maps 22, 23*
Masséna, André (1756-1817), 338
Matabele tribes, 938
mathematical instruments, **563-4**, *563*
Matilda, Queen (d. 1167), 633
Matisse, Henry (1869-1954), 516
Matthias I Hunyadi *or* Matthias Corvinus, King of Hungary (1458-90), King of Bohemia (1478-90), **564**
Mau Mau, 504, **564**
Maurice of Nassau (1567-1625), 617, 658
Mauritania, *Map 7*
Mauritius, 119, **565**, 616. *Map 565*

paper money, **686**
Papua New Guinea, **686**
papyrus, **686**, *686*
Paracelsus, Philippus Aureolus (1493-1541), **687**
parachute, **687**, *687*
Paraguay, **687**. *Map, see endpapers*
parchment, **687-8**
Paris, 331, **688-9**, *688*; exhibitions, 298, 901;
  founding, 335; siege (1870-71), 79, 334;
  university, 963
Paris, Matthew (*c.* 1200-59), 174, 555
Paris, Peace of (1856), 212, 527, 624, 760
Paris, Treaties of: (1396), 434; (1763), 25, 136,
  594, **689**, 833; (1783), 962
Park, Mungo (1771-1806), 6
Parliament, 208-9, 371, **689-91**, *690*
Parliament Act (1911), 198
Parry, Sir William Edward (1790-1855), 732
Parnell, Charles Stewart (1846-91), **691**
Parsons, Charles (1854-1931), 887
Parthia, 680. *Maps 15, 701*
Pascal, Blaise (1623-62), 131, 356, **691**; Pascal's
  calculating machine, *132*
Pasternak, Boris (1890-1960), 810
Pasteur, Louis (1822-95), 74, 534, 574, **691-2**, *692*
Patagonia, **692**. *Map, see endpapers*
Paterson, William (1658-1719), 80, 225
Pathan, **692**, 703
Patriarch, 667, **692**
patrician, **692**
Patrick, St (*c.* 385-461), 371, 471, 595, **692-3**
Patristic Age, 301
Paul III, Pope (1534-49), 208, **693**, *693*
Paul IV, Pope (1555-59), 186
Paul VI, Pope (1963-   ), **693**, *693*
Paul, St (d. *c.* AD 64 or 67), 282, 411, 561, 595,
  694. Plate 46
Paul of Yugoslavia, Prince Regent (1934-41), 501
Paulinus, Archbishop of York (AD 625), 998
Pavlova, Anna (1885-1931), 223
Paxos, 469. *Map 468*
Paxton, Joseph (1801-65), 298
Pearl Harbour, 487, 589, 623, 676, **694**, 993.
  Map 994
Pearse, Padraic (1879-1916), 473
Peary, Robert E. (1856-1920), 734
Peasant's *or* Great Revolt (1381), 99, 328, **694-5**
Pedro II of Aragon (1276-85), 847
Peel, Sir Robert (1788-1850), 446, **695**, 735, *695*
Peking, 168, 614, **695-6**, *696*; Peking man, 166
Peking, Treaty of (1860), 168
Pelagius (4th-5th cent.), 301
Peloponnese, 375
Peloponnesian War (431-404 BC), 59, 291, 376-
  77, 469, **696-7**. *Map 696*
Penang, **697**
penicillin, **697**
Peninsular War (1808-14), 381, 545, 616, **697**,
  926. *Map 698*
Penn, William (1644-1718), 21, 341, **698**, 707,
  919, *698*
Pennsylvania, USA, 21, 341, 588, 698, 707, 919.
  Maps 22, 23
pensions, **699**
Pepin *or* Pépin le Bref, King of the Franks
  (AD 752-68), 161, 330, 422
Pepys, Samuel (1633-1703), 114, 560, 572, **699-
  700**, 805, *700*

Pergamum, 53, 282, 377-8, 407, 688
Pericles (*c.* 495-429 BC), 59, 243, 290, 376, **700**
Perkin, Sir William (1838-1907), 916
Perpendicular style, 368, 985
Perret, Auguste (1874-1954), 465, *466*
Perry, Matthew Galbraith (1794-1858), 481, **700**,
  998, *487*
Persepolis, *map 15*. Plate 47
Pershing, General (1860-1948), 514
Persia, **700-1**. *Map 701*. Plate 47
Persian Empire, 73, 282, 448
Persian Wars (499-449 BC), 58, 290-1, 375-6,
  411, **702**. *Map 701*
Peru, 532, 647, **702**; Spanish conquest, 237, 277.
  Map 868 and endpapers
Perugia, **702**
Perugino, Pietro (1445-1523), 702
Pescadores, 487. *Map 486*
Peshawar, 505, 512, **703**
Pestalozzi, Johann Heinrich (1746-1827), **703**, 824
Pétain, Henri Philippe (1856-1951), **703**
Peter I the Great, Tsar of Russia (1689-1725),
  271-2, **703-4**, 799, 809, 834, *703*. *Map 704*
Peter Claver, St (*c.* 1581-1654), **704**
Peter the Hermit (*c.* 1050-1115), 215, 660, **705**
Peter, St (d. *c.* AD 64 or 67), 411, 561, **703**
Peter, King of Yugoslavia (1941), 501
Petition of Right (1628), 96, **705**
Petra, 31. Plate 32
Petrarch (Francesco de Petrarca, 1304-74), 328,
  705
Petrie, Sir William Matthew Flinders (1853-
  1942), **705**, *705*
Petrograd (*now* Leningrad), 526, 645, 958
Petsamo *or* Pechenga corridor, 311
Phaestus, 593
phalanx, 14, 15, 46, 156, **706**, *706*
Pharaoh, **706-7**, *706*. Plates 14, 31
Pharos, The, **707**, 15, *832*
Pharsalus, Battle of (AD 48), 740
Pheidippides (5th cent. BC), 557
Pheidon (7th cent. BC), 375
Phidias (*c.* 431-417 BC), 59, 290, 379, **707**
Philadelphia, USA, 588, **707**
Philip the Good, Duke of Burgundy (1419-67),
  316
Philip II Augustus, King of France (1180-1223),
  216
Philip IV, King of France (1285-1314), 331
Philip VI, King of France (1328-50), 331, 966
Philip, Duke of Orleans, Regent of France
  (1715-23), 666, 785
Philip II, King of Macedon (359-336 BC), 59,
  156, 377, 543, 659, **707**
Philip V, King of Macedon (221 BC), 377-8
Philip II, King of Spain and the Two Sicilies
  (1556-98), 162, 285, 343, 622, **707-8**, 876
Philip V, King of Spain (1700-46), 111
Philippa of Hainault, Queen of England (d.
  1369), 125, 175, 342
Philippi, Battle of (42 BC), 61
Philippines, Republic of the, 475, 487, 553, 674,
  676, **708**. *Map 675*
Philistines, 353, 494, **708**
Phillip, Arthur (1738-1814), 61, 110
philosophers, **708**
Philoxenus (4th cent. BC), 379
Phnom Penh, *Map 972*

Pre-Raphaelites, 602
Presbyterians, 210
President, **753**
Prester John (*c.* 12th cent.), 49, 236, 287, **753**
Pretenders, **753**
Pretorius, Marthinus (1819–1901), 938
Priestley, Joseph (1733–1804), **753**
primitive, **754**
Prince Edward Island, 136, 139, **754**. *Map 138*
Prince of Wales, **754**, *754*
Princeton University, **754**, 964
printing, 105, 307, **755–7**, *756*, *757*
priory, **758**
prisons, **758–60**, *758*
privateers, **760**
Privy Council, **760**
Privy Seal, **760**, *760*
Prohibition, 348–9, **760–1**
Prokofiev, Sergey (1891–1953), 657, 810
proletariat, **761**
pronunciamento, **761**
propaganda, **761**
proportional representation, 274–5
Protectorate, **761**
Protestant, 331, 384, 615, **761–2**, 921
protocol, **762**
Provence, **762**
Prussia, 67, 230, 338, 393, **762–3**. *Map 358*. See
  also **Austria**; **Bismarck**; **Frederick II**;
  Germany
Prynne, William (1600–69), 106
Psalmanazar, George (?1679–1763), 325
Ptolemy (Claudius Ptolemaeus, *c.* 200 AD), 56,
  232, 236, 555, 564, **763**
Ptolemy Dynasty (323–30 BC), 269, 407, 735
Ptolemy I, King of Egypt (323–285 BC), 377, **763**
Ptolemy V Epiphanes, King of Egypt (205–180
  BC), 411
Puccini, Giacomo (1858–1924), 657
Pueblo Indians, 206
Puerto Rico, **763**
Pulitzer, Joseph (1847–1911), **763**
Punic (Carthaginian) wars, 142, 148–9, 378, 388,
  763–4, 799
Punjab, 503, **764**
Purcell, Henry (1658–95), 656
Puritans, 369, 624, 715, **764**
Pusey, Edward Bouverie (1800–82), 673
Pushkin, Alexander (1799–1837), 810
Pydna, Battle of (168 BC), 378
Pylos, 379
Pyongyang, **764**
pyramid, **764–5**, *765*. Plates 6, 14
Pyramids, Battle of the (1798), 338, **765**, *765*
Pyrenees, **765**; Treaty of the (1659), 833
Pyrrhus, King of Epirus (307–302 BC, 297–272
  BC), 148, 377
Pythagoras (*c.* 580–500 BC), 356, **765–6**

Qajar Dynasty, 469
Quai d'Orsay, **766**
Quakers, 329, 340–1, **766**, 783, 858, 919, *341*
Quebec, 136, 271, **766**, 813. *Maps 137*, *138*; fall
  of (1759), 599, 766, 833
Quebec Act (1774), 136, **766**
Quebec Conference (1843), **766**
Queen Anne style, **767**, *767*. Plate 52
Queen Anne's War (1701–14), **767**

Queensland, **767**. *Map 64*
Quetta, **767**
Quiberon Bay, Battle of (1759), **767–8**, 833
quintain, **768**, *768*
Quisling, Vidkun (1887–1945), 281, 638, **768**,
  768
Quito, **768**

Rachmaninov, Serge (1873–1943), 810
Racine, Jean (1639–99), 250
racism, **769**
radio, **769–71**, 952
radio astronomy, **771**
radio telescopes, *see* **Telescopes**
Raffles, Sir Stamford (1781–1826), 854
Raglan, Fitzroy James, 1st Baron (1788–1855),
  211, *212*
railways *or* railroads, 121, 676, **771–4**, 937, 938,
  772, *773*
Rainier III, Prince of Monaco (b. 1923), 597
Rajput, **774**
Ralegh, Sir Walter (*c.* 1552–1618), 274, 416,
  774–5, 918, 924, 988, *775*
Rama IV, King of Siam (1851–68), 916
Ramakrishna (1836–86), **775**
Ramillies, Battle of (1706), **775**
Ramses *or* Rameses II (*c.* 1304–1223 BC), 221, **775**.
  Plate 14
Rangoon, **775**
Ranjit Singh (1780–1839), **775**, 852
ransom, **776**, *776*
Raphael *or* Raffaello-Sanzio (1483–1520), 320,
  477, 702, **776**. Plate 19
Rasputin, Grigori Yefimovich (1871–1916), 558,
  776, *776*
Ravenna, 81, 370, 477, 603, **777**, *777*. *Map 82*.
  Plate 8
Réaumur, René-Antoine (1683–1757), 918
Reason, Age of, 9, 106, 271
Red Army, 940, 958. *See also* **USSR**
Red Cross, International, 354, **777–8**, *778*
Reform Act (1832), 826
Reformation, 9, 230, 271, 359, **778–80**, 855, *779*,
  780. *See also* **Christianity**
Reformed Church, **780**
reformers, religious, **780–1**
reformers, social, **782–4**, *783*, *784*
refrigeration, 321–2, **784–5**, 930
Regency, **785–6**, *785*. Plate 52
regicide, **786**
regnal years, **786**
Regiomontanus (1436–76), 233
Regulating Act (1773), 261, 399, 450
Reichstag, **786**, *786*
Reign of Terror *or* The Terror, **786–7**, *786*
Reims *or* Rheims, **787**; Cathedral, *787*
Relativity, Theory of, 273
Religion, Wars of, **787**
Rembrandt Harmenszoon van Rijn (1606–69),
  623, 742, **787–8**, *788*. Plates 51, 53
Renaissance, 9, 291, 306–7, 319–20, 328, 465, 477,
  788–9. Plates 18–20, 34, 36–7, 46, 60–1
Rennell, James (1742–1830), 556
Rennie, John (1761–1821), 729
Renoir, Auguste (1841–1919), 287, 444
reparations, **789**
Republican Party, *see* **USA**
Restoration, **789**; Restoration drama, 250

566; kings, 385; Moorish influence, 328–9; rule of Naples, Sicily, 477; slave trade, 67; trade routes, 930; Visigoth rule (*c.* 500–711 AD), 370. *Map 875.* Plates 13, 56. *See also* **Armada, Spanish; Franco; Spanish Civil War**
Spanish–American War (1898), **877**
Spanish Armada, *see* **Armada**
Spanish Civil War (1936–39), 129, 333, 545, **877**
Spanish Inquisition, 67, 463, 495. *See also* **Inquisition**
Spanish language, 518
Spanish Succession, War of (1702–14), 54, 175, 550, 623, **877**
Sparta, 375–7, 409, 696, **878**, 918. *Maps 376. 696. See also* **Peloponnesian War**
Speed, John (*c.* 1551–1629), 556. Plate 37
Speke, John (1827–64), 902, 954
sphinx, **878**, *878*
Spice Islands, 261
spies, **878–9**
Spithead Mutiny (1797), 613
spoils system, **879**
sports and athletics, **879–83**, *881*
Spurgeon, Charles Haddon (1834–92), 660
Sri Lanka, **883**. *See also* **Ceylon**
Stalin, Joseph (1879–1953), 463, 501, **883–4**, 907, 958, 960, *525*, *884*
Stalingrad, *now* Volgograd, **884**, 993
Stamp Act (1765), **884–5**
Standish, Miles (1584–1656), **885**
Stanley, Sir Henry Morton (1841–1904), 6, 8, **885**, 902, *885*
Stanton, Elizabeth Cady (1815–1902), 784
Star Chamber, 521, **885**
stars and bars, **885**, *885*
stars and stripes, **886**, *885*
Star-spangled Banner, **886**
Stationers' Company, 105–6
Statue of Liberty, **886**, *886*
Statute of Labourers (1351), 328
steam, 9, **886–8**, *887*
steel, **888**, *888*
Steele, Sir Richard (1672–1729), 625
Stefan Dusan, King of Serbia (d. 1355), 76
Stephen, King of England (1135–54), 174, 294, 306, 498, 633
Stephen, St (AD 977–1038), 561
Stephens, James (1824–1901), 303
Stephenson, George (1781–1848), 771–2, **888–9**
Stevenson, Robert Louis (1850–94), 266, 417
Stilicho, Flavius (*c.* AD 360–408), 82
Stirling Bridge, Battle of (1297), 977
Stockholm, **889**. *Map 821.* Plate 55
Stoicism, Stoics, 377, 407
Stone Age, 8, 34, 752–3, **889**, *889*; paintings, 516
Stonehenge, **889–90**, *890*
Stormont, Northern Ireland, 955
Stowe, Harriet Beecher (1811–96), 859, **890**
Stradivari, Antonio (1644–1737), 610
Straits Settlements, 550
Stralsund, Siege of (1370), 921
Strasbourg, **890**. *Map 358*
strategy, **890**
Stravinsky, Igor (b. 1881), 810
strikes, **890–1**, 900, 932–3, *891*
Strindberg, August (1849–1912), 897
Strongbow, Richard, Earl of Pembroke (*c.* 1130–76), 471

Strutt, Jedediah, 39, 295
Strutt, William, 295, 405
Stuart, Charles Edward, the "Young Pretender", "Bonny Prince Charlie" (1720–88), 484, 753, *484*
Stuart, James Francis Edward, the "Old Pretender" (1688–1766), 483, 753, *892*
Stuart, Stewart *or* Steuart, House of, 271, 789, **892**, *892*. *See also* **Pretenders**
Sturge, Joseph (1793–1859), 859
submarines, **893**, *893*
Sudan, **893–4**. *Maps 7, 830*; French Sudan, *see* **Mali**
Sudetenland, 219, 608
Suez Canal, 141, 527, 631, **894**, 930. *Maps 475, 476. See also* **Aden Protectorate; Disraeli; Egypt**
Suez crisis (1956), 353, 617
Suffragette movement, 178
sugar, **894**, 930; Sugar Act (1764), 668, 894
Sui Dynasty, 370
Suleiman I, the Magnificent, 670, **895**, 946, *670*
Sulla, Lucius Cornelius (138–78 BC), 671
Sully, Maximilien de Béthune, Duc de (1560–1641), **895**
Sumatra, 455, **895**. *Maps 456, 818*
Sumer, 49, **895**; Sumeria, 456, 581. *Map 55*; Sumerian alphabet, 17; Sumerian language, 33, 518, 581; Sumerians, 54, 72, 935
Sun Yat-sen (1886–1925), 165, 168, 512, 554, 614, **895**
Sung Dynasty (AD 960–1280), 166, 516, 591, 949
Sunningdale Agreement (1973), 637
Supreme Soviet, **895–6**
Surinam, **896**
suttee, 451
Sutton Hoo, 34, 492, **896**, *492*, *896*
Suvaroff, Alexander (1730–1800), 338
Swabia, 286, 381, 419; Swabian army, 46; Swabian League, 930
Swan, Sir Joseph (1828–1914), 442
Swaziland, 119, **896**. *Maps 7, 896*
Sweden, 230, 271, 384, 730–1, 834, **896–7**. *Map 821.* Plate 55
Swift, Jonathan (1667–1745), 625
Switzerland, **897–8**. *Map 898.* Plate 57
Sydney, 62, 111, 467, **898**, *62*, *467*
Sylvester I, Pope (AD 314–315), 422
Sylvester II, Pope (AD 999–1003), 787
Syracuse, Battle of (413 BC), 87
Syria, **898–9**; Roman occupation, 385, 407–8

Tacitus, Gaius Cornelius (AD 55–118), 10, 28, 305, 357, **899**, *899*
tactics, **899**
Taft, William Howard, US President (1909–13), **900**
Taft–Hartley Act (1947), 891, **900**, 933
Tagore, Sir Rabindranath (1861–1941), **900**
Tahiti, 676. *Map 675*
Taiping Rebellion (1850–65), 53, 367, **900**
Taj Mahal, **900**. Plate 57
Talavera, Battle of (1809), 697. *Map 698*
Talbot, William Fox (1800–77), 710, *711*
talking machines, **900–1**
Talleyrand-Perigord, Charles Maurice de (1754–1838), **901**, 971
tallies, talley sticks, **901–2**, *901*

Trabzon, *see* **Trebizond**
trade marks, **927-9**, *383, 928*
trade routes, 815, 923, **929-31**
trade unions, **931-3**, *932*
Trades Union Congress (TUC), 890, 932-3
Tradescant, John (1608-62), 609
Trafalgar, Battle of (1805), 27, 87, 101, 616, 621, **933-4**
Trajan, Roman Emperor (AD 98-117), 220, 313, 385, 722, 874
tramways, **934**, 937, *934*
Trans-Jordan, 498. *Map 475*
Transkeian Territories, **934-5**
transport, **935-7**, *935, 936, 937*
transportation, **938**
Trans-Siberian Railway, 676, 974, 811, **938**, 989
Transvaal, **938**. *Maps 7, 867*
Transylvania, *Map 669*
Trasimene, Lake, Battle of (AD 217), 149, 392
Trebia, Trevia, River: Battle of the (218 BC), 157; Battle of the (1799), 338
Trebizond *or* Trabzon, Empire of (1204-1461), 946. *Map 946*
Trent *or* Trento, Council of (1545-63), 208, 646, 798, 855
Trevelyan, G. M. (1876-1962), 415-16
Trèves, 330
Trevithick, Richard (1771-1833), 872, 886, *772*
Trieste, **938-9**
Trinidad, 339, 985; Trinidad and Tobago, 119, **939**, 986. *Map, see endpapers*
Trinity House, 531
Triple Alliances, **939**; (1668), 129, 386; (1717), **939**; (1882), 76, 282
Triple Entente (1907), 282
Trojan War, 379, 423, **939-40**, *939*
Tromp, Maarten Harpertszoon (1597-1653), 100, **940**
Trotsky, Leon, *or* Lev Davidovich Bronstein (1879-1940), 645, **940**, *645*
troubadours, **940-1**, *941*
Troy (Ilium), 5, 33, 423, 646, 940, **941**, 973. *Map 376*
Troyes fair (Troy-weight), 297
Trucial States, Trucial Oman, Trucial Coast, **941**
Trujillo, General Rafael (1891-1961), 247
Truman, Harry S., US President (1945-53), 618, 690, **941**. Plate 3
Tsar, Tzar, Czar, **941**
Tsushima, Battle of (1905), 676. *Map 675*
Tudor, House of, **941-3**, *942*
Tuileries, **943**
Tuke, William (1732-1822), 574, 783
Tull, Jethro (1674-1740), 10, **943-4**
Tunisia, **944**. *Maps 7, 576*
tunnels, **944**, *944*
Turin, **945**
Turkestan, 923, 929, **945**
Turkey, 262, **945-6**. *Map 946*; earthquake, 260, *259*
Turkic language, 904; tribes, 945
Turkish empire, 16, 78, 130, 469, 809; invasion of India, 448; occupation of Greece, 378, 526
Turner, John Mallord William (1775-1851), 516
turnpikes, **946-7**
Turpin, Dick (1706-39), 412, *412*
Tuscany, 288. *Map 66*
Tutankhamun, Tutankhamen, etc (ruled 1352-43 BC), 34, 269, 492, 707, **947**. Plates 14, 31

Twain, Mark (1835-1910), 953
twelfth century, **947-50**, *948*. Plates 7, 10
twentieth century, **950-3**
Twenty-one Demands (1915), 198
Tyler, Wat (d. 1381), 328, 694-5, 739
Tyndale, William (1494-1536), 95
typewriter, **953**
tyranny, **953**
Tyre, 256, 523, **953**; Battle of (332 BC), 14. *Maps 15, 135*

Uccello, Paolo (1400-75), 320. Plate 19
Udall, Nicholas (1505?-56), 249
Uden, Lucas van (1595-1672), 317
Uganda, 119, 504, **954**. *Map 7*
Ukraine, **954**
Ulm, Battle of (1805), 616
Ulster, **954-5**. *Map 636. See also* **Northern Ireland**
Ulyanov, Vladimir Ilyich, *see* **Lenin**
Umayyad Caliphs, 31, 220, 874-6, 899
Umbria, 713. *Map 685*
underwater exploration, **955-7**, *955, 957*
UNESCO (United Nations Educational, Scientific and Cultural Organisation), 37, **957-8**
Union, Acts of: (1707), 225-6, 371, 825, 958; (1801), 371; (1840, Canada), 136
Union Jack, 371, **958**
Union of Soviet Socialist Republics (USSR), 277, 525, **958-60**. *Map 959*; space exploration, 244; World War II, 360
United Arab Republic, *see* **Egypt**
United Kingdom, *see* **Great Britain and Northern Ireland**
United Kingdom Atomic Energy Authority (UKAEA), **960**
United Nations Organisation (UNO), 389, 817, 828-9, 951, **960-1**, 997; Charter, 164; Court of Justice, 210; Declaration on Human Rights, 179; Food and Agriculture Organisation (FAO), 300; Security Council, *see* separate entry; World Health Organisation (WHO), 404
United Provinces, **961**
United States of America, **961-2**. *Maps 22, 23.* Plates 3, 41; American Federation of Labor, 993; armed forces, 558; Bill of Rights, 199; budget, 123; cabinet, 129; census, 160; civil rights, 179, *179*; civil service, 179-80; coast-guards, 184, *532*; dams, 221, *221*; Democratic Party, 482, 738-9, 902; Depression, 223, 231; dockyards, 242; Federal Bureau of Investigation, 310; federal government, 302; 49th Parallel (1846), 136; hillbillies, 304; historians, 414-15; hospitals, 429; immigrants, 632; judges, 499-500; monopolies (trusts), 598; museums, 609, *609*; negroes, 415, 512; newspapers, 626, *110*; pensions, 699; place-names, 722; postal services, 746-7; prisons, 759; public records, 37; railroads, 772, 774, *773*; Republican Party, 738-9; roads, turnpikes, 795, 947, *795*; slavery, 306, 396, 857-9, *858, 859*; Supreme Court, 561; taxation, 446; women's suffrage, 276, *277*; World War II, 360. *See also* **American Civil War; American War of Independence; Congress; Constitution; Declaration of Independence; Political parties, US**
universities, 660, 677, 920, 924, 950, **962-4**. Plate 45

Acknowledgements

The publishers wish to thank the following for allowing us to reproduce copyright illustrations in black and white: Aerofilms Ltd: page 2, 538, 551, 688; Aldus Books Ltd: page 856; J. Allan Cash Ltd: page 165, 168, 229, 488, 524, 547, 609, 623, 643, 652, 667, 679, 684, 718, 749, 785, 794, 801, 804, 806, 814, 816, 839, 857, 886, 890; Edizione Alinari: page 320, 333; Courtesy of the American Museum of Natural History: page 974; Architect of the Capitol: page 196; Archives Photographiques: page 172; Art-Wood Photography: page 115; Associated Press: page 179, 768; Atlantic Press: page 20; Australian News and Information Bureau: page 412, 467; Austrian National Tourist Office: page 971; Barnaby's Picture Library: page 6, 8, 12, 26, 28, 36, 41, 154, 244, 282, 298, 406, 413, 467, 599, 777, 787, 792, 795, 823, 849, 871, 873, 878, W. F. Meadows 976; Barnardo Photo Library: page 784; B. T. Batsford: page 71, 555; Bethnal Green Museum: page 245; Blenheim Palace: page 100; The Curators of the Bodleian Library, Oxford: page 97, 159, 739; British Aircraft Corporation Ltd: page 70; British Library Board: page 169, 222, 256 MSS Royal 15E III f269-690; British Lion Films Ltd: page 605; Trustees of the British Museum: page 33, 47, 49, 54, 71, 72, 94, 110, 120, 257, 258, 268, 272, 289, 294, 297, 298, 342, 344, 351, 379, 390, 440, 447, 490, 492, 508, 515, 519, 529, 566, 586, 591, 600, 625, 633, 690, 705, 720, 748, 807, 896, 913, 935; Trustees of the British Museum (Natural History): page 235; British Olivetti Ltd: page 295; British Railways Board: page 773; British Red Cross Society: page 778; Camera Press Ltd: page 4, 165, 221, 259, 277, 352, 419, 445, Mike Andrews 466 and 968, Karsh of Ottawa 504, 522, 526, 543, 544, 570, 573, 589, 617, 693, 694, 696, 714, 720, 748, 754, 847, Paul Almasy 995; Campagna dei Giovani: page 251; Canadian Pacific Railroad: page 140; Central Press Photos: page 190; Church Information Service: page 143; Church of Jesus Christ of Latter-Day Saints, USA: page 602; Colorsport: page 881; Master and Fellows of Corpus Christi College, Cambridge: page 586; Council of the Institution of Mechanical Engineers, from "Engineering Heritage": page 92; Courtauld Institute of Art: page 284, 517; Courtaulds Ltd: page 915; Crown Copyright: page 205; Culver Pictures: page 388, 485, 580; Dominic Photography: page 657; Esso: page 648; Mary Evans Picture Library: page 182, 188, 542; Fishbourne Roman Palace and Museum: page 34; Fort Ticonderoga Museum Collection: page 599; Fox Photos: page 231, 245; John R. Freeman and Co.: page 485, 625; Lucie Freud: page 339; The Frick Collection, New York: page 601; Genehmigung des Museums für Volkerkunde: page 90; Stanley Gibbons Ltd: page 746; Government Information Service, Crown Copyright: page 424; Greater London Council Fire Brigade: page 313; Guildhall Record Office: page 383; Hale Observatories: page 643; Paul Hamlyn: page 15; Fritz Hansen, Denmark: page 344; B. J. Harris (Oxford) Ltd: page 99; Frederick Hill Reserve Collection, courtesy American Heritage: page 533; Hirmer Fotoarchiv, München: page 58; Historical Pictures Service, Chicago: page 370; Historical Society of Pennsylvania: page 698; Michael Holford Picture Library: page 285; Dr L. H. Hurrell: page 715; Hydatum, J. Baker and J. Scheerbohm: page 743; Imperial War Museum: page 200, 253, 729, 992; Instituto Nacional de Antropologia e Historia, Mexico: page 71; Israel Museum: page 227; Italian State Tourist Office: page 304; The House of Thomas Jefferson, Monticello: page 489; Jodrell Bank, Cheshire: page 643; A. F. Kersting: page 154, 246, 255, 480, 497, 995; Keystone Press Agency: page 538, 546, 554, 566, 605, 644, 653, 712, 758, 776, 796, 802, 837, 873, 884, 891, 926, 955; The Library of Congress, Washington: page 110, 529, 625; Lloyd's of London: page 536; London Express: page 178; The London Planetarium: page 724; Los Angeles County Museum of Natural History: page 453; Lowell Observatory: page 387; The Mansell Collection: page 3, 4, 5, 9, 11, 12, 13, 14, 18, 38, 39, 61, 68, 69, 75, 78, 94, 103, 104,

107, 109, 115, 124, 129, 130, 144, 146, 147, 152, 154, 156, 175, 176, 177, 178, 179, 180, 186, 195, 197, 201, 202, 211, 227, 231, 237, 247, 251, 254, 262, 272, 295, 303, 307, 310, 314, 320, 332, 340, 344, 348, 357, 385, 401, 410, 418, 423, 425, 427, 439, 452, 456, 477, 479, 481, 487, 499, 505, 511, 512, 526, 544, 553, 567, 571, 583, 586, 596, 598, 602, 603, 661, 666, 672, 673, 693, 695, 703, 705, 711, 715, 717, 719, 723, 728, 747, 772, 773, 779, 789, 804, 813, 819, 823, 827, 832, 833, 835, 836, 840, 851, 858, 863, 864, 881, 885, 887, 888, 889, 893, 925, 934, 935, 936, 937, 970, 989; Mercedes Benz (GB) Ltd: page 606; The Monotype Corporation: page 756; Montagu Motor Museum: page 323; Musée Cantonal d'Archeologie, Neuchatel: page 913; Musée des Arts Decoratifs: photo Giraudon: page 344; Musée Royale des Beaux-Arts: page 556; Museo del Prado: page 256; Museum of Fine Arts, Boston: page 110, gift of Maxim Karolik: page 344; Museum of Modern Art, New York, gift of Edgar Kaufmann, Jr: page 344; NERC copyright. Reproduced by permission of the Director, Institute of Geological Sciences: page 285, 327; National Film Archives: page 427; National Galleries of Scotland: page 508, 825; National Lifeboat Institution: page 531; National Maritime Museum, London: page 40, 163, 398, 839, 840, 843; Maritime Museum of Sweden and the warship *Wasa*: page 957; National Portrait Gallery: page 73, 88, 181, 210, 213, 242, 248, 267, 329, 364, 367, 515, 535, 621, 626, 645, 659, 673, 682, 690, 695, 700, 718, 719, 754, 775, 779, 783, 807, 826, 836, 837, 861, 892, 942, 987; National Theatre: page 251; National Tourist Organisation of Greece: page 251; The Nobel Foundation, Stockholm: page 632; Novosti Press Agency: page 205, 244, 301, 510, 809, 810, 831, 873, 993; Ore Mining Corporation: page 592; Overseas Containers Ltd: page 580; P. and A. Photos: page 680, 681, 687, 706; Phaidon Press Ltd: page 88; Photographie Giraudon: page 307, 332, 390, 492, 540, 557, 615, 650, 665, 686, 692, 709, 765, 786, 792, 805; Popperfoto: page 363, 605, 677; Port of London Authority: page 240; From *The Darien Disaster* by John Prebble, by courtesy of Simon Prebble: page 226; Public Archives of Canada: page 139; Public Record Office, London, Crown Copyright: page 760, 780, 827, 828, 901; *Punch*: page 277; By gracious permission of Her Majesty the Queen: page 390, 942; Radio Times Hulton Picture Library: page 27, 29, 62, 83, 84, 107, 125, 212, 253, 336, 354, 374, 381, 399, 403, 412, 473, 485, 506, 510, 527, 534, 536, 558, 562, 573, 602, 608, 613, 641, 645, 670, 672, 683, 745, 746, 758, 776, 778, 786, 793, 802, 839, 899, 911, 912, 932, 934, 944, 990; RIBA Library: page 350, 351; Rijksmuseum, Amsterdam: page 436, 659; H. Roger-Viollet: page 466; Royal Commission of Historical Monuments: page 528; The Salvation Army: page 815; Crown Copyright, Science Museum, London: page 56, 60, 89, 266; Science Museum, London: page 10, 89, 132, 193, 233, 274, 275, 346, 430, 617, 711; Shell: page 647; Skyfotos: page 532; E. A. Sollars: page 586; Staatliche Museen zu Berlin: page 14; Staatsbibliothek, Berlin: page 996; Städtische Galerie in Lenbachhaus München: page 98; Statens Sjonistouska Museum, Sweden: page 957; Syndication International: page 501; Swiss National Tourist Office and Swiss Federal Railways: page 548; TMM (Research) Ltd Museum: page 206; TWA/Photri: page 812; The Tate Gallery: page 419, 517; E. Piccaglioni, Teatro alla Scala: page 656; Tennessee Valley Authority: page 221; Tourisme-Franceschi: page 467, 524; United Kingdom Atomic Energy Authority: page 436; United Nations: page 390; United Press International: page 219; United States Coast Guard: page 532; USIS: page 221; University of Reading Museum of English Rural Life: page 525; University of Washington, USA: page 507; Victoria and Albert Museum, Crown Copyright: page 122, 173, 245, 248, 278, 287, 344, 365, 414, 450, 481, 492, 559, 561, 767, 914, 981; Volkswagen Motors Ltd: page 295; Weidenfeld & Nicolson Ltd: page 245; Fraser, *History of Toys*, 311, 344; Dean and Chapter of Westminster: page 268; Roger Wood: page 917; WHO: page 404.

The publishers wish to thank the following for allowing us to reproduce copyright illustrations in colour: Acropolis Museum, Athens: plate 1 *bottom right*; Actualit: plate 16 *top* and *bottom left*; J. Allan Cash: plate 4 *middle*, 40 *bottom left*, 45 *top left* and *right*, 47 *bottom right*, 57 *top right*; Ashmolean Museum: plate 31 *bottom*; Peter Baker: plate 57 *bottom*; Barnaby's Picture Library: plate 4 *top left*, 6 *bottom right*, 12 *bottom*, 14 *middle left*, 38 *bottom*, 42 *top*, 52 *bottom*, 55 *middle* and *bottom*, 57 *middle*; Trustees of the British Museum: plate 5 *bottom*, 11 *top right*, 13 *middle left*, 14 *bottom left* and *right*, 22 *top left*, 28, 32 *bottom right*, 37 *top*, 46 *bottom right*, 49 *bottom left*; Camera Press: Wim Swaan plate 44 *top left* and *bottom left*, 46 *middle*, 59 *bottom*, Bernard Silberstein 60 *top left*, 63 *top*; By courtesy of Christies: plate 62 *top left*; Douglas Dickens: plate 22 *top* and *middle right*, 23 *bottom left*, 30 *bottom left*; By permission of the Governors of Dulwich College Picture Library: plate 51 *bottom left*; French Government Tourist Office: plate 9 *top*; Galleria Uffizzi: plate 19 *top left*; HMSO: plate 31 *top right*; Hirmer Fotoarchiv, München: plate 5 *top*, 6 *bottom left*, 38 *top right*; The John Hillelson Agency Ltd: plate 50 *top*; Michael Holford Library: plate 14 *top* and *middle right*, 22 *bottom*, 30 *top left*, 44 *top right* (Gerry Clyde), 47 *bottom left*, 52 *top*, 53 *bottom*, 54, 56 *top left* and *right*, 58 *bottom left*; By courtesy of the Italian State Tourist Office: plate 62 *bottom*; Japan Information Centre: plate 30 *top right*, *middle left* and *bottom right*, 63 *bottom left*; A. F. Kersting: plate 7 *top*, 23 *top* and *bottom right*, 64 *bottom*; Keystone Press Agency Ltd: plate 35 *bottom*, 63 *bottom right*; Lord Chamberlain's Office, Crown Copyright: plate 20 *bottom*; Mauritshuis – Den Haag: plate 26 *bottom right*; Mittet Foto A/S: plate 41 *middle* and *bottom right*; Musée De L'Homme: plate 1 *top left* and *right*; Musées Nationaux, Paris: plate 29 *top*; Museo del Ejerhito: plate 11 *bottom left*; Museum Boymans: plate 17 *top*; The National Galleries of Scotland: plate 17 *bottom*; Reproduced by courtesy of the Trustees, the National Gallery, London: plate 19 *top right*, 26 *middle left*, 29 *bottom left* and *right*, 33; National Maritime Museum: plate 35 *top*; The National Portrait Gallery: plate 23 *bottom left* and *right*, 32 *top*, 38 *top left*; New Hampshire Historical Society: plate 2 *bottom*; Julian Nieman: plate 49 *bottom right*; Norwegian Embassy: plate 50 *bottom left* (Aldus Books); Oesterreichische National Bibliothek, Vienna: plate 10; P. and A. Photos: plate 42 *bottom left* and *right*, 49 *top left* and *right*; Philadelphia Museum of Art: gift of Edgar William and Bernice Chrysler

Garbisch, plate 2 *top*; Photographie Giraudon: plate 21 *top*, 27, 34, 36, 41 *bottom left*, 48 *top left* and *right*, 58 *top*, 61 *top*; Lauros-Giraudon: plate 15 *bottom*, 41 *bottom left*, 59 *top right*; Photri: plate 41 *top*, 55 *top*; Picturepoint: plate 4 *top right*, 12 *top left* and *right*, 32 *bottom left*, 44 *middle right*; George Rainbird Ltd (F. L. Kenett photo): plate 31 *top left*; William Rockwell Nelson Gallery of Art: plate 9 *bottom left*; Royal College of Surgeons: plate 11 *bottom right*; Scala Istituto Fotografico Editoriale: plate 8, 11 *top left*, 13 *top*, 15 *top left*, 16 *bottom right*, 18, 19 *bottom left*, *middle* and *bottom right*, 20 *top*, 37 *bottom*, 40 *top*, 43 *bottom*, 45 *middle right* and *bottom*, 46 *top* and *bottom left*, 48 *bottom*, 50 *bottom right*, 51 *top*, 53 *top*, 56 *bottom left* and *right*, 59 *top left*, 60 *top right*, *middle* and *bottom*, 61 *bottom*, 62 *top right*; Staatliche Museen, Berlin: plate 6 *top*; Stock Exchange Club, California: plate 40 *bottom right*; Swiss National Tourist Office: plate 57 *top left*; The Tate Gallery: plate 26 *top* (John Webb), Francis Bacon plate 51 *bottom right*; The Victoria and Albert Museum: plate 1 *bottom left*, 9 *bottom right*, 12 *bottom left* and *right*, 13 *top right* and *middle right*, 16 *middle left*, 26 *bottom left*, 39, 47 *top*; The Wallace Collection: plate 24 *top*; Courtesy of Wedgwood Ltd: plate 64 *top left* and *top right*; Reg Wilson: plate 43 *top left* and *right*; Weidenfeld & Nicolson Ltd/Yigal Yadin: plate 4 *bottom right*; Woodmansterne: plate 21 *bottom left* and *right*, 58 *bottom right*: the illustration for Heraldry is based on information supplied by P. A. Burgoyne and *The Dictionary of Chivalry* by Grant Uden (Kestrel Books).

The illustrations by Anthony Colbert are based upon information from the following sources: *Age of Kings*, Time Life Books (Time Life International); *Annals of Printing*, Turner and Poole (Blandford); *Armour and Weapons*, Paul Martin (Herbert Jenkins); *Arms and Armour*, Vesey Norman (Weidenfeld & Nicolson); *Assyrian Palace Reliefs*, R. D. Barrett (Batchworth); Bibliotheque Nationale, Paris; British Museum; *British Trade Marks and Symbols*, David Caplan and Gregory Stuart (Peter Owen); *Castles, An Introduction* (HMSO); *Country Life*; *The Early Motor Bus*, Charles E. Lee (British Rail); *Encyclopedia Brittannica*; *A Glossary of Arms and Armour*, G. Cameron Stone (Jack Brussel, NY); *Greek Pottery*, Arthur Lane (Faber and Faber); *Greek and Roman Life* (British Museum Publications); *A History of Architecture*, Bannister Fletcher (Batsford); *History of Mankind*, J. Hawkes and L. Woolley (Allen and Unwin); *The Horse Bus as a Vehicle*, Charles E. Lee (British Rail); *I See All*, Arthur Mee (Amalgamated Press); *Illustrated English Social History*, G. M. Trevelyan (Penguin); *Industry and Technology*, Chaloner and Musson (Studio Vista); *Life and Work of the People of England*, P. Hartley and M. Elliot (Batsford); *Life Science Library* (Time Life International); *The Making of Books*, Sean Jennet (Faber); *Musical Instruments Through the Ages*, A. Bains (Penguin); *New Architecture of London*, Sam Lambert (British Travel Association); *Odhams Illustrated Encyclopedia*; *Pictorial Knowledge* (International Learning Systems); *Plough and Pasture*, E. C. Curwen (Colwell Press); *Scientific Instruments in Art and History*, Henri Michel (Barrie & Rockliff); *Soldiers Soldiers*, Richard Bowood (Paul Hamlyn); *The Styles of Ornament*, Alexander Speltz (Dover Publications); *The Universal Encyclopedia of Machines* (Allen & Unwin); Victoria and Albert Museum; *Watermarks in Paper*, W. A. Churchill (Menno Hertzburger and Co).

Arctic

GREENLAND

Alaska

CANADA

Hudson Bay

ICELAND
NORWAY

SWEDEN

UNITED
KINGDOM
North Sea 7
IRELAND
(EIRE) 15 8
12 9 11 6
19 3
FRANCE
2 14 18
SPAIN ITALY
Mediterranean 13
GIBRALTAR *Sea*
TUNISIA

UNITED STATES
OF AMERICA

BERMUDA

AZORES
PORTUGAL

MADIERA

MEXICO
Gulf of Mexico
BAHAMA
ISLANDS
CANARY
ISLANDS

MOROCCO

ALGERIA LIB

SPANISH
SAHARA

CUBA
1 JAMAICA
HAITI
DOMINICAN
REP.

MAURITANIA
MALI
NIGER

CAPE
VERDE
ISLANDS

SENEGAL 12
4
5 PORT.
GUINEA GUINEA NIGERIA
SIERRA 6
LEONE 7 IVORY
COAST 10
CAMEROON

3 4
7 5
2
6

Caribbean Sea

WEST
INDIES

TRINIDAD &
TOBAGO
GUYANA
SURINAM
FRENCH
GUIANA

Atlantic Ocean

VENEZUELA

COLOMBIA

EQUATORIAL GUINEA
GABON 3

ECUADOR

PERU
BRAZIL

Pacific Ocean

ANGOLA

BOLIVIA

SOUTH
WEST
AFRICA

PARAGUAY

URUGUAY

ARGENTINA

CHILE

FALKLAND ISLANDS
SOUTH GEORGIA

Antarctic Ocean